DANCING *in the* DARK

ALSO BY MORRIS DICKSTEIN

A Mirror in the Roadway:
Literature and the Real World

Leopards in the Temple:
The Transformation of American Fiction, 1945–1970

Double Agent:
The Critic and Society

Gates of Eden:
American Culture in the Sixties

Keats and His Poetry:
A Study in Development

EDITED BY MORRIS DICKSTEIN

The Revival of Pragmatism:
New Essays on Social Thought, Law, and Culture

Great Film Directors:
A Critical Anthology
(coedited with Leo Braudy)

DANCING

in the DARK

A Cultural History of the Great Depression

MORRIS DICKSTEIN

W. W. NORTON & COMPANY / NEW YORK LONDON

Since this page cannot legibly accommodate all the copyright notices, pages
565–68 constitute an extension of the copyright page.

For information about permission to reproduce selections from this book,
write to Permissions, W. W. Norton & Company, Inc.,
500 Fifth Avenue, New York, NY 10110

For information about special discounts for bulk purchases, please contact
W. W. Norton Special Sales at specialsales@wwnorton.com or 800-233-4830

Manufacturing by RR Donnelley, Harrisonburg
Book design by Ellen Cipriano
Production manager: Julia Druskin

Library of Congress Cataloging-in-Publication Data

Dickstein, Morris.
Dancing in the dark : a cultural history of the Great Depression /
Morris Dickstein.
p. cm.
Includes bibliographical references and index.
ISBN 978-0-393-07225-9 (hardcover)
1. Popular culture—United States—History—20th century.
2. United States—Civilization—1918–1945. 3. United States—Intellectual
life—20th century. 4. United States—Social life and customs—1918–1945.
5. Depressions—1929—United States. 6. United States—History—1933–1945.
7. United States—History—1919–1933. I. Title.
E806.D57 2009
973.91—dc22
2009017389

W. W. Norton & Company, Inc.
500 Fifth Avenue, New York, N.Y. 10110
www.wwnorton.com

W. W. Norton & Company Ltd.
Castle House, 75/76 Wells Street, London W1T 3QT

1 2 3 4 5 6 7 8 9 0

To Evan, Adam, Simon, and Anya,

citizens of the future,

and in memory of Stanley Burnshaw,

in whom the 1930s lived on

CONTENTS

PART ONE   DISCOVERING POVERTY

PART TWO   SUCCESS AND FAILURE

PART THREE   THE CULTURE OF ELEGANCE

PART FOUR   THE SEARCH FOR COMMUNITY

PREFACE

As I completed this book, the United States was entering its worst economic crisis since the Great Depression of 1929 to 1941. References to the 1930s blanketed the airwaves, the newspapers, and the online blogs, as well as the press conferences of politicians, the testimony of federal regulators, and the oracular pronouncements of economists. Because of structural reforms enacted then and bolstered by subsequent administrations, this was never supposed to happen again. But even before our latest economic crisis, the painful conditions of Depression years continued to haunt us: as distant memories fading into myth, as a stern warning that tough times might return, and, finally, as a blow to America's sense of itself as a land of endlessly open possibilities. Every postwar recession, every economic crisis, inevitably triggered fears going back to the 1930s.

Surprisingly, the Depression was also the scene of a great cultural spectacle against the unlikely backdrop of economic misery. The crisis kindled America's social imagination, firing enormous interest in how ordinary people lived, how they suffered, interacted, took pleasure in one another, and endured. It might seem unusual to approach those calamitous years through their reflection in the arts, but the art and reportage that helped people cope with hard times still speak to us today: strangely beautiful photographs documenting the toll of human suffering; novels that respond to the social crisis, sometimes directly, often obliquely; romantic screen comedies whose wit and brio have never been surpassed; dance films that remain the ultimate in elegance and sophisticated grace; jazz-inflected popular music that may be the best America has ever produced. Combining the truth of art with the immediate impact of entertainment, these works give us intimate glimpses of the inner history of the Great Depression, including its plaintive longing for something better, that place at the end of the Yellow Brick Road. They provide us with singular keys to its moral and emotional life, its dream life, its unguarded feelings about the world.

The thirties were also the testing ground for political debates that continue to this day: about totalitarianism and democracy, about the relations between social welfare, individual initiative, and public responsibility, about the ideologies of the twentieth century. Along with other leading intellectuals, some of my best teachers received their baptism of fire in those debates, and I undoubtedly soaked up some of this influence. But this book is not about thirties intellectuals and their ideas, which historians and critics have covered extensively, but about the arts and society, the crucial role that culture can play in times of national trial. What first drew me to the period were the movies, still wonderfully watchable, although the techniques and the scale of film production have altered dramatically. Moviemaking then was dominated by individual studios, each with its distinct style: the punchy and

topical films of Warner Brothers, "ripped from the headlines of today";
the Frank Capra comedies, with their unique common touch, that put
Columbia Pictures on the map; the European romantic sophistication
that Ernest Lubitsch brought to Paramount; the stylish Germanic horror films made at Universal; the Astaire-Rogers films and romantic comedies that floated RKO.

Some of these films are visibly marked by the Depression, others
seemingly not at all, at least until we look at them more closely. This
book examines the rich array of cultural material—books, films, songs,
pictures, designs—to fathom the life and mind of the Depression. But it
also brings history to bear on these peerless works to understand where
they came from—to listen to their dialogue with their own times. Great
art or performance helps us understand how people felt about their lives;
it testifies to what they needed to keep going. This why we return again
and again to classic American social novels, from *Uncle Tom's Cabin*, *The
House of Mirth*, and *The Jungle*, different as they are, to *The Great Gatsby*
and *The Grapes of Wrath*. Each in its own way enables us to feel the pulse
of society from the inside. *Dancing in the Dark*, then, shows how the arts
responded to a society in upheaval and, at the same time, how they altered
and influenced that society, providing a hard-pressed audience with pleasure, escape, illumination, and hope when they were most needed.

No two views of the 1930s are entirely the same. The critic Alfred
Kazin, who saw the thirties as decisive for his own life, expressed one
deeply felt view many years later. "No one who grew up in the Depression ever recovered from it," he wrote in 1980. "To anyone who grew up
in a family where the father was usually looking for work, every image
of the thirties is gray, embittered."[1] My own father was not scrambling
for work then; he had a steady job throughout the decade, low-paying
but decent enough for my parents to marry in December 1938. But he
once told me that every Friday when he picked up his paycheck he looked
for the pink slip telling him he was laid off. This steady drip of anxiety
eroded his confidence and instilled lifelong habits of caution, an undying
concern about security so typical of the Depression generation. For him
these fears may have been there already, since my father grew up in a poor
immigrant family, the son of Yiddish-speaking parents who never fully
adapted to living in this country. As with the many writers who came
from impoverished backgrounds, the Depression made him a specialist

in economic anxiety. Unfailingly generous to his family, a devoted union man, he remained thrifty, self-denying, pessimistic about the future, and very conservative about risk and change. Until his death, in 1992, he followed the stock market every day as a spectator sport but, always averse to risk, never invested a cent after pulling out in 1928.

Not everyone looked back at the thirties in this worrisome way. In the 1980s, when I occasionally taught undergraduate courses on the Depression years, the first assignment was to interview someone who actually remembered those times. Students gained a visceral sense of what it was like to live through the period but an even greater feeling for the variety of people's experience. Some had suffered, others had thrived. Some had been utterly wiped out, others had bought businesses, properties, or even stocks at bargain rates and eventually did well. Many of those interviewed looked back at the thirties with unabashed nostalgia: they were young then, and remembered the period as the time of their lives. The price of everything was low; if you were single and unencumbered, you could live on almost nothing. Others insisted that those who had grown up amid postwar prosperity understood nothing; hard times were bound to come again.

Because the Depression was a national trauma, we have a mother lode of personal testimony: interviews and oral histories; reports and studies commissioned by the government; poignant letters to many officials including the president and the first lady; memorable photographs, documentaries, newsreels, and other reportage. Few other periods of American life are as well documented. To gain support for unprecedented New Deal programs, the government, for the first time, sent out writers, photographers, and filmmakers to canvas the land. Newspapers and magazines also sent writers to do fieldwork. Others simply explored the country on their own or as working journalists; at no other time have writers been so consumed by how their fellow citizens were doing. They crisscrossed America, writing books and articles about what they saw, what people told them. They turned the interview into a richer cultural form, focusing not on prominent men but on the drama of everyday life. This you-are-there documentation soon infiltrated the arts. The art and entertainment of the thirties developed unusual forms of witness designed to comfort, enlighten, or distract a troubled nation. Today we have all sorts of books investigating the economic issues of the Depression, the politics and programs of the New Deal, or the travail of the common man and the typical family. The testimony of the arts sheds a different light on how people felt about themselves and about their lives. It offers us access to some of the innermost feelings of the age.

For most critics and cultural historians, the great modern flowering of the arts in America belongs to the freewheeling twenties, which produced novelists like Sherwood Anderson, Sinclair Lewis, Ernest Hemingway, F. Scott Fitzgerald, Willa Cather, and William Faulkner, along with canonical modern poets such as T. S. Eliot, Wallace Stevens, Robert Frost, Edna St. Vincent Millay, Marianne Moore, and William Carlos Williams, writers we still read and teach today. It was the era of the Harlem Renaissance, the spectacular emergence of jazz, the great ferment of European modernism, and the arrival of a new, profoundly American group of young composers, including Aaron Copland and Virgil Thomson, who trained in Europe yet would go on to explore their native roots. The mood coming out of the First World War was existential, disillusioned, not only for the expatriates but also among many who stayed home. If theirs was a wild party, booze-soaked and bohemian, it was played out over a void. These innovative artists were highly critical of American life as they pursued daring new forms and breached old moral barriers. This booming decade, not the sorely beset thirties, has always been seen as the creative peak of the twentieth century, the first modern decade, the breakthrough era that transformed the arts for many years to come.

The biting social criticism and creative daring of these artists would carry over, often subtly and covertly, into the 1930s, when the arts took off on an adventure all their own. As the Depression deepened, artists entered a dialogue with history that helps us to understand those distressed years, but also to appreciate what these thirties artists themselves achieved. As the art historian Matthew Baigell has written of the painters of the 1930s, "the imperatives of place, politics, social change, and history replaced individual consciousness as sources of motivation. Once again, art was to become a vehicle for recording things more permanent and concrete than movements of personal experience, insight, and feeling."[2] This points well to the social imagination of these artists, but it speaks less for writers than for painters, since writers could rarely sacrifice "personal experience, insight, and feeling" without dooming themselves to topical relevance and rapid oblivion. Rarely have artists—or Americans in general—identified so strongly with ordinary people and their needs. If

art has the power to move people, to survive its time, even to provide genuine witness, it can only be through personal identification with real people's problems in a convincingly realized time and place. At once social
and personal, the arts of the thirties give us a richly subjective understanding of the mind and heart of the Depression, a moment of American
history that resonates strongly today amid new economic troubles.

The 1930s offer an incomparable case study of the function of art and
media in a time of social crisis. As Walter Benjamin demonstrated in his
classic 1936 essay "The Work of Art in the Age of Mechanical Reproduc-
tion," this was a time when technology altered the arts and tremendously
expanded their reach. The transitions from vaudeville to radio, from
silent film to talking film, from live music and sheet music to recorded
and broadcast music, all gave impetus to a more pervasive popular culture
that reached a huge new audience. Because they were ready-made for propaganda, these forms of communication also proved a boon for dictators
and democrats, aggressive journalists and creative advertisers. The living-
room intimacy of FDR's fireside radio chats and later the orotund periods
of Churchill's stirring oratory were matched by the malignant power of
Hitler's hypnotic speeches. From his parish near Detroit, Father Charles
Coughlin, the populist priest, could use the radio to stir up grievance and
resentment, but it also enabled FDR to create the feeling of community,
a shared perception of crisis, hope, or reassurance, a sense that someone
cared and was not daunted or afraid. The many genres of the classic Hollywood cinema, from gangster films and backstage musicals to monster
films and screwball comedies, arose not simply as the studios' way of coin-
ing money and dodging bankruptcy but in response to the needs and anxieties of the Depression. It's conventional to call these movies escapist, but
they are imbued with the real concerns of the beleaguered audience.

Often these worries are displaced onto stories that seem to have little
to do with hard times—stories of *other* hard times set in the past, like *Gone
with the Wind*; in the realm of fantasy, like *The Wizard of Oz*; or the carefree
lives of the very rich, as in screwball comedies—but escape is not their main
purpose. In many popular standards of the period, a song about frustrated
love can stand in for other forms of unhappiness, providing an emotional
catharsis, a temporary resolution, a satisfying moment of uplift. They take
us "somewhere over the rainbow," to a land where lowering clouds are dispelled, "where troubles melt like lemon drops" and wishes might come true.

This may account for the power of the male torch songs that Bing Crosby sang in the darkest days of the early thirties, melancholy numbers like "I Apologize" and "Just One More Chance." Crosby was the most popular entertainer of the decade, when his best work ranged from the stark social protest of "Brother, Can You Spare a Dime?" to the sense of vulnerability evoked in "Dancing in the Dark." The latter, a great 1931 ballad by Howard Dietz and Arthur Schwartz, is a song about a community of two surrounded by a great darkness, a moment of tenuous joy whose backdrop is impermanence and insecurity, "the wonder of *why* we're here . . . and gone."

The arts in the 1930s at once deflected people from their problems and gave them vicarious experiences, an alternate world, that could help them bear up. This was as true for timely, topical stories as for seemingly escapist fare. We read *The Grapes of Wrath* today, or watch the unusually faithful movie version, or look at the photographs of Walker Evans or Dorothea Lange, or listen to the songs like "Brother, Can You Spare a Dime?" not so much to document the Depression but to experience it, to understand the feelings and touch the human tragedy, full of shock, hope, pain, and plaintive longing. Paradoxically, the Depression also left us with the most buoyant, most effervescent popular culture of the twentieth century. Screwball comedies, dance films choreographed by Astaire or Busby Berkeley, folk ballets by Aaron Copland, crackerjack performances by Cary Grant and a legion of other young stars, swing music by Duke Ellington and other maestros of vastly popular big bands, or the new, streamlined consumer products by Deco designers—all these offered wit, energy, class, style, and movement (above all, movement) to people whose lives were stagnant, fearful, deprived of hope, people who often took to the road but really had nowhere to go. "Just going," one of them told an interviewer who asked about his destination.

As a song about the magic of movement, the wonder of simply being together in dark times, living in and for the moment, "Dancing in the Dark" is one of the motifs echoing through this book. And dark times they were, especially in the first half of the decade. For those of us born after 1940, the Depression seems to have unfolded in somber tones of black and white, thanks to the films and photographs that documented it. Historians have long known that the Depression did not begin suddenly with the 1929 Crash but developed like a rolling swell over a lengthy period. The agricultural sector was in depression all through the 1920s.

The stock market did lose $14 billion in value on October 29, 1929, and a full $26 billion within the next two weeks. But the economic impact spread gradually. Though precise unemployment statistics are hard to pin down, there were perhaps three million people out of work in December 1929, eight million by the winter of 1931–32, ten million by early 1932. During the punishing winter of 1932–33, just before FDR took office, a quarter of the American workforce was out of a job, up from a little over 3 percent before the Crash. Companies cut wages as well as jobs. Industrial output went down precipitously. Banks began failing in large numbers in the last two months of 1930 and continued all through 1931. By 1932–33 the whole banking system was in collapse. A bank holiday designed to shore up confidence in the financial system was Roosevelt's first order of business. Mortgage foreclosures, especially on farms, kept pace with bank failures. Some sixty thousand farmers lost their land to foreclosure between 1929 and 1933. No less than 40 percent of Mississippi's farms were on the auction block when Roosevelt was inaugurated.

In a handful of movies, novels, and works of reportage, these statistics were played out in individual lives, though many newspapers, magazines, and politicians ignored or played down what was happening. The Depression put a strain on families, undermining the breadwinner and placing more pressure on the wife to bring in money and hold the family together. Stories describe single men, whole families, and even children taking to the road when their homes, farms, or jobs have been lost. But many other stories deal with the Depression glancingly, such as the showgirls rehearsing a garish number called "We're in the Money" before the sheriff closes the production down (in *Gold Diggers of 1933*), or rich society types on a treasure hunt searching for a Forgotten Man (in *My Man Godfrey*). The first of these films concludes with one of Busby Berkeley's greatest numbers, "Remember My Forgotten Man," focusing on unemployed war veterans whose plight had drawn attention in 1932 when a veritable army of them came to Washington, demonstrated at the Capitol, and encamped on the Anacostia Flats to press for promised bonuses, only to be driven out with tear gas by troops led by General Douglas MacArthur.

Joblessness is a conduit to poverty; the shock and daily reality of poverty is the opening theme in this book. The poor became a test of our common humanity; their plight was an index to the state of society. As Caroline Bird wrote in *The Invisible Scar*, "before the Crash, it was easy for the middle classes to forget about the poor, because soon everyone was going to be rich." In addition, "the poor themselves thought they were exceptions, or victims of bad luck, or that it was true they did not deserve any better." "Before the Crash," she says, "nobody suspected how many Americans were poor."[3] The poor then were recast as heroic figures, coping with inconceivable burdens; they were not seen as hapless victims or as deficient people responsible for their own sorry state. Americans gradually came to identify with the worst off among them, but the poor also stood in for everyone else's economic anxieties. To many they showed that capitalism was doomed, that the American system had failed, including many of its cherished ideas: unbridled individualism, self-reliance, the entrepreneurial spirit, the promise of prosperity and social mobility, the open horizons once represented by the frontier, by virgin lands, and by the sheer size of the continent.

These promises had crystallized into the myth of the American Dream, a phrase that first came into common use in the 1930s, when it was also most sharply questioned. In the arts this led to a fascination with success and failure, highlighting the insecurities of the middle class rather than the destitution of the poor. With the economy in shambles and recovery ever more elusive, a dream of elegance, a longing for ease and motion, took the place of the dream of success. By the midthirties an idea of community and interdependence, a fascination with the People, along with a new faith in planning and government, began to replace the reliance on individual enterprise. In the growth of union membership, especially the industrial unions that embraced blue-collar workers, in the programs of the New Deal, in the ideals of the Popular Front, and in populist works like The Grapes of Wrath, a message of solidarity, or common responsibility for the nation's well-being, made it clear that the individual could not go it alone. We had obligations to each other, and especially to the least fortunate among us. As the historian David M. Kennedy writes, summarizing the long-term effects of the New Deal, "ever after, Americans assumed that the federal government had not merely a role, but a major responsibility, in ensuring the health of the economy and the welfare of citizens."[4] This was not how the American government had previously been seen, or had seen itself. Through agencies like the Public Works Administration and the Works Progress Administration, the New Deal also altered the very landscape of America, creating a solid infrastructure of dams, bridges, parks, roads, playgrounds, hospitals, post offices, and other public buildings, besides supporting writers, artists, musicians, and theater professionals. It made the case that providing for the welfare of individuals could benefit the well-being of the nation.

A key feature of the cultural life of the thirties was the fascination with America itself—its history and geography, its diverse population, the songs and legends of its folk culture, its heroes and social myths. If the twenties artist looked inward, many thirties artists looked socially inward, seeking neglected sources of national strength in turbulent times. They aimed for clarity, simplicity, and accessibility, qualities usually shunned by the avant-garde. Many writers moved left but the Popular Front turned them toward a "progressive" Americanism rather than a faith in revolution. Caught up in the moment, many works inspired by the social muse did not outlast the decade. Committed artists had nowhere to turn when war, postwar prosperity, cold war, and anti-Communism replaced the economic crisis and the reform mood of the Depression years. The public art of the New Deal—the vast murals, for example—did not win much respect from postwar artists, even from those who had helped execute them. ("Post Office art," the abstract expressionists would call it.) But the best of what the thirties produced in the cultural sphere proved as long-lasting as its political and economic achievements. The work of John Steinbeck, Richard Wright, Frank Capra, Cole Porter, Walker Evans, and many others gives us both a sense of the times and a sense for all times. Other enduring writers of the thirties were fully appreciated only later, including Henry Roth, Nathanael West, William Faulkner, James Agee, and Zora Neale Hurston. In exploring this body of work, I have tried to choose not only representative examples but those that continue to matter to us today. I made no effort to cover everything; this was a series of strategic choices, focusing on work that genuinely engaged me.

I've often been drawn to periods when art and social crisis come together, when politics fires the imagination and social needs call for creative solutions, yet initially I resisted writing about the 1930s. I had already done a book about the sixties: did this decade raise too many of the same issues? Besides, I wasn't born until 1940—how could I capture the pulse of the times? I soon discovered that the issues were different: it was a time of economic crisis rather than discontent amid prosperity, of the rise of fascism rather than the resistance to an unwinnable war, of concern with the dilemmas of ordinary people, not with personal liberation and self-expression. Moreover, so many others had borne witness to the "feel" of it that I could count on their testimony. But, above all, I was interested in how they assimilated the scene before them, the social anguish that could blunt or ignite the imagination. They gave Americans a collective portrait of themselves yet consoled them for all that made the picture disheartening. Artists with the pen, the brush, or the camera reported on American lives, often grimly, but also brightened American lives with restored hopes and irrepressibly high spirits. Like FDR himself, they boosted the people's morale, supplying a charge of social energy that also illuminated their works and days. They gave us an exemplary lesson in the relation between artistic expression and social purpose. Their responses should resonate with us again today as we go through the stresses and anxieties that remind us too much of the Great Depression.

—New York, January 2009

DANCING *in the* DARK

CHAPTER 1

Introduction:

DEPRESSION CULTURE

CULTURAL HISTORY IS COMMONLY SEEN as soft history, an exploration of what falls between the cracks: sensibility, moral feelings, dreams, relationships, all hard to objectify. My subject here is at once concrete—the books, the films of an era: the stories they told, the fears and hopes they expressed— and yet intangible, the look, the mood, the feel of the historical moment. Most of us think we *know* what the thirties were about. Its iconic images remain with us: apple sellers by their pushcarts, tenant farmers in their shacks, families trudging through dust clouds swirling over parched land. Like the 1960s, the thirties belong not only to history but to myth and legend.

To this day the period remains our byword for economic crisis, a historical marker of what could happen again. Every serious economic reversal since then has elicited dire comparisons to the 1930s. It was not, of course, the first economic depression. Nineteenth-century economic history is punctuated by repeated episodes of "panic," a word that suggests headlong, contagious, irrational anxiety: the Panic of 1873, the Panic of 1893–94. But it was the 1929 Crash, not the bank run of 1907, that was on everyone's mind when stocks plummeted in the fall of 1987. It remained an unspoken fear during the long, intractable recession that began in 1989 and left many Americans without jobs and with diminished hopes, a downturn that doomed the presidency of the first President Bush. Similar fears surfaced in 2007 when the housing bubble burst, leading to widespread mortgage foreclosures and explosive pressure on banking and investment firms.[1] As the credit markets dried up in 2008, there was a near-meltdown of the whole financial system, followed by a renewed fascination with every facet of the Depression and the New Deal. But these problems did not begin in 2007–08. In the preceding decades we witnessed a contraction not only of American industry but of the old sense of unlimited possibility in American life. My theme, however, is psychological and personal rather than strictly economic: not the loss of jobs but the state of mind that accompanies the lowering of economic horizons. My goal here is to explore the role of culture in reflecting and influencing how people understand their own lives and how they cope with social and economic malaise.

The mood of the Depression was defined not only by hard times and a coming world crisis but by many extraordinary attempts to cheer people up—or else to sober them up into facing what was happening. Though poor economically, the decade created a vibrant culture rich in the production of popular fantasy and trenchant social criticism. This is the split personality of Depression culture: on one hand, the effort to grapple with unprecedented economic disaster, to explain and interpret it; on the other hand, the need to get away, to create art and entertainment to distract people from their trouble, which was in the end another way of coming to terms with it. Looking at both sides of this cultural divide, we can see how closely linked they are.

Thanks to the new media created by early twentieth-century technology, the thirties proved to be a turning point in American popular culture. Radio had grown exponentially in the late 1920s. By the early 1930s it came of age, binding together audiences living far apart with shared amusements as well as anxieties. Photography, photojournalism, and newsreels provided visual images, all in stark shades of black and white, that even those great radio voices H. V. Kaltenborn from civil war Spain, Edward R. Murrow from London under siege, Orson Welles from Mars—could not convey. This was also the era that saw the consolidation of the Hollywood studio system and the classical style of American sound films. The great movie genres of the thirties the gangster movie, the horror film, the screwball comedy, the dance musical, the road movie, the social-consciousness drama, the animated cartoon—came to domi nate American filmmaking over the next decades. Significantly, they still influence the way movies are made, while the old films themselves remain objects of nostalgia or affectionate imitation.

In 1985, for example, Woody Allen looked back at the 1930s in his ingenious movie *The Purple Rose of Cairo*, a pastiche of Depression clichés that lovingly portrays the Janus-faced culture of the era. Mia Farrow is a waitress in a jerkwater town who lives out her fantasies by going to the movies, while Danny Aiello plays her unemployed husband, a blue-collar lout representing the drab and boring life she's trying to forget. Jeff Dan iels portrays a character who literally steps off the screen to add a little magic and romance to her pinched world.

If you look at the movie within the movie, the film she keeps going back to see, you'll notice Woody Allen's send-up of the fantasy itself. There are incoherent glimpses of wealthy, frivolous idlers making silly banter on movie sets designed to look like cavernous living rooms, glitzy nightclubs, or "Egyptian" tombs. This cheesy but exotic setting parodies the famous Depression idea of the careless rich living a life of pure swank and style. But Allen's movie also shows us the other side of the story: the small town so idle and empty that it looks like a picture postcard; the husband out of work, supported by a waif-like wife as he hangs out with the boys; the movie theater as the scene of communal daydreaming where ordinary people feed on escapist images of wealth, adventure, and romance.

Woody Allen was always a master at manipulating movie clichés, simplifying them, satirizing them, infusing them (like Chaplin) with his own kind of little-man pathos. Dennis Potter did the same thing for the English common man, Depression-style, in his wildly original series *Pennies from Heaven*. There Bob Hoskins played a sheet-music salesman with a bossy, repressed wife and a shy, dreamy love for the music and lyrics that light up his gray, constricted world. They're his romantic outlet as he lip-synchs his feelings to the incongruous sound of the old recordings. He looks longingly to America as the place the best songs come from, but also as the fantasy land where those songs actually come true.

Psychological studies of the Depression have shown how economic problems were complicated by emotional problems, since hard times, whatever their origin, undercut their victims' feelings of confidence, self-worth, even their sense of reality. "The Depression hurt people and maimed them permanently because it literally depressed mind and spirit," according to Caroline Bird. "Hoover chose the word 'Depression' in 1929 because it sounded less frightening than 'panic' or 'crisis,' the words that had formerly been used for economic downturns."[2] The psychological anguish was worsened by the American ethic of self-help and individualism, the remnant of a frontier mentality—the same dream of success, dignity, and opportunity that had inspired immigrants, freed slaves, and natives alike. But it made people feel responsible when their lives ran downhill. *Purple Rose* and even *Pennies from Heaven* are stories about fighting off depression, in every sense of the word. In *Purple Rose*, as in *Zelig*, Woody Allen showed a special affinity for people who feed on borrowed lives. Out of the clichés of movie fandom and Depression escapism—far less escapist than he suggests—Woody Allen fashioned a complex fable of art and life, the wounded self and the projections that help sustain it. This exploration of dream life and fantasy is indeed a Depression theme, though seen through later eyes.

As the Depression wore on, fewer people believed the assurances of America's hapless thirty-fifth president, Herbert Hoover: they saw that the economy was *not* "fundamentally sound," that prosperity was *not* "just around the corner." Despite how the public remembers him, Hoover himself was a progressive whose activist policies in combating the Depression actually paved the way for the New Deal. He was anything but aloof, but his chilly demeanor lacked empathy. He was incapable of doing what was needed to boost the nation's morale, and he resisted intervening in important areas of the economy, such as the creation of jobs. The Depression was more than a temporary setback: though the word was coined to minimize the crisis, it seemed like a betrayal of the American Dream, the deeply felt promise of American life. As individualism lost its glow, certain varieties of collectivism, including the Soviet model, became attractive to many American intellectuals, some of whom had been drawn to the Russian experiment since the 1917 revolution.

Yet this economic morass also fostered a communal feeling far more widespread than Marxism or nostalgic agrarianism. There was a growing fascination with regional culture and folklore. Exploring popular culture, Constance Rourke unearthed tall tales and legends and studied the roots of American humor; anthropologists such as Zora Neale Hurston recorded the folkways of backwater towns whose way of life would soon be threatened; Ruth Benedict's 1934 book *Patterns of Culture* became a bestseller, as did Margaret Mead's studies of growing up in Samoa and New Guinea; musicologists like Charles Seeger and John and Alan Lomax, traveling with rudimentary tape recorders, unearthed a treasure trove of folk music that had been passed on in prisons, on chain gangs, and in remote country settings. But the thirties also witnessed the momentous growth of a new kind of popular culture in America: national rather than regional, amplified by technology, creating new folkways in a country still relatively isolated from the world.

It has been forcefully argued that during the thirties more people, especially the poor, lived vicariously by turning on the radio than by going to the movies. (The movie audience actually peaked in 1946, shortly before the full arrival of television.) Woody Allen complemented his picture of the Depression in *Purple Rose* with his more autobiographical treatment of a noisy Jewish family in Brooklyn in *Radio Days*, a tribute to the role radio had played in forming a larger community out of an ethnic stew. The nightly fifteen-minute dose of the tribulations of *Amos 'n' Andy*, which was often piped into theaters—otherwise few would have gone to the movies—propelled traditional dialect humor onto a national stage. New York's mayor, the inimitable Fiorello La Guardia, himself a salad of ethnic differences, read the comic strips over the radio on Sunday mornings. Franklin Roosevelt's fireside chats gave people a feeling of intimate connection with their more activist government; radio, by intervening so widely into people's lives, thus became the electronic equivalent of the New Deal. It eased their anxieties and contributed to lifting their spirits; it helped fashion the nation's collective mind.

For all its roots in minstrel humor, *Amos 'n' Andy* was an ongoing epic of daily life, setting off the practical man against the quixotic dreamer whose schemes, especially moneymaking schemes, were always going awry. Behind the laugh lines, it was a program about ordinary people trying to get by. This was typical of Depression "escapism": reflecting people's deeply felt concerns yet also channeling and neutralizing them, spinning out problems to show they could somehow be worked out. This was not so different from the way Roosevelt himself, despite his patrician tones, put a warm human spin on the news of the world. He spoke with authority but simply and directly, as if to each listener individually. By showing he cared, he fostered a renewal of hope after the deepening despair of the Hoover years. While giving a human touch to the new federal role in people's lives, he reaffirmed traditional values. Taking full advantage of the new media, he helped navigate the nation through this troubled decade.

Though movie newsreels, like illustrated magazines such as *Life*, were important vehicles of information in the thirties, movies were inherently a fictional medium. With their dreamlike qualities, which film aestheticians had long emphasized, they offered appealing fantasies to counter social and economic malaise. But the myth of the thirties was far more than the sum of its movie images and radio sounds. A legion of gifted photographers helped create the indelible galaxy of images that we'll always associate with hard times: the urban and rural poor, the bread lines and the homeless, families camped out in Hoovervilles at the edge of towns and cities; southern chain gangs and haggard but dignified sharecroppers. Epic scenes from the Dust Bowl are part of our permanent shorthand for rural poverty and natural desolation. Much that we know about the human spirit in adversity can still be seen in Dorothea Lange's "Migrant Mother," the great 1936 photograph of a woman whose brow is furrowed like tractored-out land, with a look on her face more pensive and distant than pained or troubled. Two children, with their back to the camera, have nuzzled into her shoulders, and the bony fingers at her chin seemed to extend from some armature sculpted to support the weight of her head. Like migrants in other Lange photographs, she is all angles, a zigzag of intersecting lines. Anxious but reserved and self-contained, she speaks to our humanity without soliciting sympathy. Yet she has a look of distress, of entrapment, of someone with her back to the wall.

As we look back at it today, the Depression is a study in contrasts. At one extreme the "look" of the thirties is in the flowing Art Deco lines of the new Chrysler Building, the Radio City Music Hall, the sets of Astaire-Rogers musicals like *Top Hat, Swing Time,* and *Shall We Dance.* At the other end is the work done by photographers like Lange, Walker Evans, Marion Post Wolcott, Russell Lee, Arthur Rothstein, and Ben Shahn for Roy Stryker's photography unit of the Farm Security Administration, conceived as a way of bringing home the unthinkable pain of rural poverty to urban Americans. If the FSA photographs give us the naturalistic art of the Depression at its most humane, the Astaire musicals convey an elegant, sophisticated world in which the Depression is barely a distant rumor. Yet the two are equally characteristic of the period.

The FSA photographs, along with Pare Lorentz's government-sponsored documentaries *The Plow That Broke the Plains* (1936) and *The River* (1937), with their images of drought, flood, and other rural calamities, helped Gregg Toland (the cinematographer) and John Ford (the director) give authenticity to their 1940 screen adaptation of Steinbeck's *The Grapes of Wrath.* (Indeed, the poetic narration and visual beauty of the Lorentz films actually influenced Steinbeck as he was writing the original novel.) The Ford film, in turn, fixed the iconography of the thirties for future generations. We can see its long afterlife in films like Hal Ashby's 1976 biography of Woody Guthrie, *Bound for Glory.*

Surprisingly, this look was more meaningful to posterity than to the people of the period. In his fine book *Documentary Expression and Thirties America,* William Stott described how the government, business leaders, and even economists suppressed or sweetened the unpleasant facts during the early years of the Depression. Until *Fortune* published an article in September 1932 called "No One Has Starved," establishment newspapers, magazines, and radio programs downplayed or ignored the Depression and portrayed the country, as Hoover himself did, in business-as-usual terms.[3] For years the Depression was underreported; it went against the grain of laissez-faire optimism, a widespread belief, revived in the 1980s and 1990s, that the system was self-correcting.

This virtual blackout of bad news gave impetus to the documentary movement, to radical journalism, and to independent films like King

Vidor's pastoral fable *Our Daily Bread* (1934), which shows the old American individualism giving way to a utopian sense of community on a Russian-style collective farm. A few years later, an upbeat *Life* magazine, founded in 1936 as the vehicle for a new photojournalism, complained that "depressions are hard to see because they consist of things not happening, of business not being done."[4] Needless to say, *Life* published none of the stomach-churning pictures of rural misery taken by its star photographer, Margaret Bourke-White, in 1936 and 1937. They appeared instead in a book she wrote with Erskine Caldwell, *You Have Seen Their Faces*, whose accusing title reminds us that a great deal of suffering, poverty, and unemployment *was* invisible, except to those who cared to look for it, and look *at* it. In his second inaugural address, on January 20, 1937, FDR described it this way:

> I see millions of families trying to live on incomes so meager that the pall of family disaster hangs over them day by day.
>
> I see millions whose daily lives in city and on farm continue under conditions labeled indecent by a so-called polite society half a century ago.
>
> I see millions denied education, recreation, and the opportunity to better their lot and the lot of their children.
>
> I see millions lacking the means to buy the products of farm and factory and by their poverty denying work and productiveness to many other millions.
>
> I see one-third of a nation ill-housed, ill-clad, ill-nourished.[5]

Trying to grasp the essential spirit of the thirties would seem to be a hopeless task. How can one era have produced both Woody Guthrie and Rudy Vallee, both the Rockettes high-stepping at the Radio City Music Hall and the Okies on their desperate trek toward the pastures of plenty in California? To readers of the journalist Eugene Lyons's 1941 bestseller it was the "Red Decade." Revisionist historians like Warren Susman and Loren Baritz countered by drawing attention to the conservative heartland of the middle class, with its deep economic fears yet also its interest in sports, mystery novels, self-improvement, and mass entertainment. Liberal historians such as Daniel Aaron, James B. Gilbert, and Richard Pells focused on the intellectual history of the thirties, analyzing the radicalism of the era in terms that reach back to prewar socialism and progressivism. Other writers, in the popular tradition of Frederick Lewis Allen's best-selling *Only Yesterday* (1931) and *Since Yesterday* (1940) or Robert and Helen Merrell Lynd's *Middletown* (1929) and *Middletown in Transition* (1937), concentrated on the social history of everyday life. Still others (like Arthur Schlesinger Jr. in the three volumes of his *Age of Roosevelt*) centered on the administrative and political history of the New Deal and the dramatic figure of Roosevelt himself, whose dominating presence became a force of mythic proportions. More recently, feminist scholars emphasized the unsung role of women writers in bringing gender issues, family histories, and deep personal emotions into the committed fiction and journalism of the era. Radical scholars have assiduously excavated the proletarian writing of the 1930s and explored the culture of the Popular Front, in part because they feel it has been unjustly neglected but also because they identify with its political direction.[6] My own approach in this book is to focus on unusually complex, enduring works for what they reveal about the age—books, films, music, and photographs that speak for their times yet still speak intimately to us today.

When I was in college in the late 1950s, the thirties appeared to us in the hazy distance as a golden age when writers, artists, and intellectuals developed strong political commitments and enlisted literature on the side of the poor and the destitute. We were able to mythologize the thirties because we had never read much of what was written then. (Most of it was long out of print.) But we managed to dig up records by Paul Robeson, Woody Guthrie, even the Red Army Chorus, all red meat for armchair revolutionaries. We recoiled from the blandness and repressive limits of the political culture of the fifties, and looked back wistfully at the excited ideological climate of the thirties, about which we knew next to nothing.

Years later, when I finally looked into some of the ideological debates of the thirties, whose radical intensity I had admired from afar, I was horrified by the brutality of many sectarian polemics; they seemed more concerned with doctrinal purity than with promoting any real social change. For all their dialectical ingenuity, the Stalinists, Trotskyists, and other left-wing factions seemed deaf to the free play of ideas; their work breathed an atmosphere of personal aggression and fundamentalist dogma. Yet this was also a period when writers as well as photographers keenly pursued an interest in the backwaters of American life: the travail of the immigrant, the slum, and the ghetto, the failures of the American Dream, and, above all, the persistence of poverty and inequality amid plenty—a subject with few but significant parallels in earlier American literature.[7]

The discovery of poverty had been a great theme of the naturalist writers of the 1890s. It had roots even earlier in the nineteenth century, in some of the lesser-known works of Herman Melville and the sensational popular literature on the "mysteries of the city," with its teeming social underground. In the nineties this fascination was summed up in the title of Jacob Riis's landmark work of documentary muckraking, *How the Other Half Lives* (1890). In the same year William Dean Howells published a great fictional study of class and social conflict in New York, *A Hazard of New Fortunes*. The protagonists of both works are social tourists in the best sense, curious about how poverty and plenty live side by side in the great metropolis. Howells had moved down from Boston to live and work in a more vibrant modern city. Riis was a Danish immigrant who became a journalist and followed the police in their raids in New York's most dangerous neighborhoods, such as the notorious Five Points. Training himself to become a photographer, he took advantage of new flash techniques to take pictures in dark, crowded rooms and dank cellars, often terrifying his hapless subjects and once, inadvertently, setting fire to their digs. He used these crude but powerful photographs to give slide lectures, which may have influenced writers, including Stephen Crane, but also to produce a text-and-pictures book, *How the Other Half Lives*, that anticipates one of the main genres of social reportage in the 1930s. In some ways this is where our story begins, in a city of immigrants, a turbulent social cauldron at the turn of the twentieth century, an era well remembered by the writers of the 1930s.

WORLD'S HIGHEST STANDARD OF LIVING

There's no way
like the
American Way

PART 1

DISCOVERING POVERTY

CHAPTER 2

The Tenement and the World:
IMMIGRANT LIVES

IN THE 1880S AND 1890S, especially after the financial panic of 1893 sent the nation reeling, a new generation of writers emerged in the wake of social changes that caused widespread human misery. The migration of young people from farms to cities, the arrival of wave after wave of immigrants, the working conditions of industrial and sweatshop labor, the exploitation of women, children, and foreign-born labor, the overcrowded slums of the

rapidly growing cities, and the hardscrabble lives of small farmers—
all these helped inspire a different kind of literature, brazen, frank, and
unsettling. Following the example of Dickens and the industrial novelists
of the 1840s and 1850s, a handful of American realists like William Dean
Howells, Stephen Crane, Hamlin Garland, Frank Norris, and Theodore
Dreiser brought home the sufferings, hopes, and crushing disappointments in ordinary American lives.

The Great Depression that followed the stock market crash of 1929
proved even more severe and enduring than the economic crisis of the
1890s. It too began with a financial panic, but this Depression centered
not on working conditions but on *non*-working conditions, since a quarter of America's labor force was out of work by the winter of 1932–33;
not on the living conditions in slums or on farms but on the disruption
of living conditions, with tenement evictions, farm foreclosures, and
the dislocation of families as men and boys took to the road. Above
all, it centered on hunger and fear, the nagging hunger of the poor-
est Americans, and the sense of insecurity that took hold of the lives
of those just above them. "Like a cold bay fog, fear of the bread line
drifted up into the middle class," wrote one historian.[1] At the edges
of many towns and cities, tin shacks and makeshift tents sprang up to
house the homeless and unemployed, including those who, after the
dry summer of 1934, were displaced from their farms by drought and
dust, by bankers and bailiffs.

The human cost of the Depression dawned on writers only gradually.
At first some of them were elated by the collapse of a business civilization
whose values they had long despised. "To writers and artists of my generation who had grown up in the Big Business era," the critic Edmund Wilson wrote later, ". . . these years were not depressing but stimulating. One
couldn't help being exhilarated at the sudden unexpected collapse of that
stupid gigantic fraud. It gave us a new sense of freedom, and it gave us a
new sense of power to find ourselves still carrying on while the bankers,
for a change, were taking a beating."[2] Feeling they were witnessing the
imminent demise of capitalism, many writers moved left, some because
their working-class origins helped them identify with the dispossessed,
others because they saw socialism or Communism as the only serious
force for radical change, still others because it was the fashionable thing

to do: they went where the action was. A few like Mike Gold and John Dos Passos had become radicals even before the Crash.

As in the 1890s, the new radicalism most influenced the work of fiction writers, since the social novel could give a powerful actuality to pressing public problems. In periods of economic crisis, fiction falls in with journalism and photography as a way of documenting human misery and sometimes sentimentalizing its victims. We don't know for certain whether Stephen Crane was inspired by the muckraking articles and slide lectures of Jacob Riis or the illustrated reportage in *How the Other Half Lives*. Yet Crane's first novel, *Maggie: A Girl of the Streets*, and his sketches of homeless men seeking shelter in "An Experiment in Misery" and "The Men in the Storm" give us a Riis-like ethnography, complete with sharp visual impressions, of the squalid Lower East Side slums.

Stephen Crane was too ironic to become socially committed; he was primarily an adventurer whose cool detachment heightened his feeling for extreme situations, including the condition of the poor. But like Jack London a few years later, he felt he had to experience poverty at first hand in order to understand it. In "An Experiment in Misery," a Dantean descent into the lower depths, a young man separates himself from his comforts and spends a night among society's outcasts in a dark and foul-smelling flophouse. Guided only by a wretched beggar who has the wild look of an assassin, he comes to understand their hopelessness and degradation from the inside looking out.

From their point of view, which he now feels himself, "social position, comfort, the pleasures of living were unconquerable kingdoms." As he emerges into the morning light, the skyscrapers around him suggest "a nation forcing its regal head into the clouds, throwing no downward glances; in the sublimity of its aspirations ignoring the wretches who may flounder at its feet." Even the noise of city sounds becomes "a confusion of strange tongues, babbling heedlessly; it was the clink of coin, the voice of the city's hopes, which were to him no hopes." What began for him as an experiment, an act of social tourism propelled by little more than curiosity, has become a heavy burden, a sense of desperation he cannot easily shake off.[3]

Despite Crane's own aesthetic distance, he became a prototype for thirties writers drawn uneasily to confront the hunger, poverty, lassitude, squalor, and fear that festered during the Depression. A host of talented writers and photographers, from Edmund Wilson to James Agee and Walker Evans, took to the road to see how ordinary people were coping with hard times. Their travels and reportage bolstered the programs of the New Deal, which sometimes funded their efforts. As we shall later see, even poets, whose writing is usually more lyrical, private, and introspective, signed on for social movements that drastically affected their work.

Some writers who had grown up in poverty, such as Michael Gold, Henry Roth, and Tillie Olsen, refracted the concerns of the Depression by writing about their parents' difficult lives. They recalled the tenements, farms, and sweatshops of their childhood, taking readers back to the challenges once faced by immigrants with a precarious toehold in the new world. Others like John Steinbeck focused on the conditions of the moment: drought, hunger, crop failure, exploitation. Richard Wright did both, writing about present-day Chicago in *Native Son* and the Deep South of his childhood in *Black Boy*. Some like Gold, Steinbeck, and Wright tilted toward naturalism and protest, portraying poverty as a social pathology, with their characters as its hapless victims. Others, deeply influenced by the modernist sensibility of the 1920s, were more engaged with individual lives and families within a culture of poverty, including the Lower East Side of Henry Roth in *Call It Sleep*, the rural South of Faulkner's *As I Lay Dying* and *Light in August*, the sharecropping world of James Agee and Walker Evans's *Let Us Now Praise Famous Men*, and the all-black Florida communities in Zora Neale Hurston's novels and stories. Where one group of writers directs attention to how people are suffering, how they are exploited and dehumanized, the others explore the psychology of individuals and their resistance to being stereotyped as victims rather than autonomous agents; they point to the pockets of humanity and community that the poor can create even under deprived conditions. But these contrasting approaches overlap, for both belong to the 1930s' fascination with the lower depths, with people rendered invisible by our almost religious faith in American prosperity, equality, and social mobility. In the following pages I have paired some of these observers to show how they complement and contradict each other, demonstrating the great range of their interest in a population whose vulnerability reflected a whole society's fears.

Michael Gold's Book of Nightmares

In everything but his lifelong loyalty to the party, Michael Gold was the representative Communist intellectual of the twentieth century. Born Itshok Isaac Granich to an immigrant family on the Lower East Side in 1893, he Christianized his name to Irwin Granich until about 1920 when he began writing as Michael Gold, a name he borrowed from an old veteran of Lincoln's army. Unlike other American writers who flirted with Communism only at the height of the Depression, Gold came to the party early and stayed late. He died in 1967.

Converted to radicalism when he heard the fiery Elizabeth Gurley Flynn at a Union Square rally in 1914, he bought his first copy of the insurgent journal *The Masses*, began to contribute poems and stories, became an anarchist and got to know the whole Village bohemian world of Max Eastman, Floyd Dell, and John Reed, studied briefly at Harvard, fled to Mexico to avoid Wilson's draft, and returned to join the Communist Party around 1920. While Gold was away, *The Masses* was closed down by the government for opposing the war; its editors were put on trial twice in 1918 for conspiring to obstruct recruitment, charges that resulted each time in a hung jury.

The defunct magazine quickly had a successor, *The Liberator*, its title inspired by the abolitionist newspaper of William Lloyd Garrison. At first it tried to revive *The Masses*'s style of irreverent, freewheeling radicalism despite the impact of the Bolshevik triumph in the Soviet Union. Socialism now had a geographical base, even an imperfect image of the promised land, but not yet a monolithic orthodoxy. Gold was an independent radical, not a commissar when he became an editor of the *The Liberator* in 1920. He soon published a dithyrambic, Whitmanesque manifesto, "Towards Proletarian Art," that expressed an almost mystical affinity for the common man, the lowly bottom dogs of society, a commitment that went deeper in him than Marxism or any other ideology.

In many ways it is a callow document, youthful, poetic, immature, eulogizing the Revolution as a form of pantheistic reverence for life. The text breathes an Emersonian euphoria rather than a Marxian logic. ("The Social Revolution today is not the mere political movement artists despise it as. It is Life at its fullest and noblest. It is the religion of the masses, articulate at last.")[4] But Gold's deterministic message stood Emerson on his head, for he saw the artist as a creature of society, the articulate voice of the mass of men who spoke through him, the conditions that produced him. When Gold talks about the tenement world he came from, his woolly, lyrical language takes on a momentary authenticity:

> I was born in a tenement. . . . The sky above the air-shafts was all my sky; and the voices of the tenement neighbors in the airshaft were the voices of all my world. . . .
>
> All I know of life I learned in the tenement. I saw love there in an old mother who wept for her sons. I saw courage there in a sick worker who went to the factory every morning. I saw beauty in little children playing in the dim hallways, and despair and hope and hate incarnated in the simple figures of those who lived there with me. The tenement is in my blood. When I think it is the tenement thinking. When I hope it is the tenement hoping, I am not an individual; I am all that the tenement group poured into me during those early years of my spiritual travail. (64–65)

At this stage of his life Gold, though already a Communist, was more a literary figure than the political person he would subsequently become—first as an editor of *The New Masses*, then (after 1933) as a workhorse *Daily Worker* columnist, the most reliable and vituperative of Stalinist hatchet men. But the Gold of 1921 was still the bohemian, a Greenwich Village original who was writing experimental plays for Eugene O'Neill's Provincetown Players. After he suffered a nervous breakdown and left the editorship of *The Liberator* in the early twenties, he objected strongly when the magazine was turned over to the Communist Party and when he heard that one of the editors was giving up literary work to become a party functionary.

Soon Gold was in correspondence with Upton Sinclair about starting up a new magazine that would be genuinely literary, that would print proletarian prose and dredge up mute, inglorious Miltons from the depths of the working class. In 1930, as editor of *The New Masses*, he attacked the party publishing house for putting out dull doctrinal works in economics rather than taking chances on the creative outpourings of the masses. At this point—the year of *Jews without Money*, his only successful book—

Gold was a proletarian writer and critic rather than a Communist Party spokesman. The stereotyped image of him as a venomously obedient apparatchik scarcely fits the Gold of this period.[5]

The later Gold was undoubtedly a nasty propagandist who swallowed every shift and betrayal, every violent twist of policy the party sent his way. Thanks to these sharp turns, nearly all his writer friends from the teens and twenties (when he knew everyone) fell off the train of History. And Gold was there to wield a particularly brutal style of invective to castigate them all as renegades; indeed, as more writers left, apostasy became one of his chief obsessions.

With his tough-guy manner and hard-boiled, telegraphic prose, Gold could have become an American Brecht, but he lacked the German playwright's instinct for survival and his canny ironic temperament, which complicated every proletarian pose into an avant-garde gesture. In his trajectory from expressionist playwright to East German institution, Brecht held on to his West German publisher and kept his eye trained ruthlessly on his craft and his career. At some cost, he evaded the paralyzing orthodoxies that enveloped Gold and snuffed out his artistic energy.

For all his gruff, truculent demeanor—like Brecht, he kept himself rough and dirty on principle—Gold was sentimental about the tenement, sentimental about art, and sentimental about the Revolution. But only the first of these offered him a real subject, though it belonged to his distant past. Gold's first sketch toward a Lower East Side novel came out in 1917 in *The Masses*. Pieces of *Jews without Money* appeared in magazines during the 1920s, at the height of Gold's career as an imaginative writer. Additional sketches, as good as anything in the book, appeared as a series of ten newspaper columns as late as 1959. Gold's childhood lasted him a lifetime; the New York slums of the turn of the century became his imaginative capital, his obsession, the ground of his religious attachment to the Revolution. He became a thirties writer by excavating the poverty, emotional misery, and millenarian hopes of his own past. Gold singlehandedly shaped an agenda for the writers of the new decade.

On the last page of his novel, describing his sudden conversion to Communism, he addresses the Revolution as a divinity that had dispelled his dark spirits and answered to his inchoate messianic longings: "O workers' Revolution, you brought hope to me, a lonely, suicidal boy. You are the true Messiah. You will destroy the East Side when you come, and build there a garden for the human spirit."[6] Others who had grown up poor shunned even the memory of poverty and sought comfort and security. For Gold the commitment to revolution was his way of keeping faith with his early life, remaining true to the mother who fought boss and landlord and pawnbroker to protect her brood. "She would have stolen or killed for us," he says. "She would have let a railroad train run over her body if it could have helped us." This leads to a revealing, overheated apostrophe: "Mother! Momma! I am still bound to you by the cords of birth. I cannot forget you. I must remain faithful to the poor because I cannot be faithless to you!" (158). The ghetto, with its dreadful miseries and deep communal loyalties, held the key to his radicalism; his intense emotion, sometimes hard to take, was the engine that gave it literary power.

Just as the Lower East Side represented everything the revolution promised to obliterate, its horrors justified everything done in the revolution's name. When Trotsky was in favor, Gold wrote about him as the Leonardo of the revolution. After his fall Gold confessed, "I, for one, can shed no tears for him; I care for something greater than Trotsky's fate; the proletarian revolution" (Folsom, 194). Telling the truth was only the first casualty of this overriding dedication. Some would say that Gold's work is fatally damaged by the ethical morass into which this blind faith led him; most of it is. But until the last past page, Gold was able to keep outright politics and ideology out of *Jews without Money*. He turned his recollections into grimly effective vignettes without belaboring their message. To an unusual extent for a Communist writer, he let the material speak for itself.

Despite its sociological title, the book has the power of a series of hallucinations, especially in the opening chapters. Though *Jews without Money* was the first of the proletarian novels of the thirties, and one of the very few to succeed commercially—it went through eleven printings in the first nine months after publication—Gold's feverish prose set his work apart from other proletarian writers, who mimicked the flatness of Hemingway without his implied depths of feeling.

We can hardly avoid being prejudiced against the later Gold as an apologist for party hacks and progressive, "enlightened" murderers. But the tenement world of *Jews without Money* imposes itself with the same urgency that enabled it to dominate him. From the opening sentence— "I can never forget the East Side street where I lived as a boy" (13)—we feel that a demon has gripped Gold by the throat and forced him to testify. In Gold's apprentice sketch for *The Masses* in 1917 this material was safely distanced and stiffly literary, as if Gold had been trying to validate an undignified subject with polished writing. In *Jews without Money* this literary texture is stripped away like superfluous insulation.

When his memories take possession of him, Gold, like the old epic writers, becomes the vessel of his muse; he slips into the second person, addressing his characters directly as if he had raised them from the grave. One chapter begins with just such a summoning:

> Joey Cohen! You who were sacrificed under the wheels of a horse car, I see you again, Joey! I see your pale face, so sensitive despite its childish grime and bruises. (50)

At another point young Mikey Gold (named for Gold's pen name, not for Granich) actually *dreams* the world that surrounds him, as all the tenement families spend a stifling summer night on the roof:

> I woke one hot choking night and saw it all like a bad dream. I saw the mounds of pale stricken flesh tossing against an unreal city. I was frightened, and didn't know where I was. Then I cried, and wondered what would happen if I jumped off the roof. My mother heard me, and soothed me, and I went back to sleep. (126)

In Gold's hallucinatory vision, the immigrant families squashed together on the airless roof are like the mass of blighted humanity in the ghetto itself—"mounds of pale stricken flesh tossing against an unreal city." Gold's memories, with their echoes of Baudelaire and T. S. Eliot, are vivid but emblematic; they yield a half-demented poetry of human wretchedness. Only the gentle strength of the tenement mother can soothe the suicidal fears of the morbid, tormented youth.

These brutal snapshots of street and tenement life are pretty much all that happens in *Jews without Money*, for the book is less a story than a series of dreamlike memories leading to a final awakening. We move from the whores and the street gangs to the dreadful decline of Gold's father, a gregarious storyteller and hapless businessman, who gradually succumbs to lead poisoning after years of work as a housepainter. As he fades, Gold's mother emerges as the strong one, the family breadwinner, an instinctive radical who wills Gold her toughness as his father wills him his imaginative gift. But all this is less important than the social material and the atmosphere: the impassioned, exclamatory way Gold recaptures his poverty-ridden childhood.

Even if we grant, as few critics have done, that Gold created a powerful style of his own, a style sharply different from documentary naturalism or socialist realism, this doesn't explain why *Jews without Money*, set at the turn of the century, should become a seminal text of the Depression years. Though the book was completed by the end of 1928, well before the Crash, its appearance early in 1930 helped place poverty, ethnicity, and human misery on the cultural agenda, just as the Depression was putting them on the political agenda. The patrician Henry James, after his return visit to America in 1904, reported on his tour of the East Side with a fascinated horror. He had been away for twenty years, and this teeming polyglot world was not the America he recognized, but he saw it prophetically as the face of the future. By 1930 that future had arrived, and, as the critic Marcus Klein argued in *Foreigners*, cultural outsiders like Gold were better equipped to write about it than the sheltered scions of New York or New England gentility. The ghetto of 1900, once barely visible to the larger world, suddenly spoke volumes to the acute social distress of 1930.

Poverty was an alien subject for most middle-class authors. With the exception of possessed writers like Dickens or Hardy, those who had grown up poor preferred to forget their early struggles and humiliations. The persistence of want amid the blessings of progress is readily forgotten yet continually rediscovered—by Melville, Hugo, and Eugène Sue, along with Carlyle, Marx and Engels, in the mid-nineteenth century; by Zola and Gissing in the 1880s; Jacob Riis, Stephen Crane, and Hamlin Garland in the 1890s; Theodore Dreiser, Jack London, and Upton Sinclair in the first years of the twentieth century; and, much later, by empathetic social observers like Oscar Lewis and Michael Harrington amid the affluence of the late 1950s.

The poor may always be with us, but we seem to notice them at thirty-year intervals, like spoilers at a party for people of good conscience. The Depression was one of those moments of visibility, when many in the middle class were impoverished, too, and often proved less able to deal with it than the chronic poor. The specter of poverty, the fear of falling, haunted the decade. As a witness from the lower depths, Michael Gold was a forerunner of Depression writing who had nurtured angry memories and a lonely radicalism through the postwar boom. In a tribute to one of his favorite writers, Upton Sinclair, Gold found in his books

> a faint trace of the Protestant minister that I can't enjoy. It is my only quarrel with this great writer. I do not relish these easy victories of virtue. There is nobility in the revolutionary camp; there is also gloom, dirt, and disorder. . . . I dislike pictures of cheerful and virtuous poverty such as Upton often draws. (Folsom, 169)

Exposing the gloom, dirt, and disorder bred by poverty became Gold's specialty, his mission, his "own obsession," he called it. The stalwart workers and happy peasants of Soviet film and fiction were not his glass of tea.

As Gold was writing, the Jewish ghetto was already being burnished with nostalgia by many who had done all they could to get away from it. This process has accelerated ever since. Gold stressed the opposite, the fifty-cent-a-night whores who swallowed carbolic acid, the bedbugs that even a Jewish mother could not eliminate. After being told by his pious mother that God made everything in the world, he wonders,

> Did God make bedbugs? One steaming hot night I couldn't sleep for the bedbugs. They have a peculiar nauseating smell of their own; it is the smell of poverty. They crawl slowly and pompously, bloated with blood, and the touch and smell of these parasites wakens every nerve to disgust.

Gold adds a rare sociological comment, in parenthesis, as if to supply his recollections with a theme, a justification:

> (Bedbugs are what people mean when they say: Poverty. There are enough pleasant superficial liars writing in America. I will write a truthful book of Poverty; I will mention bedbugs.)

A paragraph later Gold concludes by hinting at the radical implications he will hammer home at the end of the book. His mother ("as clean as any German housewife") repeatedly changes the sheets, sprays the mattresses, douses the beds with kerosene, but to no avail. Tinkering and reform were not enough; on her own the individual could do little to improve the conditions of the ghetto:

> The bedbugs lived and bred in the rotten walls of the tenement, with the rats, fleas, roaches; the whole rotten structure needed to be torn down; a kerosene bottle would not help. (71–72)

"The whole rotten structure needed to be torn down"—not a fashionable view today, even of urban renewal, but it became one of the battle cries of the 1930s. Many other episodes were parables pointing in the same direction, toward the revolutionary turn on the last page of the book, which critics have always dismissed as a deus ex machina. But Gold's conversion was foreshadowed on every page. He wasn't a writer who adopted revolutionary ideas when they were fashionable or abandoned them when they had gone out of fashion. The revolution was betrayed, but not for him. The pogroms of Europe were still buzzing in his ear, and new horrors were already on the horizon. The Jew as victim had merged in his mind with the proletarian as victim. His memories of the ghetto were reshaped into a hatred of capitalism. He had seen the poison of poverty make young people desperate, middle-aged people old and sick before their time, and old people grotesque and deformed. The hope of revolution had allayed the fever in his own blood.

Jews without Money could easily be renamed, after Sherwood Anderson, "The Book of the Grotesque" (the original title of *Winesburg, Ohio*), but Gold's repulsively vivid characters are much more colorful and exotic than Anderson's small-town eccentrics. "He was a bum in moldy, wrinkled clothes saturated like a foul kitchenrag with grease," as Gold describes the man who soon tries to molest little Joey Cohen. "His rusty yellow face was covered with sores. He was gruesome. He was like a corpse in the first week of decomposition" (58). Gold's old Hebrew teacher fares no better: "The man was a walking, belching symbol of the decay of orthodox Judaism. What could such as he teach anyone? He was ignorant as a rat. He was a foul smelling, emaciated beggar who had never read anything" (65). A newly arrived immigrant who freeloads on Gold's family, Fyfka the Miser, seems hardly distinguishable from an animal:

> He was squat, with a glum black muzzle, and nostrils like a camel. A thatch of black uncombed hair fell down his forehead, over small eyes, too bright and too morbid, like a baboon's. One arm was twisted, and he never smiled, he never said a pleasant word, he was always scratching himself, he never cleaned his nose. (74)

These three characters aren't entirely representative: all are sadistic, ungenerous, warped in their sexuality—pure products of poverty and ignorance, even in their physical deformities. A certain sameness, a badgering insistence, creeps into these portraits, as if Gold, with uncontrolled disgust, were exorcising figments of his childhood as Gothic nightmare. At other moments a vein of tenderness and sentiment infuses all this ugliness with lyricism, as in Gold's apostrophe to the rare open lots that gave children a respite from the claustral tenements:

> Shabby old ground, ripped like a battlefield by workers' picks and shovels, little garbage dump lying forgotten in the midst of tall tenements. O home of all the twisted junk, rusty baby carriages, lumber, bottles, boxes, moldy pants and dead cats of the neighborhood— every one spat and held the nostrils when passing you. But in my mind you still blaze in a halo of childish romance. No place will ever seem as wonderful again. (46)

Perhaps on the basis of such passages, the few able literary critics who remember Gold attack him as a sentimentalist and bad stylist. ("Gold was a writer whom almost any student of literary style can criticize," wrote Allen Guttmann in *The Jewish Writer in America*.)[7] To me Gold's work at such heightened moments takes on some Homeric qualities he assimilated from two of his favorite writers, Whitman and Tolstoy. From Tolstoy he learned simplicity, directness, a preternatural clarity of outline. (He always insisted that Tolstoy was Hemingway's true teacher.) From Whitman he borrowed the direct Homeric apostrophe, the rolling catalog, the tenderness toward creatures and things that, like this *unforgotten* junkyard, become emblematic of all despised rejects who make up the ghetto.

Despite these influences, Gold does not sound much like any writer before or since. When I first tried reading him in the truncated edition Avon published in paperback soon after the publisher's success with Henry Roth's *Call It Sleep* in 1964, I was put off by what seemed like a lack of texture: the staccato paragraphs, the flashing succession of sharp little pictures that are meant to feel raw and authentic—as if a prose less jagged, more fluent, would inevitably have been less honest. ("All these things happened," he says, after describing the prostitutes of Chrystie Street. "They were part of our daily lives, not lurid articles in a Sunday newspaper" [35].)

Later I came to realize that his abrupt, impacted sentences and paragraphs were long-limbed lines of prose poetry, overheated, feverishly autobiographical, charged with hyperbole for all their would-be realism. Gold was the missing link between the plebeian Whitman, whom he idolized, and the youthful Allen Ginsberg, who must have read him as a Young Communist in the 1930s or early 1940s. Once this is noticed, it's hard to imagine the impassioned, surreal language of poems like *Howl* or "America" or "Sunflower Sutra" without thinking of certain slightly nutty passages like this one in *Jews without Money*:

America is so rich and fat, because it has eaten the tragedy of millions of immigrants.

To understand this, you should have seen at twilight, after the day's work, one of our pick and shovel wops watering his can of beloved flowers. Brown peasant, son of thirty generations of peasants, in a sweaty undershirt by a tenement window, feeling the lost poetry. Uprooted! Lost! Betrayed! (41–42)

Ginsberg, like Gold, was a Jewish visionary touched by messianic hopes, a reader of Whitman and Blake mesmerized by the American junkyard and its outcast inhabitants. Ginsberg's long lines echo Gold's staccato paragraphs and exclamatory fervor. As a child of the postwar era, son of a mad Communist mother, Ginsberg looked at the revolution not as the promised redeemer but as the God that failed; like the elder Blake, he looked instead to a revolution in consciousness, fostered by visionary experiences and sublime writing. He also leavened his dithyrambs with the kind of humor that, in Gold's case, was strictly unintentional, buried in an agonized solemnity.

For Gold, America was still essentially the golden land immigrants dreamed about, a country that could yet fulfill its own idea. Tom Paine, Whitman, Lincoln, and Jack London were as important to him as Marx and Lenin. But there was also the other America he knew from the tenement, the one he wanted the world to notice and change. ("My parents hated all this filth. But it was America, one had to accept it" [30].) For him the uprooted, the lost, the betrayed were still real people in a social landscape, memories that could not be put by; for Ginsberg, the postwar writer, they are figures in a personal rhetoric, elements in a quest for spiritual self-realization.

For Gold and his family, still pressed by the struggle for survival, poverty is a curse, the ghetto a trap. "The city is locked against me! I am a man in a trap!" his father groans in his humiliating slide from businessman to housepainter to street peddler, and from health to illness, as he is no longer able to support his family. For Ginsberg and his Beat friends, poverty was a set of voluntary vows, the rejection of a money culture; ironically, Gold's decrepit Lower East Side was their chosen refuge from consumerism, family life, and upward mobility.[8]

Gold, like Ginsberg, created a style of his own but his purpose lay beyond language; his newspaper column was called "Change the World!"; altering consciousness was a means, not an end. The contrast between him and Ginsberg measures the distance between the social radicalism of the thirties, still dreaming of an equality achieved through political upheaval, and the cultural radicalism of the sixties, adrift from the historical certitudes of Marxism, inventing its own personal legends, conjuring up more private forms of community and utopia.

The Idea of Poverty

In 1935, then in the long twilight of his novelistic career, Theodore Dreiser published some lightly considered remarks about Jews that made Mike Gold "want to howl like a dog with rage and fight" (Folsom, 226). The older writer, a favorite of the Left, an untouchable ally of the party, castigated Jews in stereotyped terms as wealthy and "money-minded," the very clichés Gold had tried hard to demolish in his book five years earlier. As Gold saw it, the rise of Hitler now made these clichés pregnant with murder. Gold himself had given Dreiser a tour of the ghetto ten years before, then had taken him for a Sabbath meal to his mother's home on Chrystie Street. So he replied to Dreiser's bigoted remarks with one of his most stinging essays, "The Gun Is Loaded, Dreiser!," a far cry from his good-natured criticism of Upton Sinclair in 1928.

Although he pays tribute to the Hoosier-born Dreiser in conventional terms as "our outstanding symbol of the literary artist who brings his genius to the aid of the oppressed," his choler rises as he turns to address him directly:

> Shame on those who insult the poor! More shame to you Mr. Dreiser, born in poverty and knowing its bitter humiliations! Don't you know, can't you understand that the Jews are a race of paupers?

Though banking was a field from which Jews in America were almost totally excluded, anti-Semitic prejudices about Jewish bankers and Jewish wealth remained impervious to reason and statistics, even on the left. As he had done in his book, Gold wants to draw attention from medieval moneylenders and modern capitalists to the mass of the Jewish poor.

> What did you see on the East Side, Mr. Dreiser? Do you remember the block of tenements I pointed out to you, famous among social workers as having the highest rate of tuberculosis per square foot of any area in the world. Do you remember the ragged children without playgrounds who darted among the streetcars and autos? Do you remember the dark, stinking hallways, the hot congested ant-life, the penny grocery stores?
>
> This was only one Jewish ghetto. All over the world the mass of Jews live in such hell-holes of poverty, and have been living in them for centuries. The ghetto has been the historic home of the Jewish race, and the ghetto is not picturesque. I can assure you; it is bedbugs, hunger, filth, tears, sickness, poverty! (Folsom, 226)

(Gold writes polemics with the same feverish intensity he brings to his fiction. His later Stalinist invective has more than a passing family resemblance, stylistically at least, to his best writing. But because of clichés about Jewish wealth and Jewish moneygrubbing, the real poverty of Jews evoked a special feeling.)

To Gold, poverty is not simply an economic fact but a soul-destroying malaise that infects its victims with hopelessness and depression. This was something he knew from his own life. Thirty years before Michael Harrington and Oscar Lewis put the neglected conditions of poverty back on the map, Gold discovered not only the "invisible" poor but also the "culture of poverty," a tissue of attitudes bred by powerlessness and virtual incarceration. "Yiddish literature and music are pervaded like the Negro spirituals with all the hopeless melancholy of ghetto poverty," he tells Dreiser. Those who survive, as he has, often become radicals: "the first spiritual operation a young Jew must perform on himself, if he is to become a fighter, is to weed out the ghetto melancholy, defeatism and despair that centuries of poverty have instilled in his blood" (226).

Gold's commitment to revolutionary struggle as an antidote to despair was only one of many views of poverty embraced by those who had lived through it, but it was especially dear to intellectuals and radical organizers in the 1930s. While seeming to dissolve the individual into the collective, Gold's viewpoint in fact is highly individual, for it envisions radicalism as a transformative therapy, a way of submerging personal unhappiness in utopian effort and mass action. Gold himself had a strong depressive streak. Others who grew up in the ghetto became fighters of a different kind, struggling to amass wealth and to escape by seizing their own opportunities and grasping at the American Dream. Jews who moved from the Lower East Side to the Grand Concourse, then later to Queens, Westchester, or Long Island, Okies who journeyed from the Dust Bowl to California, indigent farmers who came to find jobs in urban factories, black sharecroppers who created new northern ghettos and, eventually, an expanding Negro middle class, Puerto Ricans who made their way from San Juan to New York—all were responding to harsh necessity but also to the lure of American enterprise and mobility.

In the thirties and again in the sixties, there were liberal programs to solve the problem of poverty through government action. The perceptions of the poor that writers helped to create had a significant impact on laws and agencies that intervened in their lives, just as poets, economists, and utilitarian social thinkers had contributed to debates over reforming the English Poor Laws in the early nineteenth century. Michael Harrington's seminal book *The Other America: Poverty in the United States* (1962) drew attention to the survival of poverty within a society that imagined itself to be affluent. At a time when many believed that America's economic problems had already been solved, the book argued that New Deal programs had benefited mainly the middle third of the population, that the new poor had "missed the political and social gains of the thirties," and that their poverty was insular, politically invisible, and resistant to the old forms of individual incentive and government assistance. "These are the people who are immune to progress," Harrington wrote, anticipating the harsh obituaries later written for the Great Society's War on Poverty that his book inspired. "The other Americans are the victims of the very inventions and machines that have provided a higher living standard for the rest of society. They are upside down in the economy, and for them greater productivity often means worse jobs; agricultural advance means hunger" (19).

Harrington's new poor were not, as he suggested, immiserated by a general crisis of society, as in the Depression, but impoverished by their own dated skills, which society no longer needed, by their skin color or ethnic identity, to which society refused equal opportunity, by region, or even by old age and illness, which society put "out of sight and out of mind" (13). The old poverty, he argued, still permitted hope of improvement by way of personal effort or the general advance of society. "But the new poverty is constructed so as to destroy aspiration; it is a system designed to be impervious to hope" (17).

In *The Other America* Harrington is eloquent on the need for a more personal, more inward and novelistic treatment of the lives of the new poor. There is, he argued, "a language of the poor, a psychology of the poor, a world view of the poor. . . . The poor can be described statistically; they can be analyzed as a group. But they need a novelist as well as a sociologist if we are to see them. They need an American Dickens to record the smell and texture and quality of their lives. . . . I am not that novelist" (24).

Such a novelist never came along in the relatively affluent 1960s, though he or she had published with some frequency in the 1930s. The widely read anthropologist Oscar Lewis was not that novelist either, though he certainly came close for the Spanish-speaking subcultures in which he worked. Yet he saw these people through the eyes of the 1960s as sexy, primitive, violent, and spontaneous.

Many thirties writers and filmmakers portrayed life in boxcars, in hobo encampments, and on the open road with a mixture of fondness and horror, but the people involved were seen as wretched rejects of society rather than as models of instinctual liberation, as Lewis saw them. Gregory La Cava's 1936 film *My Man Godfrey*, a combination of social consciousness and screwball comedy, is lethal on the subject of idealizing the poor and making them chic. Here the encampments of the poor become objects of refined slumming, starting with a scavenger hunt for a "forgotten man" and ending with a nightclub for social tourists called "The Dump," a pure (and wonderfully daffy) product of the American genius for commercial exploitation.

Only in the 1950s did the idea of poverty, as revived and adapted by the Beats, lose its political edge and become once more a chosen bohemian "lifestyle," a way of thumbing your nose at the middle class, to which one could of course return at any time. (Kerouac always had his mother to fall back on, as he did toward the end of his life. Neal Cassady, a genuine orphan, always took jobs, haphazardly supporting wives and children. Kerouac's *On the Road*, which idealizes Cassady's spontaneity and mobility, has its roots in the road novels of the Depression but is more about joyriding than about authentic social desperation, something unknown or unnoticed in the postwar years.)

In other words, there were as many ways of dealing with poverty as people writing about it, and the differences were political as well as cultural. Oscar Lewis summarizes it this way in the preface to *La Vida*:

Throughout recorded history, in literature, in proverbs and in popular sayings, we find two opposite evaluations of the nature of the poor. Some characterize the poor as blessed, virtuous, upright, serene, independent, honest, kind and happy. Others characterize them as evil, mean, violent, sordid and criminal. These contradictory and confusing evaluations are also reflected in the in-fighting that is going on in the current war against poverty. Some stress the great potential of the poor for self-help, leadership and community organization, while others point to the sometimes irreversible, destructive effect of poverty upon individual character, and therefore emphasize the need for guidance and control to remain in the hands of the middle class, which presumably has better mental health.

These opposing views reflect a political power struggle between competing groups.[9]

The politics of poverty in America has always been difficult and complex, ranging from the radicalism of the Populists of the 1890s and the Wobblies of the Industrial Workers of the World to the federal initiatives and evocative rhetoric of FDR and the New Deal ("I see one-third of a nation . . ."). The spectrum extends from the inspired demagoguery of Huey Long to the "community control" principle of the Kennedy-Johnson War on Poverty; from the sociological approach of the controversial 1965 Moynihan report to the "trickle-down effect" of supply-side economics and Reaganite conservatism, which sought to turn back the clock to the unbridled economic individualism of the Gilded Age. Once in power, Republicans stressed voluntarism, faith-based initiatives, welfare reform, the privatization of government programs, and individual benevolence, under deceptive slogans like "a thousand points of light" and "compassionate conservatism."

In the nineteenth century the industrialization of society into large urban agglomerations created new ways of making people poor—new ways of using their labor while housing and feeding them in wretchedly unhealthy conditions—but it also created a new moral awareness of poverty and its dehumanizing effects. The poor had always had their place as objects of charity within the moral framework of Judaism and Christianity, but the nineteenth century developed a profound secular critique of social inequality, industrialism, and laissez-faire economics. In *The Idea of Poverty*, Gertrude Himmelfarb traced this development as a milestone in intellectual history, just as E. P. Thompson in England and Louis Chevalier in France explored the growth of working-class consciousness as a revolution in modern social history.

Though Chevalier makes pointed use of literary sources, such as the writings of Victor Hugo, it would be fair to say that until the nineteenth century poor people played only bit parts on the great stage of literature and the arts. They were the cannon fodder of early epic and adventure, mere backdrops for the heroism of their betters; they were the clownish rustics and faithful servants in Shakespeare, the ennobling occasions for sentiment and morality by poets like Thomas Gray (in his famous "Elegy Written in a Country Churchyard") and Oliver Goldsmith (in "The Deserted Village"). Not until the French Revolution—and what William Hazlitt described as its literary equivalent, the leveling Romanticism of Wordsworth and his *Lyrical Ballads*—did the sans-culottes and the rural poor take center stage as sources of power, pathos, and moral value.

Wordsworth at the turn of the century was attacked by liberals and conservatives alike for maintaining that the language of rural life, seemingly untouched by an encroaching urban industrialism, was more authentic than the chaste language of classical decorum or the more sensational language of Gothic Romanticism. His leading critic, the lawyer and haughty liberal editor Francis Jeffrey, wrote in the *Edinburgh Review* that the poor could serve in literature as *objects* of interest but never as dignified *subjects*, fully human agents of a worthy destiny. "The poor and vulgar," he wrote in one of his attacks on Wordsworth, "may interest us, in poetry, by their situation; but never, we apprehend, by any sentiments that are peculiar to their condition, still less by any language that is characteristic of it." The poor, *as* poor, fall short of the generalized humanity of the classical ideal, for "poverty makes men ridiculous" and "just taste and refinement are rarely to be met with among the uncultivated part of mankind."[10] The violent attacks on Courbet and other French realist painters after 1848 were based on the same political ideas disguised as classical values. Such people, and the dignity accorded to them, were seen as outside the ken of serious art. In Courbet, as in Wordsworth, the very portrayal of the poor without stylization or condescension seemed to smack of Jacobinism.[11]

As a reform-minded upper-class liberal, Jeffrey allows for a literature of social consciousness and personal pathos, but he rejects Wordsworth's insistence that the poor live closer to the bone of human feeling; indeed, he rejects the notion that their special feelings, defined by their degraded condition, can signify anything of general human interest. In the 1930s, too, there was a tendency to think of the poor as social cases, as specimens of the structural problems of society. But this environmental approach was not the whole story of thirties writing. The same national crisis that helped revive naturalism and stir up a new literature of social protest also stimulated other approaches to characters who had barely been on the fringes of literature—or of national attention—in the 1920s.

As Alfred Kazin remarked in *Starting Out in the Thirties*, the new writers themselves seemed to come from anywhere, which meant nowhere; they had no mainstream lineage, no family pedigree.[12] Far from sounding only a note of angry protest, their work could be more modernist, more satiric, more subjective, more humorous, or even more politically detached than the main current of social writing in the thirties. In some cases they were not fully appreciated until many years later, when critics and the reading public finally caught up with them.

Writers like Henry Roth, Henry Miller, Nathanael West, Daniel Fuchs, and James Agee are almost the creations of a later era, yet they also represent vital countertendencies in the mind of the 1930s. Their work shows us strikingly different ways to bring marginal lives into the public consciousness. Their characters are often the urban slum dwellers, sharecroppers, and down-and-outers of thirties legend, but these writers are not muckrakers or social activists. Despite their own radical affiliations, their writing tended to be more personal or more ironic, more attuned to psychology or more comically irrepressible. They were more influenced by the modernist writers of the twenties than by Zola and Dreiser. Though at first they reached a small audience, they were attuned to some of the deepest vibrations of the age, as posterity has come to recognize. They complicate our picture of the social imagination of the 1930s.

The Ghetto as a State of Mind: The Case of Henry Roth

Henry Roth is almost the archetype of the neglected and rediscovered writer in the twentieth century. He was born in Galicia in 1906 and was brought to New York as a young child. While yet an undergraduate at City College, he fell under the spell of his best friend's professor, Eda Lou Walton, a well-connected poet and critic, twelve years his senior, who taught at New York University. She nurtured his talent, supported him financially, exposed him to many modern writers, and encouraged him to turn his early life into fiction. Roth lived with her for ten years—his prime years as a writer—beginning in 1928. He began writing his first novel, *Call It Sleep*, a few months after the success of *Jews without Money* in 1930, as if determined to tell a far different version of the same story. (In interviews in the fall of 1987, Roth told me he had not read Gold's novel, though he surely knew of its success, but had read other treatments of the same milieu, such as Anzia Yezierska's *Bread Givers* [1925], which he felt would have profited from a more rigorous concentration on the Lower East Side experience.)[13] Roth's novel received modest attention, including some very favorable reviews, but his publisher went bankrupt and the book was largely forgotten within a few years after it appeared in 1934.

Roth was unable to complete two other novels he began in the 1930s, one a proletarian novel about a tough midwestern worker who becomes a Communist, the other a projected autobiographical novel about his adolescent years, which would have taken up where *Call It Sleep* left off. Over the objections of Eda Lou Walton, who felt it would destroy his talent, Roth joined the Communist Party shortly before the publication of *Call It Sleep*. Like Michael Gold, Roth remained a faithful Communist long after most of his fellow writers had abandoned the party—in his case until the trauma of de-Stalinization in the late fifties and finally the Six-Day War of 1967, which reawakened his long-buried ethnic loyalties toward the Jews.

Roth kept politics out of his novel even more thoroughly than Gold had done, but no discussion of proletarian fiction in the thirties can afford to ignore *Call It Sleep*. The reviewer in *The New Masses* complained that "it is a pity that so many young writers drawn from the proletariat can make no better use of their working class experience except as material for introspective and febrile novels."[14] This obtuse response, typical of the radical aesthetics of the so-called Third Period, drew such protest from Roth's admirers that the magazine was forced to reconsider the book and review it more favorably.

Though Roth himself disappeared from the literary world after 1940, despite having been signed up for a second novel by Maxwell Perkins, Hemingway's and Fitzgerald's editor, a few influential critics like Alfred Kazin and Leslie Fiedler never forgot *Call It Sleep*. The explosion of Jewish-American fiction after the war created a new context for the novel. Suddenly, proletarian naturalism was passé, ethnic subjects were in, psychological, introspective fiction was the norm, and Roth's novel, republished first in 1960, went on to sell more than a million copies. By that time Roth himself was raising waterfowl on a farm in Maine.

Though Michael Gold was a passionate follower of Whitman and an experimenter in various literary forms in the teens and twenties, in fiction he admired the fluent left-wing storytellers of the prewar years, especially Jack London, Dreiser, and Upton Sinclair. The most modern influence on his work was probably Hemingway, a writer of a different emotional cast. But like many early readers he saw Hemingway, despite his pared-down, naturalistic technique, as the epitome of the fashionable romantic despair of middle-class youth right after the war. Eventually he attacked Hemingway as yet another apostate, despite Hemingway's romance with the Popular Front during the Spanish Civil War.

Henry Roth, under Eda Lou Walton's tutelage—his novel is dedicated to her—came out of another tradition, less naturalistic, more modern, more inward and subjective. *Call It Sleep* recalls the emotional intensity of D. H. Lawrence, the role of memory in Proust, the language of Joyce, and the symbolism of Eliot. It is an immigrant *Sons and Lovers* by a writer who has also read *The Waste Land*, *A Portrait of the Artist as a Young Man*, and *Ulysses*. It deals with a childhood in the ghetto at the turn of the century strictly, almost claustrally, from the viewpoint of the child ("this six-year old Proust," *The New Masses* called him), not from the usual angle of the grown-up writer evoking his early years.

Gold's book had managed to cover his first twenty-one years, until the moment his conversion to Communism in 1914 brought the whole first phase of his life to an end. But Gold's subject is not so much the person he *was* as the world he grew up in, the tenements that created him, the parents who nurtured him, who were themselves (as he saw it) the living results of conditions that spoke through them. Whatever the inner pressures that compelled him to write—we can feel them in the vocative intensity of his prose—Gold is freely fictionalizing his own experience to document a milieu and drive home an argument; his title suggests an essay, not a novel. Aiming (like Maxim Gorky in *The Lower Depths*) to excavate a new subject, an "unliterary" subject dredged up from his own life, he seems almost incidentally to have forged a new style. Art for art's sake was abhorrent to him, the height of decadence. The title of his book emphasizes its polemical side—the Jewish poor as a social type.

Roth, on the other hand, covers only three years in the life of his protagonist, David Schearl, three years from the ages of six to eight when the boy's sense of place, his comprehension of his parents' lives, could only be precocious, fragmentary, and myopic. As the book's poetic title implies, David's world is intimate, lyrical, and endowed with a dark and dreamlike vividness. (Twenties Freud and Yiddish literature and drama brood over the book as much as any modernist writers.)

Gold's stories of filth, prostitution, and gang warfare in the slums are tabloid horrors that take us back to the age of Progressive muckraking or the reports of Victorian social reformers. His accounts of the wasting illness of his father, his deteriorating morale, and the accidental death of his sister belong to the pathos of immigrant life; they could have come from the famous *Bintel Brief*, the personal letters column of the *Jewish Daily Forward*. Roth, on the other hand, portrays the world of the ghetto through the prism of the family romance. The brutal, explosive father, the placid, seductive mother, the magpie aunt and her henpecked, milquetoast husband are creatures out of Yiddish melodrama, especially when the plot begins to turn on revelations of the mother's hushed-up love affair with a church organist in the old country and his father's suspicions that David is not actually his own son.

Rarely has a novel focused so unflinchingly on childhood as sheer terror: the fear of the alien streets, the bullying crudeness of other children, the trauma of early sexual experiences, the constant looming threat of a parent's anger and violence, the inchoate spiritual longings that lead to a brush with death toward the end of the book. At first the world appears as a stinging lash to the boy's poetic soul. But gradually we move outward from David Schearl's enclosed maternal world, confined by immigrant isolation and the limits of the Yiddish language, to encompass school life and street adventures that create a stronger sense of the whole ghetto, with its tremendous cacophony of ethnic tribes and languages.

The four sections of the novel, "The Cellar," "The Picture," "The Coal," and "The Rail," influenced by the emblematic method of *The Waste Land*, open outward in widening circles from the frightfully small breathing space that David has at the beginning of the novel. As the social terrain shifts from Brooklyn to the Lower East Side, from the apartment and the tenement to the whole neighborhood, David's emotional terrain expands: from the Freudian cellar in which he cowers in fear, to the cornfields of the picture that take him back in time to the rural world of Europe and his mother's love affair, to the coal that links the dark underworld of the cellar to the bright dream of purity, the hint of divine vision, that he senses in the words of Isaiah, to the actual illumination he experiences in nearly electrocuting himself on the rails of a tram with an ordinary milk ladle.

This network of signposts is much less cumbersome than it sounds. Only on rereading do we discover how much *Call It Sleep* is really *written*, not only in its intensely worked prose but in this tissue of motifs that support the narrative with a luxuriant underbrush of symbolism.

Call It Sleep was unfashionably "literary" for its day, and it has perhaps become unfashionably dense and literary again today, despite the continuing vogue for magic realism and historical fantasy. As an old man, in interviews and in his late autobiographical novel *Mercy of a Rude Stream* (1994–98), Roth himself renounced it as a falsification of his life and a prettification of its sensitive young hero, whom the elder Roth loved to mock.[15] The book belonged to the first wave of Freudian and modernist literary influence in America, and its symbolism might have seemed intrusive and self-conscious if its story had not been so directly gripping. Though published in the proletarian thirties, *Call It Sleep* partly belonged in spirit to the era dominated by *Ulysses* and *The Waste Land*; these were works with a great deal of literary scaffolding (as Eliot pointed out in his self-serving essay on Joyce's "mythical method"). The portentously significant milk ladle, for example, might refer to the father's livelihood as a milkman, or to his anger and male violence (for the boy has seen him wield it as a fierce weapon against thieves), but also to the mother's protective feminine nurture, which the boy has begun to outgrow.

The progress of the characters gains resonance from the progress of its key emblems. By moving from the darkness of the cellar to the sparks of light that explode from the tram rail, the book shows how growth and illumination, even transcendence, are possible in the mean world of the cheder and the immigrant slums—the very world Mike Gold had wanted to tear down. Gold's book ends in a leap of revolutionary faith, Roth's in the bildungsroman's promise of individual growth.

Yet this contrast can be unduly stressed. Just as *Jews without Money* is far from being a strictly sociological novel, *Call It Sleep* is not simply the poetic or subjective work it was once imagined to be. For all his admiration of Joyce and Eliot, Roth gives us a distinctly quotidian, post-1930 mutation of what they were doing. He avoids allusions and devices that would call attention to themselves, and was determined (as he told me in 1987) to keep his symbols from slowing down the flow of the narrative. Roth, who eagerly devoured the prose of *Ulysses* in 1925 after his benefactor smuggled it into the country, saw Joyce not merely as the inventor of new fictional techniques, some of which—stream of consciousness, for example—he adapted to his own use. He also saw him as the inspired explorer of the subliterary reaches of everyday life, a man who had written an immense book about things that happened to ordinary people in the course of a single day.

Ulysses, like *Call It Sleep*, was a great evocation of the modern city, gritty, ugly, even banal. Joyce showed Roth how to turn the mundane and the ordinary into art by filtering them through a rich language of subjective perception. For the naturalistic writer, the plain documentary truth validated an author's vision. (Upton Sinclair prided himself on never being corrected on any matter of fact.) For a modernist writer all truth was personal and mediated by language. Just as Sherwood Anderson told the young Faulkner to write about what he knew, Joyce taught Roth that literature was inside him and around him if only he could lay hold of it, articulate it. Reading Joyce gave Roth, as he told one interviewer, "this awed realization that you didn't have to go anywhere at all except around the corner to flesh out a literary work of art—given some kind of vision, of course. In stream of consciousness I recognized that my own continual dialogue with myself could be made into literature."[16] Humble as it sounds, this respectful attention to the ordinary was a great leap forward for the thirties writer, as it had been for painters like Courbet, Winslow Homer, and Thomas Eakins.

Despite our metaphor of the avant-garde, art is rarely a series of breakthroughs and advances on the old model of scientific progress. Once we recognize that modernism is less a method of technical experimentation than a form of release, a new way of giving expression to individual perception, we can begin to understand the tension in the 1930s between a resurgent naturalism and a subterranean modernism, between a desire to bear witness to the social fact and an insistence on the individual character of all witness, all perception. This dialectic was at the heart of the portrayal of poverty in the 1930s.

The economic crisis of the era gave impetus to those who were eager to document how life was actually lived in neglected, almost invisible corners of society: on remote southern farms, in factories and mills, in teeming urban ghettos, in lower middle-class tenements and row houses, and among drifters who had lost all sense of "place," the flotsam of the new society. For some writers this interest did not run deep; it was simply a new literary trend, or was triggered by a radical agenda far from any creative necessity. Writers who a year earlier had been sipping bubbly in Paris now set out with their notebooks for Harlan County to see how the other half lived. Some of those reports, such as the ones Edmund Wilson collected in his *American Jitters* (1932) and *Travels in Two Democracies* (1936), bore powerful witness, testifying to a depth of social curiosity and genuine commitment. Other travel reports made a fetish of flatness and impersonality to replace the scorned literary showmanship of the 1920s, as if the writer could efface himself in the service of the common man, trying to highlight what he observed by obliterating the observer.

Yet some of the most ambitious works of the thirties straddle this line between naturalism and modernism, as Joyce himself (that great admirer of Ibsen) had done in parts of *Ulysses*. In *Studs Lonigan*, often taken as the epitome of the social novel of the 1930s, James Farrell had borrowed Joycean interior monologues and Joycean irony to build up an acidulous portrait of a Catholic lower middle-class family; in effect, he had assimilated Joyce to his own autobiography and subdued modernism to his minute reconstruction of everyday life. Studs, like John Updike's later Rabbit, is what the author himself might have become had he not left home, not become a writer. Studs was an emblem of his class at a certain time and place—a world literature had largely ignored—yet also a cautionary parable full of personal power.

In *U.S.A.* (1930–36) John Dos Passos created a mosaic of interconnected stories that mingled private and public lives, historical and contemporary realities, emblematic and narrative techniques, in which no single character or story was allowed to carry the whole thread of the novel. His attempt to write a collective novel, a panoramic portrait of the American scene, was a typical ambition of the 1930s. His interplay of personal histories, blaring headlines, cinematic montage, and Whitmanesque biographies of famous people gave his novel a modernist cast and an exuberant variety of narrative angles, though it lacks the inner resonance of an authentic modernism. (Sartre remarked that "Dos Passos reports all his characters' utterances to us in the style of a statement to the Press.")[17] Yet his large legacy to the young war novelists who followed him and read him avidly, especially Mailer, was a form of perspectivism, made up of naturalistic documentation without omniscient authority, fragmented into multiple points of view.

The most rigorous element in Henry Roth's memory novel is his concentration on the child's point of view. If Michael Gold's perspective is that of a man looking backward, hallucinating his own family history and the scenes of his early years, Roth re-creates the limited purview of the perpetually frightened child. The difference is a matter of language. The young Mike Gold is largely an observer of his own life, not really a character in it. He is like the subjective camera eye of Dos Passos, taking in people and images visually, as if from a distance. The exceptional intensity of his language, with its telegraphic immediacy, shows us more of what the older man remembers than what the young boy experienced. As a character the boy doesn't reverberate; he is somehow less real than everyone around him.

Young David Schearl, on the other hand, almost shimmers with sensitivity. In an interview almost forty years later, Roth described this portrayal of his childhood mockingly as "simply an idealization based on the notion that I was a much finer sensibility than what was around me—so fine that I was being persecuted and victimized" (Lyons, 160). This was what the critic in *The New Masses* meant by "this six-year old Proust," but it's a reductive caricature of how the book works. Since Roth makes sure that David misunderstands or half understands what happens around him, this narrative is as fragmentary, mysterious, and overpowering as the world around him.

David's perceptual field *is* the novel. His domain is feeling, not doing. His lyrical intimacy with his mother fortifies him against the brutality of his father—like Paul Morel in Lawrence's *Sons and Lovers*, Roth doesn't try to see anything at all from the father's alien point of view. Similarly, the boy's spiritual longings, first crystallized when he is drawn to the passage in Isaiah, elevate him over the coarseness of the kids around him. This is his calling; it marks him as a future writer. The novel is, among other things, a portrait of the artist as a (very) young man.

From the cellar scenes early in the book to the orgasmic blowup on the electrified rail, *Call It Sleep* is drenched in the sexual fear and curiosity of boyhood. David recoils in horror from his sexual initiation with a deformed tenement girl, but he envies his father's rippling muscles and bathes in the glow of his mother's dreamy tenderness. He loathes the man who pays court to his mother and sees him with dread as a sexual intruder. But in return for some rosary beads that feed his mystical desires, he half consciously collaborates when his precocious friend Leo, a gentile, "plays dirty" with David's cousin in yet another Freudian cellar. As Leslie Fiedler remarks, "No book insists more on the distance between the foulness man lives and the purity he dreams; but none makes more clear how deeply rooted that dream is in the existence which seems to contradict it" (Lyons, 150).

The same split—between coarseness and purity, earth and sky, sex and love—finds expression in the most famous feature of the book's language, the contrast between the poetic riches of the characters' "translated" Yiddish and the barbarous crudeness of their broken English. Neither style was in any way given to Roth, for all their appearance of mere transcription. He heightens the first by seeming to translate literally, so that ordinary phrases take on an ineffable strangeness, and he exaggerates the second with a phonetic literalism that almost insults the page it's printed on. The first kind of dialogue is remarkably literary: David's mother at times seems like an emanation from the Song of Songs, while his glowering father echoes the terrific imprecations of the Hebrew prophets. This is closely related to the book's own narration, which echoes the sublime terror of Blake and Milton in the boy's moments of fear. See, for example, the truly awesome scene in which the father beats David with a coat hanger:

> Answer me, his words rang out. Answer me, but they meant, Despair! Who could answer his father? In that dread summons, the judgement was already sealed. Like a cornered thing, he shrank within himself, deadened his mind because the body would not deaden and waited. Nothing existed any longer except his father's right hand—the hand that hung down into the electric circle of his vision. Terrific clarity was given him. Terrific leisure. Transfixed, timeless, he studied the curling fingers that twitched spasmodically, studied the printer's ink ingrained upon the finger tips, pondered, as if all there were in the world, the nail of the smallest finger, nipped by a press, that climbed in a jagged little stair to the hangnail. Terrific absorption.
> *The hammer in that hand when he stood! The hammer!*

There may be too much self-conscious virtuosity in these lines—this is, after all, a first novel, written under strong modernist influence—but it shows how Roth, like Faulkner, uses literary language, full of stylistic echoes, to convey a strikingly individual point of view.[18]

On the other hand, the "English" dialogue is resolutely antiliterary, a slap in the face to all polite diction in well-mannered novels, as if in fulfillment of Henry James's dire prophecy that the sounds that assaulted him on a visit to the Lower East Side would someday alter the literary language as he knew it. In *The American Scene* (1907) James had described the teeming immigrant cafés as "torture-rooms of the living idiom," but he also heard in them "the accent of the very ultimate future," adding, in his anxiety as a writer, that "whatever we shall know it for, certainly, we shall not know it for English—in any sense for which there is an existing literary measure."[19]

The crude, limited English of the immigrants is a shock when we encounter it on the page—hard to understand, outside the range of fiction as we generally know it. This is not the rich but difficult idiom of dialect fiction, as we find it in Zora Neale Hurston's *Their Eyes Were Watching God* (1937), but an alien tongue that maims self-expression. Thus Roth shows us his characters from both inside and out, contrasting their vivid inner lives and fluent intercourse with each other with the drastically confined ways they interact with the outside world. And as David begins to connect more with other kids, he slips timidly, and with immense revulsion, into the barbarous street talk of the immigrant children.

In one of David's first external encounters, his friend Yossie tells him how his parents set rattraps, and it's hard to tell whether the fastidious David, still delicate like his mother—they are both natural aristocrats—is more disgusted by what he says or by how he says it:

Foist yuh put sompin ove' hea, on iz' liddle hook. An' nen nuh rat gizzin. Dey uz zuh big rat inna house, yuh could hear him at night, so my fodder bought dis, an' my mudder put in schmaltz f'om de meat, and nuh rat comes in, an' inna mawingk, I look unner by de woshtob, an'ooh—he wuz dere, runnin' dis way like dot. (49)

On one level the rats feed David's fears of the cellar, of death, of sexuality. (In an oft-quoted scene that soon follows, David first learns of sex in the same grim language, with deliberate associations with the rattrap. [53–54].) On another level the rats belong with Mike Gold's bedbugs: a way of facing the dark, unpoetic side of ghetto life, except that Roth goes further, to make the language itself as revolting as what it describes.

No doubt it was Joyce who helped Roth to this mimetic notion of style, just as Faulkner might have licensed him to interrupt a flowing narrative prose with this tortured colloquial idiom. Thanks in part to such influences, Roth was able to do in fiction precisely what James feared, something for which there was almost no "existing literary measure." Yet it follows, too, from James's own practice in fiction, which was to avoid omniscient narration and to filter the action through a consistent point of view. In his lecture called "The Art of Fiction," James had defended the novel of inner experience by insisting that "the moral consciousness of a child is as much a part of life as the islands of the Spanish Main"[20]—a line Roth might well have borrowed as an epigraph for his own novel.

Along with writers like Anzia Yezierska in the twenties, Clifford Odets in the thirties, and (eventually) Bernard Malamud in the fifties, Roth invented a new idiom that sounded like a colloquial Yiddish-English but was actually a stylized poetic construction quite unlike actual immigrant speech. Though he is a much heightened character, seen through the eyes of a small terrified boy, David's father is hardly given to poetic turns of phrase. But when he speaks, his language cuts across the page— and through the people around him—like a whip. "Shudder when I speak to you," he snaps at David (77), for he is always on the verge of going out of control. He speaks of someone else whose palate is "jaded with delicacies" (73), and his paranoia gives him many other fierce turns of speech that are Roth's haunting fantasias from the Yiddish. His clumsy flashes of anger are reflected in his abrupt rhythms and odd diction: "There's a good beating in store for you! I warn you! It's been gathering for years" (80).

The father's ferocity, the mother's sensuous pagan warmth, her sister's ribald obscenity and earthiness, the cheder teacher's biblical cadences: all these traits are expressed in a "Yiddish" as different as each of their personalities. Unlike Yezierska and Mike Gold, whose characters all speak in one style, who are revealed by *what* they say, not by *how* they say it, Roth invents a translated voice for each of them. Their nuanced, varied speech discloses the humanity imprisoned within the immigrant stereotype, for these people are all locked into an alien language, hemmed in by poverty, overwork, and daily necessity. Very little of this humanity breaks through when they stumble into fractured English, which filters out everything subtle, complex, and individual about them, and turns them simply into greenhorns, strangers in a strange land.

It's not simply that Roth uses language in a more complicated way than Gold or Yezierska; his novel is partly about language itself, which is another one of its affinities with modernism. As David's range of language relentlessly widens, as it takes in more about the people that formed him, the texts and voices that excite him, and the ghetto that surrounds him, he is gradually becoming the person who could someday write this book. The book is at once the story of a calling, of an initiation, and of the rebarbative world that would serve as its inspiration. The rich literary idiom of the novel springs partly from the rocky verbal soil of the ghetto.

It's hardly possible to do full justice to the role language plays in *Call It Sleep*.[21] Like the modified stream of consciousness Roth uses in the narration, the characters' language is subjective in the ways it expresses the complexity of their lives. Though poststructuralist literary theorists have argued that language is conventional and duplicitous, an arbitrary set of signifiers, and that selfhood is little more than an illusion sustained by language, Roth's mentors were the first-generation modernists who taught him to use language to convey the shape and rhythm of individual awareness. This enabled him to keep his characters from being reduced to stereotypes of the poor, from being turned into social data, which is what some thirties writers, turning back to naturalism, had begun to do.

But there was also a Dickensian side to Roth's writing, a sheer pleasure in the variety of language as social notation. He saw that language, besides revealing personality, was also the most important social fact of immigrant and ghetto life. It was the barrier to acculturation that left the newcomer permanently divided between the world of his childhood and the accents of an alien land. David's mother cannot pronounce her own address; this effectively confines her to her home, a small circle of streets nearby, and to her pleasant memories of rural European scenes. As David learns English, the forbidding streets in which he once got lost become familiar to him and he ventures outside the cocoon of his dependence and maternal influence.

A surprising number of other languages appear in the book besides the musical Yiddish and the guttural English. Several of them hold magic and mystery for David, such as the Polish his mother speaks to hide her sexual secrets from him, and the scriptural Hebrew that tantalizes him with its spiritual secrets. These spheres of language are associated with the web of symbols I described earlier, especially images of darkness and light: the sexual darkness of the cellar and the sexual brightness of the painted cornfields (which remind his mother of her old affair), the visionary radiance of the coal that emanates from its carbon blackness, the electrical sparks from the rail that can destroy, uplift, and purify David, yet finally, on the last pages of the book, allow him his first moments of ordinary calm.

Between the inferno of sexual terror and the paradise of transcendent possibilities, there is a Dantean middle realm—the streets of the Lower East Side—where a babble of languages initiates David into everyday life. In an old East Side tradition, still practiced when I was a kid in the 1940s, the boys have made small fires to burn the last of the unleavened bread on the eve of Passover. When the Italian street cleaner objects, treats this as trash, a Jewish butcher comes to their rescue:

> "Fav'y you push dis, ha?" The butcher flung an angry hand at the choked, smouldering embers mixed now with rubbish and manure.
>
> "Wadda you wa-an?" The street cleaner stopped angrily, black brows leaping together as stiff as carbon rods under the white helmet. "You no tella me waddaduh push! I cleanuh dis street. Dey no makuh duh fiuh hea!" His intricate gestures jig-sawed space.
>
> "No? I ken't tell you, ha? Verstinkeneh Goy!" The butcher planted himself directly before the mound upon the shovel. "Now moof!"
>
> "Sonnomo bitzah you! I fix!" He leaned viciously on the shovel-handle. The smouldering hummock sprang forward. The butcher leaped sideways to avoid being mowed down into the variegated debris.
>
> "You vanna push me?" he roared. "I'll zebreak you het."
>
> "Vai a fanculo te!" The sweeper threw down the shovel. "Come on! Jew bast!" (244)

In the contested space of the immigrant streets, different languages and ethnic groups compete ferociously for the same turf. As Bonnie Lyons remarks, "Polish, Yiddish, Hebrew, Italian, German, and many dialects of English all go into the mixing bowl, and the result is a novel that breathes the complex social and ethnic reality of New York" (65).

This is a world in which children and adults are constantly playing at different languages as if the right words could somehow save them. "Talk

Hungarian," says one kid. "Sure like dis. Abashishishababyo tomama wawa. Like dot" (250). The fragmentary utterances of the characters, who grasp at English words as if they were jagged shards of rock, are punctuated by a narrative diction that is shockingly formal and literary ("the smouldering hummock," "the variegated debris"), as if to separate the grown-up author from the street world he still shudderingly remembers some thirty years later. Young David, always the victim, always put upon—perhaps he is the heir to his father's rampant paranoia—has finally escaped from his childhood into literature, which enables him to give names to his own fears.

At a time when many writers were turning away from subjective, autobiographical themes to deal with the immediate social crisis, sacrificing their individuality on the altar of class consciousness, Roth portrays the scene of poverty as a scene of memory. Unfashionably, he makes his language a vehicle of self-analysis, almost a Freudian case study. Yet *Call It Sleep* never evades the social meaning of its material, but insists that it can be approached only by way of the individual experience. Like Mike Gold but with still greater power, he imported his childhood memories of the ghetto into the dire new social realities of the Depression. Through the mediation of Freud, and helped by the examples of modernist poetry and fiction, fueled by his own indelible recollections, which only then became suitable material for literature, Roth gave the proletarian novel its richest and most haunting text.

CHAPTER 3

The Starvation Army

Proletarians

THE DEPRESSION LENT NEW MEANING to the childhood memories of Michael Gold and Henry Roth by making the poor, even of past times, a subject of vital, immediate interest. But many writers made a much more self-conscious attempt to craft a new, more contemporary, more engaged Depression literature. Most of these proletarian novels focused on industrial conflict and were set in the present or the immediate past. They amounted to a middle-class experiment in creating militant, revolutionary fiction about the condition of the working class. These books have never been widely read, but in recent years they have elicited a revival of interest from radical scholars. At least six of them dealt with the same strike in the cotton mills of Gastonia, North Carolina, in 1929. If Gold and Roth in different ways turned fiction into thinly disguised autobiography, other writers reshaped journalistic material into ideological fables. In this they were encouraged by the Communist Party; during its militant phase in the early thirties, it saw literature as a weapon, a device that could foster class consciousness. Debates on proletarian writing proliferated in left-wing journals in the early 1930s, with some critics discounting books that merely focused on working-class life without stressing its revolutionary potential.

The standard view of these novels was expressed by Malcolm Cowley, who drew a composite sketch of their plots as follows:

> A young man comes down from the hills to work in a cotton mill (or a veneer factory or a Harlan County mine). Like all his fellow workers except one, he is innocent of ideas about labor unionism or the class struggle. The exception is always an older man, tough but humorous, who keeps quoting passages from *The Communist Manifesto*. Always the workers are heartlessly oppressed, always they go out on strike, always they form a union with the older man as leader, and always the strike is broken by force of arms. The older man dies for the cause, like John the Baptist, but the young hero takes over his faith and mission.[1]

Described in this reductive and amusing way, the novels seem even more formulaic than they actually were. Partly inspired by Soviet experiments in proletarian art in the heady years after the Russian Revolution, they have never fared very well with ordinary readers. Most of these novels sold few copies, despite all the critical attention they received. Philip Rahv, who was a theorist of proletarian writing from 1934 to 1936—the period when, as a young Communist editor, he published some of it in the early issues of *Partisan Review*—would by 1939 dismiss the whole experiment as "the literature of a party disguised as the literature of a class." Rahv had once urged working-class authors to learn from the great novelists of the past. Now he complained about their lack of formal innovation and their reliance on "the bourgeois creative mode."[2]

After 1935 the Communist Party itself would lose interest in the proletarian experiment, aiming instead, as part of the program for the Popular Front, to attract the support of fellow-traveling middle-class writers
like Hemingway and Steinbeck. They might prove unstable allies, but
their names were expected to do more for the cause, especially among
liberals, than Mike Gold's mythical "Shakespeare in overalls." (As Rahv
wrote in 1939, "the official Left is today primarily interested not in literature but in authors.") Yet proletarian writing continued to appear all
through the 1940s, influencing not only war novels like *From Here to Eternity* and *The Naked and the Dead*, gritty novels of urban realism such as
Richard Wright's *Native Son*, Ann Petry's *The Street*, Willard Motley's
Knock on Any Door, and Ira Wolfert's *Tucker's People*, but also works as different as Arthur Miller's *Death of a Salesman* and Bernard Malamud's *The
Assistant*, where economic privations are abstracted into a timeless vision
of loneliness, futility, and failure.

Proletarian writing not only had a long afterlife but was part of a
much wider tradition of thirties and forties literature than the critics of
the official "proletarian novel" were willing to acknowledge. Many works
of Depression journalism and social documentation are almost indistinguishable from proletarian fiction, which also overlaps with mainstream
social novels like *Studs Lonigan* and *U.S.A.* that have few working-class
characters and no simple conversion fable. Mac, the first major character in *U.S.A.*, anticipates the classic itinerant figure of thirties fiction, the
drifter who gets a dose of radical politics. There are also strong resem-
blances between proletarian fiction and the 1930s road novel, the hard-
boiled crime fiction of writers like James M. Cain and W. R. Burnett, and
their ubiquitous Hollywood progeny. Stylistically, they all came out of
Hemingway's sleeve.

Malcolm Cowley welcomed many proletarian novels when they first
appeared but later complained about their "monotony of tone"; he boiled
them down to a simple formula by confining "the proletarian novel" to
works erected on that formula, especially strike novels. In *Part of Our
Time* (1955), the first important postwar look at thirties culture, Murray
Kempton also insists that the "canons" of the proletarian novel were as
rigidly circumscribed as older cultural traditions. Writing from the anti-
Stalinist left, he suggests that "the standards of the proletarian novel
were so demanding as to amount almost to a conspiracy against the

writer." "The proletarian novel was thus rooted in the American tradition of bad literature," he says, asserting that the leading social realists of the decade, such as Farrell, Richard Wright, and Nelson Algren, never wrote one.[3] This is proletarianism by exclusion, the 1950s view that only bad books can be described as proletarian, while better books by definition transcend the category. No such compunction prevented a scholar like Walter Rideout, a year later, from singling out *Call It Sleep*, influenced by Proust and Joyce, with a child as its protagonist, as an extraordinary piece of proletarian fiction.[4]

Despite the limitations of Cowley's stress on the strike novel and its conversion formula, Cowley's books and articles on the 1930s, from the influential *Exile's Return* in 1934 to *The Dream of the Golden Mountains* in 1980, rightly laid emphasis on the conversion experiences of artists and intellectuals who were at first apolitical but were catapulted into radical awareness by the economic crisis. This is a pattern driven home in every memoir of the period. This wave of political conversions was highlighted ironically in James T. Farrell's posthumous novel about a group of young radical intellectuals, *Sam Holman* (1983): "It came as a big surprise to Frances Holman that her husband had become a revolutionary. She had gone to bed one night not knowing it. The next night she had gone to bed knowing. . . . It wasn't only Sam. Most of the people she knew were talking differently from the way they had talked a year ago."[5]

One result of such an awakening was a tremendous interest in what Edward Dahlberg had called the "bottom dogs" of society, the down and out characters at the bottom of the social ladder, who became the subject of a different kind of "proletarian" novel from anything in Cowley's definition. Reading Dahlberg's novel *Bottom Dogs* (1929) not long before his death, D. H. Lawrence was horrified and fascinated by what he took to be the latest wave of American primitivism, a brutal reduction of the human animal to "a *willed* minimum." "The next step," he prophesied, "is legal insanity, or just crime."[6] Besides Dahlberg's, this raw, grim vein of writing includes books like Edward Anderson's *Hungry Men* (1935) and Tom Kromer's Kafkaesque *Waiting for Nothing* (1935), both republished and well received in the mid-1980s.

Nelson Algren was the best of these writers; Walter Rideout described his first novel, *Somebody in Boots* (1935), as "fascinatingly hideous" (185). It anticipated the work of hard-boiled pulp writers like Jim Thompson. But

Algren himself was anything but a product of the lower depths. Partly Jewish, partly Scandinavian in origin, his real name was Nelson Algren Abraham; he had been to both college and journalism school. For him, becoming a writer meant taking to the road to see how the other half lived: riding boxcars, cadging meals, stopping in hobo jungles and Salvation Army soup kitchens, and learning which towns threw drifters in jail for vagrancy.[7] Many men and even children took to the road simply because there were no jobs, or because their families were disintegrating around them. (It was not the first time this had occurred. Americans had taken to the road in large numbers after the financial panic of 1893–94.)

In later interviews Algren estimated that there were a million people out on the road in the early thirties. Falling into their world made Algren a writer. "The experience on the road gave me something to write about," he told H. E. F. Donohue.

> You do see what it's like, what a man in shock who is dying looks like. He knows he's going to die, and he's shocked by the idea that he's dying. Or you're waiting for a boxcar and it seems to be going a little too fast and some kid makes a try for it and you see him miss and then you get the smell of blood and you go over and you see it sliced off his arm. And all the whores in New Orleans. And all the tens of thousands of Americans literally milling around at that time trying to survive. (53)

The road, says Algren, not only gave the young writer something to write about; it conditioned his attitude toward the larger society.

> Everything I'd been told was wrong. That I see with my own eyes. I'd been told, I'd been assured that it was a strive and succeed world. What you did: you got yourself an education and a degree and then you went to work for a family newspaper and then you married a nice girl and raised children and this was what America was. But this is not what America was. America was not socialized and I resented very deeply that I'd been lied to. (54)

In his tough-guy manner Algren may have romanticized his life on the road. But because it was based on experience, not formula, it became a truer act of discovery than the contrived conversions that abound in the strike novels.

The empathetic writer, burdened by a guilty sense of privilege, was invariably radicalized by what he saw on the road, by his exposure to so many marginal and miserable people, the detritus of the American dream. While few women took to the road like Algren, they often had the same experiences in bread lines, on picket lines, or among the homeless. They too got involved in the labor wars, witnessing factory lockouts and seeing goons beat up strikers to prevent unions from organizing. Writers moved back and forth between journalism and fiction or poetry. Steinbeck's *Grapes of Wrath* emerged directly out of the wrenching articles he wrote about the conditions of migrant labor. Often the writer became a Communist, or worked with the Communists, not because he or she was strongly political but simply because the Communists, especially at the local level, seemed the most committed to changing society and helping those at the bottom.

Thus writing in the thirties was in many ways an experiment in downward mobility. Only a few of the "proletarian" authors, such as Jack Conroy and Tillie Olsen, actually came from the working class. Other writers felt ashamed of their own background and upbringing. Still others (like Algren) may have been seeking adventure and risk in the style of Hemingway— then writing about it, often in Hemingway's style. (Quite a few writers followed Hemingway to Spain after 1936.) Though some middle-class or ethnic authors and filmmakers grew up in circumstances that were but one step above poverty, their education vaulted them into the ranks of the privileged, though it didn't assure them a regular income.[8] Many sloughed off the comforts of the middle class, if only for short periods of time, to explore a way of life that seemed more authentic, more emblematic of Depression America. They went where it was all happening.

The Lower Depths

No doubt there was a comic side to this quest for the lower depths when so many were desperate to leave it behind. More writers nurtured their radicalism in the Hollywood hills than in riding the rails. As the Depression ended, Preston Sturges brilliantly satirized Hollywood social consciousness in *Sullivan's Travels* (1942) by sending a frivolous director of inane comedies (played by Joel McCrea) out on the road looking for the poor, with an entourage of studio retainers following close behind. Instead of another edition of *Ants in Your Pants*, his usual kind of work, McCrea wants to make a serious epic of social concern. It's to be called *O Brother, Where Art Thou?*, even though his thoughtful butler warns him that only "the morbid rich" have an interest in poverty, which is really a plague to be shunned at all cost.

At first the director's cushioned life and his absurd playacting prevent him from making even superficial contact with the poor. (A limousine ferries him to where he can hop a freight train.) But then, in a series of circumstances that could happen only in a movie, he loses his memory and his identity, is given up for dead, gets railroaded by the judicial system somewhere in the South, and is propelled without appeal into a world of "real" suffering—that is, the chain gang world of movies like *I Am a Fugitive from a Chain Gang*, with a chorus of prisoners singing "Go Down, Moses."

In the most deft way possible—a silent montage of McCrea's sudden changes of fortune, almost too stereotyped for dialogue—Sturges shifts from satirizing social-problem movies (and the Hollywood types who make them) to reenacting them in a setting of dreamlike intensity. Sturges traps his well-meaning director in just the kind of movie he wanted to make, a stylized world of arbitrary punishment and grim endurance. After merely slumming in social misery, he is swallowed up by it, with no lifeline to his familiar world.

But the movie doesn't end here. On Saturday night McCrea, along with his fellow prisoners, gains momentary relief watching cartoons of Mickey Mouse and Pluto. *This* is what the Depression audiences really needed, says Sturges: escape, lighthearted enjoyment. The point is pungently philistine and a trifle complacent: Sturges the comedy director is telling us that laughter, not lower-depths sociology or protest, is the universal solvent. It's the entertainer, not the plebeian revolutionary, who truly has the common touch. Comedy eases the burden of even the most wretched of the earth, and unites the privileged artist for a brief moment with his suffering brother, that thirties myth, the common man. Yet *Sullivan's Travels*, though self-congratulatory, pays handsome tribute to the genre it satirizes and re-creates, the lower-depths movie. For the comic artist, as Chaplin showed, the way down is the way out, into life's pratfalls and social embarrassments.

The kinds of protest movies Sturges had in mind stretch from the Warner Brothers problem movies of the early 1930s, such as *I Am a Fugitive from a Chain Gang* (directed by Mervyn LeRoy in 1932) and *Wild Boys of the Road* (William Wellman, 1933), to the grand summation of the decade's social consciousness on film, John Ford's unusually faithful 1940 adaptation of *The Grapes of Wrath*. Significantly, all three of these films are road movies, not about observers doing research on the poor but about ordinary people uprooted from a stable life, forced to wander in search of something better, only to find more hellish conditions among other displaced, unwanted, or viciously mistreated people. The social disintegration, violence, and human isolation we see in these films are closely related to the gangster films from which they emerged, some of them made by the same men, often at the same studio, Warner Brothers. (Meryn LeRoy directed *Little Caesar*, Wellman directed *The Public Enemy*, and Paul Muni starred in *Scarface* shortly before he made *I Am a Fugitive*.) Hard-boiled drama and hard-boiled comedy, quick, crisp, and topical, edged over easily into social protest, Warner's-style; the booming receipts saved the studio from the Depression, while other studios went broke.

Like some of the gangster films, *I Am a Fugitive* traces the roots of social turmoil back to the Great War, which had exposed the men who fought in it to violence and carnage but also to a wider world than the one they came from. In a later, elegiac gangster film, *The Roaring Twenties*, made at the end of the 1930s, Jimmy Cagney returns from the war to find his place taken by men who didn't go off to fight. His reluctant career in crime begins when he can't reclaim his niche in the old order. *I Am a Fugitive*, based on a controversial magazine serial that was turned into a novel, shows us how James Allen (played by Paul Muni) returns from the war to face a different world, a family that can't understand what he's been through or how he's changed. This is exactly what happens in Hemingway's great story "Soldier's Home." Just as Hemingway's returning soldier, having seen what he's seen, can no longer summon up the will or purpose to do *anything*, Muni finds his old factory job confining. After so much army regimentation, he recoils at the rigid industrial routine. He doesn't want to be a "soldier of peace," a soldier of anything. He wants to be creative, an engineer who can work with his hands and build projections of his own dreams. Instead, he's chained to his desk, to a job he can do with his eyes closed. His brother, a minister, speaks for conventional society and preaches personal submission; he cannot understand his malaise. "The army changes a fellow," Muni tries to explain. "I've changed . . . been through hell."

So he leaves his steady job, crisscrosses the country, gradually becoming a hobo as he's unable to find work. He tries to pawn his war medals—at a pawnshop that already has a case full of such medals. Evidently, many others have been brought to the same pass. The time frame is vague, but we're still in the early 1920s, a relatively prosperous period (though there was indeed a postwar recession between 1920 and 1922). We soon understand that the film is projecting the social crisis of the Depression onto the earlier decade, thinking about the twenties in thirties terms: scarcity of work, a mobility born of ambition but soon fueled by desperation, the disruption of social bonds and the promises embodied in the discarded medals, which speak to us of discarded values, dreams, and ideals.

Soon, caught up in another hobo's stickup attempt, Muni is railroaded by a crude legal system into ten years on a chain gang. We see, as Andrew Bergman remarks, "the process by which an individual could move outside the law by standing still." Thus the first of the great social-protest movies of the 1930s doesn't deal directly with the Depression, for what happens to James Allen can hardly be seen as a result of hard times. Nevertheless, the film couldn't have been made without the Depression frame of mind. As Bergman adds, "the forces that continually disrupt Allen's life are invisible but all-powerful: implied were a decaying economy and a rigid, depersonalized legal structure."[9]

What made the movie famous was something more visceral and concrete: the concentration-camp atmosphere of the prison barracks, the casual brutality of the overseers and the chain gang itself, the wasting away of a desperately ill prisoner who is forced to work, the torture of the sweatbox and the inedible food, and the excruciating feat of the escape, from removal of Allen's leg irons with blows from a sledgehammer to the flight through the swamps pursued by vicious armed guards with snarling dogs. These scenes have the sensory yet social immediacy of the early Soviet films on which they were modeled. This imagery was so memorable that it could be quoted effortlessly in later films, from *Sullivan's Travels* to *Cool Hand Luke*, a Paul Newman vehicle, to Jim Jarmusch's indie *Down by Law,* set in the Louisiana bayous. Like *The Jungle* and *The Grapes of Wrath, I Am a Fugitive* was one of the works that actually made a difference in the real world, exploding in violent controversy that led to reform of the grotesque system of "justice" it vividly exposed. But the really radical twist in the movie has not been fully understood.

After escaping north and reversing his two names, James Allen manages to invert his position in society as well. He gets the job in construction he's always wanted—a job that his work on the chain gang had obscenely parodied—and between 1924 and 1929, in Chicago, under his new identity, he builds himself into one of the upstanding citizens of the community. Blackmailed and eventually betrayed by a woman he is forced to marry, he returns voluntarily to the South, by agreement, to serve out a symbolic ninety-day sentence. But the unnamed state—actually Georgia—goes back on its word, subjects him to more brutality than before, then refuses to release him at the promised time.

Those who could not believe he would agree to go back are proven right. His only way out is another escape. Now, at top speed, all he did before must be done again. But the frenzied, desperate, utterly disillusioned creature who escapes a second time is not the cocky, confident person who broke out before. During the escape he loses the old man who embodies the only bit of humanity he's ever encountered on the chain gang, the cynical realist who was stunned that he had willingly returned, but also the living symbol of his own dwindling humanity and resilience.

Careening along with a truckload of dynamite, James Allen has gone from being an unfairly victimized citizen, still resourceful and full of hope, to an explosive desperado hell-bent on freedom or self-destruction. Now there's no question of putting his life together again, not simply because of the Depression but because of his own grim depression. His self-assurance has crumbled with his trust. The man who was stupid enough to walk back into the chain gang now sees through everything: "The state's promise didn't mean anything. . . . Their crimes are worse than mine." The bedrock faith in the system, which brought him through the war, which survived poverty, injustice, and physical torture, has now disintegrated, leaving him a haunted and a haunting man.

The last lines of the movie are a famous exception to the Hollywood cult of the happy ending. He appears in the shadows, a shadow himself, for a furtive goodbye to his second wife. "How do you live?" she asks him. A hollow, frightened voice hisses, "I steal." His crazed eyes tell us that his second escape, for all its reckless bravado, didn't really take. He's a wreck of a man, unable to function except as the criminal and fugitive he was falsely accused of being. Quite literally, society has made him what he is: a man who, in his half-demented, half-realistic fears, sees through society, sees the lie of its official values. The unusual title of the film, like Muni's last line, places this man in an ongoing, open-ended, unresolved present: I *am* a fugitive, I still am. He points a finger at us, for he is the homeless, shadowy outcast we would all prefer to forget. The movie ends but his flight continues. It would be a long time before another American film ended on such a hopeless, accusing note.

Subsequent films like Wild Boys of the Road *and* The Grapes of Wrath, made during the Roosevelt presidency, have a quite different tone. Though they show us a society deeply disrupted by the Depression, both films make room for benign government officials with more than a passing resemblance to FDR. The understanding judge in the first film sits beneath the Blue Eagle of the NRA (National Recovery Administration), leavening justice with a social worker's caring insight. The government camp administrator in *The Grapes of Wrath*, whose pince-nez bespeaks benevolent dignity, provides the individualistic Joads with clean, well-run quarters that restore their self-respect and allay their suspicions of bureaucracy and authority. Like many other Depression stories, both films try to show how the old American individualism can't really solve the economic crisis. Everyone is in the same boat. The representatives of the law who bulldoze their homes and rout them out of makeshift camps have families of their own, children who also need to be fed. The only solutions are collective ones. The migrants must help themselves by banding together and recognizing their common plight. They must learn to accept the aid filtered down to them through the New Deal.

Wild Boys of the Road is a slight film with an unconvincing ending, yet because it is about children rather than grown-up hobos, it movingly evokes the meaning of the road for the disrupted families of the 1930s. The film begins in a Hardy Boys world of small-town adolescent problems familiar to us from a thousand other movies. These are people who won't admit to poverty, won't take charity, yet are increasingly unable to support their own children. Our adolescent hero, sensing his father's quiet anguish, makes the ultimate sacrifice and has his cherished jalopy dismantled. Finally he takes to the road to give them one fewer mouth to feed, and soon joins a virtual army of wayward adolescents whose folks can no longer manage to care for them. Harassed wherever they turn, the kids learn not to trust authority, only each other. They come up against a respectable world of towns and cities that, behind barricades of law and order, turn a deaf ear to their human needs. Yet they also meet some benevolent adults who help them when they're in trouble, anticipating the thoughtful judge who sympathizes with them and gives them a break at the end of the movie.

One feature of the movie is the way young people band together in improvised Hoovervilles to form small societies of their own. This is the recurring thirties vision of an alternative community that would some-how free us of our worst social inequities.[10] The government camp in *The Grapes of Wrath* with its wise administrator and modern sanitary facili-ties is just such a well-planned arrangement, a kind of Americanized communism from above, with family life intact. In both *Wild Boys* and *Grapes* these model encampments are hated and often physically attacked by the hired mercenaries of bigotry and capitalism who surround them. The people living in them, weak as they are, represent a challenge to the system of competition and exploitation that rules the larger world. (In their pitched battles with railroad detectives, police, and vigilante goons, they have the look of a ragtag army that hints at revolutionary possibili-ties.) Thus, along with the mythology of the road, with its hardships and manly liberties, there developed a mythology of the free and poor society of equals, a society born of desperation as much as of dreams, where the gruff and timid, the maimed and the hardy, could live together in some kind of rough harmony.

Out of Work, Out of Luck

According to a 1935 book by Kingsley Davis called *Youth in the Depres-sion*, *Wild Boys* was not quite accurate in at least one respect. Though many men and boys did take to the road, the young ones, instead of forming communities of their own, usually traveled in twos and threes and attached themselves to the hobo jungles of older men. The adult equivalent of *Wild Boys of the Road* was a crisply written novel by Edward Anderson, *Hungry Men*, that won a prize from its publisher, Doubleday, Doran, in 1935. (Promptly forgotten, it was reprinted by Penguin fifty years later, after the success of William Kennedy's *Ironweed*, a modern tale of a Depression bum.) Born in Texas in 1906, Anderson cut his teeth as a small-town reporter, a boxer, an itinerant hobo, and a pulp writer channeling stories directly from the police blotter. His work, like Tom Kromer's, conveys the unique flavor of being down and out during the Depression. Anderson was one of the promising young writers of the late 1930s, but he faded soon after the 1937 publication of his second and final novel, *Thieves Like Us*, a Bonnie and Clyde story that has survived in numerous film versions, including Nicholas Ray's *They Live By Night* (1948) and Robert Altman's *Thieves Like Us* (1974). Anderson himself failed as a screenwriter in Hollywood and went back to journalism. He died in obscurity in 1969, in Brownsville, Texas, where he edited a local newspaper.

Until quite recently *Hungry Men* was not mentioned in any standard account of the proletarian novel, for it exploded the narrow limits that had been laid down for such fiction. With its generic title (like Michael Gold's), it could easily be mistaken for a piece of sociology or Depression journalism, which it partly is. Though the book does contain an older worker (a veteran sailor named Boats) who spouts revolutionary phrases, and is killed for his pains, and a younger protagonist, Acel Stecker, who takes over a few of his ideas, the proletarian conversion formula, along with politics in general, remains quite peripheral to the book, taking up barely a handful of pages.

Buried somewhere in *Hungry Men* is a mild revolutionary anger, but the book is so pared down and subdued that it flares up at only a few points, and then quite ambiguously. Though Boats fits the part as the Communist martyr, Acel takes on merely a fragmentary, inarticulate version of his faith. In a rare moment of political discussion he says, "They can call it what they want, Communism or Bolshevism or Socialism, but there is going to be a change. Men are not going to keep bumming or work in flop houses for ninety cents a week forever." But a page later he wonders whether the *Lumpenproletariat* make any kind of material for a radical upheaval: "A revolution never will start among a bunch of bums. Sometimes I wonder if it's worth your time to talk to them about it all. . . . But there's a million men in this country on the road, and if these men were organized, or prepared to follow some organization, it'd be something."[11]

These pages, far from typical, are among the weakest in the book; they project a political consciousness onto rudimentary characters in a fake, condescending way. Far from being a party novel, or even a political novel, *Hungry Men* is a book about hunger and about the road, both of which Anderson had studied firsthand between 1931 and 1934. Unable to sell his stories, he had taken to the road, as Algren had done, to learn something about life in Depression America. Like Algren's *Somebody in Boots*, the book is rooted in what the author found while he was bumming around. It is written with the mannered simplicity of so many proletarian novels, a style that suggests the influence of Hemingway yet lacks the deeper resonance, the suggestiveness that makes Hemingway seem more a prose poet than a fiction writer in his short pieces. Where Hemingway is taciturn, keeping his emotions under fierce control, the prose of *Hungry Men* simply feels uninflected, perhaps emotionally wounded, more like later minimalist writers than like Hemingway himself. This seems to be the case even when Acel Stecker is telling us what he supposedly feels:

> I'd like to get a hundred dollars. . . . With a hundred bucks I could get a new suit and new shoes and have fifty bucks in my pocket. With a new suit and everything and money in my pocket I'd feel different. This is what has been the matter with me. It's psychological. A man can't get a job looking like a bum or feeling like one. (52)

There's something numb yet also numbing about these short sentences with their repetitions and conjunctions, their avoidance of long words and metaphors, or subordinate clauses. Yet Acel Stecker is not really a bum, he isn't even a proletarian; as an unemployed musician and a "college man," he is a declassed member of the middle class, as Anderson himself was when he hoboed around the country, as any middle-class author is when he writes this kind of plebeian novel. The book's strength is in the wonderfully authentic atmosphere and details, not in its characters. Though Anderson may be simplifying himself when he gets into Stecker's mind, he is being true to his own experience of living and writing this novel. If you call it an educated man's *nostalgie de la boue*, you must add that the Depression gave it a timely meaning.

The problem with Acel Stecker's "psychology," from our point of view, is that it's a social psychology rather than a personal one. It's meant to account for a whole class of men trapped in a general crisis, not for the wrinkles of an individual mind. Anderson's characters are not the hopelessly derelict—those who have fallen through the bottom of society—but those just surviving on the margin, always looking for a break, blaming their hard luck, wondering where they'll find the next meal, the next place to sleep. Anderson's rival as the laureate of the lower depths, Tom Kromer, complained that he had softened the picture, not shown how bad it could get.[12] One cardinal rule that few of these drifters can follow is that "a man should keep up a good front," for he can't even think of landing a job or shacking up with a woman unless he has a clean shave and a decent suit. When Acel is arrested, he worries about his appearance. "If I could just have shaved this morning I wouldn't look so much like a tramp" (174). But he hopes his way of talking will rescue him:

> The judge will know I am no ordinary bum when I address him. He will know that by the language I use. *Your honor, my companions are here in the courtroom now, and they will testify that we were just walking along there, minding our own business, and this man steps out and starts trouble.* The judge will know by the language I use that I am no ordinary bum in court for fighting on the street. . . . (175)

Instead, in an ironic twist that ends the novel, Acel and his friends get credit off for their patriotism, having refused to play the Marxist "International" with their little street band. The final pages of the book shift into a political cartoon as the group, now safely anti-Communist, promises to prosper as The Three Americans, playing war songs at veterans' smokers. The rudimentary growth of their radical ideas has now been stunted into class betrayal.

Acel has already remarked to himself that stories of hoboes riding freight trains and getting run in by the police don't really interest many people. "These stories had to have surprises at the end." But this particular surprise, which could have come from tongue-in-cheek novels like Nathanael West's *A Cool Million* or Ralph Ellison's *Invisible Man*—books

built on surreal or ironic reversals—hardly belongs in a work as straight
and as somber as *Hungry Men*, which has nary a shred of a plot and whose
real strength comes in exposing how life feels in the nether reaches of
society. There's a good deal of talk about hunger itself that convinces us
that Anderson is speaking from firsthand knowledge:

> "You know when I was a kid," Acel said, "I used to think hunger was
> something like a toothache, only worse. I mean when you went a
> long time. But now I know there isn't much to it."
> "All hunger is, is your belly muscles drawing up."
> "Yeah, a man could starve to death and not know it." (10)

Anderson not only gets the feel of things right; he gets the feelings too.
"After he had eaten, Acel got up and stood at the edge of the highway.
He felt strength in the breadth of his chest and the slope of his shoulders, in the steadiness of his legs and the firmness of his stomach" (16).
Yet hitchhiking is humiliating to him; it subjects him to the harangues
that the respectable world pours into his captive ear, usually a dose of the
bootstraps philosophy that has little relevance to a man in Acel's position.
When he takes food and shelter from the Salvation Army, Acel is in the
same vulnerable situation, bending his knees and listening to sermons as
the price for a bowl of soup and perhaps a pair of shoes.

By taking us aimlessly from scene to scene across the country, Anderson is trying to paint the whole picture of the hungry man's world. Good
as he is on the will-o'-the-wisp of landing a job, he is even better on the
challenge of finding a woman. When Acel gets to New York, he falls for a
girl named Corinne, but after they take a cheap hotel room he drives her
away by being suspicious and surly. Like so many of the Depression's victims, Acel's self-confidence has been badly bruised, and he expresses his
insecurity by taunting her and imagining how many other men she's had.
Later, with some money from his friend Boats, they set up house together,
simulating middle-class marital respectability. But Acel eventually drifts
away to look for work, and he writes Corinne out of his mind by assuming she has slipped into prostitution. "I heard a girl say one time that a
down-and-out man became a bum and a woman turned whore" (143). In
a short chapter set in New Orleans he meets another girl, they plan to get
together, but this time she turns skeptical and disappears. This self-con-

tained little sketch, full of the understated poetry of missed connections and unlived lives, could easily pass for a short story by Sherwood Anderson or Hemingway. Better than most Depression writers, Anderson shows how social problems translate into psychological problems: loss of confidence, self-accusation, and throttled, helpless anger. As social rejects, his characters don't have the luxury to be individuals, but they usually react to their plight in fresh and unexpected ways. Out of some fear of reading like a novel, *Hungry Men* doesn't allow itself the indulgence of a plot, as if the mechanics of narrative closure would undermine the authenticity of its social observation. Thus, as a road novel, the book imitates the structure of its characters' shapeless, distended lives. Their motto is: "Just keep moving and you will always run into something. That was what that old bum in Omaha said. Just keep moving and something will turn up—a flop, a handout, a ride, a cigarette, a piece of change. All you had to do was keep moving" (134).

The historian William E. Leuchtenburg has written,

> As the depression years wore on, the jobless adjusted to a kind of purposeless motion, like the music in the favorite song of the day that went 'round and around, like the marathon dancers who shuffled listlessly around the dance floor barely able to keep their bodies moving, like the six-day bike riders who spun endlessly around an oval track, anesthetizing spectators by the relentless monotony of the circular grind.[13]

Incessant, often aimless movement was at once a key metaphor of the 1930s and a pervasive social reality. Many were simply dancing in the dark, heading nowhere, or pushing hard just to keep going.

One chapter of *Hungry Men* is called "On the Road," but that phrase could apply to much else in the novel. There are even passages to make us think of Kerouac:

> I have walked down a lot of streets, just moseying around like this. In Frisco and Minneapolis. In Denver and St. Louis. In little towns like Paducah and Ranger and St. Augustine. I have kind of liked them all and sort of hated to leave them. Each new town makes me forget the other. They're like girls. (134)

Reading Kerouac's *On the Road*, like hearing the rhythms of Mike Gold in Ginsberg's poetry, reminds us of how much the Beat writers, in their recoil from what they took to be the respectability of postwar writing and the conformity of postwar society, modeled themselves on the writers of the thirties. Kerouac began as a direct imitator of Thomas Wolfe. As the Depression loosened the social bonds of family life and ties to the workplace, the road and the drifter became metaphors for a community in disintegration. The critic Yvor Winters once wrote an attack on Robert Frost called "The Spiritual Drifter as Poet." He thought emotional confusion could be toxic to a writer. Even writers who did not write road novels became spiritual drifters, emotional vagabonds like William Saroyan, moral expatriates like Henry Miller—two other thirties prototypes for the Beat writers. In a period filled with collectivist solutions that seemed to go against the American grain, writers like Saroyan and Miller relished an anarchic individualism that gave a different accent to the idea of the common man. The Beats, who found themselves not in a society coming apart but in one that seemed too tightly held together, transformed the privations, the desperate marginality of the 1930s, into a willed and voluntary poverty, just as they turned life on the road from an economic necessity into a spiritual adventure. The Beats reached back to the myths and rhythms of the 1930s to act out a criticism of postwar America, which had either forgotten the Depression or remembered it all too well.

In the end, however, *Hungry Men* has an entirely different feeling from a book like *On the Road*. To Anderson the small-town Depression newspaperman, the world out there really exists; it is not a function of his own need for excitement or his sheer love of aimless velocity. In a notorious passage in *On the Road*, Sal Paradise, Kerouac's alter ego, writes, "At lilac evening I walked with every muscle aching among the lights of the 27th and Welton in the Denver colored section, wishing I were a Negro, feeling that the best the white world had offered was not enough ecstasy for me, not enough life, joy, kicks, darkness, music, not enough night." Though Sal himself is a somewhat dim figure, with a strong sense of his inner fear and dependency, his dream is to become expansive and spontaneous like Dean Moriarty, and this wish is embodied in the narrative flow of the novel. Acel Stecker, on the other hand, is only trying to get by, and the flat, hard-boiled style of the novel reflects his pinched horizons. The same imperative that made Thomas Wolfe the right model for Kerouac made Hemingway the necessary example for Anderson and other proletarian authors. Just as Hemingway's story "The Killers" taught thirties crime novelists like Dashiell Hammett, James Cain, and W. R. Burnett to write lean, tough, suggestive dialogue, other stories like "The Battler," in which Nick Adams is menaced by a punch-drunk old prizefighter turned hobo, gave lessons in laconic writing to lower-depths novelists like Edward Anderson.

We can see the overlap between these two kinds of Hemingway-induced fiction especially in the handling of women, as in the following passage:

> Acel pulled out cigarettes, and Corinne took one. The match he held for her trembled. "That's what you are doing to me," he said. "I'm falling for you, honey."
>
> "You certainly are different."
>
> "I'll bet you got a kick out of me choking up the way I did when I asked you if you ever had any experience. I didn't know but what you taught a Sunday school somewhere. I'll bet you got a kick out of that."
>
> "You are sweet."
>
> "I'm gettin' fogbound over you, if you want to know." (67)

This slightly absurd exchange, with its dated slang and choked (or doomed) romanticism, already belongs to the fatalistic crime world of *Red Harvest* and *The Maltese Falcon* that Anderson would soon try out in *Thieves Like Us*. Along with the proletarian novelists, many of the hard-boiled writers were leftists. So were the screenwriters who would later adapt those books into the films noirs of the 1940s. Some had begun their careers as journalists, just as Hemingway did, and they respected a fact when they saw one. Just as crime movies led directors toward social problem movies, crime fiction was an apolitical version of the lower-depths novel, especially because the criminal was frequently seen as the product of the society that spawned him. (*They Made Me a Criminal* was the title of one late-thirties movie.) Yet the audience was also made to identify with the criminal, as the guardians of public morals often complained in the first years of the decade. The characters played by Edward G. Robinson, Jimmy Cagney, George Raft, Paul Muni, and later Humphrey Bogart were embattled outsiders clawing their way to the top, never white-collar criminals who ruled impersonal organizations. In the violent ways they amassed wealth and power despite their humble origins, they were fantasy figures for people suffering through hard times. Their cause was themselves, not politics or revolution, yet they served as the focus of rebellious energy at a time when many felt helpless before larger forces. They had style, panache; they knew the moves, inventing themselves as they went along; they made a mark on their world before they went under.

We can distinguish between the hard-boiled crime novel, with its atmosphere of double-dealing and corruption, and the gangster movie of the same period, where the criminal often emerged as an ambiguously heroic and tragic figure. As Lincoln Kirstein wrote about Cagney in *The Hound and Horn* in 1932: "Cagney may be a dirty little low-life rat, a hoodlum, a small-time racketeer, but when his riddled body is propped up against his mother's door, mummied in bandages and flecked with blood, we catch our throats and realize that this is a hero's death."[14] No such claim can be made for the dozens of criminals who kill each other off in Hammett's *Red Harvest*, or even for the private dick who maneuvers them into doing it. Even today there is something distinctly modern about the nihilism and disillusionment of the hard-boiled novel of that period. Though rooted in the effect of World War I on the Hemingway generation, this mood has worn better than the sodden pieties of the Popular Front or the revolutionary Left. It created a bleak picture of contemporary America that radicals could live with. Unlike the proletarian novel, however, it was well suited to the violent and melodramatic formulas of popular culture. The growth of pulp fiction, especially crime fiction, in the 1930s created an alternate image of American life that was relatively free of the censorship of moralists of both left and right, at a time when the "serious" novel assumed a heavy burden of social responsibility. Yet the lower-depths novel, with its indelible portrait of hunger, poverty, rootlessness, and psychological malaise, gave an original though little-recognized flavor to proletarian fiction. At its best it combined the down-and-out tradition of Jack London, Maxim Gorky, and Knut Hamsun with the stylistic restraint of Hemingway to give us an illuminating image of Depression life.

Steinbeck Country

John Steinbeck was virtually the only proletarian writer who achieved enduring popular success. His novels are all in print today—even more widely read than they were by the end of the 1930s, the era to which he is usually relegated. My encounters with John Steinbeck's work began, like most people's, when I was young, with wonderfully readable short novels such as *The Pearl*, *The Red Pony*, and *Cannery Row.* There was something elemental about them, a rich sensuous simplicity that also led many readers to leave Steinbeck behind as an enthusiasm to be outgrown. Since I was never required to read him in high school or college, his more ambitious books were not spoiled for me by bad teaching or premature exposure. But Steinbeck seemed no more than a strong regional writer who had taken possession of a small corner of California, including the Salinas Valley, where he was born, and the Monterey peninsula, with its canneries and colorful paisanos. This had enchanted me early on, and I sought it out again, with nostalgia, while I lived in northern California with my wife and kids in the summer of 1973, when we visited Monterey and Cannery Row.

When I began to examine the effects of the Depression on American culture, another side of Steinbeck took hold of me: the books of reportage and protest that earned him a central role in the social conscience of the Depression. Along with the work of the photographers of the Farm Security Administration, such as Dorothea Lange and Walker Evans, and documentary filmmakers like Pare Lorentz, who inspired him and helped him see, Steinbeck developed into one of the key witnesses to those years of trauma and social suffering. With the exception of Harriet Beecher Stowe in *Uncle Tom's Cabin*, Upton Sinclair in *The Jungle*, and perhaps Richard Wright with *Native Son*, no protest writer had a greater impact on how Americans understood their own country. The plight and migration of the Joads, as conceived by Steinbeck and filmed by John Ford, the parched world of the Dust Bowl, the loss of a family home, the trek in search of work, the awful conditions for migrant farm labor, the struggle to keep the family together, became a metaphor for the Depression as a whole. It aroused sympathy and indignation that reached beyond literature and became part of our social iconography. It was as if Steinbeck had been reporting on a real family, which in a sense he was.

Unfortunately, his success as a protest writer undermined his literary standing, especially after the war, when that commitment looked narrow and simplistic. The Nobel Prize for Literature usually elicits a brief burst of national pride, but after Steinbeck was named, in 1962, the *New York Times Book Review* published a sharp dissent by Arthur Mizener under the heading "Does a Moral Vision of the Thirties Deserve a Nobel Prize?"— one of several attacks that, along with the prize itself, made it more difficult for him write to another novel before he died in 1968. From the time of early critiques by Mary McCarthy, Edmund Wilson, and Alfred Kazin, Steinbeck had never been a favorite of the intellectuals or even of his fellow writers. It's no surprise that the *Times* attack was written by F. Scott Fitzgerald's biographer, since Fitzgerald himself, though unfailingly generous toward most writers, was annoyed by Steinbeck's success, dismissing him in his letters as little more than a plagiarist who borrowed freely from his betters, including Frank Norris and D. H. Lawrence.

Fitzgerald had his reasons: Steinbeck was the kind of socially committed writer who had displaced him in the 1930s and made his own work seem like a back number. Fitzgerald's untypical rage at Steinbeck was a dirge for his own troubled career. Yet Steinbeck, with his remarkably simple, concrete, and accessible style, remains virtually the introduction to literature for many younger readers. Thanks to his earthiness, sensuous immediacy, and sheer storytelling ability, Steinbeck's work has not dated like that of more ambitious or grimly topical contemporaries.

While there is little doubt that Steinbeck did his greatest work in the 1930s, most of what he wrote then had little connection to social protest, or even to the realism and naturalism to which his name has been attached. He first achieved modest fame and sales not as a social critic but with his lighthearted evocation of the paisanos of Monterey in *Tortilla Flat* (1935), a book that echoes Malory's Arthurian legends. He had a huge commercial success with *Of Mice and Men*, the least political of his three novels about migrant farmworkers, which went in rapid succession from Book-of-the-Month Club choice to Broadway play to Hollywood movie. In many ways this is less a social novel than a tissue of symbolic relationships; it fits quite well with his short fiction of the early thirties, including *The Pastures of Heaven*, *Tortilla Flat*, and the stories in *The Long Valley*. To explode the received wisdom of Steinbeck as a protest writer, one could locate the authentic Steinbeck in this prepolitical work, where I first discovered him. We might see these early books as his real imaginative center, even as his oblique response to the Depression (which scarcely figures in them at all), and argue that he was sidetracked into a social consciousness that was not natural to him.

In this reading, the core of Steinbeck's work would be his feeling for the land, his evocation of his native California as a natural paradise, his hatred of middle-class acquisitiveness and ambition, and his warm sympathy for outsiders who form a natural community built on impulse and fellow feeling. Like nature itself, these instinctive anarchists mock the values of commercial society by remaining oblivious to them. By emphasizing works with strong mythic underpinnings, this approach would link Steinbeck not with proletarian writers or social realists, with whom he felt little affinity, but with the free-spirited low-life explorers like William Saroyan, Nelson Algren, and Henry Miller, whose heroes are footloose individualists, vagabonds who live by their own code—live by instinct, apart from the social values that constrain most other people. This sort of untamed creature is certainly close to Steinbeck's heart, the emotional ground from which he sets out. There is a Rabelaisian strain in his work, an affection for hell-raisers and troublemakers who act out nature's mutiny against all social codes. This core of rebellious naturalism, rooted in the instinctual life, explains why he responded so strongly to writers as different as Frank Norris, Sherwood Anderson, and D. H. Lawrence. Yet he also had a near-mystical feeling for the soil, which, though often muted into comedy, gave his books their strong sense of place. It's hard to pass through Monterey or the Salinas Valley, changed as they are, without thinking of them as Steinbeck country and looking around for some of his people.

One of the features of Steinbeck's work that nettles humanists and idealists is his insistence on the animal basis of human life, as seen in our fundamental need for food, shelter, physical expression, and, above all, tenderness and companionship. For better or worse, Steinbeck leaves man's more sublime aspirations to writers of cosmic or tragic ambition. In his letters he frequently sets aside such grand aims to stress the palpable and immediate. Asked by a friend in 1934 what he really wants out of life, he provocatively answers in strict biological and physical terms:

As an organism I am so simple that I want to be comfortable and comfort consists in—a place to sleep, dry and fairly soft, lack of hunger, almost any kind of food, occasional loss of semen in intercourse when it becomes troublesome, and a good deal of work. . . . I don't want to possess anything, nor to be anything. I have no ambition because on inspection the ends of ambition achieved seem tiresome.[15]

Steinbeck's modesty extends to his work, which also seems to belong to the biorhythms of his nervous system rather than to any higher goals as an artist. In a 1933 letter, long before he was gripped by a social conscience, he writes, "I work because I know it gives me pleasure to work. It is as simple as that and I don't require any other reasons. I am losing a sense of self to a marked degree and that is a pleasant thing." This is reminiscent of Keats's famous notion of Negative Capability, the writer's loss of identity in his immersion in subjects outside himself. Keats attributes this chameleon quality above all to Shakespeare, but Steinbeck disclaims being anything but a minor writer, a smooth, self-gratifying professional.

A couple of years ago I realized that I was not the material of which great artists are made and that I was rather glad I wasn't. And since then I have been happier simply to do the work and to take the reward at the end of every day that is given for a day of honest work. . . . I have a book to write. I think about it for a while and then I write it. There is nothing more. When it is done I have little interest in it. By the time one comes out I am usually tied up in another. (87)

These letters are typical. Steinbeck was no intellectual heavyweight, and even at the peak of his career he was plagued by doubts about his own abilities. His description of himself as a physical animal, a simple organism, is consistent not only with his self-portrait as a writer but with the view of humanity that emerges in his early work. It also helps explain why those early books, all brief, episodic, and unambitious, were spun off with such facility. The writer himself was penniless and unknown, with no expectation of ever making money from his work. He was partly supported by his father, at some cost to his self-respect. He wrote *Tortilla Flat* as a refuge from the illness and constant care of his parents, who were both dying. "Its tone, I guess, is direct rebellion against all the sorrow of our house" (89–90). The unexpected success of the book, published five days after his father's death, would enable him to take on more ambitious projects, including *The Grapes of Wrath,* but his sudden popularity would complicate his life with a self-consciousness he had tried to avoid and could not bear. "I'm scared to death of popularity," he writes, soon after *Tortilla Flat* appeared. "It has ruined everyone I know" (111–12). It endangers a writer's honesty, besides making it more difficult to lose himself in his material. When he wins a prize for *Tortilla Flat*, he is loath to collect it in person. "The whole early part of my life was poisoned with egotism," he explains, "and then gradually I began to lose it." As a result, he claims, "in the last few books I have felt a curious richness as though my life had been multiplied through having become identified in a most real way with people who were not me." "If I become a trade mark," he fears, if he emerges from behind his work, "I shall lose the ability to do that" (119). Explaining his refusal to attend book luncheons, give interviews, appear on radio programs, or even turn up to collect an award, he tells his agent, "I simply cannot write books if a consciousness of self is thrust on me. Must have some anonymity" (138).

The small fame and income that Steinbeck achieved after *Tortilla Flat* was nothing like the fame and wealth thrust upon him four years later, in 1939, with the success (and notoriety) of *The Grapes of Wrath,* but these fears were prophetic of the terrible conflicts, the erosion of self-confidence he felt while writing that book and the sense of decline, of anticlimax, he felt after publishing it. "This book has become a misery to me because of my inadequacy," he wrote in his journal in 1938. By then it was his larger ambitions, his determination to do justice to a great subject, that brought him so much misery. To focus exclusively on the early books that preceded that fame would take him at his word as a minor professional writer, who later happened to cause a sensation with some quasi-journalistic fiction that touched on burning social problems. It would beg the question of how those simpler, more casual works, which gave him such pleasure to write, set the stage for the larger books, which, with all their flaws, brought him into angry collision with some of America's cherished values and with the forces that shaped society during the Depression.

For all his attraction to biological theory, which led him to use fiction to probe notions like "group-man" and the "phalanx," Steinbeck was anything but a rigorous or systematic thinker. In gauging his response to the Depression, the subject for which he will surely be remembered, we grapple with many seeming inconsistencies. How was the rich valley of

The Pastures of Heaven of 1932 transformed into ugly scenes of labor conflict and exploitation of *In Dubious Battle* in 1936 and *The Grapes of Wrath* in 1939? How did the carefree poverty of the paisanos in *Tortilla Flat* of 1935 turn into the wretched, heartsick poverty of *The Grapes of Wrath*? How did the bohemian contempt for ownership, possessions, and steady work in *Tortilla Flat* give way to the Joads' desperation for work or George and Lennie's poignant dream of self-sufficiency, of owning "a little piece a' lan'" and raising rabbits, which is at the emotional core of *Of Mice and Men*? And finally, how did Steinbeck's almost clinically objective sympathy for the strikers in *In Dubious Battle* and his mixed feelings about their calculating Communist organizers turn into his impassioned advocacy for the Joads in the epic and poetic pages of *The Grapes of Wrath*? Even in the natural paradise of the early books, people are gifted at making themselves unhappy. But how did the serpent of American capitalism, self-interest, and exploitation find its way into Steinbeck's California Eden, making it such a grim and miserable scene? Some answers to these questions must wait until I turn to *The Grapes of Wrath* later in this book.

Steinbeck's initial vision of California as a fertile garden is the background against which his Depression drama is played out. *In Dubious Battle*, *Of Mice and Men*, and *The Grapes of Wrath* give us three versions of this story, supplemented by the bleak articles Steinbeck wrote about the conditions of migrant farmworkers for the *San Francisco News* and *The Nation* in 1936, which mark his transformation from a detached observer who sees a strike as the crucible of a larger metaphysical conflict to an indignant muckraker and reformer exposing the human costs of the system. The fruit of American plenty on the California trees and vines is exactly the fruit that the beleaguered migrants cannot have, the dream that will never be realized. It hangs on the trees all around them, but they cannot enjoy it. The simple organic needs that John Steinbeck shares with the paisanos of Monterey are precisely the needs that loom so large for Lennie and George or for the Joads when they are thwarted by a selfish, competitive, manipulated system. Surrounded by hostility amid plenty, Steinbeck's characters are brought together by dreams never to be realized. "Ever'thing in California is owned," someone tells Tom Joad. "They ain't nothin' left. An' them people that owns it is gonna hang on to it if they got ta kill ever-body in the worl' to do it." Ownership turns people ugly. There are huge concentrations of agricultural wealth that need workers but also keep them close to starvation. This system deprives people of basic hope, human dignity, animal satisfaction, and even the means of survival, amid great natural abundance. The seeming contradictions between Steinbeck's pastoral works and his protest novels are parts of a jigsaw puzzle that in the end fit neatly together, though, as reviewers noted from the beginning, he never wrote two books that were exactly alike.

What kind of books were these? What use did Steinbeck make of the material that the Depression belatedly sent his way? Steinbeck did not seek out the subject of migrant labor because he was a committed reformer or because he saw it as the poisoned apple in his California garden. "Steinbeck was always on the lookout for a story," says his biographer Jackson Benson.[16] In quick succession he had found and used one set of stories in *The Pastures of Heaven*, another in the cycle that became *Tortilla Flat*, yet others for the stories that would fill out *The Long Valley*. But the story behind his first real Depression novel, *In Dubious Battle*, was more topical and urgent. Though it is rarely included in the canon of proletarian writing, *In Dubious Battle* takes up the strict formulas of such fiction for its own use. It is a strike novel set among the migrant apple pickers in the fictional Torgas Valley in California. Furthermore, the relation between veteran Communist labor organizer and a young initiate is central, though here it's the younger man who sacrifices himself to the cause.

The story of *In Dubious Battle* is quickly told. Mac, the older Communist, and Jim, the novice, serve as catalysts for a strike they know will fail, as a way of radicalizing the otherwise docile migrant farmworkers. Instead of leading it themselves, they single out "natural" leaders among the men, such as Dakin and London, and gain their confidence. In this world the forces of the law are entirely on the side of the large agricultural producers, so the organizers know they'll take serious casualties, which they plan to turn to their advantage. Admirably self-sacrificing, they are also coldly fanatical, quite ready to sacrifice others for the cause without their consent, for they are sure they know the workers' interests better than they themselves do. It adds up to a remarkably ambivalent portrait on Steinbeck's part, though it is not entirely realistic.

Steinbeck didn't consider himself a social realist. Each of his books has mythic underpinnings from sources as different as the Bible, the Arthurian legends, and Milton. He was a student of biology, and his mentor, a marine biologist named Ed Ricketts, served as the model for several wisdom figures in his books, such as Doc Burton, the health officer in *In Dubious Battle*, who aids the strikers from the detached position of a nonparty sympathizer with strong ideas of his own. He articulates some of Steinbeck's pet ideas about mass behavior yet refuses any full ideological commitment, out of his faith in scientific observation and concern for moral ambiguity. "I don't want to put on the blinders of 'good' and 'bad,' and limit my vision," he tells the older Communist, Mac. "If I used the term 'good' on a thing I'd lose my license to inspect it, because there might be bad in it." When he expounds his idea of the collective biological creature he calls "group-man," Mac tells him "You're too God-damn far left to be a communist. You go too far with collectivization."[17]

Doc's ideas, murky and confused as they are, add a wrinkle of complexity and doubt to a novel that, like so much proletarian fiction, often feels too didactic. Steinbeck always seems to be looking for little pictures to convey the big picture, little words to project big ideas. Though the book is like a Baedeker of farm exploitation and party organizing tactics, Steinbeck insisted adamantly that his interest lay elsewhere. In a 1935 letter he wrote that he'd originally "planned to write a journalistic account of a strike. But as I thought of it as fiction the thing got bigger and bigger":

> I have used a small strike in an orchard valley as the symbol of man's bitter, eternal warfare with himself.
>
> I'm not interested in strike as means of raising men's wages, and I'm not interested in ranting about justice and oppression, mere outcroppings which indicate the condition. . . . The book is brutal. I wanted to be merely a recording consciousness, judging nothing, simply putting down the thing. I think it has the thrust, almost crazy, that mobs have. (*A Life in Letters*, 98)

He adds that the title comes from *Paradise Lost*, which he sees as an account of man's struggle with himself, as symbolized by a war in heaven, the rebellion of Satan. This is pretentious and not deeply relevant. Though some critics have tried to develop some detailed parallels between the novel and Milton's epic, the only effective element that *Paradise Lost* contributes is the ambiguity of Steinbeck's title, which is a phrase used by Satan himself to describe his struggle. *In Dubious Battle* was labeled a piece of pro-Communist propaganda by some early reviewers, but "dubious" bolsters our sense of Steinbeck's own political misgivings, for it can mean many things, from "of doubtful purpose" to "uncertain in outcome." The crux of the matter can be found in Steinbeck's subtle portrayal of Mac and Jim, the key Communist organizers.

According to Benson, early in 1934 Steinbeck met two fugitive union organizers and, with a nonfiction book initially in mind, arranged to buy the rights to their story (291). One of the two, Cicil McKiddy, became a major source for the novel. Steinbeck's strike in the Torgas Valley's apple orchards was loosely based on a prolonged and bitter 1933 cotton pickers' strike in which McKiddy was involved, as well as a peach pickers' strike that was won after four days. The modest, temporary gains achieved in these strikes incited the large fruit growers to band together to shut out unions, harass and arrest organizers, and keep labor costs down to near-starvation levels. The cotton pickers were paid $1.50 for putting in a ten-hour day, and in Steinbeck's novel it is a five-cent cut to fifteen cents an hour that triggers the strike. Benson describes succinctly how this wage-level could be sustained:

> Wages could be kept low and living conditions could remain miserable because with the Dust Bowl migrants entering the state in large numbers, joining the already more than sufficient Mexican and Filipino workers, there was a large surplus of farm labor. Many of the Dust Bowlers were so desperate that they would work for almost nothing. . . . The power of the growers' organizations, nearly always supported by local authorities, was nearly absolute, and that power, in combination with an almost inexhaustible supply of scabs, made union organizing extremely difficult and dangerous. (301)

The living situation of these men and their families was as bad as their economic plight. The popular social historian Frederick Lewis Allen described it this way in *Since Yesterday*:

> Huge farms were in the control of absentee owners or banks or corporations, and were accustomed to depend upon the labor of migratory "fruit tramps," who had formerly been mostly Mexicans, Japanese, and other foreigners, but now were increasingly Americans. Those

laborers who were lucky enough to get jobs picking cotton or peas or fruit would be sheltered temporarily in camps consisting typically of frame cabins in rows, with a water line between every two rows; they were very likely to find in their cabin no stove, no cots, no water pail. Even the best of the camps offered a way of life strikingly different from that of the ruggedly individualist farmer of the American tradition, who owned his farm or else was preparing, by working as a resident "hired man," or by renting a farm, for the chance of ultimate ownership. These pickers were homeless, voteless nomads, unwanted anywhere save at the harvest season.[18]

The film version of *The Grapes of Wrath* in 1940 made these living conditions far more widely known. Though the same conditions had affected Mexican and Filipino workers, it was the oppression and dreadful living conditions of *white* workers that would eventually arouse the national conscience. Rather than aspiring to own their own land, many of these pickers had already lost their farms, driven off by crop failures and dust storms, by foreclosures, or by loss of tenant rights thanks to federal payments made only to landlords to limit acreage and crop production. For them the trek west was not a move forward but a last hope, and their meager wages for seasonal work stood between them and starvation. This was when a maverick socialist writer, Upton Sinclair, won the Democratic nomination for governor in an evangelical crusade to End Poverty in California (EPIC), a campaign which, though it finally failed at the polls in 1934, helped push the so-called Second New Deal of 1935 to more radical measures.

In the light of the growers' power—and his own suspicion of Communist tactics—Steinbeck makes his fictional strike more futile and tragic that the ones it was based on, just as he makes his organizers and strike leaders a good deal less heroic than their real-life models. Steinbeck was not thinking politically when he wrote this book. Instead, with the Miltonic echoes heard in the title, he portrays the strike as a struggle against overwhelming power and gives the whole story a flavor of fatality, reminiscent of earlier works of literary naturalism. This dark, deterministic strain would carry over into the cruelly dashed hopes in *Of Mice and Men*, where the malevolent Curley, the boss's pugnacious son, and his lonely, seductive, unsatisfied wife trigger a catastrophe that seems inevitable from the first page. Yet there is never any doubt that Steinbeck's sympathy in his strike novel is entirely with the exploited men and their families, whom he never manages to individualize. He will begin to do so only in *Of Mice and Men* and *The Grapes of Wrath,* which helps explain why *In Dubious Battle* has never matched the popularity of Steinbeck's other work and, rare for his novels, has never been adapted into another medium. Instead of becoming characters in their own right, his strikers are the famous thirties "masses," victimized by their bosses, brutalized by callous authorities and vigilantes, and, crucially, manipulated by their own selfless but unscrupulous leaders, who are intent on grand strategy, not individual well-being. But this demands a brief digression.

The Crowd

Like so many other thirties-inspired works, starting in 1932 with José Ortega y Gasset's haughty *Revolt of the Masses* and culminating thirty years later with Elias Canetti's *Crowds and Power, In Dubious Battle* is a study in mass behavior. Already in the 1920s there was a great interest in mass psychology. H. L. Mencken and Sinclair Lewis saw the timid conformism of Babbitry as a species of the herd instinct. The growth of a consumer society, recorded in *Babbitt* with such uncanny precision, gave rise to modern advertising and the new science of public relations, one of whose founders, Edward Bernays, was Freud's American nephew. The indefatigable Bernays wrote books about "engineering social consent" like *Crystallizing Public Opinion* (1923) and *Propaganda* (1928), which were admired by Goebbels and Hitler.

The patriotic carnage of the Great War and the frightening rise of mass movements like Bolshevism and Fascism created a widespread fascination with mass psychology. Yet if upholders of traditional values saw themselves stranded in "the century of the common man," the worldwide Depression caused younger writers and thinkers to turn to collectivism as the only solution to intractable economic problems. Writer after writer set about to mock the premises of American individualism and the promises of the American dream. Even Hemingway, whose anxious, taciturn heroes inherit the full burden of self-created Emersonian man, lent his prestige to the Communists in the late 1930s. In *To Have and Have Not,* his stab at Depression fiction, he has his badly injured hero Harry Morgan blurt out the book's feeble moral: "A man alone ain't got no bloody fucking chance." The Depression years were perhaps the first period in American culture when images of collective activity overcame the cherished myth of "a man alone," represented not only by Emerson but by Thoreau at Walden, or in his justifying acts of civil disobedience; by Ahab shaking his fist at the whale; by Whitman absorbing the world into his own body; even by Emily Dickinson, alone with her conscience and consciousness in her room in Amherst. In 1928 King Vidor had made a great film, *The Crowd*, about a young couple poignantly adrift in the brave new world of the modern city. Six years later, against all odds, he made a wooden sequel, *Our Daily Bread*, stocked with an assortment of character actors who represent the Hollywood image of the common people. They play cigar salesmen, hoodlums, and violinists who all get a chance to submerge their atomized urban identities by working the soil and contributing selflessly toward common goals. A wanted man, tough and taciturn, straight out of a classic western, turns himself in so that the reward money can bail out the farm. Only a narcissistic femme fatale refuses to do her share and nearly gets the hero to run off with her. (He resists settling down, but his desires, though not quite eliminated, have been sublimated into work.)

In the film's last and most memorable scene, borrowed directly from the montage techniques of Eisenstein and the Russian revolutionary cinema, the whole commune works feverishly together to build an irrigation ditch that will save the crops from a killing drought. The scene is conceived musically as a visual hymn to collective effort. From a low angle in what feels like slow motion, we see their hammers on the horizon, their shovels and pickaxes interweaving as they lend their bodies to something larger than themselves. The scene is corny but enormously powerful, strikingly cinematic, influenced by the great Russians yet curiously American in its optimistic trust in teamwork and physical know-how.

Though the message of *Our Daily Bread* was a long way from revolutionary, this independently made film was a landmark of the Depression cinema's aborted utopian potential. Yet its predecessor, *The Crowd*, though it came out in 1928, seems somehow the more authentic Depression film. Avoiding the pitfalls of Hollywood optimism, it sees the problems of life as far more intractable. "It breathes hopelessness and despair," said one contemporary reviewer.[19]

If King Vidor's *Our Daily Bread* was a remarkably sunny and innocent film, despite its focus on the Depression, two other filmmakers unconsciously explored the darker side of thirties collectivism, though this was far from their conscious intent. Leni Riefenstahl's *Triumph of the Will*, made in the same year as Vidor's film, was perhaps the only artistic triumph of Goebbels's propaganda machine. It presents itself duplicitously as a mere record of the 1934 Nuremberg congress of the Nazi Party, but in fact the whole event was staged as a spectacle for the camera, using the largest cast ever assembled for any film. Just as Vidor shows his communards subduing their individuality to the collective effort, Riefenstahl dramatizes a mass of young Germans subjugating theirs to the will of the Maximum Leader. From the Wagnerian opening picturing Hitler's plane flying like an eagle through the clouds and mist toward a new Germany, the film goes on to scan the rapt faces of the people welcoming their charismatic chief, then hundreds of thousands of "workers" with their "shovels" chanting in unison. Every image in the film is cunningly designed for indoctrination into the new order: the melding of people from different parts of the land, the faces in ecstatic submission, the top-down view of enormous masses of soon-to-be mobilized humanity, seen from the air, and the men washing themselves for a clean break with the past.

The rally itself is the culmination of this genuinely Fascist piece of filmmaking. Not only do we see Hitler from below, standing behind his massively monumental podium—the very image of the godlike, distant figure—but his vast army of worshippers is organized into strict geometrical formations that subsume individual humanity into one collective, and frighteningly impersonal, mass. Down the center aisle of this gigantic phalanx, Hitler and two of his henchmen move slowly, as if they were the only living things within a geometrical grid, as if they belonged to a different order of being from their inert followers. In creating this mythic image of the Fascist collective, Riefenstahl also tells the truth about the dehumanization it inevitably entails.

The other director who matched this appalling choreography of human masses was in fact a choreographer, Busby Berkeley. Berkeley, who single-handedly created the 1930s Hollywood musical, arrayed his chorus girls in machinelike formations as depersonalizing as Riefenstahl's, minus the menacing grandeur and intimidating scale. Berkeley was a true filmmaker, not an adapter of Broadway material; he learned his visual craft from the same directors and cameramen as Riefenstahl: from Fritz Lang, Friedrich Murnau, and other German expressionists. Lang's massive *Metropolis* (1927), for example, is a forerunner of Depression filmmaking in its portrayal of the dehumanizing effects of the labor process, with men marching to work, heads bowed, like a phalanx of spiritless drones; then descending to airless depths to submit their limbs to the machine, becoming slavelike armatures of a Faustian yet Satanic technology; and finally rioting self-destructively when they are inflamed by a seductive female robot who spouts Marxist slogans about exploitation. René Clair (in *À Nous la Liberté*) and Charlie Chaplin (in *Modern Times*) may have learned to satirize the assembly line from this frightening film, but for Berkeley it was something else, a poetry of mass movement and abstract design. What he borrowed from the stylized fantasy world of German expressionism was the submission of the human body to the technology of staging, camera movement, and visual montage.

Some of the same effects of precise uniform motion could be achieved on the stage. The high-stepping Rockettes, so perfectly synchronized, who drew crowds to the new Radio City Music Hall in New York, were a typical creation of the 1930s. There's an exhilarating aura of kinky sexuality about Berkeley's kaleidoscopic overhead shots, which resemble the opening and closing of rose petals, and his traveling shots between women's legs, which depersonalize them vertiginously into detached limbs. Sometimes the effect seems deliberately orgiastic, at other times weirdly abstract, as in the big "I Only Have Eyes for You" number in *Dames* (1934), in which Ruby Keeler's face and eyes are endlessly replicated in the constantly shifting patterns of Dick Powell's imagination. For Berkeley, as for Riefenstahl, the human form, whether individual or en masse, is merely the raw material for new technical effects, whether of propaganda or visual stylization. The purer the film imagination, the more complete the manipulation. No wonder the medium became such an important tool of mass indoctrination. The very things that Lang and his humanist successors like Clair and Chaplin protest, Riefenstahl and Berkeley celebrate: for them, modern society with its new technology can diminish individuality by welding men into an undifferentiated mass, a new collective creature that left the individualism of the nineteenth century behind.

This excursus into film may seem to take us far afield from Steinbeck's *In Dubious Battle*, yet both that novel and *The Grapes of Wrath*, like Dos Passos's *U.S.A.*, are experiments at seeing man in the collective terms the Depression seemed to demand. This conflicted sharply not only with America's habitual, ingrained individualism but with a novel's need for vivid, well-defined characters who have some chance of being agents of their own destiny. When Alfred Kazin complained in *On Native Grounds* (1942) that "Steinbeck's people are always on the verge of becoming human, but never do," he was pointing to a weakness that was also, at some level, a deliberate intention.[20] Steinbeck touches on this point in *Working Days*, the journal he kept while writing *The Grapes of Wrath*: "Make the people live," he says to himself. "Make them live. But my people must be more than people. They must be an over-essence of people." For Steinbeck, realism had been more a commercial obligation than an article of faith. "I am writing many stories now," he said in a letter a few years earlier. "Because I should like to sell some of them, I am making my characters as nearly as I can in the likeness of men. The stream underneath and the meanings I am interested in can be ignored" (94). It was this symbolic or allegorical dimension, the story behind the story, that most engaged him.

Strike!

When he wrote *In Dubious Battle*, Steinbeck did not yet feel that individualized characters were essential to his work. As we've already noted, he was more influenced by biology than by psychology and saw free will as a widespread illusion. Just as Dos Passos refused to mitigate his panorama of defeat and pessimism in *U.S.A.* by giving the trilogy an individual hero, Steinbeck saw mass man as an ecosystem that lived and moved by different rules, especially under Depression conditions of want and powerlessness. A very perceptive admirer of *In Dubious Battle*, André Gide, remarked in his journal in 1940 that "the main character is the crowd." The novel is punctuated by descriptions of mass behavior, not in the conservative tradition of Gustave Le Bon and Ortega y Gasset, which depicts the masses as a dangerously irrational beast, but with a different emphasis.[21] Steinbeck shows us how weak and hopeless the workers are individually, how strong they can be when united, almost unconsciously, by some sense of common purpose. When one of the strikers is killed, the crowd is roused from its habitual fear and torpor: "A strange, heavy movement started among the men. . . . The guards aimed with their guns, but the line moved on, unheeding, unseeing. . . . The guards were frightened; riots they could stop, fighting they could stop; but this slow, silent movement of men with the wide eyes of sleep-walkers terrified them" (148). This larger-than-life picture, with its preternatural clarity of outline, could almost have come from one of the 1930s muralists. The crowd seems to move with a life of its own. In the novel's outbursts of violence, Steinbeck, like other observers of mass behavior, stresses the heavy, ominous quality of this mass of men as well as its strength. His novel is remarkably ambivalent about the proletarian formulas that it appropriates.

On the one hand, Steinbeck gives us little didactic portraits that stress the perils of going it alone. Crusty old-timers like Dan or Jim's father, who fought their own fights angrily, bitterly, and, in the end, hopelessly, become cautionary lessons in the futility of prickly independence. We first encounter Jim himself alone with his thoughts in a rented room, like the Swede waiting resignedly for death in Hemingway's stark story "The Killers." Thus the novel begins with a 1920s pattern highlighting an individual destiny, only to show us Jim's conversion to solidarity, hope, and self-abnegating activism as he joins the Communist Party. Individual leaders and battles may be lost, men martyred, but the fight goes on. Steinbeck's focus on Mac and Jim, the veteran union organizer and the diligent novice who learns from him but goes beyond him, reveals that his interest lies less in the crowd than in how it can be molded and manipulated. His Reds keep their eye on long-term goals, shaping the men into an angry mass, a unified force, with little regard for their immediate human needs. To Gide the book was "the best (psychological) portrayal" of Communism that he knew. He read it in the aftermath of a bitter controversy on the French Left over the mixed impressions he published after his long visit to the USSR. Unlike many worshipful literary pilgrims, Gide had become disillusioned. His incisive comments emphasize the "dubious" side of Steinbeck's attitude, which paralleled his own mixed observations of Soviet life. The strikers' needs and claims, he remarks, are

presented so fairly that one cannot take sides for or against the flood of demands any more than the author has done. The legitimacy of these demands, like the outcome of the struggle itself, remains "dubious." Especially dubious the legitimacy of using treacherous means to bring about the triumph of even the most legitimate cause. (*Journal*, 4:48)

This reading, personal as it is, feels more accurate than the reaction of American readers, who initially saw Steinbeck as a fellow traveler who idealized the union struggle and supported the Communist line, but more recently have gone to the other extreme to exaggerate the negative side of his portrait of Mac and Jim. An otherwise careful Steinbeck scholar, Richard Astro, for example, claimed that "though we are prone to identify with their struggle against the ruthless agri-businessmen of the Torgas Valley, Steinbeck demonstrates that Mac and Jim are obdurate men to whom the human virtues of friendship, tolerance, and brotherly love are platitudes to be voiced when politically expedient, but are actually impediments to the real business of fighting a revolution."[22]

This exaggerated negative tenor is an offshoot of the cold war years; it tries to bring the Steinbeck of the 1930s into line with a later anti-Communist orthodoxy—to sanitize him politically. Gide goes awry as well, for nowhere does Steinbeck show the least theoretical or political interest in Communism. Though he was wooed by the Popular Front, though he wrote hard-hitting journalistic pieces on migrant farmworkers, though *The Grapes of Wrath,* which emerged from the those articles, became a canonical text of left-wing protest literature, Steinbeck himself played no role in the ideological debates of the 1930s. What interested him in this novel was not Communism but Communists as character types, behavioral specimens— not the chiefs who passed along Moscow's orders from offices high above Union Square, not the urban intellectuals who debated Marxist principles in dingy all-night cafeterias, but the foot soldiers in the field whose lives could be as stripped down as the paisanos of Monterey.

Mac and Jim are not strike "leaders," in Steinbeck's view, but men who somehow manage to tune in with the rhythms of group life, who become adept at using the material at hand, including their own human losses, as a means of playing on people and welding their anger into an iron fist. The intellectual Doc Burton, based on Steinbeck's friend Ed Ricketts, manages to be a skeptic and activist at the same time, dispassionate like Steinbeck himself, but the two Reds, Mac and Jim, have little patience with ideas. As purely practical men, organizers building a movement, they find Doc's intellectual detachment alien and disturbing. They dismiss his "high-falutin ideas," and he suggests that even they are merely specialized cells of a larger organism.

In a bizarre letter explaining his phalanx theory, Steinbeck, clearly influenced by the mass bloodshed of World War I and the mass movements that succeeded it, argued that the group had a life of its own that submerged the will of the individuals within it. "Hitler did not create the present phalanx in Germany," he says; "he merely interprets it" (80). Such a view, if taken seriously, would do away not only with free will but with all moral responsibility. Fortunately, the novelist in Steinbeck has the upper hand over the homespun theorist of "group-man." *In Dubious Battle* zeroes in on Communist organizing tactics and motives, bringing in Doc Burton's biological notions as an occasional chorus, not a definitive explanation.

As Mac educates Jim in his methods, we cannot avoid seeing how manipulative he is. First he wins the trust of the men and their "natural" leader, London, by delivering his daughter-in-law's baby, though we later discover he knew nothing about obstetrics. In one of several scenes of graphic violence, he coolly breaks the nose of a young strikebreaker with surgical precision, to make him a walking lesson to others. "I want a billboard," he says, "not a corpse" (247). Elsewhere he says, "I can't take time to think about the feelings of one man. I'm too busy with big bunches of men" (183). In Ralph Ellison's *Invisible Man*, which deals satirically with Communism during just this period, another veteran organizer warns the newcomer, "You mustn't waste your emotions on individuals, they don't count." Mac's masterly orchestration of groups puts him in the position of the film directors discussed earlier, concerned not with the individual but with larger formations. He pursues distant ends by using whatever comes to hand. "There's just one rule," he tells Jim early on. "Use whatever material you've got." He has little faith in the success of this strike, but he's thinking ahead to other strikes and hardly cares who gets hurt along the way. His best bit of material is the fresh corpse of one of his own men, ironically named Joy, a scarred veteran of many labor battles, whose joyful martyrdom he turns to full advantage to sow indignation among the men. The ultimate irony is that his last bit of material is provided by his young acolyte Jim, over whose body he intones what is virtually the Communist motto in this book: "Comrades! He didn't want nothing for himself—" (313). On this open-ended line the novel ends. By then, martyrdom is the only weapon the strikers have left.

This is where the special human drama of *In Dubious Battle* unexpectedly slips in. In most proletarian novels, the solidarity between the hardened Communist and the young initiate is a doctrinal one. Here it grows personal as well. Late in life Jean-Paul Sartre confided to Simone de Beauvoir that much as he had written in support of the Communists, as individuals he had found them automatons, humanly inaccessible, personally inauthentic. In the growth of Mac's tender feelings for Jim, in his discomfort that Jim is learning his lessons too well, Steinbeck exposes the private vulnerability behind the impersonal façade. Though he orchestrates powerful emotions in ordinary men, Mac rejects them when they show up in himself. "I'm no good. The Party ought to get rid of me. I lose my head." By his inhuman definition, his pupil is now a better Communist than he is, more daring, more selfless, more fanatical. He is not only frightened for Jim but frightened at the kind of man he has become. He hears his own ideas emerge from Jim's mouth with the icy intensity of total commitment. "You're getting beyond me, Jim. I'm getting scared of you" (249). They are tender comrades now, and his protective fears for his apt pupil get in their way, for now he has something he's not prepared to lose.

Jim, for his part, becomes as impervious to argument as he is to fear. He argues with Doc about ends and means, but finally insists, "Your words don't mean anything to me. I know what I'm doing. Argument doesn't have any effect on me." If he adopts Mac's anti-intellectualism, he also assumes the dead Joy's impulse to martyrdom. "I wanted you to use me," he tells Mac. "You wouldn't because you liked me too well. . . . That was wrong." Though already wounded, he refuses to hang back. He *wants* to be used. Just before he is killed, we are told, "his face was transfigured. A furious light of energy seemed to shine from it." Mac does finally use him, but not in the way he had hoped to do. His faith, like Steinbeck's, that the individual person scarcely matters, is put to its most severe test. The book develops its own fictional logic apart from any ideas of "group-man." An older ethic of personal loyalty and honest emotion clashes with the new vision of collective man.

Writing a novel on a burning social issue of the day is a process of simplification—giving narrative shape to what is amorphous, making the part stand for the whole. When Steinbeck wrote *In Dubious Battle*, the violent labor battles in the California valleys had been breaking out for five or six years. Like the problems of poor tenant farmers in the South, the struggles of the California pickers had already received journalistic attention; they occupied a corner of the national consciousness. Steinbeck wrote his novel in a stark Dick-and-Jane manner made up largely of dialogue of the simplest kind. Just as Mac, among the workers, becomes a plain man of the people, so Steinbeck is didactic without too obviously writing down. Carey McWilliams's 1939 book *Factories in the Field* details a long history of feudal ownership, industrial methods, vicious exploitation (especially of minorities), and union-busting violence. All this made the California valleys a notorious scene of labor conflict, helpless victimization, and grinding poverty.[23] And it was unfolding in the promised land that Steinbeck had already staked out as his literary territory. When the spirit of radical protest and proletarian conflict possessed Steinbeck, he did not have to look very far for a subject.

Telling such a story in fiction requires an art of finding examples that count, without making them too obviously representative or typical. Were there ever Communists as transparently calculating as Mac, as fanatically selfless and devoted to the cause as Jim? When Mac speaks of the need for organization and discipline, he speaks for all Communists of the period, who threw their best energies into labor organizing, often against overwhelming odds. This was the heroic, the empathetic side of the Old Left. Memory is a perilous thing, but here is what one Communist organizer told Vivian Gornick over four decades later:

> The years with the fruit pickers became a world within the world, a microcosm of feelings that never left me, even when I left them. I lived with the pickers, ate, slept, and got drunk with them. I helped bury their men and deliver their babies. We laughed, cried, and talked endlessly into the night together. And, slowly, some extraordinary interchange began to take place between us. I taught them how to read, and they taught me how to think. I taught them how to organize, and they taught me how to lead. . . . [T]hey were—there's no other word for it—noble. Powerful in struggle, no longer sluggish with depression, they became inventive, alive, democratic, filled with an instinctive sense of responsibility for each other.
>
> . . . . It was my dream of socialism come to life.[24]

These may be idealized memories but they feel real to me. Steinbeck catches such details—the deaths and births, the shift from cowed depression to hopeful solidarity—but little of the passion and spirit. The one character who would fit this recollection, Joy, the most zealous of old Communists, is already cracked in the head when we meet him, and is soon killed off. By choosing to focus on a figure as shifty as Mac, Steinbeck gives full play to his own ambivalence, not about the plight of the pickers but about the Communists' way of alleviating it. This complication, which Steinbeck saw as scientific neutrality and skepticism, was certainly a rare feature of Depression naturalism and proletarian writing.

Steinbeck was fascinated by how a small number of Communists could be the yeast for a large body of powerless, unorganized workers. But he almost leaves out the feelings that would make this effort human rather than dehumanizing. This is where his own relation to the struggle would evolve, and where *Of Mice and Men,* the *San Francisco News* articles, and especially *The Grapes of Wrath* would mark a departure from *In Dubious Battle*, which is finally a catechism on Communist tactics that gives short shrift to the workers themselves. "We got to take the long view," says Mac. "A strike that's settled too quickly won't teach the men how to organize, how to work together. A tough strike is good. . . . There's nothing like a fight to cement the men together. . . . [E]very time a guardsman jabs a fruit tramp with a bayonet a thousand men all over the country come on our side" (27–28). Steinbeck sees callousness and condescension in the way Mac and Jim approach these benighted men, treating them as an unleavened mass ready to rise, needing only be hurt, angered, and radicalized. Yet, to a degree, his novel treats them the same way, as disposable cannon fodder, not fully human beings.

This finally is the problem with Mac, as with so many of Steinbeck's characters: he is too theoretical. Far from being unrepresentative, he is too representative. Steinbeck had a good eye for types but it could lead him astray. Mac is less a person than the crystallization of Steinbeck's keen observations about Communists' strategy and psychology. His view of them is a complex one but it is precisely that, a point of view. Behind the fictional trappings of *In Dubious Battle* lay a shrewd essay on an urgent subject: How were men to live when, even in the midst of natural plenty, they were oppressed by arbitrary economic power? How were they to survive when their most ardent defenders cared less for them as people than as bearers of the revolutionary cause, mere embryos of a better world? As the "dubious" ending of the novel shows, the migrant workers of the Depression years were largely powerless pawns, exploited on all sides, caught between a rock and a hard place.

CHAPTER 4

The Country and the City

Tenant Farmers: Words and Images

RURAL POVERTY WAS ONE OF the critical social problems of the Depression but also the occasion for some of the decade's most memorable words and images. Just as the New Deal tried from its first days to cope with the farm crisis, so writers and photographers from Edmund Wilson and Steinbeck to Pare Lorentz and Walker Evans set out to document the blight and human misery that city dwellers rarely associated with rural life. After the expansion of acreage and output to meet the enormous demands created during the First World War, the farm economy had virtually collapsed during the first half of the 1920s. Between 1919 and 1924, 13 million acres were "abandoned to brush," according to the historian William E. Leuchtenburg, who asserts that although "the poverty of farmers in the 1920s has been exaggerated," they rightly felt "they were not sharing the new urban prosperity. . . . The farmer felt that he was losing out, that the country was being industrialized at his expense."[1]

But once industry began to collapse, the agricultural sector fell even further. The realized net income of farmers had plummeted by 1932 to less than a third of what it had been in 1929, while farm prices fell more than 50 percent.[2] Despite all the efforts of the Roosevelt administration, farm income was not to regain its 1929 level until 1941, when another war was on. Among the most important New Deal attacks on the farm depression was the creation of the Agricultural Adjustment Administration (AAA) in 1933, which paid farmers to reduce production, and the Resettlement Administration (RA) in 1935, renamed in 1937 the Farm Security Administration. The latter agency tried directly to rescue the poorer half of the farm population, which earned only 10 percent of all farm income, through various schemes of relocation and retraining.

Those in charge of the agricultural and rural policies of the New Deal were among the most radical figures in the Roosevelt administration. The secretary of agriculture, Henry A. Wallace, whose father had been secretary during the Warren Harding years, had an almost mystical feeling for the land and a burning desire to help the destitute farmers. The administration of the AAA from 1933 to 1935 was in the hands of idealistic young radicals like Jerome Frank, Lee Pressman, and Alger Hiss, several of whom eventually became ardent Communists. When they were purged from the Agriculture Department in 1935, their patron Rex Tugwell, one of the most brilliant counselors in FDR's so-called Brains Trust, which went back to the president's days as New York's governor, was appointed to head the Resettlement Administration. By 1940 the government had managed to enlist some six million farmers in its subsidy programs, which reduced the production of staple crops, brought up prices, and encouraged the planting of "soil-conserving" crops instead.

The New Deal changed the face of rural America on many fronts, by way of agencies such as the Tennessee Valley Authority, the Civilian Conservation Corps, and the Rural Electrification Administration. Through the Subsistence Homestead Division of the National Recovery Administration, the New Deal built about a hundred new communities in the early years of the Roosevelt administration. Under Tugwell the Resettlement Administration built "greenbelt" towns near Washington, Cincinnati, and Milwaukee that represented major efforts of social planning.[3] As Leuchtenburg notes, Tugwell "sought to move impoverished farmers from submarginal land and give them a fresh start on good soil with adequate equipment and expert guidance. But he never had enough money to do very much. The RA, which planned to move 500,000 families, actually resettled 4,441." The most urgently discussed farm problem of the mid-1930s was the condition of sharecroppers and tenant farmers, whose plight had been inadvertently worsened by subsidies that caused some landowners to drive them off their land, and who were little helped by these relocation efforts.

The federal government had appointed a committee to study farm tenancy in 1936. Its report led to the passage of the Bankhead-Jones Farm Tenancy Act of 1937, which created the new Farm Security Administration (FSA). This "was the first agency to do anything substantial for the tenant farmer, the sharecropper, and the migrant; by the end of 1941, it had spent more than a billion dollars," says Leuchtenburg, on items like rehabilitation loans to farmers, long-term, low-interest loans to some tenants to enable them to buy their own farms, and sanitary camps for migrants (like the one memorably portrayed in *The Grapes of Wrath*). Because such government interventions in the nation's economic life were controversial, the FSA created the Photography Unit under Roy Stryker to build support for New Deal policies by documenting the grim realities of the rural Depression. (This had begun as part of the Information Division of the RA in 1935; Stryker had been Tugwell's teaching assistant at Columbia.)

Despite the journalistic nature of this photographic work, the thirties were a period when journalism and art grew closely intertwined. Photography itself had a long history of documenting social ills, going back to Jacob Riis in New York's worst slums and to Lewis Hine's recording, with powerful reserve, the arrival of immigrants at Ellis Island and later the conditions of child labor. During the Depression this documentary approach took on tremendous new importance.[4] Along with the arts projects of the Works Progress Administration (WPA) and the Post Office murals, this Photography Unit proved to be a fateful partnership between government and art—something unique in American history. The work of the FSA photographers is not only the best-remembered art of the Depression—seeming greater today than it did then—but also the way we are likely to remember the Depression itself, the very look and feel of the period.

The work that photographers like Walker Evans, Dorothea Lange, Marion Post Wolcott, Carl Mydans, Russell Lee, Ben Shahn, and Arthur Rothstein did for the RA and the FSA, of course, took place not in isolation but within the larger documentary context that included Pare Lorentz's government-sponsored films, *The Plow That Broke the Plains* (1936) and *The River* (1937), and many other efforts to put the realities of American life on record, most notably the American Guide Series of the Federal Writers' Project. The collaboration of writers and photographers led to the creation of a new kind of journalism epitomized by Henry Luce's new *Life* magazine. Luce's employees helped create a new genre of text-and-pictures books, which began with *You Have Seen Their Faces* (1937; text by Erskine Caldwell, photographs by Margaret Bourke-White) and reached its late apogee with *Let Us Now Praise Famous Men* (1941; text by James Agee, photographs by Walker Evans). Both books deal with the living and working conditions of southern tenant farmers; both were based on field visits to the South in the summer of 1936, when national concern about the lives of these farm tenants was great, though accurate knowledge of their lives was rudimentary. Agee and Evans were on assignment from *Fortune*, but the extremely long article Agee wrote (now lost) never appeared in the magazine, whose editorial direction had shifted by the time the piece came in. Margaret Bourke-White was already Luce's most celebrated photojournalist, turning her attention from industrial photography, which had first made her famous, to human misery. Erskine Caldwell, then at the height of his fame as a novelist, had recently written a series of articles for the *New York Post* on the plight of the sharecroppers. They returned to the South in the spring of 1937 to complete their work for the book, which appeared in November.

A comparison of these two books reveals much about how the 1930s imagined its own social reality, particularly the horrendous poverty that had existed earlier but was deepened by the Depression. Today, when the South has turned into the Sun Belt, transformed by air-conditioning, and has grown much more urban and industrial than even the prophets of the New South ever dreamed—when it has shaken off many of its old racial attitudes, elected conservative Republicans as well as black candidates, and joined the Union at long last—it is hard to recall how different this region once seemed, and in some ways still is.

To many urban northerners and westerners, the South was indelibly associated with ignorance, backwardness, poverty, and prejudice.[5] In politics Dixie had nurtured not only corrupt bigots like Senator Theodore Bilbo of Mississippi but also a vigorous populist tradition embodied in men like Tom Watson of Georgia and Huey Long of Louisiana, whose demagogic national movement gathered strength until its chief's assassination in 1935. The romantic myth of the antebellum South, with its fatherly plantation economy, its loyal, loving slave population, and chivalric gallantry out of Sir Walter Scott, was everyone's favorite escape reading. While Agee, Evans, Caldwell, and Bourke-White were searching out poor sharecroppers along the dirt roads of Alabama, the whole nation was reading about Scarlett O'Hara and Rhett Butler—*Gone with the Wind* had been published just a few weeks earlier—just as it had thrilled to D. W. Griffith's *Birth of a Nation* twenty years before, with its racial stereotypes and sympathy for the white-hooded Klan.

Erskine Caldwell had already done much to create a powerful image of poverty and degradation in the contemporary South. *Tobacco Road* (1932) and *God's Little Acre* (1933) had made his literary reputation, and a stage adaptation of *Tobacco Road* that had opened late in 1933 would become the longest-running play on Broadway (it ran for seven and a half years). It is tempting to say that Caldwell was responsible for the most graphic portrayal of rural destitution in the 1930s. As late as 1939, in his literary farewell to the 1930s in *The New Republic*, Malcolm Cowley described *Tobacco Road* as the "first and best" of the sharecropper novels, an ambiguous distinction.[6]

Caldwell's books, festooned with lurid covers, sold many millions of copies in cheap paperbacks in the forties and fifties, but they were read more as wild, grotesque, lubricious comedy than as literary sociology. His work is unfairly neglected today, although "Tobacco Road" remains a byword for a rural slum. Caldwell always described himself modestly as a storyteller and entertainer rather than a didactic writer.[7] Yet the extreme cruelty in *Tobacco Road* has a special thirties resonance to us today. Farming for cotton on hopelessly used-up land, Jeeter Lester and his family have gradually lost connection to any human emotion except hunger and lust. When Jeeter's son-in-law Lov comes by with a sack of turnips, which he has no intention of sharing, the family turns into a pack of leering, scurrying little animals, like the creatures Jeeter fears will eat *him* after he dies, the rats that nibbled away at his father's face before they managed to bury him. (Now there's so little to eat that even the rats have abandoned the farm.)

The turnips, the rats, the automobile that keeps disintegrating each time it's taken out, his daughter Ellie May's harelip, which Jeeter has somehow neglected to repair, his twelve-year-old daughter Pearl's refusal to sleep with Lov, her husband—all these become Dickensian leitmotifs in a comedy all the more horrific for being told in a tone of deadpan neutrality, as if Caldwell himself were no more than the anthropological observer of a strange, alien form of life. Only a misplaced emphasis would enable one to say that these characters and stories strain credibility, for they come out of the world of tall tales, legends, and regional humor, not social reporting. There is the daughter-in-law, Bessie, the sex-hungry lady preacher—she happens to have no nose, only two dirty-looking holes in the middle of her face—who spends a night in a whorehouse, thinking it's a very hospitable hotel. There's the old grandmother whom the Lesters ignore completely, even when she's been run over by Bessie's car:

> "Is she dead yet?" Ada asked, looking at Jeeter. "She don't make no sound and she don't move. I don't reckon she could stay alive with her face all mashed like that."[8]

For one gruesome paragraph the old lady tries to move. Then, dead or not, they bury her in a shallow ditch.

> She had lived so long in the house with Jeeter and Ada that she had been considered nothing more than a door-jamb or a length of weather-boarding. . . . Even when she was hungry, or sick, no word had passed her lips. . . . If she had said anything, Jeeter or Ada would have knocked her down. (131)

This exaggerated cruelty originates in comic stereotypes—the kind we still see in Road Runner cartoons and other forms of knockabout farce—yet it also transcends them. Caldwell takes material from jokes and folktales and combines them with his own precise memories of the Georgia cotton country to achieve at times a surreal effect. If his deadpan neutrality makes us think of Kafka, his outrageousness foreshadows Terry Southern and other black humorists of the 1960s. Caldwell confects full-length novels that still have the quality of wild oral anecdotes, and characters whose grotesque behavior, entertaining as it is, bears all the marks of the pathetically marginal lives they lead. He turns cruelty and inhumanity from a joke into a bitter joke indeed.

There's only one thing besides hunger that moves these characters—and obviously moves the author as well—their love for the land. The smell of burning broom sedge keeps Jeeter alive, though the fire he set finally kills him. An old habit that dies hard—this is how it's always been done—the fire represents his absurd, lingering hope of farming the land his grandfather and father owned and gradually lost. Even his landlord has long since given up and gone to Augusta, taking his credit with him—Jeeter is a sharecropper with no crops to share, a tenant without benefit of a landlord.

While his own children run off to work in the cotton mills, Jeeter still has a physical need to find seed and guano to put in the depleted ground. "He was going to plow and patch to raise some cotton on, if he never did anything else as long as he lived" (127). This is almost his last thought, and, according to Caldwell, this absurd persistence amid sheer desolation was the key memory from which the novel originated ("Advertisement," 11–12). "He was a man who liked to grow things in the ground," says his son-in-law. "The mills ain't no place for a human who's got that in his bones" (131).

This is the sentimental kernel within the hard-edged modern novel, despite Caldwell's later disavowal of any purpose beyond plain storytelling. It led Caldwell to write extensively about sharecropping with an insider's knowledge of the South and a set of strongly held views that belied the air of cruel indifference and tragicomic inevitability we find in his fiction. Though it is scarcely 50 pages long—something we can read through in an hour or two—Caldwell's text for *You Have Seen Their Faces* delivers more solid information about sharecropping than we can easily ferret out of the 471 dizzying pages of *Let Us Now Praise Famous Men*. Yet, with Bourke-White's riveting photos dispersed throughout, their book feels more like a picture book, even a coffee-table book, than Agee and Evans's work could ever be. At one time there must have been a copy of the cheap edition of *You Have Seen Their Faces* in every "progressive" household in America, and in many other homes as well, if only as an act of piety toward the southern poor. Yet I wonder how many people actually read the book, as opposed to simply taking it in. Caldwell's modest text was not what they were looking at.

Those who did read it would have found something exemplary of its kind: a clean, understated piece of writing that belongs securely in the annals of protest and muckraking journalism, not literature. It is divided into six short chapters, the first of them a short history of land use and sharecropping in the South, especially the cotton country; this opening is closely related to the bits of social documentation tucked into *Tobacco Road*. The next five chapters, each beginning and ending with a long, anonymous quote from a farmer himself, deal with a whole range of topics—the depletion of the land, the departure of the landlords, the desperate feelings of the farmers, their failure to achieve even a minimum level of subsistence, their scapegoating of Negroes, the need for unionization and for some kind of federal commission to study the problem—just the kind of liberal "solutions" James Agee hated.

Caldwell writes with a somber simplicity that has a touch of grandeur about it. He writes as a novelist with a primary interest in people rather than in statistics. But what strikes one most about this text today is its generality. The second and third chapters are case studies that still have names attached to them, but by the fourth chapter we are given a composite portrait of a "typical" sharecropper, which leads us on to things-in-general: a sweeping picture of the overall "condition" of these hapless tenants. Near the end we get a hopeful, "epic" note reminiscent of the last page of *Jews without Money*, but without its frank, underlying desperation:

> Ten million persons on Southern tenant farms are living in degradation and defeat. They have been beaten and subjected. They are depleted and sterile. All has been taken away from them and they have nothing.
>
> But they are still people, still human beings. They have life. . . .
>
> The youth of the South can succeed where their mothers and fathers failed if they refuse to raise another man's cotton while hun-

gry and in rags. With hope and a dream before them they can change
a hell into a living paradise.[9]

The tone of the book is set not so much by this kind of valedictory
rhetoric as by the first-person testimonies that introduce and conclude
each chapter, and by the fictitious quotations that Caldwell and Bourke-
White conceived as captions for all the pictures. Since this last bit of invention has been hotly criticized, it is worth citing Caldwell's prefatory note
explaining this practice: "No person, place, or episode in this book is fictitious, but names and places have been changed to avoid unnecessary individualization. . . . The legends under the pictures are intended to express
the authors' conceptions of the sentiments of the individuals portrayed;
they do not pretend to reproduce the actual sentiments of these persons."

Here we have two of the most ambiguous keystones of the documentary tradition of the 1930s: the need to center on individuals but without
"unnecessary individualization," and a willingness to introduce elements
of fiction without acknowledging how the result can become "fictitious."
There is a sort of ventriloquy about the book, which marks and mars
more than a few of the interview books, the "people talk" genre, that
became so popular in the 1930s—a need to hear the very voice of the
common man, even at the cost of putting words in his mouth. The book
reads like a series of interviews without real interlocutors, a collection of
portraits whose outlines are blurred and softened.

This is why Bourke-White's pictures are so much more arresting than
Caldwell's thoughtful, sensitive text, and why, I suspect, many people
who bought the book "read" only Bourke-White. The book's title puts all
its stress upon the images while pointing an accusing finger at the spectator, who must now rise to the moral challenge of those faces he has seen.
These photographs are rich in the kind of precise, grotesque detail that
reminds us more of *Tobacco Road* than of Caldwell's present text. With its
many stomach-churning images of disease and deformity, this must be
the most gruesome series of pictures before those of Diane Arbus. It's not
exactly the stuff of *Life* magazine, which rejected this material and preferred a more upbeat image of American life.

Despite the strong initial impact of these photos, it doesn't take long
for us to realize that they are quite as generalized as Caldwell's accompanying text, and far more rhetorical in their way. A comparison with

Walker Evans and Agee helps us grasp the highly stylized quality of Bourke-White's vision. The captions are but one device by which the spectator is emotionally manipulated. Bourke-White loves low-angle shots that infuse drama into the image by making people loom up over us, like the opening picture of the young man plowing. Evans just as insistently shoots head on, at chest height or eye level, as if to establish a clear parity between the subject and the viewer.

Already legendary for her energy, persistence, and fearlessness, Bourke-White boasted about stealing her way into a Negro church and about how she got her pictures of a chain gang, as if her own derring-do were the most important part of the story. Like Jacob Riis before her, though with far greater photographic skill, she loves the effect of catching a subject unawares, even when a picture is obviously posed or staged for maximum effect. Evans avoids "candid" shots as though there were something prurient about them: a voyeuristic intrusion into the subject's private space. Peering straight into the camera, his people pose for him, often in their Sunday best, which still reveals a great deal about them: how they array themselves for the camera, yet also how vulnerable they can still be.[10] In effect, Evans played Lewis Hine to Bourke-White's Jacob Riis. Where Hine, with patient understatement, documented the arrival of immigrants or the conditions of child labor, Riis made sensational forays into New York's most wretched slums. Not surprisingly, Hine's earlier work was rediscovered and acclaimed in the 1930s, the last decade of his life.

The word most often used for Evans's people is "dignity," as when Lionel Trilling says of one woman, "The sitter gains in dignity when allowed to defend herself against the lens."[11] Agee himself talks of the "weight, mystery, and dignity" of characters who are not imagined, as in a novel, but simply *exist*.[12] It is not as often remarked that Evans allows exactly the same dignity to his people's homes and possessions, a dignity of modest personal spaces; they too peer back at us with an uncanny look of unassailable pride. Evans grants an unusual integrity to the world of objects. It is not for nothing that his shot of George Gudger's work shoes has been compared (favorably!) to the peasant shoes of Van Gogh.[13] "Without doubt," wrote John Szarkowski in 1971, "Evans' pictures have enlarged our sense of the usable visual tradition, and have affected the way we see not only other photographs, but billboards, junkyards, postcards, colloquial architecture, Main Streets, and the walls of rooms."[14]

In their deeply affecting transformation of the commonplace, they bring to mind the seemingly flat but numinous realism of Edward Hopper's paintings. His influence on later vernacular photography was enormous and beneficial. Robert Frank's 1959 masterpiece *The Americans* testifies to his influence. Trilling comments on the "perfect *taste*" of Evans's work, a tact and delicacy that he praises as a "tremendously impressive moral quality."[15]

Evans's pictures, like Frank's, have the casual yet stiffly formal look of amateur snapshots; his lens searches out the ordinary and is itself a heightened version of the ordinary eye. (He even gives us a photo of two snapshots nailed to the wall of a shack, which serves as a dark ground that frames them like the page of an old photo album.) Bourke-White, on the other hand, is the consummate professional, famous for the glossy, almost unearthly sheen she could give to the surface of inanimate objects. Even her sympathetic biographer Vicki Goldberg acknowledges a degree of truth in the common description of Bourke-White as "a photographer of things," a photographer of objects, even of people as objects.[16] The very qualities of design and composition, the surface play of light, which lend her industrial images the brilliance of abstract paintings, also dehumanize her photos of people. Her chain gang pictures, besides being familiar images to audiences weaned on movies like *I Am a Fugitive*, focus more on the play of shadows across the convicts' stripes than on the plight of those wearing them. "When we first discussed plans for *You Have Seen Their Faces*," she wrote at the end of the book, "the first thought was of lighting" (51). Her dramatic landscape shots, with their spectacular sky and beautifully etched horizon, reveal the influence of Soviet silent films. Evans's pictures foreshadow the more modest imagery yet authentic look of Italian neorealism.

Before she took these sharecropper pictures, it was largely technology that attracted Bourke-White, even on her pioneering trips to the Soviet Union; she photographed people largely for scale. In many cases her industrial style involves the suppression of the human vantage point entirely. With striking analogies to abstract art, we see an endless repetition of mechanical forms with no localizing context, no sense of scale or frame of reference.[17] But her growing left-wing politics made Bourke-White want to do something, in her own way, for the betterment of the downtrodden.

There are plenty of striking images in *You Have Seen Their Faces*. The weathered face of a man from Tupelo, Mississippi, that reappeared almost fifty years later on the cover of William Kennedy's *Ironweed*, was an instantly readable icon of poverty in the 1930s. Other images, especially when combined with their captions, betray the substitution of sentimentality for feeling, humanitarian cliché for social observation. A close-up of a young black man behind bars bears the legend "I've only been misbehaving." Two gaunt, statuesque old women sitting on a porch are said to bring forth this just-folks line: "There comes a time when there's nothing to do except just sit." Even the chassis of an old car, looming in the foreground of a rural shack, can be sentimentalized into this: "I remember when that automobile was a mighty pretty thing to ride around in."

The sequence of images is even more manipulative than the individual words and pictures. Evans's pictures, without identifying captions of any kind, are detached from the text and coequal with them; they appear in a batch before the title page like a separate book or mysterious set of frontispieces. It takes hundreds of pages before we can identify all the people with any assurance. The only order, as far as I can tell, is that of an inventory, like Agee's verbal inventories, or a family album. (The three tenant families in *Let Us Now Praise Famous Men* are all related by marriage.) We move in turn from pictures of the families and their dwellings to pictures of the wider world: the surrounding land and community. By contrast, Bourke-White, whose picture are interspersed in groups throughout the text, takes us inexorably from images of "normal," even happy life—plowing, fishing, eating watermelon, working the land—to images of sullen misery, deformity, hardship, and blight. At first we see families, even smiling children, with only the captions to tell us how bad things *really* are. But these are soon replaced by the lined, craggy faces of people old before their time, faces etched with weariness, hopelessness, hunger, and disease.

No one can fail to be moved by this collective blight, but it lacks all reticence and specificity. We feel the photographer is somehow cheating: taking images of old age and passing them off as illness, presenting images of disease, some of them quite ghoulish, as more typical and hopeless than they really were. These people express no emotions that would individualize them, usually no emotions at all; instead, they come across as passive victims whose ravaged features, shorn of "unnecessary individualization," serve as emblems of their general condition. As Vicki Goldberg remarks about *Life* during this period, "Photojournalists were always eager to record the large and readily identifiable emotions, such as grief, fear, and joy, but psychological nuance was not considered the crux of their stories until after the Second World War." Of Bourke-White's photos she adds, "Like *Life* itself, these pictures often tend to repeat a stereotype in a more visually compelling form than it usually commands" (190).

The degree of selection and manipulation is especially evident when we compare a later Caldwell/Bourke-White collaboration, *Say, is this the U.S.A.* (1941), a curiously contradictory title. Here the two authors, now married to each other, join the new wartime mood of national celebration with a vengeance. Though poor harvests and unemployment are briefly mentioned in the text, the key themes here are patriotism, small-town color, and a bursting sense of national vitality. Disease is out of the question: old, lined faces are almost banished from the book, replaced by soldiers and sailors training for the defense of the native soil. One or two photos of black boys in prison are almost the only reminder of that earlier world. Caldwell gives the last words to a taxi driver who tells him the Depression's over and everyone is making lots of money. On the opposite page, ambiguously, is a picture of some well-dressed men peering at job notices. In case this worries us, the last picture shows us the Statue of Liberty from beneath its skirts, holding its torch and book aloft. An age of anxiety, dogged by want and fear, has given way too precipitously to an age of exuberance, of reassurance. A muckraker's exposé has been displaced by propaganda for the American Way. Evidently, America needed a boost of confidence to face the coming war.

Looking for Salvation: James Agee's Quest

This was the bright new atmosphere in which *Let Us Now Praise Famous Men*, long delayed, finally appeared. It proved to be one of the spectacular publishing flops of 1941. (Though generally well reviewed, it sold only a few hundred copies before being remaindered.) If *You Have Seen Their Faces* and its immediate successors had not cornered the market on sharecroppers, who in any case were no longer in fashion, then *The Grapes of Wrath* would have exhausted the last shred of interest in the poor, round-ing off a decade that had begun with Michael Gold's immigrant world in *Jews without Money*. Even before Steinbeck's Dust Bowl novel, not only had *Fortune* failed to publish Agee's original article but Harper and Brothers rejected the resulting book without revisions the author refused to make. The marks of Agee's obstinacy and excruciating integrity can be found in the book itself, surely one of the most self-conscious, involuted contributions to American literature since the later novels of Melville.

In a period when so many writers cultivated a simple, declarative prose, like camera eyes humbly observing their subjects, *Let Us Now Praise Famous Men* is an unashamedly difficult book. It took me years to learn my way around it. When I've assigned it to undergraduates, the results have been disastrous. Strange to say, this was largely Agee's own doing. In his determination to forestall "the emasculation of acceptance" (13), he stipples the text with the jejune, dated mannerisms of the twenties avant-garde, echoes of Blake and Lawrence, imitations of Faulkner and Joyce, poetic resonances from Hart Crane and the Bible, innumerable prefaces, statements of purpose, confessions of failure—a whole range of personal interventions that envelop the subject and make it problematic. His integrity is a gauntlet Agee lays down before the unwary reader.

Unlike most documentary writers and filmmakers, Agee takes full account—too full, some would say—of the relation of the observer to the thing observed. Like many other modernist works, this is a book struggling visibly to get itself written. The author's soul-searching gives it much of its tormented quality. As Lionel Trilling remarked in his original review, "too much of our attention is taken with subtracting Agee from his record."[18] This autobiographical prism foreshadows the first-person journalism of the postwar era, especially books like Mailer's *Advertisements for Myself* and *The Armies of the Night*, but with significantly less ego and a fine moral seriousness.

In the way he writes about his three tenant families, and about his own exaltations and misgivings, Agee transposes the whole decade's concern with the poor onto another plane, sometimes displacing his actual subjects. Dealing with the Gudgers, the Ricketts, and the Woods, all fictitious names, he stresses repeatedly, almost obsessively, that he is writing about real people, not imagined characters, "an undefended and appallingly damaged group of human beings" (7) whose lives, so distant from the imagination of the urban middle class, are at once naked and inconceivable. But he turns that real presence into an idea. In his preamble to book two (essentially, there is no book one) and in the first part of a section called "On the Porch: 2" (Agee's structural high jinks are confusing, even sophomoric), he gives much thought to what separates any artist or journalist from the truly wretched of the earth, lamenting the futility of trying to capture any living thing in mere words.

Here is a specimen of Agee in his reflective vein ("I am the sort of person who generalizes," 220–21), when he is not simply trying, in documentary fashion, to catalog the minute details of his tenants' lives:

> The one deeply exciting thing to me about Gudger is that he is actual, he is living, at this instant. He is not some artist's or journalist's or propagandist's invention: he is a human being: and to what degree I am able it is my business to reproduce him as the human being he is; not just to amalgamate him into some invented, literary imitation of a human being. (216)

The striking thing about this passage, so typical of the book, is how Gudger himself—a fictional name, after all—disappears in the violent assertion of his actuality. The very words "Gudger" and "human being" appear here like incantations that will transport Agee and his readers beyond the bounds of mere representation. Agee is determined to avoid both the artifice of fiction and the patronizing stereotypes that pass for social consciousness: this is the "amalgamation" we have already observed in *You Have Seen Their Faces*. Yet "Gudger" signifies what this writer can rarely deliver: a convincing human being who seems to live and breathe on his own, as characters in novels somehow manage to do.

Agee perversely places one of the book's strongest, most novelistic sections, called "Inductions," near the very end. Here he tells us what we needed to learn first, how he came to know these families, to live with one of them and share their food, how he tried working with them in the hot fields, and how the indestructible lice and fleas and bedbugs in their shack nearly devoured him alive. ("I will write a truthful book of Poverty," said Michael Gold. "I will mention bedbugs.") Without providing a context, Agee had given us some of what he actually *wrote* in their cabin some three hundred pages earlier. (His model for this reversal is a modernist text like *The Sound and the Fury*, a book that initiates us confusingly in the scattered mind of an idiot, leaving its straightforward storytelling for a later stage. Much of Agee's writing is Faulknerian as well.)

Yet in this last section he makes his frankest confession of failure: "But somehow I have lost hold of the reality of all this, I scarcely can understand how; a loss of the reality of simple actions upon the specific surface of the earth. . . . I have not managed to give their truth in words" (376). This avowal of the limitations of language, or at least of his own kind of prose poetry, lyrical rather than novelistic language, takes us full circle to the futile wish he had expressed at the outset:

> If I could do it, I'd do no writing at all here. It would be photographs; the rest would be fragments of cloth, bits of cotton, lumps of earth, records of speech, pieces of wood and iron, phials of odors, plates of food and of excrement. Booksellers would consider it quite a novelty, critics would murmur, yes, but is it art. . . . (12)

This apotheosis of the real, the material, with its grave suspicion of the imagination, is typical of the 1930s. But it also points up the paradox of Agee's relation to the decade-long project of documenting the condition of the poor: on one hand his literalism, his desire to wrestle us into the presence of the thing itself; yet also his modernism, that is to say his insistence that the full consciousness of the observer must be brought to bear on the humanity and sensory reality of his material. The very syntax of the passage ("If I could do it . . .") shows us Agee's mind bending around the subject, straining at limits, interrogating his own awareness along with his given medium.

One result of this self-questioning is that the book is too much an extended rumination. Where Caldwell and Bourke-White make up words they put in their subjects' mouths, Agee rarely lets his sharecroppers speak for themselves. He fears diminishing their humanity by falling into rural stereotypes, the ones Caldwell and Bourke-White embrace with gusto. He fears dialect. He is afraid his people will sound funny or illiterate, like poor white trash or hapless social victims. As a result, the Gudger we encounter is invariably the Gudger in Agee's mind, distanced, mediated, impalpable—as far from a bit of cotton or lump of earth as possible. The "records of speech" that Agee could have given us are absent. As William Stott remarks, with some restraint, Agee and

Evans "commended the full humanity of their subjects, but they did not fully disclose it" (286).

Agee's self-lacerating complexity as a person and artist was one basis for his failure. The shrewd and sensitive Evans, whose pictures convey the reserved immediacy missing from Agee's prose, saw his writing as, "among other things, the reflection of one resolute, private rebellion" (xi). Agee was a legend in his own time: an incandescent, self-consuming personality, a bohemian in the 1920s style, by then *out* of style, a poet trapped at Time, Inc., a hard drinker and luminous talker who could describe a movie lovingly, frame by frame, yet also a Christian gentleman from Tennessee by way of Exeter and Harvard who felt impelled to do penance for his mildly privileged background. This last was a vital need among intellectuals of the 1930s, as seen from the examples of Edward Anderson and Nelson Algren. Discussing the schooling available to the tenants' children, Agee writes, notoriously, "I could not wish of any one of them that they should have had the 'advantages' I have had: a Harvard education is by no means an unqualified advantage" (282).

A more obvious parallel was George Orwell, who went from Eton and the colonial police in British India to living "down and out" in London and Paris, whose early difficulties as a novelist resemble Agee's failure as a poet, whose fieldwork among the poor in *The Road to Wigan Pier* bears comparison to Agee's explorations of the sharecropper world, whose work at the BBC parallels Agee's drudgery under Luce. There are other similarities: the fundamental decency that was larger than any specific literary achievements, the early death and posthumous fame achieved by way of late works of fiction that had wide appeal but were by no means their best writing.

Yet once we have invoked this comparison, Agee cannot help suffering from it. Orwell perfected his plain-speaking British obtuseness into an instrument of immense moral gravity; he found touchstones of simple probity that he could apply to the great political issues of the age. Agee's reach never extended this far. His film work was always direct and immediate, thanks to his intuitive, largely preverbal sense of the medium. (*Agee on Film*, including reviews and screenplays, was his other masterpiece.) Otherwise, the sheer clarity of Orwell escaped him. An Elizabethan extravagance in Agee's language reflected less the complexity of his subjects than the inner conflicts he never resolved.

Despite Agee's shortcomings, there are few books of the 1930s as inspiriting to read and reread as *Let Us Now Praise Famous Men*. Of all the attitudes that writers and artists struck toward the poor during the Depression, Agee's was unique in his numinous sense of *awe*, his feeling of religious reverence. When, in spite of his longing to be accepted by them, he turns down a chance to stay with one of the tenant families, he goes off and runs his car into the mud. Forced to return, he will now, like a waif of fortune (or *Fortune*), have to be taken in:

> . . . and standing here, silently, in the demeanor of the house itself I grow full of shame and reverence from the soles of my feet up my body to the crest of my skull and the leaves of my hands like a vessel quietly spread full of water which has sprung from in the middle of my chest: and shame the more, because I do not yet turn away, but still stand here motionless and as if in balance, and am aware of the vigilant and shameless hope that—not that I shall move forward and request you, disorder you—but that "something shall happen," as it "happened" that the car lost to the mud . . . (373)

This is by no means the end of the sentence. The feelings it describes are equally hard to shape and delimit: sensory acuteness mingled with self-accusation, feelings of unworthiness and trembling expectancy on the momentous edge of conversion or self-transformation. Agee wants to be saved by the Gudgers, taken in by them. This is the early-orphaned boy of *A Death in the Family* whose father had died in a car crash. When they do take him in, and feed him, and come to trust and love him, their shack becomes "home" to him, the couple becomes his "brother and sister" yet also his "own parents, in whose patience I was so different, so diverged, so strange as I was" (376). "So that I could wish that all my chance life was in truth the betrayal, the curable delusion, that it seemed, and that this was my right home, right earth, right blood, to which I would never have true right" (377). In his acceptance in the house he finds "a knowledge of brief truancy into the sources of my life, whereto I have no rightful access, having paid no price beyond love and sorrow."

Were I not so moved by it, I'd be tempted to dismiss this as self-indulgent prose poetry, spirituality heightened into resonant vagueness, or as material for a psychoanalytic biography. Yet Agee escapes our reductive readings by impenitently making this his own kind of book. He risks seeming ludicrous by exposing the drama of his own need to be loved and accepted, just as he risks condescending to his subjects by hugging them to his breast as if they were precious children or playthings of his imagination. The drama of his sexual feelings for them—he is astonishingly frank about this—is played out largely in his own mind. *Famous Men* can be read only as an autobiographical meditation, for all Agee's insistence on presenting it, documentary style, as "an effort in human actuality" (xv), the verbal equivalent of the camera eye, which to him is "the central instrument of our time" (11).

Like the self-tormented Russian Narodniks who worshipped the simplicity of the peasants and their relation to the soil, Agee saw the tenant farmers as instruments of his salvation. The more he entangled them in his own ideas, the more pressed he felt to see them "as they really were"— yet at the same time to see their lives as beautiful rather than paltry, thin, and deprived.

This comes through even in the curious sections on work and education, in which he compares the look of Gudger's overalls to the blue of Cézanne and complains that the children's schooling, about which he admits he knows next to nothing, gives them little training in the sense of beauty or any facility with abstract ideas—as if these were the things they most needed, since they mattered to him, Jim Agee. With his customary rhetorical overkill, he sees even the best of their teachers as "the servants of unconscious murder" (265); having pinned the tenant families in his own fantasy of the simple life, he wants them to remain just as they were, not processed by the institutions of an imperfect civilization. He can dismiss the "advantages" of a Harvard education because he's had one.

I'm afraid I've stressed Agee's idiosyncrasy without giving full credit to his eloquence—the beauty of his meditations even when they lose touch with what they strain to bring to life. Again and again Agee wants to deliver the simple, direct truths of these tenants' lives; again and again they elude him. He cannot write "journalism," at least not in this book: his feelings complicate matters, he cannot detach himself, and he has read too much Blake and Lawrence, apostles of sensuous energy and vitality, to see these farmers as a class of people, "the poor." He treats them not as social victims but as separate, sentient universes of blood and bone, mind and will. They are no less human to him for being maimed, wounded, unfulfilled, "each in the most casual of his life so measurelessly discredited, harmed, insulted, poisoned, cheated." He wonders,

> how, looking thus into your eyes and seeing thus, how each of you is a creature which has never in all time existed before and which shall never in all time exist again and which is not quite like any other and which has the grand stature and natural warmth of every other and whose existence is all measured upon a still mad and incurable time; how am I to speak of you as "tenant" "farmers," as "representatives" of your "class," as social integers in a criminal economy, or as individuals, fathers, wives, sons, daughters, and as my friends and as I "know" you? (92)

Lathered into a kind of ecstasy of direct address, meditating on ultimate things, Agee, who more than once calls himself a communist, gives vent to a radical individualism that was unusual in a decade searching for collective solutions. Yet his prose, even with the help of Evans's magnificent pictures, cannot fully realize the individuals to whom these apostrophes are directed. His methodically detailed word pictures, such as his descriptions of the men's shoes and overalls and the wives' dresses, make only a futile stab at realizing them completely. Agee takes comfort in the example of an unnamed book, obviously *Ulysses*, a work he reads less as a modernist text than as an exhaustive epic of ordinary life. "It took a great artist seven years to record nineteen hours and to wring them anywhere near dry" (218).

Agee's wish to take hold of a small corner of the real world and wring it dry helps explain the unwieldy size of *Famous Men*, its anomalous combination of documentary detail and baroque artifice. (Some of the book is modeled on the structure of the Mass.) Influenced by the great writers of the twenties, especially Joyce and Faulkner, Agee aimed to reshape modernism to encompass the social and human urgencies of the Depression, just as he tried to stretch naturalism to embrace the complications of the individual consciousness.

Such an effort was probably doomed, and Agee will always remain a more fascinating figure than any single work he actually wrote. Yet this intransigent book stands as his major claim to greatness, besides being a benchmark for our own time on how to deal with society's victims without falling into the worn stereotypes of protest literature or the lofty condescension of middle-class sympathy. To Agee, both the system and its critics had tacitly agreed to treat the dispossessed as something less than human; his aim is to humanize them. It detracts little to note that this social agenda, if it is one, is invigorated by his own needs: knowing and helping these people will be a way to save himself. Stymied as an artist and as a journalist, Agee was drawn to the poor as a religious vocation, his way out of compromise and *Time*-serving. This set him off on a course so idiosyncratic, so out of phase with the literary moment, that it took two decades for writers to catch up with him—to free journalism from the shackles of an uncaring "objectivity" and turn it into literature.

"Desperate, Broken-hearted, Sick-of-it-all": West's Disease

From what we've said so far, it would seem that the language of social awareness in the 1930s is at least two different languages: a language of naturalism concerned with documenting social fact, and a language of modernism that plumbs the mind of the observer, translating complex states of consciousness into new narrative modes. Both of these approaches go back to earlier models. The protest writers look back to Zola and Dreiser on one level, Upton Sinclair and Jack London on another. Yet they were also deeply influenced by the deceptively plain style of Hemingway, which seemed to point them toward an illusory goal: a clean, uninflected language of social fact. The thirties modernists, by contrast, were nourished by a subterranean current that flowed from the preceding decade and would surface again after the war. In place of the simple, declarative prose of the naturalists, they substituted an ironic voice, a constantly shifting literary language, highly textured, frequently obscure, and narrative experiments that reflect multiple and overlapping subjective viewpoints.

Against the grain of the new populism, writers like Faulkner pursued formal effects that made their work seem fragmentary, discontinuous, and difficult. Their work continued to reflect not only the pessimism and widespread disillusionment of the postwar years but the epistemological crisis brought on by the new physics and the work of Freud. They avoided straight documentary writing for something more inventive and highly imagined, stressing individual minds over social types, spiritual poverty over physical poverty, the shadowy recesses of the mental landscape over the hard determinations of the economic life.

Few writers of the period were wholly of one type. We have seen how the almost hallucinatory intensity of Michael Gold's prose lent power to his naturalism, just as James Agee tried to achieve the aims of documentation by modernist means. In their great trilogies Farrell and Dos Passos were fundamentally naturalists, which helps explain why they have long since fallen out of favor, yet Farrell was influenced by Proust and Joyce, while Dos Passos, for the variety of narrative devices he uses in *U.S.A.*, was acclaimed as a daring experimenter in the 1930s. (Sartre compared him to Faulkner, Kafka, and Stendhal and called him "the greatest writer of our time." But it should be remembered that Sartre's English was poor.)

Some writers, as we have already seen, are divided against themselves. As Sylvia Jenkins Cook remarks of Erskine Caldwell, "most striking in the nonfiction is the complete absence of any comic or ironic vision of the poor, who are presented solely as victims with all ridicule stripped away. Without the earthy folk humor that acts in the novels as something of a counterforce to any completely naturalistic understanding of poor whites, they become mere sociological specimens, acting in accordance with clear economic laws."[19] The thirties writer who avoided the pitfalls of naturalistic reductionism most consistently was Nathanael West, another writer neglected then and rediscovered decades later.

Different as they were, Caldwell and West were friends in the early 1930s, when West worked as a hotel manager and, since business was poor, often allowed other writers to occupy vacant rooms for months at a time. Caldwell read and admired *Miss Lonelyhearts* in manuscript, and may well have appreciated West's "comic or ironic vision of the poor" since it was just as essential to his own early fiction, spiced with touches of ridicule the two writers shared. Both were influenced by the cultivation of the grotesque in the work of Sherwood Anderson and Faulkner, his onetime protégé. Mirroring the conversions of so many writers, West himself became increasingly radical and politicized, especially after moving to Hollywood to work as a screenwriter in 1935. But he managed to insulate his fiction from the well-meaning pressures of his friends, the stern criticisms of the literary Left, and his own growing political involvements. Mike Gold later told Jay Martin, West's biographer, "His writing seemed to me symbolic rather than realistic and that was, to me, the supreme crime."[20] But he was tolerated by the Left, rather obtusely, as the anatomist of a sick society. (This was how Leon Trotsky defended the anarchic bitterness in the early work of Céline.) Gold felt that West "was fundamentally on the side of the people," despite his resistance to message literature, agitprop, and socialist realism.

It's impossible to tell how much irony West was exercising when he piously—but firmly—defended his position to his radical friends, as in this letter from Hollywood to the proletarian novelist and editor Jack Conroy: "If I put into 'Day of the Locust' any of the sincere, honest people who work here and are making such a great, progressive fight, those chapters couldn't be written satirically and the whole fabric of the peculiar half world which I attempted to create would be badly torn by them" (quoted by Martin, 336). Since he lays it on quite thick, it's hard not to feel that West was being wickedly sarcastic in his praise of all the "honest, admirable, politically-conscious people" in Hollywood. But with this deeply ironic writer, who knows? According to his brother-in-law and close friend S. J. Perelman, "the noble piety of the Hollywood folks, as they immersed themselves in the plight of the migratory workers and the like, was pretty comical. One couldn't fault them for their social conscience, but when you saw the English country houses they dwelt in, the hundred-thousand-dollar estancias, and the Cadillacs they drove to the protest meetings, it was to laugh" (Martin, 345).

But starting in 1935, even before he left for Hollywood, West threw himself into a range of Popular Front activities all the more remarkable for one whose temperament, like Henry Roth's, seemed far from political. He was arrested in 1935 while marching on a picket line at Ohrbach's, a leading Union Square retailer; he signed the call for the radical American Writers' Congress in 1935 and the Western Writers' Congress in 1936, where he gave a talk on the topic "Makers of Mass Neuroses." Later he became very active in the embattled Screen Writers' Guild, and was eventually elected to the executive board, despite his reputation as a cynic rather than a committed revolutionary. The anti-Stalinist Left, vigorous in New York, had no presence in Hollywood, where the party and its fellow travelers represented the only entrenched political culture, and it included many of

West's closest friends. Much of this was merest fashion, though West paid his dues to it in a number of ways (even to the extent of signing a statement attacking the establishment of the commission headed by the venerable and impartial John Dewey to investigate the heinous charges lodged against Trotsky at the Moscow purge trials).[21] But West, despite his comfortable background and Ivy League schooling (at Brown), had a genuine streak of proletarian sympathy in his makeup, a bleak affinity for human wretchedness that comes across clearly in his novels.

Since West mainly kept politics out of his work, since he avoided social realism and seemed to deal with spiritual rather than economic privation, few attempts have been made to situate him firmly in the 1930s or to connect him to the social consciousness of the period. Like Roth and Agee, he found no large audience then and was not widely appreciated till his work was republished decades later, when he was acclaimed as a forerunner of black humor and a metaphysician of sordid and laughably miserable lives. Unsettled by West's bracing cynicism and startling modernity, critics looked at him through the prism of the postwar years, when W. H. Auden described "West's disease" as a timeless inner malaise, "a disease of consciousness which renders it incapable of converting wishes into desires."[22]

It is certainly true that West's people suffer not from hunger or unemployment but from boredom, deformity, and frustration. They need a New Deal of the soul, not the dole. This makes it more difficult to see how West was responding to the Depression and especially to how others were writing about it. Yet his work was more timely than his contemporaries realized.

Like the other once neglected modernists of the 1930s, including Agee, Roth, and Faulkner, West was deeply affected by the European avant-garde of the preceding decade. He remained faithful to the quest for new forms as well as the pessimism and cynicism of the expatriate generation. It would be easy to show the impact of surrealism and Freud on West's first novel, *The Dream Life of Balso Snell* (1931), a peculiar venture in jejune, sophomoric facetiousness. It's less easy to show how he leaves these influences behind in *Miss Lonelyhearts* (1933)—a book that plays devil's advocate to all populist and proletarian novels while sharing some features of their vision. In his intricate encounter with the new populism, West turned *Miss Lonelyhearts* and *The Day of the Locust* (1939) into *anti*-proletarian novels even as he made the miseries of ordinary people one of his main subjects.

Like Agee, Roth, and Faulkner, Nathanael West engaged the radical writers on their own ground while significantly altering the vantage point of the reader. As a hotel manager, he had an unusual angle on people's private lives, collecting stories he recycled into fiction (or sometimes used directly, as in the pathetic travails of Homer Simpson in *The Day of the Locust*). In Hollywood he lived modestly and loved to visit sordid neighborhoods. The glitz of Hollywood was not his beat, only the pathos of its dream factory. According to a screenwriter friend, Sy Bartlett, he spent a great deal of time with crime reporters and police officers in the homicide department, "always looking for bizarre backgrounds" and "very interested in . . . the really seamy side of life" (Martin, 272–73). Though he always insisted he was a comic writer, his was the hard-boiled LA of Chandler and Cain rather than the glitter dome of most Hollywood fiction. His film people were the disappointed extras looking for parts, the crowds at premieres hungry for a glimpse of a star; there were no tycoons, first or last, in his movie world.

Miss Lonelyhearts (1933) was typical of the populist fiction and journalism of the 1930s—especially the "People Talk" genre—since it was based on the real-life letters of actual people, letters West altered and exaggerated to heighten their effect. Miss Lonelyhearts' own description of the plot of the novel may reflect some of West's reaction to the original documents:

> A man is hired to give advice to the readers of a newspaper. The job is a circulation stunt and the whole staff considers it a joke. . . . He too considers the job a joke, but after several months at it, the joke begins to escape him. He sees that the majority of the letters are profoundly humble pleas for moral and spiritual advice, that they are inarticulate expressions of genuine suffering. He also discovers that his correspondents take him seriously. For the first time in his life, he is forced to examine the values by which he lives. This examination shows him that he is the victim of the joke and not its perpetrator.[23]

On the simplest level, Miss Lonelyhearts—we never learn his "real" name—is no more than a man having a nervous breakdown. But the terms of that breakdown are far-reaching. His anonymity and some of his misfortune may be borrowed from Kafka, his "Christ complex" and self-laceration from Dostoyevsky, but West puts these influences to strikingly original use. As this passage makes clear, the novel can be seen as a gravely flippant allegory of the twenties writer at sea in the strange new world of the Depression. Like other mocking wits whose eyes are suddenly opened to human misery, Miss L. is a failed cynic, profoundly moved in spite of himself, unable to sustain his joking detachment and sense of superiority.

Miss L. works in the *Front Page* world of the daily newspaper, at once the citadel of hard-bitten cynicism and, in the advice column at least, a focus of popular fantasy. To remind him of what he once was, his boss Shrike and his old friends at Delehanty's, their favorite watering hole, are inexhaustible parodists of the rhetoric of concern and spiritual crisis; they are childish nihilists who believe in nothing. ("At college, and perhaps for a year afterwards, they had believed in literature, had believed in Beauty and in personal expression as an absolute end. When they lost this belief, they lost everything. . . . Like Shrike, the man they imitated, they were machines for making jokes" [14, 15].) Set against this 1920s cynicism and soured aestheticism stands Betty, Miss L.'s girlfriend, whose sunny faith in country living and conventional domestic arrangements beckons to Miss Lonelyhearts without being able to satisfy or save him. ("Her world was not the world and could never include the readers of his column. Her sureness was based on the power to limit experience arbitrarily" [11].)

Between these untenable extremes of sarcasm and simplicity is a man on a rack. His torments both evoke and burlesque the new gospel of altruistic empathy imposed by the Depression:

> "What a kind bitch you are. As soon as any one acts viciously, you say he's sick. Wife-torturers, rapers of small children, according to you they're all sick. No morality, only medicine. Well, I'm not sick. I don't need any of your damned aspirin. I've got a Christ complex. Humanity . . . I'm a humanity lover. All the broken bastards . . ." He finished with a short laugh that was like a bark. (12–13)

Leagued around him are all the broken bastards, capitalized into types, clichés, people as anonymous as he is—they call themselves "Desperate,

Broken-hearted, Sick-of-it-all, Disillusioned-with-tubercular-husband"—
and he reaches out to them, as to Betty, with a vast love indistinguishable from violence. "He knew that only violence could make him supple"
(11). Betty herself is compared to "a small kitten whose soft helplessness
makes one ache to hurt it" (13). This transition from helplessness to sadistic rage recurs several times in the novel. As Miss Lonelyhearts tries to
hurt an old homosexual he found cruising in the park, "he was twisting
the arm of all the sick and miserable, broken and betrayed, inarticulate
and impotent" (18).

This transformation of weakness or sympathy into violence is like the
buried underside of the radical altruism of Depression writing, a streak of
sadism submerged within that torrent of pity. In a direct line from Dostoyevsky and Freud, West shows us that there is no simple humanitarian feeling that can be detached from irrational impulses, bursts of anger,
violence, and sheer frustration. In both Agee and West, sympathy for the
dispossessed takes on a spiritual dimension that becomes self-punishing.
In Agee's case this takes the form of guilt feelings, a revulsion at one's
own sheltered life, a tormented self-awareness.

Agee reacts to the lives of his tenant farmers as Miss Lonelyhearts
responds to his letter writers: with an emotional imbalance by turns
wildly eager, grimly depressed, and vaguely suicidal. Some have seen
Agee's driving, as described in *Let Us Now Praise Famous Men*, as an unconscious reenactment of the early death of his father. Yet a mishap with his
car finally enables him to come to live with one of his tenant families.
West, who was notorious among his friends for his careless and distracted
driving, did finally die in an auto accident with his new wife.

In a sense, Agee lived his whole life in a self-destructive rush of incandescent intensity. He kept faith with the bohemian ideal of burning with a
hard, gemlike flame. This is not to say that modernist writers, being (presumably) more inward and spiritual, were more prone to suicide, while
those who chronicled the Depression in a documentary mode knew how
to keep a stiff upper lip. Miss Lonelyhearts' problem is that he cannot
help seeing the deeper pathos behind the commonplace misery of ordinary people's lives. In him the temperament of a martyr has been superimposed on the mind of cynic. He sees through other people's dreams
and fantasies but somehow can no longer scoff at them or dismiss them.
He is now tortured by what he once found enjoyably ludicrous, the cheap

or sordid poetry of pinched, shabby lives. West's book is a piercing shriek of frustration before the depths of human misery.

When Mary Shrike, the boss's wife and his occasional paramour, tells him about her mother's miserable death, "he stopped listening and tried to bring his great understanding heart into action again. Parents are also part of the business of dreams. . . . People like Mary were unable to do without such tales" (23). Some of the proletarian writers were looking for a kind of poetry of the quotidian, but West actually found it—in the clichés of mass culture and the pathos of common fantasies. His characters' miseries are not so much documented as refracted through the tawdriness and desperation of their fantasy lives, the demotic poetry of their wishes and dreams.

West sees the common man as an instinctive artist, though often manipulated by the huckster vendors of collective dreams. His *Day of the Locust* appeared in the same year as the art critic Clement Greenberg's celebrated attack on mass culture, "Avant-Garde and Kitsch." But where Greenberg argued that "Kitsch is mechanical and operates by formula. Kitsch is vicarious experience and faked sensations. . . . Kitsch is the epitome of all that is spurious in the life of our times,"[24] West was moved by an authentic pathos at the heart of these crude formulas and fantasies, whose absurdity he exaggerated into a desperate kind of comedy. Where Greenberg is dismissive and one-dimensional, West is complex and empathetic: "It is hard to laugh at the need for beauty and romance, no matter how tasteless, even horrible, the results of that are. But it is easy to sigh. Few things are sadder than the truly monstrous" (61). Unlike Greenberg, West does not let himself off the hook. The irony of Miss L.'s "great understanding heart" cuts both ways.

West's novels are like an anthropological inventory of popular fantasy: the crudely ungrammatical yet grotesquely poignant letters in *Miss Lonelyhearts*; the Alger-like dreams of American opportunity and self-making in *A Cool Million*; the cheap movie ambitions of Hollywood deadenders in *The Day of the Locust*. But this is satire with a grim personal bite, though based on cool and cruel observation. Like all good caricature, West's work conveys the broad outlines of something recognizably solid and real, exaggerating only what is already self-exaggerated.

West's triumphant originality lies in the way he mixes comedy with pathos, a Dostoyevskian spiritual abyss with the style of a comic strip. West had planned to subtitle *Miss Lonelyhearts* "A novel in the form of a comic strip."[25] Giving this up, he hinted at an organization based on separate panels or tableaux by affixing ironic chapter titles that could belong to a diorama or the episodes of a popular serial (for example, "Miss Lonelyhearts on a Field Trip," "Miss Lonelyhearts Attends a Party"). The most important feature of West's style is its stringent economy. For an age of prose, anchored to the concrete social fact, these poetic texts were remarkably lean and intense, composed of sharply chiseled scenes and paragraphs punctuated by spare but striking images.

In *Miss Lonelyhearts* only the common folk are garrulous, for deep down, although the People Talk, the People are also fundamentally inarticulate. Miss L.'s reactions are sketched in a brutally laconic way. As Fay Doyle speaks, for example, her very words seem to press him down: "The life out of which she spoke was even heavier than her body. It was as if a gigantic, living Miss Lonelyhearts letter in the shape of a paper weight had been placed on his brain" (29). Shrike, too, the demonic tempter and parodist, makes long, brilliant speeches, as does the iconic Shagpoke Whipple, the would-be fascist dictator in *A Cool Million*. This expansive rhetorical facility is the very mark of their insincerity—the protean demagogic flow of the confidence man, *homo Americanus*.

When Miss L.—as a therapist to the masses, a secular cleric—*does* try to talk, to show how truly sincere and concerned he can be, he finds that he has "merely written a column for his paper" or, worse still, "substituted the rhetoric of Shrike for that of Miss Lonelyhearts" (49, 50). This problem of language drives West to some of his most arresting images. As the cripple Doyle speaks, Miss L. realizes that "he was making no attempt to be understood. He was giving birth to groups of words that lived inside of him as things" (45–46). Caught between the inarticulate misery of the Doyles, which leaks *through* language, and the hyper-articulate cynicism of Shrike, which is *all* language, Miss L. spirals inward toward a depressed silence that foreshadows his martyrdom.

Doyle shoots him—with a gun wrapped appropriately in a newspaper—as he is reaching out to all the miserable readers of his column without understanding them or being able to succor them, except in his salvational fantasy. His Christ dream is now more than ever the mark of his dementia:

He would embrace the cripple and the cripple would be made whole again, even as he, a spiritual cripple, had been made whole. . . . He did not understand the cripple's shout and heard it as a cry for help from Desperate, Harold S., Catholic-mother, Broken-hearted, Broad Shoulders, Sick-of-it-all, Disillusioned-with-tubercular-husband. He was running to succor them with love. (57–58)

James Agee, an authentic if besieged Christian, expressed a similar wish to hug his people, merge with them, save them, even as he envied the bare, bedrock beauty of their lives. Faced with genuine poverty or misery, Depression writers could not always maintain the prescribed attitudes of detached pity or radical indignation. They were moved to intervene, yet sometimes haunted by the hopelessness of any formulaic intervention. Abandoning the would-be objectivity of the social chronicler, Agee and West make the writer's reaction central to their subject, substituting a complex of personal emotions for any easy social or economic attitude. Their subjects' plight comes home to us more effectively as it comes to seem more tangled and insoluble.

Unlike Agee's book, *Miss Lonelyhearts* is a novel, and the central character is surely not to be confused with the author. But Miss L., like Tod in *The Day of the Locust*, is the kind of seismically perceiving sensor West needs, perhaps to balance off his own instinctive detachment and irony. In one respect, however, the character is beyond detached, in a way that connects him to the author. According to his biographer Jay Martin, who offers persuasive evidence, "guilt feelings and associations with pain and disease—these mixed powerfully in West with a personal restraint and romantic yearning—and gave a highly ambiguous and unresolved character to his sexual identity" (Martin, 134). In Miss Lonelyhearts, whose name points to sexual confusion, this is expressed in his halfhearted, mechanical lovemaking with Betty and the disgust and sexual anesthesia he experiences with Mrs. Shrike and Fay Doyle. With Betty: "He remembered that towards the end of his last visit he had put his hand inside her clothes. Unable to think of anything else to do, he now repeated the gesture" (12). With Mary Shrike: "No similar change ever took place in his own body, however. Like a dead man, only friction could make him warm or violence make him mobile" (19). With Fay Doyle: "Some fifteen minutes later, he crawled out of bed like an exhausted swimmer leaving the surf" (28). And later, another watery image, passive and disgusted: "He tried to fend her off, but she kept pressing her open mouth against his and when he turned away, she nuzzled his cheek. He felt like an empty bottle that is being slowly filled with warm, dirty water" (50).

I catalog these numb images not to illustrate West's style—though they do—or to psychoanalyze him by way of his characters, which would be perilous indeed with such a conscious craftsman, but to demonstrate the spiritual and physical depths to which his characters descend. For all the sensory immediacy of his style, West is in line with allegorical writers from Dante and Bunyan to Dostoyevsky and Kafka, writers whose concrete realism of detail serves a larger, more abstract spiritual plot. Stanley Edgar Hyman once argued, too literally, I think, that there is a homosexual subtext in the novel—between Shrike and Miss L., between Miss L. and Doyle, between Miss L. and the Dirty Old Man whose arm he twists. It seems more likely that the hero's sexual anesthesia and disgust stand for his larger deadness, his general failure of affect. Having lost his cynicism, he has lost his fix on life. The discrete chapters of the book are like the Stations of the Cross. Having taken a kind of Dantean journey and gazed into the well of human misery, he has lost the ability to take pleasure in the ordinary world. His only recourse is Not to Feel, and near the end of the book his emotional self has become "the rock," a fortified stoical entity he can observe from the outside with serene detachment:

> It was not the rock that was touched. The rock was still perfect. It was his mind that was touched, the instrument with which he knew the rock. . . .
>
> He felt for the rock. It was still there; neither laughter nor tears could affect the rock. It was oblivious to wind and rain.
>
> . . . The rock had been thoroughly tested and had been found perfect. He had only to climb aboard the bed again. (54, 55, 56)

Notebook or camera in hand, the documentary observer of social calamity or human wretchedness is a key figure of Depression culture, which West subtly undermines. He gives us instead a figure who whirls back and forth between extreme agitation and numb endurance, who has lost all faith in the language of concern or consolation he once wielded, and who has no use for the rhetoric of reform or revolutionary change.

that was on so many writers' lips. At the heart of the book is an immense futility, at once comical and horrendous, best expressed in the desperate letters that propel Miss Lonelyhearts into his own despairing state.

Ingeniously, West altered his original sources—the letters he actually saw that inspired the book—to make both the misery and the language of misery more absurd, and therefore harder to take seriously. The troubles he describes are so grotesque and comic-parodic that we hardly know what to make of them. In the most daring change, right near the beginning of the book, a girl with a "weak knee" and a "slight limp" becomes a girl who "was born without a nose," although she describes herself as "a good dancer" with "a nice shape," whose father buys her "pretty clothes."

> I sit and look at myself all day and cry. I have a big hole in the middle
> of my face that scares people even myself so I cant blame the boys for
> not wanting to take me out. My mother loves me, but she crys terri-
> ble when she looks at me. (2)

Superficially, West's changes bring to mind the controversial inventions with which Caldwell and Bourke-White cooked the documentary evidence in *You Have Seen Their Faces*, the anonymous speeches and folksy captions, making them the kinds of things no real person has ever said. But where Caldwell's inventions issued in a single repeated note of social protest and dehumanization ("It ain't hardly worth the trouble to go on living"), West's forgeries sound a more piercing cri de coeur, at once mischievously jokey and strangely touching. In a period rife with social pieties about real anguish, West escapes from formula into a realm of comic freedom. He mastered the pathos of the grotesque, not its mocking note of superiority. His humor is black and bilious like Céline's, vertiginously anarchic like Perelman's and the Marx brothers'. This is the anarchic side of the 1930s we often forget, the zaniness of *Duck Soup* and screwball comedy. It flouts taboos, making fun of children and cripples, reminiscent of the vinegary humor of W. C. Fields. It even mocks of the bad grammar of the poor, which somehow renders their misery more poignant because it is more clichéd and inarticulate. Few writers have turned ridicule to such profound (and unpredictable) use.

Both Agee and West give us protagonists who are unhinged by their subject, who pass, disastrously, beyond the limits of any documentary detachment. Agee wants to make love to his people; West's hero is deadened by them, catapulted into a realm of dementia beyond feeling. The effect in both cases is the same: a skepticism about the social analysis of human misery, a pessimism about whether anything significant can or should be changed. It is no surprise that only a later generation, schooled in the brutality of the war and its aftermath, could fully respond to their message.

The People, Yes

The work of West, Agee, and Walker Evans was rediscovered and acclaimed by later readers, when the social consciousness of the thirties had long been considered passé. In his more direct approach to social protest in *The Grapes of Wrath,* John Steinbeck, even more than Dos Passos, was the representative writer of the period itself. His book summarized many of the ambitions and contradictions of the decade and delivered them somewhat belatedly to a much wider audience.

The Dust Bowl was not a new subject when Steinbeck began writing about it in the late thirties. There had been small dust storms in 1931 and 1932 in western Kansas and eastern Colorado. By the spring of 1934 a terrible drought centered in the Dakotas had decimated farm acreage, removed topsoil, and caused enormous black clouds to blanket towns and plains throughout the West. In 1936 the Resettlement Administration sponsored a documentary by Pare Lorentz, *The Plow That Broke the Plains,* to explore the causes and dreadful effects of this natural calamity. Displaced and impoverished farmers had been adding to the pool of migrant labor in California in large numbers since 1930, reaching a climax in 1936, when more than eighty thousand migrants made the trek.

Nor was Steinbeck's treatment new in literary terms. By 1939, when the book appeared, the proletarian novel had long since lost the sponsorship of both left-liberal critics and party apparatchiks. In 1935 the worldwide policy of the Communist movement had shifted from the radicalism of the Third Period, when the party, true to its Leninist beginnings, remained a small, militant vanguard of disciplined revolutionaries, to the reformism of the Popular Front, when the party tried to build a broad-based alliance with liberals, Socialists, and New Dealers. The divisive language of class-consciousness gave way to the more fuzzy vocabulary of populism, and even Communists began referring to themselves as "liberals" and "progressives" (as some of the survivors of that period would continue to do for the rest of their lives).

The cultural policy of the Communists took a similar turn. Just as the party ditched its policy of creating parallel trade unions, working instead within the emerging industrial unionism of the Congress of Industrial Organizations (CIO), it pulled the plug on its parallel literary structures, such as the John Reed Clubs and the proletarian novel, which had in part been devoted to searching out what Mike Gold had called a "Shakespeare in overalls." Instead, it cultivated the support of widely read liberal writers and well-heeled Hollywood celebrities. At the Writers' Congresses of 1935, 1937, and 1939, attention was focused on old-line American radicals like Waldo Frank, independent-minded leftists like Kenneth Burke, and famous fellow travelers such as Hemingway rather than on militant Communists like Gold, who were identified with the proletarian movement.

John Steinbeck was never a Communist—his politics were those of a New Deal Democrat—but he grew interested in the Communists themselves as they tried to radicalize the masses of unorganized workers. When *In Dubious Battle* appeared early in 1936, it made him a kind of authority on migrant labor in California. This led him to do a series of articles in October for the *San Francisco News*, called "The Harvest Gypsies," which contained an outline of what, two years later, would develop into the final draft of *The Grapes of Wrath*. In the same year, 1938, these articles, along with a new epilogue and some photographs by Dorothea Lange, would be collected into a pamphlet, *"Their Blood Is Strong"*—printed to raise money for the starving migrants themselves.

The story of Steinbeck's evolving response to the Depression can be seen in his shifting viewpoint in the years between *In Dubious Battle* of 1936 and the final version of *The Grapes of Wrath*, which came out in 1939. Above all, he went from seeing the migrant workers from the outside as social victims, objects of pity or exploitation, to identifying with them as besieged individuals and seeing the world through their eyes. This began in a small way in the spring and summer of 1936 as he worked on his novella *Of Mice and Men*, which would become one of his most popular and accessible works. The book is about the hopes and dreams of one of the oddest couples in American literature, the canny George, who thinks he wants to be off on his own, free of responsibility, and Lennie, the lumbering giant, whose thwarted tenderness and dangerous strength are always at risk of crushing whatever he touches, whether it be mice and pups or men and women. Some readers have always found these characters too elemental, yet they reflect the primal needs that Steinbeck discovered in himself—a longing for animal warmth, the feeling of security, and the reassuring touch of other living creatures. Steinbeck was no doubt inspired by Faulkner's Benjy in *The Sound and the Fury* to create in Lennie a character who embodies the least common denominator in human longings, a baffled need for simple affection, the sense of having a place in the world. He may also represent the untested strength and capacity of feeling of ordinary, limited human beings. The strange relationship of George and Lennie, which echoes the bond between Huck and Jim in *Huckleberry Finn*, is built on a dream of independence that others around them come to share, from the crippled old Candy, who's been hurt on the job, been paid a pittance for his injuries, and fears that when he "can't swamp out no bunk houses they'll put [him] on the county," to the bowed and embittered black man Crooks, who has always been treated as a pariah. For a brief instant, these men come to share Lennie's dream of having a small homestead of their own. For Lennie and George the American Dream has become a ritualized litany, a moment of communion, that punctuates the action, meaning something different each time it is repeated: it first represents cockeyed hope, then shared possibility, then failure and disappointment. By sticking together and dreaming of their own patch of land, Lennie and George offer a glimmer of solidarity and mutual trust to lonely men who have long been scorned as human driftwood. Everyone comments on how unusual it is for two men, especially these men, to be traveling together, tied to each other, and George repeatedly laments how free and easy his life would be if he were on his own. But caring for Lennie, getting Lennie out of trouble, nurturing a pipe dream of independence that is really Lennie's, and finally saving Lennie from vigilante justice by taking his life—these are the only things that give *his* life some purpose. In a sense, George and Lennie pick up where Mac and Jim left off in *In Dubious Battle*, with another deep bond that culminates in rupture, sacrifice, and loss.

The symbolism of the novel is far too schematic. George and Lennie stand for mind and body, thought and feeling, calculation and instinctive need. The accidental deaths of Lennie's pet mice and pup, crushed in his tender grip, too neatly foreshadow the death of Curley's wife; she too dies in his strong but wayward arms. Her role was enlarged in the 1937 stage adaptation and the 1939 film version; she is another lonely soul, neglected by her brutal husband, scorned by the ranch hands, someone looking desperately for human company. More foreshadowing: when Candy's old dog must be put out of his misery, this looks ahead to the sacrificial death the old man foresees for himself, the mercy killing that George will have to provide for Lennie. In the fateful world of *Of Mice and Men*, every man must kill the thing he loves, the thing he cares for most, and every event symbolically anticipates such a dire outcome. Steinbeck, like a latter-day Thomas Hardy, put his thumb on the scales to make sure that his characters' hopes were thwarted, but he also tried hard to individualize them and see the world simply from their point of view. As he worked on the book, he wanted his people to "act with all the unexpectedness of real people," and worried that "building too carefully for an event" would be "doing that old human trick of reducing everything to its simplest design," which proved to be the real weakness of the novel. He reminded himself that "the designs of lives are not so simple." This is a far cry from what he had felt only a few years earlier when he was writing short stories, chafing at the exigency of making his characters seem like real human beings.

The real shift in Steinbeck's angle of vision began later in the year as he was visiting squatters' camps for the articles in the "Harvest Gypsies" series for the *San Francisco News*. Between August 1936, when he did this research, and February and March 1938, when he was sent to report on the flooding and starvation in Visalia, shortly before writing *The Grapes of Wrath*, Steinbeck not only went down into the trenches, as other committed thirties writers did, but grew horrified and helplessly indignant at the migrants' living conditions, which he described with awful vividness in the second of his *News* articles and in his letters. In the *News* article, one of the most effective pieces of Depression journalism, he focuses on the inexorable disintegration of three families in one of the squatters' camps. In his letters of February and March 1938, he describes the awful conditions in the interior valleys, flood and hunger, lack of medical care and sanitary facilities, government inaction, hostility in the surrounding towns, and the awful need he feels to publicize these conditions. "I must go to Visalia. Four thousand families, drowned out of their tents are really starving to death. . . . The death of children by starvation in our valleys is simply staggering."[26] When he goes there, he finds it even worse than he expected. "A short trip into the fields where the water is a foot deep in the tents and the children are up on the beds and there is no food and no fire, and the county has taken off all the nurses because 'the problem is so great that we can't do anything about it.' So they do nothing" (161).

If they would do nothing, perhaps he could. "The newspapers won't touch the stuff but they will under my byline" (159). "I want to put a tag of shame on the greedy bastards who are responsible for this" (162). Under this pressure to do something, Steinbeck shifted from observer to advocate, from would-be scientist theorizing about "group-man" to angry reformer exposing the system's abuses, but, above all, from seeing the migrants as mistreated objects to seeing them as people trying to preserve their dignity as they struggled to survive. In its final version, *The Grapes of Wrath* was not simply a new take on the same material; it was a different kind of novel, with all the strengths and flaws that came with Steinbeck's emotional identification with the migrants' plight.

Despite the accusations of those who derided him as a dangerous radical, Steinbeck actually went to Visalia at the urging of the Farm Security Administration, which wanted him to use his name to publicize what was happening there. His research for *The Grapes of Wrath* was virtually sponsored by a lower-level New Deal administrator, Tom Collins, and the accuracy of his novel was later defended by Eleanor Roosevelt herself. But he grew fascinated by the same social issues that engaged the Communists. His turn from the union organizers of *In Dubious Battle* to the saga of one migrant family paralleled the party's turn from a revolutionary program stressing class conflict toward the sentimental populism of the Popular Front, which cultivated themes of patriotism and common values and stressed its roots in American democratic traditions.

A closer look at Steinbeck's impressive journalism shows how his reporting provided him with the material for the novel. The key articles in the "Harvest Gypsies" series are the first, acquainting readers with these migrants and describing their long trek, and the second, examining the social geography and living conditions of the squatters' camps in factual but heartrending detail. (A later article explores conditions in the government camps, one of which would provide temporary refuge for the fictional Joads.) In the opening article Steinbeck tries to convince his readers that these are neighbors, people just like themselves, driven by forces beyond their control, not a pest of locusts that had simply descended upon them. "They are not migrants by nature. They are gypsies by force of circumstance." Unlike the foreign laborers of the past, going back to the Chinese who had built the railroads, these people are Americans who will not be cowed or sent away. They cannot be forced into a subhuman standard of living. "It should be understood that with this new race the old methods of repression, of starvation wages, of jailing, beating, and intimidation are not going to work; these are American people."[27]

Steinbeck appeals to his readers' moral sympathy and sense of kinship but also to their Americanism, a narrow but powerful theme in a period when all social protest was labeled Communist and Communists were labeled foreign agitators. (Thus an antilynching film like Fritz Lang's *Fury*, also out in 1936, had to focus on an unlikely white target, played by Spencer Tracy.) In *The Grapes of Wrath* Steinbeck gives a native air to the plight of the starving poor. He makes the migrants' cause feel truly American but also inserts it into a large, inexorable historical movement that will sweep everything before it.

In the novel these features are keyed into the title itself, to which the author was strongly attached. For him the image of the grapes of wrath was at once apocalyptic and quintessentially American. He urged his editor to print all the words *and* music of the "Battle Hymn of the Republic" at the beginning of the book. He sees the grapes as an image of the Edenic plenty of America, controlled by a small plutocracy while the people starve, yet also an omen of biblical vengeance coming to fruition as surely as nature itself. As pigs are slaughtered and fruit and vegetables are plowed under, children die of malnutrition and disease. "There is a crime here that goes beyond denunciation. . . . In the souls of the people the grapes of wrath are filling and growing heavy, growing heavy for the vintage."[28]

The Communists had their own version of historical inevitability, which Steinbeck occasionally echoes in the weaker interchapters of the novel. His strength is not in general ideas but in concrete, visceral evocation of things as they are: the facts of the harvest, the camps, the rotting fruit, the dying children, the listless parents, the things he saw with his own eyes. Despite his homespun philosophizing, or his reach for an epic saga in biblical, folksy, at times dithyrambic prose, Steinbeck is basically a sensuous writer, immediate and visceral in his grasp of physical reality. He has no rival in showing how things were done, how they happened. Where much proletarian fiction was willed and all too theoretical, he has a gift for absorbing data and breaking it down into something simple and direct. Nothing is more effective in *The Grapes of Wrath* than the nuts and bolts of slaughtering a pig, getting on the road, preparing a meager meal, repairing a broken-down car. This immediacy has always secured his hold on readers. Even his journalism has a narrative grasp that gives it power; his second *News* article is a classic piece of Depression reportage.

First Steinbeck describes a typical camp itself ("from a distance it looks like a city dump, and well may be, for the city dumps are the sources of the materials of which it is built"), then three of the families who live in it. The first is a farm family that once had fifty acres of land and a thousand dollars in the bank, and still clings to cleanliness, decency, and respectability. "There is still pride in this family. Wherever they stop they try to put the children in school. It may be that the children will be in school for as much as a month before they are moved to another local-ity" (*"Their Blood Is Strong,"* 6). The father has made a makeshift toilet by digging a hole near his paper house. "He is a newcomer and his spirit and his decency and his sense of his own dignity have not been quite wiped out." Yet his face is etched with a peculiar look, "not worry, but absolute terror of the starvation that crowds in against the borders of the camp" (6–7). Even their simulation of "home" has little chance to endure. "With the first rain the carefully built house will slop down into a brown, pulpy mush," just as "the clothes will fray off the children's bodies," exposing them to the cold.

A full step down, the next family, once the proprietors of a small grocery store, now lives in a tattered, rotten canvas tent. One quilt and a single piece of canvas are the only bedding for a couple and four chil-dren. The filth, the flies buzzing around the foul clothes of the children, are appalling. "This family has been on the road longer than the builder of the paper house. There is no toilet here, but there is a clump of wil-lows nearby where human faeces lie exposed to the flies—the same flies that are in the tent" (7). Another child, four years old, has recently died of fever and malnutrition. "With this death there came a change of mind in this family. The father and mother now feel that paralyzed dullness with which the mind protects itself against too much sorrow and too much pain." Even the limited earnings of the family will now be reduced, for the father "is no longer alert; he isn't quick at piece-work, and he is not able to fight clear of the dullness that has settled on him." In a stunning sentence Steinbeck adds, "His spirit is losing caste rapidly." There is a measured irony to Steinbeck's conclusion: "This is the middle class of the squatters' camp. In a few months this family will slip down to the lower class" (8).

The third family, typifying the lowest class in the camp, has built a "house" of branches and scrap with only the barest simulation of walls and a roof. It contains no bed, only a piece of old carpet lying on the ground. "To go to bed the members of the family lie on the ground and fold the carpet up over them."

> The three year old child has a gunny sack tied about his middle for clothing. He has the swollen belly caused by malnutrition.
>
> He sits on the ground in the sun in front of the house, and the little black fruit flies buzz in circles and land on his closed eyes and crawl up his nose until he weakly brushes them away.
>
> They try to get at the mucous in the eye-corners. This child seems to have the reactions of a baby much younger. The first year he had a little milk, but he has had none since.
>
> He will die in a very short time. The older children may survive.

The picture here is not very different from the faces in some of Margaret Bourke-White's photographs of southern tenant farmers, with the same touch of Gothic horror, the same generalized appeal to our emotions, especially our pity, our middle-class revulsion and sense of guilt. Yet these simple paragraphs escape the insincerity and social rhetoric we feel in Bourke-White's tour of the lower depths. Steinbeck's letters and his journal, *Working Days*, show that he was obsessed with the human wreckage he sought out in the camps of those years, and was determined to write a novel that would do it full justice. Yet he had no easy explanations or solutions. Like so many 1930s naturalists, his impulse was simply to tell us what he *saw*—as he continues here to describe the same family:

Four nights ago the mother had a baby in the tent, on the dirty carpet. It was born dead, which was just as well because she could not have fed it at the breast; her own diet will not produce milk.

After it was born and she had seen that it was dead, the mother rolled over and lay still for two days. She is up today, tottering around. The last baby, born less than a year ago, lived a week. This woman's eyes have the glazed, far-away look of a sleep walker's eyes.

She does not wash clothes any more. The drive that makes for cleanliness has been drained out of her and she hasn't the energy. The husband was a share-cropper once, but he couldn't make it go. Now he has lost even the desire to talk. (8)

This is the topical soil out of which *The Grapes of Wrath* grew. I quote the passage at length for the testimony it provides, the novelistic yet schematic way it is organized, and the peculiar emphasis that Steinbeck subtly adds to his material. Not content with description, he reaches for the type, giving us a carefully sculpted parable—which is also a parody—of a miniature society. It is divided into three classes, not so much by wealth and origin as by middle-class values like pride and dignity, as shown above all by cleanliness. (Steinbeck's insight was later confirmed from the other side of the world. We know from reports out of the Nazi concentration camps that those who stopped washing had lost the will to live, and soon died.)

Studies of the Depression have repeatedly emphasized the high incidence of emotional and marital problems among those, especially middle-class males, who lost all sense of self-worth. (Women in general, and men who had grown up poor, proved better able to adapt, often by taking more menial work.) Steinbeck had a novelist's intuition of the psychology of pride and degradation. In the third family, "the children do not even go to the willow clump any more. They squat where they are and kick a little dirt" (9). For these squatters he holds out little hope, yet they are no less than what the other families may soon become. Like the world surrounding them, which they represent in miniature, this is a society whose only mobility is downward. The Depression has set these families on a precipitous slide, a free fall, which they themselves are not strong enough to arrest. The father of the third family has lost not only livelihood but will, energy, concentration. His listlessness defines his life, as it threatens to engulf those who have not yet sunk to his level:

This is what the man in the tent will be in six months; what the man in the paper house will be in a year, after his house has been washed down and his children have sickened and died, after the loss of dignity and spirit have cut him down to a kind of sub-humanity. (9)

The miserable details in this article are more harsh than anything in the novel, in part because they are presented so barely, without countervailing moments of joy, satisfaction, or free choice. Yet they shed light on the relentless decline of the Joads after they leave the government camp, when the saga of their journey to California is long behind them. They also help explain why Steinbeck locates the emotional center of his book in two feisty, difficult characters, a mother and her eldest son, whose will to survive and to keep the family together is strongest.

Much of Steinbeck's earlier work had dealt with male relationships—Mac and Jim, Lennie and George, with women (like Curley's wife) as an intrusive, even threatening presence—but the nurturing role of Ma Joad conveys the author's emotional connection to this material. She combines toughness, endurance, and maternal empathy. This awesome female determination in terrible times resonated with Depression audiences, much as it did in *Gone with the Wind*. It would prove to be a key to the book's popular success, which far exceeded that of other proletarian fiction.

The Grapes of Wrath begins as the story of an eviction, continues with the account of a journey, the difficult passage of a family from its old world to a new one, and concludes with the disillusioning calamities that beset its members after they have reached this promised land. Steinbeck underlines the typicality of the family's fate by interspersing brief, poetic chapters of general history, as Dos Passos had interwoven newsreels, historical summaries, and capsule biographies of famous Americans into the narrative pattern of *U.S.A.* Steinbeck's novel is resonant with literary echoes. From the proletarian novel he borrowed protagonists, especially Tom Joad and Preacher Casy, who come gradually to understand the social causes of their misery and oppression; in the parlance of a later era, they get their consciousness raised.

Steinbeck understood the limited appeal of the kind of ideological novel he had already written in *In Dubious Battle*. This new work begins in the hard-boiled world of the thirties road novel, with a truculent Tom Joad hitchhiking home after a stint in prison for killing a man. But it turns out there is no "home" for him to come to—this is a rural society in disintegration. In a brilliant stroke the author transforms the individual drifter of thirties fact and legend into a migrating family that reflects that disintegration. He turns the hard-boiled loner into a tenacious upholder of family solidarity, showing how such middle-class values themselves are threatened by corporate greed and cruelty. To the respectable people along the way, the Okies are outsiders, dirty and uncivilized. ("Them goddamn Okies got no sense and no feeling," says one bystander. "They ain't human. A human being wouldn't live like they do" [301].) But Steinbeck must convince his readers that these are good country people like themselves, white Americans. So he gives them troubled families, not lone derelicts or alien outsiders.

As Malcolm Cowley pointed out in 1939, this family journey is rich with echoes of other stories, from the Book of Exodus to Faulkner's 1930 novel *As I Lay Dying*.[29] Besides the biblical resonance, the crossing of the desert in search of the promised land, the westward trek undertaken by the Joads is a central theme of American history, from the sea voyages of early explorers and the Puritan founders to the covered wagons of the pioneer days, which Steinbeck had already explored in his one of his best stories, "The Leader of the People."[30] These mythical touches help explain why the book became one of the few proletarian novels to survive its period. In addition, the great movie adaptation by the scenarist Nunnally Johnson, cinematographer Gregg Toland, and director John Ford lent a physical actuality and immediacy to the characters that Steinbeck himself could not fully provide. As a family the Joads entered American mythology even more fully than Jeeter Lester and his crew in *Tobacco Road*.

Here we come upon a paradox. Thanks to the perfect casting of Henry Fonda, Jane Darwell, and their colleagues, the Joads come through not only as a "fambly" but as sharply etched individuals. Even the vaporous, folksy philosophy of Preacher Casy—who too often tells us, in fake-sounding, down-home terms, precisely what to think—is solidly anchored to the long, lean face, cadaverous limbs, and sonorous voice of John Carradine. Yet Steinbeck's overt purpose, like Dos Passos's in *U.S.A.*, is to convince us—and his characters—that the individual, even the individual family, scarcely matters any longer. The new concentrations of economic power have made the old yeoman independence a thing of the past. Those who cannot adapt, like Granpa and Granma, die on the road, unable to enter the promised land. Even Ma and Tom, the strongest and most determined, who never lose heart as others do, are at best able to hold only part of the family together. They learn that unless they throw in their lot with others—the Wilsons early on, the Wainwrights later, the strikers whose jobs they unknowingly take—they are helpless against the large growers and their minions, the police and the vigilantes who enforce their power. The natural community of outsiders that Steinbeck identified with in *Tortilla Flat* gives way to a self-conscious community of the insulted and injured, aware of their common condition—the people whom modern society has rendered powerless.

That we should remember the Joads so well, that their story continues to summarize the Depression for us, is a sign that Steinbeck was divided against himself, for the hero of the book is not a family but more of an abstraction, the People. For all his literary echoes and political theories, Steinbeck prided himself on working close to the social misery that so troubled him. "I'm trying to write history while it is happening and I don't want to be wrong" (*Letters*, 162). He destroyed a more satiric, polemical version of the novel, though it had already been announced for publication, because it mocked the growers and vigilantes without doing justice to the humanity of the victims. "My father would have called it a smart-alec book. It was full of tricks to make people ridiculous."[31]

Like so many other writers moved by the social crisis of the 1930s, he was trying to catch history on the wing, to humanize it into a narrative everyone could grasp and feel. Despite his pessimism about migrants like the Joads, who seemed to have little power to shape their own destiny—his straightforward picture of the conditions of their lives was violently attacked by politicians, newspapers, and business interests—Steinbeck could not resist giving their grim story a heavy dose of populist uplift, in lines such as the ones Nunnally Johnson amplified into the conclusion of the movie: "Why, Tom—" says Ma, "us people will go on livin' when all them people is gone. Why, Tom, we're the people that live. They ain't gonna wipe us out. Why, we're the people—we go on" (383). In other words, the Joads may go under but the people are indomitable.

This is another difference between *The Grapes of Wrath* and most of the proletarian fiction that preceded it. Though Steinbeck was far from being a

Communist or even a consistent fellow traveler, *In Dubious Battle*, despite its coldly analytical dissection of Communist tactics, was typical of the so-called Third Period, emphasizing the strike as a means of promoting class conflict, portraying the workers as passive vessels guided by vanguard leadership and tactics. *The Grapes of Wrath*, by contrast, is akin to the post-1935 Popular Front, with its romance of the people, a novel in which the Communists are barely mentioned except as all-purpose bogeymen of the owners and their lackeys. In a famous passage Tom learns that "a red is any son-of-a-bitch that wants thirty cents an hour when we're payin' twenty-five!"—which means, "we're all reds" (407). Earlier, we had seen Tom refer to himself jokingly as "bolshevisky" (263), as he proceeded with Casy to reinvent radicalism in All-American terms. When Tom figures out that if the pickers refuse to pick the peaches, they will rot, Steinbeck is crafting a simple lesson in collective action and the power of the people. "Well, you figgered out somepin, didn' you," a young man tells him. "Come right outa your own head," he says—not from any Red radical troublemaker (336).

The novel is full of didactic little scenes like this one, where Tom learns something so that Steinbeck can teach *us* something, where little parables of capitalist exploitation or plebeian fellowship are enacted—in dialect that's supposed to make it sound like "real life."

> "An' here's another thing [says Tom's friend]. Ever hear a' the black-list?"
>
> "What's that?"
>
> "Well, you jus' open your trap about us folks gettin' together, an' you'll see. They take your pitcher an' send it all over. Then you can't get work nowhere. An' if you got kids—"
>
> Tom took off his cap and twisted it in his hands. "So we take what we can get, huh, or we starve; an' if we yelp we starve." (336)

The facts are true, much as they were denied, reviled, when the book came out. But this isn't how anyone has ever talked. The underpinnings of Steinbeck's morality play peep through, even as he gets his information—and indignation—across.

Steinbeck usually rounds off his scenes of muckraking exposure by illustrating the potential for group solidarity. When Ma Joad, with her miserable pittance but unshakable pride, is buying groceries at the company store run by the Hooper Ranch, we see how a man much like herself must glumly enforce the company's inflated prices. They come to logger-heads when she is a dime short and cannot buy some sugar for Tom's coffee, though the family will shortly be earning enough money to pay for it. Caught between Ma's simple humanity and his own fear of losing his job for extending credit, the clerk grows more and more uncomfort-able. Finally, breaking through to his own underlying kinship with her, he takes a dime from his own pocket and drops it in the cash register.

The scene is pat and contrived, though it deftly transposes the book's theme into a small dramatic encounter. But Steinbeck, with his didactic purpose, is unable to leave well enough alone. As Ma is leaving, she turns and adds, "I'm learnin' one thing good. . . . Learnin' it all a time, ever' day. If you're in trouble or hurt or need—go to poor people. They're the only ones that'll help—the only ones" (513–14). What Ma says is not far from the truth—the poor do contribute to those even poorer than themselves—but by hitting us over the head with it Steinbeck weakens the scene and damages its credibility as fiction. His anger gives the book unusual power, and he shows real feeling for these people's lives, for the touch and feel of their experience. But he cannot resist preaching at us, driving a point home, sentimentalizing his material. Like many other thirties writers, he chooses the demands of social protest over the constraints of art.

Steinbeck was a gifted mimic of country dialect, but his way of put-ting his own ideas in the mouths of simple folk can often sound phony and staged. His sympathy extends less to the people he creates than to their social prototypes, the *real* suffering Joads he had actually seen in the camps and written about in his articles.

The folksy and sentimental touches in *The Grapes of Wrath* betray its Popular Front ambience. They link the novel to the muscular regional paintings of Thomas Hart Benton, who illustrated the novel and had the same typed feeling for America's working stiffs; the songs of Woody Guthrie, who turned the whole story into a seventeen-stanza ballad; the splendid folk material in Virgil Thomson's scores for Pare Lorentz's doc-umentary films, *The Plow That Broke the Plains* and *The River*; the thirties ballets of Aaron Copland and Martha Graham; and even that coming blockbuster, *Oklahoma!*, with its celebrated Agnes de Mille choreography. Yet none of these works, except for the Lorentz films, could match the darker side of Steinbeck's novel, culminating in the disintegration of the family and the final scene in the Visalia-like flood. By the time the Rodgers and Hammerstein musical appeared in 1943, America was at war and an amnesiac mood of national self-celebration had taken hold (as we have seen in Caldwell and Bourke-White's *Say, is this the U.S.A.*). The Okies were forgotten, or working in defense industries, and the nation wanted an anti–*Grapes of Wrath*, an Oklahoma in which "the wind [that] comes sweeping down the plains" is no longer threatening, in which "the corn is as high as an elephant's eye," so no one should starve. Steinbeck's populism rings false at times, but his novel is no *Ballad for Americans*; it represents the best, not the worst, of the Popular Front sensibility.

It is Steinbeck's populism rather than his naturalistic technique that makes his work so different from that of Nathanael West, just as their images of California seem to come from different planets. Like many other protest writers, Steinbeck sees people as essentially good, though often twisted and damaged by what they've lived through, by institutions that were meant to serve them. Despite his gospel of social solidarity, Steinbeck wants his characters to remain in tune with nature: with the soil, with their animal instincts (freewheeling sexuality for the man, maternal bonding for the woman), with the agricultural rhythm of the seasons, and with the sweaty exertions of hard work. California is one of nature's favored places, a heaven on earth in the eyes of those trying to get there. "I like to think of how nice it's gonna be, maybe, in California," says Ma in a dreamy mood. "Never cold. An' fruit ever'place, an' people just bein' in the nicest places, little white houses in among the orange trees. I wonder—that is, if we all get jobs an' all work—maybe we can get one of them little white houses. An' the little fellas go out an' pick oranges right off the tree" (124).

Tom immediately corrects her with some of the bad rumors he's heard about lack of work, dirty camps, and low wages. But Steinbeck certainly leaves us with the impression that this poignant Depression fantasy is really the way things ought to be, that the social horrors the Joads encounter in the real California are a despicable—and avoidable—betrayal of the American Dream.

West, by contrast, was a close student of the fantasy lives of Depression Americans, and what he found was movingly corny, pathetic, or grotesque. Since he had already disposed of the pastoral fantasy in *Miss Lonelyhearts*, he found something monstrous about the whole migration to California, something accurately reflected in the tacky, flimsy, man-made world the migrants find when they get there. (The Garden of Eden is nowhere in sight, though the Garden of Allah is there.) It's almost as if West, with his skepticism about the common man, foresaw the kinds of "ordinary" people the Joads would become when they ceased being a cause, when the war brought them jobs and the jobs bought them those little white houses among the orange trees.

In *The Day of the Locust*, which came out the same year as *The Grapes of Wrath*, West's version of the common man is no longer the Desperate, Broken-hearted, Sick-of-it-all of *Miss Lonelyhearts* but what he describes as the people who "had come to California to die" (60). They are the trampling, soulless "crowd" of antidemocratic theorists from Plato to Le Bon and Ortega, those nightmare visions of mass society. In West's novel these are people whose dreams are banal and whose potential for boredom, disaffection, and violence is enormous. At the apocalyptic movie premiere that concludes the novel, West writes,

> It was a mistake to think of them as harmless curiosity seekers. They were savage and bitter, especially the middle-aged and the old, and had been made so by boredom and disappointment.
>
> All their lives they had slaved at some kind of dull, heavy labor, behind desks and counters, in the fields and at tedious machines of all sorts, saving their pennies and dreaming of the leisure that would be theirs when they had enough. Finally that day came. They could draw a weekly income of ten or fifteen dollars. Where else should they go but California, the land of sunshine and oranges?
>
> Once there they discover that sunshine isn't enough. They get tired of oranges, even of avocado pears and passion fruit. Nothing happens. They don't know what to do with their time. They haven't the mental equipment for leisure, the money nor the physical equipment for pleasure. . . .
>
> Their boredom becomes more and more terrible. They realize that they've been tricked and burn with resentment. . . . The sun is a joke. Oranges can't titillate their jaded palates. Nothing can ever be violent enough to make taut their slack minds and bodies. They have been cheated and betrayed. They have slaved and saved for nothing. (177–78)

Both West's and Steinbeck's novels, coming at the end of a decade of revolutionary hopes, carry apocalyptic titles; both point to the implacable vengeance of the disappointed masses. Here the similarity ends. In place of Steinbeck's image of a ripening revolutionary upsurge in the name of equity and justice, we have in West, despite his left-wing politics, an image of mindless lumpen violence fed by boredom, resentment, and a heavy diet of mass culture. Steinbeck's concern is for those who are desperately poor, trying to survive and yet preserve their dignity. West's fears focus on those who have enough to eat, perhaps just barely, but whose lives have somehow been mentally and spiritually impoverished, people who haven't the inner resources for the Joads' form of stoic heroism, the sheer endurance.

In a period of want and need, Steinbeck emphasizes *homo economicus*, the man whose state of mind is a function of his material well-being. But West, at a time when the forgotten man was idealized, mythologized, by writers and politicians alike, stresses everyman's spiritual torpor, the destructive potential of his pent-up frustrations and resentments. Both writers see California—and, by extension, America—as a betrayal of the utopian dreams that have been invested in it. But West remains a figure out of the irreverent twenties, a Jew chastened perhaps by memories of mass violence, skeptical of all utopian promises; Steinbeck sees the Edenic image of his beloved valleys spoiled by greed and inequality. True to his Dostoyevskian and modernist premises, West remains suspicious of people and nature alike; Steinbeck, with his strong feeling for the biology of man in nature, wants to see them fulfill their thwarted potential.

West's pessimism is deep-seated, expressing itself as pathos, ridicule, or contempt. Steinbeck's anger is directed at particular targets—the growers, the vigilantes, the spoilers of the land—and balanced by a theme with heroic outlines: the saga of a family's migration and its quest for survival. In the film version, as George Bluestone showed long ago in *Novels into Film*, this arduous trek became an even more dominant motif. Nunnally Johnson and John Ford produced an adaptation that was not only exceptionally faithful for its time but also unusually bold for Hollywood in its treatment of a controversial issue. Yet this did not prevent the film from toning down the explicit sexual, religious, and political dimensions of the novel. Though Steinbeck himself was then wracked with guilt when he had an affair that threatened his first marriage—his wife, Carol, had long supported and encouraged him—in his novels he usually presents men as horny, randy creatures—lusty animals bursting with natural vitality. (Tom's brother Al is the perfect example of such a type, always "tomcattin'" around, rarely capable of taking the long view, but finally, with his instinctive practical wisdom, instrumental in helping to keep the family together.) Steinbeck worked hard to prevent this side of the novel from being censored, especially the frank language, which led its being condemned for obscenity by those who really objected to its social views. Virtually none of this survives in the movie.

Steinbeck's naturalism also fuels the book's religious satire, beginning with Preacher Casy, who is estranged from his calling in part because he cannot condemn or restrain his own sexual promptings. This eventually leads him to a religion of humanity, a revolutionary radicalism that joins Emerson's Oversoul with Marx's theory of surplus value. For him, as for many newly radicalized prophets of the 1930s, the time for prayer has ended, the time for action has begun. "Almighty God never raised no wages," he says. The biological rhythms of life, the right to primary satisfactions and elementary decency, come first. "These here folks want to live decent and bring up their kids decent. An' when they're old they wanta set in the door an' watch the downing sun. An' when they're young they wanta dance an' sing an' lay together. They wanta eat an' get drunk an' work." But somehow he senses that his view of the Common Man is numbingly reductive, patronizing him in the guise of praising him. "An' that's it—they wanta jus' fling their goddamn muscles aroun' an' get tired. Christ! What'm I talkin' about?" (341). This is just the way things are; there is no moral order. Very little of this antireligious naturalism gets picked up in the movie.

In *Novels into Film* George Bluestone showed how the muckraking side of the novel is softened in the film, starting with the ingenious transformation of the historical interchapters into smooth visual montages—an inexorable rhythm of events without the ghost of an explanation. This extends to numerous lines of dialogue in which the plight of the families becomes more vague in origin yet more visceral in impact. As Bluestone summarizes it, "If the religious satire is absent and the politics muted, the love of land, family and human dignity are consistently translated into effective cinematic images."[32] Though they speak for Steinbeck too, these deeply conveyed feelings for the land and the family belong even more to the film work of John Ford. The director never claimed this film as one of his favorite works, and even insisted, "I never read the book" (Bluestone, 169), yet it contains haunting Fordian touches only dimly suggested by the novel. A few sentences in the novel (148) that describe Ma burning her keepsakes just before leaving home becomes a wordless scene of inestimable power, evoking Ma first as a younger woman, now as a mother staunchly but poignantly taking leave of the past. The Saturday night dance at the sanitary camp becomes the occasion for another privileged moment, as Tom dances with Ma to the tune of the "The Red River Valley"—a scene of intense communal and personal warmth that is not at all typical of Steinbeck, but was reprised brilliantly by Fonda and Ford after the war in the church-dedication scene of *My Darling Clementine*. It's as if Ford could lay bare the emotional core of *The Grapes of Wrath* by borrowing a page from *Sons and Lovers*. The novel is about a vast social migration; the film is about a mother and son.

By reversing the order of two episodes, and dispensing with Steinbeck's garish (and perhaps unfilmable) symbolic conclusion, which he defended stubbornly as his initial inspiration, Johnson and Ford subtly altered the pessimistic outlook of the novel. In Steinbeck everything goes downhill, and the family eventually breaks apart. But by placing the scenes at the sanitary camp *after* the miserable strikebreaking episode at the private ranch, the film in one stroke makes the New Deal, along with the communal democracy of the migrants themselves, the effective solution to the migrants' problems.[33] This optimism is enhanced by Ma's populist rhetoric, borrowed from what she told Tom earlier in the novel. Though Pa had largely been emasculated and displaced in the course of the film, she tells him, "We're the people that live. They can't wipe us out—they can't lick us. We'll go on forever, Pa, 'cause we're the people." On this note of determination the film concludes.

Steinbeck's somber ending, on the other hand, is one of those expressionist touches we often find in naturalistic novels, as Erich von Stroheim understood when he turned Frank Norris's creepy turn-of-the-century novel *McTeague* into his masterpiece, *Greed*. Having lost her own baby out of shock and malnutrition, Rose of Sharon gives her breast to a starving man, who in turn had stopped eating so his own boy could live. Both are taking refuge from the flood in someone else's barn, where they enact this small, improbable lesson in community and mutual aid that the novel has been preaching from the very start. What she does is an act of desperation, at the biological bedrock of nature and nurture, far from the reassuring populist platitudes of the movie's ending.

Finally, however, the novel and film come together as an almost seamless composite of words and images, fictional characters and performances, an indelible testament to their times. We may be tempted to look back to Steinbeck's early fiction, as we are drawn to the lively, unpretentious films that Frank Capra churned out for Columbia before he too began preaching a populist social gospel. In the end, Steinbeck's ambitious social novels fulfill the agrarian pastoral dreams of his earlier books by setting them against the awesome conditions of the Depression, which gave him the kind of subject a writer finds only once in a lifetime. Steinbeck's biblical myth of passage, his matriarchal construction of the family as a defense against disintegration, the moral indignation that gradually took the place of his scientific naturalism, the advocacy that shattered his detachment, the sense of individual life that competed with his vision of community—all these represent a full reaction to a social and economic crisis he could not avoid or ignore, one that we can't forget because he enabled us to see it.

Faulkner: All in the Family

If Steinbeck's parable of a family journey was indeed indebted to Faulkner's *As I Lay Dying*, as Malcolm Cowley first suggested, this provides us with another opportunity to compare how modernist and naturalist writers explored the situation of the bottom dogs in society. Faulkner's career sits oddly in our study, since he was by no means a "Depression author" though his best work, beginning with *The Sound and the Fury* in 1929, coincides with these years. Faulkner looms over this period from which he seems historically detached. It would be hard to imagine the prose of *Call It Sleep* or *Let Us Now Praise Famous Men* without the example he set. At a moment of profound crisis, when a journalistic model of social documentation was dominant, Faulkner gave writers like Roth and

Agee the means to locate characters precisely within a society, as he him-self did, without reducing them to their abstract social identity. Thanks to Hemingway's influence and the journalistic notion of the writer as a transparent observer, a fly on the wall, the 1930s were also the high-water mark of the Simple Declarative Sentence. Faulkner offered writers a real alternative: a complex, at times baroque prose that might permit them to do justice to the inner lives of these characters as well as their social cir-cumstances. At the same time, perhaps to their regret, he showed them how to become difficult rather than popular writers, writing books that could hardly sell.[34] Above all, he taught how to deal with the poor with-out turning them into The Poor—a constant temptation for social real-ists in the Depression years.

Published in October 1930, *As I Lay Dying* was Faulkner's most daz-zling technical experiment. "I set out deliberately to write a tour-de-force," he later remarked.[35] Even more than *The Sound and the Fury*, it could serve as a textbook example of modernist perspectivism, the splin-tering of omniscient narration into a montage of subjective viewpoints. In his earlier breakthrough Faulkner had told the same tale four times over, beginning with the most fragmentary and impressionistic version, set in the mind of an idiot, and ending with the most consecutive, objective account, as if the whole book were the process by which the story gradu-ally clarified itself. *As I Lay Dying* takes this fracturing effect even further, breaking up what seems at times no more than a far-fetched, shaggy-dog anecdote of death and endlessly delayed burial into brief interior mono-logues for no fewer than fifteen characters, including all seven members of the Bundren family—from the half-mad, clairvoyant son Darl to the whining, manipulative father, Anse, and, once only, at the center of the book, the already dead mother, Addie, the still point of this whole turn-ing world.

Superficially, Faulkner's Bundren family, with its weak father and tenacious mother, the two older sons, Cash and Darl, the headstrong younger son, Jewel, the pregnant daughter, Dewey Dell, and young boy, Vardaman, strongly resembles Steinbeck's Joads, just as the family's stu-pendous journey through flood and fire to bury Addie in Jefferson, Mis-sissippi, can be compared to the Joads' trek along Route 66 and across the desert to California. Both of these family journeys, though tinged with a mixture of heroism and comic absurdity, are rich with biblical echoes. Yet the two writers wisely avoid allegory to attend concretely to the physical and human obstacles that make passage so difficult. Steinbeck shows us exactly how an ancient tire is mended, a leaking crankcase sealed; Faulkner, how a mule-team fords a raging river. Both are road novels, both make meticulous use of country dialect—two hallmarks of the populism of the 1930s.[*]

Cleanth Brooks, the Southern born critic who devoted several volumes to Faulkner, reminds us that Faulkner's characters, though obviously penniless, aren't really that poor, since they own their own farm. What he may mean, I think, is that though they *are* poor their poverty is not the salient thing about them. Their frequent concern about money stands for something else: Anse's predatory grasping, Dewey Dell's need for an abortion, Darl's and Jewel's knowingly missing their mother's death to earn three dollars for a load of wood, Jewel's need to obtain money to buy one of the last of Flem Snopes's wild horses, which his father will make him sell for a team of mules to bring Addie to Jefferson for burial. Money stands for the way people do injury to each other, especially Anse to his children, whom he may yet wear out as he has worn out their mother.

It takes no more than a glance at these family dynamics to see where the resemblance to *The Grapes of Wrath* ends. As he did in *In Dubious Battle*, Steinbeck observes his characters strictly from the outside, behaviorally, as elements of a family unit that symbolizes a larger social reality. In Edmund Wilson's view, Steinbeck had "summoned all his resources" to humanize his people, but the result was "not quite real. The characters of *The Grapes of Wrath* are animated and put through their paces rather than brought to life."[36] The characters are once emblematic and stagy—Steinbeck had a real bent for the stage—so that the movie is already inherent in the novel, as the novel is inherent in Steinbeck's journalism. In the sweeping interchapters, Steinbeck impersonates History itself, the omniscient Hegelian *Zeitgeist*, which, often quite effectively,

---

[*] The form of Faulkner's book even anticipates the collage structure, the layers of interviews, of the "People Talk" books of the late 1930s—a form picked up in later times by Oscar Lewis and Studs Terkel—except that Faulkner has an ironic view of many of his characters. Like Flannery O'Connor with her "good country people," Faulkner harbored no sentimental illusions about the human types he knew so well, people he even loved in his way.

inserts the family into the broader social movement that its members themselves can barely begin to comprehend.

The naturalistic writer always knows much more than his characters, for they are buffeted by forces he alone understands. Faulkner, on the other hand, allows us no privileged point of view. We see the family from the inside, through its own eyes, and through the eyes of observers like Cora and Vernon Tull, who enable the author to smuggle in connecting fragments of a third-person narration. Surprisingly, however, the interior monologues that make up the book do not have the effect of turning it into a psychological novel. Though each character is a distinct type, Faulkner is far less interested in what makes them tick than in the timbre and rhythm of their perception, as refracted through his own rich language. The novel consists of a mélange of verbal styles that filter every event, as it is told and retold, through a shifting prism, as if each wrinkle of the plot, slight as it is, were merely the occasion for a kaleidoscope of contrasting perceptions.

For the less imaginative characters, like the pragmatic Cash and the sanctimonious, mealy-mouthed Anse, and for outsiders like the Tulls, Faulkner writes naturalistic, matter-of-fact monologues and ruminations that have the straightforward accents of their individual personalities. But with the visionary Darl or the wild, dreamy child Vardaman, Faulkner gives free rein to his most complex effects, in vividly sensory prose that seems intended to provide a rhythmic equivalent and poetic expansion of their precise thoughts. The writing in several of Darl's many monologues is the closest to what we think of as "Faulknerian" prose. Some of them are stream of consciousness, a technique used sparely in this book compared with *The Sound and the Fury*. One of them, improbably, is the wonderfully funny, straightforward yarn of the mysterious summer when Jewel, at fifteen, "took a spell of sleeping,"[37] for he was spending all his nights secretly earning the money to buy his horse. Some of his sections simply carry on the narrative in a high literary manner: the voice cannot *literally* be Darl's—it is far too complex, too literary—yet its distance from him underlines both his proximity to Faulkner and his curious dissociation from much of what takes place around him, indeed, his dissociation from himself. Darl is different, "sensitive," poetic, and therefore doomed. The secret sympathy between him and his mother is so great that he must try to destroy her rotting body in its coffin, a deed for which he will be sent away forever.

One of Darl's monologues, for example, begins like this: "The lantern sits on a stump. Rusted, grease-fouled, its cracked chimney smeared on one side with a soaring smudge of soot, it sheds a feeble and sultry glare upon the trestles and the boards and the adjacent earth" (71). Later on we find stunning bits of prose like this one: "Pa lifts his face, slackmouthed, the wet black rim of snuff plastered close along the base of his gums; from behind his slack-faced astonishment he muses as though from beyond time, upon the ultimate outrage" (72). Darl is so sensitive and observant that he himself is nowhere, nothing. The poignant last words of this monologue are not even his own, but an unacknowledged translation of the opening lines of Aeschylus' *Oresteia*, where they are spoken by a bit player, the Watchman: "How often have I lain beneath rain on a strange roof, thinking of home" (76). This underlines Darl's isolation and his position as an almost helpless observer of a family that Faulkner daringly compares to the murderous House of Agamemnon.

What is most Faulknerian about this language is not the allusive poetic prose per se but the author's audacity in putting it in Darl's mouth, then following it with Cash's ultra practical "I made it on the bevel," referring to his methodical work on his mother's coffin, followed by his terse series of numbered observations (77) and then by Vardaman's wild insistence that "my mother is a fish" (79), five words that make up a whole chapter. Around such leitmotifs the book is (symphonically) organized. What Faulkner gave to a writer like Agee was not just a complex, inward style but a mixture of styles that reached from inner ruminations to concrete lists and inventories, a musical way of balancing the outer and inner worlds.

Though there are elements of a brutal and powerful naturalism in his work, in books like *Sanctuary* but also in the whole project of writing a *comédie humaine* of a complete society in miniature, Faulkner fights free of all literalism and documentary fidelity. He has the traditional American romance writer's fascination with the irrational and the unknown, the shadow side of the mind. He takes his greatest liberties with characters like Darl and Vardaman whose leaps of imagination bring them close to the author and distance them from their more practical siblings.

The poetic embroidery of the interior monologues underlines the contrast between the sparseness of what these people say to each other and the rich, dense variety of their inner worlds. Faulkner's technique heightens his characters' terrifying separateness. The Bundren family is less a family than a scene of warfare, cruelty, and immense isolation. To Addie marriage and motherhood were the names for a process by which her "aloneness had to be violated over and over each day" (164), a violation masked by hollow words like "love." Her husband Anse is a taker, a survivor, who, determined never to work up a sweat himself, lives parasitically on the sweat of others. Triumphantly, he manages to end the novel with a new set of teeth and a new Mrs. Bundren.

Each member of the family has his or her own reason for going to Jefferson, a private agenda, but Anse feeds on all their wishes and dreams. He causes Cash to break his leg (again), and nearly cripples him permanently by having it set it in cement—a good example of the kind of grotesquely comic incident Faulkner works into the story, itself a wild yarn just barely credible. (Even the account of Addie's adultery with Minister Whitfield, which led to the birth of Jewel, is closer to southern folk humor than to *The Scarlet Letter*.) Anse takes away Jewel's splendid horse and Dewey Dell's abortion money, and has Darl thrown down and handcuffed in the middle of the street and committed to a grisly state asylum for life. All the while Anse is sniveling about what a "luckless man" he is, always put upon, for he is a Dickensian creature who never tires of advertising his doleful affinity for misfortune.

The only exceptional feature of Anse's life is his insistence against all obstacles, comic and tragic, on fulfilling Addie's wish to be buried away from him, away from her children, among her own people in Jefferson. This cataclysmically stubborn mission takes on absurd, even monstrous dimensions as the mishaps multiply and Addie's corpse begins to decay and stink. One bystander, Samson, attributes Anse's almost heroic doggedness to simple inertia: "I notice how it takes a lazy man, a man that hates moving, to get set on moving once he does get started off, the same as he was set on staying still, like it aint the moving he hates so much as the starting and stopping" (108). This brings to mind Anse's remarkable meditation on the ill effects that come from roads, since man, being vertical, like a tree, was obviously intended to stay put, while roads, being horizontal, like horses or wagons, were destined by the Lord for movement. His wife, he thinks, "was well and hale as ere a woman ever were, except for that road" (36)—precisely the road by which she hopes eventually to leave him, as he instinctively understands. Roads and movement of every

kind are central to thirties culture, set in a world endangered by immobility, stagnation, and decay. As the Joads are expelled from their parched
land, the stationary Anse, impelled by his wife's dying wish, somehow
gets his family moving, on a mission if not a migration.

With the help of his children, each driven by their different aims,
Anse unshakably pushes this bizarre journey to completion—of course,
without much physical effort on his own part. He is a specialist on having things done for him. But Addie, though she is already dead or "dying"
all through the novel, is very much the controlling figure in this story.
From our first glimpse of her son Cash making the coffin and holding up
each board for her inspection, to the moment when, after a dozen horrific
delays, she is finally laid to rest, the whole novel is an enactment of Addie's
wishes, of her ironic awareness of the bleakness of life, of her revenge for
the bitterness of her own life. *She* is the "I" of the title, though she herself
has only one eight-page monologue midway through the book. Her children's lives are shaped by the varying quality of her love for them and by
the effects of her adultery with Whitfield and her sullen hatred of her husband. She has learned to live by her father's maxim "that the reason for
living was to get ready to stay dead a long time" (161). This is a curious
variant on her husband's immobility, especially as she thinks that Anse
has long been dead without knowing it (165).

Her "dying" is not only what "happens" in the book but is built into
its formal syntax—the plastic and malleable time sequence, the shuffling
of subjective viewpoints. Though her "actual" death is reported early
on—by the clairvoyant Darl, who could not be there to see it—her coffin throughout is described as "she" and "her," as if it were a living presence, and Anse constantly refers to her wishes in the present tense ("I
give her my promise," he says. "She is counting on it" [133].) The novel's peculiar participial title, with its suggestion of time extended and suspended, drawn out into a pure present, accords precisely with the form
and meaning of the story. The sections of the novel fall into place like the
pieces of a jigsaw puzzle, from which a single picture gradually emerges,
full of events that are all inserted synchronically—as if simultaneously—
into her dying. As incidents are told and retold from different points of
view, events from the past return—as in Addie's own monologue—in no
sequence but that of the book's own unfolding. Addie "dead" is as vivid as
Addie alive. She dominates her family, and the book itself, as effectively as

Ma Joad dominates *The Grapes of Wrath*. Everything that happens is enveloped in a continuous present, and a point of view at the edge of the other side, an anteroom of eternity. As each piece falls into place, we sense something that can also be said of other modernist texts: that the "story" is more crucial for the *way* it's told than for what it appears to be about. Straighten out or summarize the narrative, and very little of Faulkner would survive. Without being overtly reflexive or self-referential, this is a book that seems primarily about itself. Yet the "subject" of Faulkner's book, the almost folklorish material that forms its "plot"—cannot be wholly dismissed, for in striking fashion it mingles elements of tragedy with its anecdotal absurdities and dazzling technical twists.

In *Jews without Money* Michael Gold proclaimed that he would write about bedbugs because his aim was to "write a truthful book about Poverty." Published later in the same year, *As I Lay Dying* tells another kind of truth about poverty, without Gold's capital P. As we have seen from the sharecropper books, the South and poverty were virtually synonymous, even before the worsening conditions of the Depression. Though *As I Lay Dying* can hardly be described as a "socially concerned" or "proletarian" novel, it shares one crucial feature with Gold's book: its social unit is the family and the surrounding community, not the larger society. If Gold's book, despite his doctrinaire Marxism, was a pioneering study in "the culture of poverty," Faulkner's novel adds up to a social portrait of its own. It evokes the pride, cruelty, stubbornness, complexity, viciousness, and prickly independence of a somewhat freakish family of "poor whites" who are figures of fun and sources of exasperation even for some of their neighbors. The unhappy Addie was a schoolteacher who "married down," and spent the rest of her life regretting it, like the cultivated Mrs. Morel in *Sons and Lovers*, married to a coarse miner.

If Gold's remembered family is a powerful piece of literary sociology, Faulkner's imagined family—which, as in his other novels, resonates here with the power of Greek tragedy—is almost a spectrum of human nature, as if based on some variant of the Greek theory of humors, with Darl as the imaginative man, Cash as the practical man ("I made it on the bevel"), Jewel, a kind of Hotspur, the man of spirit, Vardaman as the Wordsworthian man-child, his wild imagination not yet confined by shades of the prison-house, and Dewey Dell, pregnant, embodying a nascent and blooming femininity, as fresh and naive as her mother is bitter and disappointed. By typing them so broadly, and putting their viewpoints in separate sections and sharply contrasting prose, Faulkner emphasizes the differences that isolate them: it's hard to think of them as belonging to the same family. Yet he also gives them great individual dignity, something hardly recognized by the people around them, who see them as poor, hapless, pigheaded, and enormously irritating (though they also give them a good deal of help on their way).

Thanks to the multiplicity of viewpoints and prose styles, it would be hard to find a novel that better answers to the Russian critic Mikhail Bakhtin's description of the "polyphonic" qualities of good fiction. Where *Jews without Money* subdues its characters to the rush of Gold's own intensely emotional voice, Faulkner is a ventriloquist of many voices and many minds without literally replicating any one of them. If Gold's legacy to other writers was the intensely personal quality of his social concern— more readily picked up by a poet like Allen Ginsberg than by proletarian documentarists—then Faulkner's legacy was his mixture of voices, his layering of ironies and disparate styles.

Faulkner was a social novelist as well as an experimental writer, but the world he created was a piece of the South, then so different from the rest of the nation. Faulkner's huge influence could be fatal to later southern writers. As Flannery O'Connor famously remarked, "The presence alone of Faulkner in our midst makes a great difference in what the writer can and cannot permit himself to do. Nobody wants his mule and wagon stalled on the same track the Dixie Limited is roaring down."[38] Unable to grapple with his larger vision, later southern writers like William Styron or Carson McCullers often echoed his overripe prose or mimicked his Gothic and Grand Guignol horrors. Yet in the 1930s the richness of Faulkner's writing was a salutary alternative to the spare inflections of Hemingway's, with their emphasis on the unspoken, the unexpressed. In the hands of other writers this could simply turn flat. Both writers had a way of swallowing their band of imitators.

Faulkner and Hemingway were equally "modern" in their fashion. Both helped to overthrow a prolix Victorian idiom of omniscient narration, of telling rather than showing; both found oblique ways of exploring their characters' secretly rich inner lives, Hemingway with a deceptively bare language pregnant with implication, Faulkner with ornate rhetorical effects that crystallize the most elusive qualities of perception and feeling. Both created fictional idioms that avoided discursiveness and authorial commentary. They aimed, instead, at creating a specific—yet unstated—emotional effect in the reader, enacting emotions rather than describing them. Faulkner's big debts were to complex stylists like Melville and Joyce, virtuosos of excess like Dickens and Dostoyevsky; Hemingway's were to plain stylists on the order of Tolstoy, Twain, Stephen Crane, and Gertrude Stein, whose methods were deceptively prosaic.

Hemingway's manner proved more congenial to the journalistic and social writers who followed him, and to the creators of hard-boiled popular fiction beginning with Dashiell Hammett. Faulkner's styles, besides dominating the southern literary tradition that followed him, fed the undercurrent of modernism that coursed through the 1930s, providing writers like Agee and Henry Roth with rich alternatives to sociological reductionism. Faulkner's manner was particularly suited to exploring complex states of consciousness, helping other writers find ways of bridging the gap between surface appearances and the mesh of feeling. With its lurid exploration of endangered innocence, powerful compulsion, self-laceration, and extreme violence, Faulkner's *Light in August* was perhaps as close to Dostoyevsky as any book in English after Conrad. In *As I Lay Dying* he wrote a wildly original book about what we would later call a dysfunctional family, a story of poor people that was not a book about Poverty. In doing so, he made possible not only the grotesque comedy and rich dialect of *Tobacco Road* but other books that were more ironic and imaginative than documentary and sociological, including the sui generis stories of Flannery O'Connor, teetering between comedy and horror.

Faulkner's escape from sociology and documentation may be connected to his political conservatism and that of his region, though the links between his novels, the overlapping stories and characters, connect them to the nineteenth-century social novel, and partly explain his vast influence on later Latin American fiction. Faulkner's folkloric South, backward and half mythic, proved a perfect model for the Colombia of García Márquez. (Sartre found a deep conservatism even in Faulkner's daring treatment of time, with its emphasis on how the past continues to haunt and determine the present.)[39] As the 1930s progressed, Faulkner, with his distinguished air of a dapper, independent gentleman, a country squire, consistently scoffed at all the programs of the New Deal—without giving much sense that national politics really mattered to him. If anything, it was the race problem of the South that began to engage his fictional and finally his public attention, beginning in 1932 with *Light in August*, one of his most powerful novels, which at one level is a thriller that probes the effects of miscegenation and makes it symbolic of the mixed racial history of the region. The tormented Joe Christmas, whose conflicts of identity lead to murder, is the direct antecedent of the violently troubled Bigger Thomas in Richard Wright's *Native Son*.

Faulkner's work is so different from other main currents in the 1930s that it's tempting but misleading to push him off into a separate category of "southern writer" or "twenties modernist." I could confine this book to writers, filmmakers, and other artists who were responding specifically to the economic and social crisis that followed the Crash. This would draw the parameters of the decade to leave out its best writer. Faulkner's modernism diminished sharply after his stints as a screenwriter in Hollywood, but even in his most daringly experimental novels, including *The Sound and the Fury* and *As I Lay Dying*, a surprisingly straightforward story ultimately comes through as we unravel it. *As I Lay Dying* is at once an experiment with time, consciousness, and fragmentary narration and a barely credible folktale, the saga of a journey, and the history of a family that connects ironically to the distressed lives of so many other ordinary families in this decade. Faulkner's voice and material, like Hemingway's, add strength to the culture of the 1930s without fully entering into it.

CHAPTER 5

Hard Times for Poets

IN *WHAT IS LITERATURE?*, his postwar polemic on the social responsibilities of literature, the writer Jean-Paul Sartre insisted that writers had no choice but to commit themselves, to be "engaged," yet surprisingly he exempted poets, since their work turned more on language and technique than on social or ideological content. But the social disruptions of the 1930s were so dire that even poets were swept up by them. A considerable body of proletarian poetry appeared in left-wing magazines such as *The Anvil* and *The New Masses*, yet scarcely one of these poems made its way into the canon of modern poetry, to the frustration of recent academics who have tried to resurrect them. To make them seem more palatable, Cary Nelson, in his 1989 book *Repression and Recovery*, acknowledges that the formation of a canon of enduring works is inevitable, but insists that we should take account of other criteria besides literary quality, as readers we must "contextualize" these poems and read them for their "historical and cultural interest." In this light, he says, "some of the more well-known failures in modern poetry become as interesting as the established successes." Indeed, we "need to reevaluate precisely those texts we habitually mark as mediocre," since "we should always read what people assure us is no good."[1] This desperate strategy for reviving forgotten radical works reminded me of the senator from Nebraska who suggested that even mediocrity deserved representation on the Supreme Court.

Langston Hughes was certainly one of the best of the young poets who became radicals and firebrands in the early thirties. Even in the 1920s, when his first two collections were published with much fanfare by Knopf, Hughes was not a personal or introspective poet so much as a blues-inflected writer with a superb musical gift and a powerful identification with the black community around him. But in the 1930s, when he began to speak for the suffering masses in general, his poems lost their focus. "I speak in the name of the black millions / Awakening to action," one poem begins.[2] In one of his best-known militant poems, "Let America Be America Again," first published in *Esquire* in 1936, he grows more diffuse:

> *I am the poor white, fooled and pushed apart,*
> *I am the Negro bearing slavery's scars.*
> *I am the red man driven from the land,*
> *I am the immigrant clutching the hope I seek—*
> *And finding only the same old stupid plan*
> *Of dog eat dog, of mighty crush the weak.*
>   (190)

Since this is the Popular Front period, Hughes, instead of attacking America, tries to recall it to its own ideals, "all the dreams we've dreamed /

And all the songs we've sung / And all the hopes we've held / And all the
flags we've hung" (191), but this is so vague and insincere that it is embar-
rassing. The Depression was a cataclysm; how were poets to rise to the
occasion? Under the guise of empathizing with the poor, too many radical poets indulged a taste for social tirade and inspirational uplift.

Elsewhere Hughes becomes hortatory in a way that verges on
doggerel:

> *Listen!*
> *All you beauty makers,*
> *Give up beauty for a moment.*
> *Look at harshness, look at pain,*
> *Look at life again.*
> *Look at hungry babies crying,*
> *Listen to the rich men lying,*
> *Look at starving China dying.*
> 　("Call to Creation," 135)

These militant and angry poems work only when Hughes remains crisp,
witty, simple, and song-like, as in "Park Bench":

> *I live on a park bench.*
> *You, Park Avenue.*
> *Hell of a distance*
> *Between us two.*
> 　(183)

The brief poem concludes with the homeless man's threat to "move
on over / To Park Avenue," but even if this is little more than wish-
ful thinking—the park bench poem is a genre of its own in proletarian
poetry—the distance (yet proximity) of the park bench to Park Avenue
makes for a neat juxtaposition. Langston Hughes's gift as a poet was in
his natural, unforced fluency, his easy rapport with his readers, including
ordinary black readers, which helped make him so prolific. In this poem
we hear the voice not of a tramp who's suddenly read Marx but of a poet,
at once ironic and populist, whose rhymes had always been insouciant
and devilishly clever.

• • •

But as the American economy spiraled downward, the human toll of the Depression exerted its pull not only on young poets of Langston Hughes's generation but on the major American poets who were already in midcareer. Even Robert Frost, who was hardly a radical, found himself wondering in "Build Soil" (1932) whether matters had "reached a depth / Of desperation that would warrant poetry's / Leaving love's alternations, joy and grief, / The weather's alternations, summer and winter, / Our age-long theme, for the uncertainty / Of judging who is a contemporary liar."[3] Frost is reductive about what political poetry can do, despite his own attraction to discursive verse, his temptation to play the sage. The proletarian movement produced no great poetry; instead, the social crisis inspired a raft of prosy Whitman imitations that proclaimed undying solidarity with the common man. But some older poets (including Frost) found their assumptions challenged or galvanized by this crisis. William Carlos Williams was already past forty-five at the time of the Crash. A doctor and pediatrician as well as a poet, he had dreamed of retiring from his practice by the age of fifty to write full-time, but the money he lost in the market made that impossible.

Like many other writers of the 1920s, Williams was already something of a radical before the Crash, completely wired to the avant-garde, publishing nearly all his verse and prose with small presses and little magazines, some of which he started himself, even when he was strapped for money. Although Williams was an experimental writer, constantly trying new things all through the 1920s, he recoiled from the branch of international modernism represented by expatriates like T. S. Eliot and his old friend Ezra Pound. Williams rejected what he saw as the mandarin despair, the baffled aestheticism, of Eliot's *Waste Land*, and he repudiated the technique that projected poetry out of a tissue of literary allusions and deracinated cultural fragments. Williams aimed at a poetry more rooted in American life, more rooted in life itself, and less defined by literary antecedents. "Eliot's work stopped the development of American poetry for over twenty years by the tremendous popular success of its mannerisms," Williams wrote in 1950.[4]

Williams's radicalism was expressed less in his politics, which was always idiosyncratic, than in his restless interest in "the creation of new forms, new names for experience," as he put it in his 1923 masterpiece, *Spring and All*.[5] The book is a mixture of disjunctive, try-anything prose that proclaims the power of the imagination and pristine lyrics, among the best he ever wrote, that are grounded in the beauty of the commonplace, of ordinary things that "astonish me beyond words," as he had written earlier ("Pastoral," 1:71). This was a poetry of glimpses and impressions, of privileged yet unexceptional moments, like his celebrated view of "a red wheel / barrow / glazed with rain / water / beside the white / chickens," (1:224) a poem that rhymes visually, in its physical shape on the page, without rhyming verbally. (Each stanza has three words followed by one word, and looks, yes, like a wheelbarrow. No ideas but in things, as Williams liked to put it.)

But in the early 1930s, as he told a later interviewer, Williams grew "obsessed by the plight of the poor" and furious at the country for ignoring it. He explained how this drove him to write fiction, especially the raw stories that were torn from his daily life as a doctor among the poor.[6] Though Williams complained about the time and energy he put into medicine, his practice had taught him to observe and listen, and linked him to the circumstances of people's everyday lives. Sketches like "The Girl with a Pimply Face," "The Use of Force," "A Night in June," "Jean Beicke," and "A Face of Stone" show how much of a proletarian writer Williams could be, how attentive to meager, deprived lives. But they also show how far from any prescriptive formula his work remained and how ambivalent he was toward the stricken immigrants whose houses he visited.[7]

At the beginning of each story the doctor is always irritated by his patients, appalled by their ignorance and stubbornness, their blind and violent emotions, and fatalistic about his efforts to save their children from horrendous diseases. But in story after story they also gain his respect, even his grudging love, not as victims of society to be pitied or idealized but as feisty, ornery, demanding people whose powers of resistance he finds irresistible—including a teenage girl who seems stonily indifferent to the illness of her baby sister but eager to find some medication for her acne; a woman who has baby after baby as if her real lover were her obstetrician, not her feckless husband; and a child who fiercely shields her symptoms from her hapless parents and from her doctor's prying hands and eyes. To Williams these people have a prickly integrity that appeals to him; they may be unattractive, even self-destructive, but they lack "the rotten smell of a liar."[8] Above all, he neither pities nor idealizes them.

Surprisingly, Williams writes his most important Depression poem, "The Yachts," not in the anecdotal, minimal style of his earlier poems and stories but in the literary mode of the despised Eliot. Eliot's favorite poet was Dante, and "The Yachts" is composed in a loose version of Dante's terza rima and is based on an image from the *Inferno* itself. "The Yachts" deals with a boating regatta, evoking a world of wealth, recreational leisure, and competition. The poem begins as an impressionist canvas, but Williams soon turns the contention of the ships into a struggle between the yachts and the sea around them. Just as the miserable sinners reached out to Dante and Virgil as they journeyed through hell, here the flailing arms of the poor clutch at the prows of the sleek yachts as they sail effortlessly, skillfully, across a roiling surf. If Eliot reacted to the mass politics of the Depression by invoking Coriolanus, with his savage contempt for popular democracy, Williams, in "The Yachts," compares the beautiful, bountiful lives of the rich with the Bosch-like misery of the world beneath them, the submerged masses, to which they remain oblivious.

But "The Yachts" would be less powerful if it simply insisted on this facile comparison between the insensitivity of rich and the hardships of the poor. The poem is also about art and its relation to social suffering. Williams's image of the yachts has some of the airy grace of a seaside painting by Monet:

> they appear youthful, rare

> as the light of a happy eye, live with the grace
> of all that in the mind is fleckless, free and
> naturally to be desired.
>   (Collected Poems, 1:388–89)

By contrast, the entangled bodies of the poor, "broken, beaten, desolate," are genuinely horrible, more Gothic than Dantean. As the skillful yachts pass over this ghastly morass of human suffering, the poet cannot resist being attracted to the beauty of art over the demands of conscience and social sympathy. As Stephen Crane's young man in "An Experiment in Misery" felt repelled by his infernal descent into a cheap lodging house, Williams's allegorical language recoils in horror from his vision of the Last Judgment, which is nevertheless the strongest part of the poem:

Arms with hands grasping seek to clutch at the prows.
Bodies thrown recklessly in the way are cut aside.
It is a sea of faces about them in agony, in despair

until the horror of the race dawns staggering the mind,
the whole sea become an entanglement of watery bodies
lost to the world bearing what they cannot hold.

Williams had used a similar image in *Spring and All* where he described a young woman caressed by a "sea of many arms," that was also "the sea that is cold with dead men's tears" (1:222). Here that sexual sea, reminiscent of Whitman, turns into a sea of horrors. Just as the dumb anguish of the doctor's patients reaches out to him in his stories, drawing him in despite his annoyance and resistance, here the mass of human suffering grasps at the glittering world of art, which ignores the world around it at the risk of becoming sleekly irrelevant. As in the evocation of the Passaic River in his long poem *Paterson*, Williams finally insists on exposing himself to the mucky flow of experience.[9] But Williams also understands how art, like medicine, can also be swamped by an exacerbated social empathy, an immersion in the turbid sea of human misery.

Turning to Robert Frost, we find a poet who, despite the folksy image he cultivated, is rarely at risk of being overcome by compassion. In a letter he describes himself as someone who needs to be "orthodox in politics love religion," adding cryptically, "I can't burn if I was born into this world to shine without heat."[10] Whether we take him as the benign New England sage of the early biographies, or the brutally competitive creature depicted by Lawrence Thompson, his authorized biographer, or the more complex figure with a dark view of humanity that we find in recent studies, Frost remains a Darwinian survivor, too single-minded to go under. He could defend selfishness as a form of autonomy and integrity in the vein of Emerson's essay "Self-Reliance."

"I own I never really warmed / To the reformer or reformed," Frost writes in "To a Thinker" (298). Even if he had not trumpeted his Yankee individualism, hated the New Deal as a form of state socialism, and scorned the left-wing literary movement, Frost was not exactly a Good

Samaritan when it came to other people's problems, including members of his own luckless family. He could be neglectful of his wife and children yet intensely devoted to them. When Frost had his sister, his only sibling, committed to a mental asylum, he wrote a letter that even his most sympathetic biographer, William H. Pritchard, finds shocking. It concludes,

> And I suppose I am a brute in that my nature refuses to carry sympathy to the point of going crazy just because someone else goes crazy, or of dying just because someone else dies. As I get older I find it easier to lie awake nights over other people's troubles. But that's as far as I go to date. In good time I will join them in death to show our common humanity. (U103)

With a history of violent outbursts, Frost's sister had grown increasingly hysterical about the war, yet Frost's letter paints her as the paradigm of a liberal gone berserk, a bleeding heart who really bled. "I really think she thought in her heart that nothing would do justice to the war but going insane over it." He, on the other hand, was fatalistic and self-protective, the kind of conservative for whom there's very little anyone can do to alter the basic conditions of life, which include going crazy and dying. For his sister, he says, "one half the world seemed unendurably bad and the other half unendurably indifferent. She included me in the unendurably indifferent. A mistake. I belong to the unendurably bad."[11] "It was designed to be a sad world," he later wrote to Untermeyer; "how sad we won't keep telling each other over and over" (U259).

Unlike most conservatives—and liberals—Frost was not content to rest in his presumptions, but tested them in the metaphorical dramas enacted in his poems. One of the conditions that fascinated him was the quiet spectacle of how life simply runs down, something no social sympathy can alter. In "An Old Man's Winter Night" he describes an old farmer who is barely able to live alone yet somehow carries on, even on a fiercely cold winter night. Except for this coping, it is a poem without consolation:

> *One aged man—one man—can't keep a house,*
> *A farm, a countryside, or if he can,*
> *It's thus he does it of a winter night.*
> (106)

Frost has no faith that social institutions can mitigate the feebleness or loneliness of old age, the radical separateness of every human creature. His poems take much of their power from this sense of the inevitable, a stoic acceptance of things as they are. Each of us can only learn for himself "what to make of a diminished thing," as he says in "The Oven Bird" (116), or what we can do to "Provide, Provide" for time's erosions. ("No memory of having starred / Atones for later disregard, / Or keeps the end from being hard" [280]). In the face of other people's troubles, our defense is simply to turn back to our own affairs, like the impatient friends and mourners in "Home Burial," or the bystanders in "'Out, Out—'" who turn away after the fatal injury of a boy in a freak accident.

> The watcher at his pulse took fright.
> No one believed. They listened at his heart.
> Little—less—nothing!—and that ended it.
> No more to build on there. And they, since they
> Were not the one dead, turned to their affairs.
>   (131)

The stuttering abruptness of this ending is awkward but no doubt deliberate. Earlier Frost had speculated tenderly about this boy "doing a man's work, though a child at heart," and tried to imagine how the accident might have been avoided. Now that it *has* happened, the moment for sympathy is past. A life has ebbed away: "No more to build on there." But since "they / Were not the one dead," the onlookers resume their lives without spilling emotion over the irretrievable, as Frost himself turned away after deaths and losses in his immediate family. This is just what the husband in "Home Burial" does after burying his child; his seeming coldness infuriates his wife, who goes on helplessly grieving.

For Frost a certain selfishness (or self-protectiveness) is part of the tissue of individual life, its marrow of integrity. This is especially true for the creative writer. "All that makes a writer is the ability to write strongly and directly from some unaccountable and almost invincible personal prejudice," he wrote to the future psychologist B. F. Skinner. Those who don't hold fast to their own prejudices, he adds, simply adopt the prejudices of others, the received wisdom.[12] A strong writer—he cites Karl Marx as an example!—is one who can impose his prejudices, his ruling metaphors, on those around him, who persists and persists in the face of all rival claims. This makes creative power hard to distinguish from personal ambition.

Frost's fatalism and self-promotion make an odd combination. In his own way he was a conscientious husband and father and a deeply feeling person, yet he often saved his feelings for his work. If Frost would not squander emotion on those close to him, it stands to reason that he would expend even less on society's victims, people he didn't know. But Frost took the sufferings of the Depression as a challenge, and in "Two Tramps in Mud Time" he set out to mark the limits of benevolence and social sympathy. It appeared in his 1936 book *A Further Range* along with other topical poems like "A Lone Striker," "Build Soil," and "To a Thinker," though the book also included some of his greatest lyrics, such as "Desert Places," "Design," "Neither Far Out Nor in Deep," and "Provide, Provide." *A Further Range* won Frost his third Pulitzer Prize but also, because it ranged into issues of politics and society, was harshly attacked by angry young critics like Newton Arvin, Rolfe Humphries, and R. P. Blackmur.

Frost, after all, was not an avant-garde writer like Dr. Williams, admired by a coterie of fellow authors, but the closest thing America had had to a public poet and official bard since the death of Whitman. Frost's poetry was not only popular but, because of its surface accessibility and homespun wisdom, seemed to speak for a populism that the left-wing critics and poets claimed as their own. It was he who was the man of the people, not his intellectual critics, Frost insisted, citing *North of Boston*, his great early book of domestic portraits and dialogues.[13] Where Frost stood was not only publicly important but would help define what poetry could do at a moment of social crisis.

In "Two Tramps at Mud Time" Frost wrestles not only with the specter of the Depression but with the ghost of a great predecessor, Wordsworth. In his 1802 poem "Resolution and Independence," Wordsworth described a particularly low moment in his life, which was dispelled by his encounter with a decrepit man whose ancient, dying trade is to collect leeches on a barren moor. Seeing someone who survives so close to the margin of human existence yet remains content, certainly not brooding about it, the poet, with a shaft of sympathy yet also a glimpse of the very bedrock of humanity, gains the strength to go on with his own life.

Just as the leech gatherer seems to materialize almost supernaturally before Wordsworth, two strangers arise "out of the mud" as Frost is splitting wood. Frost describes the glorious day, as Wordsworth did, but this one hovers precariously between two seasons, between the chill of winter and the spring thaw, like the opposing values that will hang in the balance later in the poem. The two men are loggers, obviously unemployed, part of the driftwood of migrant labor during the Depression years. They disturb him, not with their self-sufficiency (like the leech gatherer) but with their unspoken need for work, exactly the kind of work the poet is doing. Initially, he finds, they "put me off my aim," but soon, as if to prove his need to do the work himself, his right *not* to employ them, he's splitting the wood as if he were born to it, as if it were the perfect expression of all he is and all he can do.

> Good blocks of oak it was I split,
> As large around as the chopping block;
> And every piece I squarely hit
> Fell splinterless as a cloven rock.
> The blows that a life of self-control
> Spares to strike for the common good
> That day, giving a loose to my soul,
> I spent on the unimportant wood.
>   (251)

Something in the poet wants to spite the men, confound their implied demand on him, and refute the notion of benevolence that would force him to hire them to work in his stead. Yet the ambiguous word "spares" turns in both directions, for and against the claims of "the common good." Abstractly, the poet accepts what they ask of him:

> My right might be love but theirs was need,
> And where the two exist in twain
> Theirs was the better right—agreed.
>   (252)

But this imposes itself on him with little conviction and much resistance, as if his *poetic* life were at stake, not simply his wood-chopping, as if his whole need to be self-directed were the issue. Every square hit on the "unimportant" wood unblocks his soul, as though each "splinterless," perfectly cleaved log were the right word in a poem, the exact metaphor that releases him and articulates his way of seeing. To Untermeyer he wrote, "My object in life is to be first-hand with some things of the senses and the mind and to strike no false personal note to set my nerves on edge" (U257).

Frost will not give over his work to the tramps, will not dispense social welfare, because the work fulfills and expresses him, very much as his poetry does. The last stanza hangs on the dubious assertion "My object in living is to unite / My avocation and my vocation." More than most of the proletarian poets, Frost is a poet of labor, of satisfying work, going back to early poems like "A Tuft of Flowers" and "Mending Wall," with their play on working together and working apart. He sees poetry itself as performance, a piece of work well done. Frost balks at any demand, however morally just or socially beneficial, that does not arise out of some inner necessity.

Poetry, he says elsewhere, comes from our griefs, not our grievances, out of the ineluctable sorrow of existence, not the social complaints of the moment, which are better expressed in prose.[14] Unfortunately, the poem's moral about combining love and need, work and play, is a logical quagmire, a message too weakly founded on his encounter with the two tramps. It's a grievance, not a grief, a strained protest against the impositions of the liberal imagination.

"Two Tramps in Mud Time" too adamantly insists on individual autonomy and self-sufficiency in the face of all progressive claims for social improvement, as if poetic power were the model for all that mattered in life. Yet Frost, with only a few notes of sarcasm, could take the other side as well. "I don't mean it is humanity not to feel the suffering of others. The last election would confute me if I did," he wrote in 1936. "I judged that half the people that voted for his Rosiness were those glad to be on the receiving end of his benevolence and half were those over glad to be on the giving end. The national mood is humanitarian. Nobly so—I wouldn't take it away from them" (U284–85). Because of phrases like "over glad," this is less generous than it looks. But Frost never tired of debating this point, which suggests a degree of social guilt, a touch of bad conscience, that he took pains to mock or deny. The two tramps allow him to make his case, but he scarcely permits them to make theirs.

To a young poet Frost wrote, after complimenting him on his work,

> You wish the world better than it is, more poetical. You are that kind of poet. I would rate as the other kind. I wouldn't give a cent to see the world, the United States or even New York made better. I want them left just as they are for me to make poetical on paper. I don't ask anything done to them that I don't do to them myself. I'm a mere selfish artist most of the time. I have no quarrel with the material. The grief will be simply if I can't transmute it into poems. (*Selected Letters*, 369)[15]

For Frost the role of the writer is not to improve the world but simply to write, or rather to improve the world *by* writing—if indeed the world is at all amenable to improvement.

Wallace Stevens was the last poet of the 1930s whom anyone would have expected to move left, to feel any degree of responsibility for the poor, or to change his writing to encompass the social unrest of the period. For him the greatest poverty is sensory, imaginative: it is "not to live / In a physical world, to feel that one's desire / Is too difficult to tell from despair."[16] To many readers of his first book, *Harmonium* (1923), he was the ultimate mandarin—rarefied, playful, recondite—the complete aesthete, with an exotic vocabulary all his own. The young radical critics of the thirties were no more sympathetic to him than to Frost, even if they could understand what he was doing. The publication of his second book, *Ideas of Order*, in 1935 thus became a defining moment, much like the appearance of Frost's *A Further Range*. Stanley Burnshaw's review on *Ideas of Order* in *The New Masses* was a flash point, the most celebrated review Stevens ever received, largely because it got under his skin. (He wrote a nearly impenetrable long poem, "Mr. Burnshaw and the Statue," responding to it.)

Yet Burnshaw grasped what most later critics missed, that Stevens, almost in spite of himself, was reaching out for a new fix on things, that *Ideas of Order* could prove be a turning point in his work. After writing what Burnshaw calls "sense poetry" in *Harmonium*, Stevens in his new book was "a man who, having lost his footing, now scrambles to stand up and keep his balance."[17] My only quarrel with Burnshaw's keenly perceptive review, which has been expounded at length in an excellent book by Alan Filreis,[18] is that it overstates the extent of Stevens's confusion. All through *Ideas of Order* Stevens knows exactly what he's doing, which is to bid farewell to the lush and musical world of *Harmonium* with an eye to the suffering masses he was accused of ignoring. Stevens wrote very little poetry in the decade after *Harmonium*, but by 1934 he felt a burst of creativity that lasted throughout the decade, thanks to the poetic challenge of the Depression, but also because he himself was aging and changing and could no longer rest in the exuberant play of language and invention that had once animated his work. "My old boat goes round on a crutch / And doesn't get under way," he says in "Sailing After Lunch." He feels like "a most inappropriate man / In a most unpropitious place." Like Williams with his yachts, he longs to give "that slight transcendence to the dirty sail, / By light, the way one feels, sharp white, / And then rush brightly through the summer air" (99–100).

Repeatedly in *Ideas of Order* Stevens strikes a mournful, elegiac note. The Knopf edition of 1936 begins with "Farewell to Florida," that is, farewell to the tropical South of Stevens's luxurious imagination and welcome to the harsh leafless North of cold necessity, with its "wintry slime / Both of men and clouds, a slime of men in crowds" (98). There's hardly a poem in *Ideas of Order* that doesn't find some metaphor for this sense of a world transformed: the sharp, frosty air of autumn replaces the fragrant promise of spring; the voices of human calamity displace the sounds of nature; the moon of the imagination gives way to the sun of harsh reality; and, above all, in poem after poem, a certain music can no longer be heard, in part because it is muted or drowned out but more because Stevens himself no longer has an ear for it.

Death hovers over this world, not as "the mother of beauty," as in "Sunday Morning," but as a marker of disintegration: "A little less returned for him each spring. / Music began to fail him." "His spirit grew uncertain of delight, / Certain of its uncertainty" ("Anglais Mort à Florence," 119). If the spirit of Wordsworth's "Resolution and Independence" influences Frost's "Two Tramps in Mud Time," then Wordsworth's other poems of decline and renewal, especially "Tintern Abbey" and the Intimations ode, lie behind *Ideas of Order*, as in the conclusion of "Anglais Mort à Florence": "He was that music and himself. / They were particles of order, a single majesty: / But he remembered the time when he stood alone. . . .When to be and delight to be seemed to be one, / Before the colors deepened and grew small" (120).

Sometimes age and temper can account for this sense of decline. In "The Sun This March" spring itself seems like an intrusion on the poet's wintry mood: "The exceeding brightness of this early sun / Makes me conceive how dark I have become" (108). Keats's nightingale has become "not a bird for me / But the name of a bird and the name of a nameless air / I have never—shall never hear" ("Autumn Refrain," 129). In other poems, like "Mozart, 1935," the sense of personal loss takes the form of an insistent pressure to face up to the world as it is. The miseries of the age are knocking at his door. He begins, "Poet, be seated at the piano. / Play the present." This is 1935, he says, and "they throw stones upon the roof / While you practice arpeggios." But instead of countering this with nostalgia, with some "lucid souvenir of the past" or "airy dream of the future," he echoes Shelley's fierce "Ode to the West Wind":

> *Be thou the voice,*
> *Not you. Be thou, be thou*
> *The voice of angry fear,*
> *The voice of this besieging pain.*
>
> *Be thou that wintry sound*
> *As of the great wind howling,*
> *By which sorrow is released,*
> *Dismissed, absolved*
> *In a starry placating.*
>   (107–8)

Could the sumptuous poet of "Sunday Morning" really become the intimate "thou": the voice of angry fear, the voice of this besieging pain, the wintry sound by which this sorrow is released? In an early journal he wondered (like Frost) whether he was "too cold to feel deeply the human destitution."[19] But this was precisely the task he set for himself in "Sad Strains of a Gay Waltz," Stevens's key poetic encounter with the Depression. As strikingly as "The Yachts," which it complements, the poem signifies the emergence of the masses into the reluctant awareness of the literary imagination:

> There comes a time when the waltz
> Is no longer a mode of desire, a mode
> Of revealing desire and is empty of shadows.

> Too many waltzes have ended.

The self-contained formality of the waltz, which belongs to an older world of love, social ritual, gaiety, and gemütlichkeit, no longer answers to any contemporary reality, a world in which "the streets are full of cries." Neither does the romantic figure of "that mountain-minded Hoon," an Apollo-like poet of pure imagination, "who found all form and order in solitude, / For whom the shapes were never the figures of men." Now

> The shapes have lost their glistening.
> There are these sudden mobs of men,

> These sudden clouds of faces and arms,
> An immense suppression, freed,
> These voices crying without knowing for what,

> Except to be happy, without knowing how,
> Imposing forms they cannot describe,
> Requiring order beyond their speech.
>   (100)

According to Stevens's biographer Joan Richardson, this poem was inspired by the sight of crowds of men out of work in Florida, once such an exotic paradise.[20] Yet it's difficult for Stevens to describe common people without melding them into a threatening and anonymous mass. In poem after poem he returns to the motif of the "slime of men in crowds" or the "sudden mobs of men," freed from their immense suppression, longing inarticulately to be happy. In "The Man with the Blue Guitar" they will become a mass of "mechanical beetles" creeping across the earth, and "a million people on one string" (137, 136), meaning a string that connects them like puppets or pearls, but also a string of the blue guitar, which raises the question of what kind of music, what kind of art, can reflect the lives of ordinary people without dehumanizing them. Stevens is reaching out to common life, to the mass of men, at the same time he is repelled by them.

This mixture of fascination, repugnance, and a sense of discovery colors the concluding stanzas of "Sad Strains of a Gay Waltz":

> *Too many waltzes have ended. Yet the shapes*
> *For which the voices cry, these, too, may be*
> *Modes of desire, modes of revealing desire.*

Just as Wordsworth in "Tintern Abbey" and the Intimations ode had dedicated himself to a more mature poetry, somber and tragic rather than youthfully ecstatic, Stevens suggests that the cries of ordinary men, their miseries and yearnings sharpened by hard times, may soon find their poet, though he does not say whether he is that man. That which is inchoate must find its form: the inarticulate need only find its voice.

> *Some harmonious skeptic soon in a skeptical music*
>
> *Will unite these figures of men and their shapes*
> *Will glisten again with motion, the music*
> *Will be motion and full of shadows.*
>   (100–01)

Out of the social sufferings of the Depression can come a new kind of music, which Stevens had already applauded in the work of his friend Dr. Williams. In a preface to Williams's *Collected Poems* in 1934, Stevens, to his friend's great annoyance, described him as "more of a realist than is commonly true in the case of a poet" yet also a sentimentalist who invested deep feeling in the "anti-poetic," someone for whom "the anti-poetic is that truth, that reality to which all of us are forever fleeing."[21] When Stevens came to write a jacket statement for *Ideas of Order*, he simply rephrased the same thought with a different emphasis, calling it "essentially a book of pure poetry" yet also a work that "attempts to illustrate the role of imagination in life, and particularly in life at present. The more realistic life may be, the more it needs the stimulus of the imagination" (*Opus Posthumous*, 223).

As Burnshaw saw clearly in 1935, *Ideas of Order* testified to Stevens's huge effort to "play the present," to combine reality and imagination in a fresh way. This was why he reacted so strongly to Burnshaw's review. "It placed me in a new setting," he wrote. "I hope I am headed left, but there are lefts and lefts, and certainly I am not headed for the ghastly left of MASSES."[22] His move toward realism flowed not from Marx but from the Nietzschean premises of his own *Harmonium*, with its pagan assurance that this is the only world there is. But in *Ideas of Order* the gorgeous and sensuous world of Stevens's earlier imagination, which reflected his rich inner life, gives way to the spare, somber realities of the Depression. Where Williams's fancy yachts remain oblivious to the sea of arms around them, Stevens deliberately capsized his craft, though he hardly knew how to swim in such turbulent waters.

Stevens never returned to the lush style of *Harmonium*, but neither could he become the voice of life's ordinary miseries, or the unhappy consciousness of the masses, or of *The New Masses*, any more than the chastened Wordsworth could. Unlike Williams or Frost or the realists of the 1890s, Stevens could not make the descent into the maelstrom of the mundane; his mind required richer fare. Yet the Depression altered his work for good, and he achieved exceptional eloquence just by consecrating himself to a new course.

Stevens is amused by how the world around him has changed; his mood can turn witty as well as elegiac. He jokes that "Marx has ruined Nature, / For the moment" (109). The long poems of *Owl's Clover* (1936) make heavy weather of the tension between democracy and poetry. (Stevens eventually dropped them from his *Collected Poems*.) But in the thirty-three short variations that make up "The Man with the Blue Guitar," written soon afterward, poetry becomes a sparkling "duet with the undertaker," and Stevens plays wonderful changes on the relation of the imagination (the blue guitar) to "things as they are," a phrase that harks back to the revolutionary turmoil of the 1790s. These poems deserve far more attention than I can give them here. "Do not speak to us of the greatness of poetry, / Of the torches wisping in the underground," he writes. "The earth, for us, is flat and bare. / There are no shadows" (V).

But what seems like poverty can yield a poetry of its own, a pagan poetry of the real, "without shadows, without magnificence, / The flesh, the bone, the dirt, the stone" (XXI). This, not *Owl's Clover*, is the finest fruit of Stevens's new mood.

The following year Steven wrote "The Poems of Our Climate," a kind of epilogue to his work in the 1930s, in which he sets aside a beauty purified of pain, circumstance, and contingency. "One desires / so much more than that," he says. "The imperfect is our paradise" (178–79). In contemplating the stresses of "things as they are," even from a distance, Stevens touched a vein of humanity that deepened his work.

> It needed the heavy nights of drenching weather
> To make him return to people, to find among them
> Whatever it was that he found in their absence,
> A pleasure, an indulgence, an infatuation.
>   ("Like Decorations in a Nigger Cemetery," 128)

For Stevens, as for Williams and Frost, the challenge of the Depression was not how to live or how to save the world but how to go on writing. The thirties did not turn him into a popular or demotic poet, a social realist, or a guilt-ridden spokesman for the wretched of the earth, but it linked him to people in an unexpected way, opening a dialogue with the world that inflected everything he subsequently wrote.

CHAPTER 6

Black Girls and Native Sons

How Bigger Was Born

"THERE IS SOMETHING ABOUT POVERTY that smells like death," Zora Neale Hurston wrote in her 1942 autobiography, *Dust Tracks on a Road*. "Dead dreams dropping off the heart like leaves in a dry season and rotting around the feet; impulses smothered too long in the fetid air of underground caves. The soul lives in a sickly air. People can be slave-ships in shoes."[1] Hurston's metaphorical language draws our attention less to a social condition than to a state of the soul, a spiritual condition heavy with a sense of illness, decay, and entrapment. Hurston draws her images from nature but she is no naturalist. What interests her most is not the caste or class system that may produce poverty but the feelings of hopelessness that flow from it. Though critics still identify Depression writing with direct, politically engaged social criticism, the work of Hurston and her most powerful rival, Richard Wright, shows how much more is involved.

There is no single work of art or literature that summarizes the deep concern with poverty or the new fascination with the lives of ordinary Americans in the 1930s. The work of documentary photographers like Walker Evans may come the closest, in part because the unvarnished humanity of their subjects seemed to transcend its historical moment. Thanks to the faith in economic individualism and Social Darwinism, the poor had often been blamed for their lack of initiative or their defective morals. But the economic crisis of the thirties drew attention not only to the miserable lot of the poor, but to the daily experience of other people also coping with tough times. Writers and photographers appealed not to middle-class pity or charity but to the widespread fear of falling, the deep sense of insecurity that had corroded the American Dream. The common man became a subject of intense interest at the same time it became a political slogan.

What began with Gold's *Jews without Money* in 1930 culminated with the surprising commercial success of *The Grapes of Wrath* in 1939 and *Native Son* in 1940. The radical novel came of age at the very moment when it was set to expire, undone by the patriotism and prosperity ushered in by the war. In Steinbeck's book the familiar hero of proletarian fiction, defeated yet dauntless even in death, is replaced by the down-home American family, coming apart, losing its land, yet also learning how the world works, even reconstructing a shattered sense of community as it struggles to survive. Only the pictures of Evans, Dorothea Lange, Ben Shahn, Carl Mydans, Arthur Rothstein, Marion Post Wolcott, Russell Lee, Jack Delano, and other photographers for the Farm Security Administration could compete with Steinbeck's story and its peerless film version in offering vivid images of marginal lives during the Depression.

In this constellation of works that rounded off the decade, Richard Wright's books occupy a special place, for they brought the Depression home to the cities and highlighted the special disabilities of race, which even the sharecropper images had largely sidestepped. Evans and Agee, avoiding the question of race entirely, portrayed three white tenant families in *Let Us Now Praise Famous Men*. *Native Son*, with its thriller plot and visceral violence, its wide circulation thanks to the Book-of-the-Month Club, shocked the nation with bad news about ghetto conditions and black fear and hatred of whites that most Americans had never imagined. It also brought home the inner experience of poverty in an indelible way.

In a decade when many Americans did badly, blacks did worse. The jobs they sought by migrating north throughout the 1920s had disappeared. Some of those jobs fell to poor whites. At the peak of the Depression in the winter of 1932–33, when 25 percent of Americans were unemployed, 50 percent of blacks had no jobs. The Roosevelt administration could not or would not confront such inequities directly because it depended politically on its southern base, but New Deal housing, slum clearance, employment, and relief programs helped, since they were applied without consideration of race. According to the historian William E. Leuchtenburg, "in many areas, Negroes, hit harder than any group by the depression, survived largely because of relief checks."[2] Agricultural subsidies, on the other hand, went only to landowners. Paid to withhold land from cultivation, they often let their black sharecroppers go, worsening the rural Depression for many of their tenants. Efforts to create a tenant farmers' union were ruthlessly put down by local authorities and night-riding vigilantes. "The New Deal was not to blame for the social system it inherited," say Leuchtenburg, "but New Deal policies made matters worse. The AAA's reduction of cotton acreage drove the tenant and the cropper from the land, and the landlords, with the connivance of local AAA committees which they dominated, cheated tenants of their fair share of benefits" (137).

Richard Wright, by contrast, was determined to make not only the condition of blacks but their masked inner lives visible to white Americans, perhaps for the first time. Most directly, in one of the last major works on poverty and the Depression, he described the plight of both rural and urban blacks in the text he wrote to accompany Edwin Rosskam's extraordinary selection of FSA photographs in *12 Million Black Voices* (1941). His commentary covered every phase of black life, but it was especially riveting in describing the typical "kitchenette" of Chicago's Black Belt, the rat-infested, privacy-deprived, one-room slum apartment that incubates disease, prostitution, and the sullen antisocial violence of a Bigger Thomas.

Thanks to the range and acrid depth of his experience, Wright was uniquely situated to write this book, a collective portrait of black Americans. Born in Mississippi in 1908, the son of an illiterate sharecropper and a schoolteacher mother, he had lived in the rural South, in Mississippi and Arkansas, and in larger cities like Memphis and Jackson before migrating with his family to Chicago in 1927. Poverty and illness kept them on the move. Wright's father had abandoned the family before Richard turned six, and his mother fell gravely ill two years later, often requiring the care of her parents, her sisters, and her growing children. In Jackson, in Memphis, and later in Chicago, Wright, to provide support for his family, took jobs that exposed him to both the racial oppression of the South and the subtler economic and social segregation of the North; his family's dire situation finally forced him to leave school after junior high.

In Chicago he became a writer and a Communist, and by the mid-1930s he was a key figure in the city's vibrant left-wing literary life and the only black supervisor working in Chicago's WPA Writers Project. He moved to Harlem to work for the party in 1937, but his experiences in the South and in Chicago gave him the material for his three major narrative works. *Native Son* was preceded by an incendiary collection of long stories, *Uncle Tom's Children* (1938), and followed by *Black Boy* (1945), a memoir of growing up in the South. Under the title of *American Hunger*, the original memoir had gone on to include his northern experiences in Chicago and in the Communist Party, which ended with his disillusionment. But this final third of the book was cut at the urging of the Book-of-the-Month Club, which was also responsible for censoring *Native Son.**

Wright was a classic radical writer, one of the few whose work still reverberates strongly with its passion and bitter intensity. Far from undergoing a conversion from middle-class comfort to middle-class conscience, his own life had made him a social critic. His experience in the party gave him his political education, but it was never free of tension and ambiva-

---

* Some pieces of the suppressed portion of *Black Boy* were soon published separately in magazines and in a widely read 1950 book, *The God That Failed*, a collection of essays by former Communists, edited by Richard Crossman. The whole latter part appeared as a separate book called *American Hunger* in 1977, and the full original text was restored by the Library of America in 1991.

lence, since the political line of the party never spoke fully to his experience as a black man. He was very much a Communist when he wrote the
stories in *Uncle Tom's Children*, a fierce indictment of the murderously brutal treatment of blacks in the South.

The role of Communists as radical organizers figures prominently in
the last two stories of the enlarged edition of 1940, "Fire and Cloud" and
"Bright and Morning Star." Local white authorities are convinced that
these "outside agitators" have stirred up trouble among their own happy
and docile Negroes, and they crack down viciously against any trace of
opposition (as they had actually done with organizers of the Southern
Tenant Farmers Union). After the Popular Front policy was proclaimed
in 1935, the party's cultural commissars had turned away from the proletarian novel, with its emphasis on class conflict. They toned down their
message, gave it a patriotic spin ("Communism is twentieth-century
Americanism"), and cultivated alliances with middle-class liberals. But
Wright, though by all reports surprisingly gentle in person, was an angry
man, and there was every indication that he would become a naturalistic
writer in the proletarian mode, a social novelist who would turn his lens
on race as well as class.

This bore the seeds of his future troubles with the party, since any
stress on race undermined the Communist view that the radical movement should be color-blind. (One of their slogans was "Black and White
Unite and Fight.") This becomes an important issue in "Bright and Morning Star," since Sue, the heroine, distrusts her two sons' collaboration
with white activists, one of whom, with the loaded name of "Booker,"
turns out to be a police spy who betrays them. In his important 1936
manifesto called "Blueprint for Negro Writing," written at the outset
of his career, Wright carefully negotiated this issue of race. Skirting the
officially ordained, race-blind emphasis on class issues, he argues, on the
one hand, that Negro writing had to be deeply grounded in Negro folklore, which embodied "the collective sense of Negro life in America," and
in Negro social institutions, including the church, the press, the social
and business world, and the school system. Conscious of overstepping
the party line, determined to avoid the charge of "black chauvinism," he
also insists that "Negro writers must accept the nationalist implications
of their lives, not in order to encourage them but in order to change and
transcend them. They must accept the concept of nationalism because,

in order to transcend it, they must *possess* and *understand* it."[3] This suggested that he would not be able to finesse the issue much longer. Even at the height of his Marxist commitment, his break with the party on racial issues looked inevitable.

Uncle Tom's Children not only illustrates Wright's ambivalence—the tightrope he was walking as a black Communist—but provides a superb introduction to his strengths and limits as a writer. Though it represents Wright's apprentice fiction, and its graphic violence at times makes it almost unbearable to read, it remains a cunningly crafted work, especially in its expanded 1940 version. The book loosely follows the template of proletarian fiction, moving its protagonists from sheer blind victimization and desperate flight in the first two stories to rebellion and impassioned conversion in the third and fourth stories and finally to determined, costly opposition in the final tale—a resistance foreshadowed in all the previous stories. The greatest strength of the book is in the physical immediacy of its writing and Wright's astonishing empathy for the feelings of black people caught in a system that allows them no rights, living among people who accuse them without cause, beat them without mercy, and kill them without compunction or fear of punishment.

Wright is drawn to extreme situations that strain his characters to the breaking point. He found his strength in portraying the physical and mental anguish of people in a state of panic, terror, or entrapment. Typically, he shows, they're stricken with a sense of numb helplessness. They feel completely overwhelmed; their world has spun out of control: "He felt giddy and a nervous shudder went through him. He rubbed his eyes. Lawd, Ah got fever. His head ached and felt heavy; he wanted sleep and rest."[4] This tells the story of a man caught in a flood, overwhelmed and exhausted by the sheer effort to survive, but his physical ordeal also serves as a metaphor for his besieged life. Besieged by conditions they are unable to control, Wright's characters feel engulfed as they realize that their fate—rape, sadistic physical punishment, even imminent death— has already overtaken them. To save his family, including his pregnant wife, from the rampaging waters, Mann has stolen a boat, then spontaneously killed the man who tried to claim it. Now he feels completely done in. "Mann rowed: he heard Grannie crying: he felt weak from fear: he had a choking impulse to stop: he felt he was lost because he had shot a white man: he felt there was no use in his rowing any longer: but the current fought the boat and he fought back with the oars" (80–81). This sequence of interlocking phrases, connected only by colons, builds to an unbearable intensity: the very syntax enmeshes this archetypal "Mann" in some iron law of consequences, gripped by a fate he cannot elude.

In these situations Wright's characters turn passive and numb or else feel impelled to strike out violently, taking their tormentors down with them. As the stories progress, this reflex morphs from a daydream of vengeance to a spontaneous act of violent resistance, however futile. Each of these reactions will be more fully developed in *Native Son*: not only terror and flight but the defensive, suicidal act of violence that shatters the limits of a lifelong confinement and becomes an act of self-definition. Living under inhuman pressure, Wright's people rarely choose to kill, but feel no moral compunction for having done so. They kill only when they're cornered, as if the troubles of a lifetime have converged on a single moment. Theirs is not a moral action based on any rational plan but an existential gesture that sums up and transforms them.

The sequence of stories in *Uncle Tom's Children* takes its characters from being victims to becoming agents of their own fate, from a passive sense of helplessness to an authentic if foolhardy gesture of opposition. At first merely instinctive, it soon grows more deliberate, as if to say, as Martin Luther did, "Here I stand, I can do nothing else." This creates the pattern for Wright's later fiction, especially *Native Son*. From story to story the act of resistance takes on a broader meaning, becoming more self-conscious and premeditated. As the mother of two young Communists in the final story, Sue has been threatened and even beaten. One son has already been taken, but she sets out to protect her remaining son's friends from being exposed to the sheriff and his goons, though she knows it may cost his life, and her own.

> She was consumed with a bitter pride. There was nothing on this earth, she felt then, that they could not do to her but that she could take. She stood on a narrow plot of ground from which she would die before she was pushed. And then it was, while standing there feeling warm blood seeping down her throat, that she gave up Johnny-Boy, gave him up to the white folks. She gave him up because they had come tramping into her heart demanding him, thinking they could get him by beating her, thinking they could scare her into making

her tell where he was. She gave him up because she wanted them to know that they could not get what they wanted by bluffing and killing. (239–40)

Hurling insults at the sheriff and his minions even as they depart, she goads them into beating her again. Finally, when she learns that this son has been caught, she conceals a gun in a winding sheet, not to protect him but in simple hope of killing the boy before he can be tortured. She also aims to kill some of their persecutors, including the spy who betrayed them, and, most likely, to forfeit her own life in doing so. Wright had once heard such a story—he reported it later in *Black Boy*—but here he turns it into an almost biblical parable of maternal resistance and self-sacrifice. Like Bigger Thomas in *Native Son*, but more consciously, more foolishly, more heroically, "she had in her heart the whole meaning of her life; her entire personality was poised on the brink of a total act" (253).

Such passages of fateful choice show us why Richard Wright could not remain a Communist writer, or even a strictly social novelist, as he is still conventionally seen. Wright's emotional stress on victimization is not compatible with the program of a political party, not even with the bare minimum of activism and optimism required of any radical movement. To authenticate his harsh portrayal of race relations in the South, Wright prefaced the 1940 edition of these stories with a brief memoir, "The Ethics of Living Jim Crow," offering glimpses of the personal history that would later develop into *Black Boy*. He describes how his younger self was hemmed in and hounded at every turn by the capricious authority attached to white skin. Thanks to this autobiographical overture, the protagonists of the first two stories, Big Boy (in "Big Boy Leaves Home") and Mann (in "Down by the Riverside"), become case studies in the workings of Jim Crow ethics, extensions of the real-life author we have just encountered.

These chilling stories are anecdotal but, in Wright's telling, take on an archetypal power. After trespassing harmlessly with other boys at a swimming hole, Big Boy sees two of his friends shot. In a spontaneous act of self-defense, he takes down the man who killed them. The remaining boys are hunted down by an angry mob, and from his hiding place he sees a boy horribly lynched, though he himself manages to escape. In the next story Mann, caught in the flood, trying only to save his sick and pregnant wife, is also provoked to kill a man who tries to kill them. After losing his wife, he too is hunted down and destroyed. In "Long Black Song," the third story, we meet Silas, the rare black man who is actually prospering—he owns his farm and is just back from selling his crops. But his world comes apart when he too kills the man (a traveling salesman) who raped his wife while he was away. Under siege, surrounded yet determined to hold out, he goes up in the flames that consume his home. In a sense he commits suicide as a form of moral reckoning, the desperate act of a man who has nothing more to lose.

There can be no doubt that blacks were treated miserably in the South, subjected to an iron caste system that gave them no recourse to the law, with periodic lynchings to keep them in their place. Yet these stories are also fueled by paranoia, rage, nauseatingly vivid violence, and a self-destructive stoicism that owes more to Christianity than to Marxism. Wright exposes the racial sickness of the South with a feverish loathing that limits the range of his work and constricts the humanity of his characters. Surely the worst feature of proletarian writing is not the predictable formulas—Wright's work transcends these—and not the sacrifice of a complex world on the altar of social protest, but the surprising fatalism, the ideologically enforced pattern of victimization, which Wright's stories exemplify yet struggle to overcome. Having killed the oily intruder who preyed on his wife, even as she tried to stop him from exacting vengeance, Silas (in "Long Black Song") sees that he has thrown away everything he worked for: his home, his land, his wife and child, his own life. Done in as much by his hatred of white people as by what they have done to him, he has "a deep and final sense that now it was all over and nothing could make any difference."

Silas voices one of the themes of the book: "The white folks ain never gimme a chance! They ain never give no black man a chance! There ain nothin in yo whole life yuh kin keep from em! They take yo lan! They take yo freedom! They take yo women! N then they take yo life!" His only resolve is that "Ef Gawd lets me live Ahm gonna make em *feel* it!" (152–53). Silas's point has already been made by his helpless wife, who, like Euripides' Trojan women, serves as the chorus helplessly observing the fatal last act of the drama: "Dimly she saw in her mind a picture of men killing and being killed. White men killed the black men and black men killed the white. White men killed the black men because they could, and the black men killed the white men to keep from being killed" (146–

47). Once again, the rolling rhythm of Wright's style projects an aura of inevitability, a sense of fate at once Greek and Faulknerian. "When the killing started," she sees, "it went on, like a red river flowing. Oh, she felt sorry for Silas! Silas. . . . He was following that long river of blood. . . . And he did not want to die; she knew he hated dying by the way he talked of it. Yet he followed the old river of blood, knowing that it meant nothing" (153–54).

Intent on showing how people like Silas and Sue surrender their lives to exact revenge and recover a morsel of their dignity, Wright introduces, but fails to pursue, motifs that would complicate this picture. Silas's wife not only stands apart from his resistance; she herself did not entirely resist her white attacker, for he excited her sexually and may have reminded her of another man she loved before marrying the solid, dependable Silas. In the concluding story, Sue's most convincing moments come when she feels poignant maternal pangs about losing her sons, not when she courts martyrdom for the sake of an abstract goal. On the surface her goal seems to be radical solidarity, the defense of a political cause to which her sons have introduced her, despite her skepticism. In fact, her goal is Wright's own, metaphysical, existential; he pushes her to an act of violent self-affirmation that would lay the groundwork for Bigger Thomas in *Native Son*. So we learn that Sue has her back to the wall but, even more than with Silas, "her entire personality was poised on the brink of a total act."

In both *Uncle Tom's Children* and *Native Son*, Wright takes the radical conversion plot of proletarian fiction and transforms it almost beyond recognition. The old pattern can be seen in the fourth story, "Fire and Cloud," which centers on Taylor, a minister who has always gotten along with local white leaders and enjoyed their condescending respect. He sees himself as a man with a calling, a black Moses shepherding his people and leading them to salvation. But his people are hungry; they live beneath a yoke worsened by the Depression. The white authorities want him to disavow a protest march being organized by Communists; when he is unwilling to do so, they treat him with overt contempt. He has long been their lackey and now he knows it, temporizing, bowing and scraping before their brutal authority. Eventually, in the dark of night, he is kidnapped and mercilessly beaten, then forced to his knees in a mockery of prayer. But he is also transformed by his own powers of stoic endurance. Taylor realizes he has spent his whole life on his knees, "a-beggin and a-pleadin wid the white folks. N all they gimme wuz crumbs! All they did wuz kick me! N then they come wida gun n ast me t give mah own soul! N ef Ah so much as talk lika man they try to kill me . . ." (209). This blinding realization does not turn him into a Communist; like Wright in his "Blueprint," his loyalty is "wid the *people*. . . . Its the *people*! Theys the ones that mus be real t us! Gawds wid the people! N the peoples gotta be real as Gawd t us!" (210). His children, the next generation, reject the old-time religion, as Wright did, but he has somehow fashioned his own synthesis of Christianity, political resistance, and black populism. "He was the same man, but he was coming back somehow changed" (212).

Superficially, Reverend Taylor's and Sue's conversion to the militant stance of the younger generation seems stereotyped and predictable, a cliché of the radical writing of the 1930s. Wright fashions an argument for Communism that uneasily assimilates elements of Christian spirituality and Negro nationalism. But nowhere is the ground more clearly laid for his later differences with the party than in the gruesome, gut-wrenching violence of these last two stories, for they tap into a rage that cannot be contained by any party program, certainly not one as shifting and tactical as the agenda of the American Communist Party. All through *Uncle Tom's Children* and *Native Son*, white people not only are malignant and unspeakably evil but appear to blacks like Sue as "a vast white blur" that looms over them, an undifferentiated force that has always dominated their lives. To Sue the treacherous Booker takes on the look of a "huge white face" that conjures up "the fear of all the white faces she had ever seen in her life" (242). In *Native Son* whites appear to Bigger Thomas as "two vast looming white walls," their faces little more than "white discs of danger." Wright's black characters take in these faces as an undifferentiated menace, scarcely human, a wall or mountain that presses in upon them.

When they beat Taylor and Sue to punish and intimidate them, when they torture Sue's son Johnny-Boy to make him talk, first breaking each of his knees, then bursting his eardrums as his mother looks on, whites become stick figures of beastliness, lacking any trace of pity or humanity. The history of race relations yields up many such sadistic tales, but literature demands something subtler than cartoonish villainy: a treatment complicated by insight into motive and meaning. A literature focused on victims obscures any human grasp of those who torment them. Though many of Wright's readers, including Eleanor Roosevelt, found this violence exceptionally disturbing, Wright felt he had let them off too easily and was determined to be tougher next time. "I found that I had written a book which even bankers' daughters could read and weep over and feel good about. I swore to myself that if I ever wrote another, no one would weep over it; that it would be so hard and deep that they would have to face it without consolation of tears."[5]

Wright accomplished this by substituting the ambiguous, at times despicable figure of Bigger Thomas—a man no one could weep over—for victim-heroes like Silas, Taylor, and Sue, humble yet noble figures who elicit pathos and admiration. Though the writing of *Uncle Tom's Children* had been rich with sensory detail, its roots lay in the bone-crushing violence of hard-boiled fiction in the 1930s. The new tough-guy writers like Dashiell Hammett and other contributors to *Black Mask*, along with crime writers like W. R. Burnett (author of *Little Caesar*) and James M. Cain (author of *The Postman Always Rings Twice*), were the proletarians' dark twin, peopling their work with drifters, short-order cooks, and petty criminals in grim, tawdry settings rather than workers and bosses locked in economic conflict. Though many of these writers (like Hammett) were leftists, they pictured a world of double-dealing, violence, and corruption so pervasive that it could hardly be blamed on any economic system or power structure. There was no solution to be found in the revolutionary potential of the party or the working class. The scarcely heroic figure who exposed these conditions—the private detective, the insurance investigator—was often himself implicated in the corruption, and he cleaned house by means that were hard to distinguish from those of the villains. Hammett made this a key theme of his first novel, *Red Harvest* (1929).

Superficially, Bigger Thomas and his poolroom friends belong to the street-corner society of James T. Farrell's *Studs Lonigan* trilogy (1930–35) and the work of Chicago's new urban sociologists, such as Robert Park. But Richard Wright was also influenced by the tainted protagonists of hard-boiled novels and their thriller plots and lurid situations, as well as sensational cases that made newspaper headlines. Bigger's sexual attraction to his new employer's daughter, Mary Dalton; his half-accidental murder of her when he suddenly fears being found in her room; the gruesome dismemberment and burning of her body in the house's furnace; the terrible suspense Wright builds up, reaching into Bigger's nerves and bones, as her remains are accidentally discovered; his flight, the even more gratuitous murder of his girlfriend when he fears she might expose him, and his capture within a police cordon that surrounds the black ghetto—all these were the kind of potboiler and tabloid material that Wright brilliantly used for serious purposes. He knew how starkly, how emotionally they would grip his readers.

By way of this sensational plot, Wright would make his white readers see the world through the eyes of a despised, threatening, vulnerable figure. He challenged them to comprehend what made Bigger—which rhymes with "nigger"—the man he was, and why he did what he did. If a young black rapist and murderer was the white reader's worst nightmare, Wright would sound the depths of his frustration and rage yet show how society had created him. Wright would frighten his readers with the specter of Bigger's hatred yet finally dare them to understand and even sympathize with him.

French writers like Camus and Sartre were drawn to hard-boiled writing because of its pervasive nihilism; it plunges us into a world untouched by "culture" and conventional values, almost beyond good and evil. Breaking free of all easy psychological explanations, Camus's affectless hero Meursault (in *The Stranger*) conveys a sense of weightlessness and marginality. Like Bigger Thomas, he defines himself by a random, arbitrary act, by killing and by being killed. The proletarians and the crime writers were both influenced by Hemingway, especially a story like "The Killers," but proletarian writers borrowed only his flat, understated manner and undercurrent of violence; the hard-boiled writers understood his deeper pessimism, his sense of nada, of isolated men in a world stripped of stable values and idealistic goals, who could justify themselves only by individual acts of self-definition: acts of courage, grace, brutality, or fortitude. For the French, hard-boiled writing became one of the flash points of existentialism, a scene from which all traditional moral constraints, all idealistic motives and transcendental sources of meaning had been excised. As Camus and Sartre were inventing existentialism with the numb, aimless heroes and flat emotional landscapes of *The Stranger* and *Nausea*, Richard Wright arrived at a similar worldview in *Native Son*, set in the violent black slums of Chicago.

Wright grasped how other writers had put lurid material to serious use, especially Dostoyevsky in *Crime and Punishment*. He had a real-life model in the Leopold-Loeb case, in which two wealthy (and gay) young Chicagoans had abducted and killed a boy simply for thrills, putting themselves beyond moral inhibition as they tried to commit the perfect crime. (This case is mentioned several times in *Native Son*.) He also had a model closer to home in the Nixon case, the story of a Negro on trial for murder in Chicago, who was tried in the press as well, and subsequently executed. In "How 'Bigger' Was Born," the lecture Wright wrote and published soon after the book appeared, he gives many examples of obstreperous young blacks he knew growing up in the South, instinctive rebels who resisted Jim Crow, "bad Niggers" who rebelled and were eventually crushed. Wright stresses that he wanted Bigger to be both an individual and an archetype, a symbol of resistance latent everywhere in the black psyche.

Wright always tried to create representative figures to convey the whole condition of his people. In *Uncle Tom's Children* he calls his characters Big Boy and Mann, taking the reader from the innocence and fears of boyhood through the stresses of besieged manhood—a rocky transition for powerless black men—and finally to the hard-won wisdom of older people. In an unusual twist, the elders are forced to learn from the toughness and impatience of their grown-up children as the young try to usher in a different world. As biographers and critics have shown, in writing *Black Boy*, Wright shapes his memories to turn his past into the prototypical experience of a black boy growing up in the Jim Crow South. In his text for *12 Million Black Voices*, which bowled over his young protégé Ralph Ellison, Wright crafts a Whitmanesque prose poem in the first-person plural, trying to speak for his people in a collective black voice. It can be seen even in the sequence of the picture captions:

> Our lives are walled with cotton /
> We plow and plant cotton /
> We chop cotton /
> We pick cotton /
> When Queen Cotton dies . . . /
> . . . how many of us will die with her?[6]

Wright was far from sympathetic to the black church. With characters like Bigger's God-fearing mother, he treats religion as a narcotic that allays black suffering without challenging it, but for *12 Million Black Voices* he deploys the hypnotic rhythms of the pulpit to evoke the bare, exposed lives of black people. In a powerful passage on "kitchenettes"— the squalid one-room flats in which families like Bigger's live—Wright punctuates the stomach-churning photos with a series of staccato paragraphs that continue for seven pages:

> The kitchenette blights the personalities of our growing children, disorganizes them, blinds them to hope, creates problems whose effects can be traced in the characters of its child victims for years afterward.
>
> The kitchenette jams our farm girls, while still in their teens, into rooms with men who are restless and stimulated by the noise and lights of the city; and more of our girls have bastard babies than the girls in any other sections of the city.
>
> The kitchenette fills our black boys with longing and restlessness, urging them to run off from home, to join together with other restless black boys in gangs, that brutal form of city courage. (110–11)

This is almost a commentary on the beginning of *Native Son*, which unfolds in a room exactly like the ones pictured here, with a similar impact on Bigger and his peers.

Wright hit upon the opening scene only after he had written more than half the novel, but it struck exactly the right note. As a piece of urban realism and social criticism, it introduces us not just to the family's poverty and pinched living conditions but also to Bigger's violence, rebelliousness, and offhand cruelty. The scene could be described as a rude awakening. It opens with the crude, disruptive sound of an alarm clock; this stands in for the book itself, which Wright hopes will serve as a wake-up call to his genteel readers. The slum building is rat-infested, and the rat that scurries around the room highlights the vulnerability of the family and the squalor in which it is forced to live. But when Bigger chases and kills it we sympathize with the rat, for its trapped situation points us toward the family stuck in this room, the black community locked into the segregated world of the ghetto, and Bigger himself in his later flight from the law. When he is surrounded and hunted down, he will envy the freedom of a rat that can slip easily through a hole in the wall.

But even this scene and the poolroom scenes that follow, all typical of ghetto sociology, introduce touches that will make this novel different. The Bigger who corners and kills the rat, who is surly toward his mother and teases his sister with the rodent's carcass, is fearless, mischievous, and uncontrollable, a disaster waiting to happen. But he is also a caged animal with few options and a large potential for trouble. "We wouldn't have to live in this garbage dump if you had any manhood in you," his mother tells him.[7] With a spell of reform school already behind him, he is taking a job reluctantly as a chauffeur for the Daltons; if he doesn't look for work, his family will be thrown off relief. In a limited way, he understands his predicament: "Yes, he could take a job at the Daltons and be miserable, or he could refuse it and starve. It maddened him to think that he did not have a wider choice of action" (456).

But Wright is not content with what Bigger thinks about it; he wants us to understand it in a larger way. So he begins a chorus of explanation that will punctuate the novel, introducing a reflective voice in which the insight of the author, articulate and analytical, fuses with the partial awareness of the character, which pulses through his nerves and muscles rather than his conscious thoughts. Violating a cardinal rule of modern fiction, one he himself underscored as the need "to *render, depict,* not merely to tell the story" (878), Wright set out to explain and explain and explain, elaborating on Bigger's point of view in ways Bigger himself could never do. The first of these commentaries comes a few pages after the book begins:

> He hated his family because he knew that they were suffering and that he was powerless to help them. He knew that the moment he allowed himself to feel to its fulness how they lived, the shame and misery of their lives, he would be swept out of himself with fear and despair. . . . He knew that the moment he allowed what his life meant to enter fully into his consciousness, he would either kill himself or someone else. So he denied himself and acted tough. (453)

Straining at the limits of Bigger's conscious awareness—indeed, trying to account for why he closes off his thinking—Wright heightens the reader's horror—the moral horror, as Wright later described it—at how the family lives. He shifts his subject to the mechanisms of Bigger's mind, his fear, shame, distance, toughness, and potential for violence.

At first Wright seems too analytical, providing the meaning along with the scene. His initial commentaries are slightly clumsy, but eventually they set a tone for the novel, a meditative air of the tragic and the inexorable. For all of Wright's suspicion of the black church, they owe a great debt to the way preachers preach, the way their sermons dilate upon texts. As *Native Son* proceeds, these reflections merge more convincingly with Bigger's point of view. Later he will structure *Black Boy* as a series of scenes and lessons, with each vignette brought home by interpretive comments. In Tolstoy's comparison of the fox and the hedgehog—the fox who knows many things (like Wright's fluent, versatile rival, Langston Hughes) and the hedgehog who knows one big thing—Wright is the hedgehog. With Bigger he found his one real subject, the extreme psychological stress of being black in America, and the rest of his work became a commentary on it, beginning within the novel itself.

Eventually Wright overreached himself. The "choral" passages in the first two-thirds of the book are very effective, but the last part, especially the courtroom speeches of Bigger's "progressive" lawyer, Boris Max, breaks down into an expository coda, a series of awkwardly dramatized perspectives on the preceding action. As if this were not enough, Wright went on to write "How 'Bigger' Was Born," then *12 Million Black Voices*, and ultimately *Black Boy (American Hunger)*, in which, as the critic Robert Stepto has observed, he set out to "authenticate" *Native Son* (just as the selective reminiscences in "The Ethics of Living Jim Crow" served to authenticate the climate of terror in *Uncle Tom's Children*).

Younger black writers, from Ralph Ellison and James Baldwin to David Bradley, found Bigger Thomas a burden, an albatross around their necks, since this was not a black man they could identify with. Bradley shuddered at the thought of a Bigger Thomas living in his neighborhood. Ellison and Baldwin wondered why their mentor, who had opened a door for them to a large reading public, had not invested himself in a character as complex and subtle as Richard Wright. But even in his autobiographical writings, Wright aimed at something more elemental. Earlier black writers like James Weldon Johnson in *The Autobiography of an Ex-Colored Man*, Nella Larsen in *Quicksand* and *Passing*, and Langston Hughes in *The Ways of White Folks* had written about exceptional blacks—some light-skinned enough to pass, others educated and ambitious enough to belong to a cultural elite—who still come to grief on the shoals of prejudice, blind hatred, and their own conflicts of identity. Wright had little interest in the conundrums of W. E. B. Du Bois's talented tenth or the disappointments of the black middle class. "Well-to-do Negroes lived in a world that was almost as alien to me as the world inhabited by whites," he wrote in *Black Boy*.[8] Nor would he rest with documenting the miserable lot of the black poor, made worse by the Depression. Only after coming north, he recalls, could he begin to understand Negro life in America "not in terms of external events, lynchings, Jim Crowism, and the endless brutalities, but in terms of crossed-up feeling, of psychic pain."[9] Gaining distance from the world he had grown up in, he found something seething in himself that he was sure every black man shared, something incendiary from which genteel literature and white society had averted their eyes. This was not rage so much as an unspeakable inner tension more explosive than rage.

Bigger Thomas feels this tension in the poolroom scenes that originally opened the novel, when he and his friends are discussing plans to rob a white storekeeper. Here Wright demonstrates the dynamic of pressure and blockage, of fear turning into violence, that will take hold of Bigger's mind through all his dealings with the Daltons, through the two murders he commits and the flight and subsequent manhunt that leads to his capture. Wright in *Black Boy* recalls this unbearable tension from his own youth whenever he was directly confronted by white people. It drove him not to violence—in the South that would have been suicidal—but to his escape to the North. Like Bigger, he assumed an impenetrable mask in their presence, an inviolable detachment he had trouble discarding in the North, even with white people he could trust, who cared about him and treated him as a human being. Caught in a venial lie by some Jewish storekeepers he worked for, who treated him well, the young Wright digs himself in deeper and deeper until he leaves the job out of sheer embarrassment. Telling the truth seemed unthinkable; he's too uncomfortable, too suspicious to do that, even when he knows he could safely open up.

Bigger experiences whites not as individuals but as a completely alien entity. "To Bigger and his kind white people were not really people; they were a sort of great natural force, like a stormy sky looming overhead, or like a deep swirling river stretching suddenly at one's feet in the dark" (550). Here the dire flood that enveloped everyone in "Down by the Riverside" becomes a metaphor for undifferentiated danger, an alien force that threatens to engulf him. He needs to keep away from it, or shield himself when he comes too close. But even at a distance it instills a "tight morass of fear and shame that sapped at the base of his life" (551).

This becomes clear in the poolroom scenes, which give us an early intimation of how Bigger's fear and self-hatred flash out into murderous violence. No whites are nearby, only the *idea* of robbing a white man, just a plan, but this builds up a physical tension in Bigger, a tight knot in the muscles of his stomach. Pulling a knife and pressing it to his friend Gus's throat, he projects his own terror onto his friend, reducing him to a whimper. Unable to admit his fear, he comes within an inch of killing Gus, just to create a nasty scene that will ensure that the job doesn't come off. "Confidence could only come to him now through action so violent that it would make him forget."

Bigger becomes someone else when he half-knowingly murders Mary Dalton, who has toyed with him and inflamed him without really seeing him. He has worn a mask of indifference with the well-meaning Daltons and remained sullen and uncommunicative with Mary and her Communist boyfriend, Jan, when they tried to befriend him. Their clumsy attempts to put him at ease only make him more miserable. This token egalitarianism, a luxury of the rich and radical, heightens the shame of his poverty. His sexual attraction to Mary, which was largely suppressed in the original edition of 1940, seems so futile that he feels effaced in her presence. "He felt he had no physical existence at all, right then; he was something he hated, the badge of shame which he knew was attached to a black skin" (508).

Mary and Jan make love in the back seat of the car as he drives them around, nullifying his humanity as if he simply were not there, or not a real person. When Bigger takes the drunken girl home and puts her to bed, he is nearly overcome by the sheer physical proximity to her—it violates a deep racial taboo. Faced by the "white blur" of her blind mother in the doorway, he smothers Mary out of fear of being found in her room. He will be convicted of rape without having raped her and convicted of murder without having intended to kill her. In a paradoxical twist that makes the novel so original, he accepts responsibility for his deeper wishes as if they were symbolic acts, and feels strangely liberated by his crimes. *Native Son* becomes a novel about a man who is reborn.

Bigger's tension is dispelled by his terrible crimes; they become his armor against the world but also his mark on the world. He is now the

subject of lurid newspaper stories, the object of a vast manhunt, a figure of fear and the centerpiece of a stagy trial. Bigger's violence resolves
the conflict between who he is and how he is seen, "that constant sense
of wanting without having, of being hated without reason," as Wright
describes it in *American Hunger* (254). Bigger "had murdered and had created a new life for himself. It was something that was all his own, and it
was the first time in his life he had had anything that others could not
take from him. . . . He felt that all of his life had been leading to something like this. . . . The hidden meaning of his life—a meaning which others did not see and which he had always tried to hide—had spilled out."
(542) The novel is less about Bigger's deeds than about the meaning of
his life, which his deeds are meant to convey. It is intended to shock and
frighten readers just as Bigger's actions frighten the community.

Bigger's elation, his sense of being reborn, is an astonishing turn. It
thrusts Wright into strange fictional territory, in the footsteps of Nietzsche's critique of slave morality and Dostoyevsky's portrait of Raskol-
nikov in *Crime and Punishment*; of Leopold and Loeb and of Gide's *acte
gratuite*. It anticipates not only Sartre and Camus but the Norman Mailer
of "The White Negro" and the Franz Fanon who developed a theory,
endorsed by Sartre, of the purgatorial uses of violence for the colonial
subject. At the same time that he explored this new psychology, turning
rape and murder into virtual metaphors for the black man's condition,
Wright did not completely abandon a traditional sense of moral responsibility for the individual act. Rich, progressive, and hypocritical, the
Daltons are stick figures for whom the reader feels little sympathy—we
experience Bigger's fear more intensely than Mary's death or her parents'
grief. But Wright describes the dismemberment and burning of her body
in gruesome detail, just as one of his favorite writers, André Malraux, had
highlighted the sheer physical resistance of human flesh in *Man's Fate*. In
a brilliant stroke, Wright adds another crime to Bigger's ledger, his deliberate murder of his hapless girlfriend, Bessie Mears, immediately after he
has made love to her. This goes far to making Bigger despicable, setting a
limit to our identification with him.

"Love" is scarcely the right word for what Bigger does to Bessie. If
Bigger embodies the unbearable tension of the black male, Bessie stands
for the pathos and vulnerability of the black woman he needs yet victim-
izes. Her world is a round of hard work and misery, alleviated only by

drink. To Bigger, newly empowered by having killed, she is merely blind and limited, like his own benighted family. "He felt the narrow orbit of her life: from her room to the kitchen of the white folks was the farthest she ever moved." On Sunday afternoons, her only day off, she looks for fun, "something to make her feel she was making up for the starved life she led." For Bigger she is a target of opportunity, someone he uses to release his tension and supply moments of warmth: "She wanted liquor and he wanted her. So he would give her liquor and she would give him herself" (573–74). As Wright sees it, through the lens of his residual Marxism, liquor and fun to Bessie are what religion is to Bigger's mother, sheer palliatives, the opiates of the downtrodden.

Though the prosecution cares little about the murder of a black woman except to paint Bigger as a monster, Wright makes every effort to link the two crimes. Mary leads Bigger around against his will; *he* intimidates Bessie into doing his bidding. Bigger neither rapes Mary nor kills her deliberately, but he forces himself on Bessie and then kills her out of fear that she might give him away. Mary is in a drunken stupor when she dies; Bessie drinks to find oblivion, but also because Bigger plays on her weakness. For the prosecutor Mary's death is all that matters; for Wright, Bessie's death matters more. If the whole meaning of Bigger's life spills out in his acts of violence, the whole meaning of Bessie's life—her passivity, her lack of power over the circumstances of her life—spills out in her death.

One axis of the novel can be seen in pervasive images of fire and snow, heat and cold. Mary's body burns in the Daltons' own blazing furnace, which represents their social power and Bigger's inner turbulence. As the snow covers the city with a white blanket, Bessie freezes to death in the air shaft of an abandoned building, where Bigger has left her for dead after smashing her head in with a brick. As an actual person, now gravely wounded, she simply "did not figure in what was before him" (665). Dying under a symbolic blanket of snow, she is as much the victim of white domination as of black violence; both have rendered her helpless and hopeless. Nothing is more poignant in the book than her token resistance, her passive acceptance of her fate: as Bigger moves to enter her, "he heard her sigh, a sigh he knew, for he had heard it many times before; but this time he heard in it a sigh deep down beneath the familiar one, a sigh of resignation, a giving up, a surrender of something more than her body. . . . [N]ot a word, but a sound that gave forth a meaning of horror accepted" (663–64).

Bessie's pointless death makes Bigger a reprobate and gives him his only touch of remorse. Yet in the scheme of the novel, she died helpless while he will die free. This is the subject of the third part, "Fate." Beginning with Wright's friends and editors who saw *Native Son* in manuscript, readers have balked at this denouement. There is almost no action. A good deal of what does happen—scenes in Bigger's cell where the novel's whole cast of characters improbably assembles, the inquest in which Bessie's battered body is wheeled in, the speeches at the trial, contrasting the defense attorney's "progressive" rhetoric with the prosecutor's lurid demagoguery—fails to meet even the minimum standard of verisimilitude (as Wright himself tacitly acknowledged in "How 'Bigger' Was Born"). Some of this, especially the prosecutor's vile speech, is a regression to the agitprop writing of *Uncle Tom's Children*, and it shows how hard it was for Wright to create a convincing white character.

This material not only feels stagy but indicates to what extent Wright must have conceived the novel as a three-act play. Soon afterward he worked unhappily with the playwright Paul Green to adapt it for the stage, and years later, when he was far too old, he played Bigger in a cheaply produced film version shot in Buenos Aires. If nothing else, this shows Wright's identification with Bigger, including the Bigger who comes to understand the meaning of his life, as Wright himself thought *he* did in going north and becoming a writer. Separating himself from his well-meaning lawyer, who sees Bigger simply as a product of his environment, he says, "I didn't mean to kill! But what I killed for, I *am!*" (849). The lawyer—whose name, Max, associates him with Marx—recoils from Bigger's frank confrontation with death, for he is more at ease with Bigger as a symbol of his race and class than as an individual man. Wright's intuitive existentialism trumps his Marxism: Bigger's new sense of freedom empowers him to look death in the face.

Once I thought that the third section was simply a superfluous accumulation of commentary on a novel that had essentially ended. It is more accurate to say that another novel began supervening on the first, a novel about a man finding a new life. But it was layered awkwardly onto a more effective novel about a man in a mask, a man in a trap, a man exploding. Bigger's gradual enlightenment, his not always convincing new acceptance and understanding of himself, brings the latter part of the book closer to Ralph Ellison's *Invisible Man* than to a black version of *Studs Lonigan*, where it had begun. Bigger's determination to grasp what happened to him reflects Wright's desire to plumb the meaning of his own experience, which links *Native Son* to its autobiographical sequel, *Black Boy (American Hunger)*. "His crimes were known, but what he had felt before committing them would never be known," thinks Bigger. "The impulsion to try to tell was as deep as had been the urge to kill" (733). But this is the writer's motive, not Bigger's.

What Bigger cannot convincingly express, his Jewish lawyer Boris Max and the author try to say for him. Max's arguments were drastically cut for the first edition (then restored in 1991), but he sounds notes that Wright deemed vital to the novel. "Your Honor," says Max addressing the court, "remember that men can starve from lack of self-realization as much as they can from lack of bread! And they can *murder* for it, too!" (820). Murder, like rape, can be symbolic as well as literal. "He has murdered many times, but there are no corpses. . . . Every time he comes in contact with us, he kills! . . . *His very existence is a crime against the state!*" (821). This reflects something we have already seen: the dawning of Bigger's sense that he had somehow actually raped Mary, for "every time he felt as he had felt that night, he raped. . . . He committed rape every time he looked into a white face. . . . [I]t was rape when he cried out in hate deep in his heart as he felt the strain of living day by day" (658). This was not the rape for which he will be condemned.

Wright's reading of Bigger's mind is imprinted on the novel long before Max's interminable speeches. Bigger "had killed twice, but in a true sense it was not the first time he had ever killed. He had killed many times before, but only during the last two days had this impulse assumed the form of actual killing" (670). Strangely, he felt empowered by this, though he knew it would destroy him. "*He* had done this. *He* had brought all this about." Never before had he felt this sense of agency, or felt so fully alive. Even in desperate flight "he was living, truly and deeply, no matter what others might think, looking at him with their blind eyes. Never had he had the chance to live out the consequences of his actions" (669–70). Earlier his life had been "a strange labyrinth" to him, "a chaos," divided between what he daily confronted and what he felt. "Only under the stress of hate was the conflict resolved" (670).

The alternative to this hate, the alternative to rape and murder as Wright sees it, is Bigger's thwarted longing for a fully human life, for "that sense of fulness he had so often but inadequately felt in magazines and movies" (583). It confronts Bigger in the comfort and security of the Daltons' home, a state of mind he has never known. In his dreams of escape Bigger feels "a certain sense of power, a power born of a latent capacity to live" (598). Wright lends Bigger what must be his own "deep yearning for a sense of wholeness," which he feels even in the black religion and church music he despises. The last part of *Native Son* is Wright's attempt to take Bigger beyond hatred and violence, beyond race and poverty, "beyond category" (as Duke Ellington liked to put it), and to allow him to become, just before his death, a human being. Bigger's deepest regret at the end, foreshadowing Ellison's *Invisible Man*, is in the thought of going to his death "feeling and thinking that they didn't see me and I didn't see them" (845).

Wright had first created a Bigger who could shock the world into a visceral awareness of black pain and black rage. Combining introspection with social reportage, he turned him into a dire warning, an apocalyptic prophecy. Bigger is a great character but a generic one like "Mann" or "Black Boy," not exactly a flesh and blood human being. James Baldwin later complained that "we know as little about him when this journey is ended as we did when it began."[10] But he is more a vehicle than an individual: his rage and fear, his inner conflicts, his frustration and capacity for violence, are meant to plumb the black male psyche. Wright provides Bigger not only with his own racial awareness but with his literary ambition of assaulting his readers, getting under their skin. Before he is captured, Bigger imagines the impact of his crimes on the white public: he relishes "the keen thrill of startling them." "He wished that he could be an idea in their minds," that his gory deeds "could hover before their eyes as a terrible picture of reality which they could see and feel and yet not destroy" (565). This was the picture presented by *Native Son* itself, which so startled American readers in 1940.

But in a striking if not entirely believable turnabout, Wright ends with Bigger at peace with himself, beyond rage. "He was not stoop-shouldered now, nor were his muscles taut. He breathed softly, wondering about the cool breath of peace that hovered in his body. It was as though he were trying to listen to the beat of his own heart" (781). Facing execution "he had to weave his feelings into a hard shield of either hope or hate." This redeemed Bigger chooses hope, which Wright thinks could take him beyond race onto the terrain of a common humanity. Does this surprising turn stem from the remains of Wright's Marxism? Is he substituting his own dream of moving beyond race for the thinking of a character less articulate, less self-conscious than he is? "For the first time in his life he had gained a pinnacle of feeling upon which he could stand and see vague relations that he had never dreamed of." Bigger wonders: what if "that white looming mountain of hate were not a mountain at all, but people, people like himself, and like Jan"? Many readers have found this scarcely credible. In a review of Chester Himes's *Lonely Crusade*, Baldwin described Bigger as a man "gone to his death cell, inarticulate and destroyed by his need for identification and for revenge, and with only the faintest intimation in that twilight of what had destroyed him and of what his life might have been."[11] This may be an unlikely turn for the brutish Bigger, but it is just the self-knowledge Wright has in mind. Wright fuses a Marxist universalism that looks beyond race with a nascent existentialism of his own making, leading toward self-realization. Together they point *Native Son*, an otherwise dark and violent book, toward a surprisingly hopeful recognition of common humanity.

"How It Feels to Be Colored Me". Zora Unbound

If that was Wright's message, the book missed its mark. As a wake-up call describing how blacks lived in the North and how they really felt about whites, *Native Son* had tremendous impact, which continues to reverberate today. Bigger's graphic murders—and the bottled-up violence that pushes him close to the edge even before he kills—were frightening; his fear and flight, with which we cannot help identifying, felt overpoweringly real. But Wright's symbolic treatment of rape and murder as steps toward Bigger's full humanity touched a nerve more in existentialist Paris than in segregated, race-conscious America. Wright's literary progeny were both tough and tender: urban naturalists like Chester Himes and Willard Motley but also restive protégés like Ralph Ellison and Baldwin, who were drawn to his courageous truth telling and keen psychological penetration before rebelling against his angry example. But since the 1970s his most important rival—and now the most widely taught black writer in America—has been the one he most sharply attacked, Zora Neale Hurston. She responded to the young Wright's dismissive review of *Their Eyes Were Watching God* in *The New Masses* with a damning piece on *Uncle Tom's Children* in a more mainstream publication, the *Saturday Review*. Though there is surely room for more than one vision of the black experience in America, their differences have come to seem archetypal. As Hazel Rowley wrote in her biography of Wright in 2001, "the Hurston-Wright controversy continues to this day."[12]

Hurston's work was almost completely forgotten between the late 1940s and the early 1970s, when it was rediscovered by feminists. But as she exchanged salvos with Wright she was already a celebrated figure, one of the best-known black writers. Born in Alabama in 1891, a date she kept buried all her life, she grew up in the all-black town of Eatonville in central Florida; her father, a preacher, served three terms as the town's mayor. She dealt with her parents' courtship, her father's troubled ministry, his infidelities, and her mother's early death in her lyrical first novel, *Jonah's Gourd Vine* (1934), but her central subject, in both her fiction and her anthropological work, was the inimitable language, lore, humor, and folkways of the Eatonville Negroes among whom she had grown up.

Hurston had an amazing ear, as she noted that Wright did not—he tended to write dialogue in standard English and "correct" it later into colloquial speech—and the oral quality of her work tilts toward the poetic, not the naturalistic. Even as a child she dazzled visitors and townspeople with her ingratiating cleverness, polishing her talent for mimicry and storytelling. The same gifts helped make her perhaps the most colorful figure in the Harlem Renaissance; she was widely seen as a born performer, irresistible to white patrons but too impatient, too undisciplined ever to write very much.[13] Hurston's early admirers and patrons were legion. They included Annie Nathan Meyer, a founder of Barnard College, where Hurston was the only black student in the late 1920s; Alain Locke, who published an early story of hers ("Spunk") in the landmark anthology *The New Negro* (1925); Langston Hughes, with whom she wrote a play, *Mule Bone*, before they fell out bitterly; Fanny Hurst, the popular novelist who befriended her and hired her as an assistant, though her clerical skills were minimal; Franz Boas, who encouraged her anthropological work and wrote a preface to her *Mules and Men*; Charlotte Osgood

Mason, the wealthy and proprietary Park Avenue "Godmother" who supported Hurston, Locke, Hughes, and other Harlem Renaissance writers; Nancy Cunard, who published her work in her massive *Negro: An Anthology* (1934); Henry Allan Moe, head of the Guggenheim Foundation, which gave her fellowship support for ethnographic research; and many others, who were all charmed by her quick intelligence and vast command of southern Negro folklore and dialect.

One of Hurston's charges against Wright was that he was so obsessed with how black people's lives were dominated by whites, so determined to expose their core of hatred, fear, and powerlessness, that he paid little attention to how they lived among themselves, how they had evolved a rich, nurturing folk culture of their own, and, above all, how they actually spoke. Hurston blamed this on Wright's adherence to the Communist Party line on southern racism, but of course it was deeply ingrained in the fears he imbibed in his own upbringing. She begins her review by complaining that "this is a book about hatreds" and, after praising some of the writing, ends with the hope "that Mr. Wright will find in Negro life a vehicle for his talents." The gender difference is also one of the keys to their enduring rivalry. "There is lavish killing here," she writes, "perhaps enough to satisfy all male black readers." For her, Wright's parables of violent oppression and revenge scanted not only the internal culture of black people—their relations with each other but their responsibility for their own lives ("state responsibility for everything and individual responsibility for nothing, not even feeding one's self," she wrote).[14] Baldwin made the same charge more than a decade later, claiming that because Wright in *Native Son* had turned Bigger into a "social symbol," a prophecy of impending disaster, "a necessary dimension has been cut away, . . . the relationship that Negroes bear to one another, that depth of involvement and unspoken recognition of shared experience which creates a way of life."[15]

That "way of life" is what we call a culture; exploring it, especially from a woman's viewpoint, was the whole raison d'être of Hurston's fiction and ethnographic work. In an astonishing 1928 essay called "How It Feels to Be Colored Me"—a title that, but for its insouciant tone, its bubbling egotism, could have been plastered across Wright's collected works—Hurston claims she scarcely knew she was colored until her thirteenth year, when she was sent away from her all-black town after her mother's death to live with a brother in Jacksonville. But even when the presence of whites reminds her that she *is* black, and is treated differently, she insists, "I am not tragically colored." It is no source of sorrow, or protest, or any sense of inferiority; the deep sources of life, she feels, are within—she echoes Emerson here—and the only loss comes from being forced to feel any confining sense of race at all, something many black people do to themselves. "Sometimes, I feel discriminated against, but it does not make me angry. It merely astonishes me. How *can* anyone deny themselves the pleasure of my company! It's beyond me."[16]

These lines are typical of the exuberant, mischievous Zora of the Harlem Renaissance, the performing self who seemed larger than life.* Hurston did not imagine that her brimming self-confidence, her buoyant American optimism and individualism, would solve all our social problems. But she did feel that blacks, especially blacks "farthest down," had cultural resources that gave them surprising strength and vitality. Hurston and Wright could agree that black people lived behind a mask—behind a "veil," as Du Bois put it. She felt that poor people in general "are most reluctant at times to reveal that which the soul lives by. And the Negro, in spite of his open-faced laughter, his seeming acquiescence, is particularly evasive."[17] But where Wright saw hatred, fear, and rage behind the polite front, Hurston heard the intonations of a tremendous oral culture—competitive storytelling, resourceful folk knowledge, delicious gossip, outrageous boasting, silver-tongued preaching. The "culture of poverty," as Hurston saw it, was not a set of social pathologies but an organic body of common wisdom, a poetics of everyday life.

Wright's criticism of *Their Eyes Were Watching God* brings its differences with his own work into sharp relief. "Miss Hurston can write," he says, "but her prose is cloaked in that facile sensuality that has dogged Negro expression since the days of Phyllis Wheatley." Though *Native Son*, especially in its uncensored version, is daringly explicit about black male sexuality, even at the risk of confirming a racist stereotype, there was a deeply puritanical streak in Wright. Like many attracted to the Communist Party, including those who were drawn to its freewheeling sexual

---

* From Wright's point of view, the essay would exemplify how the Harlem writers, whom he disliked, played to whites, entertaining them while assuaging any guilt they might feel.

milieu, Wright saw sex and pleasure as political liabilities; like the consolations of religion, they siphoned off discontent and kept the masses docile. For whites the vicarious projection of black sexual freedom was at
once a naughty diversion and a hideously condescending form of primitivism; blacks represented the savage state from which they themselves
were barred by middle-class inhibition.

In the 1920s many whites were indeed drawn to the Harlem Renaissance writers, as they were enamored of jazz, for its "primitive" qualities:
raw energy, physical vitality, unguarded emotion, erotic freedom. (The
French adored jazz—and made a sensational cult of Josephine Baker—
for the same reason. Indeed, they saw American culture in general as an
escape from their own overrefined civilization, which smothered them
in moral hypocrisy.) It's also true that many black writers and performers
played to this appeal, as Hurston did in her vast and amusing repertoire
of Eatonville stories.

As a creature propelled by her own remarkable gifts, Hurston really
did feel free, but she did not feel in the least primitive. Stories of rural
black life were in vogue—by 1935 DuBose Heyward's *Porgy* had gone
in quick succession from a novel to a successful Broadway play to a
Gershwin folk opera—and among the Harlem writers she had the deepest roots in southern life and lore. To the politically committed Wright
this was little more than a minstrel show, a blackface entertainment.
"Miss Hurston *voluntarily* continues in her novel the tradition that was
forced upon the Negro in the theater, that is, the minstrel technique that
makes the 'white folks' laugh." In "How It Feels to Be Colored Me,"
Hurston had thrilled to her own powers, her performance, whatever the
cost had been: "Someone is always at my elbow reminding me that I am
the grand-daughter of slaves. It fails to register depression with me. . . .
Slavery is the price I paid for civilization, and the choice was not with
me. . . . No one on earth ever had a greater chance for glory. The world
to be won and nothing to be lost. . . . It is quite exciting to hold the center of the national stage with the spectators not knowing whether to
laugh or to weep" (827). Wright throws this back at her from the point
of view of an angry new generation: "Her characters eat and laugh and
cry and work and kill; they swing like a pendulum eternally in that safe
and narrow orbit in which America likes to see the Negro live: between
laughter and tears."[18]

Wright's criticism of Hurston was prefigured by his attack on the Harlem Renaissance writers in his 1936 manifesto "Blueprint for Negro Writing," a classic example of how the committed writers of the 1930s mocked the aesthetic values of their predecessors. These writers had tried to elevate the race and gain respect by showing that Negroes too could produce poems, novels, and plays—in short, a high culture. Wright depicts them as "prim and decorous ambassadors who went a-begging to white America.... [D]ressed in the knee-pants of servility, curtsying to show that the Negro was not inferior, that he was human, that he had a life comparable to that of other people."[19] But once Wright gets beyond ridiculing this appeal to whites, which he sees as shameful and humiliating, his essay takes a curious turn. Negro writing, at its best, he says, has rarely been "addressed to the Negro himself, his needs, his sufferings, his aspirations." Blacks have a culture of their own stemming mainly from "the Negro church" and "the folklore of the Negro people." He wonders why Negro writers, taking the high road of genteel art, have not exploited and tried to deepen this folk tradition, with its oral culture, which "embodies the memories and hopes of his struggle for freedom" and "the collective sense of Negro life in America" (198). Instead of this communal work through which they might have achieved "artistic communication between them and their people," they had "the illusion that they could escape through individual achievement the harsh lot of their race."

Hurston no doubt believed that she and her work were irreducibly individual. But the material she used was precisely what Wright recommends: Negro speech and the Negro church in *Jonah's Gourd Vine*, which concludes somewhat abruptly with a magnificent sermon that she herself had once heard preached; Negro folklore and the mores of Eatonville in *Mules and Men* and *Their Eyes Were Watching God*. Her best work reads like a response to Baldwin's later complaint against *Native Son* and Wright's own prescriptions for Negro writing. Wright himself did little with the folk culture he praises so eloquently, nor was his work primarily addressed to black people and their relations with each other. He too appealed mainly to white audiences, not to impress them but to throw down the gauntlet to them. The inner strengths of black life, the riches of its vernacular culture, largely pass him by. His "Blueprint" reads more like a manifesto for Hurston's work, or Ralph Ellison's, than for his own, since their books were enriched by the folkways of the black masses. Her subject was not the effects of racism but the inner life of the race, not the terrible lot of the rural black poor but the tang and flourish of their language and culture.

Wright was certainly on target in stressing the sensuality of Hurston's novel, which she conveyed through lush imagery and a boldly romantic, iconoclastic story. As Hurston's insightful biographer Robert Hemenway was one of the first to show, *Their Eyes Were Watching God* develops more along a symbol-laden axis of metaphor than through the linear thread of its plot. The basic narrative of the discontented woman locked in an unsatisfying marriage or simply looking for love and fulfillment was something Hurston inherited from works of the 1920s by Sherwood Anderson (*Winesburg, Ohio*), Sinclair Lewis (*Main Street*), Willa Cather (*A Lost Lady, My Mortal Enemy*), Nella Larsen (*Quicksand*), and even Faulkner in *As I Lay Dying*, with its echoes of *The Scarlet Letter*. The women in these works were restive, thwarted, sexually unrealized. Underlying their stories was not only an implied feminism that saw marriage as a trap, even a form of servitude, but something deeper, a vitalism influenced by the vogue of Nietzsche, Freud, and D. H. Lawrence, a cultural fascination with the new psychoanalysis. It underscored every individual's right to personal realization and looked to sex and love, to the overthrow of Victorian cant and repression, as the royal road to happiness. The blossoming pear tree that is the emblem of Janie Crawford's sexual awakening becomes the grail she seeks in her search for a full life. It recurs as a leitmotif in each of her relationships with men.

Hurston's introduction of this image echoes Keats and Lawrence in its breathtaking sensuality, yet it is daringly explicit and vivid in describing this sexual yearning from a woman's point of view:

> She was stretched on her back beneath the pear tree soaking in the alto chant of the visiting bees, the gold of the sun and the panting breath of the breeze when the inaudible voice of it all came to her. She saw a dust-bearing bee sink into the sanctum of a bloom; the thousand sister-calyxes arch to meet the love embrace and the ecstatic shiver of the tree from root to tiniest branch creaming in every blossom and frothing with delight. So this was a marriage! She had been summoned to behold a revelation.[20]

At sixteen Janie, her senses now fully alive, feels a mingled sadness and longing, a hunger for life: "Oh to be a pear tree—*any* tree in bloom! With kissing bees singing of the beginning of the world! . . . Where were the singing bees for her?" (25). Certainly not with the shiftless boy who plants the first kiss, or with the hardworking farmer whom her grandmother, frightened by her sexual awakening, presses her to marry. Born into slavery, the old woman has learned how the explosive chemistry of sex and male dominance leaves many women defenseless, including herself and Janie's mother, who ran off after she was raped and bore a child. In her mind, the only protection against the caprice of passion and abandonment is not love but marriage, "a house bought and paid for and sixty acres uh land on de big road" (41). Otherwise, "de nigger woman is de mule uh de world so fur as Ah can see" (29). "Dis love!" she says. "Dat's de very prong all us black women gits hung on" (41).

Nanny's view, with its hard-won caution and cynicism, forms the prologue against which Janie's fate is played out; the old woman speaks the bitter lessons of experience that must be understood and then unlearned.* For Nanny marriage is a worthwhile bargain, a social and economic shield that puts the woman in a "high chair"; sex and love merely ensure that she will be used and eventually discarded. But Janie, without quite knowing it, wants happiness, not security, an inner ripening, not status. She waits patiently for love to blossom, but neither of her first two marriages satisfies the inner woman. The prospect of one of them seems to be "desecrating the pear tree" (28); she marries the second although "he did not represent sun-up and pollen and blooming trees, but he spoke for far horizon. He spoke for change and chance" (50). Janie, like her ambitious creator, longs for the immediacy of true romance but also the more distant prospect of self-transformation. All this unfolds in Hurston's wonderfully orchestrated images.

After being initially attentive to her, Janie's first husband, Logan Killicks, treats her like the proverbial mule, a beast of burden. Her second husband, Joe Starks, who helps found Eatonville and becomes its mayor and principal storekeeper, puts her on a pedestal, which also keeps her in her place, though it's an elevated one. He tries to control how she dresses,

---

* Ralph Ellison borrowed this strategy with the dying grandfather's cynical advice to the young protagonist to live a double life at the beginning of *Invisible Man*.

how and when she speaks. Repeatedly, he humiliates her in public, taunting her about her age and looks, until "the spirit of the marriage left the bedroom and took to living in the parlor." Soon "the bed was no longer a daisy-field for her and Joe to play in. It was a place where she went and laid down when she was sleepy and tired." In short, "she wasn't petal-open anymore with him" (111). When he dies, deeply bitter at her for challenging him, she plays the role of the bereaved widow but is inwardly unmoved. "Inside the expensive black folds were resurrection and life. . . . She sent her face to Joe's funeral, and herself went rollicking with the springtime across the world" (136–37). Only her third husband, the much younger Tea Cake, allows her to open up and bloom, kindling her sexuality into a fierce passion yet also treating her instinctively like an equal, a vital, independent human being.

Each of these motifs—the blossoming pear tree that represents her vital inner flame; the "high chair" that stands for protection and acquired social status (married to mayor Joe, Janie "slept with authority"); the mule, half beast, half legend, degraded but indestructible, the least common denominator of ordinary humanity; and the horizon, introduced in the book's opening lines as the ultimate goal of a rich and complete existence—is developed musically as a set of themes and variations, sometimes in concert with each other. Nanny pushes Janie toward the "high chair" of security over the will-o'-the-wisp of sexuality embodied in the pear tree, with its seductive promise of natural fruition. "She was borned in slavery time," as Janie later realizes, "when folks, dat is black folks, didn't sit down anytime dey felt lak it. . . . Dat's whut she wanted for me—don't keer whut it cost. Git up on uh high chair and sit dere." Janie achieves Nanny's goal with her marriage to Joe, a "big voice" in his world, a man who radiated authority. "But Pheoby," she tells her friend, "Ah done nearly languished tuh death up dere" (172).

Hurston plays the same changes around the image of the horizon, which she had introduced at the outset as the locus of "every man's wish" (9). Instead, by following her grandmother's advice, she found herself in a series of traps, as if they were plots to remind her of human limitations. "Nanny had taken the biggest thing God ever made, the horizon—for no matter how far a person can go the horizon is still way beyond you— and pinched it in to such a little bit of a thing that she could tie it about her granddaughter's neck tight enough to choke her" (138). The horizon, the pear tree, and the high chair are further linked by the inside/outside dichotomy. Instead of living the split between the socially sanctioned role—being the obedient granddaughter, the proper wife, the widowed woman who merely "sent her face to the funeral"—and her own feelings, Janie longs for a unity of seeming and being that eludes most people, whose tongues wag with envy when they see it. Instead of immuring herself in the show of widowhood, she feels that "mourning oughtn't tuh last no longer'n grief" (143). She looks inward for the treasure buried or tarnished by her first two marriages. "She had found a jewel down inside herself and she had wanted to walk where people could see her and gleam it around. But she had been set in the market-place to sell. Been set for still-bait" (138). Nanny has turned her into a poor black version of Edith Wharton's Lily Bart, in *The House of Mirth*, a woman up for bids in the marriage market. Only with Tea Cake, working together down in the muck of the Everglades, can she "show her shine" (139).

Married to Tea Cake, Janie reenacts the social descent Hurston herself had mapped and lived out in her writing. Just as Hurston had gone back to Eatonville for her ethnographic research, then carried it over into fiction flush with folklore and dialect, Janie abjures the social status of the wealthy, respectable widow, first by taking up with a much younger man, then by basking in an erotic and romantic dream, and finally by descending physically to a life of difficult labor among ordinary people amid the mud of the swamp. Hurston based the novel on her own brief love affair with a younger man; the whole second half of the book is drenched in an older woman's pride in her beauty, her personal freedom, and her inalienable right to grasp life by the horns, even in the face of social censure.

Working alongside her young husband and the seasonal workers picking beans in the Everglades, Janie finds happiness in the communal warmth and rich poetic speech that envelop her. When she first meets him, she sees that "he could be a bee to a blossom—a pear tree blossom," but she remains wary. She knows stories of foolish widows exploited and abandoned by young lovers. She confronts him with their difference in age—she is forty, he no more than twenty-five—but his honied speech wins her over. "Ah done thought all about dat and tried tuh struggle aginst it," he tells her, "but it don't do me no good. De thought uh mah youngness don't satisfy me lak yo' presence do" (159–60). He comes to her in the morning so that she can know him not simply as a lover but as a person. "Ah see yuh needs tuh know mah daytime feelings. Ah can't sense yuh intuh it at night." (161) When Janie turns jealous about a much younger woman down on the muck, Tea Cake tells her, "Whut would Ah do wid dat lil chunk of a woman wid you around? . . . You'se something tuh make uh man forget tuh git old and forget tuh die" (206). His feeling for her is inescapable, an opening to life: "You got de keys to de kingdom" (165).

Radiating an attraction that would be hard to counterfeit, Tea Cake's captivating language reassures Janie in just the way the novel's rich dialect and lush imagery stroke and seduce the reader. "Listenin' tuh dat kind uh talk," says Janie at the end, "is jus' lak openin' yo' mouth and lettin' de moon shine down yo' throat" (285). The dense underbrush of her dialogue, with its phonetic spelling, can initially be a barrier for some readers. (My students testify to this.) Once they yield to it, though, they enter a different world, at once rich and strange. The reader's descent from the literary to the colloquial parallels Janie's (and Hurston's) reversion from the genteel to the "primitive." Like so many modern classics, *Their Eyes Were Watching God* is a journey through the lower depths.

When Hurston wrote this book, the Harlem Renaissance was already defunct, done in by economic needs and the new social themes of the Depression, but the novel brilliantly redeems the fascination with the primitive, the dream of downward mobility, the *nostalgie de la boue* that marked the work of these and other twenties writers and artists. This vision, however, was grounded in an appeal to authenticity that could turn into a romantic dream of violence, a rejection of civilization. But *Their Eyes Were Watching God* is no crude idealization of the unspoiled state of nature or the sterling virtues of the simple and the poor. Just as Hurston ultimately broke off with her younger lover when he felt threatened by her career, Janie must kill Tea Cake, bitten by a rabid dog, when he loses his mind and turns on her. This has sometimes been seen as a hasty resolution of the plot, but it may be the novel's most brilliant turn.

A fierce hurricane strikes the Everglades, as if to show that this idealized tropical paradise, like nature itself, has a dark and dangerous side entirely out of our control. In the course of the ensuing flood, Janie and Tea Cake must flee. A mad dog threatens Janie but actually bites Tea Cake when he bravely rescues her. His madness, though it was contracted in this loving, self-sacrificing way, indicates that he too has his dark side—

jealous, irrational, violent. Tea Cake has taught Janie to shoot, and when he tries to kill her she shoots him. His friends, who made up such a supportive black folk community, turn on her crudely for this deed, but she is exonerated by a white court.

Hurston evokes this wild, ungovernable side of nature with the same eloquence with which she conjured up its potential for fruition and erotic transcendence. When the hurricane comes up, the poor blacks on the muck know they're in the grip of a larger force, pitiless and impersonal. The storm creates a different kind of community, threatened and vulnerable, as those in its path try to read meaning into the assault of the elements:

> The wind came back with triple fury, and put out the light for the last time. They sat in company with the others in other shanties, their eyes straining against crude walls and their souls asking if He meant to measure their puny might against His. They seemed to be staring at the dark, but their eyes were watching God.

Outside, in a swirl of wind and water, fish and animals, God seems to be reenacting Noah's flood, but arbitrarily, without any clear path to survival. People can only try to fathom it. Nature has overturned the human order, taken its revenge. "As soon as Tea Cake went out pushing wind in front of him, he saw that the wind and water had given life to lots of things that folks think of as dead and given death to so much that had been living things. Water everywhere. Stray fish swimming in the yard" (236). Later, when Tea Cake is pressed into service to collect and bury corpses—caskets for whites, quicklime and mass burial for blacks—he finds the victims stunned by the inscrutable power that has overtaken them. "Some bodies with calm faces and satisfied hands. Some dead with fighting faces and eyes flung wide open in wonder. Death had found them watching, trying to see beyond seeing" (252).

This motif of "watching" is Hurston's last and most resonant metaphor. She had introduced it in the opening sentence, with people watching distant ships on the horizon, vessels carrying all their human wishes. She complicates it repeatedly with a chorus of watchers who observe Janie disapprovingly all through the novel—when she first returns to town after Tea Cake's death, when she joins him on the muck, when she sits in court accused of killing him. As Richard Wright complained about earlier black writers, Janie, like her creator, pursues her destiny as an individual, in the teeth of these faultfinding watchers, who make up a social consensus deformed by envy, timidity, and conformity. Hurston too, for all her generous patrons and her own devil-may-care persona, felt under the eye of these censorious watchers. Gossiping maliciously, taking pleasure enviously in her troubles, they sit in judgment over her, and the novel is her proud apologia.

Hemenway, Hurston's biographer, usefully summarizes various criticisms of her anthropological work in *Mules and Men* for avoiding politics and racism, for idealizing the folk culture of Eatonville from her childhood but making no reference to contemporary atrocities perpetrated on blacks in the South. These included the sensational trial of the Scottsboro boys in 1931 and a well remembered 1920 riot and lynching not far from Eatonville itself. After criticizing *Their Eyes Were Watching God*, Richard Wright sketched an unforgettable picture of these horrors in *Uncle Tom's Children*. Even her former patron Alain Locke, in a brief notice that enraged her more than Wright's review, urged her to take up "political and social document fiction," something that never attracted her interest.

But Hurston's work on folklore was anything but a carryover from the individualistic 1920s. Even before the cultural policy of the Popular Front was unveiled by the Left in 1935, ethnographers and musicologists like Charles Seeger and Alan Lomax were trawling the rural communities of the South for folk songs, legends, dialects, and other oral traditions. The dire economic conditions of the Depression led not only to a political concern for the poor and destitute but to a cultural interest in their lives and traditions. Both as novelist and as anthropologist, Hurston was in the vanguard of this populist turn, which was first frowned upon but later adopted by political intellectuals on the left. By 1941, with the text and photographs in *12 Million Black Voices*, even Richard Wright belatedly contributed to this cultural shift, which he had actually praised five years earlier in his "Blueprint for Negro Writing."

Wright's focus on the bitter racial divide between blacks and whites would seem to make *Native Son* the antithesis of *Their Eyes Were Watching God*. But the arc of the two novels is similar enough to suggest that he may have been influenced, almost in spite of himself, by Hurston's greatest book. Throughout *Native Son* Bigger is haunted by something denied to him, a sense of the fullness of life. He feels "a certain sense of power, a power born of a latent capacity to live." This is the intimation that Janie receives from the blossoming pear tree. Early on, both characters are divided between what they feel and what is demanded of them, the social face they must put on. In both novels they move from alienation to agency, to a fuller, more undivided sense of identity, and both must kill along the way. For both of them, the way down is the way up: they achieve transcendence not through obedience or respectability but by way of a downward mobility, through scorned acts of violation or transgression.

Janie is not truly a killer like Bigger, but she can be ruthless in pursuit of the authentic life that eludes her. Like Bigger, she moves from confusion to determination, from other people's plans for her to her own. She abandons her first husband without a qualm, humiliates her second husband by publicly exposing his loss of manhood, and cruelly forces him to face up to his impending death. In effect, in the name of a implacable honesty, she finishes him off just as she will later have to kill Tea Cake. We may recall that Hurston's two great early stories, "Spunk" and "Sweat," are both revenge fables ending in violent death. In one a hardworking wife turns the tables on her errant, abusive husband, killing him with the rattlesnake he hoped would make short work of her. In the other, the ghost of a betrayed husband takes gruesome revenge on the man who stole his wife and took his life. The buoyant atmosphere of these ersatz folktales takes on a defiant feminist coloring in *Their Eyes Were Watching God*. The sense of power, the fullness of being that Janie achieves, is not so different from the authentic humanity that Bigger feels for the first time after he kills and is publicly excoriated and condemned. Wright saw this breakthrough, as he had seen Bigger's early misery, in psychological terms; Hurston saw it in naturalistic terms reflected in her images of blossoming and fruition. Her husband Joe is a "big voice" in his community but gradually turns empty inside. Janie finds happiness by being in tune with nature, even with the price it exacts and the terrors it brings.

"Live all you can—it's a mistake not to," says one of Henry James's characters, delivering the message of *The Ambassadors*. Hurston's novel concludes with the same do-it theme, a Lawrentian credo of living life fully, to the hilt. It flies in the face of all "political" responses to the Depression or to America's racial divisions. It emphasizes the experiences of individuals, not the grievances of the group. It puts its faith in personal courage and adventure. "It's uh known fact," Janie tells her friend Pheoby, "you got tuh *go* there tuh *know* there. Yo' papa and yo' mama and nobody else can't tell yuh and show yuh. Two things everybody's got tuh do fuh theyselves. They got tuh go tuh God, and they got tuh find out about livin' fuh theyselves" (285). Typically, Hurston realizes this by reprising the novel's opening image. "Ah done been tuh de horizon and back and now Ah kin set heah in mah house and live by comparisons. Dis house ain't so absent of things lak it used tuh be befo' Tea Cake come along" (284). Having been to the mountaintop with Tea Cake, Janie can return home and live contentedly. On this lyrical note the novel ends:

> Of course he wasn't dead. He could never be dead until she herself had finished feeling and thinking. The kiss of his memory made pictures of love and light against the wall. Here was peace. She pulled in her horizon like a great fish-net. Pulled it from around the waist of the world and draped it over her shoulder. So much of life in its meshes! She called in her soul to come and see. (286)

PART 2

SUCCESS *and* FAILURE

Beyond the American Dream

Success Myths and Depression Realities

AS WE HAVE SEEN, THE DEPRESSION drew unprecedented attention to the once invisible America inhabited by the poor—to the warped lives in all the suffocating ghettoes, past and present; to destitute tenant farmers, cultivating the depleted soil; to migrant families and itinerant children, and to their ramshackle Hoovervilles, which caricatured the very idea of home and shelter. Caroline Bird goes so far as to insist, with some hyperbole, that "the

Depression did not depress the conditions of the poor. It merely publicized them. The poor had been poor all along. It was just that nobody had looked at them."[1] Depression culture provided a way of paying attention. It changed the subject for thinking people concerned about what was happening to American lives.

But the economic collapse that squeezed the poor also seriously damaged the lives of the middle class and even of the rich, who, because they had already enjoyed so much of the promise of American life, had more to lose, including their self-respect. As Robert and Helen Lynd wrote of Muncie, Indiana, in 1937,

> While nearly every family in Middletown has met reverses of sorts in the depression, for a considerably greater proportion of the working class these reverses have not been the novel experience they have been to the business class. The latter do not have so much habituation to living close to sudden shattering changes like unemployment, and their personal identifications with the big-symbol world of "Progress" and "Opportunity" have in the past been more continuous and confident.[2]

This is somewhat patronizing, for it underestimates how much the members of the working class had to lose; with long-term unemployment, they had no cushion, nothing to fall back on. Theirs was a dilemma of survival, not status, a fear of homelessness and even starvation.

"Fear was the great leveler of the Great Depression," writes T. H. Watkins.

> It haunted the dreams of the African-American sharecropper in the South who held a fistful of barren dust in his hand and wondered what the system would do now to cheat him and his family of life. It stalked the middle-class white merchant in Idaho who had seen decades of work destroyed when his once-friendly banker coldly forced him into bankruptcy. It whispered terror into the ear of the Mexican-American foundry worker in Detroit who had put his future in the hands of the *coyote* who brought him north from Mexico into this strange cold place and who now found his job had vanished. Fear shattered all the fine Anglo-Saxon certitudes of the Great Plains farm

wife who watched black clouds of dust roll up on the edge of the horizon and knew that her dreams would soon be sucked up into that boiling mass.

Worse still, the Depression seemed to have no visible end. "I thought it was going to be forever and ever and ever," said a Chicago schoolteacher. "That people would always live in fear of losing their job, you know, fear."[3] Like many others who belonged tenuously to the middle class, my father, who worked for a middleman in the clothing industry, kept his small paycheck throughout the Depression but, as he told me much later, was never free of the anxiety that he would lose his job.

The specter for the middle class, Caroline Bird writes, was a pervasive "fear of falling": "Middle-class horror stories of the Depression run to the humiliation of 'coming down in the world.' One woman remembers the first morning her husband ever put overalls on to go to work. Another woman remembers pawning her engagement ring. A man remembers putting his hand five times on the knob of the door of the relief office before getting the courage to open it."[4] To many who believed that the United States was essentially a middle-class nation, a land of progress and opportunity in which everyone could *become* middle class, the Depression not only challenged America's economy and its political system, but also undermined the central myths and beliefs on which the system was founded.

In some ways these beliefs were well founded. Through much of American history, some avenues of progress and opportunity were readily available. My own parents and grandparents came here from the shtetls of the Ukraine and the small cities of southern Poland in search of just such opportunities, for their children if not for themselves. The offspring of southern European peasants and Confederate slaves migrated for the same reasons, but prejudice and discrimination, though it also affected Catholics and Jews, made life even more difficult for people with brown or red or yellow skin. Nevertheless, despite racial exclusions, nativist prejudice, and sometimes vile working conditions, there was cheap, abundant land as well as industrial work in an expanding economy. The labor could be backbreaking, the working hours appalling, but the social mobility was real.

In theory (and often in practice too), America was born of the secular pluralism of the Enlightenment and the revolutionary ideal of the career

open to talents, not simply birth or wealth. Since it had no hereditary aristocracy, since its class structure was porous, America loved to imagine
that it had no classes. "The United States was never a feudal nation," said
one editorial in a Muncie newspaper at the height of the Depression, to
explain why no revolution could ever occur on these shores. "As a result,
while some became very rich and others very poor, the sovereign authority rested with a great middle class, whom we like to term typical Americans. . . . It is from the children of these middle-class families that our
industrial and political leaders have come. . . . So long as the United States
eschews class division and maintains this great middle-class America, we
shall be free of such troubles as now beset unhappy Spain" (*Middletown in
Transition*, 446).

Another editorial insisted that, in a sense, everyone in America was
"working class," since our rich work hard too, and our poor, if industri-
ous enough, can eventually become rich.

> In the United States . . . every man has worked who had the ambition
> and the opportunity to do so. There has been no class of idle rich.
> The average industrialist has put in as many hours as the salaried
> man or wage earner, and he often points with pride to the number
> of jobs he has been able to afford for others through the effort of his
> own thrift, intelligence, and industry.
>
> Abraham Lincoln put it well when he said: "There is no perma-
> nent class of hired laborers amongst us. Twenty-five years ago I was
> a hired laborer. The hired laborer of yesterday labors on his own
> account today, and will hire others to labor for him tomorrow."
>
> Here is embodied the true American principle of progress. It is in
> recognition of such a principle that we have builded the greatest eco-
> nomic empire ever known to man, in a little more than a century
> and a half. (*Middletown in Transition*, 447)

A timeless, nakedly exposed quality of traditional Americana informs
these documents. (The deliberate archaism of "builded" in the final sentence is especially revealing.) But it's hard to ignore the defensive tone
that belongs specifically to the Depression, when this optimistic view of
mobility and America's economic destiny was under siege as never before.
The editorials proceed from naive professions of faith to attacks on those

who preach class consciousness and the "redistribution of wealth through increasingly high taxes," on the Russian model. They were reacting to the New Deal by reasserting older ideals of individual opportunity that were undergoing their most severe challenge.

A great deal has already been written about the documentary impulse in the 1930s, the widespread effort to examine people's real lives to show how they were coping with adverse conditions that seemed unprecedented. But the Depression also challenged key tenets of the American ideology. Longstanding beliefs were called into question, especially the myth of success enshrined in the notion of the American Dream. The thirties was the first period in which the phrase "the American Dream" was commonly used, just when its premise of limitless opportunity and economic abundance seemed suddenly in doubt. There had been many earlier recessions and even depressions in the American economy, but none had lasted so long and cut so deep—and, above all, none exerted the immense psychological impact of the Great Depression. The Depression weakened many Americans' most common assumptions: that reverses in the business cycle were brief and temporary, that jobs would always be available to those willing to work, that businessmen were the oracles and seers of society, that the younger generation would always be able to come up in the world and do better than its parents.[5]

The roots of these convictions have been studied exhaustively by cultural historians. The success myth goes back to the Puritan belief in work as a secular calling and in wealth as an outward manifestation of inner grace. In his widely read *Autobiography*, and in works like *Poor Richard's Almanack*, "The Way to Wealth," and "Advice to a Young Tradesman," Benjamin Franklin secularized this notion of a calling even further, moving toward the ideal of the self-made man. Franklin's own rise from poverty and obscurity to greatness was the stuff of legend, which many of his readers transformed into a fairy tale that stressed wealth as the only index of success. Franklin's "Advice to a Young Tradesman" was written on his own retirement from business to a life devoted to science and public service, but it seemed to embody a simple faith in the efficacy of character, cunning, and persistence to achieve riches: "In short, the way to wealth, if you desire it, is as plain as the way to market. It depends chiefly on two words, *industry* and *frugality*; that is, waste neither *time* nor *money*, but make the best use of both."[6] The great sociologist Max Weber made

Franklin his key exhibit in establishing the link between the Protestant ethic and the spirit of capitalism.

Despite his importance in propagating this myth of open advancement, Franklin was not the sole inventor of the self-made man, nor did he limit his notion of self-improvement to the work of the entrepreneur. Its growth in the nineteenth century, when hundreds of writers, preachers, and lecturers expounded the gospel of success, was deeply rooted in American individualism, in popular religion, in highly simplified versions of Emersonian "self-reliance," and, above all, in the realities of a growing capitalist economy. A nation shifting from an agrarian to an industrial economy, from a rural to an urban society—a nation whose class lines were fluid and whose official faith was populist and democratic—provided the material base for an ethic of competitive individualism.

The catchy, formulaic titles of Horatio Alger's novels tell the whole story: *Struggling Upward, Do and Dare, Fame and Fortune, Strive and Succeed, Luck and Pluck, Bound to Rise.* These novels, published between 1867 and 1899, were the epic material of the Gilded Age, not a realistic portrayal of social change but a richly developed metaphor for what was happening in the industrial economy, which was expanding aggressively. As John Cawelti points out in his *Apostles of the Self-made Man*, Alger himself knew little of the immense concentrations of economic power that were building up in the late nineteenth century. His economic model still belongs to an older world of small business.[7] The world of Frank Norris's muckraking novel *The Octopus*—the world of railroad barons, powerful monopolies, and industrial giants—was utterly foreign to him. But the myth of individual opportunity he helped propagate was the perfect ideology of an era of production and laissez-faire expansion, precisely the myth that the Depression would later bring into question.

Foreign observers and jaundiced American intellectuals were always fond of describing success as the religion of American life. William James once said, "The exclusive worship of the bitch-goddess Success is our national disease." The German economist Werner Sombart, with a dose of European condescension, noted: "The life ideal of the Americans is not found in the pleasurable development of self, nor in the beautiful harmony of a well-rounded life, but only in 'getting ahead.'"[8] The notion of the self-made man, however, had originally been a democratic ideal, a dream of social mobility—and even of *Kultur*—not simply for a small elite but for the common man. As Richard Huber comments, "the poor boy who made good was a powerful weapon to fight a haughty European air of social and artistic superiority." Thus, "the Jeffersonian concept of leadership based on an aristocracy of virtue and talents was beaten down by a Jacksonian belief that anyone could rule."[9] This common-man, log-cabin-to-the-White-House ideal reached its apogee in the career and the subsequent mythology of Abraham Lincoln. It was only after the Civil War that the self-made man became virtually synonymous with the businessman. As the political and cultural aspects of this ideal—the model of the great statesman, the great writer, the great orator—began to diminish, the myth took on a strongly conservative, even philistine coloring; it became a defense of the status quo, a way of blaming the victim, the loser. This was the heyday of Social Darwinism and the influence of Herbert Spencer, who coined the term "the survival of the fittest." In the ruthless, competitive climate of the Gilded Age, the idea of success hardened into a Darwinian formula that condemned the poor as either lazy or inferior. This moral translation of Manifest Destiny identified success with virtue, with character, and with individual effort.

In the large body of success literature in the late nineteenth century, a remarkable proportion of writers and propagandists had begun as clergymen.[10] According to the tireless Matthew Hale Smith, a onetime minister who became a lecturer and Wall Street journalist, "Whoever writes the history of our merchant, mechanical, or agricultural life, must write the history of religion." Smith himself gave a Franklinesque description of the road to achievement: "Industry, honesty, perseverance, sticking to one thing, invariably lead to success in any reputable calling."[11] At the height of the post–Civil War fascination with success, Smith published books like *Twenty Years among the Bulls and Bears of Wall Street* (1870) and *Successful Folks* (1878). Another clergyman, Wilbur F. Crafts, became the would-be sociologist of the success phenomenon. In 1883 he published *Successful Men of To-day and What They Say of Success*, in which he polled hundreds of distinguished leaders on the keys to fame, fortune, and achievement. Crafts's secular oracles gave an impeccably moral coloring to the quest for worldly goods. They preached the unlimited capacity of the individual and laid almost a divine sanction on personal effort. As Franklin Carter, the president of Williams College, wrote to Crafts, "Every man [is] the architect of his own fortune. . . . No, I will take that back. . . . God makes capacity, man makes character." "You cannot dream yourself into a character, you must forge yourself one."[12] This was the material for thousands of sermons, commencement addresses, newspaper editorials, and popular lectures like Russell Conwell's *Acres of Diamonds*, which the Baptist minister and philanthropist, who founded Temple University, delivered more than six thousand times, to enormous acclaim, between the 1870s and the 1920s.

"I say that you ought to get rich, and it is your duty to get rich," Conwell told his audiences. "Money is power, and you ought to be reasonably ambitious to have it. You ought because you can do more good with it than you could without it." He told them that they didn't have to become adventurers and cross the world in search of wealth: their own society, their own city, their own backyard, was the perfect place to build a fortune. "Never in the history of the world did a poor man without capital have such an opportunity to get rich quickly and honestly as he has now in our city."[13] In a rough-and-tumble era when large numbers of ambitious men were given over to the unbridled, sometimes cutthroat pursuit of wealth and power, clergymen and publicists like Smith, Crafts, and Conwell gave this quest an exemplary moral tone, an aura of duty defined by the noble "stewardship of wealth" rather than the nasty Darwinian struggle for survival. Despite its trappings of social science and opinion research, Crafts's book fed the self-help mania of a period of social and economic mobility, which rewarded some with great fortunes but punished others with unspeakable miseries, the by-products of progress. Crafts's book belonged to the busy culture of popular biography and soothsaying, which cast the blessings of morality and secular grace, even divinity, on the yearning for worldly success.

As in the many mythmaking biographies of the period—Horatio Alger himself wrote three, on Lincoln, Garfield, and Daniel Webster—Crafts's subjects were models for emulation, idols of the laissez-faire mentality, like the best-selling Lee Iacoccas and Donald Trumps of our own time. During the period between the Civil War and the stock market Crash, the respected figure of the businessman was the major icon of popular envy and imitation, the shining example of competitive triumph that was also wise, ethical, and beneficial to society. This is the faith that still echoes thinly, unconfidently, in those editorials in the Muncie heartland of 1937. The need to restore "confidence" was a universal theme of the early Depression years, starting with Herbert Hoover, who kept insisting that "conditions" were "fundamentally sound" and the effects of the Crash were largely a problem of morale. Advertising agencies encouraged more promotion by insisting that the Depression was mainly a *spending* problem: worried consumers had simply become too tightfisted. According to Roland Marchand, to encourage businesses to advertise, they "preferred to portray depression consumers not as impoverished or unemployed but as hoarders who resisted spending their money."[14]

The other side of the confidence problem was the equally universal theme of fear, most famously articulated in Roosevelt's confidence-building 1933 inaugural address: "First of all, let me assert my firm belief that the only thing we have to fear is fear itself—nameless, unreasoning, unjustified terror." This fear had reached a climax in the virtual collapse of the economy in the four months between the 1932 election and FDR's inauguration in early March, culminating in the bank crisis, which had been building for two years and is today considered the linchpin of the Depression, even more than the stock market Crash. "In Hoover's last days in office, the old order tottered on the brink of disaster," notes Leuchtenburg, and by inauguration day thirty-eight states had closed their banks.[15] An early (and relatively conservative) member of FDR's Brains Trust, Raymond Moley, later likened the whole Depression to a bank crisis: "A Depression is much like a run on the bank. It's a crisis of confidence. People panic and grab their money."[16] This historical overview is too lofty and olympian, too insensitive to the real human lives that were at stake in people's fears. A more apt psychological analogy was made by one observer in the *New York Times* in 1932, who likened the mood of the time to the depressive phase of the manic-depressive cycle, marked by hopelessness, panic, listless inactivity, and deep apprehensions about the future. He even compared "the current forecast of permanent depression" with "the fear of the patient that he will never recover."[17]

This is perhaps facile, like Moley's image—as if the fault lay in people's minds alone, not in their real condition—but it does hit upon a crucial feature of the years after the Crash. In the inner lives of Americans, a deep strain of depression was one mark of the Depression, a tendency for people to turn the crisis inward, to blame themselves, to target their own shortcomings and failures, not those of the system. This self-blame, rooted in American individualism and self-reliance as well as in Protestant notions of personal accountability, was where the still-dominant

American success ethic played its baneful and destructive part. As one psychiatrist who had trained with Freud later told Studs Terkel, "Everybody, more or less, blamed himself for his delinquency or lack of talent or bad luck. There was an acceptance that it was your own fault, your own indolence, your lack of ability. You took it and kept quiet." Thanks to this "kind of shame about your own personal failure . . . there were very few disturbances." A bartender who was very young then tells Terkel a similar story, repeated in many other accounts of the period. He remembers the worry and sense of relief he had overheard in adult conversations in the farm belt, "the fascination with catastrophe" as mortgages were foreclosed and other farmers were forced off the land: "The dominant thing was this helpless despair and submission. There was anger and rebellion among a few but, by and large, that quiet desperation and submission."[18] Unlike Europeans who turned to Fascism, Communism, or militarism in those hard times, most Americans remained passive, even self-accusing, in the face of Depression conditions. They neither rebelled nor submitted to the despotic rule of a would-be savior. This looks even more remarkable today than it did then.

Thanks to both the economics and the psychology of depression, the early 1930s saw a decline in the marriage rate, the divorce rate (people couldn't afford to separate), the birthrate, and even, as far as it can be known, the frequency of sexual relations. "Sketchy evidence suggests that due to the tensions of hard times, sex within marriage decreased," writes Susan Ware. "Fear of pregnancy was a major factor, but feelings of inadequacy on the part of the male and lack of respect for the unemployed man from his wife also played roles."[19] One woman told Lorena Hickok of her fear of pregnancy, balanced by a fear of withholding sex from her depressed husband: "I suppose you can say the easiest way would be not to do it. But it wouldn't be. You don't know what it's like when your husband's out of work. He's gloomy and unhappy all the time. Life is terrible. You must try all the time to keep him from going crazy. And many times—that's the only way."[20]

The historian Robert S. McElvaine studied the enormous cache of letters that ordinary citizens wrote to Eleanor Roosevelt, to the president, and to other public officials; out of this and other personal materials, he constructed a portrait of the inner lives of working-class Americans during the Depression. Of their "family troubles" he writes,

Unemployment upset the traditional roles of father, mother, and children. Since the father's position was based upon his occupation and his role as a provider, the loss of his job was likely to mean a decline in his status within the family. The man who was without a position was, well, without a position. . . .

Being "on relief " stigmatized an entire family, but most especially the father.[21]

In one scene McElvaine describes the typical humiliation of applying for relief, which involved being questioned and processed in a way that confirmed a man's degradation and pauperization. Such an ordeal was a far cry from the middle-class "fear of falling."[22] An article by Joseph Heffernan in the *Atlantic* of May 1932 also strikingly accented the psychological effects of the way relief was doled out: the precipitous "descent from respectability," the built-in humiliation. "This is what we have accomplished with our bread lines and soup kitchens," he concludes. "I know, because I have seen thousands of these defeated, discouraged, hopeless men and women, cringing and fawning as they come to ask for public aid. It is a spectacle of national degeneration. This is the fundamental tragedy for America."[23] A woman in *The Grapes of Wrath*, describing the relief work of the Salvation Army, expresses the same horror at becoming an object of charity and impersonal manipulation: "We was hungry—they made us crawl for our dinner. They took our dignity" (432). The recently pauperized classes were poor but still proud. They needed to be helped, but charity was not the way.

The receiver's sense of shame, like the donor's unconscious need to humiliate, was built into America's self-help mentality and grounded in its success mystique. McElvaine describes self-blame and the sense of personal failure as "the Depression's most significant psychological problem" and argues that women, who usually held lower-level jobs—including domestic service, primary teaching, and clerical jobs—and had less emotional investment in work, were more insulated from the Depression and from this terrible guilt syndrome. The Depression "placed women in a relatively better position for obtaining work—poorly paid, of course—than men." On the other hand, "the economic collapse hit hardest just those sectors of the economy (especially heavy industry) that had barred women workers."[24]

Most observers agree that women fared better than men during the Depression, indeed, that many women were thrust into the role of both supporting their families, often with menial jobs, and holding them together emotionally, while the men, unmoored and rudderless, were beginning to break up. This is confirmed in novels of the period, most memorably in *The Grapes of Wrath*, built around the strong mother; we hear repeatedly that "the fambly's breakin' up" and that Pa has "lost his place," meaning not just his home and work but his position in the family, in the world, his place in a stable universe. "Seems like times is changed," says Pa sarcastically. "Time was when a man said what we'd do. Seems like women is tellin' now." "Sure," Ma says to Tom. "Take a man, he can get worried an' worried, an' it eats out his liver, an' purty soon he'll jus' lay down and die with his heart et out" (481). Later she insists, "Woman can change better'n a man" (577).

But books like *Jews without Money* and *The Grapes of Wrath* portray the protective, indomitable mother from the male point of view—essentially, the idealizing son's point of view. The protracted agony of this heroism can look very different from the woman's angle, as we can see in Tillie Olsen's unfinished *Yonnondio*, written then but published much later, where the brutish husband, terribly undermined at work, unmanned by the conditions of his life, unable to provide, becomes like another demanding, insensitive child, another burden for the barely coping mother to nurture and placate, despite her own exhaustion. Ill, this woman continues to function in a stupor of routine and automatic activity. "Remote she fed and clothed the children, scrubbed, gave herself to Jim, clenching her fists against a pain she had no strength to feel."[25] Simply, she works till she drops. This is a far cry from Ma Joad's famous but stereotyped description of how the vulnerable male "lives in jerks," while for the woman, who embodies the resilient spirit of the People, "it's all one flow" (577).

The conviction that women fared better during the Depression means not that they didn't suffer but that they weren't prevented by pride from taking low-paying service jobs. They weren't crippled by the success ethic, though they paid the emotional price for its effects on their husbands. It's revealing that Busby Berkeley's famous Depression number "Remember My Forgotten Man" (the finale of *Gold Diggers of 1933*) is set to a torch song by Al Dubin and Harry Warren, the piercing lament of an abandoned woman twice deprived of her man—first when he was sent off to war, then at home when he has been stripped of all dignity.

Perhaps the usual emphasis on women's moral strength was itself a challenge to the mystique of success and failure that preoccupies the mind of the Depression. As serious writers began to emphasize the limitations and distortions of the American Dream, popular artists became obsessed with fantastic, even magical images of success. In the first category were writers like Clifford Odets, F. Scott Fitzgerald, Nathanael West, James T. Farrell, John Steinbeck, and John Dos Passos. Buoying up the popular culture were gangster films and backstage musicals that reinvented rags-to-riches fantasies in terms the Depression audiences loved and needed. Meanwhile, many New Dealers and radical intellectuals were trying to redefine American individualism in communitarian terms that played down individual effort and competitive achievement. They insisted on a new ideal of mutual welfare just when the New Deal was priming the capitalist pump and creating federally funded make-work jobs to restore individual self-worth. At the heart of the New Deal was a tension between individualism and community, between private initiative and public planning. Out of this conflict capitalism was saved, in the modified form of the welfare state; the success ethic survived, but the federal government began to take a far more active role in most Americans' lives. A new ethos took hold, not to be seriously challenged until the 1980s, when Ronald Reagan set out to convince Americans that greed was good, wealth was no embarrassment, and government itself was the problem.

The Gangster and the Showgirl: From Cagney to Berkeley

Because of the economic crisis, because the sufferings of the Depression eroded confidence in the whole system, including its dominant myths, the overriding fascination with success and failure ran deep in the culture of the thirties. It formed a link between the psychology of the era and its reexamination of cultural myths. There were no more ardent believers in the American Dream than immigrants who had pursued it to these shores and done well. Gangster films were largely immigrant fables, as well as wild, almost parodic versions of Horatio Alger stories. Because of this linkage, Andrew Bergman suggests that these films "only reinforced some of the country's most cherished myths about individual success." This is unconvincing, for Bergman must add, "That only gangsters could make upward mobility believable tells much about how legitimate institutions had failed."[26] The classic gangster films made in the years 1930–32, before the heavy hand of the official morality fell upon them, were thrilling stories, brisk, immediate, electric. But they are tellingly ambivalent toward success and the American Dream.

The three best-known crime pictures of the period, *Little Caesar* (with Edward G. Robinson), *The Public Enemy* (with Jimmy Cagney), and *Scarface* (starring Paul Muni), were all built around the explosive figure of the gangster himself, loosely based on the meteoric career of Al Capone, by then a kind of outlaw folk hero and one of the most famous men in America. (As *Scarface* was made, Capone himself was trying to get into the movies; two of his henchmen, and perhaps even Capone himself, came to look the business over to be sure he got a fair shake.)[27] Andrew Bergman wittily demonstrates how Rico's rise in *Little Caesar* closely follows Andrew Carnegie's celebrated precepts for success in business. The gangster film became a contemporary version of the gospel of the Gilded Age. But the gangster film always dealt with both rise and fall; when the gangster, sitting on "top of the world," dies spectacularly alone, his success proves hollow and short-lived, like the great bubble of prosperity in the 1920s. He is at once self-made and self-defeated, a tragically ambiguous tribute to the success mystique.

The gangster film in the classic period is not moralistic; despite the forced disclaimers prefixed to these films, the stories themselves induce the audience to identify with the flawed protagonist, not just with his success but with his style and audacity, his gift for bold gestures and self-dramatization. But as Robert Warshow showed in his classic essay "The Gangster as Tragic Hero," the gangster's career belies the supposed optimism of American popular culture. "The whole meaning of his career is a drive for success," he says, but the films also show that "one is *punished* for success," that "failure is a kind of death and success is evil and dangerous, is—ultimately—impossible." This dilemma explains why, in his view, the films give "a consistent and astonishingly complete presentation of the modern sense of tragedy."[28]

Besides being distorted versions of the Horatio Alger myth, these stories are also closely linked to the monster films of the period, which deal with creatures—King Kong, the Frankenstein monster, the Invisible Man—who are not so much intrinsically evil as thwarted in their need for love or acceptance. Unlike the monsters of a later period—the fifties, for example—these are not invading aliens, utterly different, unredeemably evil; we fear them but know them, we can connect with them, marvel at them, pity them. They have their reasons; society has made them what they are. Like these menacing figures, the gangster becomes an outsized, fearsome creature who terrorizes society. In the lightning course of acquiring wealth, notoriety, and beautiful women, the gangster not only kills others but undoes himself, destroying his nearest and dearest but also sacrificing his own humanity. It didn't take much alteration for a clever screenwriter to turn *Macbeth* into a gangster film.

Cagney's career as a star began with *The Public Enemy*, directed by William Wellman in 1931. He started the film as the hero's bland sidekick, but his acting apparently burned up the screen in the first days' rushes. So he took over the leading role and gave it all the coiled energy and insouciance, all the astonishing bits of business that made the performance famous. Instead of starting with Cagney as an adult, the film parallels the Alger pattern by giving us the boyhood that helped make him who he was; this reflects the social and environmental approach that would grow in importance all through the 1930s. In a solemn opening admonition, no doubt pasted on afterward, this becomes the excuse for the movie as a whole: the film's goal is "to depict an environment . . . rather than glorify the criminal."

In the early scenes set before the world war, we get a strong sense of the Irish family, the urban setting—the crackling tension, movement, and sounds of city life—along with the first baby steps in the life of a tough guy, "the meanest boy in town." As a boy he's already a thief, already mean to girls. When he's beaten by his father with a strap, he is proud of his stoical capacity to withstand pain without flinching or yielding. There's a Fagin character ("Putty Nose") who sets the boys off on a life of crime—sings them smutty songs, gives them their first guns, acts as a fence, but disappears when the heat is on. For this, long afterward, Cagney kills him as the man desperately appeals for his life, singing and playing a song at the piano for old time's sake. In this brilliant scene, the actual killing takes place off camera: we hear the pleading, hear the gunshot as the music ends and the body slumps down on the keyboard. What we see instead is the blank but riveted face of Cagney's friend Matt, staring intently at a man he never knew before. In Matt's blank gaze we see Cagney becoming a cold-blooded, implacable murderer. He kills his own adolescence, represented by the music, kills whatever softness or sentiment he has left, yet at the same time takes revenge on the man who made him a criminal.

The same issue is highlighted in *Little Caesar* when a jealous, angry Edward G. Robinson, determined to show that nobody ever quits him, sets out to destroy his oldest friend, his only friend. The man has betrayed him by falling in love, by coming under the influence of a woman and her values: he now wants to leave the mob to become a full-time dancer. Completely fearless and ruthless, Rico has made it to the top by his willingness to use his gun, to stop at nothing, and his downfall begins when, for the first time, he cannot kill. In a great scene, the old friend bravely stands his ground, ready to die, while the camera gives us a rare close-up of Robinson's twisted face, tormented, retreating, slipping out of focus. If Cagney's downfall can be gauged by his loss of humanity, Robinson is brought down by a residual trace of human feeling.

In *The Public Enemy*, as Cagney's personality becomes more baroque, he's set off against straight-arrow figures like his weaker friend Matt, who gets killed out of simple loyalty to him, and his brother Mike, who avoids all the shortcuts to success and takes the prescribed Horatio Alger route of hard work and study, industry and frugality. To Cagney this is the "road to being poor." Similarly, Cagney can't follow Matt in marrying and settling down. Like most movie gangsters he treats women as trophies, easily disposable. In an unusual twist, the brooding Mike is actually a stronger figure than his kid brother: he takes a straight course, goes off to war, rejects Cagney's tainted money, and even knocks him down once or twice. But he is boringly solemn and humorless, even in his way of getting ahead. "In 1931," says Andrew Bergman, "one did not go to movies to see trolley conductors working their way through night school."[29]

Cagney has everything these bland figures lack, everything Depression audiences demanded: a nervy style, vitality, pugnacious charm. Like all the great gangsters, he sees himself as a dramatic character. When he pushes the grapefruit into Mae Clarke's face, it feels as if he's improvising for the camera. After shooting up a rival gang single-handedly, he staggers out, riddled with bullets, onto a rain-swept film noir street and says, "I ain't so tough." From his hospital bed, swathed in bandages, he can still give his mother a poke in the chin, half loving, half aggressive; it's the trademark gesture expected of him. Even in death he makes a dramatic entrance, wrapped up like a mummy, some artifact of an ancient dynasty. And all this energy is outside the law, enabling the audience at once to root vicariously for the outlaw and to see him brought to heel.

It would be hard to find more highly charged, more wildly mannered performances than the ones Cagney, Robinson, and Muni give in these three films. Muni's stagy antics have not worn as well as Cagney's spit-fire delivery and Robinson's whiney gutter snarl, but all three leap out at us beyond any naturalistic framework. Yet the classic gangster is just one example of the pervasiveness of "personality" in the films of the 1930s, in which a constellation of "stars" were surrounded by a galaxy of character actors, that stock company of almost anonymous but unforgettable Dickensian creatures with their craggy features, awesome behavioral tics, and great radio voices. Compared with these colorful cartoons of ordinary American types, the stars, proverbially larger than life, inhabit a more remote, even forbidden region of personality. No one would want to compare Bette Davis to Cagney, but her willingness to play difficult, overbearing, even monstrous characters like Regina in *The Little Foxes* appealed to the iconoclastic side of the thirties. (For another part of the audience, there were always perfect paragons like Shirley Temple, and later, Deanna Durbin.)

No one, to my knowledge, has ever compared Clark Gable to Cagney, but part of Gable's power as a sexy leading man was that he played something of an outlaw, a man from nowhere with a barely restrained potential for (sexual) violence. The erotic charge of his more explicit pre–Production Code films like *Red Dust* still survives in *It Happened One Night*, in *San Francisco*, and especially in his daring Rhett Butler, surrounded by Selznick's soapy fantasy of the Old South. *Gone with the Wind* is carried not by its sentimental links with *The Birth of a Nation* and the mythology of the Old South but by Gable's portrayal of an outlaw and adventurer, perfectly matched with Vivien Leigh's quirky, mannered, risk-taking performance as an outrageous woman free of some conventional scruples of her class. Like Cagney, they are surrounded by pious and predictable people, "good" people, whose blandness forms the backdrop for their own grasping will and energy, their surplus of personality.*

Gone with the Wind, like the gangster films, shows how ambiguous the thrust of Hollywood's values could be in the 1930s. The crime genre was contemporary, topical, and immediate—"Ripped from Today's Head-lines," Warner Brothers boasted—while the historical romance seemed the height of escapism. Yet both portray a turbulent, violently disrupted world that is partly a metaphor for Depression America (though neither is "about" the Depression).† Once I asked a film class to compare *Gone with the Wind* to *The Grapes of Wrath*: social catastrophe, family disintegration, a world held together, but just barely, by a grimly determined woman. The relevance of *Gone with the Wind* is more striking because less obvious: both Rhett and Scarlett are survivors, strong personalities who batter their way through terrible times. Rhett is a social outcast, already notorious in his native Charleston. After denouncing his fellow southerners' illusions about the coming war, he makes his fortune as a blockade-runner. Scar-lett, the true Horatio Alger character, grows from a petulant, immature girl into a scheming, successful woman, far more interested in status and money than in sex. Though determined to rebuild Tara, she avoids the traps of womanhood and "romance." Free of all nostalgia for the old order, she spunkily embodies the commercial awakening that came to be called the New South. For her, indeed, "Tomorrow is another day."

Some Depression-oriented movies like *I Am a Fugitive* or Fritz Lang's *You Only Live Once* portrayed the individual as helplessly entrapped by the conditions of a callous and unjust society; a few others like *Our Daily Bread* exchanged larger-than-life characters for collective action. But most Hol-lywood movies, by centering on larger-than-life personalities, confirmed both the conservative and the radical dimensions of America's individu-

---

* In MGM's *San Francisco*, on the other hand, Gable, also playing the reprobate and womanizer, is badly matched with the bland Jeanette MacDonald. He must get a dose of Hollywood religion to become worthy of the love of the parson's daughter.

† The point could be applied to many other romantic adventure fables of the period: *San Francisco* (instead of the Civil War, the famous 1906 earthquake), *The Wizard of Oz* (a cyclone), John Ford's *The Hurricane*, even *Mutiny on the Bounty*, which fed the 1930s appetite for rebellion against unjust authority. For one cogent view of the timeliness of *Gone with the Wind*, see Lawrence W. Levine, "American Culture and the Great Depression," *Yale Review* 74 (Winter 1985): 209.

alist tradition: an admiration for rebels and outcasts, for prickly, trouble-some personalities, went hand in hand with the received wisdom that all success, all achievement, must be seen in individual terms.

Yet this was a period when the new mass media, especially radio, did much to keep the nation together in the face of economic disaster. Like the proliferation of spectator sports in the 1920s, the mass media gave people an emotional outlet and a collective mythology, besides becom-ing a vehicle for all kinds of political influence, from FDR's reassuring fireside chats to Father Coughlin's venomous radio preaching.[30] Still, dur-ing a time of communitarian experiments associated with the New Deal, Hollywood's commercial dependence on the star system, featuring color-ful brand-name personalities, was a conservative social force, even as it stimulated hope and ministered to people's need for variety, passion, and emotional energy in their Depression-pinched lives.

It follows that no easy contrast can be drawn between escapism and social relevance—the standard line on Depression culture. Collective escape and entertainment can be just as revealing as solemn social criti-cism. If many people were dancing in the dark, their desperate or spirited steps were as important as the surrounding shadows. There's a great deal of fantasy and melodrama in the best of Hollywood's social films, and a rich lode of meaning in its "escapist" and genre films, formulaic as they usually are.[31] In the early thirties the same studio, Warner Brothers, cre-ated the new crime film and backstage musical but also, starting with *I Am a Fugitive from a Chain Gang*, *Heroes for Sale*, and *Wild Boys of the Road*, the hard-hitting social movie, made with the same gusto, which more directly reflected the conditions of the Depression; in a sense, this became another definable genre. These topical films were directed by some of the same studio pros who handled the genre films—William Wellman, Mervyn LeRoy—and had the brisk, snappy rhythm and inexpensive look of Warner's emerging house style.[32]

The subjects and stories of Warner's genre films belonged as much to the Depression as the up-to-date films of social protest. There were backstage musicals on Broadway all through the twenties, and in Hollywood all through the thirties, first at Warner, later at MGM, especially after Busby Berkeley moved there in 1939. But the cycle reached its peak in 1933 and

1934 during the transition from the Hoover era to the early New Deal. It took on its greatest cultural meaning when Depression-influenced success stories, the staple of popular magazine fiction, were joined with Berkeley's ingenious and stupefying choreography, which was marked by its bizarre, collective, abstract, often dehumanizing visual patterns. This choreography itself was a reflection of the fantasy life of the Depression. The prototype for these movies was *42nd Street*. Its surprising success (mirroring its theme) single-handedly revived the fortunes of the Hollywood musical, which had largely failed after the novelty of the first talkie revues had worn off.

The supposed escapism of these films is a misnomer; topical allusions help give these films their Warner's bite. The original poster for *42nd Street* describes it as "Inaugurating a NEW DEAL in ENTERTAINMENT." (With the promise of "14 STARS" and "200 GIRLS," this seems like a pretty good deal.) The standard work on Busby Berkeley gets it wrong in suggesting that "the frothy backstage was perfect escapist entertainment for the early years of the Depression, but as economic conditions improved, the public expected musicals with a little more reality." Since the strong Depression touches in the early films disappeared later on, this is a strange definition of "reality."

The same authors praise the "successful formula of breezy comedy and elaborate production" in *Gold Diggers of 1933* as "just right for the escapist fare that people craved in the dreary 1930's."[33] Yet this is a film about a man (much like Berkeley) trying against the odds to stage a musical about the Depression, which he brings off only in the closing number. Paradoxically, these complacent remarks are illustrated by scenes from the hilariously surreal "We're in the Money" routine, full of curvaceous women scantily clad in garish arrangements of gold coins. But even before the number ends the chorus girls are thrown out of work; the sheriff closes the whole show down because the producer can't pay his bills. Suddenly this *is* the Depression: they're not in the money after all. Escapist illusions are what this number is *about*—pretending you're in the money when there isn't any. In *Footlight Parade* they have to call off a "Prosperity" number. Even earlier, we hear the dancers have been complaining about their glum choreographer: "How can we look Prosperity when he's got Depression all over that pan of his?"

These are not just glib, up-the-minute lines; they go the heart of the Gold Diggers series, inherited from the frivolous 1920s. The theme was first introduced in a 1919 play and had already been filmed more than once. But in the Depression the well-worn cliché that all showgirls are looking for rich sugar daddies took on new meaning. It becomes a different form of escape: from hunger and insecurity for those who had only their bodies to offer. In these films, show business is more a way of selling your body than of displaying your talent—selling it to a fickle, anonymous audience, to slave driving showmen, or, privately, to lecherous but sexless old millionaires. Each of these became a comment on the Depression. If "We're in the Money," with its abrupt termination, is escapist fare, then this can be said of any dance and music, even the 1933 film's tour de force, "Remember My Forgotten Man," Berkeley's astounding attempt to choreograph the entire look and significance of the Depression.

This remarkable number uses 150 extras first as marching soldiers, then as hungry, unemployed veterans roaming the streets, standing in breadlines, pleading for work in visual patterns borrowed from contemporary newsreels yet also from stylized expressionist films of the 1920s, especially Fritz Lang's 1927 *Metropolis*, which also deals with working conditions and the relations between labor and capital. In a backdrop behind the pleading men, who are grouped around a female figure out of *Metropolis*, is another Langian image of American doughboys marching in kaleidoscopic patterns. The music is inspired pastiche, a mixture of torch song and marching song, and the result is in some sense ludicrous—the Depression as *decor*, as oral and visual phantasmagoria. Yet this is a powerful number, a gigantic, slightly nutty extravaganza on a serious theme, inspired by the real protests of the Bonus Marchers (World War I veterans demanding early payment of their promised bonuses) and the serious drama of *I Am a Fugitive*, which also drew attention to the plight of decorated veterans in the postwar years.

To appeal specifically—and from a woman's viewpoint—for what the nation owed to its citizen soldiers was a way of saying that the unemployed were not aliens or misfits but simply mainstream Americans down on their luck. It is a choreographic version of the popular 1932 song "Brother, Can You Spare a Dime?" Men who had risked their lives for their country were now done in by the system they had fought to defend. Berkeley's technique was stylized, fantastic—the explosions of a surreal imagination bursting the naturalistic frame of the "all-talking" picture—but in his own way he was trying to humanize the victims of the Depression.

Though the much scorned plot lines of these movies were directed separately from the big production numbers, they contributed to the immediacy of backstage musicals. The success motif links them to the gangster films. Just as the beer wars and bootleggers of the Prohibition era became metaphors for the Depression, just as the depredations, so long ago, of Sherman's march through Georgia stood in for the catastrophic disruptions of the 1930s, show business became an ideal metaphor for the boom-and-bust experiences of the Depression. The high-stakes, high-risk ambience of the backstage musical was perfect fare for a post-Crash world beset by radical changes of fortune. In the make-or-break jungle of show business, closer to gambling than to art, Ruby Keeler can be catapulted from fainting on the chorus line out of sheer hunger to becoming the latest star in the Broadway firmament. With the unexpected success of *42nd Street*, this was what actually happened to the careers of Keeler, Berkeley, the songwriters Dubin and Warren, even to the Warner Brothers studio, which would otherwise have fallen into bankruptcy. These movies belong to the precarious hit-or-miss world that gives them their theme. This last-ditch venture in pluck and luck is exactly what happens *within* the movie to Warner Baxter, the director of a show called *Pretty Lady*.

As *42nd Street* begins, Baxter (Julian Marsh) is a veteran director at the end of his rope. The New York skyline we see from the air is as magnificent as ever, but Baxter, like Broadway itself, is losing his grip. He's had one too many flops, and given away all he's made. He's already had one nervous breakdown, and *Pretty Lady*, he knows, is his "last shot." All through the movie he's hard-driven, intense, on the ropes; he desperately needs a hit, needs to make a bundle. His star, Dorothy (Bebe Daniels), has a sugar daddy (the ineffable Guy Kibbee) who is bankrolling the whole show, but she also, secretly, has an old partner and lover (George Brent), whose career has languished since vaudeville days while she has become a temperamental star. Here is yet another mark of male failure in this largely female success story.

Tired of skulking around, Brent is having a "sudden attack of manhood" and wants Daniels to quit the stage and retire into marriage. To protect the show's investment, Baxter has him warned off by gangsters—the usual thirties form of polite pressure. (Crime and gangsters were so much in the public eye that they pop up in musicals and comedies.) Like the gangster film, the backstage musical is an urban genre—that's where the action is—cued to the quick rhythms and daily hazards of city life, which Berkeley evokes in his big "42nd Street" number and again two years later with the whirling, finally tragic euphoria of "Lullaby of Broadway" (in *Gold Diggers of 1935*). In "42nd Street" there's a well-filmed murder that foreshadows the famous "Slaughter on Tenth Avenue" ballet in Rodgers and Hart's *On Your Toes*, the young George Balanchine's choreographic tribute to the crime movie and to New York's mean streets. The gangster film itself is a piece of urban choreography; it's no accident that men like Cagney and George Raft, along with Robinson's fictional sidekick in *Little Caesar*, doubled as hoofers and gangsters. As in show business, survival in the city demanded fancy footwork.

When the star, Daniels, breaks a leg, literally, Ruby Keeler, playing a raw but innocent ingénue who has been thrust into the chorus *just* as a pair of legs, gets her chance to go on. It's a fairy tale: unlike the hard-bitten, cynical, tough-talking girls around her, who've seen everything, Keeler is a novice. She has "youth, beauty, freshness." In a bruised and jaded world, spiced with tart pre-Code dialogue, the winsome Keeler stands for a new beginning. She has the support of the leading man, played by Dick Powell, whose career as a boyish, collegiate, apple-cheeked young crooner also dates from the success of this movie.

Though there was a lascivious edge to his bursting "Young and Healthy" image, Powell's screen personality was bland. (Later he turned up unexpectedly in films noirs of the mid-1940s, starting with Edward Dmytryk's harsh, Chandler-inspired *Murder, My Sweet*.) In these early musicals, the bemused, unforced sweetness of Ruby Keeler is more affecting. Always a bit surprised at where she finds herself, Keeler brings off the Cinderella theme with effortless grace and charm. Audiences in the early thirties readily took to this fresh young couple, as they took to a story line that involved dramatic turns of success and failure. They also appreciated the racy dialogue of the tough chorus girls and their crude paramours—the whole casting-couch side of show business— which would be cleaned up as the decade wore on. Under the thumb of censorship and a new puritanism, the screwball comedy of the late thirties would work by suggestion and innuendo. Even the witty dialogue of Gregory La Cava's breezy *Stage Door* (1937), the most crisp of the backstage comedies, would finally turn mawkish in the more sentimental, straitlaced phase of the 1930s.

In the early Berkeley films, the uninhibited dialogue is of a piece with the lubricious choreography, which subdues individual women to kaleidoscopic masses of impersonal flesh, opening and closing like flowers, at once pornographic and deliciously naive, parodic, pre-Freudian. This softcore stuff is linked with the bouncy songs of Al Dubin and Harry Warren, such as their jaundiced look at marriage, honeymoon, and divorce, the famous "Shuffle Off to Buffalo." Aboard the honeymoon train, the well-named Niagara Limited, with its army of couples performing in lockstep, we learn that "Matrimony is baloney. / She'll be wanting alimony. / In a year or so." In *Footlight Parade* the same coy, slightly off-color routine would be recycled as "Honeymoon Hotel"; in *Gold Diggers of 1933* it became "Pettin' in the Park"; Warner and Berkeley had no qualms about repeating winning numbers.

All the separate elements of *42nd Street* came together—the story, the music, the acting, the dancing—but the real triumph was Berkeley's. In the course of this movie, he re-created the film musical by emancipating it from the stage and reconceiving it in cinematic terms. The greatest weakness of backstage musicals, as we see in the early parts of *42nd Street*, was the way they used music and dance realistically, as literal show-biz situations, not dramatically, as something expressing the characters. They give us music only when they're rehearsing numbers or performing them before an audience. The musical numbers are tied to the rhythm of the theater. They don't serve to advance the action or convey inner thoughts and feeling, like operatic arias, or interior monologues, or Shakespearean soliloquies. (This is why Laurence Olivier, in his great 1948 film, projected Hamlet's soliloquies in voice-over, as silent ruminations.)

In typical backstage musicals, the numbers were public performances, hemmed in by the spatial limits of the rehearsal studio and the stage. But as he gains confidence, Berkeley choreographs for the camera eye, not for a live audience. With his tricky overhead shots and close-ups and traveling shots, he puts us in positions no theater audience could ever have. Berkeley helped teach Fred Astaire how to choreograph on film, but Astaire's is a dancer's choreography, always respectful of the whole body in motion, while Berkeley's is a showman's bag of special effects, an eye-popping spectacle. As a film editor, he revels in technical tricks, the effects of lighting and splicing and multiple exposure that go back to the magic of the French filmmaker Georges Méliès, not to methods of stage production, not even to the extravaganzas of Flo Ziegfeld that he tried hard to surpass.

Numbers like "42nd Street" and "Shuffle Off to Buffalo" begin on a stage, among constructed sets, but the action expands beyond what any stage could accommodate; as the camera moves spectacularly in and around it, the illusion of a stage gives way to the vast cinematic space of a soundstage: film revels in its technical advance over live production. I defy any viewer to make sense of *Pretty Lady*, the show this cast is supposedly putting on. (I suppose you could call it a revue.) By the end it's entirely left behind, and all we know is that after starting out sluggishly, lifelessly, it somehow clicked; it went on to become a HIT(!). This coming together (a key Depression motif) is reflected in the rhythm of these films, in which, after all the botched rehearsals and human complications, the real numbers come toward the end, complete and perfect, with little reference to the messy run-throughs we've already seen—usually rehearsals of unrelated material. The big musical payoff, inseparable from the thrill of success, made Depression audiences exceptionally tolerant of these small bits of incoherence.

We can't help wondering at the patience of the audience during a film like *Footlight Parade*, where all three big Berkeley "prologues" conclude the film in a blaze of music, spectacle, and dance. Until then nothing much happens, or at least nothing goes well, but this is just the point. The show *does* go on, and the show itself is the main success story, embracing the individual triumph of everyone who made it. This is a perfect thirties paradox: success in show business is individual, but the overall triumph, at least in Berkeley's vision, belongs to the ensemble, the collective effort.

Berkeley's imagination was so abstract, so given over to larger patterns and ensembles, that it was amazing that he was ever able to integrate Warner-style Depression material. He was a control freak; the house style was offhand, topical, and raw, and it was scarcely touched by the sheen and finish laid on at MGM. Benefiting from a creative autonomy that was rare at the height of the studio system, his work was an island of outrageous surrealism and blatant, fleshly sensuality in a sea of increasingly naturalistic filmmaking. His skill at orchestrating grouped masses in precise formations belonged to the collective side of the 1930s outlook, like the real-life choreography of the Nazi filmmaker Leni Riefenstahl. Berkeley went his own way; his numbers were like self-contained films. There was something frightening, dehumanizing, about the way he used people—as cogs in a wheel, interchangeable units of a grand design. He took the philosopher Henri Bergson's definition of comedy—the intrusion of the mechanical into the sphere of the human—and made something scarily impressive out of it.

Berkeley's best work paralleled the early, NRA phase of the New Deal, with its devotion to planning and social consensus, not Keynesian pump priming. Despite the individual success stories, Berkeley's films, on the formal side, were hymns to collective planning and precision movement, not to individual initiative. In *Footlight Parade*, perhaps to please Jack Warner, a friend of FDR's, he includes a tricky series of overhead shots in which a marching chorus first forms an American flag, then, superimposed on the flag, a reassuring image of Roosevelt himself, then a huge NRA eagle (which pops up in other Warner's films of the period, such as *Wild Boys of the Road*). Berkeley too could play the Depression game with timely plots and topical allusions. Without the breadlines, Berkeley's films would lose some of their point.

Working on as many as eight movies at once, pushing Warner Brothers to unheard-of levels of extravagance, he became in a sense one of the largest employers in Hollywood. Like the New Deal, he gave jobs to all those starving chorus girls, whatever their own pluck and luck. But apart from these good works, he was also the crazy visionary who choreographed vast ensembles of tall buildings, white pianos, man-made waterfalls. For all the Depression touches, his most daring and surreal numbers (such as "I Only Have Eyes for You," in *Dames*, and "By a Waterfall," from *Footlight Parade*) were presented as dream sequences, exempt from the burdens of reality and probability, like the spectacular stunts in Buster Keaton's 1924 masterpiece, *Sherlock Jr.*

If show business fed the wild, kinky side of Berkeley's imagination, it was also his metaphor for the Depression. In his zany way, he conveyed the urgency of success and failure, fame or disaster. For his hard-driving producers the big jackpot was a Hit. For his showgirls the payoff could also be marriage—escape from the uncertainties of show business itself. During a period when the old success formulas seemed useless, when business and entrepreneurship no longer provided any sure route to achievement, the worlds of crime and show business—which were not always easy to distinguish—offered Depression audiences some quasi-magical alternatives. Their fix on success had many ambiguous implications, but like most popular entertainment, they provided avenues of wish fulfillment that highlighted what the audience lacked and sorely needed.

Just as the fall of the gangster was already implicit in his rise, stardom for a few meant failure and frustration for the many. Even successful performers burn out in spectacular ways, much to the fascination of their fans. The early deaths of Charlie Parker, James Dean, Jackson Pollock, Janis Joplin, Jim Morrison, Jimi Hendrix, John Lennon, Rainer Werner Fassbinder, John Belushi, and Jean-Michel Basquiat became part of their legend, evidence of their risk-taking intensity, the completion of what they stood for, how they lived. The most affecting moment in Busby Berkeley's career came in his brilliantly inventive tribute to New York nightlife, "Lullaby of Broadway." This appears in one of his lesser films, *The Gold Diggers of 1935*, when a singer and night crawler falls to her death from a skyscraper in the wild forest of bright buildings that is New York after dark. This fall is choreographed to the simple strains of "Lullaby of Broadway." It's the kind of ending gangster films such as *White Heat* specialized in, the spectacular fall from the top of the world. Like "Remember My Forgotten Man," this eerily effective number was anything but an escape from reality, despite its surreal imagery.

By the late thirties the showgirl was a tired stereotype, and the gangster was a figure of obsolescence whom audiences associated with the rough-and-tumble days of Prohibition. Though the restraints of the Production Code did not really kick in until 1934, by 1932 a new moral censorship forced studios to cut the gangster down to size. All through the late 1930s, Humphrey Bogart's career flared and sputtered as he played such constricted roles: the nervous, hard-bitten outcast in *The Petrified Forest* (1936), the psychotic loner, produced by the slums, rejected by his own mother, in *Dead End* (1937), the treacherous, back-stabbing, cowardly operator in *The Roaring Twenties* (1939). In this last film, it was left to Cagney to hold on to the heroic mold of the gangster, yet his character also betrays and softens it with his poignant longing for respectability. Worse still, in Warner's *Angels with Dirty Faces* (1938), Cagney (like Clark Gable in *San Francisco*) comes under the sanctimonious influence of a smooth-talking priest, his friend, played by Pat O'Brien, who convinces him that he's a poor role model for the Dead End Kids. He urges him to die badly, to turn yellow before getting the electric chair, and hence to shatter his own image, which the kids so much admire. "You're asking me to throw away the only thing I got left," he tells the priest. But his compliance is ambiguous; we see it only in silhouette. The priest triumphs through a ruse, a hypocritical piece of manipulation, and the movie itself dramatizes the social pressure on Warner Brothers to cut the gangster down to size. They puncture the myth by falsifying and diminishing it.

What undid the gangster was less the influence of morality than the new atmosphere of enlightened social improvement fostered by the New Deal. Despite the ambiguities of the gangster as a success figure, he is nothing if not an individual, at once sordid and larger than life. The New Deal helped propagate a more corporate ideal of success, a sense of collective responsibility for social welfare; this was the liberal's version of the collectivism that attracted the decade's radical intellectuals. Andrew Bergman describes the viewpoint of films like *Dead End* and *Angels with Dirty Faces* as "environmentalism": the sense that crime is a social problem, a product of poverty and slums.[*] This is a major theme of the thirties, beginning with books like *Jews without Money*, and it issues in the utopian optimism inherent in all social engineering: we can deal with this problem, we can fix it. At the end of *Jews without Money*, Mike Gold sees the revolution as "the true Messiah," tearing down the slums to "build there a garden for the human spirit." Bogart's antagonist in *Dead End* is an architect-dreamer, played by Joel McCrea, who wants to tear down and rebuild the city in just this way. When crime becomes a social problem, optimism breaks out and the classic gangster, a mythic and tragic figure, cannot survive.

The decade's soured romance with the gangster ended with two elegiac films directed by Raoul Walsh, *The Roaring Twenties* and Bogart's last and best gangster film, *High Sierra* (1941). Both portray the gangster as a disappearing species, the almost extinct artifact of an earlier era. (Carlos Clarens succinctly calls such movies "twilight-of-the-gangster pictures.")[34]

---

[*] Bergman, *We're in the Money*, 149–65. The whole theme is summarized in the title of John Garfield's first film, *They Made Me a Criminal* (1939), directed by none other than Busby Berkeley, doing his first "straight" film and his last for Warner Brothers before going to MGM. Garfield was an icon of thirties radicalism from his work with Clifford Odets and the Group Theatre. The movie also featured the Dead End Kids, who played in so many of the environmentalist movies about crime and delinquency.

The brisk March of Time–style prologue in *The Roaring Twenties* reviews the history of the gangster going back to World War I and the coming of Prohibition. "This film is a memory," it tells us. Despite its crisp dialogue and quick rhythm, despite Cagney's superb performance, the film clouds his role in a haze of nostalgia and makes him at once too noble and too pathetic. In *Little Caesar* and *The Public Enemy*, the ambiguous figure of the gangster was both appealing and amoral, immensely vital and immensely vicious. Here the central figure is split into the good gangster, an old-style man of the streets (Cagney), and the bad, psychopathic gangster, in a treacherous new boardroom style (Bogart).

Cagney longs to get out of the crime business. He idealizes the down-home girl who wrote to him when he was a GI, who ends up married to a district attorney. Like other capitalists, he's been ruined by the Depression, especially by the end of Prohibition. The criminals are washed up; the new era belongs to the suburbs and the DA's office. The gangster is outdated and irrelevant because "people are *building* things now." As the optimism of the New Deal and the Popular Front have taken hold, Cagney is reduced to a drunken stumblebum. But at least he dies grandly, staggering in the snow on the steps of a church. "What was his business?" someone asks. "He used to be a big shot."

Bogart too dies well in *High Sierra*, trapped in the mountains like some primeval beast, almost extinct. The role he plays has the same underlying nobility, the same archaic irrelevance as Cagney's. Graying at the temples, looking completely out of place, the aging Roy Earle, whose very name suggests class, emerges from prison into a world different from what he left behind. He is told that all the A–1 guys are gone, dead or in Alacatraz. His old boss is sick and dying ("My life's catching up with me"), and he's bored by the adulation of the young hoods, who see him as a living legend. Like Cagney, he focuses his longing for unspoiled purity on a "decent" girl, while ignoring a tough, loyal woman (played here by Ida Lupino) who's very much his female counterpart. When he pays for an operation to have the girl's clubfoot corrected, she loses the only thing that distinguished her. In a brilliant twist, she not only turns on him but, worse still, turns ordinary. She wants only to have "fun," to be like everyone else. She foreshadows the banal postwar world that's already doing him in.

In the face of this numbing post-Depression normality, with its tawdry middle-class values, Roy Earle is nowhere. This is a melancholy movie, a classic of brooding masculine fatalism. Like all the great gang-sters, Roy is "rushing toward death." On the same note of fatality, no one's love for another person is here reciprocated; everyone longs vainly for someone else. But Roy finally does what he's wanted to do from the beginning: he "crashes out." Rising higher and higher on curving roads into the foothills of the Sierras, he breathes clean air as the law closes in on him. This is a different sense of the "top of the world" from Raoul Walsh's later, Freudian *White Heat* (with Cagney, 1949), not an apocalyp-tic world in flames but a mythic translation into a sort of transcendence in the clear mountain air.

These late gangster films show how much the success mystique belonged to the *early* thirties, when the Depression was at its worst. By the late thirties, with economic fears somewhat allayed, success was asso-ciated with normality and ordinariness, with the coming postwar world of prosperity, "fun," and family life. Here the classic gangster would have no place. With Bogart taking refuge in the mountains, *High Sierra* ends more like a western than a gangster film, for the western imagery better suggests his irrelevance to the new order. Even at the beginning he was already the aging gunfighter, out of place. Here this consciously myth-making film differs from the classic pattern. As Jack Shadoian puts it in *Dreams and Dead Ends*, "Here it is no rise and all fall, but by falling the hero rises. He does not die squalidly, in a gutter, but nobly, at the foot of a mountain, and his death is equated with freedom."[35]

Fitzgerald's Second Act

These late and melancholy films show the gradual convergence of pop-ular culture and serious art in their portrayal of success. It would be far too simple to say that popular artists fed Depression audiences fantasies of success while serious writers explored the grim realities of failure. In these terms, the later films are closer to the writers than to the ear-lier filmmakers. Starting with business novels like Howells's *The Rise of Silas Lapham* (1885) and Abraham Cahan's Howellsian *The Rise of David Levinsky* (1917), writer after writer equates material success with spiri-tual impoverishment and failure. This anticipates the more critical atti-tude toward capitalism and middle-class life that came in with *Babbitt* and twenties modernism. In the famous ending of *David Levinsky*, the hero looks back on his business career with unease, puzzlement, a sense of disconnection:

> I don't seem to be able to get accustomed to my luxurious life. I am always more or less conscious of my good clothes, of the high quality of my office furniture, of the power I wield over the men in my pay. As I have said in another connection, I still have a lurking fear of restaurant waiters.
>
> I can never forget the days of my misery. I cannot escape from my old self. My past and present do not comport well. David, the poor lad swinging over a Talmud volume at the Preacher's Synagogue, seems to have more in common with my inner identity than David Levinsky, the well-known cloak-manufacturer.[36]

During the Depression, for obvious reasons, writers were less concerned with the hollowness of success than with wrenching failure, including the kind of inner failure Levinsky describes here. Because of the economic crisis and its challenge to the American Dream, virtually every serious writer of the 1930s grappled with success and failure, but a few, like F. Scott Fitzgerald, James T. Farrell, Nathanael West, and Clifford Odets, made it the armature of their work, revealing much about themselves while illuminating the values of the surrounding culture. Fitzgerald was America's greatest novelist of the dream of success and the inevitability of failure; he enacted both with striking symmetry in the two halves of his own career, which stretched from 1920 to 1940. For many he remains an icon of the twenties, his years of fame, when his writing was in vogue. Yet in one sense he came into his own when his career began to falter, when the magazines that had supported him began rejecting his work, indeed, when the writing itself no longer flowed and his life edged into the downward drift of some of the most affecting stories he had already written.

Like many writers, Fitzgerald had a personality that was a rich yet fertile tissue of contradictions. He was a midwestern provincial from St. Paul who adored Princeton, from which he never graduated, and a perpetual adolescent who wrote more maturely about love than any other American novelist. His ambivalence toward the rich was the subject of a famous gibe by his treacherous friend Hemingway. He was an

Irish-Catholic moralist who was prudish about sex yet also an unabashed romantic who popularized the "flapper" and became a spokesman for the scandalous youth culture of the Jazz Age. His marriage to Zelda Sayre, a great southern belle from Birmingham, came a few days after the publication of his first novel, *This Side of Paradise*, in 1920. She had at first rejected him—his prospects were poor—and a nostalgic sense of romantic disappointment, even decline, already colors the book. But it became a bestseller—for many it served to define the new generation—though his college friend Edmund Wilson would describe it two years later as "one of the most illiterate books of any merit ever published." Like Byron in 1812, he awoke and found himself famous, and the Fitzgeralds became the most sought-after young couple of the decade. It was a fairy tale, a more uncomplicated success story than any he ever wrote.

They seemed to live for glamour, style, and kicks. He was not yet twenty-four and already a legend: the devil-may-care side of postwar youth personified. She was a great beauty whose personality, letters, and diaries were his best source of material. It must have seemed like a wonderful lark when Zelda reviewed his second novel for the New York *Tribune* and accused him breezily of lifting many of her own words. "In fact," she said, "Mr Fitzgerald—I believe that is how he spells his name—seems to believe that plagiarism begins at home." This was amusing at the time—it was her first published piece—but it foreshadowed the tension, bitterness, and competition that later developed between them, especially when she set up as a writer, and he accused her of poaching on *his* material. Later, he would try to convince even her psychiatrists that his work was more important than hers ("because my writing kept the mare going, while Zelda's belongs to the luxury trade"). But long before she broke down in 1930 (as if to mark the end of an era), their marriage foundered on too much drinking, too much competition, too little support and mutual understanding. Beside squandering all he earned, they were prodigal spenders of their own youth, beauty, and talent.

The spectacular and tragic curve of their marriage and his career provided an eerie parallel to the general collapse of the economy and the near-total shift of sensibility between the two decades. Fitzgerald was considered a wash-up through much of the thirties, especially when his "Crack-Up" articles in *Esquire* in 1936 burst upon an audience that had little experience with confessional journalism. Embarrassed, even shocked by his candor, the world took his self-portrait as self-pity, precisely the opposite of what he was saying. He was dedicating himself to a new beginning, *as a writer.* The symbolism of his early death in Hollywood at the end of 1940 encouraged obituary writers to put their seal on this legend. "Roughly, his own career began and ended with the Nineteen Twenties," said the *New York Times.* "The promise of his brilliant career was never fulfilled."[37]

Though the Fitzgerald revival began soon afterward with Edmund Wilson's publication of his unfinished novel, *The Last Tycoon* (in 1941), and *The Crack-Up*, a somber collection of articles, letters, and journals (1945), there is still a tendency for biographers to anchor Fitzgerald's career symbolically in the 1920s, to treat the succeeding decade as a dreadful epilogue of disintegration and decline.[38] Yet the opposite case can also be made: for Fitzgerald as a developing writer who reached his maturity in the 1930s. It was then that the disasters of his life enabled him to pursue darker themes that were there from the beginning. Fitzgerald was acutely aware of the analogies between his own life and the larger society. In later years, whenever he wrote about the boom and the Crash, as he often did (in essays like "Echoes of the Jazz Age" and stories such as "Babylon Revisited"), he was musing on his own boom and crash as well. In the ledger for his thirty-third year he noted, *"The Crash! Zelda + America,"* almost a formula for his later work.[39] By 1931 he understood that as a chronicler of the Jazz Age, who invested sophomoric fantasies with an iridescent romantic sheen, his work was as irretrievably remote as the era itself.

But as early as 1922 in a story called "Winter Dreams," and again in stories like "'The Sensible Thing,'" "Absolution," and "The Rich Boy," and, above all, in *The Great Gatsby* in 1925, Fitzgerald began to infuse an elegiac and tragic note into his characters' dreams of love and success. In the generally disillusioned years that followed the Great War, a period whose literary tone was set by the grotesque misfits of *Winesburg, Ohio*, the savage satirical gusto of Mencken and Lewis, the desiccation and despair of *The Waste Land*, and the bleak mood of the early Hemingway, Fitzgerald gave a shimmering glow to the bright, impossible longings of the younger generation, as writers like Goethe, Schiller, Byron, Keats, and Shelley had done before him. He understood these writers better than most of his critics, for in his plots, and in the feelings that animate

them, he reminds us of how Keats and Shelley had joined the disenchantment to the dream, the inevitable failures to extravagant hopes.

Remarkably, Fitzgerald wrote about failure, loss, and disappointment before he had experienced them. By the time his life was on the
skids, along with the rest of American society, Fitzgerald was ready to
handle it all in fiction. Looking back on his early work, in an article called
"Early Success," Fitzgerald observed, "All the stories that came into my
head had a touch of disaster in them—the lovely young creatures in my
novels went to ruin, the diamond mountains of my short stories blew
up, my millionaires were as beautiful and damned as Thomas Hardy's
peasants. In life these things hadn't happened yet, but I was pretty sure
living wasn't the reckless, careless business these people thought—this
generation just younger than me."[40] Those early stories demonstrate this
especially well, for they are essentially Horatio Alger fantasies projected
through a tragic prism.

In "Absolution" (1924), said to be material first written to fill in the
early life of Jay Gatsby, we encounter the boy sleeping "among his Alger
books" or else daydreaming of a different life entirely, aristocratic, triumphant. In this alternate identity (in which he's called "Blatchford Sarnem-
ington") "a suave nobility flowed from him." Meanwhile, his deeply
religious father, a failure like Fitzgerald's, clings to his own distant model
of success in the figure of James J. Hill, the railroad builder and banker
who dominated St. Paul from the time of his arrival in 1870 to his death in
1916. Enveloped in his harsh Catholicism and his hero worship, the father
"had never in his life felt the balance of any single thing in his hands.
His weary, sprightly, undersized body was growing old in Hill's gigantic
shadow. For twenty years he had lived alone with Hill's name and God."
He takes out his frustrations in his rigidly repressive behavior toward his
son. ("It was not so much the beating he dreaded as the savage ferocity,
outlet of the ineffectual man, which would lie behind it.")[41]

In Alger's books there's usually a surrogate for the absent or inadequate parent, often a benevolent businessman (like Mr. Greyson in *Ragged
Dick*) who guides the youth toward higher things. Here the role is played
unwittingly by a Catholic priest. Unwittingly, because he has his own
problems: he is even more tormented by the conflict between restraint
and desire than the boy. He's a living admonition of what the boy might
become if he remains his father's son. But the priest's self-lacerating sense

of guilt somehow speaks to the boy; his terrible breakdown, though hard to comprehend, helps liberate this younger version of himself. Babbling, he tells the boy to go to an amusement park ("like a fair, only much more glittering"), tells him not to worry about having lied in the confessional. The boy is amazed to see this man, a figure of austere authority, crumble before his eyes. "But underneath his terror he felt his own inner convictions were confirmed. There was something ineffably gorgeous some where that had nothing to do with God" (150).

As usual, Fitzgerald conveys this dream life in terms of light, glitter, and radiance, even in terms of art: "He no longer thought that God was angry at him about the original lie," for he "had done it to make things finer in the confessional, brightening up the dinginess of his admissions by saying a thing radiant and proud." His lying was creative, imaginative, his projection of an alternative life for himself. The priest's delusions, the involuntary expression of his repressed feelings, confirm the boy's inchoate longings for another life; they alleviate his growing sense of guilt, which is destroying the priest. In this way, paradoxically, the older man, so troubled himself, provides the boy with the absolution he needs.

Thus, like so many Fitzgerald works of this period, "Absolution" is both a success story and a failure story. As the priest disintegrates, the boy is set free. This mixture of success and failure is even more marked in other works of the 1920s, such as "Winter Dreams," "'The Sensible Thing,'" *The Great Gatsby*, and the especially fine story that immediately followed *Gatsby*, "The Rich Boy." Seen in terms of the idea of success or failure, these stories lend a fascinating twist to the Horatio Alger pattern. Fitzgerald saw *himself* as an Alger character, an outsider, but his stories, which turn on the relationship between love and money, show that he measured success not by wealth or fame but by his pursuit of the ideal woman. She answers to the dream of an unattainable fullness of being, one that combines romance and class, perfection of feeling and perfection of status. The money itself seems casual, instrumental, just a way of winning her—this material success is sketched in a few lines—while the love dream, the purpose of the money, proves impossible to have and hold.

The idea of the American Dream was ingrained in Fitzgerald; he turned to it but frequently in his own way. Even at the beginning of "The Crack-Up," his most explicit chronicle of failure, he writes, "One should . . . be able to see that things are hopeless and yet be determined to make them otherwise. This philosophy fitted on to my early adult life, when I saw the improbable, the implausible, often the 'impossible' come true. Life was something you dominated if you were any good."[42] This project of mastering life was in the American grain; it was a confident notion that the 1930s—and Fitzgerald's own 1930s—brought sharply into question. But he was already questioning it in showing us the fate of "all the sad young men" of the preceding decade.

"Winter Dreams" gives us the prototypical pattern. Dexter Green, whose father owns "the second best grocery-store in Black Bear," caddies at a local club, where he falls in love with Judy Jones, a popular, mercurial, well-to-do girl who becomes his dream object. Through many ups and downs, she will not have him, for his career "is largely a matter of futures," yet this only fuels his ambition. "But do not get the impression," Fitzgerald tells us, "because his winter dreams happened to be concerned with musings on the rich, that there was anything merely snobbish in the boy. He wanted not association with glittering things and glittering people—he wanted the glittering things themselves." In a few deft but scarcely credible sentences, he grows wealthy enough to have almost anything he desires. "He made money. It was rather amazing. . . . Before he was twenty-seven he owned the largest string of laundries in his section of the country."[43]

But he still cannot have her. He's drawn to her charm, her beauty, above all her inaccessibility, and she treats him "with interest, with encouragement, with malice, with indifference, with contempt," inflicting on him "the innumerable little slights and indignities possible in such a case—as if in revenge for having cared for him at all."

> She had brought him ecstatic happiness and intolerable agony of spirit. She had caused him untold inconvenience and not a little trouble. She had insulted him, and she had ridden over him, and she had played his interest in her against his interest in his work—for fun. She had done everything to him except to criticise him—this she had not done—it seemed to him only because it might have sullied the utter indifference she manifested and sincerely felt toward him. (67)

She pays attention to him, briefly, only after he gives her up and settles on someone else. She loses interest, of course, the moment that planned wedding is off. Dexter sells his business and leaves for New York, but Fitzgerald saves the best for last. Years later, Dexter hears by chance that she has married badly, to a man who mistreats her, and has even lost her looks, grown merely ordinary. Now, instead of experiencing revenge or vindication, he feels his loss for the first time, as if some light in the world had gone out, as if life had passed him by. "The dream was gone. . . . For the first time in years the tears were streaming down his face. But they were for himself now" (75).

Biographers have traced this story to Fitzgerald's own rejection by Ginevra King, and critics have rightly seen a sketch here for Daisy's final rejection of Gatsby.[44] Though Gatsby's early life is left in shadow, he is just as much an Alger character as Dexter Green or as the boy Rudolph Miller in "Absolution." Even more than Ragged Dick's transformation into Richard Hunter, Esq., the molding of James Gatz into Jay Gatsby is a remarkable piece of self-invention (like the career in salesmanship, the keen business sense, of Bruce Barton's Jesus in *The Many Nobody Knows*, the success bible of the 1920s, published the same year as *Gatsby*): "His parents were shiftless and unsuccessful farm people—his imagination had never really accepted them as his parents at all. The truth was that Jay Gatsby of West Egg, Long Island, sprang from his Platonic concep tion of himself. He was a son of God—a phrase which, if it means any- thing, means just that—and he must be about His Father's business, the service of a vast, vulgar, and meretricious beauty."[45] It is hard to re-create the shock and daring of these lines, perhaps too often quoted.

Like Alger's heroes, Gatsby is not entirely self-created. He finds his surrogate father in Dan Cody, a Gilded Age buccaneer who is an adven- turer version of the James J. Hill figure, "a product of the Nevada sil- ver fields, of the Yukon, of every rush for metal since seventy-five, . . . the pioneer debauchee, who during one phase of American life brought back to the Eastern seaboard the savage violence of the frontier brothel and saloon" (106–7). Like his mentor, Gatsby will eventually be done in by a woman, but his success too is a version of Cody's. In Gatsby's deal- ings with Wolfsheim—based on the Jewish gangster Arnold Rothstein— Fitzgerald anticipated the vogue of crime films in the early thirties. He understood, above all, that the gangster and the bootlegger were contem- porary versions of the classic American entrepreneur. Just as Bruce Bar- ton, by making Jesus a genius at marketing and promotion, was adapting the success gospel from an era of production to a culture of consumption, Fitzgerald makes Gatsby a conspicuous consumer, one of the vulgar rich, who, like Citizen Kane, looks to wealth as a means of finding love.* If Barton's Jesus, a back-slapping Babbitt, was "the most popular dinner guest in Jerusalem," Gatsby was the Trimalchio who gave parties that were tawdry emblems of the era, yet meant nothing to him except as a way of recapturing Daisy.

After Gatsby's death, when his real father unexpectedly arrives on the scene, awed and befuddled by the scale of his son's life, we get a precious glimpse of an earlier Gatsby, who was much closer to the original Alger model. He has left behind a notebook he kept as a boy, with a strict daily schedule for self-improvement, along with "general resolves" like "Bath every other day" and "Read one improving book or magazine per week" (180). The father suggests that "if he'd of lived, he'd of been a great man. A man like James J. Hill. He'd of helped build up the country" (175). Instead, nobody shows up for Gatsby's funeral.

Fitzgerald gives the time-honored language of the success gospel a comically bleak, disillusioned cast. He lampoons Wolfsheim as an illiterate who is afraid to come to the funeral, and satirizes the partygoers who used Gatsby while he was alive but haven't quite realized "the party was over." Through Nick Carraway's Conradian narration, he gives us a chilling portrait of the rich themselves, of Tom and Daisy as "careless people" who "smashed up things and creatures and then retreated back into their money or their vast carelessness, or whatever it was that kept them together, and let other people clean up the mess they had made" (186). Above all, through Nick, Gatsby's chronicler and alter ego, he provides a

---

* See Warren I. Susman, *Culture as History: The Transformation of American Society in the Twentieth Century* (New York: Pantheon, 1984), 122–31. Echoing a distinction Malcolm Cowley had developed in *Exile's Return*, Susman says that Barton's "version of the success story helped ease the transition from an older, more producer-oriented system with its traditional value structure to the newer, more consumer-centered system with its changed value structure. Barton's inspirational writings (and in a way that includes his brilliant advertising copy) found a way of bridging the gap between the demands of a Calvinistic producer ethic with its emphasis on hard work, self-denial, savings and the new, increasing demands of a hedonistic consumer ethic: spend, enjoy, use up" (123). In many ways, of course, nothing better exemplified these new imperatives than the youth culture of the early 1920s, with Fitzgerald as its chief spokesman and interpreter.

mixed verdict on Gatsby himself, respectful of his dream, his unshakable fidelity to his grail-like quest, but insistent on its tissue of illusions, the hollowness of its object. Daisy is finally as unworthy of his dream as Judy Jones, something unutterably lovely that was created by the fevered mind of a poor boy from the Midwest.

Using Nick as his narrator, Fitzgerald distances us from Gatsby's hopes and failings. Nick has been clear-eyed about Gatsby from the start, first seeing him "as an elegant young rough-neck . . . whose elaborate formality of speech just missed being absurd" (54). But he's gradually converted to Gatsby's viewpoint, his romantic largeness of vision, balancing his "appalling sentimentality" against his "incomparable" sense of wonder (118). In his poetic treatment of Gatsby's dream and ultimate loss, Fitzgerald veers close to the clichés of romantic fiction yet somehow eludes them entirely.

Fitzgerald can write gorgeous prose about Gatsby's need to "suck on the pap of life, gulp down the incomparable milk of wonder" (118). But when his dream comes to grief on the shoals of Daisy's weakness and Tom's hardness, colliding with barriers of class that money can't breach, Gatsby's constructed personality falls apart, as if Richard Hunter would dissolve back into Ragged Dick. He then tells Nick the story of his youth, "told it to me because 'Jay Gatsby' had broken up like glass against Tom's hard malice, and the long secret extravaganza was played out" (154).

As Westerners, Nick later muses, "perhaps we possessed some deficiency in common which made us subtly unadaptable to Eastern life" (183). Like so much else in the novel, this feels like Fitzgerald himself speaking. By balancing Gatsby's "corruption" against his "incorruptible dream" (160), Fitzgerald preserves an equilibrium between his own lyrical longings for "the glittering things themselves" and his cold-eyed realism about how much they cost and what lies behind the glitter. Even the famous conclusion about the Dutch mariners first glimpsing the new continent has a hard, tragic edge. It places their awkward sense of wonder in the dim past, and grimly stresses what the continent later became.

Other Fitzgerald stories of this period, such as "'The Sensible Thing'" and "The Rich Boy," lack the cultural reach of *Gatsby*, its deft allusions to broader currents of American life, but they reveal other facets of Fitzgerald's sharp interrogation of the success myth, though written long before he made failure one of his central themes. Both tales show how the evanescence of love renders worldly success hollow. Instead of seizing the day, sweeping the girl off her feet, the poor boy in "'The Sensible Thing'" goes off like Dexter Green to make his fortune. To the girl he loves this seems like "the sensible thing." He grows rich easily—this is a given—and when he returns he actually wins her back. But the moment for love has somehow passed them by. "He knew that that boy of fifteen months before had had something, a trust, a warmth that was gone forever. The sensible thing—they had done the sensible thing. He had traded his first youth for strength and carved success out of despair. But with his youth, life had carried away the freshness of his love" (103). He had missed the moment of passion, achieved an empty "success" by doing the sensible thing.

In the long story "The Rich Boy," written right after *Gatsby*, Fitzgerald shows how the wealthy can wall themselves off from life as fully, and as fatefully, as the striving poor. Where "'The Sensible Thing'" is little more than a sketch, "The Rich Boy" has the patient buildup of a short novel. Forsaking the gaps and quick cuts of *Gatsby*, whose mysterious hero we see only by glimpses, this story foreshadows the way Fitzgerald will portray the gradual, almost imperceptible disintegration of Dick Diver in *Tender Is the Night*. Anson Hunter, based on one of Fitzgerald's classmates, has everything going for him: money, connections, pedigree, charm, a gift for both work and friendship. But he too, perhaps out of some inbred sense of superiority, fails to grasp the moment that could have turned unruly desire into a bond of enduring love. This elusive bond is something the woman herself does find (with someone else) before she dies in childbirth. At the end Anson himself is not only isolated, overweight, and deeply morose—a mere shadow of himself—but he's had the bittersweet mortification of seeing her happy, and then seeing her disappear.

For all his social gifts, for all his advantages, there's something about Anson that prevents him from taking hold of his experience, possessing it. Fitzgerald's theme is closely akin to the chilling evocation of the unlived life in late Henry James, the theme of *The Ambassadors*, "The Jolly Corner," and, above all, "The Beast in the Jungle." But Fitzgerald avoids James's melodramatic effects. In its knowing tone and fine social texture, even in its theme, "The Rich Boy" is closest to Edith Wharton's stories of old New York, probing the constraints and disabilities imposed by money and character on the chances of living a full life.

Wharton's heroes are often crippled by the "the prudent old New York way," the code of discretion in which they were reared, which enforces a reticence and emotional timidity that can leave everything important in their lives unspoken. Thus Lawrence Selden in *The House of Mirth* finds the right words to say to Lily Bart only when she's just died, and Newland Archer in *The Age of Innocence* gives up Madame Olenska though she offered him his "first glimpse of a real life." Archer's inward musings, which echo the theme of "The Beast in the Jungle," could easily be applied to Fitzgerald's Anson Hunter: "His whole future seemed suddenly to be unrolled before him; and passing down its endless emptiness he saw the dwindling figure of a man to whom nothing was ever to happen."[46]

Fitzgerald underlines this connection to Wharton's world near the very beginning, in a passage made famous by Hemingway's rejoinder:

> Let me tell you about the very rich. They are different from you and me. They possess and enjoy early, and it does something to them, makes them soft where we are hard, and cynical where we are trustful, in a way that, unless you were born rich, it is very difficult to understand. They think, deep in their hearts, that they are better than we are because we had to discover the compensations and refuges of life for ourselves. Even when they enter deep into our world or sink below us, they still think they are better than we are. (239)

Fitzgerald's carefully etched point of view, as in *Gatsby*, makes this special and different. Wharton never pretended to see New York society from the angle of the poor, or even of the ambitious young man from the provinces. Such characters (like the Jew Rosedale in *The House of Mirth* or the midwestern parvenu Moffatt in *The Custom of the Country*) do figure in her work, but only as vulgar, predatory outsiders. But Fitzgerald, though criticized for his fascination with the rich, deliberately wrote about them from the viewpoint of the outsider: the middle-class provincial, or the poor boy striving for a foothold in a world beyond him.

In a sense, Anson is yet another victim of the drive for success, since he, like certain Wharton heroes and heroines, is impaired by not having or needing it. Wealth proves as disastrous for him as poverty was for Gatsby. If Gatsby became the victim of his dreams and illusions, Scott Donaldson observes, "Anson Hunter's money confers on him a fatal incapacity for illusion" (111). Like the protagonist of "'The Sensible Thing,'" like some of the focal figures in Wharton's work, the comfortable Anson simply cannot seize the day; nothing drives him, nothing impels him to it. He acts out his resistance by getting drunk, missing engagements, behaving badly. "His despair was helpless before his pride and his knowledge of himself" (247). Finally the moment has passed—only then can he truly understand it.

Anson begins to live vicariously through his friends' lives, but as they marry and have children, their worlds draw apart from his. Invoking the honor of the family, he cruelly destroys an aunt's illicit affair, isolating himself even further from the kind of love he himself let slip away. Turning to other women, he discovers "the rarity, in a single life, of encountering true emotion" (260). The odd phrase "in a single life" has, I suspect, a double meaning here: "the life of a single person," someone linked to others only in casual encounters, but also "in any one lifetime," suggesting the rarity of love for anyone at all.[47] In all these stories Fitzgerald seems to be saying that genuine love, if it comes at all, comes only once, and must be caught on the wing before it becomes earthbound. "April is over, April is over," he says at the end of "'The Sensible Thing.'" "There are all kinds of love in the world, but never the same love twice" (104).

To make this clear, Fitzgerald constructs these stories in terms of the double take: the second attempt to realize a love, that heartbreakingly caricatures the first. In conversation, Edith Wharton's biographer R. W. B. Lewis reminded me that she had used such a device in a story called "The Long Run" (in *Xingu and Other Stories*, 1916). Just as the young couples in Fitzgerald, by doing "the sensible thing," wait until it's too late, the man in Wharton's story holds back all too properly when the woman he loves, who is unhappily married, places herself in his hands. Precipitously, she offers to leave her husband and move in with him. All too mindful of the mores of society, he temporizes; they decide to see what happens to them "in the long run." Years later, after her husband dies, he tries but fails to ask her to marry him. "But there, between us, was the memory of the gesture I hadn't made, forever parodying the one I was attempting." In time, she falls into another unsuitable marriage, and he, like Anson Hunter, retreats into a hollow shell of himself. Now they meet only at dinner parties, where they make conversation and play bridge. The fatal phrase recurs: "The long run, well we've run it, she and I." As Fitzgerald would later put it, there are no second acts in American lives, though he himself had one in the 1930s.

Anson Hunter's collapse into dissipation and depression foreshadowed the fate of Fitzgerald's later protagonists. In a 1931 essay, "Echoes of the Jazz Age," he described how remote the great orgy of the twenties seemed, and how some of his contemporaries had begun to come undone long before it ended. A classmate kills his wife, another kills himself; two are killed in speakeasies, while another is murdered in an insane asylum. "These are not catastrophes I went out of my way to look for—these were my friends; moreover, these things happened not during the depression but during the boom."[48] In "Babylon Revisited," a great story of the same year, which anticipates "The Crack-Up," Fitzgerald, with strong autobiographical overtones, gives us a case study of a figure of the twenties, a reformed alcoholic, trying to put his life together again.

Far more harsh and bitter than "Echoes of the Jazz Age," the story is an epitaph for the expatriate life in Paris during the twenties, portrayed as one endless spree of drinking and spending. "He suddenly realized the meaning of the word 'dissipate'—to dissipate into thin air; to make nothing out of something. . . . He remembered thousand-franc notes given to an orchestra for playing a single number, hundred-franc notes tossed to a doorman for calling a cab" (214–15). This was the world in which Charlie Wales, a businessman, had lost his wife, his health, and, when the Crash came, his fortune. Now, shaky but recovered, he has returned to Paris to reclaim his daughter from the stern clutches of his hostile sister-in-law, who had assumed custody when he was in a sanatorium. His mission ends in failure when a drunken pair of old acquaintances appears on the scene, an ill-timed reminder of his former life.

The first thing we notice about this story is the tough, spare writing, which reflects the hard-won self-knowledge that went into it. There's scarcely a remnant of the old iridescent shimmer, that romantic glow; at issue in Fitzgerald's later work is no longer the dream and disappointment but simply survival, pasting it together. Charlie Wales allows himself only one golden memory, really a memory of Scott and Zelda: "We were a sort of royalty, almost infallible, with a sort of magic around us."

But this recollection hurts him with his sister-in-law, and even the good times are spoiled for him now. "In retrospect it was a nightmare," he says, recalling his own earlier pranks (225).

"Babylon Revisited" makes use of the same doubling effect as the earlier stories, but here it's not a single relationship but a whole culture replayed before us. The chastened hero returns to the Paris of his drunken, madcap years. Reclaiming his daughter, he tries to salvage something of love and family from the wreckage. Instead, he's taunted by his sister-in-law and revisited by "ghosts out of the past," *revenants*, who remind him of the man he once was. Everything serves to heighten the feeling that much has changed, yet the past seems inescapable. The return is a disaster, but the story ends on a note of determination. "He would come back some day; they couldn't make him pay forever" (230).

Fitzgerald strains to achieve the same upbeat tone in the three "Crack-Up" articles of 1936, written after he had gone through the kind of alcoholic breakdown foretold in "Babylon Revisited." Zelda had first been hospitalized in 1930; she had attempted suicide several times since. *Tender Is the Night*, nine years in the making, was finally published in 1934, to a very mixed reception. Portraits of the expatriate rich were no longer in fashion; psychological fiction was no longer in fashion—Henry Roth's feverish, Proustian *Call It Sleep* failed to find an audience that same year, though it was set in the immigrant slums of New York's Lower East Side.

To many, Fitzgerald seemed like a figure left over from a distant time. Writing in the *Daily Worker*, the young critic Philip Rahv, who cofounded *Partisan Review* as a Marxist literary journal that year, called on Fitzgerald to come in from under his beach umbrella; the world of the expatriate rich along the French Riviera was no place for a thirties writer. A young admirer, John O'Hara, who also published a remarkable failure novel in 1934, *Appointment in Samarra*, later wrote that Fitzgerald's book "came out at precisely the wrong time in the national history. No matter how good it was, it was about the Bad People, the well fed, well housed, well educated, well born—the villains of the depression. It was a time for Odets and the imitators of Odets, and of Steinbeck and the imitators of Steinbeck."[49]

This reads like personal apologia, since O'Hara had already begun to make the malaise of this prosperous class the basis of his work, while Odets and Steinbeck were as yet completely unknown in 1934. But surely it conveys part of the truth and helps particularly to account for the book's grudging critical reception. Worse still, it was becoming increasingly difficult for Fitzgerald to sell his stories, which were his real bread and butter, to the usual commercial magazines. His drinking worsened. His marriage to Zelda had long since become a nightmare, yet he still felt an enormous responsibility for her, even as he continued to undercut and undermine her. To each other and to her doctors and even in rival works of fiction, they kept trying brilliantly to justify themselves, to take control of the contested narrative of their marriage, which had long since edged over into a public mythology.[50] Finally, in 1935, Fitzgerald gave way, suffering what Bruccoli calls "a lesion of confidence": his most precious resource as a writer was slipping away. This was the context in which Fitzgerald wrote "The Crack-Up," which so embarrassed his friends. By creating the impression that he was washed up, it only served to worsen his problems.

Fitzgerald doesn't tell the whole story in "The Crack-Up"—he lies outright about his drinking—but the essays tap into a vein of harsh honesty and rueful irony that adds something new to his work. Fitzgerald's self-knowledge had always been at the heart of his talent. It allowed him to turn his experience into fiction with amazing speed and insight. He could pin a character in a phrase, evoke a feeling in a way that makes the reader vibrate. During the happier years, this emotional honesty was a key to the sinuous brightness of his prose—the elegiac, romantic tone that enabled him to strike a balance between dream and disillusionment, between utopian reverie and an incipient hard-edged realism. Now Fitzgerald describes his old gift for happiness as a "talent for self-delusion," and dedicates himself to a more thoughtful, clear-sighted wisdom. The old prospective language of pleasure and anticipation gives way to the sober consolations of the writer's professional responsibility, political conscience, and intellectual maturity.

This happens to be the pattern of Fitzgerald's favorite poetry, the great Romantic poems of self-examination, such as Wordsworth's Immortality ode and Keats's nightingale poem, which the novelist incorporated into his own imagination. He refers directly to Shelley's "Lines Written among the Euganean Hills" and, in his eloquent conclusion, virtually paraphrases Wordsworth's famous prose gloss on his great ode. There, looking back late in life, the poet described the ecstatic experiences of his boyhood, which were so powerful that they eclipsed his grasp of the material world. "My own happiness in the past," Fitzgerald writes, "often approached such an ecstasy that I could not share it even with the person dearest to me but had to walk it away in quiet streets and lanes with only fragments of it to distill into little lines in books." Now Fitzgerald finds such feelings "an exception," a kind of freakish immaturity that happened to be in tune with the expansive world around him: "It was not the natural thing but the unnatural—unnatural as the Boom; and my recent experience parallels the wave of despair that swept the nation when the Boom was over."[51]

As if to cheer himself up, Wordsworth in his ode had portrayed the loss of the "visionary gleam" as a growing-up experience, an advance toward maturity and realism. Fitzgerald strains to give the same hopeful accent to his litany of breakdown, failure, and despair. Like Wordsworth embracing the consolations of the "philosophic mind," he tells us he has learned to think, learned more about society, and, above all, given up his claims to personality, "the old dream of being an entire man in the Goethe-Byron-Shaw tradition." Instead, he will become more selfish with his time and energy, less ingratiating. "I have now at last become a writer only" (419). His final, unfinished novel, *The Last Tycoon*, would be a more detached, less self-mythologizing book than any he had ever attempted. But for now he is trying to see his predicament in historical terms, making his problems seem typical of the traumatic shift from the boom decade to the Depression, stressing above all the depressive side of the Depression, its psychological impact. As he said elsewhere, astutely but also defensively, "I am part of the break-up of the times."[52]

Even in its pressure to be cheerful, "The Crack-Up" is an exceptional Depression document, for this was a period when people were indeed trying to cheer themselves up. The New Deal itself provided grounds for hope where none had existed before; it gave substance to Hoover's empty reassurances, convinced people that *something* could be done. But "The Crack-Up" is also interesting as an epilogue to *Tender Is the Night*, Fitzgerald's greatest contribution to the literature of success and failure. In the essays he insists that he was no uncritical admirer of the rich, which should have been clear enough from the novel. Among the disappointments described in "The Crack-Up" was his initial rejection by Zelda, "one of those tragic loves doomed for lack of money," from which money soon saved him. This left him, he says, with an "abiding distrust, an animosity, toward the leisure class—not the conviction of a revolutionist but the smouldering hatred of a peasant" (413).

Tailored for the Depression audience, this last touch—Scott the antinomian radical, the angry peasant—was probably one of Fitzgerald's least credible pieces of self-projection. Yet it shows how he examined the rich from below, as an outsider. If the literature of the thirties was a literature of outsiders—as Kazin says, of new writers who "came from anywhere"[53]—then this Irish American boy from St. Paul, a Princeton dropout, a soldier who "never got over," felt as provincial as any of them. For all his longing for "the glittering things themselves," the author of "Winter Dreams," *Gatsby*, "The Rich Boy," and especially *Tender*—with its harsh portrayal of Nicole's family and its satire on the whole Riviera set—has few illusions about the rich, except for the illusions that the stories themselves dismantle. Fitzgerald strikes a balance a few lines later in his essay, when he describes himself "distrusting the rich, yet working for money with which to share their mobility and the grace that some of them brought into their lives." This is the part of the success ethic he still shares, an insistence on money and mobility as the economic basis for a rich inner life. Like Henry James in *The Portrait of a Lady*, he sees how leisure and culture are intertwined, though he's hardly convinced that one assures the other.

Tender Is the Night is primarily about money and society as a trap, a temptation, especially for the gifted man. When the wealthy Warrens buy themselves a doctor for their sick daughter, they set in motion an inexorable process by which he will decline as she rises; he'll slowly come apart as she comes together. Dick Diver is a promising psychiatrist who can almost taste the fatality of getting involved with his helpless patient and her arrogant family. This establishes our sense of the inner weakness of this ingratiating man, who at first resists, then too easily falls in love with the woman he has been treating. Fitzgerald may not have a full grasp of the ethics of psychiatry, but he shows how Dick compromises his professionalism as he erodes his independence.

We first observe the marriage of Dick and Nicole through the eyes of an innocent young starlet, Rosemary Hoyt, who sees only the charm, glamour, and sophistication of their lives, none of the inner mystery or potential for corruption. Rosemary is the enchanted outsider through whom we witness the public face of the Diver marriage, just as it begins to lose its fine equilibrium. For the time being, Rosemary is the Nick Carraway of the novel, the imperfect observer whose partial view both colors and distances us from the action. With her astonishing early success in the movie *Daddy's Girl*, she's also Fitzgerald himself, young and newly famous, cavorting in the fairy-tale world of Gerald and Sara Murphy's expatriate salon. But as Daddy's Girl, tempting Dick with her freshness and adoration, Rosemary reminds us too of an earlier, more helpless Nicole, whose problems began when she was sexually abused by her domineering father.

The novel's technical problem was Fitzgerald's inability to maintain Rosemary's point of view, his shift to Dick Diver's own angle of vision, and finally to Nicole's, to describe Dick's background and eventual decline. As Nicole breaks down, as the marriage and Dick's morale begin to come apart, the starry-eyed Rosemary recoils from a reality she can't comprehend. Avoiding the deft trompe l'oeil strokes of *Gatsby*, which give us Gatsby's progress in flashes, Fitzgerald, like an older-style realist, gives us the full inner history of the Diver marriage. In her congratulatory letter on the publication of *Gatsby*, Edith Wharton had complained that "to make Gatsby really Great, you ought to have given us his early career . . . instead of a short résumé of it. That would have situated him, & made his final tragedy a tragedy instead of a 'fait divers' for the morning papers." Then, mindful of the literary generation gap, she added, "But you'll tell me that's the old way, & consequently not *your* way."[54] Fitzgerald responded to her complaint with a profusion of circumstantial detail in his Whartonesque story "The Rich Boy"; he followed up with other tales of slow disintegration that foreshadowed *Tender*, such as the painful story "One Trip Abroad," made up of scenes from a marriage inspired by what had been happening in his own life;[55] above all, through some seventeen drafts of the novel itself, he responded by giving essentially the same story a long trajectory, a novelistic richness, closer to traditional fiction yet more ambitious than anything he'd ever written.

When I first read *Tender Is the Night*, I was surprised by some of the "modern" elements in it: the portrayal of the hero as a psychiatrist, the explicit treatment of incest and sexual abuse, Fitzgerald's daring transposition of Zelda's ongoing illness and their troubled marriage directly into fiction, and his insistence on Diver's inexorable decline, despite the book's autobiographical implications. This was not exactly confessional writing:

it wasn't boastful or exhibitionistic, and it was not motivated by revenge or self-exculpation. But it presupposed an intimate, almost undefended relation between life and art, paying little heed to the public pressures on art in the 1930s. Fitzgerald had always husbanded his own experience and projected himself into his work, even in *Gatsby*, where he begins to take over the main character, to fill him out, as the book goes on. There was always a personal stake in his work, even at its most commercial. But as writing became more difficult for him, as his life ran downhill, he began to use fiction as a vehicle of personal crisis, just as Lord Byron had used poetry, playing on his own fame and notoriety, when *his* marriage was failing. "Fitzgerald was, in effect, living the novel he was writing," James Mellow comments. He notes that this interplay could be damaging to the novel, a book that no new version could ever quite pull together, despite Fitzgerald's efforts at revision. "The problem with *Tender Is the Night* is that Fitzgerald tried to solve in literary terms the problems he could not resolve in private life."[56] For all the distance he does achieve, this is not exactly Wordsworth's emotion recollected in tranquillity.

Dick Diver is not wholly credible as a psychiatrist, in spite of the German treatises he writes, as well as Fitzgerald's many futile exchanges with Zelda's eminent doctors. Fitzgerald doesn't fully understand the crucial notion of transference (as Jeffrey Berman points out in *The Talking Cure*),[57] and he tends to talk about patients in ways that must have sounded odd even then, after the vogue of popular Freudianism in the 1920s. "She's a schizoid—a permanent eccentric," Dick says early on of Nicole.[58] But as a novelist, not a diagnostician, Fitzgerald is wholly credible on mental illness and its effect on marriage. Under stress, Nicole can turn quickly from Dick's wife into an object of his care or pity, a medical case that needs special handling. "The dualism in his views of her— that of the husband, that of the psychiatrist—was increasingly paralyzing his faculties" (208). Fitzgerald's dealing with Zelda had given him painful new insight. "Nicole was alternately a person to whom nothing need be explained and one to whom nothing *could* be explained. . . . The brilliance, the versatility of madness is akin to the resourcefulness of water seeping through, over, and around a dike" (211).

One sign of weakness in this novel is that Fitzgerald analyzes and explains too much, bridging gaps, filling in for things we haven't seen— the "real" experiences that underlie the book's vitality and immediacy.

Some of these passages, though they overleap the action of the novel, are astonishingly eloquent about marriage and feeling, markers for scenes Fitzgerald never wrote; other passages simply point outward to Scott and Zelda themselves, as when we hear that "the people she liked, rebels mostly, disturbed her and were bad for her—she sought in them the vitality that had made them independent or creative or rugged, sought in vain—for their secrets were buried deep in childhood struggles they had forgotten" (200). This is psychoanalytic with a vengeance, unassimilated into a fiction whose reach is occasionally beyond its grasp.

Dick's decline, on the other hand, though explained in any number of provisional ways, is more vivid and convincing to us than Nicole's virtually inaccessible state of mind. His stations of the cross are firmly anchored in the book's action, nearly always in small, incremental touches: his drinking, his loss of professional discipline, the silly brawl in Rome, the belated little affair with Rosemary, his break with his old medical colleague Franz, the beginning of his physical deterioration, his abuse of the charm and "pleasingness" that had once served him so well. Fitzgerald's strength is his subtlety, his sense of mystery, his avoidance of the obvious. There's no cheap melodrama in the way Dick loses his grip; his progressive disintegration is both oblique and enormous.

Though Dick in the end is a failure like his father, he is not simply a man who sold out, who found shelter under the umbrella of Nicole's money as he sheltered her from her inner demons. For the longest time he genuinely loves her, as she loves him; in spite of the luxury that envelops him, he works hard to keep up his "qualified financial independence" along with the professional morale that depends on it. Fitzgerald is at his best in the intermediate state between success and failure, when Dick Diver is still able to keep up a good front, hiding his decline even from himself. "Did you hear I'd gone into a process of deterioration?" he says to Rosemary toward the end. "The change came a long way back, but at first it didn't show. The manner remains intact for a long time after the morale cracks" (304). This final recognition is apt, momentous, for the book had begun with appearances, begun with Rosemary on the Riviera beach: that is, with the beautiful couple seen through the eyes of the young innocent, who has now herself gotten older and perhaps wiser.

To politically committed readers in the 1930s, such as Philip Rahv, this subtle focus on morale and appearance was itself a luxury, as people were starving and the system itself seemed to be breaking down. More than many readers, Rahv understood that Fitzgerald wasn't glamorizing the rich but wondered why he was still caught up with them and the little disturbances of their inner lives. But, as we found earlier, problems of morale and appearance were central to the psychology of the Depression. With low morale, even the working man could not find a job or keep it. "A man should keep up a good front, all right," says one of the unemployed in Edward Anderson's proletarian novel, *Hungry Men*. He's referring to his clean shave and decent suit but his point runs deeper. "It's psychological. A man can't get a job looking like a bum or feeling like one."[59] Without unlimited confidence himself—both Zelda and Hemingway knew exactly how to cut him down—Fitzgerald understood the relation of self-confidence, pride, and appearance to social functioning. Like Dos Passos in *U.S.A.* and Farrell in *Studs Lonigan*, he deliberately set his final scenes after 1929, so that Diver's nosedive would parallel the effects of the Crash. He charted the feelings of his characters in tandem with the larger movements of society.

In the novel Dick's decline becomes a touchstone, and other characters see it in their own way. For Franz and his wife, so very European, Dick "is no longer a serious man" (359). Yet, as Fitzgerald shows, their own needs and animosities push them to expel him from his clinic and from their lives. For Baby Warren, the family enforcer, who expresses the viewpoint of the rich, Dick proved in the end an overreacher, someone who aspired beyond his birth and breeding, then couldn't keep it up: "When people are taken out of their depths they lose their heads, no matter how charming a bluff they put up" (331). Like Franz's judgment, this is essentially true, yet it ignores her own role in taking him out of his "depths," which were far deeper than she knew or cared.

In this prism of explanations, Fitzgerald himself seems to favor the emphasis on Dick's "pleasingness" and charm, his need to be loved and used, which makes him inwardly complicit with the people who try to own him. Significantly, he attributes this trait to himself in the "Crack-Up" essays, where he makes fun of his own soothing smile and voice, always eager to please, and promises to defend himself in the future with "that polite acerbity that makes people feel that far from being welcome they are not even tolerated and are under continual and scathing analysis at every moment."[60] Under the old Alger dispensation, so central to the self-image of the Gilded Age, the poor boy could make good by way of hard work, by way of industry and frugality. Fitzgerald's more contemporary characters depend instead on their fatal charm, their need to be well liked. This reflects the new success ethic of the 1930s, as articulated by Dale Carnegie in his famous *How to Win Friends and Influence People* (1936). If *The Great Gatsby* suggested fictional parallels to Bruce Barton's huckster Jesus, then *Tender Is the Night* provides an eerie equivalent to Carnegie's glad-handing specimen of the personality ethic—though in each case Fitzgerald adds a tragic, monitory edge.

The progress from the Darwinian values of Andrew Carnegie to the social ethic of Dale Carnegie is also the difference between Diver's father's failure and his own. Fitzgerald's father died in 1931, and Fitzgerald sailed home from Europe to bury him, as Dick Diver does in *Tender*. In an unpublished essay, some of it transposed directly into the novel, Fitzgerald says his father "came from tired old stock with very little left of vitality and mental energy but he managed to raise a little for me."[61] In the novel, as in the essay, he pays tribute to the old man as a moral guide, someone to whom he instinctively referred his own inner judgments. But in worldly terms, he tells us, "he was one of those about whom it was said with smug finality in the gilded age: 'Very much the gentleman, but not much get-up-and-go about him'" (224). In that Social Darwinist world embodied by James J. Hill, where energy and aggression counted for more than morality, the father was disabled by his traditional values, which he passed on to his son. Significantly, Dick's real violations of his own code—his affair with Rosemary, his imbroglio in Rome—come only after he bids the old man farewell: "'Good-bye, my father—good-bye, all my fathers'" (225). On the book's last page, as Dick drifts ever more indistinctly from town to town in upstate New York, his aimless progress becomes a parody of the "get-up-and-go" his father never had, the success ethic that served them both so poorly.

As if to drive home this point, Fitzgerald drops in a crucial reference to Grant at Galena—the quiet middle years of General Grant after he had left the army in the 1850s, when he toiled anonymously in his brother's general store, awaiting the moment that might never come, the call to greatness. Fitzgerald had already pointed us toward Grant's Alger-like history when he first began to fill in Dick's background. "The foregoing has the ring of a biography," he wrote, "without the satisfaction of knowing that the hero, like Grant, lolling in his general store in Galena, is ready to be called to an intricate destiny." With delicate irony he adds, "Best to be reassuring—Dick Diver's moment now began" (22). Even in the reprise on the last page, Fitzgerald will not say that all hope for him is lost. Instead, we see him through the eyes of a fully healed Nicole: "Perhaps, so she liked to think, his career was biding its time, again like Grant's in Galena" (334).

Dick's "moment" ultimately led nowhere—his failure was definitive—but perhaps Nicole needs to hold out hope, as Fitzgerald would tentatively hold out hope for himself at the end of "The Crack-Up." In *Tender* Fitzgerald tried to define himself by creating a gifted man, not just a snake charmer but an American who typically dreamed of having it all. He tells Franz at the outset that he wants to be "a good psychologist—maybe to be the greatest one that ever lived" (37). Franz, on the other hand, has a European sense of limits. Yet even at this early stage Dick's aims contradicted themselves: "he used to think that he wanted to be good, he wanted to be kind, he wanted to be brave and wise, but it was all pretty difficult. He wanted to be loved, too, if he could fit it in" (39). Eventually, his need to be loved undermines all his other needs. Because Dick is a kind of artist of human consciousness, his terrain of ambition is spiritual and moral, not financial; so is his failure. This made the radical critics of the thirties suspicious, as if Dick's troubles were a piece of authorial self-indulgence, too rarefied for the Depression. It would have been easier if Dick had simply been the victim of the Warrens, the plaything of the predatory rich, instead of sharing responsibility for his own downfall.

Tender Is the Night is finally a curious mixture of two seemingly antithetical literary models, the international novel of Henry James and the success-and-failure novels of Dreiser. Fitzgerald acknowledged his relationship to James when he wrote to the critic Van Wyck Brooks in 1925 that both had "love as a main concern since our interest lies outside the economic struggle or the life of violence,"[62] but this applies more to *Gatsby* than to *Tender,* where the economic factor becomes more important. With its incest theme furnishing an aura of capitalist decadence, *Tender* is a Freudian or Lawrentian version of *The Golden Bowl,* with Mr. Warren as a more sinister edition of Adam Verver and Nicole as a more helpless, more passive Maggie Verver. As the Warrens buy a doctor in Europe, the Ververs, more subtly, acquired a title, in the time-honored way of rich American families.*

Yet Fitzgerald crosses James with Dreiser by making his protagonists outsiders, as he had been, people who are hungry for a larger piece of the world, yet who also can easily lose all the world they have. *Sister Carrie, An American Tragedy*, and other Dreiser novels provided prototypes for many later novels about success and failure. The story of Clyde Griffiths, whose craving for wealth and status leads to his execution for a murder he only half intended, is a Horatio Alger tale in reverse, with a weak hero who does little to determine his own fate. The horrendous deterioration of Hurstwood in *Sister Carrie* was a grimly influential account of inexorable decline and disaster, a permanent rebuke to the optimistic strain in American popular culture. This part of the story became especially meaningful to the writers of the thirties and forties, who had lost some fundamental faith in the promise of American life. In *Tender* Fitzgerald also borrows the star-is-born structure of *Sister Carrie*: as Hurstwood descends, Carrie rises; as Dick Diver fades, Nicole gets stronger—the same seesaw pattern the director William Wellman would use brilliantly in the first version of *A Star Is Born* in 1937.

In real life, of course, Zelda did not get better, but Fitzgerald sensed that she was feeding off him, that she had somehow gotten stronger at his expense. He felt that her passion to be creative, to compete with him, was a caricature of the mad, glamorous life they had led together. The twenties style he turned into myth had now, with his active collaboration, consumed him. In *Tender Is the Night*, as in his other writings of the 1930s, such as "One Trip Abroad," "Babylon Revisited," "Crazy Sunday," and "The Crack-Up," he tried to build a new career by exploring the ways in which he had been overextended, self-destructive, like America itself during the Boom years. Though few could see it at the time, Fitzgerald made his personal plight—the disintegration of his marriage, his health, and his career—somehow definitive of the age. Comparing himself as usual with Hemingway, he wrote to their editor, "I talk with the authority of fail-

---

* The mythically powerful father and monstrously corrupt daughter in Norman Mailer's *An American Dream* would become a later variant of this motif. So would the incestuous father played with menacing charm by John Huston in Roman Polanski's *Chinatown*.

ure, Ernest with the authority of success." During the Depression years at least, this was an authority that demanded to be heard.

The Hollow Men: Studs Lonigan and His World

The authority of failure: here we have one crucial side of the Depression mind. In their own lives, in their work, the writers and artists of the Depression era wanted to succeed as much as anyone. Yet because so many bright promises made to their generation had come to naught, they were drawn to the notion of failure as an inescapable contemporary theme. One of them, James T. Farrell, wrote a powerful essay in 1938 about how he had come to write the *Studs Lonigan* trilogy. The piece deals with the young writer's fear of failure, his wild swings between exalted ambitions and spiritual miseries.

> One moment the young writer is energetic and hopeful. The next he
> is catapulted into a fit of despair. . . . He measures himself, with his
> few unpublished manuscripts, against the accomplishments of the
> great writers, and his ambition seems like insanity. Even though he
> is not particularly conscious of clothes, there are periods when he
> gazes upon his own shabbiness—his unshined shoes, his worn and
> unpressed shiny suit, his frayed overcoat, his uncut hair—and he sees
> these as a badge of his own miserable mediocrity. A sense of failure
> dogs his steps. Living with himself becomes almost unendurable.[63]

As Farrell describes it in this essay, the young writer, by his very appearance, is already on the road to failure. Bored by the college routine, he has been doing badly in school. He is shaggy, bohemian, unkempt. He comes from nowhere. He cannot or will not keep up a "front," yet neither can he be sure that he possesses an inner gift that redeems the external trappings of poverty. He cannot play the game of economic competition and advancement as his forebears did. "Most of them were poor immigrants. Some of them could not read or write. . . .They struggled upward in American society just as have other immigrant groups and races before and after them. . . . . Their lives were dedicated to work, to advancing themselves, to savings and thrift, to raising their families." Though they reached the goals America had promised them, the results were hollow (as they had been for Cahan's David Levinsky). "They believed in the American myth of success and advancement. They believed in the teachings and dogmas of their church. They believed that with homilies, platitudes about faith and work, and little fables about good example, they could educate their children." What this means is that, despite their achievements, "their spiritual resources were meager" (87). They had no good example to pass on to their children, no way of truly educating them. That condition of "spiritual poverty" is the subject of *Studs Lonigan*, a once-famous, now half-forgotten trilogy of novels set in Chicago.* It shows how the lives of the young reflect the bankruptcy of the older generation, the thinness of the nation's ideals, the shallowness of its spiritual culture. The novel begins in 1916 as Woodrow Wilson is renominated for the presidency and the nation seems at its peak. But as the Depression sets in by the third part, aptly called *Judgment Day*, the economic bankruptcy merely exposes the condition of spiritual bankruptcy; the young and their bewildered parents have no firm values to fall back on. Those who survive grow fat, complacent, and lower middle-class, like their parents. By the end we see them *becoming* their parents, going back to the church, mouthing the platitudes they once rebelled against. They are as lost as those fated to die young, like Studs himself. Nothing in their formation, nothing in their environment, can truly sustain them.

Like *Winesburg, Ohio, Main Street*, and other books of the World War I generation, *Studs Lonigan* is the work of a man separating himself from his background—obsessed with it yet burning to demolish it. Behind the writer is always the man running away but also looking back in anger, the man who never forgot anything he saw. Farrell's own surrogate in the book, Danny O'Neill, plays a marginal role as a budding intellectual on the fringes of the street gang, the goofy kid who was never accepted, the one who got away. In a famous passage, he promises himself that "some day he would drive the neighborhood and all his memories of it out of his consciousness with a book,"[64] but the book itself, the evidence of his anger, is also the first sign of his failure: again and again Farrell had

---

* The novels, each longer and more ambitious than the last, were first published as *Young Lonigan* (1932), *The Young Manhood of Studs Lonigan* (1934), and *Judgment Day* (1935).

to keep rewriting it. Rather than driving it out of his consciousness, he was never done with it, and his vast, numbing body of work eventually sapped his literary standing.

The theme of the trilogy is already there in "Studs," the 1929 story from which it all germinated. It's set at the wake of a street-corner tough guy. The slightly younger narrator once looked up to him and his gang; now, all too explicitly, the grown man looks down on them. Like Updike's Rabbit, they are what he himself might have become had he stayed at home. On the last page he tells us exactly what he thinks: "They kept on talking, and I thought more and more that they were a bunch of slobs. All the adventurous boy that was in them had been killed. Slobs, getting fat and middle-aged, bragging of their stupid brawls, reciting the commonplaces of their days." In that sense Studs was lucky: "He, too, was a slob; but he died without having to live countless slobbish years."[65] By the time he wrote the novel, Farrell had better learned his craft: the "slob" element—the outright denunciation, the strained sense of superiority, the nervous declaration of independence—is nowhere to be found, yet it can be read everywhere between the lines. This is a rigidly confining, soul-destroying world, an offshoot of Joyce's *Dubliners* set in Chicago's Irish streets, with its sense of moral paralysis intact.

The novel will always be of extraordinary interest as an immense documentary account of ethnic, urban, lower middle-class Catholics. But what gives it vitality is more than Farrell's power of recall and the profusion of naturalistic detail. Compared with apprentice work like "Studs," Farrell not only keeps himself out but, in a different sense, puts himself in; he identifies with Studs as his doomed alter-ego and builds him up as the troubled, confused spirit of the neighborhood. Much of the book is Studs's reveries: first his boyish dreams of making something of himself, of becoming the cock of the walk, and then, as he begins going downhill, his nagging sense of nostalgia and regret, his rueful feeling that, young as he is, the best is already behind him. "He tried to think of himself as a hero. He was a hero in his own mind. He was utterly miserable" (182). Through it all we sense his longing to be somehow pure and free, his recurring fears of death, his guilt-ridden sexual fantasies, his ambivalence toward his body, and his growing disappointment and self-pity. "He was sad because he had grown up, and because the years had passed like a river that no man could stop." As he half listens to the Mass, he's overtaken by this sadness. "His thoughts were vague. His body and mind seemed separated, his mind swimming away free and in a sea of melancholy, his body heavy and sluggish like a dragging weight" (306). Like young David Schearl in *Call It Sleep* (published the same year), Studs has inchoate spiritual longings. But they are not to be fulfilled by the church itself, which has helped make him so tormented and divided, so uncomfortable with himself. As far back as his grade-school graduation, a pompous priest had foretold his fate with a gloomy, rhetorical sermon on the theme of *"Tempus fugit!* Time flies," time as a "thief in the night" robbing us of our youth (33).

Later he comes to know the feeling well: "All his hopes were gone, like they'd dropped into a sewer" (207–8). The whole book is methodically structured in terms of dream and disappointment, hope and decline. Originally it was to have led up to Studs Lonigan's wake—the material of the original story—at the end of what is now the second novel. But Farrell, like Fitzgerald in *Tender Is the Night*, must have seen that what he had was more than a biography, more than personal history. Surrounded by a whole society in the throes of crisis, he gives Studs a temporary reprieve and writes the third novel, *Judgment Day*, as a Depression documentary, complementing Studs's life with films, newsreels, headlines, references to Mussolini. He shows us Studs and his father losing their shirts in the stock market, and makes Studs's disintegration stand for something more than their soulless neighborhood, the inexorable aging process, and a Catholic sense of guilt and melancholy. He makes it stand for the decline of America and its ideals, for the spiritual poverty inherent in the failed promise of material affluence, the shattered dream of success.

What Fitzgerald did implicitly, obliquely, Farrell, like other documentary novelists, insists on too strenuously, too directly. *Studs Lonigan* is about the destruction of the American Dream, but poor Studs can hardly bear the weight Farrell has put on him. His losses in the stock market and his admiration for Mussolini are never convincing. They're too marginal to his character, too representative. Farrell makes him and his friends the mouthpiece for whatever he dislikes in America, including anti-Semitism and racism. He toys with the notion of making these people the raw material for a native American fascism. Like the naturalists of the 1890s, such as Frank Norris, the author also stacks the deck against Studs, boxes him in too mercilessly. Dick Diver's decline, though inexorable, was at least partly of his own making. But Studs, manipulated by the author to make his points, is mainly the product of the conditions that created him. As Lionel Trilling observed of Farrell's stories, "Whoever reads about these people is accepting an invitation to regard them with sympathy but always at a remove, from above looking down."[66] A certain detachment, even condescension, was built into Farrell's project.

By implication, both Farrell and Fitzgerald respond to the American dream of success with the idea of art, a notion of spiritual self-fulfillment through craft and creative effort. Danny O'Neill's escape to write a book is also Dick Diver's early promise as a psychiatrist; it's the "genius" of the books he writes and could have written. This notion of art as a form of freedom and salvation was more credible to the rebellious generation of the twenties and thirties than it has since become. Fitzgerald brings it into question in the book itself, showing us a man who, in the end, had only two or three ideas, a man whose "spear has been blunted" (221), who simply peters out. With our contemporary "hermeneutics of suspicion," we have come to see the worship of art and genius as a piece of dubious idealism, if not ideology, a cover for mixed motives and social contradictions. But in the twenties and thirties it still represented an escape from small-minded (if not always small town) American values. The artist, seeking fulfillment through freedom of expression and an almost utopian fullness of being, was projected as the antithesis of provincial values.

This is how the writers could dream of their own success while rejecting the American worship of success. What Fitzgerald means by "the authority of failure" is really a Dostoyevskian (or Flaubertian, or Joycean) idea of success: we lose the world but gain our souls—through poverty and self-denial, through humiliation, through devotion to art. Rather than filthy lucre, we amass what the French social scientist Pierre Bourdieu called "cultural capital," which should not be reduced to a matter of prestige, or even fame. If it is true, as Nathanael West suggested, that "Alger is to America what Homer was to the Greeks"—the man who best defined the epic enterprise of self-improvement and commercial ambition—then writers like Dostoyevsky, Joyce, and Flaubert defined the contrary goal that young Americans pursued when they took up the artistic life: a bohemian ideal, a spiritual ideal, within what they took to be a philistine society. This dream of escape into art dimmed in the thirties as the Depression worsened. More precisely, it oriented itself toward immediate social material. But the older notion still can be found in the angry judgments that underlie a book like *Studs Lonigan*, by writers incensed by their middle-class origins, looking elsewhere for a spiritual homeland.

As late as the 1960s, artists and intellectuals were united in their disdain for the hard material realities of American life, so that in *Making It* (1967), a precocious autobiography, Norman Podhoretz could proclaim that he was exposing a "dirty little secret" that would shock the literary world: that "it is better to be a success than a failure."[67] Ultimately this embrace of success won out: the lines grew blurred between art and commerce, between intellectual ambition and social ambition. The Freudian axiom triumphed: that writers write and painters paint in the pursuit of money, fame, and love. The idealized notion of art as a calling was deconstructed as mere mystification. By the 1980s, the age of Andy Warhol and Ronald Reagan, artists courted money and celebrity openly and flaunted the spoils they had gained in the marketplace. At the same time, confessional writers, blurring the lines between public and private, tried to turn the base metal of failure into the jingling coin of notoriety. They learned that addiction, alcoholism, and sexual abuse could pay.

This takes us far afield from pure-minded Farrell, with his theme of "spiritual poverty," attacking the shoddy dreams and values of the Lonigans and their friends. Farrell may have modeled his book on Flaubert's *Sentimental Education*, with its circular, ironic structure. In Flaubert the protagonists look back wistfully in the last two chapters at a simple early experience—a visit to a whorehouse. Nothing in the interim has really reached them; their sentimental education has been no education at all. In the same way Studs's only triumphs come at the beginning: the day he sat in the tree with Lucy Scanlan, singing "The Blue Ridge Mountains of Virginia," the day he won the respect of the other kids by whipping the local bully, Weary Reilley. These are the glowing moments that always come back to haunt him, the recollections that highlight his failures and disappointments. Across the vast expanse of some nine hundred pages, it is as if only a few things actually happen to Studs. His life and mind are built up out of a handful of leitmotifs the author recycles from chapter to chapter. Despite Studs's decline, no book has ever offered so little real progression; his stations of the cross, unlike Dick Diver's, are all the same.

Grounded in the new urban sociology of the Chicago school, represented by researchers like Robert Park, *Studs Lonigan* is also closely connected to the gangster films and tough-guy novels of the early Depression years. This was the time not only of the classic crime movies, many set in Capone's Chicago, but also of the novels of Dashiell Hammett, the first novels of James M. Cain, the early stories of Raymond Chandler. In *Judgment Day* Studs goes to see a gangster movie, released by the "Grandiose Film Corporation," called *Doomed Victory*—a wonderful play on the success-and-failure theme of these pulpy classics. He identifies with the tough hero but is annoyed at the downbeat ending. As I indicated earlier, the hard-boiled fiction of the period, with little reference to the Depression yet closely akin to it, lays bare a world of universal cynicism and corruption, exposed by a "hero" who is partly implicated in that corruption.

Studs is an adolescent parody of this tough-guy model. Fitzgerald in the twenties had helped put youth on the agenda, making it the vanguard of something racy and new, a different morality. Farrell gives us another side of youth, "rebels without a cause," their swagger pointless, their rebellion empty. From the very beginning at the age of fifteen, Studs prides himself on not having "mushy feelings"; like Jean-Paul Belmondo aping Humphrey Bogart in *Breathless*, Studs gazes in a mirror with a cigarette dangling from the corner of his mouth. "He looked tough and sneered" (15). As it turns out, Studs is anything but hard and self-confident. Lucy is his core of romantic sentiment, as the brutish Weary Reilley exposes his kernel of desperate insecurity, which would be given a racial coloring by Richard Wright in *Native Son*.

This hollow core is Farrell's main point: behind the increasingly threadbare façade of his bravado and rebellion, Studs, like almost everyone else in his world, is hopelessly conventional. His dreams are as pathetic as his little triumphs. Despite his would-be toughness, Studs is another version of the "little guy" so dear to the thirties, like Chaplin's tramp and the hero of Hans Fallada's best-selling *Little Man, What Now?* (1933). As Studs grows paunchy and his health fails, he grows fearful of everything. Beaten up by his old nemesis and even by his contemptuous younger brother, he can barely maintain a surface pride. But Farrell refuses to sentimentalize his inadequacies. Studs's goals in life prove not unrealizable but cheap and unworthy. As Farrell sees it, unforgivingly, the Depression delivers a coup de grâce to an already weak structure of values—hollow, blustering, sanctimonious, superficial, materialistic—the qualities that link the doomed Studs to his small-minded parents, weak-minded friends, and narrow-minded church. The Depression simply provides additional material for the author's furious declaration of independence, his payback, framed as a re-creation of the hated world from which he sprang.

Go West: Sending Up Horatio Alger

In 1931 a young man still in his twenties published a bitter autobiographical essay in the prestigious pages of *Scribner's Magazine*. It described how, six years earlier, he had gone directly from college to work in the advertising department of a large corporation; it itemized the frustrations he and his eager co-workers had encountered. Full of fresh ideas, ready to conquer the world, they couldn't get their ideas off the ground. They felt tightly constrained by the timidity of those above them, who feared lawsuits, feared offending distant markets, distrusted anyone who wasn't a team player. Advertising was an exciting new game then; the expanding business world had the appeal of power and adventure. These recruits had been attracted to the corporation because of its modernity and dynamism, "the subtle feeling of power" that emanated from it, but the power seemed to be floating far above them, mysterious and inaccessible. "Foreign companies, great areas of men and shops were bought and sold in the quiet upper offices. Yet the tempo of our work was so slow and undetermined we smarted in harness."[68]

These young men, he says, had seen vast changes in the structure of society since the war. The small town had been overtaken by the big city, small business swamped by big business: "The municipal power plant was absorbed by a utility. Automobiles and hard roads overcame the peculiar barriers of small towns. Chain stores took over ancient mercantile establishments. We saw corporation initials tacked to coal-mines, hardware stores, steel-mills. The small town became a subsidiary of the city." Thus were ambitious young men attracted to "the Armageddon of the world— big business," from whose ranks came many of the heroes, the role models, on whom they were encouraged to pattern their lives.

The author of this essay never made it into the ranks of big business. He was the future film critic and documentary filmmaker Pare Lorentz, whose rhythmical, incantatory narration of *The River* and *The Plow That*

Broke the Plains may have borrowed something from the despised techniques he learned in advertising. He speaks in this essay as a typically disillusioned young radical, but his aim is to expose not just the corporation but the whole American ideology of success. Lorentz and his co-workers had entered corporate life because it was powerful, because it had been widely idealized, but also because it seemed to offer the greatest field of activity. It seemed like the modern equivalent of the frontier. "It never occurred to us that we were temperamentally unfit to work for corporations. . . . We still thought we were two-gun men pushing back the frontiers of the world and we serenely wrote advertisements telling the public how our company was pioneering for humanity and tried ourselves to believe we were covered-wagon drivers."

Instead, they found fear, competition, mutual distrust. "A staff of lawyers examined every line of advertising that left the offices." Above all, they found the path to advancement blocked, partly by the rigidity of corporate life, partly by their own unsuitability. "They discovered a world of highly geared machines, not an open wilderness." They had been enticed but then tripped up by "the great American myth," that is, "the ubiquitous legend of working up from the bottom." The large corporate enterprise, which had redefined the very terms of success, had cloaked its novelty in the old American ideology, so well articulated by writers ranging from Franklin to Alger. The faith in hard work, individualism, and mobility was now simply decorating the corporate framework, falsifying its real nature. Lorentz's essay is a young man's declaration of disenchantment. "America is no longer the land of opportunity for a young man of honor and decency. The man who starts at the bottom of a corporation to work his way up is a fool."

Did Lorentz and his friends really still believe in this Franklin-Alger vision at precisely the moment when structural changes in the economy were rendering it irrelevant? Did they honestly think the corporation was the modern version of the frontier, or was this analogy no more than a sweeping rhetorical convenience to sharpen their criticism? Were they naive, or were they simply rewriting their experience after the fact? It turns out, as we'll later see, that the frontier analogy was remarkably interwoven with the whole ideology of success in the 1930s, just when the frontier itself was becoming a distant memory, increasingly enveloped in a haze of myth. It's worth noting that Lorentz blames not the Depression but, like many young radicals, the basic catch-22 structure of the economy. "Every business, every profession has been affected. . . . Invent a device for a plane, a ship, a railroad engine. Without capital you cannot compete. With capital you are controlled."

Lorentz's conclusion reveals his nostalgia for an older kind of rugged individualism. He longs for power, for the scope to make his own mark; as a well-trained son of the middle class, he wants to be where the action is: "No youngster of any ambition cares to bury himself in the minor activities of a small town when college has given him the urge to go out and battle in the high places." But now, he laments, "the great American game of starting from scratch is definitely over." It certainly was. The New Deal, though it tried to regulate the power of business, if anything, made the federal government itself a large corporate enterprise. Lorentz would later do his own best work as a filmmaker in the employ of this government.

As we have seen all through this chapter, Lorentz was not the only writer to criticize the American ideology of success. Horatio Alger's most authoritative biographers show that though his wide readership as a boys' writer belongs to the period before World War I, his "enshrinement as a cultural hero," the key to understanding our national ideals, was largely a later development. "The radical transformation in Alger's reputation, his canonization as an American success mythmaker, occurred largely after 1920 as his books declined in popularity and eventually lapsed from print." Thanks to the business ideals of the 1920s—the very values Pare Lorentz was attacking by 1931—"Alger's stock hero was reinvented during this decade as a business tycoon. . . . The phrase 'Horatio Alger hero' obtained popular currency in the language during the 1920s—its first appearance in print may have occurred as late as 1926, even as more libraries were removing Alger's books from their shelves."[69] This belated canonization made it inevitable that the young men of the next decade would focus their attacks on Alger as the ideologist of American capitalism and individualism.

It was Nathanael West who wrote, "Only fools will laugh at Horatio Alger, and his poor boys who make good. The wiser man who thinks twice about that sterling author will realize that Alger is to America what Homer was to the Greeks."[70] West published the most savage and cynical failure novels of the decade, too savage, in fact, for most contemporary readers to accept. Unlike Alger's fame, his popularity was a posthumous one; the tone of his work was more in tune with the apocalyptic black humor of the sixties than with the prevailing naturalism of the thirties. The only one of his books that has *never* been properly appreciated is *A Cool Million*, his 1934 satire on a Horatio Alger novel. (It appeared in the same year as *Tender Is the Night*, *Call It Sleep*, and *The Young Manhood of Studs Lonigan*, none of which were really welcomed when they first appeared.) Though West's method is different from Fitzgerald's or Farrell's, he too focuses on dreams and illusions, especially the dream of success. As we have previously noted, all three of West's mature novels deal with cultural myths; they are rooted in his ambivalent fascination with American popular culture. *A Cool Million* was his only outright parody, and, with its ultimate focus on the rise of a homespun American fascism, his only book that could remotely be described as a political novel.

As a parody, *A Cool Million* takes us into the territory of West's wacky, gifted brother-in-law, S. J. Perelman, who was already well known as a *New Yorker* writer and occasional scenarist for the Marx brothers during their best period. When *Miss Lonelyhearts* appeared the preceding year, Perelman wrote a wildly surreal Swiftian sketch of West, describing him as "only eighteen inches high": "He is very sensitive about his stature and only goes out after dark, and then armed with a tiny umbrella with which he beats off cats who try to attack him." (This is virtually a treatment for a scary horror film made more than twenty years later, *The Incredible Shrinking Man*.) Perelman's specialty was not simple parody but Homeric riffs in which the language takes off on its own wild trajectory: rolling catalogs full of odd taglines, majestically purple prose, and ripe clichés torn from their banal context. His sketch of West ends with the following piece of sheer anarchy, where words cut loose from all referential meaning:

> What I like about him most is his mouth, a jagged scarlet wound etched against the unforgettable blankness of his face. I love his sudden impish smile, the twinkle of those alert green eyes, and the print of his cloven foot in the shrubbery. I love the curly brown locks cascading down his receding forehead; I love the wind in the willows, the boy in the bush, and the seven against Thebes. I love coffee, I love tea, I love the girls and the girls love me. And I'm going to be a civil engineer when I grow up, no matter WHAT Mamma says.[71]

Perelman, like West in his first novel, *The Dream Life of Balso Snell*, takes us back to the Dada and surrealism of the 1920s, but Perelman's nihilism always seems more harmless than West's: wholly intoxicated with language, it affords us a subtle pleasure without offending anyone. Reveling in clichés, exquisitely literary, Perelman points toward the later *New Yorker* sketches of Woody Allen and Donald Barthelme, while West anticipates the more somber satirical spirit of Flannery O'Connor's *A Good Man Is Hard to Find*, Thomas Pynchon's *The Crying of Lot 49*, and Ralph Ellison's *Invisible Man*. Yet both Perelman and West belong to the playful, anarchic side of the early thirties that cultivated the wild antics of the Marx brothers and W. C. Fields along with the sexually suggestive comedy of Mae West, before Hollywood's Production Code kicked in, when movies still exuded some of the free spirit of vaudeville and burlesque. This kind of humor, which mocks everyone and everything with gusto and abandon, belongs to the low point of the Depression, when anarchy was a safe form of cultural rebellion but also a reflection of American life on a roller coaster of uncertainty. Even before this humor turned zanily political, as it does in 1934 with *Duck Soup* and *A Cool Million*, it was all at once a mode of dissent, of national expression, and of sheer escape into lunacy. (After 1934 it gave way to something different: a more oblique and reserved lunacy anchored in class: screwball comedy.)

A Cool Million, subtitled "The Dismantling of Lemuel Pitkin," is a Horatio Alger novel in reverse—using some actual fragments of Alger's books, so that Alger's biographers perversely describe it as a plagiarism, not a parody.[72] But *A Cool Million* has many other literary models, especially the classic literary attack on optimism, Voltaire's *Candide*. West models his book on Alger's basic plot: the young lad from the provinces setting out to make his fortune. Lionel Trilling once singled out this theme as a key feature of the major European novels of the nineteenth century. In a famous essay, he described the protagonists of these novels, characters like Stendhal's Julien Sorel and Balzac's Rastignac, as legendary, romantic figures whose dreams, conquests, and failures reflect the new fluidity of society after the French Revolution:

From the late years of the eighteenth century to the early years of the twentieth, the social structure of the West was peculiarly fitted—

one might say designed—for changes in fortune that were magical and romantic. The upper-class ethos was strong enough to make it remarkable that a young man would cross the borders, yet weak enough to permit the crossing in exceptional cases.[73]

Trilling goes on to cite Rousseau and Napoleon as real-life paradigms for these fictional creations. America, with its openness and professed egalitarianism, was the perfect venue for a meaner version of this success story, based not on Rousseau but on Emerson's (and Samuel Smiles's) gospel of self-reliance and self-help. The young man in Horatio Alger's fables takes none of the moral liberties of Julien Sorel or Rastignac, but he too gets an education in good and evil, and learns to make his way in the modern jungle. He depends too much on patrons and chance encounters to be described as wholly self-reliant. An Alger biographer, Ralph D. Gardner, has composed an amusing synthesis of the typical plot complications that helped inspire West:

> Scoundrels conspired to waylay the hero by chloroform, slugging, drugging, or shanghaiing. They tried to steal his wallet, and he was occasionally thrown into an abandoned well. Between daring escapes he performed heroic deeds, rescuing a child from the path of a runaway horse, jumping into the East River to save a life, flagging down a speeding train or preventing an old man from being black-jacked or robbed.[74]

In Alger these horrendous twists and turns, besides being the staples of popular adventure fiction, were tests of character. His hero's bravery and initiative brought him recognition and reward, putting him on the path to stability as well as respectability. As Gardner adds,

> He was rewarded with cash (which was wisely invested) and a better job, perhaps as a clerk earning as much as ten dollars a week. Because he showed initiative and shrewdness, he was sent on a confidential and perilous journey. This mission was always a triumph and in its course he may have discovered some secret that cleared up the mystery of his own identity or accidentally met the man who helped

282 DANCING in the DARK

recover his legacy. While the hero most often had not achieved great wealth, he was well on his way with the clouds past and a bright future predicted at the inevitable happy ending.

For this bright march toward success, West substituted an inexorable decline and disintegration—literally, because Lemuel Pitkin, losing one limb after another, simply comes apart as the book goes on. Like so many of the young men in Alger's novels, Lemuel Pitkin—his name is a facetious linkage of Swift's hapless Gulliver with an avenue in Brooklyn—sets out to make his fortune in the land of opportunity. But in the process he loses his teeth, his eye, his leg; he gets scalped, gets beaten up every night as a vaudeville "stooge," and is finally shot through the heart by an assassin in the audience.

Lem's "dismantling" transcends West's parody of success novels: it's his audacious conceit for the body politic, for a nation coming apart during the depths of the Depression. The authorities themselves are often the agents of Lem's deconstruction, as when he is first thrown into jail and gets all his perfectly healthy teeth pulled. At other times the catastrophes occur in comically violent set pieces out of Hollywood films and pulp fiction: West has feeble fun with Wild West clichés but does better with the ripe Oriental stereotypes that were popular in the thirties, thanks in part to the daily diet of war news from China and Japan, which had invaded Manchuria in 1931. (Following the success of Joseph von Sternberg's *Shanghai Express*, Frank Capra's *The Bitter Tea of General Yen* had just been shown as the opening attraction at the new Radio City Music Hall in New York's Rockefeller Center. Other Oriental-themed movies later in the decade would range from *The Good Earth* to the popular Charlie Chan detective series.)

The "inscrutable" Oriental, which allows West some funny moments, was as much an expression of America's isolationism as of its nativism or racism—a sense that the world out there was distant, different, exotic, and essentially unmanageable. West's crafty Chinamen rub their hands gleefully and smile inscrutably, but his favorite motif is the pop fantasy of white slavery. Dropping his much abused heroine into Wu Fong's House of All Nations, West perfectly imitates the mixture of lubricity and moralism in so much pulp fiction, which reflects both the hypocrisy of our puritan culture and the poverty and half-suppressed violence of our fantasy lives.

The main object of lust in *A Cool Million* is Betty Prail, the pure but endlessly beleaguered maiden of all popular serials, whose repeated rape, abuse, and enslavement run parallel to the hero's dismemberment. West had considered calling *Miss Lonelyhearts* "a novel in the form of a comic strip," but *A Cool Million*, its very title a Perelmanic cliché, is his real venture in cartoon writing, especially in the "literary" touches that adorn each peril and pitfall. As Miss Prail is about to be raped, with her all-American attacker standing over her ("His little pig-like eyes shone with bestiality"), the lip-smacking author, as beady-eyed as the character himself, discreetly draws a curtain across the scene: "It is with reluctance that I leave Miss Prail in the lecherous embrace of Tom Baxter to begin a new chapter, but I cannot with propriety continue my narrative beyond the point at which the bully undressed that unfortunate lady."[75]

At times West seems just as implicated in the lechery and violence as the sanctimonious "author" he is parodying. Though Lem and Betty are little more than coefficients of a wildly proliferating plot, the humor of their interminable travail can seem sadistic—when it's not simply crude and sophomoric. Trying to save Betty from yet another rape, for example, Lem is caught in a bear trap:

> Its saw-toothed jaws closed with great force on the calf of his leg, cutting through his trousers, skin, flesh, and halfway into the bone besides. He dropped in a heap as though he had been shot through the brain.
>
> At the sight of poor Lem weltering in his own blood, Betty fainted. In no way disturbed, the Missourian went coolly about his nefarious business and soon accomplished his purpose. (153–54)

This kind of grotesque violence and melodramatic euphemism has always been a staple of popular culture, reflecting our own repressed fantasies. The main conceit of the novel, however, is that these people, like the eternally hopeful Candide, or the creatures in Road Runner cartoons, are impervious to anything that befalls them. Though they come apart physically, they learn nothing from being thwarted and knocked about, not even to cultivate their own gardens. As Candide is armored with a philosophical optimism, Lem is fortified with the clichés of individualism and opportunity.*

Lem's teacher, like Candide's, was a philosopher, one "Shagpoke" Whipple, former president of the United States and small-town theorist of the American Dream. In Whipple, loosely based on Calvin Coolidge, West parodies the "Log Cabin to the White House myth" that enjoyed such a long run in American politics.[76] Whipple's speeches offering fatherly counsel to Lem burlesque the rhetoric of all those success sermons since the Civil War, such as Russell Conwell's ubiquitous *Acres of Diamonds*. "America is still a young country," Whipple says.

> Office boys still marry their employers' daughters. Shipping clerks are still becoming presidents of railroads. Why, only the other day, I read where an elevator operator won a hundred thousand dollars in a sweepstake and was made a partner in a brokerage house. Despite the Communists and their vile propaganda against individualism, this is still the golden land of opportunity. Oil wells are still found in people's back yards. There are still gold mines hidden away in our mountain fastnesses. (102–03)

Of course, Whipple takes Lem and his widowed mother for everything they have; this too belongs to "the golden land of opportunity," opportunities for con artists. Lem next meets him in prison, but this is just a temporary setback, another turn of the wheel of luck or fate that plays such a large role in success preaching, including Alger's books. Whipple is simply the first and biggest of the many con men and hypocrites Lem meets along the way; in this West is faithful to the gritty side of Alger's vision that cultural historians tend to neglect. Alger's novels are a wonderful guide to the seamier side of city life, especially the rich Dickensian population of sharpies who lay cunning snares for the ever gullible hero. West adores these smooth-talking tricksters who repeatedly fleece poor Lem of everything he has, but they also epitomize the entrepreneur-

---

* Ralph Ellison would later adapt the *Candide* model for *Invisible Man*, as Kurt Vonnegut would for *Slaughterhouse-Five* and other novels. It became a staple of the revival of the picaresque, a recurring portrait of injured innocence in a cruel and sadistic world.

ial spirit preached by Whipple and practiced by Wu Fong in his House of All Nations. West shares with Alger a love of rapscallion vitality: these tricksters and hucksters, with their ingenious rap and their sly, exuberant energy, embody his sense of the city. As self-created figures staging their own lives, they represent a typical American personality.*

Yet the city for West is also a scene of poverty, misery, and violence. When Lem finally hobbles into New York, the Depression renders him invisible: "Times had grown exceedingly hard with the inhabitants of that once prosperous metropolis and Lem's ragged, emaciated appearance caused no adverse comment. He was able to submerge himself in the great army of the unemployed." Lem himself has become a physical emblem of the disintegration of Depression America; West presents this, ironically, as some kind of virtue, a way of going unnoticed, almost a form of solidarity. Though in bad shape, he's a cut above his fellows: "For one thing, he bathed regularly. Each morning he took a cold plunge in the Central Park lake on whose shores he was living in a piano crate." West's sentences have a special way of detonating before they end. "Also, he visited daily all the unemployment agencies that were still open, refusing to be discouraged or grow bitter and become a carping critic of things as they are" (168). West might have known that "Things as They Are" was the subtitle of a great revolutionary novel of the 1790s, the radical philosopher William Godwin's *Caleb Williams*. Like Dickens's

---

* Ralph Ellison, like his friend Saul Bellow, shared West's attraction to con men and tricksters. Besides updating *Candide* in *Invisible Man*, Ellison may have leaned on West along with black folk materials when he created his own trickster figure, the ubiquitous Rinehart, who epitomizes the shifting dodges and identities that enable a man to survive in the fluid street world of Harlem. He certainly noticed Lem's glass eye, which tends to pop out at inconvenient times, since this also happens at a crucial moment to Jack, who recruited Ellison's hero into the Brotherhood, Ellison's broad take on the Communist Party.

All in all, *Invisible Man*, set in the 1930s, is a remarkably Alger-like novel, not only in its sense of the city. Like *A Cool Million*, it is a tongue-in-cheek bildungsroman about a young man from the provinces who is abused and misused by everyone he meets. Ellison, like West, crosses Alger with *Candide*, and his book turns eventually into a political novel. The wide-eyed hero's ultimate disillusionment, his retreat to his underground lair, from which he narrates his story, is Ellison's comment on a naive American optimism and on the American Dream of success and mobility—For Whites Only. Having completed this exorcism, he promises to emerge.

mid-Victorian *Hard Times*, that indictment of the industrial system whose very title became synonymous with the Great Depression, Godwin's and West's fables focus less on the system itself than on its intellectual under-pinnings. Dickens's broad burlesque of the utilitarianism of Jeremy Ben-tham is, like West's travesty of Alger, an assault on rugged optimism and its indifference to human misery. Unlike Ellison's hero, who grows dis-illusioned, Lem maintains his optimism to the end, at the very moment that many intellectuals were radicalized by the Depression and became fierce critics of capitalism.

West shows prophetically how discontent with the Depression could also lead in a quite different direction. Ominously, the last part of *A Cool Million* focuses on Lem's martyrdom and Whipple's transformation into the führer of a homegrown American fascism. The novel becomes a study in the politics of resentment, showing—as West does in *Miss Lone-lyhearts* and *The Day of the Locust*—how mass fantasy can explode into vio-lence. It's important to understand that this book was written in 1933, the year Hitler took power in Germany. (While writing it, West intui-tively boned up on *Mein Kampf* as well as on Horatio Alger.) In conjur-ing up the "Leather Shirts," West comments farcically on Mussolini's and Hitler's rise to power but also imagines a possible native variant. In one swoop he foretells two oddities of the 1950s, the John Birch Society and the Davy Crockett craze. Describing his National Revolutionary Party, "popularly known as the 'Leather Shirts,'" Whipple says, "The uniform of our 'Storm Troops' is a coonskin cap like the one I am wearing, a deer-skin shirt and a pair of moccasins. Our weapon is the squirrel rifle" (113). Could Thomas Pynchon's vision of Southern California as a cabinet of cults and curiosities be far behind?

Whipple points to a long line of the unemployed. "These men," he says, "are the material from which I must fill the ranks of my party" (113). Whipple blames "the Jewish international bankers and Bolshevik labor unions" because there are so few jobs. Like many real populist demagogues, Whipple taps the justified resentment of the unemployed and directs it toward the usual scapegoats. In the fate of Lemuel Pit-kin, West farcically but horrifically portrays the descent into chaos and despair in the 1929–33 period as well as the promise of order that was one key to the appeal of fascism. Lem's physical dismemberment feeds the imagery of disease, decadence, and decay that figured so significantly in the rhetoric of fascism. In this rhetoric the Jew was the bacillus that was poisoning the body politic, as the Red was the rotten member that needed to be amputated.

The novel ends with Lem as a vaudeville clown being beaten nightly until he simply falls apart:

> For a final curtain, they brought out an enormous wooden mallet labeled "The Works" and with it completely demolished our hero. His toupee flew off, his eye and teeth popped out, and his wooden leg was knocked into the audience.
>
> At the sight of the wooden leg, the presence of which they had not even suspected, the spectators were convulsed with joy. (171)

This was a period when roving thugs were liberally administering beatings in the streets of German and other cities. After Lem is assassinated, he is translated into myth, like Horst Wessel, the Nazi "martyr," or John Birch, or like the "Horatio Alger hero." The National Revolutionary Party takes possession of his history, and the novel ends with Whipple's speech over what remains of his body, a speech that mingles the clichés of the American Dream with the clichés of fascist demagoguery. He speaks of "the right of every American boy to go into the world and there receive fair play and a chance to make his fortune by industry and probity without being laughed at or conspired against by sophisticated aliens." He lovingly details the stages of Lem's "dismantling" and concludes with a mock-peroration:

> "But he did not live or die in vain. Through his martyrdom the National Revolutionary Party triumphed, and by that triumph this country was delivered from sophistication, Marxism and International Capitalism. Through the National Revolution its people were purged of alien diseases and America became again American." (176)

His followers respond by shouting, "All hail, the American Boy."

West's "inverted fable" is absurd in both the good and the bad senses. Like many thirties leftists who had none of his literary talent or audacity, West saw Americanism as an incipient or potential form of fascism. Despite the ferment of right-wing populists and demagogues all through the thirties, despite the history of the Ku Klux Klan, the Huey Long movement, Father Coughlin, and the isolationists of the America First group, there was little that subsequently happened to bear this out. But *A Cool Million* is also brilliantly absurd in its grasp of the fundamentals of an American mythology enshrined in popular culture, a know-nothingism, a sanctimonious hypocrisy and love of violence, a belief in the manifest destiny of individuals to work out their own fate by whatever means they can muster. He felt that the Depression had dealt a staggering blow to this entrepreneurial mentality, but, with his congenital pessimism and suspicion, he feared that the result would be not social revolution but resentment, scapegoating, and xenophobia. After one of Whipple's flowery speeches, a riot ensues: "Barricades were thrown up in the streets. The heads of Negroes were paraded on poles. A Jewish drummer was nailed to the door of his hotel room. The housekeeper of the local Catholic priest was raped" (167). Yet this seeming piece of agitprop, broader than any broadside, comes to us from the same writer who gives us a museum called the "Chamber of American Horrors," full of objects culled from the popular art of the country, whose main exhibit is "a gigantic hemorrhoid that was lit from within by electric lights." At demented moments like this, the proletarian novel shakes hands with Kafka and Philip Roth.

West sees the work of P. T. Barnum and Horatio Alger in an apocalyptic light, not simply as examples of popular pathos and vulgarity but as omens of collective violence. Like F. Scott Fitzgerald and James T. Farrell, he builds his story around the promises made to American youth, shoddy promises, false promises. Like Farrell, he sees the American epic not as a history of success but as a story of failure, a drama of "spiritual poverty." But West's literary method is closer to Mark Twain's regional whoppers than to Farrell's circumstantial realism. Twain's humor rests on the healthy pleasure he took in American vulgarity. In West's more ominous and jaded vein, the mountebanks and hotheads Huck Finn met along the river have turned into the operators and con men who fill out the pages of *A Cool Million*, which is, after all, an outrageous comic novel. But it's also a thesis novel; its prophetic intent sometimes sours its humor and turns it sadistic. Thanks to a drastic failure of sympathy, the book falls short not only of *Huckleberry Finn*, the prototypical boys' novel, but of West's own masterpiece, *Miss Lonelyhearts*, published the preceding year.

Miss Lonelyhearts is also a collection of failure stories. But though he caricatures the sufferings of those who write in to the newspaper column, West manages to make their miseries at once absurd and achingly real. As their troubles intersect with Miss L.'s own gloom and depression, the book attains a rare pathos on the far side of parody. West breaks through the verbal trappings of his mockery to achieve almost a visionary portrayal of religious exaltation. Even as a failure story *Miss Lonelyhearts* is more heartfelt than its relentlessly facetious successor, which always remains a satirical construct, a burlesque of how Americans use certain words as themes and myths to explain their world to themselves. Lemuel Pitkin is never more than an effect of language. Though he comes apart, he cannot really be said to suffer; we always know it's West himself who's inflicting the punishment. The Christ-like Miss Lonelyhearts, escaping irony to take on the cares of the world, is more truly miserable.

As Lem is held up in the end as some kind of martyr or hero, his fate ironically becomes a success story after all. Lem is the strangest of all the common-man heroes of Depression novels—a pure artifact of the mass mind, by a writer who couldn't abide proletarian clichés but was himself addicted to mass culture, even as he was censorious of it. As in all his books, West pays kitsch the tribute of parody and gives it an ambiguous place of pride in the mental life of the nation. He exposes his readers' longing for myth and fantasy by providing it in such a debased form. West gave the American Dream a different edge, in part because he saw dreaming and fantasy as a universal and revealing need. He intuited a desperation behind the ideology of success, as behind its twin, the dream of the West and the frontier, the dream of unencumbered freedom and new beginnings. As he says in lines quoted earlier from *The Day of the Locust,* "It is hard to laugh at the need for beauty and romance, no matter how tasteless, even horrible, the results of that are. But it is easy to sigh. Few things are sadder than the truly monstrous" (61).

Waiting for Odets: The Sour Smell of Success

Clifford Odets was the great poet of Depression fear and Depression longing, the obsession with success and the spiritual recoil from it. He has been seen as the archetypal playwright of the 1930s, but this was largely

because the instant fame of his brief agitprop drama, *Waiting for Lefty*, created a misleading image of him as a political writer, a committed radical.
Harold Clurman described the unheralded first performance at a labor
benefit at the Civic Repertory Theatre on January 5, 1935, when the audience arose at the end with a spontaneous chant of "Strike! Strike!":

> The first scene of *Lefty* had not played two minutes when a shock
> of delighted recognition struck the audience like a tidal wave. Deep
> laughter, hot assent, a kind of joyous fervor seemed to sweep the audi-
> ence toward the stage. The actors no longer performed; they were
> being carried along as if by an exultancy of communication such as
> I had never witnessed in the theatre before. Audience and actors had
> become one. Line after line brought applause, whistles, bravos, and
> heartfelt shouts of kinship.
>
> . . . When the audience at the end of the play responded to the
> militant question from the stage: "Well, what's the answer?" with a
> spontaneous roar of "Strike! Strike!" it was something more than a
> tribute to the play's effectiveness, more even than a testimony of the
> audience's hunger for constructive social action. It was the birth cry
> of the thirties. Our youth had found its voice.[77]

Clurman's account of the play's tumultuous reception was confirmed to
me by others who saw it, including Stanley Kauffmann, then a young
actor, and Stanley Burnshaw, who was the drama critic of *The New Masses*.
Burnshaw described the heated conversations between the audience and
the actors that continued long after the play ended. It's virtually impossible for us today to recapture that first enthusiasm for Odets's slight series
of sketches based very loosely on a 1934 New York taxi strike, a play that
still embodies the militance of radical theater in the 1930s.[78] Much of this
politically engaged activity was topical and ephemeral, such as the famous
"Living Newspaper" of the WPA's Federal Theatre Project. This ferment
included the International Ladies' Garment Workers' Union's popular
labor cabaret, *Pins and Needles*; Brecht's short, didactic plays like *The Measures Taken*; Marc Blitzstein's often brilliant imitation of Brecht and Weill
in *The Cradle Will Rock*, which was closed down by the WPA under political
pressure; and some of Orson Welles's and John Houseman's other exciting
Mercury Theatre productions, which culminated in Welles's departure for

Hollywood as the boy wonder who would make *Citizen Kane*. A few of these shows have seen revivals, and *The Cradle Will Rock* and the drama of its opening even became the basis for a reverential film by Tim Robbins in 1999, but *Waiting for Lefty* still stands as the epitome of this radical theater. This is partly because of its convenient title (oddly echoed by Samuel Beckett in the 1950s), which survives as a watchword of the "Red Decade," partly because of the play's success and notoriety: within months there was a Broadway production along with innumerable amateur productions by labor groups all around the country. Buoyed up by the fierce energy of the original performers and by Odets's gutsy, streetwise language, the play, angry yet hopeful, caught the emotional tenor of the times. Yet *Waiting for Lefty* was a cartoon, the dramatic equivalent of a piece of rabble-rousing oratory, and Odets never produced anything quite like it again, though he wrote a weaker one-act political play, *Till the Day I Die*, set in Nazi Germany, to accompany *Lefty* on Broadway, and worked hard in the middle and late 1930s on a much longer labor play, *The Silent Partner*, which the Group Theatre rehearsed twice but never put on. (It was finally performed by the Actors Studio in 1972.)

As later critics came to understand. Odets's real career as a playwright began six weeks after *Lefty*, on February 19, 1935, with a full-length work written two years before, a passionate, yearning drama of middle-class life, *Awake and Sing!* When Odets wrote it he was an obscure actor in Clurman's company, the Group Theatre, living in a symbiotic relationship with the more reflective director who would become at once the midwife, theorist, and most articulate interpreter of his work. One of the best passages in *The Fervent Years*, Clurman's history of the Group Theatre, describes how he and Odets roamed the streets of New York night after night during the bad winter of 1932–33, when the Depression, sinking to its lowest point, first became real to them. Clurman and his theater friends had been oblivious to the economic crisis that gradually developed after the Crash. "The twenties, you remember, was a period of parties," the book began. "Everybody who was anybody, or anybody who hoped to become somebody, threw as many parties as possible. . . . It was the time of the good time" (1). When the Crash came, he says, "it had made no strong impression on me. . . . ⌊N⌋ot only I but none of my colleagues ever spoke of the crash at this time. None of us apparently was directly involved" (50–51). Clurman had taken off for Paris in the 1920s, sharing rooms with another young expatriate, Aaron Copland, who was studying composition with Nadia Boulanger. In the 1930s Clurman and his bohemian friends, all from middle-class homes, were chronically strapped for money. But it was cheap to live, everyone shared, they all seemed equally poor, and life went on more or less as before.

But during the terrible winter of 1932–33, as economic conditions worsened from week to week, the psychological weight of the Depression, especially on the middle class, sank in for the first time. A pervasive anxiety blanketed everything.

> I could see it in my parents' home. Outwardly very little had altered since the better days, and I could not quite understand why they were unable fully to enjoy their good table, their comparative peace. Against all reason, it seemed to me, they and their friends were increasingly terrified, as if soon the walls would disappear, and they would remain naked and alone on the cold empty street of a night without a morrow. (114)

Much has been written about the desperately poor during the Depression, less about the more muted dreams and terrors of the middle class. These were people whose outward lives seemed solid but who had lost their footing, their sense of security, a certain basic confidence in their values. Even those who had work were afraid of losing it: fear had entered their lives. Their hopes and ambitions, the promises made to them, seemed built on quicksand. This was the mental atmosphere that eventually fed into Odets's plays, a world of immigrant striving, of middle-class longing, anxiety, and frustration.

> Yes, we could smell the depression in the air. It was like a raw wind; the very houses we lived in seemed to be shrinking, hopeless of real comfort. In these days of gloom and fear outside me and personal frustration in my work, I roamed the streets, where my own bleak state seemed to be reflected in thousands of faces, signs, and portents. (114)

Odets and Clurman immersed themselves in the grim nightlife of the period. "We listened to queer conversations on street corners, visited byways we had never suspected before. . . . [W]e were strangely attracted to people and places that might be described as hangdog, ratty, and low." They visited burlesque houses. "The shows had no sex lure for us; they had the appeal of a lurid dejection. Somehow we felt close to the down-in-the-mouth comedians and oddly tender about the bruised beauties of the chorus" (114–15). Their nocturnal rambles, so typical of the spontaneous fieldwork of thirties intellectuals going down among the people, rubbing their noses in the lower depths—bring out the links between depression and Depression, between personal frustration and social blockage. The first version of *Awake and Sing!*—a play about a troubled family, not about this demimonde—was called *I Got the Blues*, and Clurman would object to the gloomy fatalism of its unhappy ending, in which neither the son nor the daughter succeeds in breaking out of their constricted lives. Even *Waiting for Lefty*, a labor play that ends with that famous call to action, includes several sharp vignettes of domestic unhappiness induced by the Depression: one couple can't marry; another, married but miserable, is on the verge of splitting up. "We got the blues, Babe—the 1935 blues," says a young man, borrowing phrases from the longer play Odets was writing.[79]

Part of Clurman's own frustrations during the grim period were the troubles of the Group Theatre, which began in 1931 as an ad hoc offshoot of the Theatre Guild. *The Fervent Years*, his remarkable memoir of the years of the Group, is a chronicle of noble theatrical aspirations counterpointed with chronic money problems, endless artistic conflicts, and personal bickering. In Clurman's version, the Group was not simply a company but a way of life, the dream of community, an impossible vehicle for the utopian aspirations of a younger generation just coming of age. Held together by the enormous talent of its young, unknown actors and gifted directors (all of them just learning their craft), inspired by Clurman's vision of a collective enterprise devoted not to entertainment but to serious art as a personal and communal quest, the Group was beset, right down to its demise in 1941, by financial pressures, conflicting egos, mediocre plays, misconceived productions, and the hit-or-miss economics of Broadway. It was undone by precisely the kinds of commercial and ego traps the Group had been created to avoid.

And then there was the lure of Hollywood—for Odets, for Clurman, for nearly everyone in the company, as soon as they showed some promise. The movie studios too were under tremendous economic pressure, with some teetering on the verge of bankruptcy, but somehow movies became a significant part of how the American people adapted to the Depression. All through the thirties, thanks to the arrival of sound and the steady hum of the studio system, Hollywood developed a vast appetite for acting and writing talent, especially from the stage. Endlessly praised and attacked yet never firmly established, always losing people who were always returning, the Group Theatre, a stock company on Broadway itself, became part of a soap opera of success and failure that infused many of its plays, especially those of Odets. (In the decade after the war, graduates of the company like Lee J. Cobb and Elia Kazan would dominate both Broadway and Hollywood—a success they had never fully achieved with the Group. Others, including Stella Adler, Sanford Meisner, and Robert Lewis, would become leading acting teachers. Through Lee Strasberg's Actors Studio, a whole new generation of performers would be trained, and the famous Stanislavsky "Method"—stripped of the Group's radical politics—would become the dominant, almost suffocating production ideal.)

For Clurman the Group was more than a theater company, and *The Fervent Years* is more than a history of the Group. Just as *Let Us Now Praise Famous Men* became an epilogue to the documentary movement of the thirties, Clurman's book was a moving testament to the socially committed theater of the era: an account of the thirties that is itself part of the decade's mind. It's also the discursive parallel to Odets's plays, most of which Clurman directed. Clurman's excited account of the first-night acclaim of *Waiting for Lefty* illustrates his sense of the "fervent years": the coalescence of the "group," the abolition of the proscenium, the ecstatic, impersonal union of artists and audience in search of a better world. For Clurman this was indeed "the birth cry of the thirties."

The rapport between Clurman and Odets struck everyone. "They would talk in a shorthand of half-sentences, intelligible only to each other," says Odets's biographer Margaret Brenman-Gibson. Their letters to each other were like an internal dialogue: by turns cosy and frank, nagging and loving, coy and critical. With greater histrionics, Clurman would play Edmund Wilson to Odets's Fitzgerald. (Fitzgerald once called Wilson his "artistic conscience.") "I respect Clifford as if he were dead," Clurman quipped. According to the actors, "Harold is never so happy as when he is pregnant with a play of Clifford's."[80] Actually, the Group itself was their baby; their collaborations best crystallized the company's special vision. *The Fervent Years* gives us not only an "official" interpretation of Odets's plays, almost from the horse's mouth, but also an angle on the thirties that is quite different from the political label observers still pin on the Group and its times.

The Group expressed the utopian spirit of the decade. Its members retreated to the country for the summer to develop pieces that were as much spiritual exercises as potential productions. They became a commune devoted to theater. Lectured constantly by Clurman, whose theoretical insight outstripped his skill as a director, they were then free to interact with one another—emotionally, sexually, artistically—without the interference of spectators, reviewers, or commercial backers. Like such later experiments as the Living Theatre of Julian Beck and Judith Malina, or Jerzy Grotowski's Polish Lab Theatre, the Group was as much a religious sect as a performing arts institution.

Most contemporary observers saw Odets and the Group as radicals, Marxists, politically committed artists. Clurman thought otherwise. For him Odets and other thirties artists were inspired less by politics than by a religious and visionary humanism, an immense youthful longing. Like other utopian communities, it became an extended, often dysfunctional family, wracked by love and conflict, a haven in a heartless world. "It had to provide what society itself failed to provide. . . . [I]t had to become a society within society, a protected unit, a utopia, an oasis within the city, in which one could work out one's career and salvation" (211). "Salvation," what a curious word to link with "career"! And how very much it tells us about the era. Clurman's book was written during the war, when this movement had already disintegrated; that gives its closing pages the bittersweet eloquence of disappointed hopes. "In the thirties there developed to a high point of consciousness," he says, "the hunger for a spiritually active world, a humanly meaningful and relevant art" (283). Yet the Group never found a secure footing. Like so much else in the decade, it suffered from a "fundamental economic instability." "Its piecemeal, bread-line existence," he says, in a striking metaphor, "accounts for much of its hectic inner life" (284). In his view, the Group fell apart not from personal problems or even financial ones but because the decade itself was winding down. "The late winter and early spring of 1940 were as special a period as the days preceding the bank holiday of 1933," he writes. "The mood in New York might have been characterized as one of intense stagnation. History was marking time. . . . Everyone seemed to be waiting. Everything was in question, and all the old answers rang a little false beside the darkening reality" (261–62).

This is his explanation for the failure of Odets's 1940 play *Night Music*, which the distraught playwright himself blamed first on the obtuseness of the critics, then on Clurman's inadequate production.* By this time Odets's brief, meteoric theatrical career was already in decline—along with the decade that had created him. Five years earlier, his plays struck exactly the lyrical note of youthful longing that Clurman saw as central to the whole era. Young Ralph's closing speech in *Awake and Sing!*, like Nora's final exit in *A Doll's House*, is less a part of the play than a bold farewell to the stifling values of the middle class, a declaration of independence that is as much the author's as the character's.

Like so many stories set in an immigrant milieu, *Awake and Sing!* is a drama of generations: the idealistic but ineffectual first generation, represented by the grandfather, Jacob, with his sentimental Marxism and acute sense of failure; the grasping, materialistic second generation—the mother, Bessie (who provokes Jacob to commit suicide), and her crudely successful brother, Morty (who thinks the old man is senile); and the desperately impatient younger generation, especially Ralph and his sister, Hennie, who reject their parents' caution and fear to claim some fuller lives for themselves. The villain, if there is one, is Bessie, who smashes her father's Caruso records, his only remaining pleasure, and ruthlessly entraps an unsuspecting greenhorn into marrying her pregnant daughter. She then claims her father's insurance money, which was meant to free up the young man after his grandfather's death. This play burns with youthful anger as well as lyrical longing.

When Ralph gives up his grandfather's small legacy and Hennie runs off with her coarse but passionate lover, leaving her baby behind, they are saying no to their mother's stultifying respectability and all-consuming

---

* "Harold must lessen the gap between his first-rate critical perceptions and production intentions with a play of mine, and what he finally produces on the stage. There is something positively weird and ununderstandable about his inability to work into a production the brilliant ideas with which he starts rehearsals." *The Time Is Ripe: The 1940 Journal of Clifford Odets* (New York: Grove Press, 1988), 50.

worries about poverty. Abandoning her husband and child, Hennie chooses a crude sexual vitality over a marriage of convenience, like her mother's, to a weaker man she could dominate and emasculate. And Ralph, ineffectual as he is, hopes to be reborn as his grandfather, dreaming big dreams, eager to change the world, but without the old man's crippling timidities. "Let Mom have the dough," he says. "I'm twenty-two and kickin'! I'll get along. Did Jake die for us to fight about nickels? No! 'Awake and sing,' he said. Right here he stood and said it. The night he died I saw it like a thunderbolt! I saw he was dead and I was born! I swear to God, I'm one week old! I want the whole city to hear it—fresh blood, arms. We got 'em. We're glad we're living" (100–01). This is the genuine Odets note, with all its strengths and problems: the heated rhetoric, the stylized, slightly false-sounding colloquialism, the flawed construction, the youthful fervor, and, above all, the avid grasping for life. An actor and director could interpret this as empty bravado; Odets did not. For him this is the Blakean "I want! I want!," the mark of someone who grew up with nothing, who is afraid of going through life without having lived. Two decades later Odets would still tell an interviewer, "All my plays deal with one subject: the struggle not to have life nullified by circumstances, false values, anything."[81] Yet his text allows for different readings.

It was this absolute note of lugubrious fervor, this strained, unappeasable hunger for life, that Clurman made the key to his interpretation of the thirties and his reading of Odets—the two are not easy to distinguish. Clurman himself had encouraged Odets to revise the "masochistically pessimistic ending" of the earlier draft. Yet Clurman understood the vein of dejection and defeat, the thread of insecurity, that runs just below the surface of what Alfred Kazin called Odets's "voluntary optimism." According to Clurman,

"A tendril of revolt" runs through all of Odets's work, but that is not the same thing as a consistent revolutionary conviction. Odets's work is not even proletarian in the sense that Gorky's work is. Rather it is profoundly of the lower middle class with all its vacillation, dual allegiance, fears, groping, self-distrust, dejection, spurts of energy, hosannas, vows of conversion, and prayers for release. . . . The feel of middle-class (and perhaps universal) disquiet in Odets's plays is sharp and specific; the ideas are general and hortatory.

Still, Clurman insists that "the quality of his plays is young, lyrical, yearning—as of someone on the threshold of life" (151).

Once we notice how much this youthful rebellion is rooted in lower middle-class anxiety, it's easy to see how Ralph (Odets's idealistic surrogate) and Hennie (his sexual surrogate) resemble their grasping, domineering mother, who is also determined to take life by the horns and shape it in her own way. Odets's focus on success is one key to his work, but unlike James Farrell or Nathanael West, he strikes no easy attitude toward it. Bessie's materialism reminds us of the "spiritual poverty" of another ethnic family, the Lonigans. But Farrell and West pity the values of ordinary middle-class Americans; they surgically expose the hollowness of their pretensions and despise the pathos of their dreams and ambitions. Odets, on the other hand, is a genuine dramatist: to a remarkable degree, he is implicated in the desires of all his characters, and gives us moments when we see the world from their point of view. Finally, Bessie is *not* a villain; we come to understand (if not excuse) the fears that drive her.

This is the famous "Chekhovian" element in his work: not simply a tone of wistful longing and nostalgic regret but the pathos, frustration, laughter, and special idiom that bring his characters to life. For all the crudely dualistic symbolism of his contrast between art and material success—as if appreciating Caruso could be set off against marrying for money, or violin playing against boxing—Odets made the plays a vehicle for his own ambivalence, which, after the first flush of acclaim, he painfully acted out in his own life.

This is why Odets's characters really live onstage, and this was how he found the language for them. *Awake and Sing!* was not literally autobiographical—Odets himself didn't grow up in an immigrant family; his father was a domineering, self-made man who long outlived him—but the play's rhythms and sentiments are intensely personal. Like Chekhov's, his characters often talk past each other; behind what they say, behind the offbeat metaphors and dated slang, is the music of what they need and feel. Odets's language has the zip of the vernacular but is intensely stylized. In *Awake and Sing!* Odets created not only a credible ethnic speech but the whole hyphenated language of American-Jewish literature.

The play is best known for its delicious deformations of dialogue; later writers like Delmore Schwartz, Bernard Malamud, and Grace

Paley—and even the de-ethnicized Arthur Miller—would be inconceivable without them. When Jacob says "I gave the dog eat" or calls someone "a bum of the first water," when Bessie says "a girl twenty-six don't grow younger" or "he eats out my heart," we hear not colloquial realism, as some then felt, but a poetic alchemy upon English, a linguistic invention by Clifford Odets that sounds notes we later hear in Schwartz's, Paley's, and Malamud's stories. What the young Alfred Kazin heard from the balcony was "a lyric uplifting of blunt Jewish speech, boiling over and explosive." He felt that Odets had stolen his life, that his own family was up there on the stage, but also, in a flash of revelation, that the private world he knew might actually be material for literature.[82] As Odets eliminated the Jewish inflections from his later plays, trying to become a mainstream writer, an "American" playwright, he deprived himself of his most powerful resource.

Odets's grasp of the ethnic milieu, like Farrell's, is bound up with his stress on success. *Awake and Sing!* is above all the story of a family: the material of soap opera transformed into art. "This is a house?" says Jacob. "Marx said it—abolish such families" (55). Along with the nagging Lonigans, the idealized Joads, and the horrific Bundrens (of Faulkner's masterpiece *As I Lay Dying*), the Bergers are one of the key literary families of the 1930s. They suggest the quintessence of the Jewish immigrant middle class with all its anxieties intact. Bessie and her brother embody a Depression version of the success ethic, the immigrant materialism familiar from Cahan's *Rise of David Levinsky*, while her husband, Myron, like Pa Joad and Paddy Lonigan, is another version of the weak, undermined Depression father, an equable man who can muse on his own ineffectuality. Odets's callow description of his characters in the printed version of the play is riddled with poetic vagueness and authorial insecurity. Bessie is "afraid of utter poverty"; Myron "is heartbroken without being aware of it"; young Ralph "is trying to find why so much dirt must be cleared away before it is possible to 'get to first base'"; his sister, Hennie, "is fatalistic about being trapped, but will escape if possible. Till the day she dies she will be faithful to a loved man" (37–39). These awkward notes, based on a fear that actors and readers might not "get" the characters, betray an almost unbearable poetry of wistfulness and longing and wild generalities—the author's own.

No playwright is closer to his characters or less capable of judging them. (Among Odets's most talented rivals, compare Lillian Hellman's love of a juicy villain and a noble victim.) None was more given to using drama as a vehicle of desire, expressing what he called the "struggle for life amidst petty conditions" (37). In *Awake and Sing!* Odets combined raw family memories with the sense of desperation and defeat he found on the streets and in the burlesque houses that bitter winter of 1932–33. His most immediate inspiration was John Howard Lawson's *Success Story*, a 1932 Group Theatre production in which Odets, as an actor, understudied Luther Adler in the lead role. In the 1920s Lawson, along with Mike Gold and John Dos Passos, had written experimental plays for the avant-garde New Playwrights' Theater. By the late thirties he would become a noted screenwriter, undergo a political conversion, become the Communist Party's cultural commissar in Hollywood, and eventually, in shouting matches with the House Un-American Activities Committee (HUAC), would prove to be the most confrontational of the Hollywood Ten. (His books on the craft of playwriting and screenwriting would remain standard works even after his literary reputation had evaporated.) But *Success Story* was a naturalistic play with an ambitious, unscrupulous ethnic hero and some harsh, razor-sharp dialogue still impressive today. Despite its crudely contrived plot and two-dimensional characters, *Success Story* was, according to Clurman, a watershed for the Group, the play that established its style of cutting realism at once personal and polemical.

Prophetically, *Success Story* is set in an ad agency, that signal innovation of the 1920s; Lawson must have been one of the first writers to portray advertising as the ultimate way of selling out. Sol Ginsberg was once a radical, but now he says, "It gives me a kick to look back at the radical type we used to fall for—that stuff's a religion for misfits." After nearly losing his job, he's become all cynicism and manipulation; he sees through everything except his own unscrupulous ambition: "Most everything's bunk when you know your way round—the trick is, to use the bunk without being taken in."[83] Like some of the boardroom and workplace dramas of the 1950s, Lawson's play is built around an outsider-hero-heel who tramples on everyone to get ahead yet is eventually done in by his own amoral overreaching.

Sol Ginsberg is an unpleasant character, a crude arriviste surrounded by arrogant Wasps, but his language, his energy, his poor boy's ambition, galvanize the play. There's a woman in the office to remind him of the young "idealist" he once was, the more tender feelings he's trampled underfoot, but he neglects her. "Tell me," he asks her, "are they still at it? Do they still sweat at those crowded meetings? And we here, high up where the air is clear, we never hear a whisper!" (196). The Depression, which made others into radicals, has turned him into the consummate operator, far more adept than the Wasps around him, who gradually lose everything.

Ginsberg is now devoted solely to number one, to making it and humiliating those who once patronized him, including his former boss and an old wellborn rival, now down at the heels and at his mercy. His lust for power, his push for success, is mingled with feelings of resentment and revenge, perhaps the only real feelings he has left. Some of the Group Theatre actors thought the play anti-Semitic; a decade later this character would return as Budd Schulberg's Sammy Glick but without the crisp language, the emotional violence, and the sense of self-betrayal that was Lawson's legacy to Odets. A harsher version of *David Levinsky*, Lawson's *Success Story* is an Odets play without the poetry. Its tone is acrid, explosive, ugly: a parable of desire without the softer feelings of wistfulness and fantasy. According to Clurman, it "brought Odets an awareness of a new kind of theatre dialogue. It was a compound of lofty moral feeling, anger, and the feverish argot of the big city."[*] (150). But Odets was also fired up by the success theme: the grasping ambition fueled by ethnic, lower-class deprivation.

Compared to Odets's heroes, Sol Ginsberg is more a projectile than a character; he spits out words that lash across the stage. "I've been dead a long time!" he says at the end, after he's been shot. A genius at appearances, he tries to stage-manage his own death to make it look like suicide. "Where the Hell is that revolver? I want it in my hand. Give me that gun, we got to make it look right" (242). Yet one character describes Sol as a kind of "revolutionist": "Never content, pursuing a vision, you want to change the whole world in the image of your own ego" (183). Odets's characters too are revolutionists of the ego, not political animals

---

[*] At the opening of a 1934 revival in Boston, with Odets again understudying the role of Sol Ginsberg, he was so moved himself and so furious at the lukewarm reception ("the frozen silence, the terrorized silence . . . the antagonism of the aristocratic audience") that he returned to his hotel and dashed off some key pages of a new play, *Paradise Lost*, a scene in which a mother tells her dying son the story of Moses and the Golden Calf. See Margaret Brenman-Gibson, *Clifford Odets: American Playwright: The Years from 1906 to 1940* (New York: Atheneum, 1981), 303.

but feverish outsiders who make absolute demands on life. As with Lawson's self-loathing hero, we can almost palpably feel them wanting, striving, yielding, yearning, failing.

In Odets's *Golden Boy* (1937), the brazen Joe Bonaparte, like his imperial namesake, breaks into the fight game by sheer force of will. His old Italian father wants him to play the violin, but he's determined not to be poor, as Odets at that moment was determined to write a commercial play, though (paradoxically) one that would deal with the pitfalls of success. Appropriately it was a hit; it resuscitated the Group, though it reminded one reviewer of a "melodramatic motion picture."[84] Odets sets up the contrast far too schematically: boxing stands for fame and fortune, while music is art, self-expression. Boxing symbolizes the violence of a cruelly competitive society at home, an impending war abroad; music is the tender, poetic side of Joe's soul: "Playing music . . . that's like saying, 'I am man. I belong here. . .' I'm not afraid of people and what they say. There's no war in music. It's not like the streets" (263). Joe's father, like Sol Ginsberg's old radical girlfriend or Ralph Berger's sentimental Marxist grandfather, wants him to find not just success but "truthful success," something worthy and honorable. (He has a brother who's a CIO organizer, a good way of staying poor.) *Golden Boy* gives us Odets at the edge of self-parody, a play too pat and heavy-handed in its symbolism but striking as a personal fable.

Joe wants to be an artist, to express himself, and some of his style comes through in his boxing as well as in his music. But Joe, like so many other city boys, like the gangster heroes played by Jimmy Cagney, Paul Muni, and Edward G. Robinson, also needs acceptance. He wants to *be* someone. "Now he wears the best, eats the best, sleeps the best. He walks down the street respected—the golden boy!" (309). But he's also giddy, he wants to take chances; in the manner of so many Odets characters, he's wildly, confusedly drunk on life. "He gotta wild wolf inside—eat him up," says his father. Joe's girl answers, antiphonally, "You could build a city with his ambition to be somebody" (295).

By the end ambition has become everything to him. He's addicted to success, talks about himself in the third person: "The main thing with Bonaparte is to win" (304). (Soon we even get references to Waterloo!) He becomes a kind of gangster, like the people he's fallen in with, above all a vaguely homosexual hoodlum named Fuseli (first played, with great nervous intensity, by Elia Kazan, who had already done the malevolent Kewpie in *Paradise Lost*). Odets returns to the classic thirties metaphor for success, the gangster. Accidentally, Joe kills another fighter, a *black* fighter, ruining his own hands at the same time. But even before that, his main victim was himself. Changing your life can mean a change for the worse. "Getting to be a killer!" his girl says. "You're getting to be like Fuseli. You're not the boy I cared about, not you. You murdered that boy with the generous face— God knows where you hid the body! I don't know you" (307–8).

The self-destructive side of Joe's ambition comes out in his love of fast cars. "You can't go too fast for me," he says (277). He wants to devour life, to cram it all in. Success enables him to buy the expensive car in which he'll kill himself—"Miss Deusenberg," he calls it, in sexual terms. Once he's destroyed himself in the ring, the vehicle will become his escape, his rocket to self-obliteration. "Ride! That's it, we ride—clear my head. We'll drive through the night. When you mow down the night with headlights, nobody gets you! You're on top of the world then—nobody laughs! That's it—speed! We're off the earth—unconnected!" (316) "Top of the world": the same words would be used by Cagney in the climactic Götterdämmerung of *White Heat* in 1949. Driving—the fast track—becomes another form of fighting, another blast against anonymity, yet also a way of quitting the fray, of going into orbit. Odets's next play, one of his best, would be called *Rocket to the Moon*.

We can see how well Odets's ambition, along with his sense of himself as an ethnic outsider, meshed with the dreams and deprivations of the 1930s. Odets wanted to change the world but also to find a place for himself in it. He needed to be an artist and wanted to be a star, a figure of substance and power, like his overweening, judgmental father, who always disapproved of his life yet would hit him up for support. Such contradictory desires doomed him to fits of guilty self-execration, especially in his Hollywood years. The antitheses are often put crudely but indelibly in his plays and screenplays; they carry a poetic force in *Awake and Sing!*, which borrows its biblical title from Isaiah (26:19): "Awake and sing, ye that dwell in dust." We need to take a closer look at this play, certainly his best, to understand who he was and how his imagination flourished.

The mother, Bessie, a character even more nasty and greedy in earlier drafts, wants her son and daughter to be comfortably married, shielded from the fears that eat away at her. "Ralph should be a success like you," she tells her businessman brother. "I should only live to see the day when he rides up to the door in a big car with a chauffeur and a radio. I could die happy, believe me." Their ineffectual father, the old radical ("a man who had golden opportunities but drank instead a glass tea" [78], sees through this: "In my day the propaganda was for God. Now it's for success. A boy don't turn around without having shoved in him he should make a success" (71).

The pressure for making it comes not only from their anxious mother, or even from the conditions of the Depression, but from the dream machinery of the culture, especially the movies, which offer a rival version of Jacob's utopia: "He dreams all night of fortunes," says Jacob. "Don't it say in the movies he should have a personal steamship, pyjamas for fifty dollars a pair and a toilet like a monument? But in the morning he wakes up and for ten dollars he can't fix the teeth" (71–72). To his capitalist son, Morty, all this is "sweatshop talk," the poor man's revenge. He made it up the ladder the American way: "I started from a poor boy who worked on an ice wagon for two dollars a week" (71). To the crooked Moe, a total cynic who simply grabs for himself as much of life as he can, "it's all a racket—from horse racing down. Marriage, politics, big business—everybody plays cops and robbers" (71). Moe's final advice to Ralph is "make a break or spend the rest of your life in a coffin" (99).

Moe is a petty gangster but a doer, far removed from Jacob's ineffectual idealism. (In the first version, I Got the Blues, he's led off to jail at the end.) Yet here he echoes Jacob's biblical imagery of death and resurrection, which leads the old man to take his life so that his grandson might live: "Look on me and learn what to do, boychick. . . . Look on this failure and see for seventy years he talked, with good ideas, but only in the head. . . . This is why I tell you—DO! . . . [Y]ou should act. Not like me" (77–78). This is really not so different from what his daughter, Bessie, says. She too is future oriented, activist. But she believes only in things she can touch and feel, and has no patience for fantasy, whether it's from Hollywood or from Isaiah by way of Karl Marx:

BESSIE: With me it's one thing—a boy should have respect for his
   own future. Go to sleep, you look tired. In the morning you'll
   forget.
JACOB: "Awake and sing, ye that dwell in dust, and the earth shall
   cast out the dead." It's cold out? (83)

This is typical of Odets's dialogue: characters talk past one another, lost in their own poetic musings, each on separate tracks, at oblique angles to each other, intersecting less through dialogue than with the unspoken thrust of their whole being.

As in Chekhov, they often speak in fragments of soliloquies; their non sequiturs betray a profound isolation as well as a deep inner logic. But these rambling scenes, with their seeming irrelevancies, are also closely knit together. Jacob's suicide is foreshadowed not so much by anything he says as by an earlier bit of dialogue about those other Depression failures, the doomed capitalists:

> MOE: Still jumping off high buildings like flies—the big shots who
>   lost all their cocoanuts. Pfft!
> JACOB: Suicides?
> MOE: Plenty can't take it—good in the break, but can't take the
>   whip in the stretch. (60)

Later it's Moe who tries to protect Jacob's insurance money for Ralph by brandishing a fake suicide note. If it were real, it would invalidate the insurance policy. But it is a blank piece of paper, like the still uncut pages of Jacob's precious Marxist texts. Thus Jacob has a message for Ralph but also no message; he attacks the gospel of success but castigates himself as a failure. Similarly, Bessie tries to keep her children from getting away, from trying to fulfil themselves and be happy, but in the end confesses how she too has longed to escape. "I'll tell you a big secret: My whole life I wanted to go away too, but with children a woman stays home. A fire burned in *my* heart too, but now it's too late" (96).

This may seem like the play's transparent effort to humanize an unappealing woman. But like Jacob and Moe in their different ways, Bessie is telling her children to seize the day, to grasp at the future as she had not. It's another kind of future she has in mind, secure from money worries. For her, immigrant poverty and Depression anxiety are greater spurs than any romantic attachments or social ideals. She is a peacetime Mother Courage, caught up in the Darwinian struggle for survival: "Prospect Avenue, Dawson, Beck Street—every day furniture's on the sidewalk. . . . [H]ere without a dollar you don't look the world in the eye. Talk from now to next year—this is life in America" (95). If the Depression ignited a burning idealism in some, it induced an unappeasable hunger for money and security in others. It sharply challenged the success ethic while giving it a desperate immediacy. Long after the war, members of the Depression generation were easy enough to recognize by their social conscience or their economic fears, though their lives had long since settled into more comfortable grooves.

In the character of Bessie, played with great force by a young Stella Adler, Odets was certainly not idealizing the tenement mother, as Mike Gold and Henry Roth had done, looking back with grim nostalgia to their early years. But Odets is as much Bessie as he is Ralph or Hennie, Jacob or Moe. What makes *Awake and Sing!* the complete Odets play is that, far from being pat or moralistic, it gives full rein to the playwright's conflicted feelings. The old radical, like Chekhov's dreamers, gets most of the good lines, the poetry of the play, but it's nothing but talk: old hat, out of date. Jacob's radicalism belongs to the past, the dreamer's world of prewar immigrant socialism. He wants Ralph to "make history," to change the world, but Ralph wants to marry his girl. "There's more important things than girls," his grandfather says (76–77), but Odets sides with neither of them: he wants to be radical and yet wants to get the girls. He wants to live a full life "amidst petty conditions," wants to have money but also ideals, wants to satisfy both Bessie and Jacob.

The plays themselves explain why Odets had such trouble dealing with sudden, unexpected success. For a brief moment his harsh but lyrical voice spoke for a young generation, as Fitzgerald had done a decade earlier. But it was not a voice he could easily sustain. Even more than Fitzgerald, who began as a midwestern provincial, he was the outsider, unsure of his footing, plagued by Napoleonic dreams but equally large insecurities. After the twin success of *Waiting for Lefty* and *Awake and Sing!* he found it difficult to concentrate. Clurman was puzzled that he cared so much for the good opinion of people neither of them respected, the columnists, the slick writers, the commercial theater people. Like many thirties writers, he longed to make a difference: to convert people, not simply to impress them. But also, says Clurman, "he wanted their admiration, their plaudits, their goodwill. He needed their love; or, lacking that, power over them" (165, 180–82).

After the first two plays, critics complained when he repeated himself and complained when he changed. In *Paradise Lost* and *Golden Boy*—

the first his biggest failure, the other an immediate success—he tried to "de-Jewish" his work, watering down the ethnic flavor of his inimitable dialogue. Yet critics like Mary McCarthy (no friend to the theater of "social significance") attacked him for repeating himself: "*Golden Boy* again demonstrates the lesson of Odets's *Paradise Lost*: that this author appears to be psychically glued to the material of his first play. He cannot advance beyond *Awake and Sing*: he can only revive it with different costumes, scenery, and (sometimes) accents."* Reviewers of *Rocket to the Moon*, including some who had attacked Odets in the past for writing agitprop theater, complained that he was losing his political edge, exploring mere emotional conflicts like any other bourgeois playwright. The predictable Ruth McKenney in *The New Masses* said he was now writing plays about "problems people solved the day before yesterday." She must have thought the revolution had already arrived.

Yet this play—though set in, of all places, a dentist's office, using the material of soap opera—was perhaps Odets's most poetic statement of his characters' ineffable dreams and longings for a full life, for the moon, for something beyond. They are caught between their need for romance and their need to pay the rent. The Hotel Algiers, just beyond the dentist's office, stands for something outside the kingdom of necessity, outside their humdrum daily lives, something exotic, mysterious, dangerous. In Miss Cleo, Odets, with a surprising feminist twist, creates a remarkable woman who is the shape of everyone's desire, who awakens each one's discontent and sense of possibility but turns out to have desires of her own. She finally rejects them all, leaving each of them unsettled, perhaps changed. Confounding the iron laws of Broadway plotting, she chooses a lonely autonomy over the kind of love they offer her. She embodies Odets's longing for life in its freshest, most poetic guise.

---

* Mary McCarthy, "Odets Deplored," *Mary McCarthy's Theatre Chronicles, 1937–62* (New York: Noonday Press, 1963), 9, first published in January 1938 in *Partisan Review*, a magazine noted for its uncompromising severity toward both the Popular Front and the theater as a middlebrow institution. For example, McCarthy, in a more-revolutionary-than-thou vein, attacks the ILGWU revue *Pins and Needles* for its New Deal attitudes: "You cannot produce trenchant political satire—at least not in America in this period—if your political horizon is the Wagner Act" (22). McCarthy was surprised and a little embarrassed when she found herself actually liking Thornton Wilder's *Our Town*, with its folksy, small-town setting.

Autonomy was something Odets himself never managed to achieve. Despite his avant-garde beginnings, he needed wider success as a form of approval, a confirmation of love. Clurman says,

> Despite his success . . . Odets still felt himself excluded, special. He was not "accepted" in the sense that, let us say, playwrights like Robert Sherwood, Philip Barry, S. N. Behrman, Sidney Howard, or George S. Kaufman were. Despite his pride in being what the period was pleased to term a "revolutionary," he did not want to remain a Left playwright. He wanted to be at the very center of standard playwrights of quality. He wanted to be inside, not outside, that circle which the mass of Americans might regard as their own. In this center was safety. (181–82)

Like many conflicted writers, especially those who came from immigrant stock, Odets wanted to be revolutionary and ordinary at the same time. He wanted money and prestige but also the respect of "advanced" people, for whom money and popular acclaim—at least before they had them—were signs of failure rather than success. Odets's ambivalence inevitably attracted him to Hollywood, just as his success in the theater drew Hollywood to him. The same temptation presented itself to other members of the Group, including Elia Kazan and Odets's onstage alter ego, Julie Garfield, who had created Ralph in *Awake and Sing!*

Soon after his 1935 success Odets went to Hollywood for ten weeks, where he wrote *The General Died at Dawn* and met Luise Rainer, the film actress, who became his first wife. "For Odets at this time Hollywood was Sin," says Clurman. This was true for the whole Group: "In the Group in those days Hollywood was the symbol in the show world of moneymaking unrelated to any other ideal" (169–70). For the rest of his life he continued bouncing back and forth between New York and Hollywood, between the theater and the movies, though he lived and worked in Hollywood from 1944 to 1948 and again from 1955 until his death in 1963, raising two small children after the death of his second wife, Bette Grayson.

For a playwright in that period there was nothing remarkable about this itinerary. As Clurman notes, "From success or failure the playwright's escape is Hollywood." Odets, full of guilty ambition, was fleeing both, shaping himself into a legend. Partly because of his Depression origins as a committed writer, Odets's name became a byword for the theater man who sold out to Hollywood, the meteoric thirties figure who burned out quickly, who failed to fulfill his early promise. Being disappointed by Odets, moralizing over his decline, became a major occupation of drama critics over the next two decades. He held his own in both his private and his public testimony before HUAC in 1952, answering directly, never groveling or seeking absolution, but by his appearance he damaged himself in his own eyes, undermining his confidence and shattering the idealistic self-image he still needed. In his retreat he became a craftsman for hire, doing credited or uncredited work on other people's screenplays.

The Odets myth endured long enough to be travestied by the Coen brothers in their obtuse film *Barton Fink*, which identifies Odets mainly by his hair. (The Hollywood Faulkner is another of their cheap stick figures.) Odets himself helped feed the stereotype. On his own deathbed he delivered manic, nonstop monologues full of megalomania and self-loathing. According to one hospital visitor, "he made all kinds of 'final' statements . . . like 'I really blew it, but you've got it all, don't waste it!'" Two years earlier he had written boastfully in his diary, "I may well be not only the foremost playwright manqué of our time but of all time."[85]

Early in 1938, returning to New York from Hollywood, Odets urged writers to stay put in the theater, since the movies avoided "controversial themes" and made it "difficult for a writer to express even the simpler pains and tragedies of life—what for instance really happens between a man and woman in love." But starting with *Golden Boy*, Odets began writing stark, melodramatic plays that in a sense were already movies— indeed, that were eventually turned into powerful movies without his help: *Golden Boy*, *Clash by Night*, *The Big Knife*, *The Country Girl*. In *The Big Knife* he attacked Hollywood for destroying an idealist, a man of talent who (in Gerald Weales's words) "at once loves and hates his success."[86] Corruption became his main theme, corruption by success, corruption by failure, corruption by exerting power over others, as in his acid portrait of a vicious New York gossip columnist (played for keeps by Burt Lancaster) and his toady (Tony Curtis) in *The Sweet Smell of Success*. All the while he feared that his own success was transitory, that he would be "the boy who hit the target's heart once, never trying again," as he confided to his notebook in 1939. "America keeps you keenly conscious of success . . . there is a face to keep, a position to retain. Before you were free; you are a prisoner now." Twenty years later he was directing a (nonmusical) Elvis Presley film and, at the time of his death, writing TV scripts for *The Richard Boone Show*. Working for money but working almost incognito, he still tried to make each script a serious piece of work. On his deathbed he remained true to his self-tormenting themes: "I may fool you all . . . you know, I may live," he raged. "Then Clifford Odets will do something to redeem the last sixteen wasted years."[87] In the movie colony he was mourned by close friends, ranging from Cary Grant to Jean Renoir.

Odets's obsession with success and his ambivalence toward Hollywood were reflections of his own character, but they were also typical of the offspring of immigrants, typical of the 1930s generation for whom success and failure took on a terrible urgency. Speaking for himself, Odets also spoke for his time, as everyone in the thirties instantly understood. Nor was Odets the only one to focus on Hollywood as a success machine toward the end of the decade, when the showgirl and the gangster of the early thirties gave way to the movie starlet and the powerful tycoon, a shift that culminates in *Citizen Kane*.

The legacy of Odets and the Group can be found not only in the Actors Studio and the importance of the "Method" in postwar acting, which propelled dozens of leading actors into brilliant careers. It can be seen in the glum fascination with pipe dreams and fantasies in the best American plays of the 1940s: Eugene O'Neill's *The Iceman Cometh*, written in 1938 but first produced (badly) in 1946; Tennessee Williams's *The Glass Menagerie* and *A Streetcar Named Desire*; and Arthur Miller's *Death of a Salesman*—all of them with deep Depression roots, plays about the hollow, unfulfilled lives of those who dream and aspire, whose hopes and wistful longings are lit up with a kind of poetry but whose drab experience reduces them to prose.

CHAPTER 8

What Price Hollywood?

THE DRIVE FOR SUCCESS is deeply etched into the American mind, grounded in a faith that this country offers unlimited opportunity and social mobility. If the French Revolution propagated the idea of a career open to talents, with advancement barred to no one because of birth or class, the United States took pride in putting the ideal into practice, in spite of a history of class differences, racial and religious discrimination, longstanding inequalities, and cutthroat greed. The Depression dealt a tremendous blow to this fundamental American trust. Despite the empty assurances of politicians, bankers, and businessmen that boom times would soon return, the whole economy, far from making good on the promise of progress, seemed to be in irretrievable decline. "In the early 30's," recalled the novelist Josephine Herbst, "who did not believe the capitalist system was doomed?"[1]

A belief in the imminent overthrow or collapse of capitalism may have been the opium of the intellectuals, but ordinary Americans expressed their concerns in other ways, including support for populist mass movements led by demagogic figures like Huey Long and Father Coughlin, but also by devouring stories that compensated for their sense of powerlessness. If two young Jewish comic-book artists responded to the rise of Hitler by creating Superman—the inspiration for Michael Chabon's novel *The Amazing Adventures of Kavalier & Clay*—there were numerous other outlets for Americans stymied by the Depression and fearful of where it would lead. The 1930s saw the consolidation of what we now think of as the classic Hollywood cinema, as the film studios perfected an industrial mode of production, promotion, and distribution. Hollywood's new film genres and star personalities connected perfectly with what Americans needed during the Depression. At great risk to their independence, writers like Odets, Faulkner, Fitzgerald, and Dorothy Parker migrated to Hollywood because that's where the money was, but also because that's where the audience had gone and where the most timely stories were being told. What movies lacked in realism they supplied in fantasy— escapist fantasies with fairy-tale endings as well as more darkly etched fables that enabled people to tap into their fears and work them through. "Doubt, disillusion, despair, created psychological needs that movies seemed to fill," wrote the historian Arthur Schlesinger Jr. in his memoir *A Life in the Twentieth Century.* "It was more than the need for distraction and escape. It was the need for reassurance and hope. With the republic struck down by circumstances beyond individual control, people longed for some vindication of individual identity, for restoration of the sense of individual potency."[2] This mother lode of fantasy enabled Hollywood to take hold of the American mind in the 1930s. With their larger-than-life actors, films furnished a rich portrayal of American manners along with seductive images of romance and sophistication. Many of these movies offered audiences elaborately embroidered tales of success and failure.

That dream of success first surfaced in the early thirties in classic gangster films such as *Little Caesar* (which introduced Edward G. Robinson), *The Public Enemy* (with a fiery performance by James Cagney), and *Scarface* (starring Paul Muni and George Raft). But even in the period of these movies, between 1930 and 1932—before the Depression reached its lowest point, but also before the election of FDR offered new hope—the American idea of success was already ambiguous, and this may be why the problematic figure of the gangster loomed so large in the popular imagination. A strong ethnic cast had not yet been bleached out of Hollywood movies, and the audience thrilled not only to the crackling power of the gangster, his coiled energy and snarling charm, but also to where he came from: the urban underclass, the immigrant slums where puritan moral values had never taken hold. In a sense, the gangster was licensed to kill, licensed to do anything to claw his way up to the top. In a period of social crisis, with received values in flux, the gangster became the epitome of the self-made man. This was the American dream with a dark, violent coloring, and the gangster's rise already contained portents of his fall. From the moment a sniveling young Cagney is knocked down by his straitlaced brother, who already understands his profound corruption, from the instant a still boyish Cagney coolly murders his early mentor (a Fagin-like figure who first led him into crime), the ambiguity of the audience's identification with the gangster set in, and this has held up through *The Godfather*, *Goodfellas*, and *The Sopranos*. This complicated identification proved too subtle for the guardians of morality in the early thirties, who insisted, even in this pre-Code era, on shrinking the outsized figure of the gangster into a common (and usually despicable) villain.

As a result of this crackdown on colorful crime, the success fantasy migrated into another powerful myth, the show business story, especially the backstage drama. By 1932, when other studios had scarcely acknowledged the Depression (though they would soon face bankruptcy), Warner Brothers was turning a profit with punchy, timely stories including gangster movies, hard-boiled newsroom dramas, and a daring exposé of the worst abuses of the judicial system, *I Am a Fugitive from a Chain Gang*. Musicals, which had been exploited as technical novelties during the early sound days, had already been left for dead when the studio took a final roll of the dice in *42nd Street*. The popularity of *42nd Street*, the *Gold Diggers* series, *Footlight Parade*, and *Dames* was due to Busby Berkeley's sur-

real choreography and the memorable songs of Al Dubin and Harry Warren, but also to the topical material, snappy, often risqué dialogue, and
brisk pacing that were quickly becoming Warner Brothers' trademarks.
As cost-saving devices evolved into a studio style, Warner's fast-working
directors like Mervyn LeRoy turned the backstage musical into buoyantly reassuring Depression fables. In order to put on a show, beleaguered
directors, hard-pressed producers, lascivious backers, overworked hoofers, callow juveniles, egocentric stars, and starving chorus girls somehow
manage to pull together, overcoming not only the vicissitudes of show
business but the dire economic conditions of the Depression. When the
star of the show within a show in *42nd Street* literally breaks a leg and a
fresh and winsome Ruby Keeler, fainting from starvation, somehow manages to learn her part overnight, Depression moviegoers suddenly found
a new figure who could make them feel good about themselves.

In retrospect it seems inevitable that Depression audiences would
turn show business into a cultural metaphor, especially a metaphor for
success. The new media of the 1920s—radio, tabloids, and feature films,
along with the great surge of advertising and public relations—had catapulted movie stars like Mary Pickford, Rudolph Valentino, and Douglas
Fairbanks and sports heroes like Jack Dempsey and Babe Ruth into legends. The idea of success had once been identified mainly with commerce,
but businessman heroes were in short supply and bad odor throughout
the 1930s, though Walter Huston managed to make them seem honorable and appealing in Frank Capra's *American Madness* (1932) and William
Wyler's *Dodsworth* (1936). But these were idealized, warmly benevolent,
idiosyncratic men looking for something beyond success and profit to
give meaning to their lives. The only true business hero in the thirties
was the gangster, a man with exceptional style, who used guts, aggression, and sheer willpower to make a corrupt system work for him. Show
business success, which usually centered on a heroine, required some of
the same grit and determination—a truly phenomenal persistence, but
also sex appeal, a tincture of talent, the timely aid of some male patron,
and, most of all, the good luck to be in the right place at the right time.
Movies themselves were to become great morale builders of the Depression era.

The gangster's fearless tenacity helped viewers hold on to the idea
that, despite the odds, individuals might still somehow shape their own

destiny. But when the chorus girl vaulted into stardom and overnight
fame, there was something magical about it, like winning a lottery—a
swift change in fortune reserved for the very few. In William Wellman's
A Star Is Born (1937), Janet Gaynor, starry-eyed from reading fan magazines, which brighten up her dismal world, comes from North Dakota to
Hollywood to break into the movies. Looking for work as a extra at one
of the studios, a kindly receptionist tells her that they haven't taken any
one on for two years, and only one in a hundred thousand ever succeeds.
"But maybe I'm that one," she answers, timidly but hopefully. The movie
business was often compared to an earlier California phenomenon, the
gold rush, when people toiling side by side could get rich or go broke
overnight. "This is a tough town," says one character in Budd Schulberg's
novel *What Makes Sammy Run?* "Because it still has that gold-rush feeling . . . where so many people could hit the jackpot and the skids this
close together."[3] The striking feature of all the versions of *A Star Is Born*
is the seesaw pattern of success and failure; the plot makes clear that for
everyone who makes good, there are others who fail badly, starting with
those who get nowhere in the first place. In *Movies about the Movies*, Christopher Ames calls these movies "cautionary tales" to differentiate them
from "the more familiar rags-to-riches tale of achieving fabulous success in Hollywood."[4] This mixed message, combining magic and pathos,
glamour and sacrifice, is pitched at the point where Hollywood and the
Depression intersect. The films tease us with a behind-the-scenes look at
the moviemaking process, especially the machinery of stardom, at once
debunking Hollywood and burnishing its myths. They deal with people's
dream lives and the distorted or poignant identification they make with
images projected by the studios and their stars.

In the early 1920s, after a series of scandals, including the murder
trial of Fatty Arbuckle, Hollywood began to make self-promoting films
to remove the taint of decadence and immorality attached to the movie
colony. They revolved around ordinary people who achieve fame and
fortune in the movies. As the California historian Kevin Starr shows
in *Inventing the Dream*, these pictures were meant to convey "that the
glamour of Hollywood should not obscure its basic American decency
and opportunities for upward mobility for people possessing talent and
willing to work hard." Stardom was democratized by fan magazines
and studio publicists offering constant access to the lifestyles of the rich

and famous. "Allowed broad latitude in sexual conduct, marriage and divorce," movie stars were "required only to remain young, glamorous, and on view," says the aptly named Starr.[5] Portrayed as a natural paradise, a fountain of perpetual youth, and a wondrous chamber of illusion, Hollywood became a key element of the chamber of commerce boosterism that was selling California, and especially Los Angeles, to the nation as a new Eden. The boom fed on health faddism or land speculation. The girls who took off for Hollywood to break into pictures were part of the same migration that brought retired people and young families to California for the climate or the economic bonanza.

The Depression put a dent in these optimistic myths. California welcomed migrants who had money to burn, but in Steinbeck's *Grapes of Wrath* the promised land is a forbidding place, a scene of fabulous abundance that exploits the low-paid labor needed to maintain it. This led to fierce class conflict over union-organizing and political power, culminating in Upton Sinclair's 1934 populist campaign to End Poverty in California, with movie studios weighing in viciously against Sinclair's candidacy for governor. The new cautionary tales about Hollywood reflected a dawning realism about the gospel of success, about the Depression, and about the California paradise itself. One of the first and best of these mixed fables was the 1932 movie on which *A Star Is Born* would be loosely based, George Cukor's *What Price Hollywood?* It was made the same year as *42nd Street*, during the brief reign of David O. Selznick at RKO, but it reflected a darker vision than Busby Berkeley's. The limited realism of the Warner musicals came through in the Depression details and showbiz lore that surfaced in the racy, hard-bitten dialogue and sparkled in the bizarre effects of Berkeley's big numbers, such as "We're in the Money" and "Remember My Forgotten Man" from *Gold Diggers of 1933*. The deeper shadows in *What Price Hollywood?* begin with the question of the title, which, as David Thomson remarks in his fine biography of Selznick, "is real, sour, and still open at the end of the film."[6] When Selznick produced *A Star Is Born* five years later, this question remained open, though it finally received a more sentimental and upbeat answer. Both movies made clear that the price was high.

Just as California was identified with the gold rush, its boosters cherished the stout mythology of the pioneer. This also became part of Hollywood's (and California's) self-image as a place where adventurous souls could make their fortune. Despite the ridicule of the rest of the family, Janet Gaynor's tough pioneer grandmother provides the money for her to take off for Hollywood, but also warns her, from her own experience, that "for every dream of yours you make come true, you'll pay the price in heartbreak." This is the gist of *What Price Hollywood?* and *A Star Is Born*. In both movies a fresh-faced young woman achieves stardom almost miraculously, first by catching the eye of a powerful man, then by quickly winning the hearts of the fans. In each case her big break comes from a man who has grown jaded with his own success and cynical about the world that acclaimed and rewarded him. Too clear-eyed for his own good, he recoils from the machinery of make-believe and the thin gruel of popular adulation. His alcoholic decline, which at first looks high-spirited and amusing, reflects a disgust with the system mingled with self-hatred for being part of it. Part of the girl's attraction for him is that she is so fresh and unspoiled—outside the system, hungry to get in, yet clueless about what success would entail. He reaches out to her, just as many fans will, precisely because of this innocence, but that lifeline proves too slippery for him to grasp. His star wanes as hers rises, and in the end he takes his own life. Both are insider's movies mixing barbed truths about the Hollywood system—steamrolling producers, cynical publicists, fickle fans— with sugar-coated tales about glamour, fame, and personal triumph, along with their attendant costs. Both films begin as witty, sophisticated comedies and descend into muted tragedy, playing off a young girl's plaintive longing against an older man's bleakly truthful world-weariness.

What Price Hollywood? is the more caustic film, though it tacks on a happier ending. It has the spunky, ragged honesty of many pre-Code movies. It offers a damning picture of the magnetic pull of celebrity yet also of its power, when we achieve it, to corrode and break down our sense of who we are. When we first meet Constance Bennett, still back home, she is composing herself in front of a mirror—the first of many mirror shots in the movie—dressing up and flipping through the pages of fan magazines to find images that will fill out her fantasies. (With the mirror as her screen, she ends up in a girlish clinch with a photo of Clark Gable.) Near the end of the movie there is a matching scene in which the director who discovered her, played by Lowell Sherman (himself an alcoholic actor turned director, who would die not long afterward), gazes into another mirror to see for the first time how low he has sunk. He's no longer working, and Bennett has rescued him from the drunk tank and put him to bed in her own home. Before the mirror he sees an inscribed photo he once gave her, the debonair image of his earlier self, and in the glass, alongside his shadowed face, we see what goes through his mind, a Russian-style montage of scenes from his better days. He shoots himself in the temple and, as he heavily falls, another sputtering flash of self-images completes the album of his life.

As Bennett had eagerly composed herself into a Hollywood icon, at great cost to her own happiness, Sherman calmly and curiously stares into the abyss of his own disintegrating face. That face is dark, chiseled by time, and the whole scene eerily anticipates the look of film noir, but the movie itself is not dark. Sherman had always been ambivalent about Hollywood, and now he is grimly amused and free of illusion about his own decline, which he has done nothing to arrest. At the end of *What Price Hollywood?* Bennett, having fled to the back-lot version of the French countryside, is reunited with her divorced husband, a wealthy outsider who always looked down on the movie colony. He humbles himself and accepts her world while she looks forward to reviving her career, which came apart after Sherman committed suicide in her home.

The story ends here, on this scarcely believable note, for nothing that happened earlier allows for a happy ending. The preceding story harshly satirizes the savagery of the tabloids and the fans, who turn on her as abruptly as they had once idolized her. But it also mocks her playboy husband's snobbish condescension toward Hollywood by warmly evoking what he detests, the movie colony's streetwise ethnic roots. "You live in a world where people are cheap and vulgar without knowing it," her husband said before walking out on her. The movie makes that vulgarity buoyant, crass, and life affirming. Gregory Ratoff turns in a winning performance as her amiable, protective, good-hearted producer in the half-literate Sam Goldwyn mold. (To decide on one film property, he wants to hear the story in fifty words. "Why don't you get someone to read the stories to you before you buy them?" the director asks. "I can read," Ratoff insists in his thick accent.) It would be a long time before Hollywood would be this frank in acknowledging the immigrant Jews who invented the place as "an empire of their own."

Success and failure, stardom and decline, are even more bound up in *A Star Is Born*, since the man and woman changing places are also husband and wife. Janet Gaynor falls in love with a famous but alcoholic actor played (with wonderful comic brio) by Fredric March. She marries him and becomes his costar, only to eclipse him almost immediately. We see nothing of her acting—talent is not the issue—but we hear the audience's reaction to their first movie and soon see her billing plastered over his. (Something like this reversal actually happened after the release of Sternberg's *The Blue Angel*, when the performance of a fresh newcomer, Marlene Dietrich, overshadowed the old-style histrionics of the celebrated Emil Jannings.) March was already slipping when he met her, but now his popularity ebbs along with his dignity and self-control. He makes a drunken, self-denigrating speech as she receives an Academy Award, and soon (like the rich husband in *What Price?*) he is reduced to being her spouse and appendage. A good-hearted producer, played by Adolphe Menjou, tries to cushion his fall. (This is Selznick's congratulatory image of himself.) But the real voice of Hollywood is represented by the inimitable Lionel Stander, playing a foul-mouthed publicist who promoted March when he was on top but smashes him now that he's down. Finally, the fading star takes his own life, walking quietly into the Pacific to keep from becoming a drag on Gaynor and her new career.

Since she really loved him, she falls apart when he dies. But having sacrificed her private self on the altar of fame, she has no outlet for personal grief. The crowds mob her at the funeral, tearing off her veil, just as they mobbed Constance Bennett at her small church wedding in *What Price?* (There, after alerting the news media and turning the wedding into a Hollywood extravaganza, the producer boasted, "We broke all the house records for this church.") When Gaynor loses heart and goes into seclusion, her feisty grandma comes out to buck her up, recalling the frontier image with which she emboldened her in the first place. "There'll always be a wilderness to conquer," she had said. "Perhaps Hollywood's your wilderness," a prediction that proved more accurate than they realized. In a blatant piece of Depression sermonizing, Grandma accuses her of being a whiner, a coward, a quitter. Since "tragedy is the test of courage," she says, Gaynor must persist and look beyond her own grief. The price of Hollywood was the loss of personal life in becoming a star, an artificial creation beloved by her fans. But in her famous concluding lines, Gaynor announces herself to the audience as "Mrs. Norman Maine," keeping her husband's name alive by erasing her own identity.

It's an upbeat climax that tugs at the heart but seems untrue to the film, which kept warning us that, for a Hollywood star, private emotions could scarcely stand up to the public demands of success.

This triumph through tears, like the happy ending of *What Price Hollywood?*, is at once uplifting and unreal. Yet it was essential to the enduring impact and popularity of the story, which was famously remade, with music added, for Judy Garland in 1954 and Barbra Streisand in 1976. Depression audiences especially needed this kind of catharsis. As with gangster films, they relished fables of success even as they responded to warnings of its pitfalls. Unlike Garland and Streisand, who came to the roles as celebrated musical performers, Gaynor appealed to Depression audiences by her very ordinariness, the fragile vulnerability that first made her a star in *Sunrise* and *Seventh Heaven*, the silent films that earned her the first Academy Award ever given for best actress. *What Price Hollywood?* and *A Star Is Born* seasoned their idealized picture of show business and the pipe dreams of ordinary people with bits of cynicism, realism, and frustration. Soon after *A Star Is Born* was released, the same formula for success through heartbreak was brilliantly applied to *Stage Door*, a hit Broadway comedy by George S. Kaufman and Edna Ferber. The original play was a backstage drama about the theater, set in a boardinghouse for struggling young actresses; it carried a message against selling out to Hollywood. It was witty but snobbish—"an orgy of petty snobbery," notes Elizabeth Kendall[7]—though the authors had done quite well whenever their work was adapted for the movies. RKO turned *Stage Door* into not simply a New York version of *A Star Is Born* but a glittering ensemble piece about a brilliant group of wisecracking, self-possessed, independent women, habitually out of work and desperate for a foothold in show business. The cast, bursting with talent, was headed by RKO's two leading female stars, Katharine Hepburn and Ginger Rogers, and included Eve Arden, Lucille Ball, Gail Patrick, and Ann Miller, playing characters who, as James Harvey points out, "were related to themselves in real life."[8] Completely rewritten from the play, *Stage Door* was directed, and to some extent improvised, by one of the great comedy geniuses of the 1930s, Gregory La Cava, fresh from his screwball success with *My Man Godfrey*.

Seeing *Stage Door* is (in Harvey's words) "like going to wisecrack heaven," with Ginger Rogers as the tough working-class broad dueling with Hepburn, who plays the rich girl in need of some humility. Additional barbs come from Gail Patrick, playing the heavy (as she did in *Godfrey*), with Eve Aden as the sardonic chorus armed with zinging one-liners—she would make a career of this. None of their lines are as memorable as the atmosphere they create, a mood of droll abandon, spiced with a needling humor that keeps adversity at bay. Like *My Man Godfrey*, with its rich, silly family, bickering and dysfunctional, this comedy is richer in Depression motifs than most serious dramas of the period, including the melodrama within the movie itself. These women, hard-boiled versions of Busby Berkeley's gold diggers, are behind in the rent, desperate for work, uncertain about their next meal. Andrea Leeds won an Academy Award nomination for her histrionic role as a starving actress, last year's stage sensation, who kills herself after Hepburn gets the lachrymose part she was born to play. Where the other girls, in the classic Depression manner, use one-liners defensively to keep up a front, shielding their exposed lives, Leeds's fragile character has neither wit nor survival skills.

It is opening night, and Hepburn, like Bennett in *What Price?* and Gaynor in *A Star Is Born*, responds to this suicide by refusing to carry on. Her acting coach, in the cheerleading spirit of Gaynor's pioneer grandma, lectures her on the mores of the "theatah": the show must go on. "It takes more than greasepaint and footlights to make an actress," she says. "It takes heartbreak as well." This inspirational hokum has its effect. Shaken by the loss, supposedly knowing real grief for the first time, Hepburn takes the stage, in a part she had mangled in rehearsal, and gives a deeply felt performance. This is the girl who, with confidence bred by her patrician background, had lectured the others on their lack of spunk and initiative ("you all talk as if the world owed you a living"), and told them about *her* pioneer grandfather who had crossed the country in a covered wagon. (These movies shamelessly stole from each other.) Born with a silver spoon, secretly backed by her disapproving father, Hepburn could buy into the Horatio Alger code of strive and succeed, which was the mantra of plutocrats and Hoover Republicans during the Depression. Now, humbled and humanized, she learns how hard it is to live by her own advice.

The real heroine of *Stage Door* is not Hepburn or Rogers, and certainly not the saintly, deranged victim played by Leeds, but the group, with its plucky camaraderie. Hepburn descends into the maelstrom of Depression life, where deprivation puts on a brave front, and discovers the solidarity that was obscured by the girls' witty rivalry and bedrock need. Picking up some of the other girls' language, she even develops a little of the common touch. "Why are we always so helpful to each other when it's too late?" she wonders. As in many Depression fables, the concerns of the individual give way to a new sense of community, interdependency. Show business becomes a metaphor for working together rather than the battle-scarred site of personal triumph. The successful heroine takes heart from the failure around her. This is especially clear with Hepburn and Rogers, whose prolonged battle of wits slowly gives way to mutual respect, bridging their vast social divide. In her splendid chapter on *Stage Door* in *The Runaway Bride*, Elizabeth Kendall sees them as the equivalent of the bickering heterosexual couple in screwball comedy, with class conflict taking the place of sexual tension. This is helpful, but it shifts the emphasis from where it belongs, on the ensemble of women living together at the Footlights Club, a female community that serves as an exquisite miniature of Depression society.

Stage Door has only one significant male role: Adolphe Menjou plays a suave but deeply corrupt version of the benign producer he played in *A Star Is Born*. With his eye for showgirls, his casting couch, and his capricious way with auditions, jobs, and sexual favors, Menjou is an oily, sinister example of the authority to which these women must bend in order to survive. While other girls may needle him a little, Katharine Hepburn tells him off; she is the only one whose hopes don't hang on his patronage. Anticipating Mel Brooks and *The Producers*, he takes money from her father to put her on the stage—her father hopes she will fail and give up her theater dream—but the morale-building support of the group helps her succeed. Thus a tale that began in crackling verbal contention, female rivalry, cultural difference, and class conflict ends in solidarity and reconciliation. The girls' surface bravado and deep-rooted sentiment come together. This is the Depression message latent in the show business parable—beyond the individual dream of success, the collective effort of putting on a show, connecting with yourself, with each one another, with the audience. The women in *Stage Door* joke about the food, about their roommates, who are all in the same boat, and about how conditions are stacked against them. But even as one of them goes under, their high spirits and common humanity keep depression at bay. Movies like *What Price Hollywood?*, *A Star Is Born*, and *Stage Door* proved cathartic for Depression audiences not just by crafting fairy tales of success but by working through the anxieties that give success its resounding immediacy: fears of poverty, solitude, abandonment, loss of hope. These films lend heft to the endemic optimism of a popular medium by weighing its costs and giving it a convincing emotional truth.

The famous novels about Hollywood written in the late thirties take a different tack. These novels created the template for later treatments of the movie industry, from Clifford Odets's play *The Big Knife* (1949; filmed in 1955) and Norman Mailer's *The Deer Park* (1955) to Michael Tolkin's novel *The Player* (1988), which Robert Altman turned into one of his best late films, in 1992. Where the movies feel like the work of insiders, glorifying show business while chronicling examples of hardship and heartbreak, the literary works were begotten by outsiders, most of them writers who came for the money but felt misused by the Hollywood system. They also looked to the wider world of Southern California that enclosed the movies and matched their fantastic culture. The novels focused more on those who made the films—producers, writers, studio heads—than on those who appeared in them. Power, not stardom, was their subject; naked ambition, not the hunger for celebrity. The lives of these domineering figures were success stories of a different kind, and their moral failures ran deeper. In many cases they came from nowhere, from poverty and virtual illiteracy, yet managed, often at great cost, to find the American grain. Budd Schulberg's Sammy Glick (in *What Makes Sammy Run?*) is a product of the Lower East Side ghetto, which gives him the raw ambition and the Darwinian view of life that lifts him to power in the Hollywood jungle. F. Scott Fitzgerald's gifted producer, Monroe Stahr (in *The Last Tycoon*), is a much subtler, more idealized Horatio Alger figure, based on MGM's boy wonder, Irving Thalberg, who became a Hollywood legend long before his early death in 1936. On the other hand, Nathanael West's Tod Hackett, the protagonist of *The Day of the Locust*, is a painter rather than a filmmaker. Feeling baffled in his real calling, as West himself certainly did, he's designing sets and costumes for the movies. The strangeness of all he sees rekindles his desire to paint. Savage satirists like Goya and Daumier have replaced Winslow Homer and Albert Pinkham Ryder as his masters. As frustrated in his love life as in his work life, he remains an observer who sees all of Southern California as a vast, ominous curiosity that no artist has ever truly captured.

Fitzgerald, Schulberg, and West each had a different relation to the movie industry. Fitzgerald was down on his luck when he came to Hollywood almost as a last resort. His most ambitious novel, *Tender Is the Night* (1934), had not sold well, and he had gone public with his problems in "The Crack-Up," his confessional articles for *Esquire* in 1936. He was deeply in debt and, worst of all, had lost some of his confidence as a writer. Thanks to his fame he was paid well by MGM and enjoyed a good deal of literary cachet, yet in the end managed only a single screen credit. Schulberg, on the other hand, was a Hollywood prince whose father, B. P. Schulberg, had once been Paramount's head of production. The younger Schulberg went off to college at Dartmouth, came back to write for the movies, published short stories, and turned to the novel after being fired, along with Fitzgerald, from the film *Winter Carnival*. Their ill-fated trip to Dartmouth in February 1939 to work on that movie ended in disaster when Fitzgerald began drinking and needed to be hospitalized after a terrible bender. But their conversations gave Fitzgerald still more material for a Hollywood novel, even as they fired Schulberg's artistic ambitions. West too came to Hollywood because of his failure as a novelist. His first three books had died commercially, though one of them, *Miss Lonelyhearts*, now a classic, was extravagantly admired by discerning contemporaries like William Carlos Williams and Edmund Wilson. Fitzgerald was well rewarded by MGM, yet he felt stymied by the special demands of screenwriting, which thwarted his rich descriptive powers, and by a system that forced him to work with other writers or see his work rewritten by them. West, on the other hand, earned much less money but gained numerous credits for his work on routine programmers for lowly Republic Pictures, a back-street studio that specialized in low-budget westerns, and later for RKO and Universal.

The coming of sound gave movies a vast appetite for dialogue and narrative that only writers could supply, but the studio system also shifted power from directors to producers. They treated writers, at best, as hired hands whose work could be mixed and matched like the ingredients of a stew. (Thalberg himself was partly responsible for this system.) Fiction about Hollywood has always had touches of an ethnographer's account of the strange mores of the natives, but, almost invariably, it also became a vehicle for the writer's revenge, his simmering indignation over how he was treated. While Faulkner and West sharply separated their screen-writing from their own work, Fitzgerald was unusual among novelists in trying to learn to write for the screen as a serious craft. He was also fascinated by the role of producers in shaping stories that touched a vital nerve of popular taste, a gift he once had but now eluded him. There were hard-boiled writers with backgrounds in journalism like James M. Cain and W. R. Burnett whose work fit well into the genre categories and narrative economy of Hollywood movies. Their writing stressed action over introspection, and they quickly became seasoned Hollywood professionals. Other writers saw the producer and the studio boss as barbarians trampling on art, but Fitzgerald in *The Last Tycoon* portrayed the producer as an artist in his own right, a man of vision who edits the work of writers, directors, actors, and set designers into a unified whole that communicates visually, not just verbally.

Fitzgerald had known Irving Thalberg slightly from earlier trips to Hollywood. He was drawn less by his mystique than by his youth, his total commitment, and the sense of authority he radiated. He was impressed by the producer's decisiveness, his grasp of the whole picture, along with his ability to keep many movies in focus at the same time. *The Last Tycoon* begins with an airplane flight, and as the first chapter concludes, Stahr is compared to Icarus, who flew too high, too close to the sun, but enjoyed a breathtaking view. At the end Stahr was to die in a plane crash. Unfortunately, *The Last Tycoon* is largely an unwritten novel, much of it existing only in summary or draft, or in projections based on the author's notes and intentions. But one fully realized sequence gives us a day in the life of the producer, in which we see Stahr interacting with writers, directors, actors, and cameramen from several different productions, challenging and refining their efforts with an instinctive story sense that made Fitzgerald marvel. He lectures a writer who looks down on Hollywood, explaining to him what movies are and how they work. In the real world of Hollywood, Fitzgerald had been on the receiving end of such lessons and rebuffs, until MGM finally refused to renew his contract. Yet he admires Stahr's ability to do what eluded him: to think cinematically, not strictly in words, and to connect with popular taste as the young Fitzgerald had been able to do. By projecting Stahr as an artist in pictures, a shaper of fantasy, Fitzgerald makes him both a version of himself and his own antitype, a pioneer in the new art that Fitzgerald tried with difficulty to master.

There are many other touches of the author in Stahr, including his youthful success, which resonated with Fitzgerald, and his delicate health, which adds a poignant overtone to everything he does, colored for us by Fitzgerald's own stalwart push to write this novel in the face of debilitating illness. Stahr is in quiet but protracted mourning for his late wife, just as Fitzgerald had essentially lost Zelda, who had shared his days of fame and glory but was now confined to a sanatorium in the East. Deeply damaged by this loss and thrown into an emotional void, Stahr sees his affair with Kathleen as a chance for rebirth, and this undoubtedly reflects Scott's nurturing new relationship to Sheila Graham. ("He has an overwhelming urge toward the girl who promises to give life back to him," says Fitzgerald in one of his notes.)[9] Like Jimmy Stewart's character in Hitchcock's *Vertigo*, Stahr is a man trying to recapture something he has lost, even to re-create the very woman he has lost. The delicate chemistry of this affair shows some of Fitzgerald's old romantic magic, though his style throughout is spare and avoids all lyrical sheen.

Amid the surreal flotsam of a studio lot, flooded after a California earthquake, Stahr is drawn to this woman because she resembles his late wife. The influence of West comes through in this scene, which feels like an outtake from *The Day of the Locust*. Perched atop the huge head of the goddess Siva, Kathleen and a friend come "floating down the current of an impromptu river," drifting dreamily into his life.[10] For West the mélange of the back lot seemed grotesque and denatured, a junkyard of cultural kitsch and shabby illusion, but Fitzgerald makes it a whimsical setting for romantic recognition, as if by cinematic alchemy. Soon Stahr sees that Kathleen offers him more than a chance resemblance to someone he loved; she shakes up his world much more than the quake. Work has become his whole life—a killing fatigue has been his drug of choice—but feeling "exalted and happy" he now is "glad that there was beauty in the world that would not be weighed in the sales of the casting department" (82). As an emissary from real life, Kathleen offers him a chance for rebirth, a renewal of vitality. Despite his fabled instincts he fails to seize the moment; for reasons more complicating than credible, she marries someone else.

The same fatigue and unexpected moments of exaltation infiltrate Fitzgerald's uneven writing. The novel's swift, musing, wryly factual manner is closer to the shorthand of Fitzgerald's letters and essays than to the lush texture of his earlier fiction, but it is dotted with moments of quiet revelation. "As he walked toward her, the people shrank back against the walls till they were only murals" (89). Of Stahr at work he writes,

> He darted in and out of the role of "one of the boys" with dexterity—but on the whole I should say he wasn't one of them. But he knew how to shut up, how to draw into the background, how to listen. From where he stood (and though he was not a tall man, it always seemed high up) he watched the multitudinous practicalities of the world like a proud young shepherd to whom night and day had never mattered. He was sleepless, without a talent for rest or the desire for it. (22–23)

Fitzgerald can shift from description to a metaphor, as he does here, without sacrificing his terse, straightforward manner. The writing is elevated and condensed without losing the off-kilter flow of conversation.

This conversational tone is meant to reflect the girlish outlook of the narrator, Cecilia Brady, the daughter of the studio chief who is Stahr's unscrupulous partner and rival. Her head is stuffed with romantic ideas out of Hollywood movies like *42nd Street* (which "had a great influence on me," she says [26]). To create this character, Fitzgerald filled out his own daughter, Scottie, with the insider experiences of a real Hollywood prince, Budd Schulberg. Naive, smitten with Stahr, and overflowing with youthful energy, she comes across as another version of Rosemary Hoyt, the wide-eyed young starlet of *Tender Is the Night* who develops a crush on the hero, Dick Diver, as she contemplates the refined elegance of his marriage and manners. Like Conrad, Fitzgerald needed a narrator who would serve as our guide to his central characters while also distancing them, shielding their mystery and mystique from too close a scrutiny. This worked brilliantly in *Gatsby*, only intermittently in *Tender*. It scarcely works at all in *The Last Tycoon*, where Cecilia, like Rosemary, could not have seen, let alone understood, all the writer wants us to take in. At times she simply evaporates into an omniscient third-person narrator, then awkwardly reappears. Yet Cecilia does help justify the novel's occasionally saucy style, its slightly immature hero-worshiping tone, and the somewhat opaque portrayal of the producer, a complex figure she is too young to understand. We get to know Stahr, like Gatsby, through his works, not by way of his inner life. Creativity in Hollywood, as Fitzgerald sees it, is a matter of instinct rather than inwardness, not a feeling for art but an intuitive grasp of popular taste. In one of Stahr's discussions with the exasperated writer (based on Aldous Huxley), who feels he cannot master the movies' method of visual storytelling, the producer says, "We have to take people's own favorite folklore and dress it up and give it back to them. Anything beyond that is sugar" (125).

This surely echoes the graceless lessons administered to Fitzgerald by his impatient employers. His admiration for Stahr hardly diminishes his mixed attitude toward the movies as a mass medium. To his daughter he wrote that "it is a business of telling stories fit for children and this is only interesting up to a point."[11] At times he saw it as little more than hackwork or crowd-pleasing reverie. In *The Last Tycoon* he set out to avoid the heart-tugging pathos he disliked in *A Star Is Born*. The writing is alternately naive and disintoxicated, and he wrote notes reminding himself to avoid black-and-white characters. ("Don't give the impression that these are bad people.")[12] Though he failed to write filmable screenplays with good spoken dialogue, Fitzgerald's fascination with dreams, ambitions, and romantic fantasies gave him an instinctive affinity for Hollywood as a dream factory. This was precisely the interest it held for Nathanael West. West saw movies, as he saw LA itself, as a vast dream dump, a Sargasso Sea of tawdry longings that exposed the pinched, disappointed lives of ordinary people, much like the pitiful letters to the advice column in *Miss Lonelyhearts*. West's imagination, like Sherwood Anderson's, was ignited by the grotesque pathos of people's twopenny dreams and frustrated desires and by the explosive potential of their dumb dissatisfaction. But there was a political dimension as well: West's sense of the dynamics of fascism as a decaying populism rife with real potential for mass violence, as shown by the rioting of the crowd at the end of *The Day of the Locust*. Fitzgerald, on the other hand, saw dreams and aspirations as the vital center of people's lives, their poetry of hope and experience. He respected even the degraded dreams manufactured in Hollywood as popular art to which the Depression lent new power. To describe his literary intentions in *The Last Tycoon*, Fitzgerald drew an analogy to the frontier. In the words of Matthew J. Bruccoli in his biography of Fitzgerald, *The Last Tycoon* is set in "the last American frontier, in a boom town built on a lode of illusions and hopes." As Fitzgerald himself put it, Hollywood represents "not just the American Dream but the human dream and if I come at the end of it that too is a place in the line of the pioneers."[13] This was why Fitzgerald considered calling the novel a western, as Bruccoli subtitles it in his revised edition.

Fitzgerald, who had concluded *Gatsby* with a magical evocation of the fresh new continent, thought of Hollywood not only as the West but as the end of the line. It would have been easy for Fitzgerald to give us Stahr as an innovator, the creator of a new production system that, as Walter Benjamin argued about movies in general, alters (and industrializes) the whole nature of art. But by describing Stahr as the "last tycoon" (as in his notes he called himself "the last of the novelists for a long time now"), he chose to portray Hollywood as the closing of the West, the end of an era of individualism when the self-integrated entrepreneur could somehow do it all. This was a pervasive Depression theme: the individual was being replaced by the collective—by the impersonal mechanics of the system or the communal will of the group. Fitzgerald intended *The Last Tycoon* to be his first real Depression-era novel. As the Depression helped throw Fitzgerald's career into eclipse, the arrival of class warfare in Hollywood, with wage cuts and labor troubles, threatens to make Stahr a relic of another era. Even the stenographers have lost the "dumb admiration for their bosses they had in 1929. They've been laid off—they've seen their bosses jittery" (50–51). The deteriorating conditions of the Depression, combined with the thuggery of Brady, the Louis B. Mayer–like studio chief, becomes a reflection of Stahr's poor health and waning vitality. (In his notes for the unwritten part, the war over the pay cut would turn vicious as Brady and Stahr scheme to have each other killed.)

Stahr blocks out this gathering storm by making movies in his own way, extravagantly (in the MGM tradition), but with an eye for simple things. He is a paternalist who maintains dying standards of craftsmanship and has been defending the workers against the cuts and layoffs spreading though the industry. To them "Stahr was the hero" who "had seen that no harm came to them"; he was "the last of the princes" (37). This old-fashioned quality influences the movies he makes, which are geared to appeal to ordinary people. Pacing the floor, Stahr outlines his notion of what a character adapted from a play needs. (It is just what he needs in his own life; and soon will find.)

> She was a perfect girl with a few small faults as in the play, but a
> perfect girl not because the public wanted her that way but because
> it was the kind of girl that he, Stahr, liked to see in this sort of pic-
> ture. . . . She stood for health, vitality, ambition and love. . . . There
> was a right thing and a wrong thing to do. . . . That was the kind of
> story this was—thin, clean and shining. No doubts. (52–53)

Significantly he adds, "She has never heard the word labor troubles. . . .
She might be living in 1929." Living in 1929, of course, meant living at the
edge of a precipice, in a world before the fall. Yet this kind of innocent
character, not yet darkened by ambiguity, would survive as a staple of the
Hollywood system, just as the strong producer of the Stahr type would
survive his early death. The production system created by Thalberg and
company during the Depression lasted well into the 1950s and beyond.

In What Makes Sammy Run? Budd Schulberg actually wrote the economic novel about Hollywood that Fitzgerald failed to bring off with *The
Last Tycoon.* Like Fitzgerald's novel, it is set around 1935 ("in the very lowest time of the Depression," says Cecilia [5]), with the studios instituting
pay cuts and the writers organizing their union and worrying about their
jobs. The studios' efforts to break the union represented, as Fitzgerald
said in one of his notes, the manifestation of "a class war reaching Hollywood."[14] Above all, Schulberg writes what Fitzgerald or West could never
have written, the best reportorial novel about Hollywood, the insider's account of how the system really worked. Leaving the glamour and
hype to others, he set about to expose "the factory side" of Hollywood,
and film historians have only recently caught up with him. *Sammy* is a
muckraking novel about Hollywood as a system fueled by greed, ego,
philistinism, and betrayal. But this is not what has given a flawed novel
its enduring vitality through many editions over more than six decades.
For Schulberg, who was then a Communist, Sammy Glick epitomizes the
spirit of ambition and vicious competitition not only of Hollywood but
of the capitalist society as a whole, the war of each against all. Yet his
demonic energy drives the whole novel.

Crude but unforgettable, Sammy Glick first appeared in two stories
in *Liberty* magazine in 1937 and 1938, which, with significant changes,

became episodes of the 1941 novel. Because Sammy's hustling, coarse, fiercely combative character was so close to an anti-Semitic stereotype, Schulberg revised the stories to turn the novel's main characters, especially the narrator, into Jews. Fitzgerald, by contrast, steers clear of ethnicity in *The Last Tycoon* but is surprisingly complimentary to Hollywood's Jews. He turns Stahr's nemesis—the unscrupulous Brady, who resents Stahr's idealism and extravagance—from a Jew (based on MGM mogul Louis B. Mayer) into an Irishman. Glick is the Horatio Alger hero as hatched by the dog-eat-dog world of the ghetto. Oddly, there's nothing really Jewish about him. Ashamed of his origins, he has moved so far that his own mother scarcely knows him, as if he had realized the American Dream of giving birth to himself: "Sammy was not a real Jew any more. He was no different from the little wops and micks who cursed and fought and cheated. Sometimes she could not believe he grew out of her belly. He grew out of the belly of Rivington Street."[15] As the narrator had already been warned, "there was an epidemic raging in that neighborhood of his—more contagious than infantile—and he caught one of the worst cases on record" (90).

This environmental emphasis, so typical of the 1930s, is the key to *What Makes Sammy Run?* but also its principal weakness. *Sammy* marks a valiant attempt to write a proletarian novel about Hollywood, focusing not only on labor-management conflict and union organizing but on the social origins of the characters as the mainspring of their behavior. The narrator, a writer (and assimilated Jew) named Al Manheim, is obsessed with finding out "what makes Sammy run?" Kit, a savvy, independent woman, once Sammy's lover, has urged him to "look into the childhood," and surprisingly he does (108). Manheim first knew him as his copyboy and gofer at a New York newspaper, and after they both end up in Hollywood he has a box seat to observe his fabulous climb. Sammy uses him, discards him, and uses him again, but Al (not quite credibly) never seems able to turn his back on him. At different times he serves as Sammy's conscience, his amazed audience, his scold, his "one-man claque," his chronicler, and, in a strange way, the only friend to a man who makes no friends. But Manheim's interest turns into an obsession. When he revisits Sammy's haunts on the Lower East Side, the book turns melodramatic and unconvincing: it becomes a derivative version of Mike Gold's novel *Jews without Money*, without the passionate authenticity of

Gold's firsthand experience of growing up in the ghetto. Gold had earned the right to make the tenement the subject of his book and the agent of everything that happens in it; Schulberg had not, and the novel, indelible in its portrait of Sammy himself, declines into a sociological cartoon and a B-movie melodrama.

Though a Communist when he wrote *What Makes Sammy Run?*, Schulberg, by his own account, left the party when it tried to influence his work. According to him, the comrades criticized the book not for its stereotypes but for its bourgeois focus on individuals; they said it took no account of the good work done by Hollywood progressives. Schulberg cherished his independence; he subsequently became a fierce anti-Communist and testified in 1951 before the House Committee on Un-American Activities, where he named fifteen other former Communists. But unlike *The Last Tycoon* or *The Day of the Locust*, both by writers sympathetic to the Hollywood Left, the book is a typical thirties social novel, explaining everything in terms of environmental influence. Its flaw is that it finally answers the question posed in the title, and the answer is the ghetto, the street, the neighborhood in which Sammy was raised. Sammy runs because he was born to run, because he grew up in a Darwinian jungle where poverty made people want to get out, driving them to succeed at all cost.

Schulberg tries to mitigate the stereotype of the grasping Jew by dissipating Sammy's ethnic loyalties and by drawing stark comparisons with other Jews—his brother who remained religious, becoming a social worker in a settlement house, staying close to the family and the neighborhood; Julian Blumberg, the talented but timorous young writer from whom Sammy shamelessly steals ideas and whole scripts—but these are simply additional stereotypes. The brother is the ghetto Jew who never breaks away, while Julian is the pathetic nebbish who allows others to walk all over him. If Sammy sees life as a race, a contest, a boxing match, Julian is his antitype, "martyring himself because he couldn't learn how to run" (169). Schulberg's point is that the same environment could produce radically different types, mutations that undermine any mechanical determinism. Somewhat defensively, he tries to show that not all Jews are Sammy Glicks, not even all Hollywood Jews. Another benign Jew in the book is its Thalberg character, Sidney Fineman, a gentleman of the old school, as his name indicates—the creative producer of quality pictures, a past master of visual storytelling, who, unlike Stahr, has lost his nerve in the Depression. Hollywood has become a cutthroat world, "full of fear," but this is just the atmosphere in which Sammy Glick and his kind can thrive. For Sammy, "going through life with a conscience is like driving your car with the brakes on" (55).

As a character Sammy is always in danger of turning into an idea, too articulate to be wholly credible, yet the novel is kept afloat for us by his ferret-like ferocity, his instinct for survival in the Hollywood rat race. Schulberg is fascinated by his amoral drive, his need for success at any price. Sammy's behavior is unconscionable, his movies all schlock based on other people's stories, his love life and friendships no more than joyless ways of getting ahead. He ends up on top but alone, rattling around his empty mansion like Citizen Kane, betrayed by a trophy wife who has used him as he tried to use her. This is an ironic twist on Hollywood's myth of success, the cult of the happy ending. The industry's own Darwinian ethic belied it. Schulberg was a better Marxist than the commissars allowed, for he turned the Hollywood novel into a critique of cruelties of American individualism and capitalism, much as he portrayed immigrant life as a breeding ground for social pathologies. By simplifying Sammy and his origins into a type, Schulberg damaged the novel but launched the character as an enduring myth, a byword for the grubby ethnic climber on the slippery ladder of success. As a recognizable type, Sammy quickly transcended the book in which he appeared. This is a rare achievement, though not strictly a literary one.

Sammy's lonely fate had long since become a cliché of the inverted success story, going back at least as far as Abraham Cahan's *Rise of David Levinsky* (1917), yet against all odds the novel is alive, charged with Sammy's animal vigor, his "genius for self-propulsion" (59). The Lower East Side section fails because Sammy himself is off-stage, unable to complicate the book's social message and moral preaching with his own manic resourcefulness and vitality. The delightful *Sammy* Web site (www.what makessammyrun.net) includes a list of "Glickisms," a tongue-in-cheek lexicon of Hollywood hypocrisy disguised as the regional dialect. Words like "switcheroo" and "Happytown" help give the novel its vulgar flavor, and no one dealing with movie people can fail to notice that hype and insincerity are the coin of the realm. Yet there's also an unpredictable air of menace about Sammy, for all his flattering ways, a touch of the gangster that seems yet another extension of the ghetto and of the industry's rough early years. ("One of these days remind me to rub you out," he says playfully [129]. This is the turbulent sea in which Sammy nervously swims, under the watchful eye of the narrator, a different sort of Jew, whose horrified attraction keeps us riveted to Sammy's outrages, as when he first supports but then torpedoes the writers' union, to curry favor with his bosses.

Schulberg's writing was influenced by the clipped, ironic, voice-over manner of the hard-boiled mystery novel. "She was becoming tiresome. Her tight little world was bursting with Sammy Glick." This we hear of Sammy's adoring Jewish girlfriend, whom he dumps en route to Hollywood. As in Chandler and Hammett, the narrator-detective is a quest figure who leads us deeper and deeper into a morass of corruption. The quest begins with the title, with Sammy himself, but takes us into the heart of Hollywood.

Schulberg also borrowed this technique of using the narrator as witness and investigator—and as the reader's surrogate—from his master, Fitzgerald, especially from *Gatsby*. Manheim is cast as Nick Carraway to Sammy's Lower East Side Gatsby, and like Nick he concludes the book with a grudging tribute to his subject, in this case to a dubious character's drive and energy. But Schulberg, who clearly identifies with Manheim, never examines his self-righteous priggishness and puritanism, his condescension, or the impact of his Reform German-Jewish background, let alone the obscure impulses that draw him back repeatedly into Sammy's orbit. Certainly his motive goes deeper than curiosity. Himself the Hollywood prince who went to Dartmouth, Schulberg can see the mote in the eye of the ghetto Jew struggling upward from poverty, but not the sizable beam that blinds the assimilated Jew with his "higher" cultural values. In his zeal to turn Sammy into a social specimen, Schulberg nearly spoils the book by providing a fulsome answer to the narrator's oft-repeated question. He dispels the mystery of the Sammy's nature, as Fitzgerald never does with the shadowy Gatsby. Fitzgerald himself, who had been anxious about what his protégé would do with this Hollywood scene, was disappointed by the book, though he endorsed it in a letter written shortly before he died, which the publisher used as a promotional comment. "It's not bad but it doesn't cut into my material at all," he told his own editor, Maxwell Perkins. But privately, in his notebook, he rather cruelly and unfairly labeled him "Bud, the untalented."[16]

Fitzgerald had no doubt about the talent of another young writer as yet largely unrecognized, someone very different from himself, whom he had noticed in his introduction to the Modern Library edition of *The Great Gatsby*. Nathanael West is unique among thirties writers for the potent mixture of savagery and pathos in his work. In a letter to Fitzgerald thanking him for his support—he enclosed the galleys of *The Day of the Locust*—West described himself as a miniaturist who cannot do the big picture, the politics, the grand human stories, but only the little disturbances that come within his ironic compass. Like all satirists, he had an eye for the absurd and a gift for caricature that the foibles of Hollywood brilliantly gratified. But unlike those who look down on bad taste and human folly as a blot on society or a delicious occasion for mimicry, West was attracted to kitsch as an oblique expression of thwarted desires. To West, popular culture, including movies and vernacular architecture, was not art but a naive form of daydreaming, offering a window onto undefended lives that were desperately unsatisfied and therefore fraught with menace. The Hollywood of *The Day of the Locust* is peopled not with stars or powerful producers but with set designers who pull down thirty dollars a week, would-be starlets who turn tricks to make ends meet, washed-up vaudevillians selling miracle polish door-to-door, and cowboys looking for work as extras in horse operas. They are surrounded by even creepier types suggesting the dead end of civilization: sleazy Mexicans who stage bloody cockfights in someone's garage, dysfunctional midwesterners who've come to California for their health, crazed movie fans hungering for a piece of the stars, religious cultists consumed with messianic rage. California was the last stop in America's westward push, the place where rootless Americans reached the end of the line, facing the ocean or the desert under an incongruously sunny sky. *The Day of the Locust* takes in a broad swath of California culture outside the movie industry. West's affinity for the LA underground drew him to night court and police stations rather than to chic Hollywood parties. At first stillborn, selling fewer than two thousand copies, *The Day*

of the Locust ultimately found its echo less in Hollywood novels by disillusioned screenwriters than in tragicomedies of such apocalyptic zaniness and incongruity as Flannery O'Connor's *Wise Blood* or *A Good Man Is
Hard to Find* and Thomas Pynchon's *The Crying of Lot 49*. Like West's book,
these were satiric works with doleful spiritual echoes.

Compared with his masterpiece, *Miss Lonelyhearts*, *The Day of the
Locust* is a more ambitious, more episodic, less controlled piece of work
(somewhat like Fitzgerald's expansive *Tender Is the Night* in relation
to the spare *Gatsby*). But it accomplishes far more than its threadbare
plot seems to allow. The novel revolves around the aimless lives of five
or six men spinning in the improbable orbit of Faye Greener, a part-
time hooker, cheaply glamorous but dissociated, who is trying, like so
many hopeful heroines, to break into the movies. The men around her
include her dying father, the old-time vaudevillian; the narrator, Tod
Hackett, who is even more glumly morose than Miss Lonelyhearts; the
lanky cowboy, Earle Shoop; his Mexican friend, Miguel; a successful
screenwriter, Claude Estee; Abe Kusich, a tough-talking dwarf; and the
timid, well-heeled, sexually repressed Homer Simpson, who worked for
twenty years at an Iowa hotel until a sexual near-incident scared him
into leaving town.

Homer is the linchpin of the plot insofar as there is one. His puppyish
devotion to Faye, which only intensifies her cruelty to him, finally leads
to an explosive breakdown in which he stomps an insufferable child actor
who is baiting him. This helps incite a mob of rioters at the premiere of
a new movie. These are Homer's people, though he has no connection
to them. They're "the people who came to California to die," the bored,
dissatisfied midwestern migrants drawn to Southern California by the
relentless boosterism of its businessmen, media promoters, and real-estate
developers. "Once there they discover that sunshine isn't enough. . . .
They haven't the mental equipment for leisure, the money nor the physical equipment for pleasure. . . . The sun is a joke. Oranges can't titillate
their jaded palates. Nothing can ever be violent enough to make taut their
slack minds and bodies. They have been cheated and betrayed. They have
saved and saved for nothing" (177–78). This is from the conclusion of the
novel, just before the riot—the apocalyptic outburst to which the whole
book has been tending. The novel had once been called *The Cheated*, and
by turning these cheated, violent souls into a plague of locusts, a destruc-

tive mass, West veers close to expressing an appalling condescension toward their meager, disappointed lives.

The Day of the Locust isn't really "about" this handful of characters. Despite the photographic sharpness of the setting, all we get of them are sketches and glimpses of stunted creatures with petty, unfulfilled desires, people closer to automatons than to rounded fictional creations. Homer, for example, is a "grotesque" out of Sherwood Anderson's *Winesburg, Ohio*, so out of touch with his body that his troubling, restless hands have a life of their own; they don't even wake up when he does. "He got out of bed in sections, like a poorly made automaton, and carried his hands into the bathroom. He turned on the cold water. When the basin was full, he plunged his hands in up to the wrists. They lay quietly on the bottom like a pair of strange aquatic animals. When they were thoroughly chilled and began to crawl about, he lifted them out and hid them in a towel" (82). Everything about this passage is typical West: the simple declarative sentences with their jewel-like precision; the figure of the automaton, dissociated and only partly human, that recurs throughout the novel; and the daring image of the "strange aquatic animals," that reminds us of West's roots in French surrealism. Such emblematic images of a deformed humanity take the place of extended description or characterization. The depraved dwarf, for example, tossed out by Faye, first appears to Tod like a bundle of old clothes, before he realizes that it's a "tiny man" with a "slightly hydrocephalic head" (63).

This shrinkage of the human to the condition of an object or a mechanical figure is heightened by West's spare but telling imagery. Introducing the tall, lean cowboy, Earle Shoop, West says that "his pole-like appearance was further exaggerated by the narrowness of his shoulders and by his lack of either hips or buttocks. . . . In fact, his legs were so straight that his dungarees, bleached a very light blue by the sun and much washing, hung down without a wrinkle, as though they were empty." What seems like careful description of Earle's appearance ends by obliterating him, evacuating his body from his standard-issue outfit. We also learn that "his reddish tan complexion was the same color from hairline to throat, as though washed in by an expert, and it completed his resemblance to a mechanical drawing" (109). When Earle clobbers the Mexican as he dances suggestively with Faye, Tod "heard the crack and saw the Mexican go to his knees still dancing, his body unwilling or unable to acknowledge the interruption" (117). Like Homer's hands and Earle's jeans, Miguel's body, imperfectly joined, has a trajectory of its own. This is slapstick comedy made literal, farce turned dead serious. As automatons they can readily become part of a dangerous mass, a rampaging crowd governed by no individual will.

The Day of the Locust underlines this reduction of their humanity to gesture and empty repetition. These "characters" are oddly eccentric figures with little individual identity, mechanical types whose peculiarities suggest a haphazard maker. To West these are lives badly performed, not lives lived. For Faye's father, Harry Greener, an old vaudevillian, mugging has become as involuntary as Homer's disjointed physical movements. "When Harry had first begun his stage career, he had probably restricted his clowning to the boards, but now he clowned continuously. It was his sole method of defense. Most people, he had discovered, won't go out of their way to punish a clown" (77). Once he's begun, he cannot stop, even as his heart is giving out. "He was really sick. The last block that held him poised over the runway of self-pity had been knocked away and he was sliding down the chute, gaining momentum all the time." This is the genuine West note, at once jeering and empathetic, pitiless and piteous, like the inspired riffing around a Dickens caricature. "He jumped to his feet and began doing Harry Greener, poor Harry, honest Harry, well-meaning, humble, deserving, a good husband, a model father, a faithful Christian, a loyal friend" (91). West lets us peer behind the scrim of his characters' self-dramatizations just as we look past the papier-mâché of Hollywood's treacly illusions, less to mock than to sigh or mourn. "Few things are sadder than the truly monstrous" (61).

West's Hollywood, like his construction of the California version of the American Dream, is a collection of cheesy simulations that are amusing and outrageous but can easily take a serious turn. As Tod walks among the studio sets, we track his preposterous passage from one historical period to another; we feel their flimsy inauthenticity as he looks at their "final dumping ground," a graveyard in which "no dream ever entirely disappears" (132). With uncanny foresight, West anticipated historian Daniel Boorstin's exposition of the pseudo-event, Jean Baudrillard's notion of the simulacrum, and the postmodern sense of pastiche. Compared with other novelists about Hollywood who were merely disillusioned, he made it his mission to strip away illusions. The delusions and

self-projections of the characters are kinetic parallels to the ersatz architecture and jerry-built sets. Deprived of a chance to act, Faye plays the
role of a starlet in a way that takes on a life of its own, radically discon-
nected from feeling. "The strange thing about her gestures and expressions was that they didn't really illustrate what she was saying. They were
almost pure." Like her father's mugging, her performance is disarming
and self-protective. "It was as though her body recognized how foolish
her words were and tried to excite her hearers into being uncritical" (159).
She *does* excite them, but the effect is mechanical, disengaged. Her projection of sex makes her seem promiscuous yet inaccessible. Without feelings of her own to consult, she models herself on the fan magazines and
trade papers. Her daydreams, which she relates to Tod as movie ideas,
parody Hollywood's bottomless well of tearful, uplifting, and romantic stories, which did so much to make movies a booming business during the Depression. Working at studios on Poverty Row, West knew this
from the inside. He found Hollywood entertaining in its fakery, yet also
ominous and dispiriting.

If movies like *A Star Is Born* leaven success with loss, stardom with
heartbreak, West tries something more radical: he shows us those who
had nowhere to go, the dreamers, bit players, and hangers-on for whom
the California dream was a dead end. In place of the mansions of the
stars and studio moguls like the one in which Sammy Glick finds himself stranded, he shows us the seedy San Bernadino Arms, the apartment
where some of West's characters live. In place of the glamour of a Hollywood premiere, he focuses on the madness of the crowd, the rabid violence of the cheated, the bored, the disappointed. This violent climax is
foreshadowed throughout the novel, sometimes casually, often comically.
Tod is working on a painting called *The Burning of Los Angeles*, where he'll
depict "the city burning at high noon, so that the flames would have to
compete with the desert sun. . . . He wanted the city to have quite a gala
air as it burned, to appear almost gay" (118). The unfinished set where the
studio is filming the Battle of Waterloo collapses under an army of extras,
defeated like Napoleon's army at the original battle. "It turned into a rout.
The victors of Bersina, Leipsic, Austerlitz, fled like schoolboys who had
broken a pane of glass. . . The armies of England and her allies were too
deep in scenery to flee" (134–35). The simulation reenacts the disastrous
event itself, the first time as tragedy, the second as farce.

West's vision of violence is rarely this benign, though its horror always has this comic edge. Looking for material for his painting, Tod visits the churches of religious cults like the "Church of Christ, Physical" and the "Tabernacle of the Third Coming" ("where a woman in male clothing preached the 'Crusade Against Salt'"). Like so many oddities inside and outside the movie studios, these weird cults, which seemed to blossom under the hot sun, amused West, as they amused the immigrant journalist Louis Adamic in his 1932 memoir *Laughing in the Jungle*, which contains pages about these cults that could have been transposed directly into *The Day of the Locust*. But Adamic—especially in the 1920s, when his book is set—was an admirer of the cynical H. L. Mencken, for whom the American scene was a circus of enormities that proved an endless source of entertainment. For West, after ten years of the Depression, besides his own tendency to depression, the amusement is laced with fear and disgust. In bringing these worshippers into his painting, Tod wants to "dramatize the contrast between their drained-out, feeble bodies and their wild, disordered minds. He would not satirize them as Daumier or Hogarth might, nor would he pity them. He would paint their fury with respect, appreciating its awful, anarchic power and aware that they had it in them to destroy civilization" (142). Under the California sun, strange flowers have bloomed. These people are deformed, but the ferocity of their passion is impressive.

West always claimed—ruefully, but perhaps ironically—that he was incapable of putting his progressive politics into his fiction; his imagination ran in other directions. He wrote apologetic letters to his radical friends about his inability to mobilize his work to advance their cause. But Tod's painting, like West's novel, has a political subtext: it registers the rise of fascism as a manifestation of mass psychology, exploring resentful, frustrated lives as they ignite into mob violence. A true child of the 1920s, West was anything but a populist. In a letter to the critic Malcolm Cowley in May 1939, he uses inverted commas when he mentions the great Popular Front heroine: "Take the 'mother' in Steinbeck's swell novel—I want to believe in her and yet inside myself I honestly can't." Far from idealizing the masses in the style of the Popular Front, he was frightened by them, yet in all his books he was drawn to popular culture as a poignant expression of their needs. Tod himself reacts to his frustrations much like the cheated masses, with fantasy: he imagines dynamiting the crummy architecture and raping the inaccessible Faye, but he saves this violence for his work. At the end, during the riot, a river of mass energy engulfs him: caught up in the surging crowd, he loses control of his own body, and we get a tremendous sense of what it's like to be swept along by an uncontrollable force. To West this is where everything has led—the tacky architecture, the laughable sets, the hollow sex, the phony glamour, the sordid amusements, the jerky, mechanical physicality, the stunted humanity, the dreams, the promises, the boredom, the disappointment—to a final murderous explosion. As the Depression clamped down, Hollywood offered an alternative reality to the common man; many were nourished by it, but others had plans of their own or became part of a crowd that reacted automatically, even savagely, like the crowd that turns on John Doe, their former hero, in Frank Capra's 1941 film. The roar of the crowd at Hitler's or Mussolini's rallies had shown Americans where this surge of mass emotion, so easily manipulated, could lead.

Quite a few writers debunked the success fantasies of Hollywood and popular culture, the utopian promise of California as the last frontier. West, with greater empathy but also a sense of revulsion, made them a grotesque source of pathos and fierce apocalyptic humor. His work proved too harsh for the Depression audience, but it would appeal to more cynical readers two or three decades later, long after he died in an auto accident in 1940. In the end, almost single-handedly, he helped alter the image of Southern California from a natural paradise to a scene of freakish eccentricity, corruption, and human waste. He exposed the machinery of the dream factory and gave its surroundings a nightmarish cast. More than most thirties writers, he was a genuine American original.

CHAPTER 9

The Last Film of the 1930s;

OR, NOTHING FAILS LIKE SUCCESS

IN FREELY FICTIONALIZING THE LIFE of William Randolph Hearst, first in a script simply entitled *American*, then in the film called *Citizen Kane*, Orson Welles and Herman Mankiewicz fashioned a haunting mystery out of the multiple perspectives of different narrators. From a fabric of legends, biographical facts, and popular stereotypes, *Citizen Kane* created a myth about an American titan that subsumed the figure of Hearst, already part of the popular imagination, into a timeless American myth. It has always been seen as a landmark that influenced everything from the flashback structure and expressionist lighting of film noir to the jump cuts and personal visions of the New Wave and the independent filmmakers who followed. But this tells only part of the story. Over the past decades, through countless viewings, two things about *Kane* have dramatically altered for me: its relation to the past, especially to the 1930s, and its human resonance. As Welles himself, long such a media presence, has receded into film history, the human quality of the film has mysteriously deepened. Critics see *Kane* through the lens of what followed it; I began to wonder about the books and films that had shaped it. For most critics *Kane* has always been the first film of a new era, the progenitor of film noir and of a new auteurist independent cinema. For me it has become the last film of the 1930s, especially for the way it handles the perils of ambition, dominance, and success.

In "Raising Kane," her longest and most ambitious essay, Pauline Kael was virtually the only critic to deal with the movie's antecedents. Yet she bent her formidable descriptive talents, idiosyncratic research, and total recall of film history into a biting, witty, but ultimately unconvincing polemic. Her goal was to restore the reputation of Herman Mankiewicz by giving him more credit for *Citizen Kane* and placing it in the context of his largely forgotten career. Cynical, iconoclastic, almost comically self-destructive, Mankiewicz proved to be an entertaining subject. But few of his previous films even remotely anticipated *Kane*, and later scholars like Robert L. Carringer were able to establish that Welles's contribution to the script was far greater than Kael had suggested. In her zeal to do justice to Mankiewicz, Kael gave voice to what Carringer summed up as "a flagrant misrepresentation" of Welles's role.[1]

To show how *Citizen Kane* emerged, Kael brought up some of the thirties genres that helped inspire the script, including newspaper movies and stories centering on wealthy tycoons. But since Mankiewicz and his friends—the Algonquin wits who migrated from Broadway to Hollywood—worked largely in comedy, Kael put her main emphasis on the one thirties genre that contributed relatively little to *Kane*: madcap romantic comedy. "As a group," says Kael, the Algonquin wits "were responsible for that sustained feat of careless magic we call 'thirties comedy.' *Citizen Kane* was, I think, its culmination" (13).

Perhaps *Kane* did owe a debt to the literate, sometimes overlapping dialogue of screwball comedies, which I deal with in the next chapter; perhaps their delicious evocation of the idle rich and the war between the sexes gets played out, remotely, in Kane's two marriages. But to call *Kane* a comedy, even a "Gothic comedy" (5), points us in the wrong direction. *Citizen Kane* tells us that fabulously wealthy people aren't very happy, but this debatable truism belongs to a wider current of 1930s pop mythology than screwball comedy—where the brainless rich usually *are* pretty happy, or at least don't know they're not.

Films like *My Man Godfrey, Easy Living*, and *Bringing Up Baby* indict the rich as coldhearted or harebrained but strictly in a farcical vein. The daffy rich are silly but salvageable, even lovable, and they appeal to us—as they did to Depression audiences—as figures of spontaneity and irresponsible freedom. *Citizen Kane*, on the other hand, is closer to many literary portrayals of the very rich, from muckraking novels like Frank Norris's *The Octopus* to social novels etched in acid by Edith Wharton, Sinclair Lewis, F. Scott Fitzgerald, John O'Hara, and J. P. Marquand, which show how the rich, though immensely attractive, exercise power over others by charming them, buying them, or intimidating them. In the work of these writers, the rich are exposed, not redeemed; behind their social authority and sense of style, their lives show up as empty, cruel, or highly destructive. Sometimes they make life miserable for others, as in *The House of Mirth* or *The Custom of the Country*, or are finally devoured by their own devices, as in *The Octopus*, or, like Tom and Daisy in *The Great Gatsby*, "they smashed up things and creatures and then retreated back into their money or their vast carelessness, . . . and let other people clean up the mess they had made."[2]

In the 1930s, when the conditions of the Depression induced envy and anger toward the rich—those whom Teddy Roosevelt had called "malefactors of great wealth"—businessmen quickly became villains rather than heroes of popular culture. Kane is the most arresting of a series of tycoon figures—initially benign, increasingly malevolent—played by actors like Walter Huston, Walter Connolly (in Capra's *It Happened One Night* and *Broadway Bill*), Eugene Pallette, and, most frequently, Edward Arnold, whose character in *Meet John Doe* (released just two months before) most resembles the figure of Kane. (He too buys a newspaper, decimates its staff, and turns it into a sensational vehicle for his political ambitions.)

Even *Kane*'s use of flashbacks to expose its protagonist was mo⟨
Preston Sturges's much praised script for a tycoon film starring
Tracy, *The Power and the Glory* (1933).

The tycoon movie was a specimen of the "biopic," the kind of biographical drama that peaked in popularity in the 1930s with historical
impersonations that were the specialty of George Arliss and the melodramatic re-creations of Pasteur, Zola, and Juarez by Paul Muni. These were
films about "real" people, nearly always in the heroic mold; they transposed the Carlylean theory of the Great Man as a mover of History into
the Hollywood practice of personalizing the past into shining models of
individual courage, willpower, and charisma.

Because the economic crisis of the Depression undercut all confidence in the system, the audiences of the 1930s had a special longing
for heroes—but also an uncommon skepticism about them. Part of the
appeal of fascism was the nostalgia for a strong leader, the caudillo, a Man
on a White Horse who would dispense with the paralyzing conflicts of
parliamentary regimes and rule in the people's name by force of will.
Hearst himself had bankrolled such a quasi-fascist message in Gregory
La Cava's *Gabriel over the White House* (1933), in which Walter Huston, as
the president, saves America by declaring a state of emergency, suspend-
ing Congress and civil liberties, and using his police powers to govern by
decree. Citizen Kane, running for office as a populist reformer, ranting
demagogically against crime and corruption in front of a huge blowup of
his own image, would have become just such a benevolent despot.

Since the Depression was marked by a widespread sense of fear and
helplessness, even despair, numerous films of the period presented audiences with willful, overbearing characters, many of them psychically
wounded, who manage for a time to dominate their environment. To the
historical biopic, the tycoon movie, and political parable, we could add the
gangster film, the monster film, and the cycle of press films that comes to
a climax with *Meet John Doe* and *Citizen Kane*. As a character, Kane is made
up of bits of all these domineering yet vulnerable figures: with Hearst as
the model, he is at once the real historical agent, the daring tycoon, the
would-be politician who wants to control people for their own good, the
moral desperado whose fall is inherent in his rise, the awkward Frankenstein monster who only wants to be loved, the unscrupulous press baron
who tells people what to think.

Citizen Kane is a parable about power, the first of the many portraits of outsized personalities that would dominate Welles's later films, right up though *Chimes at Midnight* and *The Immortal Story*. Welles himself was already a legend when he arrived in Hollywood at twenty-four with a contract that gave him unprecedented freedom and control of his film projects. Faced with the obvious fact that at some level Welles *was* Kane, Pauline Kael suggested that Mankiewicz cleverly wrote him into the part. It seems more likely that Welles had already developed the ambivalent relation to his own overbearing charm that would mark his subsequent films. In interviews he unfailingly attacked the characters he played, denying any real affinity for them. Of Hank Quinlan, the corrupt cop in *Touch of Evil*, who intuitively frames suspects who actually turn out to be guilty, he told *Cahiers du Cinéma*,

> It's a mistake to think that Quinlan finds any favor in my eyes. To me, he's hateful. There's no ambiguity in his character. He's not a genius: he's a master of his field, a provincial master, but a detestable man. . . . But it's always possible to feel sympathy for a son of a bitch. Sympathy is a human thing, after all. Hence my soft spot for men for whom I in no way hide my repugnance. . . . I believe that Kane is a detestable man, but I have a great deal of sympathy for him so far as he's a human being.

Warming to his attack on these characters, Welles adds, "I've played a lot of unsavory types. I detest Harry Lime, that little black market hustler, all these horrible men I've interpreted. But these aren't small men, because I'm an actor for characters on a grand scale. . . . I always play the role of leaders, men of some unusual breadth: I always need to be bigger than life. It's a fault of my nature."[3]

While denying any ambiguity in his portrayal, Welles allows that such characters attract him on a human level. As an actor at least, he shares the scale of their ambition, if not their morality. He finds real pathos in the contrast between their size and their limitations; he sees how their need to exert control leads inevitably to a failure of control, repelling those who might otherwise remain close to them. Kane in old age, jerky and stiff in his movements, desperate in his demands, is a pathetic figure out of a horror film—a creature now too weak to be threatening—just as the massive Quinlan, lying dead in shallow water, resembles a beached whale.

Citizen Kane is about the human costs of exercising power, a theme of all the thirties genres that contributed to it. Power corrupts; it also isolates. Wanting to be loved, the protagonists manage merely to be feared. Wanting to dominate people, they end up being alone. The secret behind many of these movies, even the monster films, is the parallel between the character's public and private life, between the big figure he cuts in the world and the emotional needs—for control, for unconditional love—that he acts out in close encounters and intimate settings.

Here is one key to *Kane*. The shallow, noisy biopic view of Charles Foster Kane comes in the fragmentary history we get in the opening newsreel—the superficial public traces of the private man. From here the reporter, Thompson, takes over: he is hard-boiled, flip, inquisitive, determined to breach the perimeters of the legend, to break through the defenses of the survivors. Where the historical biopics are iconic and moralistic, rarely engaging more than the official story, the newspaper dramas are cynical and iconoclastic. These reporters see through everything; the movie sees through them.

All the press movies of the thirties come out of the sleeve of *The Front Page*, the sensationally successful play of 1928, an effective movie in 1931, an even better movie when transformed by Howard Hawks into a battle of the sexes in *His Girl Friday* in 1940. Another popular press story that began as a play was *Five Star Final* (1931) with Edward G. Robinson as a fast-talking, circulation-hustling editor and Aline MacMahon as the secretary who speaks for his deeply buried conscience, at least until he has a change of heart. The story takes place in a cutthroat world, very close to the world of gangster films and social-consciousness dramas. Reporters and editors in these films are cynical, manipulative, and utterly shameless—ready to expose anyone and everyone to sell papers. They pander to the worst in people, and manage to find the worst wherever they look. But the tough characters who populate these newsrooms are full of zip and spark. Their energy, their freedom from illusion, is exhilarating though their morality is detestable. Cynical and unscrupulous, they take no prisoners. The more they succeed the more detestable they are—exactly Welles's point about the characters he plays.

This brings us to the real genre of *Citizen Kane*, which links so many of its sources and anchors the film in the cultural outlook of the 1930s. More than anything else *Citizen Kane* is a success story, capping off a decade that had sharply questioned the older American models of success and failure. As I showed earlier, the backstage musicals that followed *42nd Street* were success stories. So were the gangster films, tycoon films, and monster films, with their mixture of horror and pathos, as well as later show business tales like *Stage Door* and *A Star Is Born*, which were honest enough to show that when someone wins, someone else loses.

This downbeat, un-American view of success became even more pervasive for the writers of the decade, as I argued in previous chapters. Their work reflects the depressive side of the Depression. Clifford Odets's plays about the strenuous longings of the children of immigrants demonstrated that you gain the world only by losing your soul. James T. Farrell's novel about the lower middle-class Irish, *Studs Lonigan*, showed how you could lose your soul even without gaining the world. Nathanael West lampooned popular fantasies of success in novel after novel, including his burlesque of an Alger novel, *A Cool Million*, and his apocalyptic portrait of Hollywood in *The Day of the Locust*. F. Scott Fitzgerald had made the poignant appeal and ultimate failure of the American Dream his specialty from his early novels and stories through Depression-era works like "Babylon Revisited," *Tender Is the Night*, "The Crack-Up," and *The Last Tycoon*. Fitzgerald's protégé and admirer John O'Hara, who had contributed to the success-as-failure genre with his first novel, *Appointment in Samarra* in 1934, mentioned his recently deceased friend twice in his brief *Newsweek* review of *Citizen Kane*.

The links between Fitzgerald and the script for *Kane* are complex yet have hardly been noticed.[4] Fitzgerald specialized in creating richly enigmatic characters like Gatsby, Dick Diver (in *Tender*), and Monroe Stahr (the Thalberg figure in *The Last Tycoon*) who are strangely appealing though morally questionable. They remain mysterious to us because we see them from the outside, from the point of view of characters like Nick Carraway who are drawn to them, intrigued and mystified by them, pondering their meaning. Fitzgerald borrowed this strategy from Joseph Conrad, who used it most powerfully in *Heart of Darkness* and other works narrated by his sea captain, Marlow, a man deeply absorbed with the almost unfathomable moral mysteries of human nature.

Welles's first project after he arrived in Hollywood was an adaptation of *Heart of Darkness*, in which he initially planned to play both Marlow (as voice-over) and the unspeakable Kurtz, the object of Marlow's quest, a man initially idealistic but ultimately poisoned and corrupted by his power over people. This film was dropped by RKO just before shooting was scheduled to begin, but, as critics have since realized, its quest structure spilled over into *Citizen Kane*. (Another aborted project, a thriller called *The Smiler with the Knife* by the English poet C. Day Lewis, also left its mark on the *Kane* script.) Between them, Conrad and Fitzgerald were the major literary influences on the script of *Citizen Kane*, not simply for the quest structure and the enigma of the central character but also in the moral pattern of Kane's rise and fall.

Most of the success literature of the 1930s, along with key film genres like gangster films and backstage musicals, deal with outsiders who make good—immigrants who claw their way to wealth or power, anonymous chorus girls who become stars, midwestern boys who conquer the big city, newspaper men who develop a stranglehold on public opinion—yet pay a steep price for their triumphs. Either they display the same ruthlessness in their private as in their public lives, or else they forget to have private lives. Sometimes they learn by the end that it's lonely at the top: they've sacrificed too much, diminished their own humanity. At other times, with what seems like a fatal inevitability, those they've stepped on in their rise to power finally band together to destroy them.

Thus Robert Warshow writes of the gangster film as a modern form of tragedy:

> No convention of the gangster film is more strongly established than this: it is dangerous to be alone. And yet the very conditions of success make it impossible not to be alone, for success is always the establishment of an *individual* pre-eminence that must be imposed on others, in whom it automatically arouses hatred; the successful man is an outlaw.[5]

In a later essay Warshow writes of the gangster that "he is wide open and defenseless, incomplete because unable to accept any limits or come to terms with his own nature, fearful, loveless. And the story of his career is a nightmare inversion of the values of ambition and opportunity" (136–

37). These comments apply not only to *Kane* but to the film cycles that led up to it: the anticapitalist tycoon stories, the newspaper dramas, the surprisingly sympathetic monster films like *The Bride of Frankenstein* that link aggression to loneliness and lovelessness.

Unlike most success stories, which chart the "rise" step by step, Kane's fortune comes to him almost magically, as Hearst inherited his wealth from his parents. His career in journalism begins without sweat, almost as a lark: "I think it would be fun to run a newspaper." The movie's early scenes are full of fun and bustle and youthful energy. But the flashback structure casts its shadow: even before the frolic begins, we've already felt the Gothic gloom of the chain-link fence around Xanadu and experienced Kane's death through a grotesque series of visual distortions. We've watched his whole career flash by in the incongruously buoyant newsreel, been rebuffed by the broken-down Susan Alexander, his second wife, and witnessed the young Kane's forcible separation from his own childhood. Even the story of Kane's best times, as "told" in Thatcher's memoirs, is rounded off by his reverses during the Depression and framed by the mausoleum atmosphere of the Thatcher Library—much the way the telegraphic newsreel was quickly undercut by the stark silhouettes of the reporters trying to make sense of it.

Kane doesn't need to fight his way to the top, but every good thing in his life quickly goes sour: his idyll as a boy in the snow, his first marriage, his appreciation of Susan's singing, his "love nest," his political career, his lifelong friendship with Jed Leland, his second try at marriage—we watch these things go awry only to start up again in the next telling of the story. In the movie's wonderfully unexpected transitions of sound and image, each intimate setting soon turns grandiose and empty, every privileged moment becomes its own parody, its undoing. These seamless but dazzling transitions make the movie. Susan's singing takes her from a modest furnished room, where she sings diffidently to a man she just met, to the well-appointed flat of a kept woman; Kane's applause for her singing turns into the audience's applause for Kane's political campaign; Leland's speech turns into Kane's speech, which then we see from the point of view of its victim and avenger, Boss Jim Gettys. This in turn will take us full circle, back to Susan and her flat, which, when exposed by Kane's own kind of journalism, will destroy both his marriage and his political prospects. When the thwarted Kane single-handedly tries to force Susan's singing on her, on her teacher, her critics, and her audience, the whole cycle begins again—evoked in the startling sound and image of one man clapping, this time in a crowded but not appreciative theater.

As Kane begins ominously to impose himself, the style and mood of the film change. Susan seems more in his shadow—literally in some scenes; the low-angle photography makes him ever more looming and menacing; the larky, spirited, comic atmosphere of his early newspaper days gives way to expressionist imagery from gangster and horror films; the deep-focus photography, which seemed innocently pictorial earlier in the film, begins to express tense power relationships. Early on, this power worked against him: framed by a window, he played outside in the snow as his fate was decided. Later, *he* is in control. When Kane appears in the background during Susan's hapless singing lesson, or in the newsroom after the opera, his small, crisply focused form and steely voice assert his domination over everyone in the room. He sets himself against them, and against reality itself, and wills them to conform: "People will think . . . what I tell them to think." The same power is displayed with Kane filling the foreground, when he casually fires Leland while completing his bad review. When Leland as an old man tells his story, he occupies Kane's place in the split frame: now *he* controls the narrative.

But in the later scenes Kane's control gradually falters. With the comatose Susan and her tainted glass gigantic in the foreground, reflecting her suicidal push to be released from his grip, he can force his way into the frame but he cannot will her back onto the stage. He becomes a recluse and imprisons his young wife with her jigsaw puzzles, but the cavernous spaces of Xanadu slip out of his grasp. His movements grow stiff, his voice hollow, his appearance grotesque, more dead than alive, and Susan finds she can pull back from under his shadow, which now suggests wraithlike helplessness rather than power. Even the pathos of his final appeal to her and the violence of his destruction of her room seem empty and inauthentic, as if no one's at home—his spirit has decamped long before she does. As he staggers from the room under the eye of his silent retainers, the corridor becomes a hall of mirrors, mutely anticipating the spectacular climax of *The Lady from Shanghai* (1947). The multiplication of his image, the enlargement of space around him, which had once (as during the election campaign) expressed his expansive ego—his baronial authority, his incontestable will, his demand for love—now seem to mock him, conveying him inexorably toward a lonely death.

Kane's downward trajectory echoes every hollow thirties "success" story, from *Little Caesar* and *The Public Enemy* to *Miss Lonelyhearts, Tender Is the Night, A Star Is Born*, and *Golden Boy*. Just as the decade's masses longed for, yet feared, the man of steel, the apostle of direct action, movie audiences dreamed of success, of magical changes of fortune, yet also identified with failure, which seemed closer to the reality of people's lives. The public loved the new comic-book hero Superman, but by the end of the decade, the obsession with success and failure, with personal power, had lost its innocence. The economy had improved as the international situation had worsened, and the strong-willed man of authority became a metaphor for fascism rather than salvation. In *Meet John Doe* Edward Arnold employs his own storm troopers and tries to enact a version of Hearst's message in *Gabriel over the White House*. "What this country needs," he says, "is an iron hand, discipline."

For Citizen Kane, politics is only one avenue for gaining love and securing power over people. Like Hearst, Kane begins as a muckraking populist and reformer, a privileged tribune of the People, but his Declaration of Principles proves as hollow as his personal relationships. His success is purchased at the cost of losing his wives, his friends, *and* his principles. *Citizen Kane's* script is unusual in making the success story retrospective, turning it into an inquest, an investigative mystery directed not to finding a culprit but to fathoming a meaning. For all the limitations of Rosebud as the McGuffin of the plot, it enables Thompson, the reporter, to collect pieces of meaning (like Susan's huge jigsaw puzzles) as he enlists each witness to unpack the enigma of a man's life. "Rosebud dead or alive," his boss tells him. "It will probably turn out to be a very simple thing." "Maybe that was something he lost," says Bernstein. "Mr. Kane was a man who lost almost everything he had." "All he really wanted out of life was love," says Leland. "That's Charlie's story. How he lost it. You see, he just didn't have any to give." Some of Welles's best critics, including André Bazin and William Johnson, have dealt with this intense feeling of loss as a mainspring of his work. But the search that structures the movie has a narrative logic of its own. It stresses the riddle itself, the mystery rather than the solution.

Another metaphor for Thompson's quest is the inventory. When Kane meets Susan, he's on his way to a warehouse to look over the stuff he inherited from his late mother; Susan's charm and innocence are thus associated with the abrupt loss of his childhood. After his death, in a long and incredibly moving tracking shot, the camera surveys all the things he collected in his lifetime, the things that remained after the people were gone. This inventory matches the opening newsreel: it surveys all he accumulated, the things that could not define him, accentuating the sense of loss. Thompson's search for a simple explanation has failed, but the audience's search is more successful. We have the powerful image of "Rosebud" burning, its secret unrevealed, but also the mosaic that Thompson and Welles have assembled. Thompson concludes, "I don't think any word can explain a man's life." The process is the explanation.

Along the way, even Kane tries his hand at explaining himself, probing his own mystery. "If I hadn't been very rich," he muses, "I might have been a really great man." This is no more definitive than any other explanation, starting with the newsreel. Explanation and the need for explanation belong with the mysteries of personality but also form part of Kane's (and Welles's) instinctive showiness. Kane behaves always as if he were on the stage, timing his words for effect, calculating the response of his listeners, leveling all resistance with overbearing force or charm. Assorted wives, old friends, employees, doctors, music teachers, even newspaper readers and opera audiences all become his satellites, the force fields in which he operates. Seducing or dominating them all, he touches none of them deeply. His subjects eventually rebel, and he is left alone among the things he never looks at.

The film ends as it began, on a Gothic note, an intimation of mystery or horror, distant and impenetrable: a chain-link fence, a "No Trespassing" sign, a fake castle, an old man's death. Behind the links in the chain is a private story more appalling than the public one. The press lord, who loved the bustle of the newsroom, the tycoon who had so many people deployed to serve him, the politician, the impresario, the monster, the charmer, the adulterer—all these characters were elements of the man who died loveless and alone. In the end, the pop stereotype of the unhappy mogul prevails, but in a deepened form. "Well, I always gagged on that silver spoon."

The thirties exploration of success as failure concludes on an spectacularly violent note in *The Day of the Locust* and a quietly reflective one
in *The Last Tycoon*, but *Citizen Kane* deepens the stereotype into pathos.
Welles invests both his grandiosity and self-loathing into all his protagonists, yet they somehow manage to hold on to our respect, even our
affection. From Kane, Macbeth, and Othello to Hank Quinlan and Fal-
staff, they do more harm to themselves than to anyone else. Starting out
in the decade of the common man, Welles repeatedly played *un*common
men with a self-protective, distancing virtuosity that elicits more wonder
than sympathy yet finally brings out both. Marlene Dietrich's tribute in
Touch of Evil, directed at the most grotesque of Welles's impersonations,
finally applies to all of them: "He was some kind of a man." But then she
adds, "What does it matter what you say about people?"

PART 3

THE CULTURE *of* ELEGANCE

CHAPTER 10

Fantasy, Elegance, Mobility:
THE DREAM LIFE OF THE 1930s

WITH ITS SERIOUS THEMES yet fireworks atmosphere, flush with technical innovations, *Citizen Kane* brought together many threads of Depression culture. The movie encompasses success and failure, power and wealth, ambition and dominance, yet it feels like a sound-and-light show, a magician's sleight of hand. Its showmanship goes back to the early years of the decade, especially the vibrant film scene, still under the influence of vaudeville. Socially committed scholars, drawn to the 1930s, have paid little attention to the seemingly frivolous, freewheeling side of the decade, the entertainment culture often seen merely as escapist. Foraging for serious political criticism, they focus instead on proletarian novels, documentaries, and socially conscious films like *I Am a Fugitive from a Chain Gang*. But despite the economic crisis, the popular art of the 1930s was striking for its lightheartedness and frivolity. This was one of the paradoxes of the decade.

During the period from 1930 to 1934, when the Depression was at its worst, Hollywood, not yet subject to the strict rigors of the Production Code, enjoyed its greatest freedom. Broadway musicals—with a few exceptions like the Gershwins' mordant but lovable satire *Of Thee I Sing* in 1931— were still afloat in the bubbly aftermath of the 1920s. Sometimes the fun in these years was anarchic in a way that bordered on savagery. The Gershwins went over the top with their sequel to *Of Thee I Sing* called *Let 'Em Eat Cake* (1933), a great musical achievement that repelled audiences with its cynical, almost nihilistic book. (Both shows were written by George S. Kaufman and Morrie Ryskind, two biting yet commercially successful Broadway satirists.) The Marx brothers were at their zaniest in the films that led up to their most madcap work, *Duck Soup*, in 1934 (their only commercial failure). One of their scenarists, S. J. Perelman, was practicing his own brand of surrealism and verbal phantasmagoria in *The New Yorker* as his brother-in-law, Nathanael West, was virtually creating black humor in *Miss Lonelyhearts* and *A Cool Million*. The snidely insinuating comedy of Mae West and W. C. Fields reached its peak before West was constrained by the censor and Fields by Hollywood's growing suspicion of physical comedy and haphazard storytelling, let alone a sly cynicism bordering on misanthropy.

At other times this popular culture was grown-up and sophisticated, as in the witty lyrics and clever patter songs of Cole Porter, Rodgers and Hart, and the Gershwins, as well as the screwball humor of *It Happened One Night*, the *Thin Man* series, and the many breakneck romantic comedies that followed. The same period that produced the histrionic Paul Muni, who clumped through *Scarface* like a childish, menacing oaf, also gave us as one of its icons, the lean, light-footed, whimsical figure of Fred Astaire, who embodied the grace and filigree of the era as definitively as Muni conveyed its heavy, brooding seriousness.

Thus the conventional picture of Depression audiences that we find in Woody Allen's *Purple Rose of Cairo* or Preston Sturges's *Sullivan's Trav-*

els, of people going to the movies or listening to the radio to escape their troubles—to daydream or simply fantasize—scarcely holds up. Though Bing Crosby sang wishfully about how his "pocketful of dreams" made up for his "empty purse," the relation of the arts to the social mood was far more complex. A culture's forms of escape, if they can be called escape, are as significant and revealing as its social criticism. Under the guise of mere entertainment, *Amos 'n' Andy* transposed people's daily problems, especially money problems, into a different key and made them seem more manageable—interminable, perhaps, but manageable. The mass audience could identify even with black people in a period when *everyone* felt beset and beleaguered.

Immensely popular historical romances like *Gone with the Wind* and *Anthony Adverse* transported readers into different eras, such as the ravaged South after the Civil War, which nevertheless had striking parallels to what they were undergoing in the Depression. Like *The Grapes of Wrath*, *Gone with the Wind* dealt with the aftermath of a social catastrophe, focusing on survival and on a strong, resourceful woman who tries to hold together her family and her world. The anarchic comedies of the early thirties, with their legendary speed, wit, sexiness, and irreverence, showed how our moral limits and social conventions had been undermined by the Depression. Finally, it's no accident that so many screwball comedies, stage musicals, and the Astaire Rogers films are set in the world of the very rich, for that world had not only the money but the mobility that was denied to most Americans during the Depression.

This is the ultimate irony, that in a world where so many took to the road, so few had any real mobility. Paul Muni's fugitive, James Allen, on his flight from the chain gang, a flight to nowhere; the men and boys hopping freights and pitching camp outside towns that didn't want them; the Joad family on its biblical trek through town and desert, Hooverville and sanitary camp: this is not travel but a way of standing still or running in place, like the marathon dancers, circling the floor in total exhaustion, almost asleep on their feet, leaning on each other in pursuit of a small prize. As Nicholas Lemann showed in *The Promised Land*, even the great black migration from the South slowed down; there were so few jobs to be found. Migrant workers like the Joads were grasping at survival, not reaching for freedom. This is one reason why photography became such a central mode of expression in the 1930s. The migrant pictures, with their sharp angles, their clashing lines, are all about going nowhere; the people are pinned like social specimens, frozen into postures that allow little movement, no escape.

The fantasy culture of the thirties, on the other hand, is all about movement, not the desperate simulation of movement we find in the road stories, but movement that suggests genuine freedom. This was why, with Busby Berkeley and Fred Astaire, with George Balanchine and Martha Graham, choreography became as important as photography for this decade. The look of the great thirties musicals is everything that Dorothea Lange's "Migrant Mother" or "Woman of the High Plains," both so angular and static, are not. It's all circle and swirl, all movement and flow. Think of it: the rose-petal effect in Berkeley's big numbers, the sweepingly elegant curvature of the Art Deco sets, the brilliance of movement of Astaire and Rogers, locked together in breathtaking dips and turns, he in top hat, white tie, and tails, she in elaborate gowns that create rococo line drawings in space.

We also forget (or underrate) the dramatic tension crucial to these films. The musical numbers are always embedded in a story line that contrives every possible conflict, hesitation, and misunderstanding to keep Astaire and Rogers apart. Like the couples in screwball comedies, they seem at first to be an incongruous pair, always at cross-purposes. Apparently, no one informed them in advance of how perfect they were together, or let them in on the critical cliché—"He gives her class and she gives him sex." Their talk is the banter of two ill-matched people, unable to agree on anything *except* when they dance. "Let Yourself Go," says one signature number; "Never Gonna Dance," says another. Dancing is not simply what they do; it's what their films are about. There may be trouble ahead, said Irving Berlin in a song for *Follow the Fleet*, but "let's face the music and dance."

And when they do dance, an astonishing transformation takes place. Feelings they could never articulate are acted out in movement. Like all genuine couples, together they are something they could never have been separately, not simply romantic, not simply a vision of swank and elegance inherited from the nightclub era of the 1920s, but a dream of motion that appealed to people whose lives felt pinched, anxious, graceless, and static.

With the arrival of sound films, the thirties also became the great age of dialogue comedy, the spoken equivalent of Astaire's dancing and

Cole Porter's songs. The great couples in 1930s comedies—William Powell and Myrna Loy, Katharine Hepburn and Cary Grant, Cary Grant and Irene Dunne, Carole Lombard and *any* of her partners—were wonderful talkers rather than ideal lovers. In the age of the Production Code, which descended like a velvet curtain in 1934, the tang and effervescence of sharp repartee and the look that accompanied this thrust and parry were the only effective ways of being sexual (rather than merely sentimental). The crackle and speed of the dialogue, like the frantic, farcical pace of the action, represented yet another form of freedom and mobility.

The screwball comedies were usually set in a comic-opera world of wealth and ease, but also a world hemmed in by stuffy conventions and rigid family proscriptions. The bubbly, unpredictable women played by Lombard or Hepburn in films like *My Man Godfrey* or *Bringing Up Baby* stood for the lure of sexual or social irresponsibility. Think of the sheer lunacy of Hepburn and Grant singing "I can't give you anything but love" to a leopard on someone else's roof. The zany freedom of their behavior is made possible by money but also by energy, spirit, insouciance, and independence, qualities with which their hard-pressed audience was quick to identify; this was the wild beast missing from their own lives. The huge dinosaur skeleton that collapses at the end of *Bringing Up Baby* represents the dry bones of the past, rigid, sexless, and sterile, while Hepburn's daffy effervescence and mobility suggests an unstoppable life force daringly oriented toward the unknown, toward the future. Many creative spirits of the Depression years reacted to the sense of stasis, the feeling of being bogged down in the intractable, with a burst of energy, lightness, and motion. The psychological impact paralleled the morale-boosting effects of the New Deal, the can-do approach taken by FDR.

This suggests that not money and success, not even elegance and sophistication, were the real dream of the expressive culture of the 1930s, but this dream of mobility, with its thrust toward the future. We can hear it in the syncopated rhythms of Gershwin's songs and piano pieces and the "topping" effects of Cole Porter's catalogs: urban, modern, smartly sophisticated. Certainly the crucial aspect of thirties architecture and design is its dedication to this dream of motion, its famous streamlining, the loops and curves of its Deco modernism, which pretended to be clean and functional but were actually so decorative and stylized. At first the completion of large projects like Rockefeller Center, the Chrysler Building, and the Empire State Building was an act of blind faith carried forward during the worst years of the Depression. But after 1933, when few large buildings were built, a new and more genuinely hopeful note enabled this architectural style to be applied to the world of consumer goods, furniture styles, and industrial design.

Streamlining was a way of putting speed and motion into consumer goods by associating them with the dynamic energy of the machine, at just the moment when consumer demand was low and so much of the workforce and the industrial plant remained idle. As Eva Weber writes in *Art Deco in America*, "The style's main function was to attract new customers by means of its persuasive allusions to modernism, high style, efficiency, and speed" (145). From the Century of Progress exhibition in Chicago in 1933 to the great New York World's Fair of 1939–40, with its famous GM Futurama, this decade of near-stagnation, in which the world was also spiraling down into totalitarianism and war, devoted itself to imagining a sleek, streamlined consumer culture that would not come into being until after 1945.

The age of industrial decline was also the golden age of industrial design. The man who took the motor off the top of the refrigerator made a fortune, for sales skyrocketed, even in the depressed thirties. The GM Futurama rightly predicted (but underestimated) the automotive America of 1960, crisscrossed by ribbons of new highways. The loops and curves of Art Deco eventually became the clover leaves of the Interstate Highway System, superseding the right-angle grid of downtown traffic patterns. Out of the stagnation of the present, the thirties had invented the future. Again Americans would take to the road, but not as drifters or fugitives. In the postwar years, with the growth of suburbia, Americans at last achieved the mobility that had been denied to them during hard times.

Thus what began seemingly as a world of fantasy, a denial of the Depression, was fundamentally a response to it, an effective antidote to it. Where did this richly articulated fantasy culture of the 1930s begin? What deep needs did it serve? Why did it flower so brilliantly at just this time? Unlike the proletarian novel or *Citizen Kane*, it was an extraordinarily commercial culture yet at the same time a truly popular kind of art, watchable, singable, unforgettable. Whatever George Gershwin's conflicts, if he really had any, between writing for Broadway or Hollywood and writing for the concert hall or the opera stage, he was a determined crowd pleaser in every one of these settings, yet also someone who elevated the taste of the crowd. In any discussion of the genius of the entertainment culture of the 1930s, George Gershwin is the place to begin, since he taught the American musical to swing, as he had already invigorated classical music by importing jazz rhythms into the concert hall.

Fascinating Rhythm: George and Ira

Born Jacob Gershwine in 1898, almost two years after his older brother Israel (Ira), he was the son of Morris Gershovitz (a.k.a. Gershvin) and the former Rose Bruskin, who had both recently emigrated from St. Petersburg to New York's Lower East Side. A completely natural performer, almost a Mozartian prodigy but without a stage father pushing him, he picked up the piano as other boys learn to play baseball and soccer. (He had some teachers as a teenager, and another years later in his thirties, but throughout his life, long after he had evolved a celebrated style of his own, he still looked to apprentice himself to masters like Maurice Ravel, Igor Stravinsky, Arnold Schoenberg, and Alban Berg who might improve his technique. Invariably, they urged him to be himself.) From 1914 to 1917 Gershwin worked for a sheet-music publisher in Tin Pan Alley, plugging new songs at the piano. He finally had a hit of his own a few years later when Al Jolson made "Swanee" one of his signature songs.

This was 1919, the same year Gershwin, who had not yet teamed up with his older brother, wrote his first (modest) Broadway show, *La-La-Lucille!* This was a period when outside influences were transforming the American musical theater and ushering in what later would come to seem like the golden era of a new, authentically American art form. Gershwin's older contemporary Irving Berlin, born Israel Baline in Russia in 1888, had had a sensational success with his snappy "Alexander's Ragtime Band" in 1911, which had little to do with ragtime but had a terrific impact on a popular music scene still dominated by music-hall material, moon-June love songs, and syrupy ballads from the Ruritanian world of European-style operettas. Berlin's hit helped set off a ragtime craze that paved the way for the huge influence of jazz and blues on the popular music of the twenties and thirties.

Meanwhile, the New York theater world had been transformed by a series of intimate, loosely assembled musicals at the 299-seat Princess Theatre—mostly written by Guy Bolton and P. G. Wodehouse and scored by the inimitable Jerome Kern—which emphasized words and music rather than stage spectacle. Despite their daffy, improbable books, which makes these shows impossible to revive, their contemporary snap and wit and lyrical grace helped make a native American musical idiom available to Broadway. Though set in a never-never land of Wodehousian whimsicality, which was part of their legacy to the American theater, these shows became more integrated vehicles for songs that were far fresher than the material in revues and operettas, where composers like Sigmund Romberg, Rudolf Friml, and Victor Herbert reigned. These songs could be miniature stories of their own. Occasionally they even advanced the plot and reflected the characters who sang them, though the integrated drama and music of *Show Boat* and *Oklahoma!* remained far in the future.

The shift was a gradual one. Richard Rodgers and Lorenz Hart were still writing varsity shows as Columbia undergraduates, as Oscar Hammerstein had done before them, as Cole Porter, born in 1891 in Peru, Indiana, had done a few years earlier at Yale. Porter's first Broadway show, *See America First* (1916), had lasted only fifteen performances, and he would not have a hit until 1928, yet he made a splash in café society during the 1920s for his private performances of his own words and music. Rodgers and Hart would not grow famous for their own brand of romantic wit and urban sophistication until 1925, when "Manhattan" became the virtual anthem of New York's cosmopolitan chic. In 1924, the year of George and Ira Gershwin's first great stage hit, *Lady, Be Good!*, the most successful musicals (out of more than forty that opened on Broadway) were Friml's *Rose Marie* and Romberg's *The Student Prince*, well-made though far-fetched operettas that are still occasionally revived in summer stock and by light-opera companies.

Lady, Be Good! was Gershwin's third musical in a year when the first public performance of his *Rhapsody in Blue* at New York's Aeolian Hall, with Paul Whiteman's orchestra, had already brought him instant fame. Thus, in a single year, Gershwin helped bring a syncopated jazz idiom into both the concert hall and the mainstream musical theater. The absurd plot and dialogue by Guy Bolton and Fred Thompson were little more than a vehicle for the dancing and singing of Fred and Adele Astaire and for the great Gershwin score, along with the specialty singing of the popular "Ukelele Ike (Cliff Edwards).* The show was notable for its continuous flow of melody, wit, and high spirits. Writing with each other inspired something in the Gershwins that they never quite achieved with other collaborators.

It could not have been easy to write a show for a pair of siblings rather than lovers, but the opening duet for Fred and Adele, "Hang On to Me," establishes the situation—their loyalty to each other—and becomes a song about dancing itself. It helped propel the Astaires to stardom. The best songs include the inimitable "Fascinating Rhythm," which established the show's jazz chops, "Oh, Lady Be Good!" (which became a byword for seduction in the decade), "Swiss Miss," and (added to the London production) "I'd Rather Charleston," in which Adele, with her girlish, high-spirited voice, sounds like the very essence of the twenties flapper. "Though several reviewers made note of the songs," says the Gershwin biographer Edward Jablonski, "they made no mention of the innovative sound, the spare, sinewy melodies, the definitely nonoperetta rhythms, the wit of the lyrics." It was "a score that scintillated and crackled with unsentimental contemporaneity" and "marked the advent of *the* Gershwin musical."[1]

The producers of *Lady, Be Good!*, Alex Aarons and Vinton Freedley, would put on all the best of the Gershwins' lighter shows, including the tuneful *Oh, Kay!* (1926), with Gertrude Lawrence and Victor Moore; *Funny Face* (1927), with the Astaires; *Treasure Girl* (1928), with Gertrude Lawrence and Clifton Webb; and *Girl Crazy* (1930), which made stars of Ethel Merman and Ginger Rogers. The last of the Aarons-Freedley productions, *Pardon My English* (1933), flopped, like *Treasure Girl*, largely because of insoluble book problems. All these shows had flimsy if occasionally witty books, which simply carried the audience from one musical number to the next. The composing team often worked with only a general knowledge of the story. "This was a common practice at the time," notes Jablonski. "Songwriters frequently worked from the merest sketch of a book, and it was not unusual for a show's final act to be written even as its first was in rehearsal" (172). Songs dropped from one show

---

* Some sense of the original production can be gained from a historical album put out in 1977 by the Smithsonian, a compilation of early recordings that almost approximates an original-cast album. There is also an excellent restored version by Tommy Krasker, conducted by Eric Stern, on Elektra Nonesuch (1992).

might pop up in another, and yet another if it didn't work there. Such replaceable parts seem primitive by post-*Oklahoma!* standards, in which songs must always express the dramatic situation, but it gave composers an autonomy denied to them in the book musical. Most of the songs of the Gershwins, Cole Porter, Irving Berlin, Rodgers and Hart, or Jerome Kern now seem to belong more to a Gershwin or Cole Porter universe than to any individual show. The composers were like film auteurs working in Hollywood studios, sometimes putting their stamp on intractable or inferior material, at other times floating high above it.

There's no denying that the American musical made a tremendous advance with the impressive drama of Kern and Hammerstein's *Show Boat* (1927), including its racial themes, and the serious nonsense of the Gershwins' political satires, *Strike Up the Band* (1927, 1930), *Of Thee I Sing*, and *Let 'Em Eat Cake*, which were strongly influenced by Gilbert and Sullivan. But the frivolity and inconsequence of the older kind of musical was part of its charm and effect. This goofy, devil-may-care quality must be reproduced and updated even when a new book is written, as it was for the smashing Lincoln Center production of Cole Porter's *Anything Goes*, which became a hit in 1987. The lyrics of Lorenz Hart, Porter, and Ira Gershwin would not have been as witty, insouciant, or topical without the "anything goes" framework of the old musicals, which were completely built around the musical numbers, with little responsibility to the ongoing plot.

The nostalgia we feel today for these rickety shows is really a longing for the freedom of songwriters who could give full play to their wit, who could explore archetypal emotions, even love, that old standby, without being hamstrung by "character development," story line, and motivation. As a result, the drama was *in* the song, not in the story around it. In later musicals the action often pauses for a song; the song is like a soliloquy, a chorus, or an operatic duet. In these shows the song (or dance) is where the action is, where character is revealed, where relationships unfold. The song itself is the story, especially in the hands of an expressive performer. Such shows are still rooted in musical revues, where everything must be accomplished within the individual number. These "standards," later enshrined as the American Song Book, not only stand on their own but are like literary classics that evolve with every fresh interpretation.

Some nostalgia for a simpler world was already an essential part of their appeal in the 1930s, when the swank, café society world of these shows—or of the Astaire films and the screwball comedies—seemed utterly removed from the realities of the Depression. The common explanations, that these shows were merely holdovers from the 1920s or that their appeal was simply a form of wish fulfillment, tell us nothing, since we can learn a great deal from the diversions that proved popular in any era. Much of the Depression audience chose to entertain itself with a memory of the 1920s, a carefree fantasy of "easy living" that was already a dream *in* the 1920s. The thirties looked to the frivolous past as a projection of the future, not the literal future but some happy valley of all utopian storytelling, the place where dreams come true, at least for a few minutes, as in Dennis Potter's universe of sad facts and enchanted musical reveries in *Pennies from Heaven*.

To shape this dream of freedom and irresponsibility into a world more attractive, the 1920s had developed a contemporary idiom in every field. Ballet, classical music, and operetta belonged safely to middle-class culture; they represented the dead hand of tradition. Ragtime, jazz, tap dancing, syncopated rhythms, blues singing—everything that could be borrowed from Negro culture—seemed more hip, less inhibited, more directly sexual, just as the minor chords lifted from Jewish or Russian music seemed more soulful. From our point of view today, this effacement and appropriation of Negro culture has its scandalous side, like the nightclubs in Harlem (such as the Cotton Club) where blacks held the stage but couldn't join the audience. But many who borrowed, adapted, and softened the black idiom genuinely loved it, and saw themselves as vehicles for bringing its thrilling and unconventional energies into the mainstream. A considerable number of them were Jewish, and their identification with black culture—and even, for a time, blackface performance—was especially intense, perhaps because, like them, it stood outside the emotional rhythms and social hierarchies of white Protestant culture.[2] In a 1927 article on Aaron Copland in H. L. Mencken's *American Mercury*, Isaac Goldberg, who would become George Gershwin's first biographer, described the "jazz" of the period as "musical miscegenation," the "musical amalgamation of the American Negro and the American Jew."[3] Many saw Jews, with their show business savvy, their performing energy, as indispensable popularizers of black rhythms.

In his introduction to *George Gershwin's Song Book* in 1932, Gershwin advised the sheet-music audience, "Our popular music asks for staccato effects. . . . The rhythms of American popular music are more or less brittle; they should be made to snap, and at times to crackle. The more sharply the music is played, the more effective it sounds."[4] Gershwin was the most creative imitator in American music, open to every influence, and just as he taught himself to write black he urged Cole Porter, the well-to-do Yalie from the Midwest, to write Jewish. "Swanee" was something of a freak for Gershwin, but his one-act Harlem opera *Blue Monday*, written with Buddy DeSylva for *George White's Scandals* in 1922 but dropped after the first performance, anticipated *Porgy and Bess* (1935), which can be seen as the first real American opera, despite its occasional Broadway touches. There, with the tight-knit community of Catfish Row and great songs like "Summertime," "I Got Plenty o' Nuttin'," and "Bess, You Is My Woman Now," the utopian dream took on a pastoral coloring. (This operatic side of Gershwin's work will be the subject of a later chapter.)

In *Girl Crazy* the Gershwins had even written a "western," for the book satirizes the vogue of dude ranches, though it also makes room for some Yiddish comedy around a character named Gieber Goldfarb, played by Willie Howard in a role intended for Bert Lahr. Such ethnic stereotypes were part of Broadway's legacy from vaudeville, where Howard had been a headliner. Some of the songs on the western theme included "Bidin' My Time," "Bronco Busters," "Cactus Time in Arizona," and (with a Latin beat) "Land of the Gay Caballero." (A few years later Cole Porter improbably wrote a cowboy ballad, "Don't Fence Me In," that later became a huge hit.) But though "Bidin' My Time" gained instant popularity, the real Gershwin standards that emerged from this show were songs like "Embraceable You," "I Got Rhythm," "Sam and Delilah," and "But Not for Me," which showed that the Gershwin voice and mood could thrive in the most unlikely setting. There was more than one kind of Gershwin song, but one of their signatures was the rhythm number like "Fascinating Rhythm" or "I Got Rhythm," where the speed and jazzy syncopation were the subject and the lyrics merely came along for the ride. In "I Got Rhythm" George and Ira turned a neat trick by writing the refrain as repetition rather than rhyme ("I got rhythm, / I got music, / I got my man"), heightening a melodic phrase in which every syllable was stressed, including *my*. In "Fascinating Rhythm" they achieved the effect of something primitive and elemental by endlessly repeating the title but varying the rhythm. Gershwin's songs often originated with a fragment of rhythm or melody that haunted him until he could work out a shape for it. Aaron Copland, who had introduced jazz elements into his *Music for the Theatre* in 1925, described "Fascinating Rhythm" (originally called "Syncopated City") as "rhythmically not only the most fascinating but the most original jazz song yet composed."[5] With their unusual chord progressions, their polyrhythms, these songs, like so many other Gershwin pieces, became endlessly attractive material for improvisations by jazz singers and musicians, demonstrating that black-derived jazz, though in some ways not jazz at all if it shunned improvisation, was more compatible with authentic black jazz than some imagined. Himself a brilliant and tireless improviser at the piano—this was how he composed—Gershwin could write music that sounded spontaneous and improvised. Gershwin's respect for jazz was reciprocated; his work used to be scorned by politically correct critics, rarely by jazzmen themselves.

"Embraceable You," by contrast, showed how George and Ira's skill at fresh, ingenious rhyming could play against a surging melodic line to create a different kind of love song. By rhyming "embraceable you" with "irreplaceable you" and even, in the encore, with "silk and lace-able you," or by rhyming "grew tipsy in me" with "the gypsy in me," they spice romantic feeling with an essentially comic flavor, harnessing wit to wooing, as Shakespeare's comic heroes always did. Like all witty lovers, he heightens the contrast between irrepressible impulse and stodgy convention (savoring the "delectable" over the "respectable"). The typical Gershwin rhyme moves hopefully from observation to action—from embraceable to embracing—with all the inevitability of a syllogism ("I love all / The many charms about you; / Above all / I want my arms about you"). As always with the Gershwins, this is a love song with a difference, combining simple yet plangent emotion with wit and sophistication.

Another kind of Gershwin song in *Girl Crazy* is "Sam and Delilah," a torchy number that shows us the lurid effects of mismatched love by retelling the biblical story of Samson as a Frankie-and-Johnny ballad. Cole Porter later included a song like this, "Solomon," in his 1933 London show *Nymph Errant*, where it was performed to great effect by a fine young black singer, Elisabeth Welch. (Some of the Grand Guignol manner of Stephen Sondheim's *Sweeney Todd* might well come out of this song.) Yet another sort of number in *Girl Crazy* is the love song with an strong dose of unhappiness, like the great "But Not for Me" or its amusing counterpart, "Boy! What Love Has Done to Me," one the story of a woman who has lost her lover, the other the curious lament of an unhappy wife. In "But Not for Me" a woman is discovering feelings she didn't know she had, and again the combination of wit and romance, melody and poetry, is irresistible:

> I've heard that love's a game;
> I'm puzzled just the same—
> Was I the Moth or Flame . . . ?
>   I'm all at sea.

The last line rhymes with the title, which itself evolves from "They're writing songs of love / But not for me" to "I guess he's not for me" to the infinitely witty conclusion:

> The climax of a plot
> Should be the marriage knot,
> But there's no knot for me.

Here's an example of a song that fits the show's gossamer plot—the character gradually realizes her mistake in rejecting the man who's courted her—but remains general enough to be sung by any man or woman separated from a lover. (There was a lovely rendition by the great Gershwin aficionado Michael Feinstein, on his first album, *Pure Gershwin*, released in 1985.) Not only do the Gershwins leaven romantic feeling and melodic flow with witty writing—in the original *Girl Crazy* in 1930, the song had a comic reprise in which Willie Howard parodied the styles of singers like Maurice Chevalier, Eddie Cantor, and Al Jolson—but the singer remains conscious of all the clichés of how the song should end, and *longs* for those clichés. The story of *Girl Crazy* may be inane, but the little plot of this song is too fresh to allow for easy resolution or a happy ending. The writing is elegant without being superficial, elemental without being simple or derivative. This is a love song for people who would never dream of singing a love song, a wistful, melancholy evocation of what might have been.[6] It is also strikingly Jewish in its evocation of this sense of loss, of being an outsider to the optimistic clichés of Tin Pan Alley. ("With Love to Lead the Way / I've found more Clouds of Gray / Than any Russian play / Could guarantee.") Working, however loosely, within a dramatic context rather than writing directly for Tin Pan Alley, the Gershwins perfected this kind of failure-of-love song that they would later use to good effect in writing the last great movie for Fred Astaire and Ginger Rogers, *Shall We Dance*.

You're the Top: Cole Porter, the Dark and the Light

The Gershwins had discovered that effortless elegance did not require a setting amid high society. It was an inner grace that could just as easily be found on Catfish Row or on a dude ranch out west. This kind of style did not put emotions into abeyance; it *was* those emotions. It was knowing rather than sentimental—adult and worldly rather than brain-dead. The Gershwins infused the 32-bar Tin Pan Alley love song with the syncopated rhythms of jazz and the delicious wit of fine light verse to create something fresh, youthful, and contemporary. Cole Porter, on the other hand, simply exploded the form of the popular song with a brio that was as infectious as it was original. Between the opening of *The New Yorkers*, two months after *Girl Crazy* in 1930, and his dreadful riding accident in 1937 that not only crushed his legs but put a sudden halt to his best period as a composer, Porter wrote a series of wonderful shows that virtually defined the frivolous, insouciant side of the culture of the 1930s, including *Gay Divorce* (1932), *Nymph Errant* (1933), *Anything Goes* (1934), *Jubilee* (1935), and *Red, Hot and Blue* (1936). Whereas the Gershwins evolved their own thirties-style social consciousness in works like *Let 'Em Eat Cake* and *Porgy and Bess*, Porter seemed like a reminder of the careless world of the 1920s, when he did some serious composing—he had more extensive musical training than any of his contemporaries—but also lived the life of a playboy expatriate and private performer during a long period when his work met with little public success.

The real toast of the 1920s, F. Scott Fitzgerald, who had given the Jazz Age its name with a 1922 collection of stories, later cited Porter as the kind of brittle Ivy League wit he himself might have become had his artistic conscience not troubled him. Through draft after draft, Fitzgerald worked harder and harder at each book, and his writing really developed, as Porter's would not. As his life took a series of disastrous turns in the 1930s, Fitzgerald brought the pain of it into his work—something that Porter, who suffered even more, never deliberately did. Paradoxically, this is what makes Porter such a classic figure of the Depression decade. In an age of adversity, he thumbs his nose at it. In a period when many rich men were taking a flying leap from high windows, when he himself—a closeted homosexual married to a woman who mothered and supported him—suffered serious bouts of depression, he behaved as if the party would go on forever.

Anything Goes, which ran for 420 performances, was Porter's greatest hit in the thirties. It was produced by Vinton Freedley, half of the Gershwins' old producing team, which had fallen apart after the failure of *Pardon My English* in 1933. Freedley conceived of *Anything Goes* as a throwback to the bubbly musicals of the Princess Theatre and the 1920s, and hired P. G. Wodehouse and Guy Bolton to write a book inspired by the new vogue of transatlantic cruise liners. He understood exactly how the shipboard setting would insulate the show from the conditions of the Depression, which already looked a little less trying in the first flush of optimism about the New Deal. (Unfortunately, a luxury liner, the SS *Morro Castle*, caught fire and burned off the New Jersey coast before the play could go into rehearsal, with great loss of life, and this required a frantic last-minute rewrite.) The show would prove to be a terrific vehicle for Ethel Merman, the sensational discovery of *Girl Crazy*, for the male quartet from that show, the Foursome, and for the comic antics of Victor Moore and William Gaxton. But what keeps *Anything Goes* alive today is the great score, probably the best Porter ever wrote, though claims could be made for his greatest postwar success, *Kiss Me Kate*, one his wittiest, most integrated shows.

Anything Goes is full of good songs—five of them were immediate hits—but it was the title number, along with Ethel Merman's great opener, "I Get a Kick out of You," and another marvelous "list" song, "You're the Top," that carried the show and gave Porter's words and music a tremendous vogue. (The 1987 Lincoln Center production imported songs from other Porter shows, including the brilliant "It's De-Lovely," from *Red, Hot and Blue*, to make the score even richer.) In all these songs Porter strikes a pose of the hedonist, the amoralist, the irrepressible pagan: "You can tell at a glance / What a swell night this is for romance, / You can hear dear Mother Nature murmuring low, / 'Let yourself go.' " This is a Porter moment, when convention and restraint give way to nature and impulse, and he gleefully tells you about it. Shock the puritans: that's his motto.

The singers are always looking for what will bring out "the gypsy in me." At the same time the characters singing these songs are no rebels: they're social animals, accustomed to holding back, feeling constrained. They're hardly free spirits. They're exhilarated yet frankly puzzled by the brave new world in which "anything goes." Both the title song and others like "Bon Voyage / There's No Cure like Travel" are works of sheer fizz and effervescence, verbally as well as musically. "Bon Voyage," like Walt Whitman's vertiginous poem "Salut au Monde!," gets a buzz out of simply bouncing through euphonious place-names like Vienna, Granada, Ravenna, and Siena and trying out travel talk in different languages. This is the world of the grand tour, the luxury cruise, the five-star hotel, with Europe at your feet. But just beneath this surface we can feel the author "fighting vainly the old ennui," looking for distraction (in "I Get a Kick out of You"). Another self, a darker mood, always lurks behind the carefree one projected.

What gives Porter's songs their special quality, what makes them impossible to imitate, is not simply the high spirits but the undertone of sadness and world-weariness behind them. Boredom, ennui, and unhappiness give an edge of desperation to Porter's bubbly world. His songs are not escapist, they're *about* escaping—and failing to escape. "I Get a Kick" mainly describes things that give the singer *no* kicks at all; the verse introduces it as a story "much too sad to be told," by someone who finds that "practic'ly ev'rything leaves me totally cold," including the champagne and cocaine that made the song sound daring, risqué, and high flying. It's a very hip song, a song about drugs, about "kicks," which is something quite different from a song about happiness or even pleasure.

All the efforts to make the song more palatable by substituting lines like "some like the perfumes of Spain" or "some like a be-bop refrain" are completely beside the point. They refuse to face up not only to cocaine but to the real refrain, which is emphatically in the negative. The rather plaintive singer reels off everything from which "I get *no* kick," except for the loved one, who doesn't reciprocate. ("I get a kick though it's clear to me / You obviously don't adore me.")

An even more extreme example of Porter's instinctive reliance on self-abasement as a backdrop for tribute is "You're the Top," where each stanza of the refrain ends with lines like "I'm a worthless check, a total wreck, a flop, / But if, baby, I'm the bottom / You're the top." Of course, nobody hears this, any more than they hear the coded sexual reference; what they hear is the constant topping, which provocatively rhymes highbrow with lowbrow references, the fashionable list that pairs a Bendel bonnet with a Shakespeare sonnet, Mahatma Gandhi with Napoleon Brandy, *Inferno's* Dante with the nose of the great Durante, a Waldorf salad with a Berlin ballad. Porter is faithful to the list songs of Gilbert and Sullivan and even to the old Petrarchan romantic tradition of praising your beloved with ever more extravagant comparisons. Yet all the words that neatly rhyme with top are its opposites: flop, pop, "de trop," stop, GOP, hop.

One great performer who heard the melancholy undertone in Porter's songs was Ella Fitzgerald. The versions in her *Cole Porter Songbook*, which inaugurated her celebrated Songbook series in 1956, sometimes sound too lugubrious. But she underlines his surprising kinship with the blues, and brings out a dark, even tragic dimension in ballads like "All through the Night," which becomes a song not just about making anonymous love but about its aftermath: waking up every day to an empty bed. The notorious "Love for Sale," a song about prostitution that was banned from the radio, shocked audiences at *The New Yorkers* so much that the producers transferred the venue to Harlem. Porter's songs were exceptionally daring for the 1930s: sex gave them their pulsing vitality, an image of high society gave them their brightness and buoyancy, and a certain self-loathing grounded in sexual unhappiness gave them heft and shading.

Love songs were a staple of any popular composer of this period—Ira Gershwin had a particularly hard time writing them—but Porter often used them to vent his melancholy. Each of Porter's love songs is a little story, a mini-drama. "Down in the Depths," a song Porter wrote for Ethel Merman during the Boston tryout of *Red, Hot and Blue*, is about feeling depressed and lonely though you're sitting on top of the world—literally, or figuratively, on the ninetieth floor, overlooking the city yet cut off from its busy life. It begins by addressing the town itself, the sophisticated heart of the city, Manhattan, with which Porter himself was uniquely identified. The singer, rejected by her lover, looks down remotely at "a million neon rainbows burning below me / And a million blazing taxis raising a roar," and imagines the crowds dancing the night away at El Morocco and the eager couples at the "21" Club—not exactly scenes of exceptional suffering during the Depression. From all this, the seeming heart of Porter's own Manhattan, the singer feels removed: "I'm deserted and depressed / In my regal eagle nest / Down in the depths on the ninetieth floor." This is, at best, a rarefied situation. Money is no problem: "When the only one you wanted wants another / What's the use of swank and cash in the bank galore?"

Whatever the personal root of Porter's problems, many in the 1930s could identify with his frustrations, for he had displaced his own depression onto the Depression and gave the social malaise a personal core, overlaid with the strenuous gaiety that was his dominant mood. During the grim early years of the Depression people could respond to this mix of feelings; only then could Cole Porter call upon them so freely. Bing Crosby's somber performances in the early thirties were hits for the same reason. The culture of elegance was always purchased at a price. The undersong, the strain, was of someone urgently trying to cheer himself up.

Despite this darker shading, with its traces of hysteria or melancholy, or perhaps because of it, audiences loved Porter; his perfectly matched music and lyrics captured the brittle chic of society. Far from celebrating or condemning it, Porter always had something of the outsider about him, the midwesterner from Peru, Indiana, even the puritan who knows he's being deliciously naughty.[7] Like Ira Gershwin and Larry Hart, Porter learned a lot from the verse of W. S. Gilbert's patter songs, but he also learned from Sullivan's seemingly monotonous but actually supportive music. The lyric of "Anything Goes" is masterly for its tone of wide-eyed surprise, beautifully grounded in pulsing musical phrases that enabled performers like Ethel Merman and Porter himself to enunciate the words perfectly. This is cabaret music, talk-singing, lyrical patter. Ethel Merman had a reputation as a belter—her pipes were one of nature's wonders—but her early recordings of "Anything Goes," "I Get a Kick out of You," "You're the Top," and "It's De-Lovely" reveal her exceptional delicacy as a vocalist, especially in her clear, nuanced phrasing. These were songs in which the words really mattered. The same could be said of Fred Astaire's immaculate, uncluttered renditions of Gershwin, Berlin, and Kern, who knew how to write for his register much as Porter wrote for Merman's.

Porter found his lilt in "Anything Goes" partly by rhyming within the line as well as at the end of it ("The world has gone *mad* today / And good's *bad* today, / And black's *white* today, / And day's *night* today . . .") and then always resolving the sequence—and the tune—with a surprise

("And that gent today / You gave a cent today / Once had several cha-teaux"). In the list songs, a certain relentlessness gives Porter his sound. Infinitely expandable, they could go on and on. The music demands that these lines be chanted rhythmically to a pounding beat rather than fully sung. Melody surrounds but doesn't fully shape or inhabit them. In lines like those above, as Philip Furia points out in *The Poets of Tin Pan Alley*, the "title itself flip-flops in meaning, from the ballyhoo years of the 1920s, when 'anything goes' was a slogan of moral abandon, to the 1930s when the phrase became a bleak reminder of the stock-market crash."[8] This is not the ordinary Depression but a fairy-tale apotheosis of it, with the rich losing their chateaux and the Whitneys and Vanderbilts short of baby clothes. Yet the song really does capture the uncertainty of the Depression years, which could be exhilarating to some even as it produced enormous anxiety in most others. This is not Yip Harburg's "Brother, Can You Spare a Dime?" but a different take on the same sub-ject. Observing the Depression scene with the eye of an anthropologist, Porter manages to turn insecurity into exuberance, as if he were danc-ing on top of a volcano.

He brings this off through the energy of language and rhythm that made the "topping" effect possible. In these songs we feel we're watching a high-wire performer, cutting a nimble figure far above our heads with-out knowing where he'll land. The topical references have no equivalent in songwriting today; in my childhood they could be found in the josh-ing poetry of Ogden Nash; their dim descendant today is the Christmas poem in *The New Yorker*, revived in 2008 after a ten-year hiatus, with its strained heartiness and mild tributes to fashionable people whose names make funny rhymes. Porter is never complacent about being "in." His sophistication is always tinged with mockery, just as his cynicism is laced with affection. In "It's De-lovely" he mocks himself even as he tops him-self, twisting and hammering the language to his purpose, reeling off all the "de-" words at the end of each stanza, delightful, delicious, delectable, delirious, until he sweeps standard English aside and lands magically at "de-lovely." The song itself gives us scenes from a marriage, just the kind of cozy, conventional, storybook marriage Porter himself didn't have; it's full of the outsider's bemused wonderment at the getting and begetting of ordinary life. Not too ordinary: this is a world in which all newly mar-ried couples pop up to Niagara Falls in a little plane!

The closest parallel to Porter's sophistication was the dancing of Fred Astaire, but not because of Porter's social references or because he dealt much with the world of top hats, white tie, and tails. Astaire actually worked more with the music of Berlin, Kern, and the Gershwins. His last Broadway show, the first after his sister retired, was Porter's *Gay Divorce*, but only one song, "Night and Day," survived the transition to film. Porter wasn't the ideal composer for Astaire, yet the surprising turns we love in Astaire's dance numbers, our sense of a man constantly outdoing himself without visible effort, offers a close equivalent to the virtuosity of Porter's nimble language and complex melodic line. In the 1930s both Porter and Astaire were reality instructors, tutors in manners and sophistication, for young people who would never set foot in their world, many of them children of immigrants or young migrants from the South and the Midwest to the fast-growing cities.

Neither man seemed conventionally suited to the role he would play. In Porter there was always a trace of the foppish undergraduate with slicked-down hair who had written two of Yale's football songs. Astaire had neither a great voice nor conventional good looks. Much of what they did had a throwaway air; they worked hard at making it look easy. But along with the great swing performers of the age, they helped define what was cool and debonair for the younger generation. Theirs was the code of the gentleman, and when that code was smashed by the violence of the Second World War they were replaced by Humphrey Bogart and others who had a different kind of cool. Though the thirties were a time of economic stagnation, a sense of limited possibilities, in their work these men seemed to be in perpetual motion. Many writers and performers responded to the Depression with keen feelings of social anguish or radical dismay—anger at the system and a fervent wish to transform or replace it; Astaire and Porter, by contrast, radiated whimsical irony and self-possession. With Ginger Rogers, Astaire created the great romantic couple of the decade; his singing and their dancing became the model for a cooler mode of romantic feeling that avoided or reinvigorated romantic clichés.

As a composer Porter came to feel victimized by the sophisticated mode. Feeling that such work had a limited shelf life, he longed to be more conventional, and eventually succeeded. "Sophisticated allusions are good for about six weeks," he told an interviewer. "Futile as presenting Sophocles in the original Greek. . . . Sophisticated lyrics are more fun but only for myself and about eighteen other people, all of whom are first-nighters anyway. Polished, urbane, and adult playwriting in the musical field is strictly a creative luxury."⁹ The mangled film version of *Gay Divorce* was an example of how mass culture could chew up and discard his work, for it was made at a time when Hollywood was still dubious about musicals and suspicious of the clever, risqué sensibility of Broadway as a source for wholesome entertainment. When the Gershwin boys were finally invited out to Hollywood, they were astonished at how little music was demanded of them, and how much of what they wrote was discarded or abbreviated. For a Broadway show they had at times written more than two dozen songs; sometimes only five would be needed for a movie.

Shall We Dance: Astaire and Rogers

After the succès fou of *Anything Goes*, Hollywood would find much more use for Porter right through the 1950s, including a 1936 film version of *Anything Goes*, with Bing Crosby, as well as many original scores and a film biography, *Night and Day* (1946), with Cary Grant and Alexis Smith, that must be seen not to be believed. (His main problem seems to be that he's a workaholic. "We haven't seen too much of each other lately," his wife says. "You've put me in a small corner of your life." We see the buildup to the success of *Anything Goes* without seeing the premiere of the show itself.) Eventually Porter's work lost the special flavor it had in the 1930s. In any case *The Gay Divorcee*, as it was renamed, was meant as a vehicle not for Porter but for Astaire and Rogers after the surprising success of their almost accidental matchup when, as supporting players, they danced "The Carioca" in a big mess of a movie, *Flying Down to Rio* (1933).

   The Gay Divorcee is more of a bedroom farce than a dance movie, yet it defined the whole series of Astaire-Rogers films that would follow.* It introduced the whole group of talented though frequently tedious charac-

---

* In the view of James Harvey, it also helped initiate the run of screwball comedy, along with three other films of 1934, Howard Hawks's *Twentieth Century*, *The Thin Man* (adapted from Dashiell Hammett's last novel), and Capra's *It Happened One Night*. See Harvey, *Romantic Comedy in Hollywood, from Lubitsch to Sturges* (New York: Alfred A. Knopf, 1987), 108–10, 125–30.

ter actors, including Eric Blore, Edward Everett Horton, and Erik Rhodes, who would lend comic relief to the couple in film after film. The story line is amusing enough. In order to get a divorce, Rogers must be caught in a rendezvous with a professional co-respondent, a harmless fool and gigolo played by the ineffable Rhodes, and she mistakes Astaire for this stock character. Since he is in love with her, he tries—within the bounds of the risqué rather than the immoral—to take on this role. "So you're the man I've been waiting for," she says, not knowing how truly she speaks. (She spits this out in a tone of contempt and disappointment, for she had already begun to think better of him.) He arrives at her room for the midnight assignation and, after much confusion, dismisses Rhodes and takes over as co-respondent. "This is *my* affair," he insists.

These sex games, rooted in traditional farce, would hardly survive into the later films, though they reappear amusingly from time to time. It was Porter, not Astaire, who specialized in the titillating, the double entendre, the sexual embarrassments. Astaire's mode was to sublimate romance and sex into the music and dancing. Yet the films would continue to weave a tissue of misunderstandings relieved only by great musical numbers, which here include Astaire's choreography to Porter's "Night and Day" and a long, wonderful sequel to "The Carioca": "The Continental," a truly cinematic ensemble piece, running some seventeen and a half minutes, that intercuts scenes involving virtually the whole cast with Astaire and Rogers dancing, leading up to an orgasmic climax that uses, among other props, revolving doors. Almost a film within a film, it's reprised at the end in private by the couple alone, transformed from mass spectacle to intimate domesticity.

The Gay Divorcee, directed by Mark Sandrich, who would go on to direct five more films in the series, set the pattern of conflict and resolution not only between Rogers and Astaire but between the films' speech world and their musical world. In the speech world everything is at cross-purposes as the films contrive a tangle of misunderstanding, hesitation, and resistance to keep the couple apart. But the films also offer us a song and dance world in which seemingly mismatched people can connect beautifully to form a little community of two, in which all awkwardness and inhibition are soon banished and all movement is unimaginably graceful, fluid, purposeful, and lovely. Though they are set in fairy-tale worlds—here, and again in *Top Hat*, a Venice borrowed from Ernst

Lubitsch and Samson Raphaelson's sublime *Trouble in Paradise* (1932)—the discord could be seen as a displaced version of the Depression, a representation of *everybody's* problems, while the concord that follows is the kind of dreamy romantic utopia in which depression and disharmony are transcended. Just as Porter's effervescence worked best against a dark background, the dancing of Astaire and Rogers was all the more effective with Depression audiences in a framework of conflict and delay.

The tone is set by a farcical misunderstanding between Astaire and Rogers when they first meet: part of her dress is stuck in a closed trunk, and he tears it in trying to help her. Miffed, she repels all his efforts to get to know her. But another tone, a tone of romantic longing, is set in the first important number, "A Needle in a Haystack." Arlene Croce described this as "the number that first defined the Astaire character on the screen. Here he is, thumping on the mantelpiece, testing the floor, vaulting the sofa, and generally behaving as if his mind were on anything but going out to search the streets for the girl of his dreams."[10] What strikes me most, though, is how the number evolves. First Astaire is sitting down, singing a rather staid ballad by Con Conrad and Herb Magidson (since RKO, as I said earlier, had dumped the entire Cole Porter score except for "Night and Day"). As he gets up and moves, the music picks up. Soon he's testing a few spots before he finds one in front of the fireplace where he can tap. The burst of energy and the complex syncopated rhythm of his dancing takes us far from the original song, like a jazzman riffing on a simple musical phrase. But when the number ends he is still alone, and this leads into the great "Night and Day" number, in which Astaire overcomes Rogers's reluctance, sweeps her into his arms, and they dance together. Even before they dance, the verse Astaire sings from "Night and Day," which is all about rhythm as a measure of longing ("the beat beat beat of the tom-tom," "the drip drip drip of the raindrops"), serves as a bridge from the solitary dancing of the preceding number. This establishes a pattern for the series: the song itself is an aria of yearning, "the hungry yearning burning inside of me"; the dance is the fulfillment, the consummation, the two-in-one. First they come together in private; finally they dance together in public, usually in a big production number.

In the backstage musicals of Busby Berkeley like *Footlight Parade*, the big production numbers were saved for the end: despite every problem, including those rooted in the Depression itself, the show finally goes on.

The Astaire-Rogers films create suspense around the couple's dancing, making the audience experience the delayed gratification of the couple themselves. Would they do it? When and how would they do it? The buzz of tension that surrounded them, fed by rumors of off-camera discord and professional rivalry, early on became part of the texture of the films, from the number "I Won't Dance" in *Roberta* to "Never Gonna Dance" in *Swing Time* (which was first called *I Won't Dance*) to the culmination of the series, *Shall We Dance*. By the time of these last two films, Astaire and his collaborators were clearly making movies about dancing itself, but the problems both on and off camera may have been too much for the audience. Box office receipts declined somewhat, encouraging RKO to separate the couple temporarily, something they themselves were eager to do—Rogers to pursue her acting career, Astaire to avoid getting locked into a team again. Though they were reunited in three later films, the magic was never the same.

The films that matter most were the six from *The Gay Divorcee* to *Shall We Dance*. Here was the essential romantic fable that brought together all the strands of the culture of elegance: the comic-opera plots about a screwball world of wealth and class, the Deco sets by the RKO art designers that helped create the aura of swank and elegance, the supporting music of all the great Broadway composers, especially Berlin, Kern, and Gershwin, who wrote some of their greatest songs for these films, the jazz-based rhythms of many of the musical numbers, which helped give them their freshness and air of sophistication, and finally the dancing, singing, and choreography of Rogers and Astaire themselves, who translated the music into movement and drama.

It was only in *Top Hat* (1935), their fourth film together, that Astaire would become the icon of class for a decade that gave it importance in every sense: social difference, economic hierarchy, personal style. For the writers who had followed the thirties injunction to "Go Left," class was an arena of exploitation, inequality, and social conflict—and, potentially, an engine of radical change. For Astaire in *Top Hat*, with the help of Irving Berlin's score, it was something quite different, a sense of class as pure style: "I'm steppin' out, my dear, / To breathe an atmosphere that simply reeks with class." There's a lovely note of self-mockery in these lines, especially in a word like "reeks," but Astaire doesn't sing it that way. Instead, he conveys an almost breathless expectation of a great night out. The song begins with an invitation, and Astaire first describes himself actually dressing, then doffing his hat and mussing up his clothes to dance, simply to dance. Astaire puts the self-mockery into his character, not into his singing. After *Top Hat* he could play with his image, often giving it an ironic twist. At the beginning of *Swing Time* we see a penniless Astaire, in top hat and tails after his wedding has been canceled, trying to get a quarter out of a cigarette machine, then taking off on the back of a freight train, that thirties symbol of bottoming out. Between these two came the underrated *Follow the Fleet*, in which the studio, fearful that Depression audiences would soon recoil at Astaire's top-hat image, tried to turn him into an ordinary guy—which, in terms of his background as Frederick Austerlitz, a brewer's son from Omaha, Nebraska, he really was.

Top Hat, says Arlene Croce, "is a Thirties' romance of the Twenties, the sins of the decade wiped clean by a flow of lyrical optimism."[11] Astaire plays a tap dancer, and tap is also what this movie is about; virtually every important scene turns on it. It begins with him frozen in the glacial setting of a London club, virtually unable to move, even to crinkle his newspaper, without disturbing someone. Being free to move, to dance, to let go—that's the theme of these films—and when Astaire escapes, he does a neat little step, speaking with his toes instead of thumbing his nose, telling us what he thinks of this kind of stuffy, purely masculine, old-world notion of class. It's a one-joke scene, but the "Thackeray Club" brings out the puckish, rebellious, "American" side of his personality. For Astaire class is motion, energy, pleasure, not static hierarchy. Unlike the upper-class swells in, say, Philip Barry's plays, Astaire is always the entertainer dressing up, relishing his role as a man of the world, never simply the rich man to the manner born. Behind the moody Petrov, the seemingly Russian ballet dancer in *Shall We Dance*, is Peter P. Peters, the ordinary American who really wants to work on Broadway. There is an instinctive democrat at work (and play) behind Astaire's joy in dressing up.

Astaire's ambivalence toward his own image can be seen most clearly in the big "Top Hat" number. He has a large male chorus behind him, all dressed, as he is, in top hat, white tie, and tails, a getup he disliked, and he wields a cane that becomes part of the tap (Astaire rivals Chaplin in his choreography of inanimate objects): he dances around it like a pivot, waves it like a wand, twirls it like a baton, taps with it like a third leg, and wields it as a rifle to mow the whole chorus down, and even as a crossbow to fell the last man. (Astaire had done a number called "High Hat," with male chorus, on the stage in *Funny Face* in 1927, and another, with lethal cane, in *Smiles* in 1930.) The whole audience is also in white tie, virtual replicas of himself, and he "shoots" at them too. Just as Chaplin's mime comes close to dancing, Astaire's choreography beautifully integrates pantomime.

If Astaire's tap dancing can turn hostile to the gentlemen of the club or the social manikins in the chorus and audience, it becomes a dance of pure seduction with Ginger Rogers. First he dances in his hotel room, alone, in the sheer burst of joy of a man who has "no strings." His friends want to marry him off, but he enjoys being on his own, playing the field, always open to romance, "fancy free, and free for anything fancy." But his irrepressible high spirits disturb Ginger in the room below, and, when she protests, he appoints himself "her official sandman," tapping softly on sand, above her head, to enable her to sleep. Dance is impulse, feeling, overflow, a kind of loving; you can even sleep to it—she trails off and so does he, secure in the new knowledge that now he *doesn't* want to be alone.

In yet another version of the man in a top hat, he masquerades as the hansom cab driver, taking her about town, but gives himself away with his tapping feet. Earlier she told him his spontaneous dancing was "some kind of affliction"; now she says, "buy yourself a new hat." Ginger's resistance, fueled by misunderstanding—she mistakes him for yet another man in a top hat, his married friend—begins to break down when they're caught in the rain and she takes refuge in a large gazebo, a picture-perfect stage set. "May I rescue you?" he asks. "I prefer being in distress," says she. But now she really is trapped—"Isn't this a lovely day / To be caught in the rain? / You were going on your way; / Now you've got to remain"—and as they dance together, the thunder becomes part of their music, and they come a mite closer to being together.

Of course, they finally do come together in "Cheek to Cheek," one of Berlin's great songs, in which the plaintive call, "*Dance* with me," which rhymes musically with the beginning of the refrain ("*Heaven!* I'm in *heaven* . . ."), serves as a lovely prologue to the dance itself. And they come together again in the closing number, "The Piccolino," a half-hearted follow-up to "The Carioca" and "The Continental," with a self-mocking set of lyrics. The dance in "Cheek to Cheek" is the height of swank and elegance, with the couple gradually separating themselves from the crowd and Rogers gradually accepting Astaire's feelings for her. She wears one of her magical dresses, a mass of ostrich feathers, organdy, with satin trim, and a rhinestone brooch. The dance is so graceful, the music so perfect, that her dress and her body become one vast swirl of form and movement, and the music continues in the background as they talk it out.

Afterward, the cross-purposes of the speech world reassert themselves: still thinking he's married, she slaps his face when he proposes to her. The suspense is whether Ginger will fall for the wrong man, Albert, her comic-Latin dressmaker, again played by Erik Rhodes, the oily gigolo of *The Gay Divorcee*, renewing the sex games of the earlier film. She actually "marries" him, but only with the help of Eric Blore, disguised as a clergyman. With Rogers already in the bridal suite, tap comes to the rescue as Astaire dances on the ceiling to disturb Rogers yet again, for he is desperate to make sure the marriage isn't consummated. Meanwhile, his friend distracts her ardent groom, until she eventually comes to her senses.

The next film, *Follow the Fleet*, finds Fred and Ginger separated again. He's joined the navy out of pique because Ginger, his dance partner, has rebuffed him and broken up their act. The main reason, though, was that the studio was looking to democratize their image in light of hard times. "RKO executives reasoned that their most popular actor might lose his appeal to the common folk if he was repeatedly seen in white tie and tails," says Bob Thomas in his book on Astaire.[12] At the end, of course, we do see him in tie and tails—the best part of the movie—but only because he's putting on a shipboard show, for charity. The fine score by Irving Berlin is used much less sparingly than in *Top Hat*, which was still stuck in the comic formulas of *The Gay Divorcee*. Here the tunes return repeatedly as dramatic and musical leitmotifs, creating a pattern for *Swing Time* and *Shall We Dance*. *Follow the Fleet* scarcely has a great plot or even effective comedy, but it's much more musical than its predecessors.

The score has great variety, beginning with a lovely Gilbert and Sullivan–style ditty, "We Saw the Sea," sung by Astaire and the sailors on shipboard. This is a *cherchez la femme* prologue to their shore leave in San Francisco, where they'll all end up somehow in the nightspot where Ginger works alone. It's followed by one of the film's jazziest numbers, "Let

Yourself Go," one of the signature themes of the series, a song about liberating yourself from your mundane personality, prosaic, weighed down with conflicts and inhibitions, into your dance personality, lightness itself, where love, freedom, and fulfillment can be found. It's also a Depression song that helps make sense of the dance crazes and swing music of the period. The lyric is remarkably therapeutic: "Relax! You've got yourself tied up in a knot"; get out on the dance floor, and leave your troubles behind. Not exactly a total solution but, like glum marathon dancing in Horace McCoy's novel *They Shoot Horses, Don't They?*, a good metaphor for the whole era.

Jazz is virtually the theme of the film, as tap was in *Top Hat*—jazz as music, as dance, as sex, as uninhibited self-expression. "Let Yourself Go," first sung by Rogers, then played in jazz time for a big dance contest, is Astaire's comment on the big-band era, and their winning dance is glorious. She dances in satin pants, with a single stripe down the side, matching his sailor suit: they're both all legs—flying legs, bouncing, jabbing, sailing—and together they create a fantastic visual rhythm. Soon afterward he tries to give shipboard dance lessons to the same tune, with half the guys playing the "Dames." ("You know," he tells them, "there's a difference between dancing and wrestling. In dancing the main idea is to keep your partner's shoulders *off* the floor.") A later number contrasts jazz rhythm with military music. The whole movie is a comparison of different kinds of music and dance, from ballroom dances, marches, and slow, soulful ballads to the hot rhythms of jazz.

Ginger hasn't been doing too well on her own. "For some reason," she says, "they're not interested in a girl dancing alone." She keeps auditioning alone, even to the music of "Let Yourself Go," but Astaire makes sure she gets none of these jobs. Astaire's joshing persona here is brash, totally confident, whimsically vague and absent, a bit ironic, and even somewhat clumsy, except, of course, when he's dancing. In one rollicking dance, to the music of Berlin's delightful "I'm Putting All My Eggs in One Basket," they remain at cross-purposes, competing, parodying each other, shadow-boxing, even knocking each other off the stage as the music keeps changing tempo, from waltz time to jazz time. As an amusing combat routine, it fits dramatically into the Fred-and-Ginger myth, which oscillates between chafing seduction, competitiveness, and spirited resistance before settling down with love.

That love arrives with the great final number, "Let's Face the Music and Dance," a self-contained dramatic playlet in which the pair finally become the perfectly *soigné* couple on the Art Deco set that the audience has been waiting for. This is the performance, the masquerade, with Rogers in a sequined dress with fox wrap, Astaire in white tie, carnation in lapel, with black tails flying. The Berlin song is a Depression piece, a moody, somber version of "Let Yourself Go." Seize the day, the song says, or rather seize the night, for there may be trouble and tears ahead; meanwhile, let's face the music and dance. Facing the music, of course, is a nicely ambiguous play on words that suggests both an escape into romance and facing up to what really matters while we still can. In the story within the story, the couple play two Monte Carlo gamblers who contemplate suicide after being wiped out—a rather melodramatic metaphor for the Depression—but console each other back into the world, save each other . . . for dancing. This in turn is a metaphor for the whole series: to face the music and dance is not to escape into superficial glitter or romance but to surmount reversals and catastrophes by finding one another, by taking beautiful steps and turns together. Dancing in the dark is a way of asserting a life-saving grace, unity, and style against the encroaching darkness. Thus the message of the series is not that different from more socially conscious hard-times fables like *The Grapes of Wrath*: separately we fail, we lose heart and fall into confusion; together we have a chance. It's only a play within a play, a performance, yet it seems more real than anything that came before.

This was the triumph of Astaire and Rogers: not only to create an irresistible image of smart elegance at an unlikely historical juncture but to make romance itself, so often cheapened by the clichés of popular culture, seem hard-won and authentic—as graceful as it was inevitable. This was what spoke warmly to the cultural moment, and it still speaks to us today. *In Swing Time* and *Shall We Dance* this myth becomes completely self-conscious. In addition, *Shall We Dance* would bring the Gershwins back to Hollywood, and back to musical comedy, for a final fling that produced perhaps a dozen of their greatest songs before George Gershwin's untimely death in 1937.

Swing Time, with a winning score by Jerome Kern and lyrics by Dorothy Fields, takes off not only from the swing motifs of *Follow the Fleet* but from the gambling theme of the play within a play. As it begins, Astaire has lost his money gambling, his wedding to Betty Furness (later the Westing-house girl of 1950s TV, still later an ardent consumer advocate) has been called off, and he must ride the rails to New York to earn enough money to restore his good name. As in *The Gay Divorcee* and *Top Hat*, Fred and Ginger are always in danger of marrying the wrong people, of settling down and becoming ordinary and never learning how good they would be together. (Ginger "almost" marries a dreadful Latin bandleader named Ricardo Romero.) The first number is "Pick Yourself Up," an upbeat Depression piece, much like "Let Yourself Go." Here we find Astaire, with two left feet, taking dance lessons from Ginger, making a pretense of learning to tap. The lyrics make this a way of learning to live, dealing with adversity. Life is full of pratfalls, he says lightheartedly, but "I pick myself up, dust myself off, and start all over again." Other great songs include "A Fine Romance," "The Way You Look Tonight," and "Never Gonna Dance," as well as a curious number in blackface, "Bojangles of Harlem," a tribute to the great black tap dancer Bill ("Bojangles") Robinson.

In "Pick Yourself Up," to win Ginger's attention, but also to drive her a little bit crazy, Fred pretends to have an ordinary, awkward, falling-down body, just like the rest of us. Her lessons fail: his clumsiness gets her fired, as in *Follow the Fleet*, but he saves her by showing the boss how wonderfully he *can* dance—to just the same music he was falling down by. It's a great jazz number and a great performance, though they dance too well together for a couple who never rehearsed. They create an illusion of intimacy that would have to be earned step by step in the course of the movie. The next number, the ballad "The Way You Look Tonight," brings them closer. He wins her with music, though her hair is in disarray, soaped up with shampoo, and then her Latin suitor sings the same song in soapy operetta fashion. Fred and Ginger move closer to intimate connection with the extremely complex "Waltz in Spring Time," which Arlene Croce describes as "a wide, white stream flowing in agile cross-rhythms, flowing without pause through so many intricacies and surprises, so many acts of mutual gallantry and faith that they can't possibly be cited, much less described." She calls it "the most rapturously sustained, endlessly reseeable of all their dances" (105). Visually, as they move behind Venetian blinds, then emerge with smiles, the number feels like the discreet climax of a love scene, using a vocabulary borrowed from the lexicon of silent film.

But they return to earth, always a bit out of synch, and after a quiet reprise of "The Way You Look Tonight" they move into a scene in the snow, to the tune of Kern and Fields's satiric "A Fine Romance," which plays on Fred's coldness, the chasteness of this cool performer's approach ("with no kisses"). The number shows how songwriters could be inspired by the couple's seemingly endless dissonance as well as their sublime moments of harmony. (Their chronic cross-purposes would prove especially delectable to the Gershwins in the next film, written when their formula was long established.) Here they're a particular boon to the witty lyricist, Dorothy Fields, writing in the Larry Hart and Ira Gershwin mode. ("You're just as hard to land as the *Ile-de-France.* / I haven't got a chance. / This is a fine romance.") Challenged to kiss, they do kiss—discreetly, behind a door, after a great teasing scene—a second climax that not only avoided romantic cliché, as Astaire insisted on doing, but kept up the dramatic tension between the couple. (Is there an outright kiss between them in the whole series? At least not until the late *Carefree*, where it would be bruited as a novelty item. The challenge of having them kiss plays on this teasing restraint.)

The remaining tension between them will be crucial to the climactic number, "Never Gonna Dance," which dramatically recapitulates bits and pieces from the earlier numbers as it reenacts the whole flow of their attraction and hesitation, love and suspicion. The spectacular two-tiered Deco set, with separate staircases, itself becomes a major player in this scene. She goes halfway up the stairs to follow his rival, then is drawn back by the pathos of Astaire's song. They dance to it, but still fail to connect; she leaves, he pulls her back, and they go up separate staircases. Both song and dance crystallize the negative energy that gives such a charge to the Astaire-Rogers relationship. The song is full of the complex pathos built into feeling rejected yet remaining obsessed. The dance turns all this into drama and movement, with a brilliant ending that avoids easy resolution. Astaire won't dance if he can't love; his refusal to dance, and the very dance in which he acts this out, makes for one of the signal moments of the whole series.

From its title alone we can see that *Shall We Dance*, the last truly extraordinary film in the series, picks up exactly where *Swing Time* leaves off. But the arrival of the Gershwins gives the film yet another layer of complexity. By this time the films were diminishing slightly in popularity but were also gaining recognition as exceptional works of contemporary art. It was now understood that dance was their subject as much as Fred and Ginger were, and *Shall We Dance* is nothing if not a reflexive film about art and dance in relation to romance. George Gershwin himself occupied an indeterminate status between art and popular entertainment, between the concert hall, the opera house, and the Broadway stage. No doubt the Gershwins in Hollywood were looking to restore their popular position after the failure of *Pardon My English* and *Let 'Em Eat Cake* and the cultural prestige (but commercial disappointment) of *Porgy and Bess*. The movie studios had never known how to use them; they considered them too highbrow, too literate, too sophisticated, to which Gershwin responded that he wanted nothing but to write hits. So, in the film, Fred Astaire plays a down-home American caught in the role of a high-culture European, a ballet dancer with a phony Russian name and atrocious accent, who's secretly drawn to Broadway and tap, as personified by the equally famous woman played by Ginger Rogers.

The film deals not only with high and low culture but, implicitly, with cinema itself, for it is fascinated by the image and its replication. Astaire falls in love with Rogers when he sees flip cards of her dancing; soon images of the two of them are circulating in newspapers, with gossip about their shipboard "romance." Later, he keeps an eerie life-size replica of her, and at the end, when she won't dance with him, he dances instead with dozens of images of her—other women in Ginger Rogers masks. With this degree of self-consciousness the series may have turned overripe, but deliciously so. Thanks to the success of Rodgers and Hart's *On Your Toes* in 1936, with its Russian ballet material and Balanchine choreography, both ballet and everything Russian were in the air. (The gigolo, or "protégé," in Gregory La Cava's great screwball comedy *My Man Godfrey*, played by Mischa Auer, had a gloomy and cultivated Russian air.)

The film begins with silhouettes of dancers. We see silly ballet dancers practicing being waves. Astaire can do this too—well enough to make Edward Everett Horton seasick—but then when we see him alone he's indulging his secret vice, the vigorously energetic, lowbrow tap he really wants to do. But the phonograph needle gets stuck in the groove, keeps repeating, then slows down and stops. His dancing with this machine is a joke-soliloquy, a private revelation. We see Rogers at the end of a show, with some stiff who tries to kiss her, other men who follow her. Both are going nowhere. Seemingly, they're at opposite ends of the cultural spectrum, but both need a partner, someone they can love as well as dance with—the two urgent needs are indistinguishable. Unpartnered, he dances with machines in the boiler room of a ship, accompanied by a black chorus. She wants to quit performing but remains the prisoner of the spotlight. They're pursued by a public that wants them together, wants to see their images joined, wants to bring them both into the same spotlight. The world sees them as madly in love; rumor has them married already—but, as in earlier films in the series, they just can't seem to get it on.

This is where the Gershwins came in, for they were inspired by the Astaire-Rogers myth to write some of the loveliest and least hackneyed love songs of all time, not only for this film but for Astaire's next (solo) film, *Damsels in Distress*, and then for a revue, *The Goldwyn Follies*, on which they were working when George Gershwin died. In *Shall We Dance* these songs aren't particularly well settled into the plot, but they're perfectly ensconced in the superplot, the overall Astaire-Rogers story that was beginning to lose its momentum. The two masterpieces are songs that, in the flow of the movie, seem to contradict each other, "Let's Call the Whole Thing Off," a wonderfully funny song about all the things that keep people apart, and "They Can't Take That Away from Me," a haunting ballad about those things that hold people together, making them inseparable even after they've parted.

The first of these could be a theme song of the ups and downs of the whole Astaire-Rogers relationship: "It looks as if we two will never be one. / Something must be done." It's more of a war-of-the-sexes song than a love song, and surely the only one that turns on differences of pronunciation, which stand for every kind of difference of class, background, and temperament. But it shifts beautifully into a love song, a version in miniature of every film in the series, with a long, plangent "oh-h-h," not once but twice: "But *oh*!, if we call the whole thing off / Then we must part, / And *oh*!, if we ever part / Then that might break my heart." This leads to the tongue-twisting and mind-bending conclusion, sung to a sharp staccato beat: "*For* we *know* we *need* each other, / *So* we better call the calling-off off," yet another turn on the calling-off theme, and nicely faithful to

the to-and-fro pattern of the series. (The pendulum is the
phor in *Shall We Dance*.)

The stabbing "oh," really a musical sob, the very so
tary bolt of feeling, links "Let's Call the Whole Thing Off to
refrain of the other song (*"No, no,* they can't take that away from me"), but
also to the equally memorable repeat emphasis of the release, or bridge:
"We may *never, never* meet again / On this bumpy road to love, / But I'll
always, always keep the memory of—." This is a wonderful transition, perfectly matched by the sequences of the refrain, which brilliantly mix the
trivial with the epochal, the little details of love with their huge effects:
"The way you hold your knife, / The way we danced till three, / The way
you changed my life, / *No, no* . . ." The Gershwins had been writing such
poignant yet smartly sophisticated love songs for some fifteen years, as far
back as songs like "I'll Build a Stairway to Paradise," "Someone to Watch
Over Me," "'S Wonderful," "How Long Has This Been Going On?," and
"I've Got a Crush on You," all written between 1922 and 1928. The Gershwins had been coming up with unexpected but remarkably unforced diction and rhymes for almost as long. But the perfect balance between the
minute and the momentous in each stanza of the refrain of "They Can't
Take That Away from Me" does more than spring surprising rhymes. This
is a poetry of love and the many obstacles to love, a musical equivalent to
the bumpy yet often sublime Astaire-Rogers relationship.

Some of these songs the Gershwins brought with them to Holly-
wood before they ever saw a script. (Everyone knew what an Astaire-
Rogers film would be about.) True to the series, these are songs about all
the things that challenge love, as well as how they are wittily overcome.
And, of course, they are often comic as well as ingenious. "They All
Laughed" is almost a Porter list song, full of bright references, ancient
and current, and an unpredictable beat. ("They all laughed at Rockefeller
Center. / Now they're fighting to get in. / They all laughed at Whit-
ney and his cotton gin.") But its basic metaphor—pioneering, invention,
skepticism—is pure Gershwin, as are the refreshing rhymes like "against
me" with "incensed me" or "Marconi" and "a phony." (Who but the Gershwins could have put Columbus, Edison, Wright, and Marconi into a love
song?) George Gershwin was not the greatest admirer of Astaire's singing, especially after he saw the finished film, but the beat of his songs

ınd the highbrow /lowbrow wit of the lyrics make a splendid match for Astaire's cool, ironical personality. Astaire always seems slightly detached from what he's doing. His romantic moods steer clear of sentimentality as his joshing "American" humor escapes vulgarity. No wonder the more single-minded Rogers often has trouble reading him right.

Shall We Dance works hard, usually successfully, to find offbeat settings for the songs and dances: the boiler room of the ship for the hot jazz number, "Slap That Bass," the dog walk (instead of dancing) for "Walking the Dog," the Central Park rotunda, with tapping roller skates, for "Let's Call the Whole Thing Off," the Hoboken ferry for "They Can't Take That Away from Me," and a bizarre stage show, half ballet, half show biz, for "Shall We Dance," which summarizes the movie the way "Never Gonna Dance" crystallized *Swing Time*. The music goes through changes that reflect the couple's feelings for each other. First Ginger, called upon to sing in a nightclub, does "They All Laughed" very straight, then Fred, called to the stage from the audience, begins to show off as a dancer, finally the music, the spotlight, the demands of the crowd (which is also the demand of their movie audience) brings them dancing together to a much jazzier version of the same song. Each number is a miniature of the movie, moving from singing alone, dancing alone, dancing with the wrong person, or dancing to the wrong music to making beautiful music together.

It's the music, the dancing, that saves all this from familiar romantic cliché. As photography documents the Depression, dance countermands it. It offers a lift to those who feel "down in the dumps," a sense of movement and relationship to those who feel hemmed in and isolated, a democratic kind of classiness, available in fantasy if not in fact, to replace stiffly hierarchical notions of class. For all Astaire's associations with "class," in *Shall We Dance* it's the upperclass twits played by Jerome Cowan and William Brisbane who are figures of fun, while Astaire wants to shuffle off his class and "culture" to go down and dirty. This is represented by his shift from classical music and ballet to jazz, tap, and musical comedy, from the grotesque Harriet Hoctor, more gymnast than ballet dancer, to the perfectly fresh Rogers, who finally emerges from behind all the images of her, the replicas that reflect merely her public personality.

This is the culmination of "Shall We Dance," the most novel of all the novel numbers. The song itself is yet another piece of Depression uplift, like "Let Yourself Go" and "Pick Yourself Up." It endorses dancing as a cure for the blues ("Shall we dance, or keep on moping? . . . Shall we give in to despair?"). But lines like "Life is short, / We're growing older" indicate the melancholy that underlies the song itself, which in retrospect we can't help referring to both the collaboration between Astaire and Rogers and the one between George and Ira Gershwin, both of which were coming to an end. The series itself was aging, elements of pathos and loss were creeping in; the audience and the stars were growing restive. After separations and reunions reminiscent of what happens in the films themselves, Astaire and Rogers made three more films together, but the most vibrant days of their partnership ended here. George Gershwin died of a wrongly diagnosed brain tumor in July 1937, two months after *Shall We Dance* was released, and the last song the brothers did together, "Love Is Here to Stay," coalesced everything that was touching and witty about their work in Hollywood. Its wistfulness connects it to "They Can't Take That Away from Me":

> *The radio and the telephone and the movies that we know*
> *May just be passing fancies, and in time may go.*
> *But oh, my dear, our love is here to stay.*

The range of reference is huge, the mood apocalyptic:

> *The Rockies may tumble, Gibraltar may crumble,*
> *They're only made of clay,*
> *But our love is here to stay.*

This was part of the music of time that soothed the spirits of the Depression years: a sense that life was transient, even catastrophic, but that a core of grace, remembrance, and connection survived. The culture of elegance, as represented by Astaire and the Gershwins, was less about the cut of your tie and tails than about the cut of your feelings, the inner radiance that was one true bastion against social suffering. They preserved in wit, rhythm, and fluidity of movement what the Depression almost took away, the high spirits of Americans, young and modern, who had once felt destined to be the heirs and heiresses of all the ages.

Cross-Purposes: The Heyday of Romantic Comedy

But the same culture of elegance is full of anarchic humor as well as grace of feeling. From *The Gay Divorcee* to *Swing Time* and *Shall We Dance*, the Astaire-Rogers series has close links to bedroom farce as well as screwball comedy. Eric Blore in *Shall We Dance* holds a certain room key, "the new key to your happiness," to be bestowed when he can determine who is actually married to whom. *Shall We Dance* belongs at the farcical extreme of what Stanley Cavell calls the "comedies of remarriage," which are among the funniest yet also most adult films ever made in America. The Astaire-Rogers series shares with screwball the basic theme of the war between the sexes, which could be handled only obliquely in the years that followed the tightening of the Production Code in 1934.

The screwball comedies are as buoyantly energetic and nimble as Astaire's tap dancing, and they too, despite their cynical edge, had a core of feeling that was liberating and romantic, though they avoid stereotypical love scenes. One defining feature of these movies is their rhythm, which could be compared to the syncopated beat and smart lyrics of Cole Porter and Gershwin. Frank Capra, who helped invent screwball comedy with *It Happened One Night* (1934), recounted in his autobiography how he had clipped scenes, dropped entrances, avoided dissolves, and speeded up the actors' delivery, giving the film the sort of zip and snap Gershwin was putting into his music. Howard Hawks went even further in *Bringing Up Baby* (1938) and *His Girl Friday* (1940) with overlapping dialogue that was not only more realistic than stage conversation but made for an extraordinary display of speed and energy that more than hinted at sheer libidinal intensity.

Of all kinds of culture discussed here, screwball comedy was the only one that originated entirely in the 1930s, since it was the coming of sound and the arrival in Hollywood of witty, sophisticated, Broadway-trained writers that made it possible. Yet the key directors like Frank Capra and Leo McCarey lacked stage experience and had actually begun their work in the silent film era, cutting their teeth on much more "primitive" and purely visual forms of comedy—Capra with Harry Langdon in films like *The Strong Man*, McCarey, along with George Stevens, in the two-reel silent comedies he crafted for Laurel and Hardy at the Hal Roach factory studio. Screwball preserved much of the anarchic flavor of early slapstick and purely physical comedy, carried along by wildly unpredictable plots but also by characters like Katharine Hepburn's in *Baby*, whose sheer lunacy is the mainspring of the action. Silent comedy endured in the thirties not just in Chaplin, who resisted the conversion to sound, but in the work of vaudeville veterans like W. C. Fields, who perfected his longtime stage routines in his films, Laurel and Hardy, whose feature films never matched the sublime effects of their early silents, and the Marx brothers, who used Harpo as the angelic and anarchic foil to their punning dialogue and malapropisms. Finally, visual comedy survived in the new thirties art of animated cartoons, with which screwball had a secret and profound kinship, as Howard Hawks showed in the cartoon credits for *Bringing Up Baby* and Blake Edwards repeated much later when he made the *Pink Panther* series.

Screwball itself has moments of pure visual storytelling, as when Jean Arthur (in Mitchell Leisen's 1937 film *Easy Living*, scripted by Preston Sturges) is in the Automat, hungry but broke, and suddenly the windows of all the tiny food compartments fly open—a great Depression fantasy with a conservative twist, since all the bums and derelicts come rushing in and wreck the place, as if this were a Laurel and Hardy destruction comedy. Silent touches could be used for indirection as well as intensification, especially since screwball comedies were always in need of oblique metaphors for actual sex. This happens at the end of McCarey's *The Awful Truth* (1937) when both cuckoos on the cuckoo clock finally wind up in the same hole, a discreet fadeout for a movie that, like so many screwball comedies, managed to be at once adult and farcical.

The unusual edge in screwball comedy came not from earlier comedies, not even from the sophisticated "Viennese" comedy that was a specialty of Ernst Lubitsch, but, surprisingly, from the hard-boiled writing that seems remote from comedy. Screwball imported into comedy the kind of unsentimental crispness and cynicism that then belonged to crime stories, detective stories, and tales of newspapermen. The explosive genre films put out by Warner Brothers in the early thirties helped pave the way for the boisterous comedies that came later in the decade; indeed, in their gestural excesses, the mannered performances of Edward G. Robinson, Jimmy Cagney, and Paul Muni in the classic gangster films, performances that exploded with coiled energy, already bordered on comedy. Certainly they anticipated the intensity and speed of the comedies. The consummate hard-boiled professional, Ben Hecht, who wrote gangster films like *Underworld* and *Scarface*, brought the same qualities into his cynical script for *Nothing Sacred* (1937). The sheer complication of plot in detective stories like Dashiell Hammett's first novel, *Red Harvest* (1929), is another element of hard-boiled writing that found its way into screwball comedy, where the stories are invariably full of baroque complications and zany reversals.

It was the runaway success of Hecht and Charles MacArthur's play *The Front Page* that made tough-talking stories about hard-boiled reporters fashionable and spawned dozens of imitations. The ingenious stroke of Howard Hawks in *His Girl Friday* was to change the sex of Hildy, the reporter, and turn the play into a major encounter in the war between the sexes. But this couldn't happen until the arrival of that great figure of the 1930s, the New Woman, including the boldly adventurous Dorothy Thompson or Margaret Bourke-White type, who asserted her professional equality, or the Dorothy Parker/Lillian Hellman type, with their barbed wit and social energy, or other types represented by figures as widely publicized as Clare Boothe Luce, who gained fame as a playwright, and Amelia Earhart, the celebrated aviator who flew solo across the Atlantic but disappeared over the Pacific in 1937. Without Dorothy Thompson there would have been no film stories built around women reporters; without Lillian Hellman, as channeled by Dashiell Hammett, there would have been no *Thin Man*, in which we can see hard-boiled writing actually turning into couples comedy, built around the verbal and even physical battles between two spirited human beings of different sexes, who find it hard to live together or to live apart.

There are, of course, no real women in the classic gangster films. For the gangster, women are a kind of chattel, and fancy women do little more than confirm his swift ascent and social power. For the ethnic gangster the real woman remains his mother, all-nurturing and all-forgiving. But the hard-boiled detective writing of the same period, coming out in magazines like *Black Mask*, took a different tack. There the subservient woman, Madonna or moll, became the difficult woman, the treacherous woman who would reappear as the femme fatale of the films noirs of the 1940s, starting with the Bogart-Huston version of *The Maltese Falcon* in 1941. But the difficult woman of screwball comedy was there first, dominating and disrupting men's lives even more fully than in film noir, where she tends to be less a real person in her own right than a figment of male fantasy, at once feared and desired.

The women in screwball comedies are not usually tough professionals like Rosalind Russell in *His Girl Friday* or working girls like Jean Arthur in *Easy Living*. More often they're the wayward daughters of the very rich, such as Claudette Colbert in *It Happened One Night*, Carole Lombard in *My Man Godfrey*, or Katharine Hepburn in *Bringing Up Baby*. Or they are elegant women like Myrna Loy and Irene Dunne who simply radiate class as well as wit and spirit. The very presence of these actresses, as alternatives to established female roles created by Mary Pickford, Lillian Gish, Marlene Dietrich, or Greta Garbo, helped make screwball comedy the mature and civilized entertainment it became. The same was true of actors beginning with Clark Gable in *It Happened One Night*, William Powell in *The Thin Man*, and Cary Grant, at once suave and radiantly physical, in virtually anything he played in the late 1930s.

Gable in *It Happened One Night* plays a tough-talking newspaper reporter right out of the *Front Page* world, while Colbert is the runaway heiress who has pigheadedly made a bad marriage to the first man she was alone with—"I come from a long line of stubborn idiots." Now, pursued by her wealthy and powerful father, who has always kept her under his control, she is trying to escape. Gable's position in *his* own world has also broken down. He's drunk, has been fired from his job, and is trying to save his pride with a blustering masculinity. Latching on to *her* story might be the scoop that provides him with the way back in. Like so many thirties fables, it's essentially a road movie, but this is a couple on the road, playing out the battle between the sexes and the classes as a way of finding each other's humanity.

Both are on a bus, down among the people, which itself sharply detaches them from their world—the detectives sent by her father can't even imagine she'd be on it—and they have very little money, which connects them to the workaday Depression characters they encounter, who are even more destitute. Compared with Capra's later movies, especially the populist trilogy, which I'll discuss in a later chapter, there's not much direct treatment of the Depression in this film. A mother who hasn't eaten all day keels over from hunger. But some of the little character bits on the bus are fine examples of Capra's common touch and sense of community—Luis Buñuel did something similar twenty years later in a little movie released here as *Mexican Bus Ride*. These touches showing ordinary people amusing themselves provide a good background for the humbling of the two proud central figures. In a surprising twist, at one low point they too find themselves hungry, foraging for vegetables in the fields, as if stripped down to their unaccommodated selves.

As in most screwball comedies, very much like Shakespearean comedy, the give-and-take between them is at the heart of the movie. Gable parodies her sense of superiority, while she softens his crusty masculinity, which has done him precious little good till now. He puts her on a budget, since she seems to be squandering the four dollars she has left. When they must share a single motel room, he famously erects a partition, the "Walls of Jericho," that epitomizes the sex games exacted by the Code. Yet it also ingeniously conveys the pattern of intimacy and separation that makes up the love minuet in these romantic comedies.

It Happened One Night is, in a sense, a movie about trial marriage: the mistaken, fortunately unconsummated marriage she has made to a stuffed shirt of her own class; the marriage of convenience she makes with Gable across the class and emotional barriers of the Walls of Jericho; even the bickering lower-class couple they play when confronted by her father's snooping detectives who are searching for her; and finally the romantic dreams Gable nurtures behind his gruff façade. When they are married for real, we only see the lights in their room go out, a fade-out very much like the oblique ending of *The Awful Truth*.

Despite the instinctive propriety of their directors, Capra and McCarey, both films are loaded with delicious sexual innuendo. The hypocritical prudery demanded by the moral guardians of Hollywood also enabled filmmakers to explore the delicate steps by which unlikely couples got to know each other. The outcome was never in doubt—the Walls of Jericho were always meant to come tumbling down—but a director like Capra could never have done his work with couples popping right into bed together. (It was daring enough to have them sleep in the same room, and to have Gable remove his shirt. His bare chest was said to have set back the sales of men's undershirts for a generation.)

The first screwball comedy was probably *The Taming of the Shrew*, followed by the comedies of Shakespeare's middle period, powered by such forceful women as Rosalind in *As You Like It* and Beatrice in *Much Ado about Nothing.* These plays did not invent the war between the sexes, which goes back at least to Aristophanes, but they provide some of the most bracing examples of verbal fencing as a form of love play between men and women. ("Rapier wit" is an exact description of the duels between Beatrice and Benedick.) *It Happened One Night* has more of a taming motif than many later screwball comedies—Gable's machismo and Capra's traditionalism made this virtually inevitable. (This would be picked up again in later films that paired Hepburn with Tracy, where the independent woman usually gets her comeuppance.) Colbert at times seems only to need the right man to take her in hand. But her role as a screwball heroine is less in her wit than in her spunk and independence, which chastens Gable's ego yet accords with his fantasy of the kind of woman he might run off or settle down with. (This was the Gable who had been paired with Jean Harlow yet also melted the resistance of the prim Mary Astor in the sizzling pre-Code film *Red Dust*, 1932.) But at the end of *It Happened One Night* Colbert again almost makes the mistake of marrying someone from her own class, a playboy who would have reduced her to the society life from which she had fled. Instead, she must break with her class and take off again, away from the big wedding she herself has planned. (Even her father, turned benign, now urges her on, partly because he sees Gable as the kind of man who can take a headstrong woman in hand.)

Frank Capra is anything but an anticapitalist, hostile to the rich, especially at this early stage of his career. His own immigrant origins and bootstrap triumphs had instilled in him a reverence for the American Dream. In *American Madness* (1932), a movie about financial panic, the hero is a sympathetic bank president, played by the trustworthy Walter Huston; here Colbert's father turns from being a figure of control to being a man who quietly abets his daughter's rebellion. Colbert brings out the sheer zaniness of the screwball heroine, which Carole Lombard would perfect in *My Man Godfrey* and *Nothing Sacred* and Katharine Hepburn would take over the top in *Bringing Up Baby*. (This last tale, directed by Howard Hawks at the breakneck speed of high farce, proved too fast and furious for its original audience, and even for some college audiences today.) In these films, rich *men* are stuffy, enervated, or domineering, but wayward heiresses are figures of impulse and irrepressible energy, a genuine life force, often misguided, always disruptive, but embodying a wild freedom. Sheltered by wealth, the heroine's cloistered innocence is itself a quickening tonic, even as it breaks down before a complicated world. It's certainly not hard to see why Depression audiences fell for this kind of character. At a time when so many people's concerns were focused anxiously on matters of necessity, even survival, this heroine spoke to them of mobility, freedom, and irresponsibility as well as class. Her high spirits, silly as they often were, proved a wonderful balm to the low spirits, the uncertainties, of people who felt nervous about the future.

To Gable in *It Happened One Night*, William Powell in *My Man Godfrey*, or Cary Grant in *Bringing Up Baby*, these women are strange, mysterious, and rather dangerous creatures. "What makes dames like you so dizzy?" Gable asks, half entranced, half aghast. The taming of the independent woman is also the socialization of the male animal, not housebroken to domesticity as in the 1950s, but softened by feminine empathy and vitality. In *It Happened One Night* this involves a man of another class, a working stiff; in *Godfrey* a man who merely seems to be lower class but is actually a wayward (once suicidal) son of the rich—the Parks of Boston, whose world is the Brahmin class gently satirized by J. P. Marquand in his first serious novel, *The Late George Apley* (1937). In *Baby* it pulls in a man from another world entirely, a dry intellectual whose sterile routine must be broken up, a timid man, under the thumb of his dried-up fiancée, who needs an infusion of the sap of life.

My Man Godfrey is one of the few screwball comedies that focuses directly on the Depression, but from the point of view of the very rich, not the poor. It begins on a junk heap, an ash pile where the refuse of society huddles together in a shantytown on the banks of New York's East River. The Bullock girls are on a scavenger hunt—for charity, of course—looking to bring back that special creature of the 1930s—the subject of the grand finale of *Gold Diggers of 1933*—a "Forgotten Man." Carole Lombard wins the contest by bringing in William Powell, a prince down in the muck, living the life of a frog. Feeling a touch of social responsibility—like her mother, Lombard wants to have a "protégé"—the Bullock family hires him as its butler. (Here the film anticipates the sublime social comedy between masters and servants that Jean Renoir would bring to the screen in 1939 with *The Rules of the Game*.)

The Bullocks themselves embody another popular motif of the 1930s, the zany family, whose members live together in perfect chaos, creatures of nature and sheer impulse. (One of the most popular plays of the decade was *You Can't Take It with You*, by George S. Kaufman and Moss Hart, which Capra would film in 1938.) Both John Steinbeck and William Saroyan, young California writers, made a specialty of chronicling such "natural" communities, idealizing people who lived outside the rigid social boundaries that, in any case, had been badly frayed by the Depression. The zany family, living on impulse, turns this theme into farce. "Hasn't anyone ever told you about certain . . . proprieties?" Powell asks Lombard. Himself born to wealthy people who "were never educated to face life," he brings both sanity and delicacy into the family, while instructing its members in a few of the realities of the Depression. Eventually, by investing some of their money on his own, he even saves them from financial ruin. This is much appreciated by the sorely tried paterfamilias, played by the great character actor Eugene Pallette (the "human bullfrog," as they called him then), who, along with the hard-boiled, wise-cracking maid, gets off some of the best lines at the expense of his wife and daughters: "This family doesn't need any stimulants," he says. And later, "If I do end up in jail, it will be the first peace I've had in twenty years." (Pallette would brilliantly reprise this role of the much put-upon patriarch a few years later in Preston Sturges's *The Lady Eve*.)

With nothing whatever to do, the women in this family are not merely eccentric and willful but infantilized. The Harvard-educated Godfrey, on the other hand, has belatedly discovered a sense of purpose. Having been saved from despair by the community of the outcasts on the shores of the river, one of the Hooverville encampments on the fringe of so many American towns and cities, he proceeds to rescue them as well by putting them to work. "The only difference between a derelict and a man is a job," he's learned. Now he gets one of his old school friends to help turn the shantytown into a theme park, a nightclub called The Dump, where derelicts can work, where the rich can patronize the poor and have fun too. They'll put in a dock for the yachting trade, and Godfrey's office is just where his little hovel once was, with a picturesque view of the Queensboro Bridge through the window. In fact, it was the neon sign of The Dump we saw behind the opening credits. The movie has come full circle. If some movie studios could turn the Depression into lucrative entertainment, why couldn't the able-bodied men in these wretched Hoovervilles also make some money off it?

This is a silly ending, though there was nothing wrong with putting people to work. Hollywood's "solutions" to the Depression, even when tossed out tongue-in-cheek, were always an embarrassment. The redemption of both the forgotten men and the spoiled children of the rich is less interesting than the idea of putting them in the same movie, a farcical anticipation of *Dead End*, which juxtaposed the rich and the poor on the same riverfront. (It was based on the actual construction in 1931 of a luxurious Sutton Place building, River House, in the midst of a notorious slum.) *My Man Godfrey* is a movie whose exuberant high spirits were a better antidote to the Depression than all the reminders of the nightclub world of the 1920s, which still lived in the imagination of Astaire, Irving Berlin, and Cole Porter but could scarcely be touted as a solution to the unemployment problem.

Hard-Boiled Love

If high spirits were what the Depression needed, at least occasionally, there was never a more manically high-spirited movie than Howard Hawks's *Bringing Up Baby*, perhaps the definitive 1930s version of the daffy rich. The film failed with its original audience but has since become a favorite of film buffs and film scholars alike, in part because it's such a cunningly constructed Freudian farce, with every detail contributing perfectly to the larger effect, which is very close to sheer madness. Hawks and his screenwriter, Dudley Nichols, were masterful at teasing and circumventing the Hollywood censors; there's hardly a scene in *Bringing Up Baby*, beginning with Cary Grant's conversation with his prudish fiancée, Miss Swallow, that isn't full of double entendres, for this film is largely about libido itself, the usually unspoken but always implied energy that drives screwball comedy. Even more than the Astaire-Rogers films, it provides a lesson in how to make a movie about sex with no actual sex in it.

Hawks was the only one of the great male action directors who was also able to create strong, independent women and give them parity with men. As a woman who was clearly both strong-willed and distinctly upper class, Katharine Hepburn was a problematic actress for a period that also loved the unspoiled but cloying innocence of Shirley Temple and Deanna Durbin. She was at her best in roles crafted especially for

her, as in *Stage Door*, but the commercial failure of *Bringing Up Baby* ended
her long career with RKO. (She would recoup almost immediately with
Holiday, *The Philadelphia Story*, and then her long collaboration with Spencer Tracy, which revived the "taming" motif that had been muted by the
intuitive feminism of the late 1930s.) Vibrant but mannered, supremely
confident in her athletic body and Brahmin speech patterns, radiating a cultivation that was light-years away from mass taste, the tomboyish Hepburn
wasn't an actress you'd immediately cast as a sex object. But this was exactly
what the conventions of screwball comedy enabled Hawks and Nichols to
bring off. Compared with Miss Swallow, who won't allow Grant to take
time off for a honeymoon, and for whom marriage will be just an extension of their scientific work on prehistoric fossils, Hepburn represents a life
of giddiness and distraction, lived entirely on whim and caprice, the kind of
thing the rich can afford more easily than anyone else.

Never has a film put anti-intellectualism to better use, not even in
Hawks's own later farce *Ball of Fire* (1941), about a nest of eggheads. We
meet Grant in *Bringing Up Baby* as an researcher named David, the cartoon of a man of science, devoting his life to reassembling the bones of
a dinosaur. Despite his halfhearted protests, his fiancée insists that their
marriage will be all business—no babies, no honeymoon, no hanky-
panky: the dinosaur will be their baby. By thoroughly disrupting his life
with adventures too far-fetched to recount here, Susan (Hepburn) will
enable him to put flesh on those ancient dry bones. With sublime lunacy,
she compromises him in every way, breaking down his dignity with her
daffiness as an instinctive method of opening him up. In place of his dinosaur bones she brings "Baby," a pet leopard, into his life, but along the way
they must also deal with another leopard, Baby's savage but almost indistinguishable double, as if to remind us that such an anarchic life force can
be threatening and destructive as well as life-enhancing. Yet Hepburn too
is Baby; for David she is an exotic species from a different world.

Though *Bringing Up Baby*, like most screwball comedies, is set among
the careless rich, many of its metaphors—as befits its Freudian theme—
are drawn from the animal world. The film is a burlesque version of *Civilization and Its Discontents*, published only a few years earlier. But where
Freud's book finally insists that renunciation is the price we pay for creating culture, *Bringing Up Baby* reminds us that there *are* leopards in civilized Connecticut, both friendly and terrible; we must come to terms

with the animal core of our own nature. The leopards are always escaping, and once they do they're hard to tell from one another. Somehow, the fearless Hepburn, sheltered by unshakable innocence and determination, manages (without realizing it) to collar and haul in even the fierce one. When the leopard is on the roof, she and Grant must try to lure it down by singing "I can't give you anything but love, Ba-by," an inspired bit of lunacy, especially since the house belongs to the movie's parody of a Viennese shrink. His all-purpose wisdom is that the "the love impulse in man frequently reveals itself in terms of conflict," a message useless in his hands but an exact description of everything else in the movie, down to its very rhythm.

For four-eyed David, lost in his work, beaten down by his fiancée, Susan and her leopard represent the return of the repressed, just as Connecticut (as the philosopher Stanley Cavell has shown in *Pursuits of Happiness*) is like the garden or forest world of Shakespearean comedy, to which we must flee or repair so as to renew our connection with nature, including our own. This is the place where the constraints of the city, the professional life, the superego, are relaxed or suspended. This is the same Connecticut where Nathanael West's advice columnist, Miss Lonelyhearts, proved impervious to the restorative powers of pastoral, which simply deepened his depression. This is where David must be stripped of his glasses, his clothes, his sexual identity. Forced to wear a woman's dressing gown, he announces to Susan's aunt that he has "gone gay." When asked "Who are you?" he answers frankly, "I don't know. I'm not quite myself today." Among the vertiginous complications, he assumes the mock identity of a big-game hunter under the suggestive name of "Mr. Bones," which also parodies his search for the one bone that will complete his dinosaur.

Though David is accidentally cast in the role of the hunter, it's actually he who's being hunted, for this imaginary Connecticut is also a playground of the rich, one of whose pastimes is big-game hunting. He meets a "real" hunter, Major Applegate, played in milquetoast fashion by Charlie Ruggles, who insists "there aren't any leopards in Connecticut," though when the major does see one, too late, he feels rather naked without his gun. These scenes include a great deal of sexual innuendo about the mating calls of loons as well as leopards. With his expert imitations, the major manages to excite not only the loons and leopards but Susan's dowager aunt. He is a beguiling parody of Hemingway-style masculinity, but also a comic affirmation of the universality of the mating instinct, even in some counterfeit forms.

From the male viewpoint, screwball comedy gives us the woman as predator, chasing the man until he catches her. She's seen as closer to nature and therefore better able to subdue it. This is also where screwball comes closest to hard-boiled writing. If *Bringing Up Baby* is a cartoon version of *Civilization and Its Discontents*, its basic story—a man gets entangled with a woman who completely overturns his way of life—is also a benign rewriting of James M. Cain's first novel, *The Postman Always Rings Twice* (1934). Along with Hammett's *The Maltese Falcon*, it was the most frequently filmed and widely imitated work of tough-guy fiction in the 1930s. (It's been filmed at least four times, including Luchino Visconti's unauthorized *Ossessione*, a wartime film that helped kick off Italian neo-realism.) Later pulp novelists and noir directors took from Cain's novel the brooding male vision of love and passion as an ineluctable fatality; screwball comedy is its dizzy twin. Compared with the treacherous femmes fatales of many 1940s movies, the Cora of *Postman* is scarcely a bad woman, though she pushes a scheme to kill her Greek husband so she can live freely and comfortably with her young lover. Her marriage to the innocuous Nick, who owns a roadside diner in Glendale, twenty miles from Los Angeles, is based on her desperate need for respectability and security. (This is, after all, a Depression novel.) The Greek physically repels her—a strong racial element enters here—and when a drifter named Frank Chambers comes along, the chemistry is instantaneous, especially for him. "Then I saw her," he tells us on the third page, assuming we'll understand how this first look leads inescapably—as it will in later Cain novels like *Double Indemnity*—to adultery, murder, mutual betrayal, and inevitable exposure and punishment. Cain was virtually the creator of the modern pulp tale of fatal passion; the same year his book appeared, screwball directors began unwittingly to transfer its vision into comedy.

Like *It Happened One Night*, *Postman* is a road story, but with an inverted plot. It's a road novel in reverse: the fatal history of a drifter who settles in. Frank Chambers has been on the road his whole adult life: he's comfortable living on the bum, hitchhiking around, riding the freights, seeing every town in the American West. He has occasionally gotten into trouble, but nothing compared with what happens when, after first seeing Cora, he accepts the job her husband thrusts upon him. The first moment Nick is gone, they couple like wild beasts. "Bite me! Bite me!" she says,[13] and he bites her so hard he draws blood and her lips are bruised for days. Sexual excitement for them is always linked with acts of violence. After they fail in their first murder attempt, Frank tries to get her to run off with him. "Just you and me and the road, Cora," he says, and for a brief time she shares his romantic fantasy. But she feels demeaned and humiliated by what the road represents: instability, beggary, the loss of what little social status she enjoyed. Unlike Claudette Colbert in *It Happened One Night*, she feels ashamed to be hitchhiking, feels like a bum, a gypsy.

As she returns home, he makes the first of several attempts to escape, only to be drawn back into her orbit, and finally into murdering her husband, which leads to their best sex. What pulls him each time, whatever his excuses, is the sheer animal attraction, perhaps combined with some irresistibly suicidal impulse. Frank sees her as some kind of wildcat, and since he's the one who tells the story—the novel is cast as his death-house confession—this image dominates the book. From the first moment he sees her, she's "a cougar," a "hell cat." Later, when she's away visiting her sick mother, he has a weeklong interlude with a woman who actually captures and trains wild cats, including tigers and jaguars, and this comes to light when she sends him one of her puma cubs. An overly curious cat had been electrocuted when they first tried to kill her husband. "Ain't that funny," Cora laughs, "how unlucky cats are for you?" (170).

Incensed by his infidelity, Cora herself has a different vision of their relationship. While they were simply together they were way up high: "We were up on a mountain" (136). But the murder, the insurance money, the legal maneuvering, even the way they seem to get away with it—all this leaves them suspicious of each other, hateful, yet inseparably bound by mutual distrust. Each feels the other will turn them in. It's a caricature of their once irresistible attraction, with fear taking the place of love. Fate still binds them, but now he realizes, "We're chained to each other, Cora. We thought we were on top of the mountain. That wasn't it. It's on top of us, and that's where it's been ever since that night" (175). This too is an illusion, for love binds them as well. In the final irony, he saves her life but is convicted of murder after she dies in a road accident—an accident very much like the one they faked to kill her husband. In the book's stormy romanticism, their love triumphs over hatred and fear, though society exacts its price for their crime. Their fate was sealed the moment they met.

This tawdry Wagnerian *Liebestod*, set in the sordid roadside world of California noir, would seem to take us a thousand miles from the culture of elegance. Yet that culture, for all its lighthearted wit and bubbly charm, is strongly grounded, like most comedy, from Aristophanes and Shakespeare, in the physical facts of our nature. The partly metaphorical hellcats and jaguars of *Postman* play the same role as the leopards in *Baby*. They're identified with the women in these stories, but they also represent a world of nature, thrilling yet dangerous, that we can never finally deny or escape. Just as the corrupt world of hard-boiled writing is grounded in animal attraction and physical force, so the worldly cynicism and satire of screwball comedy are linked with strong sexual feelings, however obliquely expressed. These currents of sexual energy are sublimated into a pas de deux of mobile, civilized wit. What Astaire and Rogers transpose into dance, what Gershwin and Cole Porter transform into verbal wit and melodic flow, screwball comedy translates into furious verbal and physical energy, propulsive in its intensity. Had this positive energy been harnessed to some larger social purpose, as the New Deal hoped to do, it might have brought the Depression to a swift end. Expressed as fantasy, it merely made those difficult years more palatable, and left us with many works that testify to the unquenchably vital spirit of those who lived through them.

Class for the Masses:
ELEGANCE DEMOCRATIZED

Mr. Lucky: The Art of Cary Grant

THE CULTURE OF ELEGANCE embraced so much of thirties entertainment that it would be hard to find its outer limits. But it's not at all difficult to locate its center: in the dancing and singing of Astaire and Rogers, the sophisticated songs of Cole Porter, the witty lyrics of Ira Gershwin and Larry Hart, the music and artistic personality of Duke Ellington, the wit and grace of innumerable Deco designers, and, perhaps above all, in the brisk energy and style of

Cary Grant, who became a star in the course of the decade. He was born Archibald Alexander Leach in 1904 to a lower middle-class family in Bristol, in the west of England. One or both of his parents may have been part Jewish; at least he thought so, since they had him circumcised. His father, who had a weakness for the bottle, was a presser in the garment industry. His mother disappeared from his life—into a mental institution, as he discovered much later—when young Archie was nine; it was twenty years before he saw her again. By the age of fourteen he had run off to join a troupe of acrobats, and at sixteen he landed in New York, where he slowly built a stage career. After 1932 he appeared in more than two dozen relatively undistinguished film roles. Along the way he changed his name and lost much of his accent without finding the screen character he would later make completely his own. His studio, Paramount, had no idea how to use him except as a gorgeous hunk with a rather passive appeal to sexually aggressive women like Mae West and Marlene Dietrich. In movies like *She Done Him Wrong* and *I'm No Angel*, dominated by West, we search in vain for the spunky, devil-may-care figure who would later prove so resilient, so irresistible to women and men alike. When his contract ran out in 1937, he went off on his own, one of the first major stars to go independent. From that point on, his career took off. The later Grant—masculine without being brutal, funny without resorting to mockery, socially poised without an ounce of superiority, at times even sexually ambiguous—would become a dominant screen presence of the late 1930s, initiating a career that, like Fred Astaire's and Duke Ellington's, would transmit the spirit of Depression elegance through the next three decades.

Paradoxically, the secret of Grant's success as a role model for men and a dream lover for women was perhaps less his man-of-the-world urbanity than some mysterious quality of coiled ease and availability. He behaved like a man with a great deal in reserve, including a past that was hard to fathom. These were qualities few would attribute to suave leading men like William Powell, Melvyn Douglas, or even the almost magically gifted but intangible Astaire, who, despite his ordinary midwestern background, seemed like another order of being entirely. Grant's audience could identify with him in a way that was closest to a performer at the other end of the social spectrum, the single most popular entertainer of the 1930s, Bing Crosby, whose laid-back personality, also created out of whole cloth, was that of the guy next door. Grant remained indelibly Grant in screwball comedies, adventure stories like *Gunga Din* and *Only Angels Have Wings*, and Hitchcock thrillers like *Suspicion*, the sublime *Notorious*, *To Catch a Thief*, and the half-comic *North by Northwest*—the precursor of the James Bond movies, in which Sean Connery does a Scotsman's imitation of Cary Grant, as Tony Curtis did an outright send-up in *Some Like It Hot*. In a similar manner, Crosby's preternatural cool and ordinary-guy charm worked well for him on radio, through innumerable movies (most of them forgettable), and in an immense variety of popular songs in which his phrasing and musicianship, to say nothing of his mellow baritone, are both inviting and impeccable. Crosby's breezy plain-man persona, which he put together well past the beginning of his career, showed how elegance could be democratized for the decade of the common man; Grant, in a different way, went on to prove his point.

The best writing on Grant tries to puzzle out his gift as a performer but also to bridge the gap between his humble origins and the person he became. Though neither he nor the characters he played were the least bit introspective, he himself was frank about his self-invention. In 1981 he told a reporter, "I don't know that I've any style at all. . . . I pretended to be somebody I wanted to be and I finally became that person. Or he became me."[1] But like Charlie Chaplin, who was somehow nourished by the appalling circumstances of his Dickensian childhood, including the breakdown of *his* mother, Grant never quite forgot the person he had been, the world he had gotten away from. He played a Cockney, opposite Katharine Hepburn, in George Cukor's disastrous *Sylvia Scarlett* (1935) and again in *Gunga Din* (1939), but after years of fame, in the early 1940s, he daringly took on two more serious Cockney roles, as a crooked gambler in *Mr. Lucky* (1943) and a footloose wastrel who returns home to care for his dying mother in *None But the Lonely Heart* (1944), a property he bought and persuaded his friend Clifford Odets to adapt and direct.* Once we notice Grant's impulse to self-exposure (including his on-screen references to Archie Leach), it helps explain the unexpected range of his more characteristic roles: the errant upper-class husband in *The Awful Truth*,

* Taken from a best-selling novel by the Welsh writer Richard Llewellyn, the story reverses the direction of Odets's best-known play, *Awake and Sing!*, where a young man, conveying the rebellious spirit of his generation, declares his independence from his cautious, controlling mother.

My Favorite Wife, and *The Philadelphia Story*; the much put-upon, nerdy scientist of *Bringing Up Baby*; the self-made man who attracts Katharine Hepburn in *Holiday*; the mind-spinningly manipulative newspaper editor and ex-husband in *His Girl Friday*; and finally the near-sinister figures he played with fiery brilliance for Hitchcock in *Suspicion* and *Notorious*.

As a key to his appeal, David Thomson pinpoints the ambiguity of his persona rather than his fabled charm and sophistication: "He can be attractive and unattractive simultaneously; there is a light and dark side to him but, whichever is dominant, the other creeps into view."[2] This is especially true in the sinister roles. Spitting out bitter words full of accusation and unspoken fury, tortured by jealousy, he nearly destroys Ingrid Bergman in *Notorious*, though he loves her. Pauline Kael puts this ambiguity differently, and more pungently, in her brilliant 1975 *New Yorker* profile: "Cary Grant's romantic elegance is wrapped around the resilient, tough core of a mutt, and Americans dream of thoroughbreds while identifying with mutts. So do moviegoers the world over." In his comic performances, Grant added brash energy and exuberance to a tumbler's physical dexterity; the lightning speed of his dialogue is anything but upper class. Kael adds, "The greatest movie stars have not been highborn; they have been strong-willed (often deprived) kids who came to embody their own dreams, and the public's."[3] Embodying dreams was especially important for Depression audiences, since the world around them held little promise.

Both Kael and Richard Schickel, Grant's biographer, point out that Grant does not steal scenes, even where he easily could. Instead, like Astaire, he invariably makes his costars look good. Watching *The Philadelphia Story* again recently, I was impressed by how confidently Grant plays straight man to the more baroque performances by Katharine Hepburn and Jimmy Stewart, conveying the inner security of a man who upsets every applecart, who is not above playing dirty tricks to win back his former wife on the eve of her marriage to another man. There is a mischievous quality in Grant that plays well against solid, reliable lunkheads like Ralph Bellamy in *The Awful Truth* and *His Girl Friday*. The dangerous glint in his eye, the ironic catch in his voice, gives promise of unpredictable adventures that the Bellamy character could never match. Like Hepburn herself in *Bringing Up Baby*, he represents what Robin Wood once called "the lure of irresponsibility," the temptations of freedom. Choosing Grant means choosing life itself, with all its charms, surprises, and pitfalls.

The Philadelphia Story is an inversion of *It Happened One Night,* since Grant's rival, played by John Howard, was once a family retainer while Grant is to the manner born. The movie's blatant snobbery gives evidence of screwball in decline, but there is no trace of snobbery in Grant's performance, just a sense of ease and superiority, whatever his human flaws. (He's loved, of course, and welcomed back by the servants on Hepburn's estate, who have no liking for the parvenu.) No patrician ever seemed more like a man of the people. As Schickel remarks, "there was always a democratic touch of common humanity in his playboys, a touch of natural good breeding in his more raffish roles" (30). This was how Grant's persona cut across the different roles he played, and this is why Depression audiences cottoned to him. His robust physicality radiated energy and movement, as did his machine-gun delivery of clipped yet crackling dialogue. He offers not chic and class but the sap of life. Grant and Hepburn made the war between the sexes seem like more fun than anyone since Shakespeare's lovers. Her new love, awed by his posh surroundings, has put Hepburn on a pedestal; Grant brings her down and allows her to be spontaneous, girlish, uninhibited. Grant humanized elegance and made it accessible. This made his upper-class role in *The Philadelphia Story* continuous with the outsider of humble origin that he played in Philip Barry's earlier *Holiday,* where, as Schickel remarks, "for the first time he was a surrogate for his democratic audience out there in the theatre, an upscale exemplar of their values" (86).

Placing Bing Crosby

If Fred Astaire and Cole Porter turned carefree elegance into art and Cary Grant lent it an aura that made it hard to resist, Bing Crosby made it seem almost too casual for either art or mystery. Born in Tacoma, Washington, in 1903 to a large Catholic family of Irish and British origins, he was an indifferent student who simply drifted into music, first locally, then in the Los Angeles area, where he and his partner, Al Rinker, were quickly discovered by Paul Whiteman, the self-proclaimed "King of Jazz." Forming a trio, the Rhythm Boys, with Harry Barris, who wrote some of Crosby's best early songs, they went national with Whiteman's jazz orchestra. Crosby performed with some of Whiteman's best players, including Bix

Beiderbecke, but he also developed a reputation for hard drinking, gambling, womanizing, and missing performances. Some dates he skipped so that he could hear musicians he admired, especially Louis Armstrong. At one point he landed in jail for weeks for drunken driving. These twenties roots in jazz and low company he never quite put behind him, though he later developed the white-bread image of a family man, a regular guy. His best biographer, Gary Giddins, attributes his shift to the populist mood of the Depression, the need to create a plain-man image and a popular music that embraced everyone. "Bing blossomed in the process," he says. "His own moralistic streak emboldened him as an actor and personality. What his singing forfeited in muscularity, it gained in poignancy." Giddins compares Bing's metamorphosis to that of Charlie Chaplin, "who reduced his Tramp's original sadistic streak in favor of a pathos that afforded him far greater nuance. Like Charlie, Bing never totally abandoned his scampish irreverence."[4] Though Cary Grant would scarcely pass for ordinary, this scampish irreverence also fed the vitality and unpredictability he brought to his best work.

Just as Bing tamped down the jazz beat of his early music, he dumped his partners in 1931 after years of friendship, when he had the chance to go off on his own. Repeatedly reinventing himself, he never looked back. Some of this was the work of his record producer, Jack Kapp, who insisted that he broaden his repertoire and go mainstream, with everything from Christmas music, which Bing resisted, to Hawaiian songs, which set off a Hawaiian craze in Southern California. With more number one hits than any other singer, Crosby ruled the charts from 1934 to 1954, influencing nearly every male vocalist who came after him. Many who preceded him were schooled in operetta or were shouters and belters who had come up through vaudeville and could project to the farthest balcony. Some of them, like Al Jolson, he deeply admired, though he went his own way. In much the way FDR used his fireside chats, Bing was one of the first to understand that the microphone enabled him to turn each song into intimate drama and emotionally heightened conversation. Like FDR too, like Jack Benny and Fred Allen, he was born for radio, where his weekly show, first live, then taped, enjoyed many years of success. His gifts included a rich baritone with a range of perhaps two and a half octaves, a genuine respect for the words and mood of a song, an unerring instinct for phrasing, tempo, and clean articulation, for which he credited his Jesuit training, and, above all, a variety of material that no other singer could match. Even as he filtered his "hot" early sound out of his style, its residue gave freshness and energy to his interpretation of otherwise buttoned-down music. In his definitive book *Jazz Singing*, Will Friedwald couples him with the artist he most admired, Louis Armstrong, as joint creators of modern American pop music. "We have to wait for Crosby," he says, "for the perfect and seamless infiltration of genuine jazz into mass-market music, but Jolson hints at what that might sound like."[5] Armstrong said that Crosby's voice was "like gold being poured out of a cup." Crosby in turn said of Armstrong that "he is the beginning and the end of music in America."[6]

All of this was lost on me when I was growing up in the 1950s. Then Crosby's crooning seemed bland and disengaged, the hit parade personified. The arrival of the Age of Rock made Bing seem lazy, old-fashioned, out of synch. Friedwald and Giddins have actually done a salvage job on a singer who, after a million replays of "White Christmas" and "Silent Night," not only had become undervalued but, as an artist, was in danger of being forgotten, though not by his popular audience, which was rapidly aging. One way to recapture Crosby in his prime is through Friedwald's (and Tony Natali's) discerning four-disc compilation *Bing! His Legendary Years, 1931–1957* (1993). It leaves out a great deal, including his early jazz recordings with Whiteman, which can be sampled on albums like *Bix 'n' Bing*, where his light voice and rhythmic energy make for a striking contrast to his mature singing. Vocalists did not yet front for orchestras in the 1920s, and Bing is not a full soloist in these numbers. His voice is part of a blend of instruments, and he often arrives very late in a number, almost like a verbal afterthought, some icing on the cake of an already established tune or rhythm. Some of the performances are wonderful, full of relaxed sexual nuance, including "You Took Advantage of Me," "That's My Weakness Now," and "Because My Baby Don't Mean Maybe Now." But the relentless Dixieland bounce makes the songs seem as dated as the recording techniques. The lyrics border on the insignificant and leave little room for personal expression, though a great deal of room for *musical* expression, especially from Bix's horn and Bing's voice, whenever they can break free for a moment. The generic character of these performances changes strikingly with Bing's solo work beginning in 1931, though echoes of their jaunty rhythm survive and sometimes resurface.

In the light of Crosby's later image as a mainstream crooner, what strikes us most in the early work he made on his own are the love songs—really loss-of-love songs—and the overt Depression material. These two strains are not always easy to distinguish. Close to half the numbers on the first disc of the Friedwald selection are songs of romantic misunderstanding, conflict, and thwarted longing. Sometimes their titles alone tell us all we need to know: "I Apologize," "Just One More Chance," "I'm Through with Love." Crosby had a grown-up's aversion to straightforward love songs—an aversion to cliché, really—but these songs, mainly recorded near the beginning of his solo career, are different, all about might-have-been and still-might-be, about betrayal, repentance, asking forgiveness. "Forgive, forget, won't you try," he pleads ("At Your Command"). "I'm sorry, so sorry, what more can I say?" he begins plaintively in "I Apologize." With a surge of feeling, he appeals to a memory of love to overcome the pain of betrayal: "Don't say that you forgot the love we knew; / After all we were *more* than friends." In some songs the singer vows to change his ways; in the haunting "Two Cigarettes in the Dark" the woman has turned to another man. For those of us who grew up with the laid-back Bing, the essence of cool, the emotional temperature of these somehow unsentimental songs comes as a surprise. Their adult frankness creates the aural equivalent of the unbuttoned pre-Code movies of the early 1930s, but the songs may also remind us of the misunderstandings and mismatched relationships that would come with screwball comedy. Some of the sources of Crosby's feeling for this material were no doubt personal. He married his first wife, Dixie Lee, in 1930; six months later she fled to Mexico, announcing publicly that she planned to file for divorce. They were reconciled, and she gradually weaned him from his bachelor ways, especially his alcoholism, laying the foundation for his new personality as an American everyman, an ordinary Joe and good family man. But in these first years of his marriage the reticent Bing, often seen as emotionally closed off, gave voice to heartache with the masculine torch song.

Yet these songs also have a larger cultural resonance, for Bing recorded them at the low point of the Depression in 1931–32, and they spoke for the nation's mood as much as for his own. This becomes almost explicit in his fiercely romantic recording of "Dancing in the Dark" (1931), from Arthur Schwartz and Howard Dietz's revue (written for Fred and

Adele Astaire—her last show) *The Band Wagon*. This song has often been performed as if it were simply about dancing, as Sinatra, of all people, recorded it in 1958. But Crosby gave full play to its darker shadings. His version encompasses, yet goes beyond, the dance floor; vividly, it evokes a sense of the darkness surrounding our lives. Working on many levels, it could refer just as easily to the darkened ballroom, our own darkest feelings, the existential limits of the human condition, or the ongoing troubles of the Depression.

> *Dancing in the dark, till the tune ends,*
> *We're dancing in the dark and it soon ends,*
> *We're waltzing in the wonder of why we're here,*
> *Time hurries by, we're here . . . and gone;*
>
> *Looking for the light of a new love,*
> *To brighten up the night, I have you love,*
> *And we can face the music together,*
> *Dancing in the dark.*

The range of emotion that Crosby brought to this song, the mixture of melancholy and hope, could not have been better keyed to the moment. The feeling is not simply in the lyric but in the surging melody that enforces the rhyme of "waltzing in the wonder of *why* we're here" with "time hurries *by*, we're here," followed, after a pause, by the inexorable "and gone." The idea that "we can face the music together" became a keystone of the New Deal as well as a pulsing antidote to self-indulgent romantic despair. Bing became master of flowing legato and lyricism he brought to perfection in works like his signature piece, "When the Blue of the Night (Meets the Gold of the Day)," his incomparable rendition of Hoagy Carmichael's "Stardust," and the superb "Red Sails in the Sunset," songs full of longing tinged with restrained melancholy.

Later, during the more forward-looking years after 1935, when he recorded Depression numbers, they tended to be songs of reassurance like "Pennies from Heaven" (1936) and "I've Got a Pocketful of Dreams" (1938). Gary Giddins suggests that he did as much to lift the country's morale as that other radio star, FDR. These numbers, trying hard to be carefree, were in striking contrast to the great version of "Brother, Can

You Spare a Dime?" by Yip Harburg and Jay Gorney, which Crosby recorded shortly before FDR was elected in 1932. Few popular standards can boast the emotional complexity of this song, especially in Crosby's full-bodied interpretation, which runs the gamut from manly pride and the memories of wartime camaraderie to protest, pathos, and a demand for simple human acknowledgment. The introductory verse evokes the promise of the American Dream; the chorus that follows describes both its accomplishments and its betrayal. "Spare a dime" really means "look at me," remember what I've done and see what I've come to now. The speaker is the generalized everyman of proletarian writing, usually a vague construct but here infused with authentic passion. He's the worker who has built railroads, built factories and skyscrapers, and slogged through the European mud, only to become the proverbial "forgotten man" who would soon help elect FDR. He's the American Dream turned nightmare, the ordinary guy now homeless and jobless. He feels baffled, thwarted, undermined. He speaks for the wounded and the vulnerable, and asks the listener to notice and take responsibility. There's nothing more radical in the song than an appeal for human community, for facing the music together, as in the dark love song of the preceding year, "Dancing in the Dark."

By the time Crosby came to make the film *Pennies from Heaven* in 1936, the Depression had lasted for more than six years, the New Deal for three. The title song, which became as much an anthem of the times as "Brother, Can You Spare a Dime?," takes account of a world of troubles as it sets out to assuage them. Hard times are as inevitable as bad weather, but so is the deep American faith that they will pass, that good times will come around again, as if there were something providential in such reverses of fortune. ("If you want the things you love, you must have showers.") The dreamlike character of this "solution" becomes explicit in later songs like "Wrap Your Troubles in Dreams" and "I've Got a Pocketful of Dreams." Never have questionable ideas been wrapped in such plangent lyrical reassurance, as wish-fulfillment touches the sublime. Thanks to Dennis Potter many years later, "Pennies from Heaven" came to stand for the whole magical dreamworld of popular music as a refuge from shabby actualities. As Potter saw it, the radio, the jukebox, and the gramophone offered the compensations of fantasy to lonely people with deadening jobs or loveless lives, to people who were deprived or emotionally starved. Bing Crosby and his lyricist, Johnny Burke,[7] were not metaphysicians like Potter, but they knew what these later, more hopeful years of the Depression needed. With the help of the composer Arthur Johnston, who had written "Just One More Chance," they gave it exquisite expression in "Pennies from Heaven."

Part of the genius of Bing's rendition is the narrative conviction he brings to the eight-line verse, which many performers drop in their rush to the melodic chorus. In the rueful love songs of the early thirties, Bing had learned to turn a single song into a highly compressed drama, using the opening verse to set the scene. Here the scene shifts back to ancient times, utopian and carefree, when "no one appreciated a sky that was always blue; / And no one congratulated a sun that was always new." Without occasional trouble, he says, we would never appreciate the good things in life. "That's what storms are made for / And you shouldn't be afraid for . . ." This flows directly into the chorus, where hard times become like life-giving rain, the April showers that bring May flowers. Not until Gene Kelly danced his way through "Singin' in the Rain" would any performer bring such sunny conviction to bad weather. "Pennies from Heaven" is a perfect antidote to the blues because Crosby's own weathered voice conveys how threatening they are and how their clouds can blot out the sky. The wistful sadness of the love songs has not quite gone away. "Pennies from Heaven" makes cockeyed optimism plausible by acknowledging the stormy troubles it tries to deny.

"Wrap Your Troubles in Dreams" offers more of the same, a simple idea wrapped in an irresistible melody. ("When skies are cloudy and gray, / They're only gray for a day, / So wrap your troubles in dreams, / And dream your troubles away.") And "I've Got a Pocketful of Dreams" adds a bouncy, syncopated lilt that melodically drives home its own message, portraying the singer as a carefree child of nature, unspoiled by money or the things it can buy. ("*I'm* no millionaire / But I'm *not* the type to care / 'Cause I've *got* a pocketful of dreams.") This is the high-spirited voice of the happy-go-lucky poor, the salt of the earth whose lives would fill out the work of William Saroyan, Henry Miller, and the early, earthy John Steinbeck. Songs like these made Crosby one of the voices of the Depression in a different key from the downbeat love songs or from "Brother, Can You Spare Dime?," which belong to a more despairing phase of the decade, before the New Deal allowed most Americans a more hopeful outlook and before Crosby himself tried to become the universal bard, the voice of everyman, singing songs that ordinary people felt they could sing just as well. The swing era had begun, and Crosby, though he had toned down his hot rhythm, was now part of its field of positive energy.

The Swing Era

Like many musical figures with roots in the 1920s, including Louis Armstrong and Duke Ellington, Crosby never fully identified himself with the swing era, though in songs like Johnny Mercer's witty, tongue-twisting "Bob White (Whatcha Gonna Swing Tonight?)" (1937), a very lively duet with Connie Boswell, he showed his jazz chops and demonstrated that he could swing as well as anyone. Swing began its roughly ten-year run with Benny Goodman's celebrated performance at the Palomar Ballroom in Los Angeles on August 21, 1935. Coming at the end of a poorly received tour for Goodman and his orchestra, it kicked off one of the periodic sensations that marked each wave of youth culture in twentieth-century America. The swing craze seemed to come out of nowhere, yet like so many other cultural phenomena of the 1930s, it had its own deep roots in the boom decade. Fletcher Henderson, a gifted black musician and arranger from Georgia, had created the first big jazz band in 1923, soon followed by Duke Ellington, whose engagement at the Cotton Club in New York from 1927 to 1931 became so fashionable that it put big-band jazz on the map, gradually displacing the symphonic jazz popularized by Paul Whiteman and his gifted arranger, Ferde Grofé, who orchestrated Gershwin's *Rhapsody in Blue*.

This was the era F. Scott Fitzgerald dubbed the Jazz Age, but there were many conflicting notions of what jazz meant. For Fitzgerald and his friends it was a larky young counterculture fueled by illegal booze, a devil-may-care spontaneity, and a hearty contempt for the straitlaced puritanism of the American middle class. It had little to do with music but everything to do with sex and morals; well-to-do kids were flaunting a new generational style. For Paul Whiteman it was syncopated music with a strong, "primitive" beat that could be melded with popular symphonic traditions.[8] This crossover also appealed to young composers with classical training, like Aaron Copland, as much as to George Gershwin, whose roots were in Tin Pan Alley. For others jazz began in New Orleans with Jelly Roll Morton, the cornetist King Oliver, and his prodigious discovery Louis Armstrong, whom he brought to Chicago in 1922 to perform with the King Oliver Creole Band. Armstrong eventually joined Fletcher Henderson's band in New York, where his talents were not fully appreciated, at least by Henderson, who would not let him sing, though his work blew nearly everyone else away. But he made jazz history back in Chicago with the Hot Five and Hot Seven recordings he cut between November 1925 and December 1928. For Armstrong, unlike most of Whiteman's crew, the heart of jazz performance was improvisation, but in these records he not only created the essentials of "hot" rhythm but built a small ensemble around the virtuosity of the individual soloist.

Classic Dixieland jazz, as reflected in King Oliver's band, had been more of a group conversation, in which the players, as Ted Gioia has written, "strived to make their instruments sound like human voices, with all the variations, imperfections, and colorations that such a model entailed."[9] Something like this almost human sound can still be heard years later in Duke Ellington's recordings in which soloists so successfully mimic vocal tones that they make actual vocalists seem like superfluous trimmings, added solely to meet popular demand. Armstrong, on the other hand, steeped in the blues, turned his own growly voice into a uniquely expressive instrument, but played the cornet or trumpet like no sound anyone had ever heard. Using simple, often bluesy melodies as a base for improvisation, a seemingly spontaneous interplay of soloists and other performers, he formalized the syntax of all later jazz performance. His scat singing highlighted rhythm and phrasing over lyrics, and he also began using popular standards (like "I Can't Give You Anything but Love") as a basis for improvisation, creating a special chemistry between the familiar and the inventively original. Through daring shifts of rhythm and intonation as well as dazzling instrumental riffs, Armstrong, like a classical master of theme and variations, could transform recognizable tunes, ranging from the trite to the transcendent, into something fresh and strange. This alchemy would continue throughout his long career.

With his funky origins as a poor New Orleans waif and his later image as an effervescent clown in the minstrel tradition, Armstrong was not a likely candidate for the culture of elegance that contributed so much to the 1930s. But the instrumental riffs that caused a sensation on numbers like "Potato Head Blues" and "West End Blues," which rank among the peaks of jazz performance, were as stylish as an Astaire dance or a Cole Porter lyric. As Ralph Ellison told an interviewer, "If Louis Armstrong's meditations on the 'Potato Head Blues' aren't marked by elegance, then the term is too inelegant to name the fastidious refinement, the mastery of nuance, the tasteful domination of melody, rhythm, sounding brass and tinkling cymbal which marked his style."[10] Above all, Armstrong taught musicians and vocalists how to swing a melody, to give it dynamism and drive by slipping it from its rhythmic foundations. The jazz critic Robert O'Meally has written, "Armstrong's sense of *timing* was at least as remarkable as his power of invention as a creator of solos. With his horn or with his voice, he could relax behind the beat, shadowing it, caressing it, playing hide-and-seek with it. He could play directly on the beat, or he could ride through it like a military bandsman with an urge to roll his hips and shoulders until the march became a dance."[11] In fact, the transformation of jazz into popular dance music was perhaps the only feature of the swing era that Armstrong did not fully anticipate, much as he may have influenced it.

If Armstrong was elegant in his music, Duke Ellington was universally seen as the definition of elegance in his style of life as well, and in the risqué aura of sophistication and glamour he developed for his band. Raised in a middle-class family in Washington, D.C., the urbane, slightly aloof Ellington was as comfortable in white tie and tails as Astaire. His band was always impeccably outfitted, and he himself was so demanding, sartorially—or so superstitious—that he would never wear an article of clothing again if it popped a button. According to his longtime cornetist, Rex Stewart, "He will purchase twenty suits at a time, designed and made to his specifications, or ten pairs of handmade shoes, or three dozen custommade shirts. And if a button should fall off a jacket, that garment is discarded."[12] To avoid segregated facilities, he traveled in his own Pullman car. He supported a large, complex domestic establishment. According to one observer, "Ellington was the epitome of black urban sophistication—he was what men dreamed of becoming, and women dreamed of possessing."[13] It is said that his appetite for food and women was as great as his need for music and for touring, which he did indefatigably until shortly before his death in 1974, having kept his band together when nearly all the other big bands had gone under. But the sheen of urban sophistication was not merely the tone of his life; it's in his music as well, which managed to be at once difficult and popular. Like Armstrong, he was one of a kind—"beyond category," to use his favorite phrase.

The small combos that Armstrong put together for the Hot Fives and Hot Sevens were not dance bands; they were carefully vetted studio groups that never performed together outside the recording studio. But at the mob-owned Cotton Club on Lenox Avenue at West 142nd Street, Duke Ellington's orchestra played dance music and accompanied other production numbers, including a chorus line, that drew whites to Harlem in large numbers. Ellington's music reached a wide audience through remote radio hookups. These were also the peak years of the Harlem Renaissance, a cultural awakening largely patronized by whites, that channeled black creative work into literature and the visual arts more than music. The black middle class, determined to achieve respectability by gaining respect, had mixed feelings about jazz, which still smacked of its low-life origins. With few exceptions (notably the populist poet Langston Hughes), the writers of the Harlem Renaissance made little use of jazz in their work as they set about gaining recognition for blacks through traditional forms of art and literature. Nor were the political intellectuals around W. E. B. Du Bois and the journal he edited, *The Crisis*, sympathetic to jazz culture as they sought to elevate the race and achieve equal rights. According to *The Crisis*, "Music should sound, not screech; music should cry, not howl; music should weep, not bawl; music should implore, not whine."* But white patrons were attracted to Harlem—including its music and its writers— not for uplift and respectability but for a delicious frisson of gaudy primitivism, like the sexy spectacles that made Josephine Baker and *La Revue*

---

* Quoted in Lawrence W. Levine, "Jazz and American Culture," in *The Jazz Cadence of American Culture*, ed. Robert G. O'Meally (New York: Columbia University Press, 1998), 437. Levine also cites a 1924 piece in the *New York Times* saying that jazz "is to real music what most of the 'new poetry,' so-called, is to real poetry. Both are without the structure and form essential to music and poetry alike, and both are the products, not of innovators, but of incompetents. . . . Jazz, especially when it depends on that ghastly instrument, the saxophone, offends people with musical taste already formed, and it prevents the formation of musical taste by others." *Time* chimed in that jazz "is merely a return to the humming, hand-clapping, or tom tom beating of savages."

Nègre the toast of Paris in the 1920s. This neoprimitivism was a key feature of modernist culture, not only in Picasso's use of African masks but in the virtual cult of Freud and D. H. Lawrence in the 1920s. This was a taste that both the Renaissance writers, with their dislike of the black middle class, and the musicians of Ellington's orchestra were willing to satisfy. But under the cover of performing "jungle music" at the Cotton Club, Ellington, like Armstrong, accomplished a cultural revolution that cut a path for the surprising new popularity of jazz during the swing era.

If Armstrong's innovation was to make music swing through an interaction, even a call-and-response, between the soloists and the sidemen, Ellington created a sound that involved multiple soloists in conversation, grounded by the beat of the strong rhythm section, rich with the expressiveness of the blues, yet moving forward with a relentless dynamic energy. Where other jazzmen used standards from Broadway or Tin Pan Alley, Ellington wrote his own music, usually in collaboration with individual players, and later with his musical alter ego Billy Strayhorn. "Everyone in the band would pitch in and help write songs," said his trumpeter Cootie Williams.[14] Armstrong brought in some hugely talented players in his Hot Fives and Hot Sevens, including the clarinetist Johnny Dodds and pianist Earl Hines, though there's never a doubt about who was in charge. But Ellington had a gift for choosing musicians and writing for their sound, like a playwright who creates parts with specific actors in mind. He had a keen ear for each of his players' gifts. One of Ellington's later masterpieces, "Main Stem," recorded at the band's peak in 1942, comes together like the branches of a tree, with seven different soloists playing eight solos, only a few bars each, the whole thing clocking in at under three minutes. Yet he could be just as generous in building a ravishing piece around an individual musician, like the complex "Concerto for Cootie," written for Cootie Williams, using his own warm-up tune, or "Cotton Tail," with Ben Webster on the tenor sax, or the lyrical "Morning Glory," showcasing the talents of Rex Stewart.

Ellington's numbers are joint efforts shaped around an individual performer or a medley of distinctive voices, yet they are also written in contrasting styles and moods. Among early pieces recorded in the late 1920s, "East St. Louis Toodle-O," the band's theme song until 1940, is built around the musical invention and trumpet work of Bubber Miley, the performer who most helped Ellington develop his "hot" style. It has a raucous, carnivalesque New Orleans quality, while "Mood Indigo," one of Ellington's most popular numbers, projects a mellow, luxurious, insinuating sound, the dreamy lyricism of Ellington in a slower tempo and more reflective mood. In his fine chapter on Ellington in *The Jazz Tradition*, Martin Williams calls these pieces "instrumental ballads."[15] They reflect the darker, more melancholy strands of Depression culture. On the other hand, a version of the "Cotton Club Stomp" recorded in 1930 is a riot of perpetual motion built around a simple, unforgettable melodic phrase and counterphrase, showing how jazz performance can make so much out of what seems at first like very little. If, as I have argued, mobility, or at least the vicarious feeling of mobility, is essential to the culture of elegance, it would be hard to find better examples of it than this "Cotton Club Stomp" or, from the later period, Strayhorn's celebrated "Take the 'A' Train," another signature piece of the Ellington band, which reproduces the literal sense of locomotion that was crucial to the swing era.

Individual musicians had their own ways of conveying this propulsive movement. Ella Fitzgerald, in a live performance of "Take the 'A' Train," begins with the verse and a bit of the song, followed by a long, increasingly wild display of scatting (her specialty, much influenced by Armstrong) that rises to an almost ecstatic climax. Like all versions of the song, but to an even greater degree, it really does feel like the inexorable forward thrust of a train. This sense of perpetual motion was at the heart of swing, as the kinetic flow of the music was translated into the literal movement of dancers on the ballroom floor or kids gyrating in theater aisles. Take Count Basie's orchestra playing "Moten Swing" with an infectious rhythmic drive, or Benny Goodman and his orchestra performing Jelly Roll Morton's "King Porter Stomp," in Fletcher Henderson's arrangement, or "Roll 'Em," in which we hear wave building upon wave, reaching higher and higher, with a topping effect, an endlessly building virtuosity, that sent audiences into delirium and dancers into a frenzy of movement. This effect of soloists and sidemen reaching for peak after peak was perfected by Armstrong riffing on his horn and riding over the ensemble like a Wagnerian heldentenor in pieces like the "St. Louis Blues." Working with Goodman, Gene Krupa, like Chick Webb before him, helped transform the drums from rhythmic backing to a genuine solo instrument, as Jimmie Blanton later did as Ellington's virtuoso bassist. In "Sing, Sing, Sing," one of the most invigorating numbers of the swing era, Goodman and Krupa helped break the barrier of the three-minute recording—it clocks in at 8:40—and gave new meaning to the term "jungle music."[16] Goodman plays the high, piercing, almost vocal wail of his clarinet solos against Krupa's charged-up drum solos to give the swing craze one of its most electric themes.

Jazz, of course, had down and dirty vernacular roots, but in the night-club world of the 1920s it was strictly luxury merchandise for well-heeled social tourists slumming in Harlem: besides the performers, no blacks were admitted. But radio brought jazz home to a growing audience that could have the vicarious experience of being at the Cotton Club or on the dance floor of one of the chic urban hotels. (Many employed their own bands.) The radio audience increased from sixteen million in 1925 to sixty million in 1930. The near collapse of the music industry in the early 1930s, as the Depression set in, forced players to work directly for radio, where they were hemmed in by the format, by time constraints and commercialism, and by limits placed on their material itself. It was not until the midthirties that jazz culture was democratized and became music for the millions. By 1939 there were some two thousand dance bands in America, sweet bands, hot bands, society bands, and everything in between. Here the parallels to the growth of Art Deco as a design style are striking. Deco too began as one-of-a-kind items for the luxury trade—with the classy French house of Ruhlmann, for example—only to be transformed first into architecture and then, in the late 1930s, into mass-produced machine products and consumer goods meant to perk up the lagging consumer demand during the Depression. If jazz was democratized (in the sense of being made widely accessible) by the radio, then by jukeboxes (invented in 1934), popular ballrooms, and big bands, the Deco fashion was spread not only by mass production but by the Deco sets of Hollywood movies, which turned them into a dream of twenties elegance and style. Jazz never made much of an inroad into Hollywood, but jazz and Deco converged in the nightclub scene and, after nightclubs had largely closed down by 1932, in the dance palaces and movie palaces that replaced them.

As Prohibition ended in most states with the repeal of the Eighteenth Amendment on December 5, 1933, and as the early initiatives of the New Deal kicked in, nightlife became profitable again and the moribund entertainment industry began to revive. Swing was the sound of that revival, as Deco served as its glamorous modern look. In this and so many other ways, 1935 was a turning point: the year of the more activist Second New Deal after a more liberal Congress had been swept into office the preceding fall; the year of the Popular Front, when the Communist Party traded its revolutionary rhetoric of class conflict for a populist appeal that reached back into America's folk culture and its political traditions; and also the year of the swing revolution, which gave America its greatest popular music.

All these developments were curiously related to one another, reflecting parallel cultural directions. The group interaction of the big bands was suggestive of the sense of community fostered by the New Deal and idealized by the Popular Front, while the growing stardom of the band leaders, the hot soloists, and the singers who began fronting for the bands could be compared to the new political leadership and burgeoning sense of restored economic competence that gave reassurance to a demoralized nation.[17] The vitality and energy of swing belonged to both the youth rebellion against the constraints of the Depression and the early stirrings of national revival. This was also the year that Washington itself began developing programs for supporting the arts—as a workfare program for artists, a means for decorating government buildings, and a way of reaffirming the national heritage. Much of the government-sponsored work, such as the Treasury Department and WPA murals, was deeply traditional. It leaned on realistic techniques, historical themes, local subjects, or traditional folklore to convey a simplified version of ordinary life in the United States. The same can be said of much of the art sponsored by the Popular Front, including Earl Robinson's famous cantata *Ballad for Americans*. This fundamental conservatism helps explain why jazz, with its avant-garde roots and daring originality, never became the official culture of either the New Deal or the Popular Front. But it achieved something that eluded those well-meaning populist efforts: it became immensely popular.

Though Ellington had anticipated the swing era with his wonderful 1932 tune "It Don't Mean a Thing (If It Ain't Got That Swing)," though he composed and recorded many popular standards throughout the 1930s, he was uneasy about swing, as he resisted every other label. His music was too complex to be at the center of the big-band era. "Jazz is music; swing is business," he said.[18] The recording industry nearly went under in the early thirties, with sales plummeting from $100 million in 1927 to $6 million in 1932.[19] Bands like Ellington's kept alive by touring, but by 1935 black bands were giving way to white bands, all still segregated. White musicians began to feed once again off black musical invention. The black bands had limited airtime on radio and were barred from lucrative gigs in fancy hotels. When Fletcher Henderson's band failed in 1934, he became a key arranger for Benny Goodman, one of the not-so-secret weapons of Goodman's success in the late 1930s. As Gary Giddins writes, "From the days of antebellum minstrel shows to the present, the point at which indigenous American music becomes pop culture is the point where white performers learn to mimic black ones."[20] This could also be seen not simply as theft or imitation but a positive synthesis of different cultural traditions, though deeply unfair in its relative rewards. Jazz itself was a melding of musical traditions—African rhythms, Delta blues, stride piano, ragtime, New Orleans brass—as Ralph Ellison frequently argued. It combined primitive energy with subtle refinement. Goodman grew up in a poor Jewish section of Chicago, the ninth of twelve children. He was one of many Jews drawn to jazz as the soulful yet stirring music of a rich outsider culture. Artie Shaw, Goodman's great rival as a clarinetist and bandleader in the late 1930s, later called Bing Crosby "the first hip white person born in the United States."[21] If that's true, then Bix Beiderbecke was the second, with Goodman and Shaw himself not far behind, and Gershwin blazing his own path somewhere nearby. And it was Goodman, in the teeth of strong opposition, who broke the color barrier by bringing jazz musicians into his small combos, later into the big band itself, just as Crosby brought Armstrong into his movies and onto his immensely popular radio program, though they did not publicly make music together until long afterward.

Goodman not only helped integrate jazz and make it popular; with the meticulous musicianship he exercised over his band, he brought it to a new respectability, especially with his celebrated Carnegie Hall concert of January 16, 1938, a marathon event that also included musicians from Basie's and Ellington's bands. It proclaimed that swing was music to listen to, not simply to dance to; in the words of Ted Gioia, it "represented a coming-of-age for jazz: not only accepted, it was all but venerated under the auspices of this symbolic home of American concert music" (152). After the concert the musicians repaired to the Savoy Ballroom in Harlem for a battle of the bands between Chick Webb, long in residence, and Count Basie, the upstart from funky Kansas City. Later that year the left-wing record producer and assiduous talent scout John Hammond, a scion of the Vanderbilts, who had helped connect Henderson with Goodman, who had promoted Billie Holiday and discovered Count Basie in Kansas City and brought him to New York, organized another Carnegie Hall concert, "From Spirituals to Swing." Sponsored by *The New Masses*, the concert tried to link jazz, previously scorned on the left as decadent, with folk music as the official culture of the Popular Front. Hammond, restless and ubiquitous, was also a great patron of folk music and ethnomusicology, and he later signed the young Bob Dylan. He was sharply critical of Ellington for his lack of race-based political commitment, a presumptuous position for any white critic, yet it may have influenced the later direction of Ellington's work.

Though his canny manager, Irving Mills, encouraged Ellington to simplify his arrangements and write for Tin Pan Alley, he was also determined to position him as an artist, not simply an entertainer, and urged him to concentrate on performing his own music. Ellington's band taught others to swing, but it would never be simply a dance band, nor would it fully regain its footing until the great period between 1940 and 1942, when the addition of Ben Webster and Jimmie Blanton, the composing of Billy Strayhorn (including "Take the 'A' Train" of 1941), and the trumpet work, among other things, of Ray Nance, created an almost magical chemistry that inspired composer and performers alike.[22] Ellington's records sold well, and he was almost universally admired, but the peak years of the swing era, and especially its hyperactive youth culture, were dominated by big bands led by Goodman, the unpredictable Shaw, the Dorsey brothers, Count Basie, Chick Webb, Jimmie Lunceford, and others, as well as the smaller combos that spun off from some of them, such as Goodman's trios and quartets. More eclectic bands like Glenn Miller's, with a more homogenized sound, and sweet bands like Guy Lombardo's Royal Canadians, also formed an important part of the dance scene.

Describing the music of all these groups would be beyond my competence and beyond the scope of this book. My horizon is limited to the cultural history of the era, not the musical history of jazz. But as a listener I find the music made by Goodman's and Shaw's bands endlessly appealing, even though they were virtually written out of jazz history in the wake of bebop, which turned jazz away from dance and popular music and toward difficult modernist experimentation, away from big bands and ballrooms and toward small groups riffing way past midnight in smoke-filled jazz clubs. So-called modern jazz was more about virtuosity than about elegance, more about intransigent art than about communal entertainment. It revived the spirit of improvisation that lay somewhat dormant in the swing era, when bigger bands and bigger halls required more arrangements, some of them written out beforehand to suggest improvisation. Yet the swing bands could also let loose and create a virtual frenzy in their young audiences, especially the so-called jitterbugs, who became their most ardent fans. In 1932 Edmund Wilson had collected his Depression journalism under the title *The American Jitters*, but the kinetic young dancers turned anxiety into activity as if, on their very own, they could get the country moving again. At one point Goodman looked out at the gyrations of his excited audience with a kind of wonder at what he had wrought. "We looked at them, I guess, [as if] they were the show and we were the audience."[23]

Despite his popularity, Goodman was nothing if not a serious musician and a highly disciplined bandleader. He could alienate people with his exacting demands. His demeanor was cool and professorial, his approach professional. Though his drummer, Gene Krupa, labeled him the King of Swing, he looked and behaved nothing like a popular idol. He did some of his best work in small groups with Krupa, the pianist Teddy Wilson, with Lionel Hampton on the vibraphone, and Charlie Christian on the electric guitar. Yet he turned his clarinet into an instrument as fiercely alive as any sound in jazz. His work ranged from the rhythmic drive of "King Porter Stomp" and "Sing, Sing, Sing" to the clean, graceful elegance of "Flying Home" and the plangent romantic sound of "Memories of You," the last two recorded in 1939 with his sextet. Artie Shaw's public personality was as different from Goodman's as his clarinet playing. Restless, erratic, he tried his hand at everything, writing, performing, composing. With movie-star good looks, he would eventually marry eight times. A perfectionist, he railed against the commercialism of the music scene and created and unmade almost as many bands as marriages. But he could play the clarinet with an almost unearthly beauty, as in his hit version of "Begin the Beguine" in 1939, the athletic twists and turns of "Non Stop Flight," the romantic sound of "Deep Purple," in which his clarinet does a duet with the vocalist Helen Forrest, and the jazzed-up version of the Gershwins' "Oh! Lady Be Good." Goodman, though unfairly dismissed as a traditionalist, was still honing his style when he died in 1986. Shaw, true to form, laid down his clarinet in 1954 and never performed again, though he lived another half century. Ted Gioia, in his *History of Jazz*, finely articulates the paradoxical contrast between the two:

> The reserved Goodman was the master of hot phrasing, a swing stylist with a concert-hall technique. Charismatic, a chameleon in both his music and personality, Shaw offered a fluid, less syncopated approach to melody. His improvised lines were varnished with a haughty elegance, submerging the emotional turbulence far below, which made even the most technically accomplished passages sound like child's play. Compare the two figures, each a puzzling compos-ite: one combined a frigid personality with a hot musical style, while the other evinced a warm-blooded temperament but a cool approach to the horn (148).

This description conveys not only the musicianship of the leading figures of the swing era but also the stardom they enjoyed. Swing jazz helped create the communal culture of the last years of the Depression. It provided an upbeat outlet for the frustrations, the thwarted energy of the young at the same time that it reflected the gradual revival of eco-nomic activity and morale, stimulated by the New Deal. It offered relief from the darkening shadows of war and the rise of fascism, yet it was not transparently ideological in the style of so much Popular Front culture, with which it shared the project of bringing together Americans of differ-ent backgrounds and diverging cultural traditions, from the children of immigrants to the children of slavery. Some of the excesses of the swing era belonged to adolescent rites of passage, a recoil against parental cau-tion and restraint, that would become even more familiar in the affluent period after the war. But some of its energies helped Americans shake off the doldrums of the Depression, preparing them for the unified effort that would be demanded in the war to come.

Art Deco: From the Carriage Trade to the Mass Market

If the big-band craze that marked the swing era helped democratize jazz culture, the new wave of streamlined design, sometimes called Depression Modern, democratized consumption. As the ethos of the jazz scene helped bury America's small-town puritanism, the modern yet decorative lines of the new design fashions made America less traditional and provincial. They infused an enormous range of products with the forward push of modernity and the futuristic lines of the machine. One feature of swing was that it was not one kind of music but a "hot" approach that could give a different rhythm to almost anything, from classical to pop, from folk to Broadway. Deco was omnivorous too, eventually transforming everything from large buildings, garish theaters, and sleek trains to farm equipment and small table radios. There were Deco skyscrapers yet also Deco kitchens. There was a modest vernacular Deco architecture, now belatedly rediscovered, in Miami Beach, or in apartment houses along the Grand Concourse in the Bronx. But there were also the Chrysler Building, the Empire State Building, Rockefeller Center, and Radio City Music Hall, all conceived before the Crash and followed through, in the early years of the Depression, with blind tenacity by wealthy men in denial about the state of the economy, or determined to get it moving single-handedly.

Much of what happened to Deco through the end of the thirties was leagues away from its formal beginnings in 1925. The launch of the Deco style, the Deco craze, is usually traced to the great Paris expo of 1925, officially called the Exposition Internationale des Arts Décoratifs et Industriels Modernes. The United States declined to participate since its secretary of commerce, Herbert Hoover, insisted it had no modern design to contribute. Scholars have shown that far from inaugurating the Deco wave, the 1925 expo consolidated decorative trends that went back to 1908 or 1910, especially in France. French Deco was symbolized by the work of Jacques-Emile Ruhlmann, who also put together the expo's most famous exhibit, the luxurious Hôtel du Collectionneur, a stunningly sumptuous model interior that later Deco shows have tried to re-create. Alastair Duncan has written, "Only the rarest and most exquisite materials were used by Ruhlmann for his furniture. Rich veneers such as palisander, amboyna, amaranth, macassar ebony and Cuban mahogany, were inlaid with ivory, tortoise-shell or horn. Dressing tables were embellished with leather, *galuchat* [sharkskin] or parchment panelling. Silk tassels applied to drawer pulls added a further touch of elegance."[24]

This is a long way from American vernacular design in the 1930s, yet the Deco impulse found its most ubiquitous flowering in the United States, albeit in the simplified, democratized form of a mischievously playful new modern style. Cultivated Americans in the 1920s looked up to everything French. A downsized version of the great expo evoked widespread interest when it traveled to eight American cities in 1926. It had an almost instantaneous effect on everything from jewelry, clothes, and furnishings to graphic design, especially posters and book jackets. The year of the expo, 1925, also saw Josephine Baker's sensational Paris debut in *La Revue Nègre*, which was trumpeted to fame by Paul Colin's brilliantly stylized posters. Their stark silhouettes and sinuous, angular curves, with their hints of the primitive and the orgiastic, in turn influenced the designs that illustrated the literature of the Harlem Renaissance, creating an international as well as interracial mix that was also typical of the expanding impact of jazz.

If the furnishings and interiors of the Paris expo affected American designers, the pavilions themselves, though soon to be torn down, had just as great an influence on America's commercial architects. Ely Jacques Kahn, a pioneer Deco architect, was deeply impressed by what he encountered in Paris and soon began applying it to commissions in New York, including in 1927 his best-known building, at 2 Park Avenue, marked by richly colored terra-cotta panels on its exterior and by a lavishly decorated lobby that included a mosaic ceiling, marble walls, bronze and glass revolving doors, ornate lighting, and bronze elevator doors decorated with bas-relief designs. Kahn was soon outdone by the gorgeous interiors, including elevators of inlaid wood veneer in geometrical patterns, and the spectacular dome of William Van Alen's Chrysler Building (1928–30), whose sunburst effect continues to light up the New York skyline. It was followed by the more spare and severe Empire State Building (1930–31) and the ensemble of Rockefeller Center, with its richly appointed Radio City Music Hall. But these are only the best-known of several hundred Deco buildings constructed in New York alone between 1927 and 1932. The Deco style spread to many other cities, and there were also more modest buildings, including apartment houses and movie theaters through which we could trace the shift of Deco from luxury design to a vernacular style still suggestive of luxury and elegance. As Rosemarie Bletter writes in *Skyscraper Style*, "while the effects were on occasion vulgar, the intention was to create a mass modern."[25] That is to say, a vulgar modernism in both senses of the word: ostentatious, but also popular, playful, accessible—a vulgate of modernism. None of this pleased the avatars of the other, more exacting and minimal modernism, the so-called International Style, which received its name at a celebrated show at the Museum of Modern Art in 1932. Curated by the young Philip Johnson and Henry-Russell Hitchcock, the exhibition and its influential catalog were part polemic, part overview of the new architecture of the preceding decade. This style, which would carry the day after the war, banned most decoration, favored glass and steel over terra-cotta and stone, and propelled American architecture toward a more austere functionalism.

Yet the minimalism of the later International Style was anticipated by developments in Deco after 1932. As the Depression deepened, the building boom of the late 1920s ended and the luxury of Deco design became an embarrassment, out of tune with the urgent stresses of the moment. In the streamlined Moderne style that soon dominated American design, Deco was transformed into something more clean-lined and horizontal, oriented less to pleasure than to speed and kinetic energy, an orientation toward the future at a time when many people were deeply fearful about what the future held in store. A new generation of designers—Raymond Loewy, Donald Deskey, Norman Bel Geddes, Gilbert Rohde, Russel Wright, Walter Dorwin Teague—began working on the cusp between pleasure palaces and a much more broad-based consumerism. Donald Deskey designed the opulent interiors of the Radio City Music Hall and the private apartment of John D. Rockefeller but also tubular furniture for the classes and the masses. Raymond Loewy virtually created the field of industrial design, reshaping a duplicating machine for Gestetner, locomotives for the Pennsylvania Railroad, refrigerators for Sears-Roebuck, and automobiles for Studebaker. He designed the bull's-eye on the Lucky Strike cigarette package and the logos for companies like Studebaker and Hoover, maker of vacuum cleaners.

In product design they used materials like chrome, plastic, and aluminum, not the precious materials of early Deco; they oversaw the transition of elegance from the luxury market to the wider world of ordinary consumption. In the process they became figures of vast cultural influence as well as commercial wizards who, in a stagnant economy, could somehow sell products that exuded elegance, optimism, and energy. It was one thing to use a sheath of metal to give an aerodynamic look to the sleek locomotive of the new Twentieth Century Limited. It was quite another to give the same look to farm equipment or to a household iron, a pencil sharpener, or a cigarette lighter, associating them too with the aesthetics of the machine, the modern, the thrust toward a utopian future. Working with curved lines, they used bullet shapes to suggest dynamic force and teardrop shapes to imply graceful flow. They could make a teapot look like Aladdin's lamp and give rounded, futuristic lines to a toaster, a mixmaster, or the Bakelite portable radios that could be found in every modest American home when I was a kid in the 1940s. These new industrial products and their designs paved the way for the postwar world by democratizing consumption itself.

"Speed is the cry of our era," wrote Bel Geddes in 1932, "and even greater speeds are the goals of tomorrow."[26] Speed lines suggesting dynamic thrust were among the few surface decorations on streamlined products, since the fantastic shape of the object was itself decorative, not strictly functional. This emphasis on speed, modernity, and the bright future was also the overarching theme of the ambitiously conceived world's fairs of the 1930s. Chicago's "Century of Progress" exhibition of 1933–34 showed a vast assortment of streamlined products, while New York's great fair of 1939–40, though shadowed by the outbreak of war, entertained legions of visitors with anticipations of "The World of Tomorrow." The fair's suggestive logo, the Trylon and Perisphere, became a ubiquitous Deco symbol, as did the widely popular General Motors Futurama exhibit, a model of streamlined design, that predicted the huge automotive surge of the postwar years. As the architecture critic Sheldon Cheney had written in 1930, "We are past the possibility of challenging the machine, of curbing it, of attempting escape from it. . . . We must move by machinery, communicate by it—live by it."[27] Like the designers of the Futurama, Cheney saw this as a utopian prospect, despite his language of resistance. "There will ultimately be machine-developed energy to solve all men's work problems," he wrote. Apparently, he did not foresee how the same energy could be used to destroy, kill, and maim on a massive, impersonal scale, as the war would show.

Streamlining, as the second phase of Deco design, preserves and transforms the original utopian impulse of Art Deco, laying its bounty before the many rather than the few. It radiates optimism and a faith in progress. So does Hollywood in the lavish Deco dreamworld it features all through the 1930s, a world of wealth and pleasure as well as speed and movement. The bewilderingly wide array of Hollywood Deco is almost too pervasive to catalog, yet Howard Mandelbaum and Eric Myers surveyed it sumptuously in their 1985 book *Screen Deco*. They trace this trend to the art directors of each studio who crafted a distinct studio style, beginning with Cedric Gibbons at MGM. A visit to the 1925 Paris expo reshaped his sense of design. He had long since banned painted backdrops for more naturalistic sets. The home he shared with his wife, the actress Dolores Del Rio, was itself soon written up as the epitome of chic and style.[28] With the coming of sound, he launched the Deco vogue both on and off the set with a 1928 Joan Crawford vehicle, *Our Dancing Daughters*. In the words of Mandelbaum and Myers, "this film's chic, soaring Deco sets depicted a dream world of the well-to-do."[29] Other art directors, including Hans Dreier at Paramount and Van Nest Polglase at RKO, followed suit, most notably in RKO's sets for the Astaire-Rogers movies, including three separate nightclub sets for *Swing Time*. Most nightclubs failed during the early Depression years, but even those that sprang up again after the end of Prohibition could hardly match their deluxe movie incarnations. Like these movies themselves, they created virtually a world of their own, free of the disturbances of the Depression yet intimately related to them. Mandelbaum and Myers describe them as "vast modern temples where passion and pleasure could be played out on a grand scale," adding, "Nightclub sets could provide any film with an injection of elegance" (102). The only grander Deco film settings were ocean liners, which were not only luxurious but altogether self-contained, like a floating parenthesis in the dreamy lives of the movie's characters. No actual nightclub or ocean liner could quite match Hollywood's vision of them, the perfect Platonic form to which they merely pointed.

But if Deco sets served as a marker for hedonism, their scale, going back to expressionist films like Fritz Lang's *Metropolis*, also dwarfed the people in them. In movies, Deco skyscrapers, office sets, hotel rooms, and apartments could be as cold as the Egyptian tombs parodied by Woody Allen in *The Purple Rose of Cairo*. (So could the hospital-white streamlined kitchen in the fashionable middle-class home.) For Woody Allen, Mia Farrow is a Depression housewife with a low-paying job who goes to the movies for escape and fantasy. But Jeff Daniels comes down off the screen for warmth and human contact, which sometimes were in short supply even in voluptuous Deco settings. When Astaire and Rogers dance—and connect—they transcend their surroundings as much as they reflect them. Even elegance has different rungs, different registers; the dancing couple has style yet their harmony of touch and movement also takes them beyond style. The same can be said of streamlining, which uses the forward thrust of speed and motion, the elegance of line, to transcend what can be sterile or geometrical in mere decoration.

The parallels with jazz and especially swing hardly need to be emphasized. From early on, jazz was sometimes mentioned, at least casually, in evoking Art Deco. One of the early terms for this design revolution, though it failed to catch on, was "jazz modern." The nightclubs and ballrooms where jazz was featured were often like Deco sets, though never as lavish or gigantic as those in the movies. But deeper parallels can be found in the work itself, particularly in its migration from the smart set to the mainstream. The syncopated rhythm of jazz and, above all, its improvisational elegance and playfulness can be compared to the ornamental riches of Deco, the inviting curlicues with which it surrounds the basic functional form of the object, whether it be a building, a stairway, or a dressing table. If jazz parlance abhors a square, the Deco designer abhors a right angle, anything that would impede the flow. Deco takes us from the linear to the curvilinear, as jazz loops around the melodic line and any conventional oompah rhythms, which it breaks down and reconstructs.

When jazz turns into swing, into dance music, it not only grows popular but assumes the very qualities of speed, motion, and forward energy that are built visually into the streamlining of Deco. In a very brief period, Deco architecture made the transition from pleasure palaces, skyscrapers, and industrial building to the kind of vernacular architecture we find in Miami's South Beach, New York's Central Park West, or the Grand Concourse in the Bronx. None of these is exactly workers' housing on the Bauhaus model, but neither are they garish, grand, or opulent. Hollywood translated Deco into mass fantasy the way radio, record players, and jukeboxes, themselves often Deco objects, transformed jazz into popular music. Both served, in tandem with the New Deal, to get people moving again, to lift sagging morale and stimulate optimism about the future.

As it turned out, the future held little place for many popular passions of the 1930s, which were so closely linked to the mind-set of the Depression. By the mid-1940s, both swing and Deco, which had once seemed like the cutting edge of modern style, came to look hopelessly old-fashioned. In part they were undone by the war itself, which gave a patriotic push to all things square, promoting a unanimity and conformity that would have an ominous and conservative impact after the war. Partly this was the result of their own success. The vogue of the big bands led many musicians to go off and form bands of their own, crowding the market. Since there was more money to be made on the road, the national touring bands competed with the many local bands, while many black bands were at a special disadvantage, especially in their limited access to radio.[30] But even at the high end, in the cultural world itself, they were rejected by adherents of a more severe modernism—including bebop, painterly abstraction, and the International Style—that mistrusted their popularity as evidence of commercialism and compromise. Once there was a great deal of money to be made, swing music *was* commercialized, as mavericks like Artie Shaw kept pointing out. All this complements the standard account that attributes the decline of the big bands and the rise of small bebop combos to the strike in the recording industry from 1942 to 1944, when young jazzmen like Charlie Parker, jamming in small groups, took daring musical directions that led toward a new bohemia, a style that thrilled intellectuals but left young dancers and the popular audience high and dry. With dazzling speed and difficult polyrhythms, they began improvising on the chord changes as much as on the melody. This is not exactly the same as the rise of the International Style, or of atonal music, or of abstract expressionist art, but each represents a modernist turn that left the populism and vernacular modernism of the thirties behind.

The pleasures and treasures of popular art and design in the 1930s could not long be forgotten. It was inevitable that even highbrow audiences would eventually grow restive under more austere and punishing forms of modernism. They would become nostalgic for narrative in literature, tuneful melodic invention in music, figurative forms in painting, or decoration and historical eclecticism in architecture and design. They would grow nostalgic for pleasure. The early greats of jazz were welcomed into a new canon that was sometimes resented by their less heralded successors. But the rediscovery of Art Deco was peculiarly dramatic because it had been so devalued by later waves of modern design. From the Deco revival shows of the late 1960s, when the style finally acquired its name, to the international sweep of the big Victoria and Albert show of 2003, Deco, even Deco kitsch, became a widely idealized cultural form, seen as the essence of enjoyment, wit, and ingenuity of design. When a version of the landmark Victoria and Albert show traveled to the Boston's Museum of Fine Arts in 2004, Ken Johnson, in an exhilarating review, highlighted the eclectic mixture of high and low, commerce and culture, and made the parallel to jazz explicit. Deco, he said, "could swallow just about any style from any period and transform it into something cool, jazzy and contemporary, and it could turn just about any commodity—even vacuum cleaners and refrigerators—into an object of desire. . . . Art Deco didn't create any new products as such, but it made familiar things look new and provoked a hunger for more new-looking things that it was happy to keep feeding."[31]

By the time I was growing up in the forties and fifties, that novelty had faded, though the consumerism it stimulated had taken off. But time showed that its spirit could be recaptured even by those with no memory of the Depression, to whom it spoke simply of the pleasures of craft and imagination, the daffy optimism, elegance, and energy that lit up even a far darker time.

THE SEARCH *for* COMMUNITY

CHAPTER 12

The Populist Turn:

COPLAND AND THE POPULAR FRONT

ONE TURNING POINT in the Depression undoubtedly came in 1933, when the economy hit bottom and the Hoover administration gave way to the first hundred days of the New Deal, which brought a host of new programs and a sharp boost in morale. Culturally, 1934 was a key year for Hollywood, since it saw both the strict enforcement of the Production Code and the beginnings of screwball comedy, which replaced direct eroticism with explosive verbal and cultural energy and made the war between the sexes an unexpected metaphor for social conflict and concord. In other ways, however, a key transition came in 1935 when the Communist parties, on a signal from Moscow, made a world-wide shift from a radical and revolutionary program to a Popular Front of all "progressive" forces against the rise of fascism. Only a year earlier, Communists had been deadly enemies of social-democratic movements, disrupting their meetings and blocking their programs, even developing parallel unions that competed with existing labor unions. Now they made common cause with Socialists and liberals, and even gave qualified support to New Deal programs and to FDR himself as the New Deal entered a more radical phase. As a result, membership in the American Communist Party ballooned in these years to over 100,000. But the cultural effects were just as far-reaching. As major artists like Hemingway were attracted to Communism, the party set aside the proletarian novel, with its emphasis on class conflict, for a vague alliance with progressive elements in the cultural community. Under the slogan that Communism was "twentieth-century Americanism," the party spearheaded an upsurge of populism and cultural nationalism that had been building since the preceding decade and would come to fruition in many forms, including the cultural programs of the New Deal. This many-sided exploration of the popular roots of American culture, from ethnomusicology to folk art, would influence the serious and popular arts for years to come. Culture itself became a source of psychological energy and social insight.

When I was growing up in New York in the 1940s and early 1950s, the remnants of Popular Front politics and culture were all around us, so much a part of the landscape that I scarcely noticed them. For my parents, who had come to the United States as immigrants when they were young, the Depression and the New Deal remained daily facts of life, fueling their anxieties and influencing their life choices. New Deal legislation dealing with housing, social security, and the rights of labor created a safety net that was quickly taken for granted, as were "progressive" ideas in general, but without allaying basic fears about the next paycheck, the next rental payment. But caution was mingled with pride, for ordinary people felt that the New Deal had offered then a new self-respect. The common man had come into his own. On the cultural side, radio programs like *The Goldbergs, I Remember Mama*, and even *Amos 'n' Andy* bolstered ethnic pride while creating cross-cultural bonds that helped bring immigrants into the mainstream, though some of the featured actors would soon fall victim to the blacklist.

New York City politics during and after the war still had a Popular Front tinge. Fiorello La Guardia, a liberal Republican of mixed Italian and Jewish background, served as mayor on a Fusion ticket from 1933 to 1945. I remember the commotion when he came to dedicate a playground near my school, a tiny piece of the vast array of public works created under the New Deal. In East Harlem, the American Labor Party (ALP), which supported Henry Wallace for president in 1948, continued to reelect a maverick congressman, Vito Marcantonio, through 1950. In every election season, banners across the *Jewish Daily Forward* building, which towered over the Lower East Side, promoted the candidates of the social-democratic Liberal Party. Heavily supported by David Dubinsky and his International Ladies' Garment Workers' Union, a New York powerhouse, it was fiercely anti-Communist and had recently split off from the ALP. At the Waldorf-Astoria Hotel in March 1949, some eight hundred cultural figures, including Arthur Miller, Lillian Hellman, Aaron Copland, the young Norman Mailer, and, from the Soviet Union a frightened Dmitri Shostakovich, met to discuss war and peace in what proved to be the swan song of Soviet-American wartime amity. A small group of intellectuals, led by Sidney Hook, Dwight Macdonald, Mary McCarthy, and the young Irving Howe, confronted the participants over the state of freedom in the Soviet Union. This was a signal moment in an atmosphere already tense with the cold war. A few months later, riots greeted those who attended a concert by one of the best-known icons of the Popular Front, the black singer and actor Paul Robeson, in Peekskill, New York.

My father, though not especially political, was a loyal member of a CIO union that cosponsored the concert. An uncle of mine, a Communist who belonged to Sidney Hillman's Amalgamated Clothing Workers, drove up to hear Robeson, whom he idolized, and to show solidarity with his old comrades. His wife, my mother's younger sister, was so terrified at the violence they encountered, which the local police did nothing to curtail, that she pressured him to withdraw from political activity. As if the Old Left were not already on the defensive, a few months later the Rosenberg spy case broke upon the world. For the next three years, until the couple was executed, their fate captured the fearful attention of immigrant Jews like no other story. Except for blacklists, spy cases, and congressional hearings, which targeted the remnants of the 1930s Left, the culture and politics of the Popular Front effectively disappeared, except in the nostalgic recollections of those involved, for whom it remained the great adventure of their lives.

For Aaron Copland, who had come to epitomize the American composer of classic music, despite his leftist associations, 1949 represented the culmination of his time in Hollywood, with his score for *The Heiress* winning an Academy Award. By 1950 his work turned quietly—but dramatically—back to the concert hall, with the first set of *Old American Songs* and the *Piano Quartet*. But soon he too was hauled before a congressional committee to account for his political leanings in the 1930s and early 1940s, when he wrote the music for *The North Star*, a pro-Soviet wartime film written by Lillian Hellman and produced by Samuel Goldwyn. Unlike some other witnesses, he gave answers that were as direct and plainspoken as his music. But as a composer for the concert hall he was much less vulnerable to being blacklisted than a Hollywood actor or director.

A few years later I became a student at Columbia University, a home to many anti-Communist New York intellectuals who had been most critical of the Popular Front, including Lionel Trilling, F. W. Dupee, Richard Hofstadter, and Robert Gorham Davis. Once sympathetic to Marxism like other writers appalled and radicalized by the Depression, they first attacked the Popular Front from the left as a middlebrow culture that had lost its radical edge, then from the right as an obedient front for Soviet interests in a patriotic American guise. In the gray mood of the late 1950s, when these issues had grown too remote for us to grasp, my friends and I were irresistibly drawn to everything that the cold war and McCarthyism had tried to banish, indeed, to whatever would annoy our teachers most. We searched for old records by Robeson and more recent ones by the Red Army Chorus, which had visited America during the cold war thaws of the post-Stalin years. By then the Robeson albums were almost impossible to find. When I inquired around 1960 at Columbia Records, once Robeson's label, a vice-president wrote to me that the company had *never* put out any recordings by him, though I later found one, which I still have, while rifling through a secondhand bin in the British crown colony of Gibraltar. This duplicity, the erasure of the past, shocked me. But I also came to share my instructors' view that most Popular Front literature was flatfooted and propagandistic in its social realism, many cuts below the intransigent modernist writing that now enthralled me.

By the 1980s, when I began studying the cultural history of the Depression years, the ambivalence I felt as an undergraduate still seemed writ large in the scholarship. In the wake of the hopes and failures of the New Left, many of us were once again attracted to the 1930s as a period of political engagement, social concern, and radical struggle. As the gap between the rich and poor began to widen and selfish greed came back into fashion, the programs initiated during the Depression shimmered like a beacon of social sympathy and responsibility. But radical work in the arts of the Depression years seemed dated by stale agitprop techniques, crippled by an aesthetic conventionality designed to appeal to the least demanding audience. In painting, in music, in literature, socially committed art seemed like a regression from the daring exigencies of modernism. Teaching this thirties material in the 1980s and 1990s required special pleading, and our students, for whom even the sixties had faded into myth or hearsay, were easily bored. At the same time, some key works produced in the 1930s seemed so unforced, so natural, that even young readers with little sense of history could connect with them immediately.

The songs of Woody Guthrie sounded musically primitive to a generation schooled on rock, but they were also bracingly direct and spontaneously appealing. The words were always fresh, and the musical idiom had survived in western ballads and talking blues, and in the work of later troubadours like Bob Dylan and Bruce Springsteen, as they often acknowledged. Dylan had arrived on the Greenwich Village scene in the early 1960s, when the folk culture, populated by aging radicals and young wannabees, was almost a lifeline back to the 1930s. This was the moment (1962) when John Steinbeck, another icon of the thirties, belatedly received the Nobel Prize for Literature. Scorned by highbrow critics, his novels retained their universal appeal, though the social situations they dramatized with gripping immediacy had long since changed. In the wake of the new civil rights movement, Richard Wright's portrayal of racial oppression and hatred in *Native Son* and *Black Boy* had lost none of its power, nor had Henry Roth's story of a boy growing up on the Lower East Side in the first decade of the twentieth century—the inimitable *Call It Sleep*. The left-wing convictions of these writers did not make their work formulaic or destroy its power to communicate across the decades.

Their social commitment, so typical of Depression writing, in no way conflicted with their artistic integrity; instead, it gave their work fire and energy. By the early sixties the revival of radicalism and the new interest in poverty and ethnicity, especially among blacks and Jews, rekindled strong interest in their work.

As I tried to show in an earlier chapter, *Call It Sleep*, one of the great novels of the century, was in many ways a special case, for it was controversial among leftist critics, then long forgotten, before being rediscovered in the 1960s.[1] Roth's conversion to Communism came only as he was finishing the book in 1933, and the political discipline that came along with his new worldview had a stultifying effect on his gift as a writer. (His next novel did not appear until sixty years later.) With its tightly woven texture, recurring symbols, and interior monologues, *Call It Sleep* showed the influence of Joyce, Eliot, and the modernism of the 1920s. As a psychological narrative, amazing in its sensitivity to a child's view of the world, it seemed self-indulgent to some Marxist critics. Yet the story, besides being deeply personal, was also a document of the recent American past: immigration, the hardscrabble life of the ghetto, with its babble—or Babel—of cultures and languages. Roth had responded not only to Joyce's experiments with language and point of view but to his keen re-creation of everyday life in a modern city.

This was a time of transition for Aaron Copland too. In 1934, the year *Call It Sleep* was published, he also struck a tenuous balance between modernism and populism. That year he wrote *Statements*, in many ways a culmination of his modernist language of the 1920s, and *Hear Ye! Hear Ye!*, the first and least-known of a series of ballets, the genre that eventually made him a household name. Along with *Call It Sleep* and other enduring works of the 1930s, Copland's music fractures our conventional narrative of the period, the one first laid out by F. Scott Fitzgerald in 1931 in "Echoes of the Jazz Age" and Malcolm Cowley three years later in *Exile's Return*.[2] In this canonical view, the twenties were the age of high spirits and expatriate adventures, reflected in wild artistic experiments, "the religion of art," as Cowley described it scornfully. In the thirties, however, the money ran out: the prodigals were forced to return home and buckle down, and most of them did. Moreover, says Cowley, "Paris was no longer the center of everything 'modern' and aesthetically ambitious in American literature" (284). The social misery of the Depression made them face up to the moral demands of American life; it pressed them to pay serious attention to an everyday world they had once dismissed with irony or contempt. Larky irresponsibility gave way to a quickened social conscience, experimentation to documentation, surrealism to a new realism. The party was supplanted by the Party.

While some careers in the arts conformed to this conversion pattern, many did not, Fitzgerald's among them; he came home, but not to become a proletarian writer. The culture of the Popular Front was long seen as a (lamentable) result of this shift, but even the turn toward populism, especially after 1935, was part of a wider development that went far beyond the new cultural policy of the Communist Party. It extended to Hollywood, which in a sense had always been populist, reaching out to the largest number of ordinary Americans, but also to a vast array of government-sponsored cultural programs, including the Treasury Department's Section of Fine Arts, which commissioned murals and sculpture for federal buildings and for eleven hundred post offices across the country; Roy Stryker's Photography Unit of the Resettlement Administration, which movingly documented the effects of the Depression in the American heartland; and, most extensively, the art, music, theater, and writers' projects of the Works Progress Administration (WPA), a relief agency. The Federal Writers' Project alone put out more than eight hundred volumes, the best known of which were guides to all forty-eight states as well as many localities. Never had Americans been so interested in themselves, in the roots and branches of a genuine American culture. Never had so much information been amassed by so many writers about the most mundane features of American life, a literary parallel to the vast array of public works that were constructed by the WPA across the nation.[3] FDR himself embarked on a more personal form of populism, using an intimate conversational tone in his fireside chats to make the chief executive a less remote figure, better able to reach ordinary Americans.

Stylistically, the new populist arts picked up important strands of modernism as well as social realism, as in such committed theater productions as Marc Blitzstein's Brechtian musical *The Cradle Will Rock* and other experimental work by the theatrical prodigy Orson Welles and his resourceful producer, John Houseman.[4] Like others in his generation, Copland fused modernism with populism, seeking a fresh, clean, spare, yet colorful sound as he turned more directly to American subjects. The focus on American life, with its creative use of native traditions, went back several decades. In the 1930s it embraced a more varied body of fiction, journalism, poetry, painting, illustration, popular music, concert music, dance, theater, film, and photography than most critics acknowledged. As early as 1942, in an eloquent tribute, Alfred Kazin devoted the concluding chapter of *On Native Grounds* to the "enormous body of writing about the American scene that is one of the most remarkable phenomena of the era of crisis." He wrote that "it testified to an extraordinary national self-scrutiny."[5] His own book, beginning with its title, belonged with this literature and arose from the same impulse. Writers like Lewis Mumford in *The Brown Decades* (1931), Van Wyck Brooks in *The Flowering of New England* (1936) and *New England: Indian Summer* (1940), and Carl Sandburg in *The People, Yes* (1936) and his multivolume biography of Lincoln (1926–39) were taking stock of neglected American traditions at a time when morale was low and faith in the system, along with any faith in the future, had taken a terrible beating. Lincoln became the epitome of the common-man hero, the rail-splitter who became president, rescued the Union, and initiated a second American Revolution by freeing the slaves. Those who volunteered for the defense of the Spanish Republic called themselves the Abraham Lincoln Brigade. John Ford's *Young Mr. Lincoln* (1939) and Copland's *A Lincoln Portrait* (1942) became enduring examples of progressive Americana.

Aaron Copland's exemplary career, so characteristic of the cultural moment of the late 1930s, needs to be seen in this political and literary framework. On the surface it seems to be an instance of the Exile's Return, the remaking of the experimental twenties modernist into the more accessible, more socially conscious thirties artist. Copland was never an expatriate, but he spent three formative years in Paris between 1921 and 1924, absorbing European culture, studying composition, and relishing the spunky novelties of the modernist scene dominated by Stravinsky, Joyce, Schoenberg, Picasso, Cocteau, Diaghilev, and younger composers like Milhaud, Satie, and George Antheil, Copland's brash American contemporary. "The sheer glamour of the period exerts a magic spell," Copland later wrote. "The very word 'modern' was exciting. The air was charged with talk of new tendencies, and the password was originality— anything was possible."[6] Yet Copland, like Malcolm Cowley, maintained

that living in Paris made him more American, stimulating him to create music that would spring from his own roots, as Europeans so clearly
were nourished by theirs. Even Stravinsky, the most influential modernist, had turned toward folk material, as Joyce relished popular songs.
At that time the French avant-garde was transfixed by all things American, which seemed to them quintessentially modern: the urban crowds,
the skyscrapers, the clean, functional lines of the machine, the informal,
egalitarian manners, the lack of tradition (or low respect for it), even the
hostility to art and culture. As they saw it, the fetishization of Art could
thwart the innovative spirit of the living. Americans were understood to
be instinctively pragmatic. Irreverence was their birthright, classlessness
their privilege: if not quite noble savages, they were happily uncultured,
even downright primitive.

As Picasso had been taken with African sculpture and masks, Copland's Paris of the twenties was enamored of blacks and especially jazz.
Soon after he and his friend Harold Clurman returned to the States, Paris
made a cult of the black American dancer and singer Josephine Baker
and *La Revue Nègre*, as pictured by Paul Colin in his strikingly stylized
modernist posters. In the same year, 1925, Copland used jazz rhythms
and snatches of familiar tunes (like "The Sidewalks of New York") in
the "Dance" section of his *Music for the Theatre*. The equally lively "Burlesque" section reminded the composer Roy Harris of "whorehouse
music." Copland was partly inspired by the vulgar but irresistible singing
and mugging of Fanny Brice (C-P 1, 120), an inspired and popular come-
dienne, whose Jewish vamps were as deliciously exaggerated as Baker's
half-naked, chocolate-colored primitives. By reaching out to the spirit of
theater, jazz, popular music, and burlesque, Copland composed a kind
of "Broadway Boogie-Woogie," with those two animated sections joined
by a bluesy interlude. This interplay of a lively voice with a somber one,
both of them clean and fresh and hard to forget, became part of Copland's
musical signature. As Copland's biographer Howard Pollack remarks, this
middle section of *Music for the Theatre* introduces that "lonely, night-in-
the-city ambience so characteristic of the mature composer."[7] By developing brief but easily recognizable melodic motifs with sparkling orchestral
color, he anticipated the ballet works of the late 1930s and early 40s that
would establish his American sound and make him a permanent classic
and a perpetual audience favorite. Like Gershwin and Cole Porter, Cop-

land captured the propulsive energy and high spirits of the 1920s and then gave it a deeper meaning in the straitened conditions of the Depression, when a choreographer like Balanchine could go back and forth between ballet and Broadway and choreography itself became an expressive way to combat inertia and get people moving.

The new interest of American artists in the neglected wealth of the American scene had been gestating all through the 1920s. On his return from Paris, Copland developed close links with the circle around Alfred Stieglitz, the great photographer and impresario of modern art, and Paul Rosenfeld, Stieglitz's loyal spokesman and eloquent house critic. Before the war, Stieglitz had promoted both European and American modernists at his celebrated gallery at 291 Fifth Avenue, which closed in 1917. But the galleries he opened from 1921 onward, including An American Place, featured only American artists, since the Europeans Stieglitz had first exhibited, among them Cézanne, Brancusi, and Picasso, had not only dominated the Armory Show of 1913 but now enjoyed worldwide renown. More than ever, American art now needed a champion. Influential cultural critics like the younger Van Wyck Brooks had argued that American life was either too genteel or too crassly materialistic to nurture great achievements in the arts, a sentiment many expatriate writers shared. (This had helped drive them away in the first place.) Stieglitz and Rosenfeld, on the other hand, looked back to Whitman for an authentic American art that rejected European models, and they were influenced by D. H. Lawrence's conviction that American writers had sounded a new note in Western culture, breaking new ground in exploring both the continent and their own psyches. Without exactly saying so, Lawrence had launched the American canon and reconfigured the classic American writers in modernist terms.

This Lawrentian argument was pursued by Rosenfeld in his most important book, *Port of New York: Essays on Fourteen American Moderns* (1924); by the poet William Carlos Williams in his ambitious prose work *In the American Grain* (1925); and by Hart Crane in his uneven Whitmanesque epic, *The Bridge* (1930). Copland was attracted to the work of Crane and Williams and grew especially close to Rosenfeld, who was primarily a music critic, though *Port of New York* focused on painters and a few writers, among them Williams, Sandburg, and Sherwood Anderson. Rosenfeld in turn became a great admirer of Copland's music. This was surprising since Rosenfeld was hostile to jazz and especially to the crowd-pleasing concert pieces of George Gershwin, to which Copland's jazz-inflected scores were sometimes compared. His 1929 essay on Copland, though written long before Copland's popular works were composed, helped set the terms by which his music would be appreciated. Rosenfeld stressed its "leanness, slenderness of sound," combined with "a strain of grandiosity." He described the liveliness, "the decided motoriness," of Copland's rhythm, even in its slow moods, and stressed the kinetic vitality that would later become a hallmark of Copland's ballet scores. "What one means by this motoriness of Copland's, is its strong kinesis, its taut, instinctive 'go.' Wistful or burlesque, slow or fast, his pieces have enormous 'snap.'" It's revealing that Rosenfeld, a mandarin stylist, reaches for colloquial terms (set off by inverted commas) to evoke this strikingly American yet also modern quality in Copland's work. He connects it to the machine ("the hiccoughing beat" of the jazzy Scherzo of Copland's first symphony, "iterated with a mad mechanic joy"), to the new architecture, with its wiry steel skeleton, and to American energy in general, "all that's swift and daring, aggressive and unconstrained in our life."[8]

While this describes what Copland had already done, it could be read as a program for work he had yet to do, from the austere virtuosity of the *Piano Variations* (1930), which thrilled young composers and performers like Leonard Bernstein, becoming a benchmark for the new music, to the folk-inspired *El Salón México* (1932–36), *Billy the Kid* (1938), *Rodeo* (1942), and *Appalachian Spring* (1944). Students of thirties culture have commonly contrasted this kind of audience-friendly populism—melodic, familiar, accessible—with the insouciant modernism of the 1920s or the aggressive experimentalism of the early 1930s, which produced not only the *Piano Variations*, a work that ordinary listeners often found forbidding, but also a great deal of severe proletarian fiction and poetry, attracting few readers. There was also a mammoth novel like Dos Passos's *U.S.A.* trilogy (1930–36), a collage of history, biography, journalism, and fiction with highly typical rather than distinctly individualized characters.

The uncompromising aesthetic radicalism of Copland or Dos Passos paralleled the political radicalism of the Left during the early thirties, the peak years of the Depression, before the official turn toward the Popular Front in 1935. Yet Dos Passos's ambitious Whitmanesque novel follows directly from the concern with the American scene promoted by the

Stieglitz circle and exemplified by writers like Williams, Crane, and even F. Scott Fitzgerald in the 1920s. For them America became a challenge, an enigma—something to be unraveled and explained by exploring its founding myths and popular traditions. They looked for the themes and folkways that might help them make sense of American culture. For Copland, as for many writers and visual artists, the burgeoning populism of the post-1935 period did not represent a sharp reversal of direction. It had deep roots in the modernism of the twenties and the radicalism of the early thirties.

Part of the turn toward populism was anthropological. Along with an interest in jazz and the blues came a recovery—or was it partly an invention?—of folk culture. Stemming from the nineteenth-century search for national roots, this fascination with folklore, which came late to the United States, took shape in the 1920s but grew in the 1930s. Ethnomusicologists like Charles Seeger, John Lomax, and his son Alan Lomax traveled through the rural South to record and transcribe music that belonged to oral traditions that might soon be lost. As early as 1927, Carl Sandburg retrieved and published a huge collection of folk songs, *The American Songbag*. Pioneering folklorists such as Constance Rourke, B. A. Botkin, and Zora Neale Hurston collected humor, tall tales, legends, and folk wisdom, including the stories Hurston brought together in *Mules and Men* (1934) under the tutelage of her mentor, the anthropologist Franz Boas. Later, after fieldwork in Haiti, she began gathering material in her native Florida for the Federal Writers' Project.

A key feature of the twenties avant-garde was a rebellion against middle-class gentility in the name of earthiness, authenticity, and frank sexual expression. These projects reflected the critical spirit of D. H. Lawrence, whose influence, along with Freud's, can be felt everywhere. Sherwood Anderson's *Winesburg, Ohio* (1919) was a deeply personal ethnography of an American town, with an accent on the unfulfilled lives of its inhabitants and the longings of its clumsy but sensitive young protagonist, who records their stories but detaches himself and escapes at the end. Jean Toomer's *Cane* (1923), an idiosyncratic mixture of poetry and prose, sank deep into the loam of the author's native Georgia in a way that fascinated both the young modernists, who brought out his work in the *Liberator*, and the future writers of the Harlem Renaissance. *Cane* found an unlikely echo in the work of an aristocratic white southerner,

DuBose Heyward, whose immersion in Gullah culture would lead to his evocative portrayal of Charleston's Catfish Row. He would see the story of Porgy and Bess through its transformations from a 1925 novel to a successful 1927 Broadway play to Gershwin's 1935 folk opera.

Of all the Harlem Renaissance writers, none better achieved a folk-like simplicity than Langston Hughes in his first two books of poems, *The Weary Blues* (1926) and *Fine Clothes to the Jew* (1927). Well before the "forgotten man"—the neglected veteran who had served his country—and the "common man" were elevated into myth by the onset of the Depression, Hughes used colloquial American speech to direct his poems and prose to ordinary readers. His language and rhythm were deceptively simple, intentionally evading the literary. Moreover, Hughes, unlike the more genteel writers of the Harlem Renaissance, tried to bring the very cadence of jazz and the blues into his jingly rhythm, as in the title poem of the first volume:

> *Droning a drowsy syncopated tune,*
> *Rocking back and forth to a mellow croon,*
> *I heard a Negro play.*
> *Down on Lenox Avenue the other night*
> *By the pale dull pallor of an old gas light*
> *He did a lazy sway. . . .*
> *He did a lazy sway. . . .*
> *To the tune o' those Weary Blues.*[9]

Another strain of Hughes's "Americanness" turned up in a poem that appeared in Alain Locke's 1925 anthology *The New Negro*. "I, too," echoed Whitman, beginning, "I, too, sing America." One of his signature works, written in the voice of the "darker brother" who is sent to eat in the kitchen, it predicts that one day he would find his place at the table (*CP*, 46). A much longer poem from 1925, "America," focuses on the "little dark baby" and the "little Jew baby" as they both struggle for acceptance. Hughes writes in lines so short, almost hypnotically repetitious, that they create a drumlike cadence: "We come / You and I, / Seeking the stars. / You and I, / You of the blue eyes / And the blond hair, / I of the dark eyes / And of the crinkly hair. / You and I / Offering hands / Being brothers, / Being one, / Being America" (*CP*, 52).

The motif of the brotherly handshake, the mutual recognition across barriers of race and class, became one of the central images of the Popular Front and part of the insignia of the industrial labor unions. Even in his best-known poem on this theme, "Let America Be America Again" (1936), whose dark refrain is "America never was America to me," Hughes concludes with the shaky confidence that the dream is not quite dead, that "America will be!" (*CP*, 189–91). This faith culminated in Earl Robinson's 1939 cantata *Ballad for Americans*, made famous by Paul Robeson, and in his 1943 anthem "The House I Live In," with lyrics by Abel Meeropol, which was sung by Robeson but also most effectively by Frank Sinatra in a celebrated short film of 1945 by that name. The introductory verse of "The House I Live In" begins, in classic Popular Front fashion, "What is America to me?" It goes on to describe the little ordinary things enjoyed by "all races and religions," all sharing the same house, the same nation. Under the banner of democracy, where each individual has "the right to speak [his] mind out," inequalities of wealth, distinctions of class, race, or religion are subdued, to be replaced by a warmhearted abstraction, the people: "But especially the people / That's America to me." In the movie—written by someone who would soon be blacklisted and imprisoned as one of the Hollywood Ten, Albert Maltz, and directed by an old Hollywood pro, Mervyn LeRoy—Sinatra sings this with such force and lyrical conviction as to make its sugary sentiments unexpectedly concrete, teaching a lesson in tolerance to a rowdy group of young boys. The message of the Popular Front, a message of unity and interdependence, of diversity within community, was rarely delivered more convincingly.

As his congressional inquisitors would later remind him, Copland, like Hughes, was a longtime fellow traveler who remained deeply involved with left-wing causes between 1932 and 1949. He even won a prize for setting a May Day song in 1934. But the motivation for his turn toward populism and Americana was not strictly political. Copland had always wanted to create an intrinsically American music, but he also came to feel that there was a limited audience for avant-garde writing, which itself had lost its keen experimental edge, in part because the Depression had altered the national mood. His response to a shifting cultural climate was typically pragmatic, as was his turn away from left-wing politics after 1949. Like the painters who grew disenchanted with museums as mausoleums for the elite, he felt hemmed in by the concert hall and looked instead to theater, films, and dance to get in touch with a wider public. To reach this audience, he accepted the artistic challenge of "an imposed simplicity" (C-P 1, 316) and the personal challenge of collaboration, even in the movies, where he knew that his music would have to play a subsidiary role. Writing his first Hollywood film score for Lewis Milestone's adaptation of Steinbeck's *Of Mice and Men* (1939), he mused that "it seemed a strange assignment to write music that is actually meant to be uninteresting" (C-P 1, 299). To make sure his music would be heard, though, he usually adapted it—especially the ballet music—into orchestral suites that proved enduringly successful in the concert hall.

When intellectuals of the 1940s and 1950s assailed Popular Front culture, they often linked it with technology, new media, and mass audiences. They saw it as hopelessly middlebrow, a dumbing down of art into toothless entertainment. To them it represented a deluge of mechanical and commercial art swamping the real thing. Some modernist critics of the twenties like Edmund Wilson and Gilbert Seldes had welcomed the new popular arts. But now, as the thirties ended, *Partisan Review* writers like Clement Greenberg and Dwight Macdonald launched attacks on kitsch and mass culture that were rooted in their anti-Stalinist politics. These became the first volleys in a culture war that would rage throughout the early postwar decades, when modernist intellectuals erected a cultural hierarchy, from highbrow to lowbrow, that made all popular art suspect.

The new avant-garde of the 1940s would define itself against post-office art, movie culture, tonality, program music, representational realism or regionalism, and progressive messages of any kind. This assault widened the modernist break between high art and popular taste. It would be pointless to decry this as a gross injustice to much of thirties art or a blind resistance to new forms of mass communication. Every modern generation defines itself against its predecessors; postwar artists, some of whom began as WPA artists and social realists, were no exception. They recoiled from cultural nationalism and from social messages. But Copland embraced the opportunity to seek out native resources to paint a picture of American life, and he set about trying to do this in strikingly novel ways, giving full play to his own distinctive musical voice. *Billy the Kid,* choreographed by Eugene Loring, was one of a series of American-themed ballets commissioned by Lincoln Kirstein's Ballet Caravan, including

Vigil Thomson's *Filling Station.* Here was a Jewish New Yorker, working on the rue de Rennes in Paris with two collections of western tunes
that Kirstein had pressed on him—achieving what the Left called a
"united front" in his own artistic identity. Copland later recalled his initial qualms: "I have never been particularly impressed with the musical
beauties of the cowboy song as such." He noted that "it is a delicate operation to put fresh and unconventional harmonies to well-known melodies without spoiling their naturalness." He kept in mind his "resolve to
write plainly—not only because I had become convinced that simplicity
was the way out of isolation for the contemporary composer, but because
I have never liked music to get in the way of the thing it is supposedly aid-
ing" (C-P 1, 279).

It was typical of the populist artist of the late 1930s to try to communicate more directly and also to undertake cooperative projects, making good use of familiar or accessible materials. Popular artists rarely saw
themselves in Romantic terms as lone creators striving for bold originality. If they were lucky and gifted, they struck a new note by combining,
synthesizing, and collaborating. Virgil Thomson undoubtedly paved the
way for Copland's use of folk material with his *Symphony on a Hymn Tune*
and especially with his wonderful scores for Pare Lorentz's government-
sponsored documentaries, *The Plow That Broke the Plains* (1936) and *The
River* (1937). Or so he often claimed. In an ambivalent but penetrating
essay on Copland in *Modern Music* in 1932, Thomson, reflecting on the
melancholy fate of the modern composer, concluded prophetically, "Simple clarity is what we need, and we will get it only by a radical simplification of our methods of composition."[10]

Clarifying and simplifying, reaching out to a wider audience, promoting some form of communal bonding, finding a distinctive native
style, and doing this with freshness and vitality—these were some hallmarks of the Group Theatre, created by Copland's lifelong friend Harold
Clurman, which sought to combine honest emotion with radical protest.
Its very name pointed to community over individuality, the collective
pursuit of art and truth over stardom or celebrity. But the populist turn
can best be seen in the New Deal arts projects, including the Treasury
Department mural commissions starting in 1934 and the WPA Arts Project starting in 1935, which decorated many official buildings all across
America with scenes from American history and contemporary life. Some

of these scenes offended local mores. Others were mocked by critics for their impersonality or figurative conservatism. In her challenging book on the post-office murals, *Wall-to-Wall America* (1982), Karal Ann Marling argues that high-art standards of aesthetic autonomy and originality are irrelevant to these works. For the painters, as for the government that commissioned them, the murals were less a work of art than a compact with the community and with popular feeling. The emphasis was on the story they told, not the form. "The mural remained a painting, but it was a painting last; first, it was a depiction of objects and scenes, a picture, a symbol, and event."[11] The artist turning from the easel to the mural was like the composer moving from the concert hall into the theater or the movie palace. This was an experiment in the democratization of art for a mass audience. Marling suggests that the murals should be compared to movies, not to paintings in museums. The murals, like Hollywood movies, relied on the "collective archetype, which aligned their aesthetic with mass culture." She argues,

Movies were successful—and profitable—in direct proportion to their ability to arouse and stimulate the latent content of the popular imagination. Movies spoke to everybody, at 25¢ a head, in a familiar tongue, the imagistic argot of the people. The cowboy, the hood, the common man, and the Midwestern farmer were instantly recognizable amalgams of operative myth, fiction, legend, and half-remembered dreams of childhood. (90)

Before the government programs, the best-known examples of such mythmaking artists were the great Mexican muralists, especially Diego Rivera, whose Rockefeller Center murals were destroyed in 1933 because he had included the head of Lenin, and the titanic midwestern populist Thomas Hart Benton, whose highly stylized scenes of ordinary Americans at work and play had a huge impact on New Deal artists. Here too we can see parallels to Copland. Benton had begun as a modernist but later turned sharply against modernism, especially abstract art, while adapting some of its techniques to the portrayal of realistic scenes. Like other regionalist painters, Marling claims, Benton worked less from life than from the stereotypes of the popular media. His figures were so recognizable in part because they were generalized rather than individualized; to achieve the typical, the sense of the collective, they relied on a stock of images familiar from films, cartoons, and photographs. In *America Today* (1930), Benton's great set of murals for the New School in New York, "the figures, drawn like animated cartoon characters, defy orthodox anatomy," says Marling. "Benton's farmers and floozies diagram kinetic energy poised for release" (40).

Copland's use of Mexican tunes in *El Salón México* and cowboy songs in *Billy the Kid* and *Rodeo* can be compared to Benton's reliance on archetypal, easily recognizable images borrowed from popular culture, though Copland, with unfailing musical taste, invariably gave them an unspoiled feeling that transcended stereotype. Both artists were reaching for the elusive figure of the common man, to whom Copland paid such dignified tribute in his famous fanfare of 1942. And both evoked tremendous energy through their use of popular material. "*America Today* is essentially plotless but achieves a comparable unity through Benton's forceful contention that energy is the hallmark of American life," according to Marling. "As the Depression deepened, the dynamism of the New School murals promised that this powerful race of doers could find a way out" (41).

Like so much populist art of the late 1930s, Copland's ballets are based on the same optimistic principle. In a period of continuing stagnation, their driving aim is to get people in motion again, to stimulate high spirits. Copland did not set out deliberately to cheer people up, only to reach them more directly, but his buoyant music, such as the "Hoe-Down" in *Rodeo*, invariably makes listeners want to kick up their heels. Copland instinctively understood why dance—from Busby Berkeley and Fred Astaire to Balanchine and Martha Graham—grew into such a passion during the Depression years, when ballet was democratized and Americanized. The figure of Billy the Kid also fits in easily with the outlaw stereotypes so popular during the Depression, such as the Bonnie-and-Clyde characters in Edward Anderson's novel *Thieves Like Us* (1937) and Fritz Lang's film *You Only Live Once* (1937), or the charismatic criminals played by Jimmy Cagney, with the same "snap," the electric sense of vitality, that Rosenfeld praised in Copland's music.

Copland's populist works, like Benton's murals, form chapters of an ongoing saga of the common man that produced not only literary creations like Steinbeck's characters but screen personalities that would endure for half a century. For Frank Capra in his celebrated populist movies made between 1936 and 1946, the common man was personified by actors like Gary Cooper and Jimmy Stewart, playing the naive but determined everyman, as well as a brilliant galaxy of character actors like Walter Brennan, while their female counterparts were the spunky working girls played by Barbara Stanwyck or Jean Arthur. In Fritz Lang's first two American movies, *Fury* (1936), an antilynching film, and *You Only Live Once*, the common man was impersonated by Spencer Tracy and Henry Fonda, whose screen personalities would become bywords for plain-man decency and rock-ribbed integrity.

John Ford would cement Fonda's image by casting him as Tom Joad and the young Abe Lincoln, the historical forerunner of the common man, as Whitman was the literary forerunner. More class-conscious directors turned to John Garfield and Sylvia Sidney as ethnic working-class figures, beloved by Popular Front audiences, who had already developed their public personalities on the New York stage. By then the Group Theatre aesthetic associated with Clurman, Lee Strasberg, and Clifford Odets was making inroads into Hollywood. It infiltrated war movies, which focused on the ordinary dogface rather than the combat hero. It would triumph after the war in the hands of Elia Kazan, Arthur Miller, Marlon Brando, and the Actors Studio, ably supported by actors like Lee J. Cobb, Karl Malden, and Rod Steiger. In different ways, Stanley Kowalski and Willy Loman brought the common man into the postwar era, while Blanche DuBois conveyed the forlorn romanticism of an earlier time.

Copland's initial film projects, his scores for *Of Mice and Men* (1939) and *Our Town* (1940), involved literary sources that exemplified the same populist bent toward Americana and the common man. Yet his music always had a singular authenticity missing from the work of composers like Earl Robinson or Elie Siegmeister, who exploited American material because they had a message to deliver or because the Communist Party steered them in that direction. Much of Popular Front art was not only message ridden but smacked of condescension and insincerity, an ersatz simplicity that patronized its subjects and came off as anything but natural. This was what makes much of the work of Copland, Benton, Steinbeck, Capra, John Ford, Walker Evans, James Agee, Marc Blitzstein, Woody Guthrie, and even Virgil Thomson so refreshing.[12] They made genuine art with what, for others, was little more than a political program, even a form of middle-class slumming.

Because Depression conditions were so extreme, social tourism became endemic to the decade. Writers and journalists of every kind were intrigued by how ordinary American were getting by. Long before the official populism of the second half of the decade, writers like Edmund Wilson, who had just published a classic work on international modernism, took to the road to report on how people were doing; he filed his stories for *The New Republic*, where he had served in the 1920s as literary editor. As published in book form, *The American Jitters* (1932) was not only the best of Wilson's travel books; along with *To the Finland Station*, his 1940 history of revolutionary ideas, it was the closest he came to writing truly effective narrative, a good deal closer than his own fiction. In one sketch, for example, "A Bad Day in Brooklyn," he explores the actual stories of three separate people who, at their wits' end, tried to kill themselves in the same day, showing how even their suicide attempts prove haplessly ineffectual. In "Two Protests" he makes a pointed juxtaposition between a protest meeting of activists and intellectuals, which he describes at considerable length, and a spontaneous act of desperation by a Sicilian immigrant, a man with a wife, an infant child, and no job, who kills his landlord when the man hounds him for the rent, an incident Wilson recounts in a few stark paragraphs almost as an afterthought. Avoiding emotion or explicit commentary, Wilson takes on the inflections of a hard-boiled writer to convey some harsh ironies that beset the lives of hard-pressed Americans during the lowest days of the Depression.

This kind of committed journalism continued in different forms all through the 1930s: in the oral histories collected by members of the Federal Writers' Project, issuing in such acclaimed volumes as *These Are Our Lives* (1939), which included thirty-five stories of southern tenant farmers; in the text-and-picture books covering some of the same ground by Agee and Evans, Margaret Bourke-White and Erskine Caldwell, Dorothea Lange and Paul Taylor, Edwin Rosskam and Richard Wright; in numerous travel books by writers on the road; or in what Marshall Berman, in an essay on Studs Turkel, called the "We-the-People-Talk book," composed of interviews and conversations in which ordinary men and women, customarily silenced by history, find their voice, as they rarely did in standard journalism, where their stories are filtered through the interpretive prose of the writer.[13] An important example was *The People Talk* (1940), by Benjamin Appel, a genuine hard-boiled writer, who took to the road by car and put together a collage of people and viewpoints so spare, so free of comment or interpretation, that it makes Wilson's bare manner look garrulous. Here the writer himself completely disappears.

Appel's book in some ways is the purest example of 1930s populism. Its dedication page reads "By the People / and / For the People," at once a political echo and an assertion of democracy, as if the people themselves could assume collective responsibility, without literary intervention.[14] James Agee had taken this documentary impulse even further when he recorded his resistance to using words at all in *Let Us Now Praise Famous Men*. Instead, he says, he would have preferred to deploy a mixture of real materials, "fragments of cloth, bits of cotton, lumps of earth, records of speech, pieces of wood and iron, phials of odors, plates of food and of excrement," as if representation itself were suspect—only the thing itself could do justice to the real.[15]

Copland's populism and his treatment of the American scene are at the farthest remove from the transcribed reality sought by Wilson, Appel, and Agee and achieved most powerfully by the great thirties photographers like Lange and Evans. When he worked on *El Sálon México* or the *Danzón Cubano*, Copland understood that he was working from the outside, not strictly as a tourist but with popular materials, which he did not hesitate to transpose into his own voice. Like Virgil Thomson, he felt that music should not simply transcribe or invent but ought to seduce. Copland's western ballets were frankly grounded in mythology, not actuality; working with Martha Graham on *Appalachian Spring* (1944), he knew he was helping her shape a myth by way of rhythm, expressive passion, and physical movement. His use of the Shaker hymn "Simple Gifts" ("'Tis the gift to be simple, 'tis the gift to be free"), which points to what was most admired about the Shaker way of life, was almost a credo for the simplifying approach to music that he had taken since the mid-1930s, and, as Howard Pollack remarks, it "had connotations relevant to the work's larger themes of peace, war, remembrance, and national identity" (C-Pol, 398). It describes a way of living as well as a way of composing.

No concert audience has ever needed to know the program of this ballet to appreciate its music, which sums up all Copland had been trying to achieve for almost a decade, and perhaps as far back as his integration of jazz and pop materials in the 1920s. "The entire score," notes Pollack, "represents an absorption of the vernacular—suitable to a script so steeped in a wide range of American myth and folklore. It often gives the impression of folk music, so much so that listeners are often surprised to discover that it uses only one folk tune" (C-Pol, 399). Where *Billy the Kid* evoked a life of risk and violent adventure and *Rodeo* had the dizzying energy of a country square dance, the music for *Appalachian Spring*, especially the variations on the Shaker melody, is stately, vibrant, often slow and tense, but always immensely dignified, with the same grandeur and solidity we hear in the *Fanfare for the Common Man*. If *Rodeo* anticipates *Oklahoma!*, also choreographed by Agnes de Mille, *Appalachian Spring* reminds me of Walker Evans's eloquent, deeply humane photographs; they make other treatments of rural folk look corny or condescending. This quiet dignity is especially impressive in Copland's original chamber score, without the color and brilliance of the orchestral suite of 1945. In either version, *Appalachian Spring* marks the culmination of Copland's populism and his exploration of American themes.

In its heyday in the 1890s, American populism was an agrarian rebellion against eastern bankers, plutocrats, and industrialists. In the Europe of the 1920s and 1930s, populism took a Fascist turn and became a frightening mass ideology of blood and soil. When Kenneth Burke, at the first American Writers' Congress of 1935, suggested substituting "the people" for "the workers" or "the masses" in the propaganda of the Left, he was reminded by one critic that it was "historically associated with demagoguery of the most vicious sort." But Burke insisted that "the symbol of 'the people'" was both "closer to our folkways" and contained "connotations both of oppression and of unity."[16] In the cultural wing of the Popular Front, a battery of socially concerned writers, artists, composers, choreographers, and photographers, abetted by the cultural programs of the New Deal, created a left-wing populism that could be urban as well as rural, that lent dignity to common people, recaptured lost elements of America's history and folk heritage, instilled energy and hope into people who were suffering from fear and privation, and tried to bridge gaps of sympathy and understanding between different races, classes, and regions. For some "the people" was an empty symbol, a tactical appeal to an undifferentiated mass that did not truly exist and to traditions that were largely imaginary or simply recast in a "progressive" image. But at its best, until postwar anti-Communism set out to destroy its influence, the new populism brought important chapters of the American past alive; it made many Americans far more aware of how others lived and suffered during the Depression; it gave political energy to a more inclusive liberal tradition, and cemented communal bonds that carried over into the national war effort. Aaron Copland was shaped by this movement as much as he helped bring it into being. He had anticipated it in the 1920s and continued to pursue it through the 1940s and even beyond. Despite the aesthetic and political backlash against populist art, his key works, like Gershwin's and Ellington's, helped create the American sound. Beloved by audiences, echoed by the younger composers he helped nurture, they became an intrinsic part of the nation's cultural life.

CHAPTER 13

Who Cares?:

THE WORLD OF PORGY AND BESS

THE TURN TOWARD POPULISM in the mid-1930s produced surprisingly few works that actually became popular, and even fewer that would stand the test of time. Copland's American ballets, Steinbeck's *Of Mice and Men* and *The Grapes of Wrath*, and Thornton Wilder's *Our Town* were the exceptions rather than the rule. It was not until the patriotic climate of World War II that a new vogue of folksy Americana, stripped of all social criticism, genuinely took hold, as seen in works like Rodgers and Hammerstein's first Broadway show, *Okla-homa!* (1943). Few would have predicted that a far less typical Broadway musical, the Gershwins' "folk opera" *Porgy and Bess*, written by George, DuBose and Dorothy Heyward, and Ira, would eventually become one of the most beloved and durable works of the century, performed repeat-edly all over the world. When *Porgy* first opened in 1935 it was rejected by the Broadway audience as too highbrow, with its all-black cast and sung recitatives, and by serious critics like Virgil Thomson and Paul Rosen-feld as too lowbrow. "Gershwin does not even know what an opera is," Thomson complained in a biting yet ambivalent essay, "and yet *Porgy and Bess* is an opera, and it has power and vigor." In words that might have wounded the composer (had his ego been more vulnerable), Thomson wrote, "With a libretto that should never have been accepted on a sub-ject that should never have been chosen, a man who should never have attempted it has written a work that has considerable power."[1]

Paradoxically, Gershwin's insistence on an all-black cast, which the powers that be at the Metropolitan Opera said could never be assembled, probably came from seeing a black cast in Thomson's own opera *Four Saints in Three Acts* a year earlier, when it migrated to Broadway after its sen-sational opening at Hartford's Wadsworth Atheneum. With a libretto by Gertrude Stein and spectacular sets and costumes by Florine Stettheimer, *Four Saints* became an avant-garde conversation piece. Completed as early as 1928, produced as a piece of modernist chic that attracted the cream of society rather than a popular audience, *Four Saints* belonged more to the expatriate decade than to the 1930s, when it unexpectedly became the fashion of the moment, as Stein herself did when she arrived in America for a lecture tour a few months later.[2] After seeing its Broadway opening, Gershwin wrote to his own librettist, DuBose Heyward, "The libretto was entirely in Stein's manner, which means that it has the effect of a 5-year-old child prattling on. Musically, it sounded early 19th Century, which was a happy inspiration and made the libretto bearable—in fact, quite enter-taining."[3] For the production of *Porgy and Bess* he borrowed not only one of the black singers in *Four Saints*, Edward Matthews, but the music director, Alexander Smallens, as well as Harlem's Eva Jessye Choir.

By taking his opera to Broadway and composing individual songs as well as complex orchestral writing, Gershwin aimed for the kind of pop-ular success that would have been inconceivable for a rarefied work like

Four Saints, which has no accessible narrative. Yet he also aimed high, seeking a genuine synthesis between opera and musical theater. Gershwin was first drawn to the story when he read Heyward's original novel, *Porgy*, in 1926, soon after it appeared. But Heyward's wife, Dorothy, an aspiring playwright, was already at work adapting it into a straight play, which had a long run on Broadway after it opened in 1927 under the auspices of the Theatre Guild. When the story of Porgy was finally free, the perpetually busy Gershwin was not. Al Jolson, at the peak of his fame after the success of *The Jazz Singer*, had also expressed strong interest in the story, but Gershwin found it difficult to imagine him in the part. "The sort of thing I should have in mind for Porgy is a much more serious thing than Jolson could ever do."[4] Jolson's rendition of "Swanee" in 1919, which became one of his signature numbers, had propelled Gershwin to fame; it was the young composer's first big hit. But Jolson's specialty was blackface and Gershwin wanted no trace of minstrelsy in his opera, despite its southern white and Jewish creators. This would not keep some musicians and critics from seeing *Porgy and Bess* as a minstrel show that stereotyped poor southern blacks and hijacked their musical heritage. "It does not use the Negro musical idiom," Duke Ellington told an interviewer. "It was not the music of Catfish Row or any other kind of Negroes."[5] Even Thomson complained of this: "Folklore subjects recounted by an outsider are only valid as long as the folk in question is unable to speak for itself, which is certainly not true of the American Negro in 1935" (26).

Unlike the minstrel performer, whose approach could range from some genuine affinity for black culture to hideous caricature and outright larceny, Gershwin aimed to achieve an authentic crossover, a synthesis of his own, not an impersonation. Unlike Copland in his American ballets or Thomson in his fine film scores, he decided not to use actual folk tunes but to write all of his own music. He had won fame by adapting the rhythms of black jazz and dance to his own voice, combining the plaintive minor keys of Jewish folk and cantorial music with the blues he heard in Harlem clubs. Out of this synthesis came some of the freshest musical sounds of the 1920s, smart, lively, hip, a voice of the new generation. We hear it perhaps in its purest form in the 1924 *Rhapsody in Blue*, especially in the melting and sinuous clarinet solo that opens the piece and some of the boisterous piano themes that follow. As much as any work of F. Scott

Fitzgerald, Gershwin's *Rhapsody* surely *is* the 1920s, for behind its surface brightness are sounds of loneliness and sexual longing that link Gershwin to Fitzgerald and makes both of them so representative of the Jazz Age.[6] For me the music evokes the smoky haze of jazz clubs after midnight. But Gershwin said there would always be something of the tenement about him; he saw himself as a melting-pot composer creating an American idiom out of a polyglot musical language. This was what drew him to make an opera of Heyward's novel and play, and it is also part of what his critics held against him. "The material is straight from the melting pot," Thomson complained. Thomson was a matchless music critic, but he could rarely resist ethnic stereotypes when writing about his more successful Jewish rivals. "At best it is a piquant but highly unsavory stirring-up-together of Israel, Africa, and the Gaelic Isles," he said of *Porgy and Bess*. He decried "the impurity of his musical sources" and, in a frank twitch of anti-Semitism, Gershwin's "gefiltefish orchestration"[7] (24, 27). As he had done with the work of Aaron Copland a few years earlier, Thomson could not resist highlighting the real or imagined Hebraic sources of Gershwin's inspiration.

Virgil Thomson was not alone in drawing attention to the eclectic quality of Gershwin's opera. For many critics it was caught between black and white culture, between Broadway and the opera house, between urban sophistication, which had been the hallmark of the Gershwins' music and lyrics, and rural simplicity. Yet such a crossover was exactly what Gershwin had in mind. As early as 1922, in his one-act opera *Blue Monday*, a tale of passion and violence set in a Harlem saloon, Gershwin had wanted to write a serious composition with a black setting. But *Blue Monday* had a risible libretto by Buddy DeSylva and was pulled from the revue in which it appeared after one performance. Though influenced by the *verismo* style of recent Italian opera, its music, especially the opening bars, anticipates the *Rhapsody in Blue* more than *Porgy and Bess*. In a different project closer to the spirit of *Porgy and Bess*, Gershwin later signed a contract with the Met to write an opera based on S. Ansky's celebrated play *The Dybbuk*, but that plan eventually foundered. He would have been reaching out to portray an archaic folk culture, as in *Porgy*, and one as remote from him as Catfish Row. His work took a different turn, however, in satirical operettas like *Strike Up the Band* (1927, 1930), *Of Thee I Sing* (1931), and *Let 'Em Eat Cake* (1933), which were partly inspired by the success of Jerome Kern's

Show Boat in 1927 in raising serious issues in a semi-operatic framework. As Gershwin's scores became increasingly complex and dramatically integrated, the stories, inspired by the Depression, became harsher, even misanthropic, thanks in part to the cynical influence of the playwright George S. Kaufman. The early thirties were a period of revolutionary despair, in which artists and intellectuals believed that the tottering system could not be fixed, only abandoned or overthrown. This was reflected in a certain intransigence in the arts, from proletarian fiction to uninhibited pre-Code moviemaking to avant-garde experiments in music and art, including Copland's most unyielding modernist scores. *Let 'Em Eat Cake*, which failed at the box office, was the Gershwin brothers' contribution to this radical mood. It was a sequel to the sublimely silly, crowd-pleasing political satire of *Of Thee I Sing*. But its elaborate musical numbers, which perform very well in concert today, marked an important step toward *Porgy and Bess*, which was in many ways a far more conservative work, bound to older traditions and simpler human feelings.

The election of Roosevelt and the beginnings of the New Deal in March 1933 opened a new vein of optimism in the public attitude toward the Depression, and many artists gradually turned from a belief in overthrowing the system toward a search for more humane forms of community. Just as the photographers and regionalist painters looked to the heartland of rural America, as the government-sponsored muralists turned to American history to seek out images of collective effort and resistance that might help people endure the social crisis, so the Gershwins and Heywards evoked the world of the Gullah Negroes of Charleston as a poetic alternative to modern lives under urban capitalism. Like the Okies in *The Grapes of Wrath*, these people are beset by poverty, by the cruelty of nature, and by capricious authorities, including the police who abuse and arrest them for no reason. They are bolstered by religious faith and a deep strain of family feeling—as husbands and wives, as parents and children—but they're also torn apart by their own weakness for violence, gambling, and sex. They fight and sometimes kill each other but also lend support to each other when they're down, raising money for a burial, taking in a baby who lost a parent, a woman who lost her husband. It is a fishing community, subject to hurricanes and other nautical disasters, and as in *The Grapes of Wrath* it is a matriarchy. Its spine of strength is the women who watch over their babies, beginning with the great opening lullaby "Summertime," or lament the loss of their men, as in "My Man's Gone Now," a song Billie Holiday found too sad to sing.

The other image of community in *Porgy and Bess* is Catfish Row itself. Few images are more dear to the populist sentiments of the 1930s than the neighborhood, the tenement, or the village square. On the stage or in the movies, these sets have windows facing one another for gossip or clothes-lines; they have doors spilling out onto a public space where neighbors interact and private joys or sorrows turn into everyone's business. They may live in a world of troubles, always close to the edge, but their lives are colorfully interwoven, not isolated from each other. Against this back-ground, Porgy and Bess stand out, for they are outsiders whose improba-ble love helps integrate them into a community in danger of falling apart. Porgy is a beggar and a cripple with a weakness for gambling. Getting around in a goat cart, he seems like a man unlikely to attract a woman. (Heyward was initially drawn by newspaper stories about just such a man, a feisty neighborhood character, who had improbably run afoul of the law for crimes of passion.) Bess is weak and dependent, a woman of dubious virtue, rejected by respectable folk, and she has lived for five years with the violent but sexually overpowering Crown. After Crown kills a man with a cotton hook in a crap game, no one will take Bess in except Porgy. Her love makes him a fuller human being, and he eventually manages to kill Crown; his love, at least for a time, makes an honest woman of her. It helps integrate her into this society, where she is gradually accepted by the chorus of wives and mothers whose very names are musical—Clara, Ser-ena, Maria. The soaring romantic feeling of Porgy's great love duet, "Bess, You Is My Woman Now"—its music recurs as a leitmotif throughout the opera—is itself a form of community, tender, intimate, redemptive. When Bess echoes this music in "I Loves You, Porgy," another touching love duet, and in "What You Want Wid Bess?," where she strains mightily to keep from returning to Crown, we feel the drama evolving not simply in the story but through the music itself, as in any genuine opera. "If you kin keep me / I wants to stay here," she tells Porgy, in words no less touching for being tentative and inarticulate.

But this fragile convergence of feeling is disrupted again and again: besieged by the brutish Crown, whom Bess admits she cannot resist, by violent death and natural calamity, by white intruders—a threatening cop and a coroner, a man running an insurance scam—but, above all, by an interloper from the North, Sportin' Life, a seductively witty Harlem pimp, gambler, and drug dealer. All through the opera he tries to lure Bess to New York, and offers her a different kind of happiness from what she has found with Porgy and Catfish Row. If Crown is one kind of drug that takes over her senses, the pimp's happy dust (cocaine) is another, and he succeeds by playing on her fear as soon as Crown is gone and Porgy has temporarily been thrown in jail.

As Deena Rosenberg showed in *Fascinating Rhythm* (1991), her book tracing the collaboration of George and Ira Gershwin, part of the drama of *Porgy and Bess* comes from the conflict between the endangered pastoral utopia of Catfish Row (the "Golden Age" that Heyward evokes on the first page of his novel) and the lure of wordliness and sophistication of New York, where Sportin' Life promises Bess he will set her up in a mansion on Fifth Avenue. Musically, we hear this as a contrast between blues or spirituals, with their rural roots (including the "shouting" Gershwin heard and absorbed on a five-week field trip to Folly Island, off Charleston), and the kind of urban jazz that had influenced his earlier work. This tension was muted because the opening scene with a jazz pianist, "Jasbo Brown's Blues," set in a dance hall, was cut when the original production came to New York, but the spirit of the big city survives in Sportin' Life's songs, which have invariably seduced audiences along with Bess.

As a tempter figure, the snake in the garden, he plays the role that Iago plays in the greatest of all operas, Verdi's *Otello*. Just as the diabolic intelligence behind Iago's nihilistic "Credo" subverts the romantic feeling of the credulous Otello, so the agnostic sarcasm and urban street smarts behind "It Ain't Necessarily So" will work against Porgy and undermine him. Though it seems to belong to another story, this teasing mockery is less a portrait of a Harlem pimp than the intrusion of a different temperament, a different language and rhythm that clashes with the music of religious faith and romantic sincerity we've heard from Porgy. The brilliant lyrics for Sportin' Life were among Ira Gershwin's main contributions to the opera, though he also rewrote many of Heyward's lyrics to make them more singable. As Heyward later recalled, "Ira's gift for the more sophisticated lyric was exactly suited to writing songs for Sporting Life, the Harlem gambler who had drifted into Catfish Row."[8] Sportin' Life had scarcely figured in the original novel—even Bess had been less important in what was essentially Porgy's story—but here he replaces Crown as Bess's seducer and Porgy's nemesis.

The opera presents Porgy as deeply spiritual and, despite his poverty—or because of it—paradoxically carefree. As the chorus of women laments the murdered Robbins ("Gone, gone, gone"), Porgy echoes their feelings by singing of "going home," which leads to the coda of the first act, a big number called "Leavin' for the Promis' Lan'." These spirituals are among the most derivative numbers in the opera but their themes are important, for they are picked up later. Home is the shelter of Porgy's house and of Catfish Row, just as heaven is seen as the final shelter for the dead; Sportin' Life offers Bess yet another deceptively attractive haven, culminating in his other dazzling number, "There's a Boat Dat's Leavin' Soon for New York." He offers her a fantasy home on Fifth Avenue, in fantasy clothes, "silks and satins / In de latest Paris styles."

> Come wid me, dat's where we belong, sister.
> You and me can live dat high life in New York.
> Come wid me, dere you can't go wrong, sister.

As he invites her to "go a-struttin'," the music echoes the dance piano of the opening scene. And his rival, after all, is a cripple in a goat cart. Sportin' Life evokes the real attractions of the city and of the music that had inspired Gershwin's best work.

But Gershwin and his collaborators also wanted to give the somber and love-smitten Porgy a lighter number, a struttin' piece of his own, to make his appeal more credible. So they wrote "I Got Plenty o' Nuttin'," which conjures up the carefree bliss of *not* having anything but the sun, the moon, and the deep blue sea: "I got my gal, got my song, / Got I lebben de whole day long." This was the Depression, after all, and having anything at all could be a dicey proposition.

> De folks wid plenty o' plenty,
>   Got to pray all de day.
> Seems wid plenty you sure got to worry
>   How to keep de Debble away.

This is still the religious Porgy but not a man too concerned about earthly possessions or last things. In the buoyant, upbeat bridge of the song, he sets these things aside.

I ain't a-frettin' bout Hell
  Till de time arrive.
Never worry long as I'm well,
  Never one to strive
    To be good, to be bad—
    What the hell! I is glad
      I's alive.

The swelling music of these last lines gives Porgy a rush of excitement, a surge of vitality. Just as Ira wrote Sportin' Life's mocking numbers, he introduced this play of wit on heaven and hell into this lightest of Porgy's numbers, to show that he too has something to offer, not only love and protection but an outlook on life that is religious in its own way, reveling in the pleasures of the earth, the senses, the ordinary—of simply being alive.

Set against this we have "It Ain't Necessarily So," a strange interlude—a "sermon," as Sportin' Life calls it—of higher biblical criticism that not only counters Porgy's appeal to scripture but directly challenges it. The figures mentioned are all from the Old Testament—David, Moses, Jonah, Methuselah, Adam and Eve, all important to both Jewish and black traditions—and the form of the lyric is, of all things, a limerick. But the attitudes are skeptical: "Dey tell all you chillun / De debble's a villain / But it ain't necessarily so." This is spoken with the charm of the "debble" himself. Even the call-and-response between him and the chorus effectively mocks the liturgical pattern. This was chanted, not sung, for the first Sportin' Life, impersonated by a crowd-pleasing vaudevillian named John W. Bubbles, was not a singer, and the character has no music in his soul.

The story of Porgy and Bess is rooted in the appeal of the simple life, Porgy's carefree faith, the rural paradise in which poverty is a blessing, not the curse it was for 1930s America. As the Harlem gambler puts it, "To get into hebben / Don't snap fo' a seben— / Live clean! Don't have no fault! / Oh, I takes dat gospel / Whenever it's pos'ple— / But wid a grain of salt!" But living with a cripple, how good could that be? And what kind of sexual attraction? You might as well live with Methuselah.

> Methus'lah live nine hunderd years,
> Methus'lah live nine hunderd years—
>> But who calls dat livin'
>> When no gal'll give in
> To no man what's nine hunderd years?

Who is Sportin' Life? He had almost no role in the novel, where he disappears early and Bess in the end goes off with some gamblers to Savannah, not to New York. I described him as an interloper from the city, but it's hard to resist the idea that the actual interloper was Gershwin himself, backed up by his clever brother back home, and that "New York" was a metaphor—or is it a synecdoche?—for Gershwin's life and music before he came upon Catfish Row. The Depression struck a blow against irony and sophistication, though it could also make them seem more attractive. The Depression brought the expatriates home and sent hard-bitten urban journalists out into the hinterland to see how the common man was faring. But it also made a hero of Cole Porter and gave fodder for cynics who made some of the best screwball comedies. In Ben Hecht's curdled script for William Wellman's *Nothing Sacred* (1937), the country rubes are as fraudulent as the city slickers, and public opinion is as gullible as the journalistic hucksters who play upon it. But in Frank Capra's populist movies like *Meet John Doe*, the "wised-up" and the sophisticated are invariably the villains, though not beyond redemption by some simple truths—unlike the plutocrats who manipulate them, who have chosen power and wealth over ordinary humanity.

So unlike Gershwin's earlier work (even *Blue Monday*), *Porgy and Bess* could be seen as his search for the common man. This is how we could describe Agee and Evans with their three tenant families, or Zora Neale Hurston exploring the folklore and folkways of her native Florida, or the many journalists and novelists who took to the road to take the measure of hard times. The values in most of Gershwin's work were anything but homely and domestic. He never married, but in his own way he was committed to family values, working in perfect harmony with his witty but phlegmatic brother. He was still living and composing amid his extended family long after he had become famous, under the eye of a matriarch as willful and self-centered as Bessie Berger in Clifford Odets's play *Awake and Sing!* (or for that matter, FDR's imperious mother, who made Eleanor Roosevelt's life a constant trial as she supervised their household from an adjoining townhouse).

Gershwin's work had never been as popular as Irving Berlin's, but his comfort with his Jewish roots, his crossover into jazz, and his affinity for black culture, to which legions of jazzmen responded in kind, had always given his music a democratic flavor, despite its sophistication. But the Gullah Negroes of Charleston and the nearby islands were another matter. Their lives and folkways, their music, demanded a different kind of immersion. "I cannot urge you too strongly to plan to come to Charleston at the earliest convenience for your visit," Heyward had written to him early in 1934. "You really haven't scratched the surface of the native material yet."[9] In his five weeks on Folly Island, where he sopped up the native rhythms with a bottomless thirst, Gershwin may have felt that *he* was the intruder from the North, the cultural tourist in the lower depths of rural poverty and a "primitive" way of life, though Heyward later recalled that he seemed perfectly at home, even competing with the "shouters" in church.

The social tourist of the 1930s, recoiling from an "advanced" society whose foundations had been shaken, would be tempted to idealize the simple life and the common man as trouble-free alternatives to modern life. *Porgy and Bess* gives us a world of community and solidarity, including the rituals of death and mourning, but also of racial oppression, constant danger, poverty, vice, temptation, violence, and physical deformity. It offers a parable of how two outcasts can redeem one another, how Porgy's crippled soulfulness can redeem Bess's weakness and need for love, which in turn allays his loneliness and gives him back his manhood. Before Bess, Porgy is alone. "When Gawd make cripple, he mean him to be lonely," he says. But just as the mother sings watchfully over her child in "Summertime," Porgy offers Bess his faith, his love, his home, morning and evening, summer and winter, while she, in a sense, puts him back on his feet. ("An' you mus' laugh and sing an' dance for two instead of one," he sings in his love song.) This is a great theme of the 1930s, getting back on your feet, dancing even—moving together toward the happiness, or simply the survival, that we can't reach on our own. Like the Astaire-

Rogers movies, the opera offers an unlikely romance, and even a meta-phorical "dance," as a synonym for solidarity.

If Gershwin's earlier jazz scores contribute to the figure of Sportin' Life, the brothers' melancholy songs of romantic loneliness prepared the way for *Porgy*, including "The Man I Love," dropped from their first important show, *Lady, Be Good*; "Someone to Watch Over Me," which anticipates the lyrics of "Summertime"; and "But Not for Me," from their sumptuous score for *Girl Crazy*. All these are love songs sung by lonely people to no one in particular, or to an ideal figure who watches and cares but who may never actually come along. *Porgy and Bess* is about two such people who find and then lose each other, but it ends on a note of quixotic determination as Porgy, learning that Bess has left, takes off on his goat cart for New York—perhaps for the very stage on which they're perform-ing, unlikely migrants from Catfish Row to Broadway. But as the fisher-man had chanted early on, "it takes a long pull to get there."

For the opera itself, the journey toward acceptance, at first aborted, required a successful West Coast revival in 1938, a Broadway revival in 1942, with much of the original cast but with spoken dialogue replac-ing the recitative, a decade of almost continuous touring in Europe and America in the 1950s, beginning with the young Leontyne Price as Bess and William Warfield as Porgy, and then, after a misconceived film ver-sion by Otto Preminger and even a boycott by some blacks in the radical 1960s, a triumphant premiere for the uncut score at the Houston Opera in 1976, leading to performances at the Met in 1985, half a century after the original production. It won over early skeptics like Virgil Thomson and Duke Ellington and inspired triumphant recordings by great jazz artists like Ella Fitzgerald, Louis Armstrong, and Miles Davis, which brought out an almost unspeakable depth of feeling in the score.[10] Since *Porgy and Bess* is now a staple of opera houses all over the world, its roots in the pop-ulist turn of the mid-1930s have understandably been obscured. It was attacked obtusely as a hybrid work but it was a hybrid work that made its own crossover—between North and South, opera and pop, sophistication and simplicity, ironic wit and romance, plenty and poverty, killing and caring, even between two ill-matched people—part of its theme.

At a time when community had been shredded by economic crisis, when writers like Steinbeck portrayed a society in disintegration, the Heywards and the Gershwins reached into a well of romantic and family feeling to come up with a great Depression theme: compassion, the secret meaning of so many of the brothers' earlier love songs. For Porgy's rich role, Gershwin wrote lonely music, triumphant music, romantic music, self-amused music, anxious music—his tones and moods are wonderfully varied—but we know why he loves and how he loves. It is never entirely clear why Bess stays with *him*, not out of pity, certainly, and not out of any obvious sexual attraction, but from her encounter with a tender inner strength she has never before seen, in which she cannot fully believe. *He takes her in*, and she takes him as he is, and so they complete each other, though the life around them finally tears them apart. They are no one's idea of a romantic couple, but who cares? As in that great Gershwin song "Who Cares?" (from *Of Thee I Sing*), he cares for her and she cares for him—in every sense of the word: tender, romantic, nurturing, empathetic—sentiments that carried over into the poignant, almost valedictory songs of Gershwin's last year in Hollywood, such as "They Can't Take That Away from Me" and "Love Is Here to Stay," songs made indescribably moving by Gershwin's early death.

CHAPTER 14

The People vs. Frank Capra:
POPULISM AGAINST ITSELF

IF THE MODERNIST AARON COPLAND discovered a popular vein with his ballet
scores in the late thirties and early forties,
while the sophisticated George Gershwin
became a kind of populist with his 1935
folk opera, what are we to make of Frank
Capra? His trilogy of common-man films
and their postwar sequel, *It's a Wonderful
Life*, seemed a world apart yet somehow
epitomized the populist turn of American
culture in the late 1930s. Like Gershwin,

like Capra's great admirer John Ford, he had no formal connection to the American Left or the Popular Front, yet despite his own conservative politics, his work was very much in tune with the cultural mood, though it is far more complex than its early critics realized. Though he had been the most successful American film director of the 1930s, a power at the Motion Picture Academy who won four Oscars for best direction, his postwar career foundered badly. As the star director of a back-street studio presided over by the autocratic and penny-pinching Harry Cohn, Capra had single-handedly put Columbia Pictures on the map beginning in the late 1920s. Between 1928 and 1931 he directed fifteen movies, gradually gaining an unheard-of authority as Cohn recognized his Midas touch and his value to the studio. Serving in the army during the war, his film unit produced the celebrated "Why We Fight" series. But *It's a Wonderful Life*, his new beginning as an independent filmmaker after the war, initially disappointed both critics and audiences, who much preferred William Wyler's ambitious portrayal of returning war veterans, *The Best Years of Our Lives*, which went on to sweep the Academy Awards. Though *It's a Wonderful Life* would later be canonized as a beloved classic, for many it epitomized Capra's sentimentality. He never recovered his footing as a director. Only in the 1970s did critical standing begin to rise again.

The charge of sentimentality brings to mind Capra's similarities to both Dickens and Chaplin. Their work too was suspected by critics for its popular appeal and its reliance on pathos and sentiment; they too had the common touch, which critics had difficulty learning to appreciate. Capra's films have the buzz of life, the sense of a peopled world that we find everywhere in Dickens. The genius of Chaplin, as a performer at the center of all his movies, is in his face; Capra's is in his actors' faces. No director uses that great galaxy of 1930s character actors, with their chiseled features and piercing radio voices, to better effect than Capra. Graham Greene, one of Capra's first and most discriminating critics, saluted "the exciting close-ups, the suddenly irrelevant humour, the delight— equal to that of the great Russians—in the ordinary human face."[1] Capra's care in casting was a byword. He delayed filming *Mr. Deeds Goes to Town* for months, at great cost, to get Gary Cooper for the lead. Character actors like Guy Kibbee, bald and weak-kneed, and Eugene Pallette, the "Human Bullfrog," achieved their apotheosis in his films, and the images of star performers like Jean Harlow, Jimmy Stewart, Jean Arthur,

Gary Cooper, Clark Gable, Claudette Colbert. and Barbara Stanwyck were molded under his direction.

An unfriendly critic might say that this epitomizes the view of character endemic to Hollywood and to popular culture, by which actors become personalities and develop recognizable images without learning to immerse themselves in difficult roles, in characters different from themselves. He might add that Capra's politics were also two-dimensional, "simplistic and shallow," as Leonard Quart says, and always the victim of the Hollywood cult of the happy ending. "In Capra's world," Quart writes, "there would be no enduring conflicts—harmony, no matter how contrived and specious, would ultimately triumph in the last frame. . . . In true Hollywood fashion, no Capra film would ever suggest that social change was a complex, painful act. For Capra, there could be pain and loss, but no enduring sense of tragedy would be allowed to intrude on his fabulist world."[2] In the same vein, the film historian Richard Griffith talked of the "fantasy of goodwill" in Capra's films, their reliance on sentimental conversion and the ultimate benevolence of ordinary humanity to resolve all deep conflicts.[3] The same criticism has frequently been leveled at the popular arts in general. Even an intelligent defender like John Cawelti, in his book *Adventure, Mystery, and Romance,* concedes that popular culture is rooted in escapism and wish-fulfillment, in "fantasies of a world more exciting, more fulfilling, or more benevolent than the one we inhabit."[4]

These criticisms imply that popular culture aspires to—yet somehow falls short of— the realistic subtleties of, say, the nineteenth-century novel. This would seem to be confirmed by the conservative plotting and characterization, as well as the general insistence on credibility and realism, of most American films before the 1960s. But most Hollywood films actually are unstable mixtures of genre formulas, repeated from other films, and realistic elements designed to make them seem believable and even unique. Filmmakers like Capra and John Ford, who rework certain patterns repeatedly with only minor variations, are especially clear in their aspiration toward myth and fable rather than lifelike verisimilitude. This is why the mythmaking apparatus of the star system, along with a stock company of secondary actors, is so congenial to them. It gives them performers who precisely do not submerge themselves in their parts, who instead come trailing clouds of association from their other parts, and whose "acting" has the bold simplicity of an icon rather than the literal detail of a photograph.

It's easy to see the mythical qualities of Chaplin's tramp or John Ford's West, for both have a timeless, emblematic quality that distances them from ordinary poverty or the historical frontier; both are allegorical ideas out of the minds of their creators. The same can be said of Capra's Hallmark version of small-town America, though it tries harder to seem lifelike and real. Hollywood's fascination with the stellar and the exotic has always been qualified by its pull toward the quotidian, the ordinary—the average American family in the average American town. Frank Capra's common touch and his vivid imagery did a great deal to form this traditional picture, which by the 1950s could be described by Robert Warshow in the following terms:

> The film [*My Son John*, a cold war movie by Leo McCarey] opens on a "typical" American town of the kind that certain Hollywood directors could probably construct with their eyes shut: a still, tree-lined street, undistinguished frame houses surrounded by modest areas of grass, a few automobiles. For certain purposes, it is assumed that all "real" Americans live in towns like this, and, so great is the power of myth, even the born city-dweller is likely to believe vaguely that he too lives on this shady pleasant street, or comes from it, or is going to it.[5]

By the 1950s, when this was written, the provincial myth of a truly native America, free of foreign influence and ethnic or urban corruption, had assumed a clear ideological purpose; by then the myth was as threadbare as the studio sets on which it had been so frequently played out. But in the 1930s and 1940s, when Capra helped create it, this vision still had the warm glow of a remembered world that belonged to a timeless, idealized past, very much like that of the western. (When Ford began filming westerns during World War I, the veterans of the actual frontier were still around, and sometimes even worked on the movies themselves.) What Andrew Sarris calls "the cinema of memory," which, for all its authentic touches, is really a cinema of myth or idealized memory, casts its radiance not only on Ford's Monument Valley but on the magical small towns of Welles's *Magnificent Ambersons* (1942), that shows us how that old world died, and on Capra's final masterpiece, *It's a Wonderful Life*, where the small-town myth found its apotheosis and critique.

Apart from this film, about a man who, more than anything else, wants to "shake the dust of this crummy town off my feet" but who never manages to get away, very little of Capra's work is actually set in small-town America. His best films, above all the social trilogy of *Mr. Deeds Goes to Town* (1936), *Mr. Smith Goes to Washington* (1939), and *Meet John Doe* (1941), take place, as their titles indicate, in the big city, the enticing Babylon where the important dramas of the modern world inevitably occur. Despite Capra's Jeffersonian suspicion of the city, the small town is already an anachronism in these films, an idea; it's where the hero comes from; its values are now embodied in his character, not in any fixed sense of place. This is how Capra brings together the two sides of Hollywood, the mythic and the quotidian, the stellar and the banal. He translated the small town—the idea of an unspoiled America—from a static tintype into flesh and blood, into Gary Cooper or Jimmy Stewart. No greatness attaches to these figures; they are not Odysseus, not Prince Hamlet, nor were they meant to be. Capra's heroes are not exceptional men, but only heightened versions of ordinary good men; they may stumble into heroism, but their myth is the 1930s myth of the common man. During a period of social crisis, this populist myth, though politically vague and ambiguous, carried nevertheless a strong political charge. It had a long history in American social criticism and popular protest.

These naive heroes come to a city where sophistication, cynicism, and corruption reign. *Sophistication* is what Capra feebly satirizes in the Algonquin-style wits and opera snobs who think they have found their mark in Mr. Deeds. Like Deeds himself, who writes greeting-card verse and plays the tuba with the hometown band, Capra always felt vulnerable to the ridicule of the café intellectuals and clever culturati. *Corruption* is embodied in various capitalist heavies impersonated with superb bloat and bluster by Edward Arnold: he plays a machine boss, Jim Taylor, in *Mr. Smith*, a Wall Street type in *You Can't Take It With You* (1938), and a media baron and would-be political strongman in *Meet John Doe*. *Cynicism*, in Capra's world, is the special style of fast-talking, wisecracking newspaper reporters, like Jean Arthur and Barbara Stanwyck, tough birds who first take the hero for a ride, only to find themselves undermined by his straightforwardness and simplicity, as he is educated by their worldli-

ness. This twin ordeal, this mutual conversion from experience to innocence and innocence to experience, is the key to Capra's surprisingly
ambivalent vision. In this chastening process, which involves much pain
and humiliation for his characters, Capra manages to reconcile the cynical and Pollyannaish sides of his sensibility. The director is able to synthe-
size country and city styles, emotional and intellectual values, in a way
that few critics have recognized and he himself never acknowledged.

There are really two Capra stories, the one he thought he had to
tell—folksy, optimistic, uplifting—which most observers long took at
face value, and the one he actually told, which grew darker and more
complicated in each new version. As he himself paraphrased his favorite
theme, it was a simple David-and-Goliath story, a fairy tale for grown-
ups: "A simple honest man, driven into a corner by predatory sophisticates, can, if he will, reach down into his God-given resources and come
up with the necessary handfuls of courage, wit, and love to triumph over
his environment."[6]

This message is foreshadowed as early as the three films Capra made
in 1926 and 1927 with the comedian Harry Langdon, the lucky simple-
ton whose persona Capra helped create when they both worked for Mack
Sennett. Langdon was one of the great silent comics, but scarcely the conscious artist that Chaplin, Keaton, and even Harold Lloyd certainly were.
He played the holy fool, the wise baby—passive, rubbery, flaccid, and
asexual, where Chaplin and Keaton were always scrappy and resourceful.
Whatever else Langdon could be, he could never be a hero, only a lucky
survivor—the man who rolls down a hill and lands, magically upright,
where his feet should have taken him in the first place. Langdon was
Capra's first plebeian protagonist.

For nearly a decade after Langdon this figure of the indestructible
innocent largely drops out of Capra's films. The hero and heroine of his
great screwball comedy *It Happened One Night* (1934) are both in their way
"predatory sophisticates," separated by class, who chasten each other in
their battle of wits and wills. Not until the story of that "simple honest
man" Longfellow Deeds, as played by Gary Cooper, did Capra find the
perfect vehicle for his new gospel, from which he claimed almost never
to have strayed. As any fairy-tale character might, Deeds inherits twenty
million dollars at the beginning of the film, a matter of remarkably little
interest to him except that it forces him to go to the city and deal with

his new responsibilities, which include a lot of "moochers" who want a piece of him.

Compared to the squishy Langdon, hardly your macho man, Gary Cooper is rather free with his fists—it's his standard way of cutting through problems; and for a supposed innocent he's surprisingly well equipped with what Hemingway and Mailer called a built-in shit detector. Only in matters of the heart is he vulnerable, a sucker, a "prize chump": where his money is concerned, he fends people off so well that he doesn't know what to do with it—until, two-thirds of the way through the film, he (and Capra) happen to notice the Depression, which had intruded only indirectly into *It Happened One Night*. This sets Deeds off doing good deeds, pursuing a somewhat New Dealish but paternalistic scheme to give away parcels of farmland. Deeds, like Capra, has at last found a purpose serious enough to justify his good fortune. In Capra's autobiography we have some deceptive clues to how he came to dramatize such a conversion. It was something, he claims, he himself had recently experienced. Capra vividly describes the physical and emotional breakdown he suffered after the unexpected success of *It Happened One Night*. Feeling a sort of Catholic remorse and unworthiness about his worldly triumphs— the film won all five major Oscars—Capra falls into a slough of morose self-pity. Unable to work, wracked by psychosomatic ailments, he visits a mysterious figure, some kind of therapist or guru with all the solidity of an apparition, who accuses him of being a coward, "an offense to God," a man squandering his native gifts. After this accusatory confrontation, which became an obligatory scene in later Capra films, the director rouses his courage, shakes off all signs of physical illness, and becomes a man with a purpose, dedicated from that point on to *saying* something, to helping humanity.

Capra was somewhat cavalier about when this illness actually occurred, but even his skeptical biographer Joseph McBride, who questions whether such an encounter ever took place, makes it clear that he did become seriously ill. All autobiographies require conversion scenes, but this one feels rather exposed without the dramatic context the films provide. Its upbeat Rotarian message would be more convincing as a new start if we hadn't already witnessed a similar despondency and renewal in Walter Huston years earlier in *American Madness* (1932), and even, mildly, in the resourceful and energetic Clark Gable in *It Happened One*

Night. Every man, at least in retrospect, invents the oracle that would do him the most good, and Capra was more than ready to invent this one before he actually "appeared" in his life. Capra's nameless daemon comes to instill the Power of Positive Thinking, to which his films were already committed, but it would be wrong to put more stress on this message than on the desperate state of mind that seemingly called it into being.

Capra's heroes beginning with Longfellow Deeds are innocents, but when the great world they enter refuses to answer to their naive expectations, they fall into bouts of serious depression that can be seen as a psychological parallel to the state of society in the 1930s. They toy with suicide, as Capra himself must have done. Walter Huston in *American Madness* has only a brief period of suicidal apathy as his bank is failing (and his wife, he thinks, is cheating on him), but Mr. Deeds sits autistically through an entire trial at which his fortune and his sanity are at stake. A Hollywood-style psychiatrist testifies in comical Viennese that he is a manic-depressive, and therefore incompetent, but Deeds's evident state of deep withdrawal confirms a good deal of the man's glib diagnosis. Jean Arthur tells him to stand up and say his piece, as she would later tell a weeping Jimmy Stewart in *Mr. Smith* not to be a "quitter." We see Stewart in powerful close-up at the Lincoln Memorial, where he has fled from his humiliation on the floor of the Senate, his face covered with gloom and shadow, his patriotic ideals shattered. By the time of *Meet John Doe* and *It's a Wonderful Life*, the heroes' impulse to withdraw and flee has escalated into a definite intention to commit suicide. In the later film the huge close-ups of Stewart's face become emblems of nightmare, and only a deus ex machina in the person of Clarence, his guardian angel, saves him from doing himself in.

This crisis of depression and self-doubt is the other story Capra has to tell, the unofficial one, which gives his positive message its drama and credibility. Capra's films are fairy tales not in the superficial sense of having unlikely stories and happy endings, but because they develop narrative archetypes rooted deep in human consciousness. Capra's heroes must undergo a *rite de passage* of trial and frustration before they take their place in society. Innocent and unprotected—"fools with faith," as Jean Arthur calls them—they come from a rural America whose values have been forgotten; the ordeal they pass through, a catharsis of pain and despair, tempers them into mature determination, a resolute spirit, and the beginnings of a knowledge of the world.

Literature and legend are full of analogues to Capra's central myth, nowhere more clearly than in Nathaniel Hawthorne's great story "My Kinsman, Major Molineux." The young protagonist, Robin, who is even more anonymous than Capra's plain-man heroes, must leave his family, cross a river from the country to the city, and witness the public humiliation of his kinsman and protector, Major Molineux, whose tar-and-feather ordeal as a servant of the crown will leave Robin on his own, more ready to grow up. As Lionel Trilling comments in *The Experience of Literature*, "the difficulties which the young man confronts suggest those trials or tests that regularly form part of the initiation rites by which primitive peoples induct the youths of the community into the status of manhood."[7] And because the major is a British colonial appointee, unseated by a popular insurrection that anticipates the American Revolution, his disgrace and Robin's new self-dependence suggest the coming of age of the nation itself.

In Capra's films something has gone wrong with this basic pattern of initiation, which supposes a legitimate social order worthy enough to command our loyalty. Capra's populist politics, complicating his bedrock patriotism, makes the opposite assumption: that American society is corrupt and decadent (though the people are good); that its machinery is meant not to integrate the newcomer and confirm his maturity but— as with Mr. Smith in the Senate—to render him harmless and superfluous—by prolonging his innocence, by debauching him with its own corrupt practices, or simply by crushing his rebelliousness, almost as a human sacrifice. All Capra's films have images of Christianity and Jesus: "I don't want any part of crucifying this boy," says Claude Rains, the Silver Knight of the Senate, once a crusading reformer along with Smith's late father, but now waist-deep in corruption, his Roman profile a dignified front for the Taylor machine, which controls not only the politics but also the newspapers and radio stations in Smith's home state. "You leave public opinion to me," says Taylor, when Mr. Smith appeals in vain from the floor of the Senate to the people of his state. When newspaper headlines and telegrams come pouring in, all hostile—public opinion has been "Taylor-made," comments one cynical reporter—Jimmy Stewart falls into a pit of despair for the second time, smashed down by a display of monolithic power that makes a charade of the popular will.[8] Only Claude Rains's last-minute change of heart—his attempt at suicide and his own confession and disgrace on the floor of the Senate—saves Stewart and his own-man crusade from certain defeat.

The ordeal of Capra's heroes becomes ever more extreme as the forces leagued against them grow more powerful. Gary Cooper in *Mr. Deeds* needs only to speak up to rout his accusers; the spectators, the judges, are all eager for him to rally his spirits. But in *Meet John Doe* Cooper is hooted down by the very people who had idolized him, whose naive faith, once so precious to Capra, now appears gullible and vulnerable, easy to manipulate for the Taylors and Nortons who control the mass media. The sea of umbrellas in the rain and gloom makes the John Doe convention look funereal even before it subjects Cooper to his ritual humiliation. Capra has written in his book of the difficulty he and his screenwriter, Robert Riskin, had in ending the film—they filmed five separate endings, none of them satisfactory: "Riskin and I had written ourselves into a corner," he says, for no triumph of the individual over the machine seemed possible (305). The ending we have merely manages to avoid Cooper's suicide, though the film still concludes on an exceptionally somber and qualified note. Cooper has been checkmated once again; his only remaining authentic gesture—his own death—has been taken away from him.

What Capra's autobiography describes as a technical problem—how to end a movie—was actually rooted in a serious shift in his own beliefs as European fascism and world war darkened the international horizon. In all his films Capra is a superb technician and entertainer. While making *American Madness* he learned to give comedy a lively pace and snap that, along with his gift for pathos and melodrama, long remained a key to his hold on the mass audience. As the film critic Raymond Carney has written, "Any account of Capra's work that leaves out the sheer sensory gusto of the films (the shapes of bodies, the timbres of voices, the movements of figures through space, the thrill of the timing and pacing) cuts the heart out of his work."[9] By the time of *It Happened One Night* and *Mr. Deeds*, he had learned to undercut sentiment with bits of comic foolishness and to deepen comedy with touches of authentic emotion. Even when they sound corny his films rarely feel dated. But *American Madness*, with its virtuoso depiction of a run on the bank, was also the first film in which Capra set out to comment on the social and economic crisis of the age. Ironically, this was not a film he originated. Under its original title, *Faith*, it was the work of the man who would become his virtual alter ego, the gifted writer Robert Riskin; Capra came aboard only after another director, Allan Dwan, had been shooting for four days.[10] But Capra relished the opportunity for social commentary. Now he had something to say, and before long critics like Alistair Cooke began complaining that he was "making movies about themes rather than about people" (just as he was entering his greatest period).

Because he repeatedly portrayed a conspiracy of money and power against the common people, Capra's films have sometimes been admired on the left (despite their remoteness from Marxism) and in recent years have come to be seen as populist, which rightly links them to the Popular Front, in which Capra played no role. His unsympathetic biographer McBride insists that he was a lifelong conservative Republican critical of FDR and the New Deal, but admits that *American Madness* "marked the beginning of a genuine, if short-lived, liberal-leftist influence on his thinking." In an atypical concession, McBride adds, "The enthusiasm and sincerity Capra brought to his direction of *American Madness* (and of later Riskin scripts) tapped into unconscious reserves of goodwill that Capra could not allow himself to express in his off-screen politics and which reflected his belated, reluctant, but nevertheless strongly felt awareness that the country's economic system needed overhauling if the American Dream was to survive" (261).

Like much of the populism of the late 1930s, this general sentiment has little connection with the historical origins of American populism, which reached its peak in the 1890s yet had an enduring life. The Populist movement, which emerged almost simultaneously in Russia and America in the late nineteenth century, was essentially an agrarian revolt against modernization, against the shift of economic and political power from the country to the city and from agriculture to industry and big capital. In Russia it was the creation of urban intellectuals who idealized the peasantry and the life of the land. In America it was a grass roots movement that sprang up in the South and Midwest and crested with the third-party presidential campaign of General Weaver in 1892—he polled 8.5 percent of the popular vote—and the Democratic nomination of William Jennings Bryan in 1896, which co-opted populism as a force for national protest and discontent.

There is very little agrarianism in Capra—his idealized past is a small-town America, not an agricultural one—so, strictly speaking, there's very little populism in him either. But as Richard Hofstadter stressed in *The Age of Reform*, populism was a cast of mind that existed long before the Populist movement and continued to reappear long after its disintegration—usually on the left, as in Jimmy Carter's acceptance speech at the 1976 Democratic convention or John Edwards's presidential campaign in 2008, but recently as often on the resurgent right, casting Democrats and liberals as elitists out of touch with the concerns of ordinary people. Populism goes back to this country's early Jeffersonian image of itself as a republic of self-sufficient yeomen free of the shackles of feudal hierarchy. The populist mood flared up again during the Jacksonian period, and in the cherished image of Lincoln as the rail-splitter raised in a log cabin. (Mr. Smith's full name is Jefferson Smith, and he worships the memory of Abe Lincoln.)

Even the Progressive movement of the early decades of the twentieth century, though largely patrician in origin, was also populist in its reliance on journalistic muckraking and its attacks on corporate trusts, banking monopolies, and corrupt political machines. And during the Depression the spirit of populism grew far more pervasive, especially among artists, than any doctrinaire Marxism. At the first Writers' Congress, in 1935, dominated by the Communists, Kenneth Burke got into hot water by urging the substitution of the broader term "the people" for divisive phrases like "the masses," "workers," or "proletariat," but within a few months the whole Communist movement, seeking an alliance against fascism, had shifted to a Popular Front strategy and a populist rhetoric. The old terminology was out, Burke's terminology was in, and by 1936 the editors of *Partisan Review*, who were still Marxists, were castigated for still pursuing an interest in something so divisive as the proletarian novel, rather than more popular works with a liberal or progressive tinge.

The Communists' remarkable tactical reversal was hardly the last of the sharp turns that eventually deprived the party of most of its American followers, but it underscores the immense prestige of the idea of "the people" throughout the culture of the 1930s. If a typical twenties writer like Fitzgerald is riveted by an ambivalent fascination with the rich, a thirties writer like Steinbeck comes into his best fiction from topical journalism without losing his burning sense of mission. Fitzgerald's 1934 novel *Tender Is the Night* is a tragedy of wasted gifts dissipated into triviality among the rich and bored. It ends with a resolute goodbye to all that: "You're all so dull," says Dick Diver, who is down but hasn't quite reached bottom. "But we're all there is!" cried Mary. "If you don't like nice people, try the ones who aren't nice, and see how you like that!" The strongest impulse among artists and intellectuals of the 1930s was precisely to "try the ones who aren't nice." The characters in a book like *The Grapes of Wrath* have so much the burden of representing the People that they are sometimes lost in epic generality.

Frank Capra was not one of the newly radicalized artists from the 1920s who discovered "the people" because they were now in fashion. He was no tortured intellectual out of Exeter and Harvard like James Agee, more like a Russian populist than an American one, a true *Narodnik* in love with the salt of the earth. Capra's feeling for ordinary life is deep and intuitive, whatever his attempts to mythicize it. But gradually, under the influence of the Depression, his fables shifted toward a genuine if vague populist politics. Besides the nostalgic idea of a golden age and the belief in conspiracy, one key notion that sets the populist vision off from Marxism is, in Hofstadter's words,

> the idea of a natural harmony of interests among the productive classes. To the Populist mind there was no fundamental conflict between the farmer and the worker, between the toiling people and the small businessman. . . . Predatory behavior existed only because it was initiated and underwritten by a small parasitic minority in the highest places of power. . . . The problems that faced the Populists assumed a delusive simplicity: the victory over injustice, the solution for all social ills, was concentrated in the crusade against a single, relatively small but immensely strong interest, the money power.[11]

Though populism could easily offend established interests by its choice of targets, this kind of dualism would prove a perfect fit for a popular art. Like Hollywood, populism has "an unusually strong tendency to account for relatively impersonal events in personal terms," says Hofstadter, especially in its fascination with individual villains, "marked with the unmistakable stigmata of the villains of melodrama" (73). Yet until *Mr. Deeds* Capra was not ready to sort out heroes and villains along populist lines. In *Tramp, Tramp, Tramp* (1926) the big shoe manufacturer is putting Harry Langdon's father out of business, but *his* dreamy wish is to marry the man's daughter (Joan Crawford), whose picture he has seen on billboards. In *American Madness* (1932) the people's tribune is none other than the bank president, who lends out money on character and battles his own board of directors. In this, his first social film, Capra would have us believe that bank panics occur because telephone operators are given to idle gossip, and spread false rumors.

Claudette Colbert's millionaire father in *It Happened One Night* is much closer to the later Edward Arnold mold. His power reaches everywhere: escaping from him is like running from the Mafia, *until* he actually finds his errant daughter. Then he becomes the world's best daddy: he saves her from a ruinous marriage and sends her off to a waiting Clark Gable, a lower-class tough guy with buried dreams, a fast-talking cynic who has given up on women until he goes soft on this one. Only in *Deeds* did Capra finally personalize the people into his common-man hero, just as John Ford would solidify the vaporous Joad family in the unforgettable immediacy of Henry Fonda and Jane Darwell.

No sooner had Capra's populist mythology found its shape in *Mr. Deeds* than it began to disintegrate. *Mr. Deeds* is the first and last film in which Capra's hero scores any easy victories. From the beginning, the director's social demonology is exceptionally vague, for all the cartoonish vividness of his bloated, menacing villains. Capra's attack on machine bosses in *Mr. Smith* has nothing to do with the Depression; it's part of the reformist litany of the earlier Progressive period. The depredations of the Taylor machine serve merely as the occasion for Capra's civics lesson about the American system, and as a metaphor for his growing sense that stifling concentrations of power threaten to make this lesson irrelevant. Capra's melodramatic vagueness about actual public issues, as well as his ambivalence toward all centralized power, makes it impossible to tell from his films what he actually thought of the New Deal. When Jefferson Smith proposes the creation of a National Boys' Camp, he stresses that he asks for no federal money, only the nickel-and-dime contributions of American boys: in effect a private, voluntarist, juvenile New Deal. But his scheme interferes with a piece of graft buried in an omnibus appropriations bill, so the machine sets out to crucify him, and nearly succeeds. Jimmy Stewart's brilliant performance helps make this the most vivid, most fully realized film in the trilogy. His boyish ideals are balanced by the agony of his protracted ordeal on the floor of the Senate, which looks ahead to the trials he would undergo in his best roles in the 1950s, under the punishing direction of Alfred Hitchcock and Anthony Mann.

In his autobiography and in numerous interviews, Capra presents himself as an incurable optimist, but his comments often veer off into the cranky and querulous. We know from his co-workers—as we know from his films—that he had a strong tendency to depression. The Manichaean vision of populism, no matter how Pollyannaish, harbors a great potential for pessimism, paranoia, and even apocalyptic anxiety. As the 1930s drag on and World War II approaches, as European dictators (and some American sympathizers) loom on the horizon, Capra's faith in the wisdom of the people wanes as their adversaries' spidery power increases. By the time of *Meet John Doe* in 1941, Capra begins to parody some of the populist attitudes he himself had promoted in the 1930s. The John Doe Clubs and "the John Doe idea," which is Capra's own cherished ideal of goodwill and benevolence, are ludicrously inadequate to the problems they face, and to the villains who manipulate them from the start. Jimmy Stewart's heroism in *Mr. Smith* is real, though ineffective; Gary Cooper has merely been cast in a role that makes him party to a kind of fraud.

Those who doubt the capacity of popular art to send itself up, to be self-ironic and multilayered, ought to look at *Meet John Doe* in the light of Capra's earlier films. As his name indicates, John Doe is very much the least of Capra's heroes, a cipher, anonymous, in Capra's own words "a bindle stiff, a drifting piece of human flotsam as devoid of ideals as he was of change in his pocket." In part he is a parody of Capra's plebeian hero; his identity, insofar as he has one, has been conjured up by a clever newspaper reporter trying to save her job. This is heightened by Gary Cooper's gawky American plainness, his baseball-player simplicity. He is the most innocent of Capra's heroes, and therefore the most vulnerable to being taken advantage of. The protest letter fabricated for him, in which he vows to commit suicide on Christmas Eve to "protest against the state of civilization," is probably the vaguest social criticism ever enunciated. The people taken in by it are good-hearted fools like him. The Cooper character accepts the role of John Doe, man of the people, simply as an actor, because he is hungry, and he is accepted by them because he looks and sounds the part. The people, more gullible than ever, take to his performance, which, in a manner familiar to Capra, warms their hearts without making undue demands upon them. They all become good neighbors; an orgy of benevolence breaks out.

In case we don't see the limitations of this reign of friendliness, Capra and Riskin, in their first independent production, provide John Doe with a hobo sidekick, the Colonel (played by Walter Brennan), who greets every sign of the new era of good feeling with a withering skepticism. To him the masses are "heelots"—greedy, materialistic, and cautiously respectable—just like the big shots and newspaper vultures. Amid the warm banalities of the John Doe philosophy the Colonel insists, "Tear down one picket of your neighbor's fence and he'll sue you." At the John Doe convention the Colonel sits alone, apart from the volatile herd, Cooper's only real friend, watching in pain as the crowd turns on him. And Capra parodies himself outright in scenes of media hype in which a buxom broad comes on as Miss Average Girl and two midgets are brought in to represent "the little people"; the woman dwarf gets turned on by John Doe and refuses to let go of him ("half a heelot," the Colonel comments).

Meet John Doe is a remarkably complex, ambivalent film, which has rarely been accorded the critical attention it deserves. It raised problems for Capra he was simply unable to resolve. Without abandoning his belief in the common people, Capra, as if in response to his intellectual critics, not only satirizes them (and himself) but shows how fickle and vulnerable they can be, how easily an unprincipled plutocrat with dictatorial ambitions like D. B. Norton (Edward Arnold) can manipulate them. Though the John Doe Clubs are supposed to exclude politics for good-neighborliness, Norton, a protofascist with his own band of storm troopers, hopes to use them as a springboard to the presidency. He believes, as many others did in the 1930s, that "what the American people need is an iron hand—discipline!" (This theme of a strong leader—the country saved by a dictator—takes us back to the 1934 film financed by William Randolph Hearst, Gregory La Cava's *Gabriel over the White House.* In *Citizen Kane* this figure becomes an egomaniac who styles himself a man of the people.) Norton's instruments, besides the newspapers, radio stations, and politicians he controls, are the gullible Mr. Doe, who delivers his prepared public speeches without reading them beforehand, and the equally unsuspecting populace, the many John Does, who are so readily swayed by demagoguery and sentimental platitudes.

Between these extremes, so dear to the populist vision, were the hinge figures whose attack of conscience or change of heart enables the hero somehow to prevail, even as it redeems them from their own cynicism. In earlier films these intermediate characters oriented Capra's plots toward conversion and redemption, balancing the ordeals his heroes suffer and the evils they confront. Here their best efforts fail. As in *Mr. Smith*, it takes a cynical newspaperman to get Doe wise to how he's being used, but in this film it's all to no avail; no real victory over the powerful mogul is possible, and the common people shout Cooper down when he tries to speak to them (just as the members of the Senate—inconceivably—tried to silence Mr. Smith). In *Meet John Doe* the individual knaves of *Mr. Deeds* and the corrupt state machine of *Mr. Smith* have ballooned into a national force whose control of the media threatens to turn democracy into a sham. Capra's and Riskin's politics have leapfrogged in one bound from the rural evangelism of William Jennings Bryan to the antitotalitarian pessimism of Herbert Marcuse and the Frankfurt school, with their sense of a world dominated by an invisible web of manipulation and control. This time the fairy tale has no catharsis, no clean resolution. By 1941 Capra's faith in the people had given way to an anxiety for their future.

This is not the place to give Capra's last great film, *It's a Wonderful Life*, the detailed treatment it demands. *Meet John Doe* is Capra's *Citizen Kane*: the two films came out within months of each other; both deal with overweening ambition masquerading as populism, and show how mass journalism and demagogic politics try to manipulate the popular will. Capra's work of postwar retrospection, *It's a Wonderful Life*, is instead a meditative film, Capra's *Magnificent Ambersons*, his *recherche du temps perdu*. Leaving politics behind to summarize his personal myth, Capra composes an elegiac footnote to the three populist films by reversing their plot. Here the young man from the provinces never leaves home, though this is his deepest wish—not even to go to war. (He is 4-F, a maimed creature like John Doe, who was a broken-down pitcher who simply wanted to get his "wing" fixed.) *It's a Wonderful Life* has a large cult following that finds it a heartwarming work, the epitome of the Christmas spirit, while others see it as sentimental. In fact, few films are more genuinely moving; I can't think of another that brings me so readily to tears, not from its uplifting ending but from the purgatorial ordeal that precedes it. When I first wrote about Capra in the late 1970s, his reputation remained low, mainly because the dark side of his work had scarcely been acknowledged. But *It's a Wonderful Life* has many of the same dark elements as *Meet John Doe*, especially in scenes that are literally dark and somber in their lighting. This is Capra's most personal film, and the psychological ordeal of George Bailey, as played by Jimmy Stewart, summarizes the fears and anxieties that had surfaced repeatedly in twenty years of Capra's spunky and effervescent filmmaking—an undertone of stress and insecurity that helped give his fairy tales their believable human solidity.

George Bailey's life epitomizes the ethic of altruism and benevolence that Capra had been preaching but also questioning since *American Madness* and all through the trilogy. At every stage George sacrifices his own wishes to the needs of others, as his selfless father had done before him. He saves his brother's life, only to see his brother go on to lead the life he himself deserved and wanted. He doesn't leave town, doesn't go to college, can't go to war, and can't even go off for his own honeymoon trip. Finally, driven to the wall by a Scrooge-like local tycoon, a bank president who is the exact opposite of the benevolent one in *American Madness*, he contemplates suicide, and is saved only by an angel who shows him what his world would have been like if he had never lived. The overall message of this part of the film is no doubt uplifting—yes, each man *does* make a difference—but the scenes themselves are nightmarish and terrifying. Bailey has been saved, but his ordeal has just begun. Stewart's agony follows directly from his near-crucifixion in *Mr. Smith*. To be purged of his suicidal wishes, the character is temporarily robbed of all identity, so that even his nearest and dearest fail to know him. It's a powerful fantasy: not to be recognized by your own mother, to find that your wife has never married but become a spinster, to stumble on the grave of the brother whose life you thought you saved. Never to have lived: in this grim vision Capra's heroes face up to the gloomy underside of their own blank anonymity. Like tragedy, the fairy tale becomes a catharsis of pity and terror.

I have stressed Capra's darker side partly to show his complexity, the kind of complication we can easily miss in this kind of popular filmmaking, but also because Capra was long portrayed—not least by himself—as a cockeyed optimist, a purveyor of marketable fantasies. If this were true, his work would not have reached people the way it still does, nor would it have connected so well with the climate of insecurity and foreboding of the Depression years. His work is both a catharsis of pain and fear and an evangel of hope. His faith in human nature is linked to an immigrant's belief in self-improvement. But Capra's work was also simple in a way that was right for him to be simple. As Robert Warshow wrote about Chaplin, "the impact of his art . . . is helped rather than hindered by a certain simplicity in his conception of political and social problems."[12] The same point could be made about Dickens. Capra's populist simplicity showed up in the way he personalized social problems into Boy Scouts and bosses, heroes and villains. But the same approach enabled him to transform America into a vivid personal myth of archetypal simplicity, affecting humor, and elemental emotional power. Like Chaplin, like Dickens, Capra remained in touch with something raw and vulnerable in himself and his audience, a memory of humiliation, struggle, and inner resolution. The coming of the Depression gave it a more than personal meaning, and helped turn it into a not always comforting social vision.

CHAPTER 15

Shakespeare in Overalls:
AN AMERICAN TROUBADOUR

UNLIKE SOME OTHER POPULISTS of the thirties and forties, Woody Guthrie was the real thing. Because of his early death and wide influence, but also thanks to the public personality he created, Guthrie became such a figure in American legend that it's hard to believe the person really existed. "This Land Is Your Land," his most famous song, became too much the alternate national anthem to seem like any one man's composition. Fabulously prolific, he wrote more than a thousand other songs, but there aren't many people alive today who heard him perform. He recorded hundreds of songs in the 1940s but they sold few copies, though some later became famous when other performers sang them. The heyday of rock left him behind, but folk singers cherished his memory. Later, Bruce Springsteen, whose roots and sympathies were blue-collar rather than folk-rural, rediscovered him for a new generation. Other singers continue to put music to the vast trove of material he left behind, including the American country and rock group Wilco, the English folksinger Billy Bragg, and a well-known Klezmer group, the Klezmatics, which added music to many Jewish songs he left behind—a surprising part of his legacy.[1]

On his recordings he is a cool, often monotonous singer and only a fair musician. But the melodic and verbal flow invariably holds us, and on the stage he could be mesmerizing, with a mellifluous speaking voice that set off his singing. He didn't read music and rarely made up his own tunes, usually adapting his words to existing songs, continually modifying both till he was satisfied with the match, never singing a song the same way twice. Sometimes it's hard to tell where the old songs break off and Woody Guthrie begins; his most original pieces often sound like traditional folk songs, while songs his mother taught him can sound like his own. Woody Guthrie has become a sort of disembodied folk spirit. Only his legend, which he cultivated, and those who sang with him, like Pete Seeger, insist that there actually was such a man.

The Guthrie legend began with the life he lived and the wonderful stories he told about it—he seemed to make himself up as he went along—but it was his long period of disease and disintegration that enabled the legend to take hold. During the folk revival of the early sixties, the guitar-strumming kids who popped up in every town, every city park, every political demonstration, were already being called Woody's children. But all that was left of Woody himself was the stories. Like a living ghost, a posthumous presence, he was wasting away with a hereditary brain disease till he died in 1967.

The folk revival, like the renewed protest politics centered on civil rights and nuclear testing, marked a return to the spirit of the 1930s; a sick Woody Guthrie was transformed into an icon, a shrine to the mythology of the Depression. Woody became the last of the Okies—drifter, troubadour, protester, avatar of the counterculture. The 1970s saw Hal Ashby's lovingly poetic film version of Woody's 1943 autobiography, *Bound for Glory*. The movie, though in color, borrowed its visual imagery from John Ford's adaptation of *The Grapes of Wrath*. Confining itself to the few years of his wanderings in the 1930s, it centered on Woody the loner, Woody the drifter. This was the Woody Guthrie that appealed to post-Beat culture. With Woody dead, the story of his life could displace his work; the myth would supersede the music.

It was only with the publication in 1980 of a biography by Joe Klein, later best known as a political writer, that the picture of Guthrie's life and art finally came into focus. Klein, with no special investment in the 1930s, the folk culture, or the Woody Guthrie legend, succeeded in telling the whole story for the first time.[2] And the truth turned out to be more fascinating than the myth. It was disconcerting to learn that Woody hated riding boxcars and took trains only as a last resort, or that this great westerner, who first went on radio singing cowboy songs, could barely ride a horse. Discarding the icon, Klein gained access to the man, thanks to his impressive research into Woody's Oklahoma and Texas background, the history of country music, the cultural policies of the Communist Party, and the medical history of Huntington's disease. Klein tracked down ancient relatives all over the country who described events from seventy years earlier; he gained the confidence of all three of Woody's wives, as well as many survivors of the left-wing folk scene of the 1940s who were later blacklisted and browbeaten into a long period of enforced silence.

Woody was the latest and perhaps the greatest ornament of the "progressive" culture created by the Popular Front, a culture of songs and books, nurseries and summer camps, radio shows and newspapers. Some of this was agitprop activity of an ephemeral kind—the handmaiden of union organizing and political indoctrination. But like the communal structures that developed within some of the European Communist parties (in Italy, for example), it was also a complete way of life, an interwoven mesh of private passions, deep-seated assumptions, social relationships, and supportive institutions, like some of the fraternal and welfare organizations of immigrant groups. What this Old Left culture produced in the arts often lacked craft and imagination, but Woody Guthrie was an exception—its natural man, its "Shakespeare in overalls."

Woody Guthrie was a Communist, a fact not convenient for most versions of the Guthrie legend. But he was a Communist from the heartland, not an urban immigrant intellectual schooled in ideology. The Oklahoma where he grew up had been a hotbed of socialist activity before the debacle of World War I. His own father, a local Democratic politician and journalist, had tried to make a reputation smearing these radicals with charges of advocating free love and sexual immorality. But the ferment of politics and even the conditions of the Depression made little impact on Woody until he hit the road in the mid 1930s to escape the dry south western towns where his family's fortunes had long been disintegrating. Drifting around, trying desperately to stay free and unattached, he stumbled into an attachment he hadn't expected.

As he picked up tunes and sang for the men in the boxcars, says Klein,

> Woody was amazed by the impact the songs had. Sometimes grown men would get all misty-eyed when he sang them, and their voices would catch when they tried to sing along. The whiney old ballads his mother had taught him were a bond that all country people shared; and now, for the migrants, the songs were all that was left of the land. . . . It wasn't just entertainment; he was performing their past. . . . An odd thought began to percolate. *He* was one *them*. The collapse of his family wasn't all that unique; these people had seen hard times too. . . . Woody had never considered himself part of any group before. But here he was, an Okie, and these were his people. (79)

This was the same message of mutual recognition and solidarity that Steinbeck worked into *The Grapes of Wrath*, a novel Woody admired so much he condensed the plot into "Tom Joad," a seventeen-stanza ballad. (He claimed he did it not from reading the novel but by seeing the movie over and over.) Yet as a loner by temperament, he himself could not fully take this message to heart. Woody had an itch to travel, to break away, especially when wives, children, and work were tying him down. He wrote that "the worst thing that can happen to you is to cut yourself loose from people" (202), but cutting loose from individual people was something he did all the time. None of his wives ever knew when he would pick up and take off, or send for them from across the country. What he meant was not people but "the people," that great thirties myth of the common man, the salt of the earth. In Woody Guthrie—with folk music as his medium—this abstract common man found a perfect spokesman.

Woody became a Communist gradually, more out of an instinctive populism than from any ideological conversion. He cared little for theory or orthodoxy but cared a great deal about social injustice. He rarely tried to versify the party line; he worked instead from the life he knew and the books he devoured. This was a time when the Communists themselves had just discovered "the people," and Woody Guthrie seemed like the genuine article. He broke into radio in 1937 on the left-wing station in Los Angeles and quickly became a local celebrity, as he would again when he arrived in New York in 1940. Soon he was receiving a thousand letters a month and crisscrossing California to sing at union meetings and radical campaign rallies. But Woody never did develop much political sense. A perverseness drew him even closer to the Communists after the Hitler-Stalin pact of 1939, just when so many others were abandoning ship. In New York he became a regular columnist for the *Daily Worker* and vaguely supported the twists and turns of party policies. When people criticized Stalin, he wrote to his wife that "the whole world cannot trick Joseph Stalin because he is too scientific for them." He stuck with the party after the fall of its general secretary, Earl Browder, in 1945, which signaled the end of the Popular Front, because, he said, "I owe them . . . the only guidance and recognition and pay that I've ever tasted" (318). But his endless flow of protest songs came from the gut rather than any calculated strategy. The Communists were right: Woody was the real thing.

By the mid-1940s, says Klein, "folk singers became part of the ceremonial trappings for any self-respecting Communist meeting" (320). But Woody's range extended far beyond protest music. His first and greatest sequence of songs, the *Dust Bowl Ballads*, is as much a thirties evocation of the open road and a hymn to the indominability of man as it is a piece of social criticism. The road means forced migration in Woody's songs, as it does in Steinbeck, but it also means freedom—a refusal to be hemmed in and regimented. The point of view of the ordinary Joe, which had eluded proletarian fiction and socialist realism, wells up in his songs like a clear spring. ("Takes a ten-dollar shoe to fit my feet," says one song. "Your two-dollar shoe hurts my feet, Lord God, / And I ain't a-gonna be treated this a way.") In both his ballads and his fine talking blues numbers—as in bits and pieces of his run-on prose—he could be a great storyteller. His songs are never nasty: even when etched in bitterness, they remain lyrical and singable, with refrains so simple and direct they are impossible to forget.

In writing songs Woody was infinitely adaptable. He could turn hillbilly music into urban songs about union struggles. His "Union Maid," with its rousing refrain, "Oh, you can't scare me, I'm stickin' to the union," became an anthem of the labor movement, a challenge to all the thugs and scabs and company spies who still tried to keep workers from organizing. Woody researched other songs from history, especially the history of labor wars, and many others he developed out of little stories in the newspapers.

Woody never tried rhyming the telephone directory, but he could make even electrification sound heroic, as he did in some twenty-six songs he wrote in a single month in 1941 while on the payroll of the Bonneville Power Administration in Oregon. The improbable subject galvanized his imagination; these were paeans to technology that also celebrated nature in the shape of the river and celebrated the ingenuity of man as embodied in the dam. One of the best of them, "Pastures of Plenty," ends with an unusual touch of overt patriotism:

> *Well, it's always we ramble, that river and I,*
> *All along your green valley I'll work till I die,*
> *My land I'll defend with my life, if it be,*
> *'Cause my pastures of plenty must always be free.*

But Woody also puzzled his radical friends by writing many songs for children that sounded simplistic or nonsensical to those who had never observed a child closely. My own children loved them when they were growing up. And many other songs he sang eschew social issues for the eternal ache of man and woman that comes close to the essence of folk music. They could be as raunchy as the blues, graphically evoking the itch of desire. At heart he was a writer. "The music usually was an afterthought," notes Klein. "The words were most important. He wrote his songs at the typewriter, it was the instrument he played the best" (97).

Typing was a medium of free association for Woody: all his life he was drunk with words. With little schooling, he had an amazing natural gift for evocative writing, abetted by the compulsive reading habits of an autodidact. "An explosion was coming in Woody's life," says Klein of the period just before he first left the Texas Panhandle in 1936. "For five years he had been sucking in knowledge like a vacuum cleaner, and now he had to let it out in some way or go crazy" (73). Woody's best stories, embroidered halfway into fiction, were about the parched, blighted Dust Bowl towns he left behind. Along with Steinbeck and documentary filmmakers and photographers like Pare Lorentz, Dorothea Lange, and Walker Evans, Woody Guthrie helped create what remains our image of rural America during the Depression, fixed forever by John Ford's celebrated movie.

Propelled by the national crisis, sometimes even mobilized by the New Deal administration, artists in every medium set out to rediscover the essence of America. In the 1890s the historian Frederick Jackson Turner had written about the closing of the frontier, but in the 1930s the vast expanse of the American continent turned into a new frontier, both for once settled migrants in search of a livelihood and once alienated artists in search of America. The horizontal extensions of physical space again became for the American imagination what the hierarchical constraints of social class were for the European: a challenge, an incitement, a field of conflict and conquest. When the Beats in the late 1950s revived the road novel and wrote Whitmanesque poems to America, they were recovering a dormant thirties tradition and giving it a sardonic or ecstatic modern twist.

When Woody Guthrie came to New York at the beginning of 1940, this popular fascination with the American heartland was still strong, especially in "progressive" circles, which included many second-generation Jews, who genuinely saw Communism as the fulfillment of American democratic values, but also among folklorists like Alan Lomax of the Library of Congress, Charles Seeger, the ethnomusicologist, and his gifted twenty-year-old son, Peter, a Harvard dropout. On February 23—the day I was born—Woody dashed off "This Land" as an angry response to the patriotic rhetoric of Irving Berlin's "God Bless America."* During his first year in New York he was lionized as a combination of Caliban (the noble savage) and Joe Hill (the proletarian saint).

---

* The song was first called "God Blessed America." It could be seen as the musical equivalent of Robert Frost's poem "The Gift Outright," which begins, "The land was ours before we were the land's."

Woody seemed nonchalant in the face of all this adulation, but a flood of creative energy poured out of him. Everything he knew and felt soon welled up to the surface. He did marathon recording sessions for the archives of the Library of Congress as Alan Lomax debriefed him of hundreds of songs and stories and encouraged him to sit down and write. For the next three or four years the world was his oyster, though that world only occasionally extended beyond the confines of the Old Left and the new young folk culture that idolized him, since he did so much to inspire it.

Woody would sing anywhere—he claims he did more than a hundred shows in his first few months in the city—but the songs he recorded were too plain to be popular, the commercial market for folk music was nonexistent, and he was constantly on guard against the slick influences of Tin Pan Alley. Instead, with Pete Seeger, Millard Lampell, Lee Hays, and others, he helped form a group called the Almanac Singers, which practiced both a communal lifestyle and endless, often naive radical agitation. (Following the twists and turns of the party line, they went from peace songs to labor songs to war songs in rapid succession.) According to Joe Klein, everyone in the group "cowered before Woody. He was the group's inspiration, the moral leader, the old master . . . and he never let anyone forget it. He was forever intimidating others with his political and musical rectitude, and his Oklahoma credentials. . . . Woody, the dust bowl refugee, was the group's repository of proletarian wisdom, the ultimate arbiter of taste" (207).

While Pete Seeger tried, without much luck, to bring some order to the group's bookings and housekeeping, Woody used his influence to insist on musical standards and to combat the group's propensity for naked propaganda. Eventually the Almanac Singers drifted apart, to be reincarnated a decade later (minus Woody, and minus much of the political bite) as the Weavers, the first group to put folk music on the national charts and make it pay. Songs like Leadbelly's "Irene" and Woody's dust-storm ballad "So Long, It's Been Good to Know You" were adapted into smooth popular hits, with most of the grit and dust removed. But the Weavers themselves soon fell victim to the blacklist, which drove the remnants of the folk culture and the Popular Front into virtual hiding or exile.

By this time Woody had begun to behave erratically and had long since lost his creative flow. Some of his behavior was caused not by alcohol, as everyone assumed, but by the early stages of Huntington's disease, which had first deranged and then killed his mother and would eventually strike at least two of his children. But in other respects Woody's career in the 1940s reads like a classic case of the inability of youthful genius to deal with sudden and spectacular recognition—to say nothing of the first signs of middle age and waning powers. Though Woody's verbal and musical sensibility, unlike his politics, was far from naive, everyone who knew him agrees that there was something childlike and innocent about him. He had what the great German poet Schiller describes (in his essay "On Naïve and Sentimental Poetry") as a spontaneous rather than a self-conscious imagination; that helped make him so prolific. It came out in his affinity for children, in his lifelong refusal to shoulder responsibility, and in the way he brought out the impulse in women to mother him and take care of him. His second wife, Marjorie, a former Martha Graham dancer, continued to do this even after they were divorced, and she remained the devoted keeper of the flame until her death in 1983. Her daughter Nora continues to play this role today; besides encouraging contemporary singers to adapt material he left behind, she has maintained a superb archive that is a boon to research and helps keep his work alive.

After the success of *Bound for Glory*, Woody set off on dozens of literary projects, none of which really satisfied him. With his astonishing fluency he could dash off half a novel only to discard it and turn to something else. He thought nothing of writing fifty-page single-spaced letters; I have seen some of them. Once, miserably trapped on an army base at the end of the war, he sent Marjorie six letters in a single day. To write his biography, Klein, with Marjorie Guthrie's assistance, went through a mountain of unpublished papers and letters, and he was able to trace Woody's melancholy descent into uncontrollable logorrhea in the last few years when he could still write. His subsequent biographer Ed Cray had even more material to work with.

Gradually, what had begun as an exuberant gift of free association dissolved into surreal incoherence. This obsession manifested itself most strangely in Woody's growing addiction to pornographic letter writing, not only to his wife but to women he had never met or barely knew. Eventually one of them complained to the law, and he was charged with sending obscene materials through the mail; when he refused to appear contrite before the judge, he was clapped in jail.

Woody had long preached the open and natural acceptance of the human body. But as he felt his sexual powers beginning to decline he became the literary equivalent of a flasher, and began to use verbal discharge as an incitement or substitute for other kinds of ejaculation. In an eerie illustration of what Jacques Derrida called "the primal scene of writing," he told his wife not to be afraid that his "love juices" were "dripping down onto pages of letters to any other girl" (338). As writing of every sort grew more compulsive and less rational for him, his work became a wild parody of the fluency of his earlier years—much as the constant random physical movements of Huntington's disease burlesqued his earlier energies.

One fresh and haunting element in Joe Klein's picture was his unflinching portrayal of Woody Guthrie's years of dissolution, starting from the late forties, which played their role in his eventual elevation from martyrdom to sainthood. The pattern of Woody's life reminds me strongly of an unlikely contemporary whose creative life was anything but fluent. Delmore Schwartz, whose dates (1913–66) are almost the same as Woody's (1912–67), was scarcely a natural. He too burst on the scene in the late thirties as a golden young talent, but sputtered within a decade into a long horrifying decline, more mental than physical. He too found it impossible to live up to his early acclaim, and what he wrote in his later years, as he turned inexorably psychotic, resembles the rambling stuff Woody Guthrie wrote during the first stages of his disease. Delmore too became a byword and a legend whose erratic life eventually overshadowed his work—which, compared to Woody Guthrie's, was more promise than performance, except for a handful of remarkable stories, poems, and essays.

What makes this parallel interesting is that Delmore belonged to exactly the opposite corner of American culture from Woody—urban, Jewish, neurotic, cosmopolitan, and modernist. The *Partisan Review* intellectuals who admired and befriended Delmore Schwartz, saw him as their golden youth, were antagonistic to everything Woody stood for, politically and artistically: Stalinism, optimism, rural populism, the democratization of culture, the Popular Front, the celebration of the American heritage, and the search for national roots. Their roots were less in America than in the European intellectual tradition, with its fascination with political *ideas*; in immigrant life, with its attendant themes of alienation and assimilation; and in the advanced styles of European modernism, which they tried to insulate from any politically motivated criticism. To them the Americanism and populism of left-wing culture was a sham, a hollow tactical masquerade that produced philistine criticism and inferior, didactic art. (Songs to cheer on union meetings were not what they had in mind when they published parts of Eliot's *Four Quartets*.)

Delmore Schwartz never wrote about Woody Guthrie—he scarcely even mentions the plebeian Whitman, one of Woody's models—and Woody probably never heard of Delmore. The New York intellectuals were surely right about much of what passed for progressive culture, such as Earl Robinson's much acclaimed cantata *Ballad for Americans*; having started as party stalwarts, even as promoters of proletarian literature (in the early Communist years of *Partisan Review*), they knew it from the inside. But their bitter hostility, so typical of converts, blinded them to genuine expressions of political art, including some of the radical painters and muralists, and of the folk spirit, like Woody Guthrie, just as it blinded them to a deep streak of idealism and radicalism in some who followed the party line through all its demoralizing "sharp turns." Like parallel lines, Woody and Delmore never met though they occupied approximately the same cultural space. They represented the yin and yang of New York left-wing culture, the one taking refuge—as many *Partisan Review* writers finally did—in art against experience, in personal meanings as against political ones, the other creating art that seemed artless and anonymous, an art like Whitman's that pretended to be all experience.

The culture of modernism had its heyday in the 1950s, an age of criticism that admired irony and paradox and pulled back from politics. The culture of populism, in disarray during the fifties, returned to the fray in the early sixties with the revival of folk music, the civil rights movement, pop art, and new bardic styles of poetry. Woody was rediscovered and hundreds of young folksingers made pilgrimages to his bedside. One of them, who called himself Bob Dylan, began by imitating Woody and sitting at his feet, but before long was writing lyrics that sounded like one of Delmore Schwartz's favorite poets, Rimbaud. Modernism went popular if not populist, much to the dismay of its older adherents. It was a fine old conflict, but its terms were finally transcended.

CHAPTER 16

Gender Trouble:

EXPOSING THE INTELLECTUALS

THIS BOOK HAS TRACED the tension in thirties culture between a naturalism or populism, with its emphasis on social reality, and a technically innovative modernism, stressing the complications of individual experience. These forms of seeing, which often overlapped, were part of a debate about the role of the arts in a period of social crisis, about the relative importance of art and politics, and about the role of witness, social observation, collective experience, and introspection in hard times, indeed, in any times. The chasm that separated Woody Guthrie, that man of the people, and Delmore Schwartz, the modernist intellectual, could also be found in the fault lines between Michael Gold's and Henry Roth's reconstructions of life in the Lower East Side ghetto, between Margaret Bourke-White's and Walker Evans's portraits of poor southern tenant farmers, between Erskine Caldwell's and James Agee's texts for these volumes, between Steinbeck's faith in the people and Nathanael West's apocalyptic view of their potential for boredom and violence, between Steinbeck's account of a family journey as an epic social tragedy and Faulkner's account as black social comedy, between Richard Wright's politically committed stories of black victimization and resistance and Zora Neale Hurston's culturally committed stories of black folkways, follies, aspirations, and triumphs. The differences among artists and writers echoed many conflicts among intellectuals: between leftists committed to social change and agrarian reactionaries looking back to earlier times, between Stalinists or fellow travelers following the line of the Soviet Union, whatever direction it took, and anti-Stalinists who had broken with Communism and were seeking a new home, somewhere between the revolutionary militance of Trotsky and the pragmatic reforms of the New Deal. The journeys of these intellectuals, an indispensable part of the cultural mix of the 1930s, unfolded in their voluminous writings and memoirs but also in a handful of works, often satiric, written in their own time.

At the tail end of the decade, in his 1940 essay "The Cult of Experience in American Writing," Philip Rahv remarks, "The intellectual is the only character missing in the American novel. He may appear in it in his professional capacity—as artist, teacher, or scientist—but rarely as a person who thinks with his entire being, that is to say, as a person who transforms ideas into actual dramatic motives. . . . Everything is contained in the American novel except ideas."[1] This is paradoxical because the United States was founded by a remarkable group of Enlightenment thinkers. Its defining texts—the Declaration of Independence, the Federalist papers, the Constitution, even the correspondence of the founding fathers—make up an immense symposium on liberty, governance, and political representation. Books about the founders have now grown popular again, yet ideas and those who live by them have rarely figured in American fiction. (Saul Bellow's work, which began appearing soon after

Rahv's essay, was a notable exception.) Perhaps because later American thinkers hardly ever exercised real power or influence, the drama of ideas rarely fired the imagination of American writers.

The opposite has been true in Europe. Especially after the Dreyfus case, around the turn of the century, the intellectual hero was a staple of French fiction, in much the way radical sects, life-and-death debates, and spiritual conversions had long been the meat and drink of the Russian novel. In these books, conflicting systems of thought were as fraught with high drama as love and death. In the more pragmatic climate of the United States, public moralists and social reformers carried some weight, and sometimes wrote novels propagating their cause (such as temperance), but ideas themselves seemed suspect, even alien. Hawthorne gently mocked the utopians of Brook Farm in *The Blithedale Romance*. A writer of metaphysical bent like Melville and a political animal like Henry Adams could grow eloquent on the subject of their own marginal position. But periods of social crisis, such as the years leading up to the Civil War or the time of the Great Depression, set off a ferment of ideas reminiscent of the early years of the Republic.

The Crash of 1929 and the worsening conditions of the Hoover years, along with the rise of European fascism, threatened to undermine the whole American system. They propelled intellectuals to the center of the national debate, both in the Roosevelt administration, with its vaunted Brains Trust, and in small circles of newly radicalized left-wing writers. One such group was made up of gifted young men such as Lionel Trilling, Clifton Fadiman, Meyer Schapiro, Whittaker Chambers, and Herbert Solow who knew each other as students at Columbia in the early 1920s. Some of them gravitated into the orbit of the *Menorah Journal*, a secular journal focused on issues of Jewish culture and identity, and they became protégés of its charismatic managing editor, Elliot Cohen, who later founded *Commentary*. After the Crash they moved left well before their contemporaries but soon broke with the Communist Party. The group fell briefly under the influence of Trotsky and eventually formed part of the nucleus of New York intellectuals around *Partisan Review*, created with Communist support in 1934 and reorganized as an independent anti-Stalinist publication in 1937.[2]

Even more than their opponents in the cultural orbit of the party, where women were often encouraged as writers and activists, these dissidents made up a heavily male group. When Philip Rahv used the masculine pronoun to refer to intellectuals, he was following the usage of the time but also assuming that an authentic intellectual was likely to be a man, and that women inevitably played a subsidiary role. Yet many young men in this circle had assertive wives with serious political commitments; some of them, like Diana Trilling, eventually became well-known writers. The first to break through, well before any of the men, was Tess Slesinger, who married Herbert Solow in 1928. Born in 1905, she had gone to the progressive Ethical Culture School in New York, then to Swarthmore College and the Columbia School of Journalism. Starting in 1930 she attracted attention with her stories, especially "Missis Flinders," a bitterly cheerful but unforgiving account of the aftermath of an abortion, published in *Story* magazine in 1932. Based on her own experience, it became the final chapter of her first and only novel, *The Unpossessed*, a book that elicited critical praise when it came out in 1934. It was soon followed by an ambitious collection of well-crafted stories, *Time: The Present*, in 1935. These mostly Depression tales were often too bright and showy, almost musical in their reliance on repeated phrases and images, but they proved unusually fresh in developing a woman's point of view. Though her novel has its flaws and is scarcely the last word, *The Unpossessed* remains the best portrait we have of the intellectual ferment of the Depression years.

Slesinger and Solow were divorced in 1933, and this rupture is reflected in *The Unpossessed*. It chronicles the disintegration of a marriage along with the more farcical collapse of a project by three friends, all political activists, to start a radical magazine. With a bow to *The Possessed*, Dostoyevsky's great novel about young Russian radicals in the 1860s, *The Unpossessed* is *The Big Chill* of the *Menorah Journal* circle of left intellectuals, etched in satire and sardonic affection rather than nostalgia. In 1935 Tess Slesinger left for Hollywood, where she had two children and wrote screenplays with her second husband, Frank Davis, including such well-received movies as *The Good Earth* and *A Tree Grows in Brooklyn* (the first film directed by Elia Kazan). She also worked on two films for one of Hollywood's few women directors, Dorothy Arzner. Slesinger died of cancer in 1945 at the age of thirty-nine.

Since there are so few good novels about American intellectuals, it's ironic that *The Unpossessed* should be so corrosive toward its subjects that it appears to dismiss them altogether. Murray Kempton later recalled that its cast of characters included "quite possibly the most unattractive specimens in American literature prior to the works of Mary McCarthy."[3] Yet the book offers a complex canvas of failed relationships between three men and their three women, along with a host of minor figures who fill in different corners of the political landscape. Slesinger makes some of her points through these bit players. They include the wealthy patron, Merle Middleton, who funds the planned magazine and sleeps with one of the future editors. Then there are the "Black Sheep," who are students of Bruno Leonard, one of the protagonists. Overflowing with "turbulent indignation,"[4] they foreshadow the more militant activism of the next generation. Finally there is Comrade Fisher, a hard-boiled Trotskyist though girlish at heart, who sleeps under a portrait of Lenin and has also slept her way through the revolutionary movement. Slesinger's sharp eye keeps these secondary figures from becoming caricatures, respectively, of the insecure rich, the hotheaded young, and the promiscuous radical girl. In his 1966 afterword to a reprint of the novel, Trilling also compared Slesinger to Mary McCarthy, seven years younger, who would make the hothouse world of thirties radical intellectuals her best subject. But whether she was writing theater reviews, short stories, or essays, McCarthy was in every way an intellectual herself, smarter and more trenchant than any of the men around her.

Tess Slesinger could be as hard on her characters as McCarthy, but at times it seems she condemns them simply for *being* intellectuals. The author and her surrogate, Margaret Flinders, recoil from the very qualities—ambivalence, reflectiveness, and self-consciousness—that make intellectuals who they are. Slesinger falls in more with the new student generation, the advance guard of a new, more militant Left, precisely for putting these deliberate habits of mind behind them. These impatient young hotheads form an alternate community devoted to direct action. At a lavish party to raise money for unemployed Hunger Marchers, their leader claims sweepingly that "intellectuals as a class are dying out, their function's dead—nobody's left to support them" (302). Disgusted with mere talk and money concerns, they leave the party to bum their way to Washington to join the march itself. With these students nipping at their heels, their elders, now in their thirties, wonder about the kids who seem determined to act rather than think: "Were they the vanguard of the newest intellectuals who, not remaining aloof with their books and their ideas, had strength to mingle with the living and bring their gifts among them?" (332). Sympathizing with their determined activism, Slesinger became a fellow traveler in her last decade in Hollywood, perhaps simply adapting to the social milieu of the film capital. She even signed a notorious letter attacking the Dewey Commission—led by the philosopher John Dewey but organized by her ex-husband, Solow—which, after extensive hearings in Mexico, exonerated Trotsky from the heinous charges of betrayal that the Soviets had leveled against him.

But gender differences are closer to the heart of this novel than political differences, for Slesinger writes more as a feminist than as a radical. The three main male characters in *The Unpossessed*—including Miles Flinders, a journalist, loosely based on Solow, Bruno Leonard, a professor at their old college, obviously modeled on Elliot Cohen, and Jeffrey Blake, a facile novelist and womanizer, perhaps based on Max Eastman—all come off as deeply inadequate. They are failures in love because they resist the intimacy of real relationships; failures in politics because, unlike the young radicals, they prefer the idea of revolution, even the idea of simply starting a magazine, to the risks of doing anything. And they are failures even as intellectuals, since they're paralyzed by scruples and misgivings and can never take an unambiguous position. As college friends a dozen years earlier, they first dreamed radical dreams and took up the cause of the downtrodden, but with no real connection to the people in whose names they hoped to speak. They show none of the organic links, described by the Italian Marxist Antonio Gramsci, between the common lives of ordinary people and the leaders or spokesmen who emerge directly from their midst. Now, though far from old, they feel haunted by premature disappointment. Each of them has already compromised: the puritanical Miles by falling in love, which opened him to the softening influences of personal feeling, as represented by his wife, Margaret; Bruno, the self-hating academic, by keeping his younger cousin Elizabeth at arm's length, though she adores him, and by becoming the flattered mentor and Pied Piper to a younger generation; and smooth Jeffrey, a creature of radical fashion, by writing glib novels and pursuing a hyperactive love life, which always leads him back to his agreeably docile wife. But the Depression demands something more from these men; they must do something to change the world. They gain the patronage of Mrs. Middleton, whom Jeffrey has enlisted between the sheets for the revolutionary cause, and the amused tolerance of her down-to-earth husband, who enjoys the spectacle of his bored wife's flirtation with high-minded characters and projects. The three friends set out to launch a magazine, for what else can such intellectuals do?

At the heart of *The Unpossessed* is Slesinger's crosshatching of the personal and the political. In real life Herbert Solow and Elliot Cohen were tormented men, though both were also effective at what they did, including editing and political organizing. Trilling describes Solow as "a man of quite remarkable intelligence, very witty in a saturnine way, deeply skeptical, tortured by bouts of extreme depression. His was the first political mind I ever encountered."[5] Trilling's relation to Cohen was even deeper, for he published Trilling's first story, "Impediments," in the *Menorah Journal* in 1925, when Trilling was still a Columbia undergraduate, and many more stories, essays, and reviews over the next seven years. Himself largely blocked as a writer, Cohen became an exceptionally gifted but sometimes intrusive editor who, according to Diana Trilling, "looked to other writers to act as his literary surrogates." As a result, she says, "one had constantly to battle the imposition of his mind and will: it was like extricating oneself from under a suffocating encumbrance. . . . There was no situation, however trivial, which he did not have to dominate."[6] After 1945, with *Commentary*, Cohen created one of the best intellectual journals of the postwar years, but he took his own life in the course of a nervous breakdown in 1958. In her memoir Diana Trilling describes her husband shaking violently and gripping the lectern with white knuckles as he tried to eulogize his old friend.

But the real-life troubles of Solow and Cohen were not exactly the psychological problems Slesinger projects onto Miles Flinders and Bruno Leonard, which allow her, often rather formulaically, to give meaning to their personal and political failures. Though Solow was as Jewish as Cohen and Slesinger, in the novel she depicts Miles Flinders as a severe Puritan, emotionally crippled by his flinty New England heritage—no doubt as a comment on the puritanical strain in the thirties Left. Miles fears that his wife's womanliness, her invitation to pleasure and a sheltering intimacy, will unman him, engulf him, and "swallow him whole." He is hobbled by his fear of the feminine, his contempt for emotion and distrust of nature. Where Miles is drawn to the world of struggle, of ideals, Margaret, like

Slesinger herself, insists on a narrower terrain in which individuals have a right to be happy. Her husband holds out against this siren song of happiness as if it were a drug. "The nearness of her female flesh, her female awareness, surrounding him with warmth he did not want, was stifling" (21). We see his wife mainly through Miles's eyes, and he is full of qualms the author projects on him to explain why he withholds himself. Slesinger was a careful reader of many modern writers, especially Virginia Woolf, and her story unfolds in the ebb and flow of her characters' minds. In this hall of mirrors we observe the marriage through the lens of a woman looking at a man as he is looking at a woman. But Miles's suspicion of women, his denial of the feminine side of his own nature, seems straight out of the diagnostic arsenal of D. H. Lawrence.

Miles's fear and self-denial come to a head in a brief chapter called "The Conscience Ticks." Returning late at night from a political meeting to plan the new magazine, he is careful not to waken his wife. Otherwise she might want him, even try to comfort him. He resists such intimacy and dependence, for he wants only to make a difference in the larger world. "Womb versus world, he thought, silently removing his shoes, his clothes, in dread of waking her." Slesinger's intellectuals are men whose heads are on distant goals, their minds a tissue of abstractions; they are unable to sustain a personal life. Women, on the other hand, she saw as grounded in biology, in feeling, in the mundane facts of ordinary experience, which intellectuals make pointless efforts to transcend. Looking down at his sleeping wife, Miles thinks that "her end was peace and his was truth and they must be enemies" (215–16). Though many young people drifted into the orbit of the activism in the 1930s in search of casual, guilt-free sex, Slesinger sees radicalism, as represented by Miles, as an impulse to escape the body, elude the lure of pleasure, resist the narcotic effect of personal happiness. Lying in bed with her body curved close to his, he pulls back from "seeking consolation . . . hiding in a woman's insides from a world he couldn't face" (217). In making its case against these confused, compromised radicals, *The Unpossessed* comes close to being a thesis novel with characters who simply stand for ideas.

To Slesinger, Miles's failure in the world is an extension of his failure as a person, a projection of his neuroses onto a larger canvas. Though Slesinger clearly writes as a feminist, she approaches the radical movement in the spirit of the 1920s, the spirit of Lawrence and Freud, for whom the revolution in human relations had to be sexual and personal before it could be political. Her satire on the utopian aims of intellectuals is based on what she understands as a woman's down-to-earth experience and a novelist's affinity for storytelling rather than abstract ideas. Jeffrey, the fiction writer, remarks that his books are about men and women, not about classes, and another character observes that all these friends, spiritually tormented, sometimes to the point of comedy, sound like figures in a Russian novel. When Miles probes the bitter memories of his own childhood, his wife breathes life into his stories, giving back to him the happy moments he forgot he had. *The Unpossessed* begins with her shopping for vegetables from the local grocer, and it ends with the fruit basket she brings back from the hospital after her abortion. Between fruit and vegetables, between sexual intimacy and the warmth of stories, she lives in the concrete, a realm he shuns as a contraction of his worldly goals. Miles imagines that his personal freedom would be compromised if they had to raise a family. He presses his wife to have an abortion, which sinks their marriage as surely as a torpedo. A genuine union of two people, says Slesinger, like a political movement, creates something greater than the individual. For Miles and Margaret that would be love: the domestic happiness they fail to find, the baby that expresses their union, which they keep from coming into being. For Bruno and his friends this new entity would be the magazine, which he aborts just as effectively.

If Miles is at the center of the marriage plot in *The Unpossessed*, Bruno Leonard is the mover of the political plot. But he is as much a basket case as his deeply repressed friend. In her psychological take on the evasions of intellectuals, Slesinger allows Miles an epiphany about himself and his friends that is all too revealing: "He saw them suddenly, coming together less from their belief in revolution (did any of them really believe a revolution would take place?) than from some terrible inner need in each of them to lay out his own personal conflicts in terms of something higher, to solve his private ends camouflaged as world-problems, secretively in public" (218). Disguised as one man's moment of recognition, this all too directly lays bare the theme of the novel. The dialogue often seems made up not of what people might actually say but of the underlying logic of their positions. *The Unpossessed* attempts a reckoning with a whole way of life but is too argumentative to be fully convincing. Though it offers a grim verdict on those who live for ideas, it is nothing if not a novel of ideas, including the idea of intimacy, the innate differences of gender, the importance of biology, and the claims of everyday life. Yet Slesinger puts these notions forward as tart rebuttals to the abstractions of intellectuals.

If Miles's problem comes from his harsh conscience, his radical ambitions, his disconnection from his body, Bruno's weakness is his egotism—much like the egotism Diana Trilling attributed to Elliot Cohen—but also his Jewish ambivalence, for Slesinger too easily conflates intellectuals with neurotic Jews. Bruno is indecisive. He thinks "it was unfortunate that all sides held truth, that sanity consisted in a constant balancing. For he agreed with Miles, he agreed with Jeffrey, agreed with the Black Sheep; and weighing their opinions, he agreed with none of them" (200). His paralyzing ambivalence extends to his sexuality. He is attracted to the Middletons' stuttering son, Emmett, who worships him, and to his cousin Elizabeth, whom he has sent off to Paris to live the free life of an artist. Through the first section of the novel he longs for her from afar, as he longs for the magazine as an idea, a kind of salvation, but when she arrives he uses both Emmett and the magazine to keep her at bay. Faced with an actual person, a creature with real needs and desires, he cannot commit and cannot act. Once she returns we see him more and more through her eyes as she grows disillusioned. Finally he sinks both the magazine and the movement with a Dostoyevskyan speech of self-loathing and self-humiliation.

In line with the liberation ideals of the 1920s, Bruno has encouraged Elizabeth to go abroad: "Don't be obsessed by inhibitions," he tells her, "don't be possessed by superstitions; you've got to be free, my dear, free, as free as a man, you must play the man's game and beat him at it" (131). But Elizabeth's whirligig of freedom in Europe turns into a round-robin of relationships that yield excitement without real satisfaction. To mimic the hectic pace of her expatriate life, Slesinger adapts a Joycean technique of breathless run-on wordplay, around the metaphor of "the fast express": "all aboard ladies and gay modern gents, try an art colony first, all aboard, no stops no halts no brooding there, all aboard the twentieth century unlimited, hell-bent for nowhere . . . the rollicking jittery cocktail express, nothing can matter so wear down, you nerves, no brakes, no goal, no love, on we go glittering jittering twittering, try and get off it kid once you're on board, it'll rattle you shatter you . . ." (131–32). This barely punctuated style imitates the perpetual high jinks of the life she leads as an artist in Paris. This is a typical 1930s view of the twenties—a moral revulsion from its devil-may-care excess, as in Malcolm Cowley's classic *Exile's Return*, published the same year.

Like Cowley's expat artists, who have run out of fun and run out of money, Elizabeth is returning to a different world: "goodbye home and hello France, goodbye France, I'm coming home—love without lust and lust without love, the country's on the breadlines, the deadlines, the redlines, have a heart America, I'm coming home to stay" (132). But Bruno, the man she's always idolized, who shipped her off to France in the first place, is somehow never available. It is no use asking whether Bruno is straight or gay: he serves as a father substitute for fragile young Emmett Middleton, who is such a disappointment to his own father, and he plays the older sibling to Elizabeth, with whom he grew up. If Miles is inhibited by morality, a masculine hardness, Bruno is held back by incestuous feelings, less transgressive than "presexual" (as Paula Rabinowitz notes in her discussion of this novel in *Labor and Desire*).[7] His ambivalence (toward Emmett and Elizabeth alike) scarcely rises to the sexual. His sexuality is treated as a facet of his larger failure.

Slesinger highlights this repressed condition by making her third male protagonist, Jeffrey Blake, so priapic and shallow. He lives only for each new conquest, cosseted by the unshakable tolerance of passive Norah, his adoring wife. Unlike his friends, he has a capacity for "uncritical enjoyment" (58). Bruno, longing "like a dead man for sensation," envies Jeffrey for "a purity of desire that he knew could never be his own. The dumb virility of the extrovert . . . needing no Idea to quicken it" (83). But Jeffrey's compulsions reflect his own watery sense of self. His lovemaking is another form of the inability to love. "When he was with one woman he would think of another" (295). He always needs "something new, someone to look at him through fresh eyes, someone through whose eyes he could see himself " (308), and this draws him finally to Elizabeth as she sees Bruno slipping away from her. "She felt a wan kinship with him, knowing him to be the same thing as herself, a weary Don Juan whose impulses having lost their freshness were the more compelling therefor" (309). Without Bruno, she feels condemned to return to the same bright, empty promiscuity she had left behind in Paris, where she grew tired of "this endless contact without benefit of soul, without benefit of love" (108).

In Bruno, Slesinger portrays the mind that always stands back, too self-conscious for real commitment. The writer's sheer technical virtuosity comes through in two long chapters, "The Inquest" and "The Party," each with a large cast of characters and multiple points of view. In the first episode, Bruno and his friends meet to make their plans for the magazine; in the second, they converge again at the Middletons to raise funds for the magazine and for the Hunger Marchers. As if to show that salvation is personal, not political, Slesinger orchestrates these scenes as collective moments of high comedy that go nowhere, blowing up in a way that mocks the aspirations of all those present. At each event Bruno remains apart, conscious of the empty farce he's set in motion. The meeting breaks up when Cornelia, one of the young Black Sheep, faints from hunger right after they have all been talking abstractly about starvation and empty bellies. Slesinger strains to drive home the point that the intellectuals cannot accommodate anything immediate. "The uncomplicated physical had no reality for them," she says. "Their busy abstract minds worked to reconcile it with some pre-accepted doctrine, some maxim of their own" (212). But to Bruno it shows that "the whole thing, the Magazine, this roomful of ghosts, his own whole life," is little more than a farce, a charade of dead souls. At the party for the Hunger Marchers, overflowing with expensive food, this hollow feeling of failure takes over his speech. Here Bruno morphs into the mouthpiece for Slesinger's message: that the intellectuals, with their cult of alienation, their hatred of their own middle-class origins, are as sterile politically as they are sexually. "We have no parents and we can have no offspring," he says. "We have no sex: we are mules—in short we are bastards, foundlings, phonys, the unpossessed and unpossessing of the world, the real minority" (327).

Turning Freudian like the author, warming to her theme, Bruno argues ponderously, "The lie in our private lives is important, it makes our public lives unreal and fraudulent—a man can't do good work with an undernourished psychic system." Their political activities reflect this illness: "Our meetings are masterpieces of postponement, our ideologies brilliant rationalizations to prevent our ever taking action." In short, "my friends and myself are sick men—if we are not already dead" (330–31). Only the Black Sheep escape this intellectual disease of reflection, abstraction, inaction. Tess Slesinger's accommodation to Stalinism in Hollywood, as well as her good work on domestic and sentimental dramas like

A Tree Grows in Brooklyn, can be seen as her farewell to the nice intellectual scruples, the constitutional ambivalence, of her friends in New York.

The concluding chapter on Margaret's abortion (which is the story from which the novel originated) points up the same argument; it makes Slesinger's case against the sterile freedom of the intellectual life and in favor of family, love, and domestic happiness. For Slesinger, as for Malcolm Cowley, the bohemian radicalism of the twenties had come to a dead end. Feminists have usually argued for abortion as a way of liberating women from the burdens of unwanted motherhood. But Slesinger's essentialist feminism—her conventional view of women as biological beings, closer to nature, grounded in the ordinary—took her down a different track. She sees Margaret's abortion as yet another way the women in the novel mold themselves to men's wants and needs. "It had been dinned into her that a woman's life was completed by her husband" (61). Margaret comes to understand her own "failure to keep her identity apart from his; she sought a thread and a meaning, and expected both of them from him" (64). Lionel Trilling has testified that the intellectuals of the thirties, especially the men, recoiled from having children as "biological traps," since children inevitably required "compromise with, or capitulation to, the forces of convention."[8] For Slesinger nothing could have served as better evidence of the intellectuals' sterile detachment from nature.

Slesinger's brief against the intellectuals was cast as a woman's innate biological wisdom as well as a deliberate break with the people she would leave behind when she left New York. But it was also a novelist's argument, the case that the storyteller, devoted to plumbing the mysteries of everyday life, makes against the abstract thinker who constructs alternate worlds. Because of the book's title, it's tempting to contrast *The Unpossessed* with Dostoyevsky's novel, since *these* characters are neither possessed by their cause nor self-possessed. But Dostoyevsky pillories his young radicals the same way Slesinger does, as people out of touch, living in a cocoon of their own making. Like the terrorists and revolutionaries in James's *Princess Casamassima* and Conrad's *Secret Agent*, they play with politics in a void. The are as ineffectual as they are inauthentic, speaking for people they do not know and don't truly care about. While the novel as a form may not be inherently conservative, it does tend to be anti-utopian and anti-intellectual, suspicious of ideas when they are not grounded in actual human situations. This is especially true of English and American novels, with their empirical traditions, and true of satire as well, going back to the fantastical scholars of Swift's Academy of Lagado. Sidney Hook, who lived for the give-and-take of controversy, said of Slesinger that "she never understood a word about the political discussions that raged around her. . . . Her book shows that. . . . Tess caught the psychological mood of some of Herbert's friends but she was a political innocent until the day of her death."[9] But it would be more accurate to say that she was a writer until the day of her death, more interested in people than in ideas. Yet in a strange way she wrote a novel of ideas, for anti-intellectualism is itself an idea.

Slesinger's work has been compared to Mary McCarthy's, partly because of her sharp satirical eye, but also because she wrote (lethally) about a similar circle of New York intellectuals. But no one would dream of calling McCarthy's work anti-intellectual. It would be a mistake even to type her as a woman writer. With brilliance and brio, McCarthy freed herself of the biologism of Lawrence and Freud, with its core notions of sexual difference. She lived by Bruno's advice to Elizabeth—to play the men's game and beat them at it. The pathos of the liberated woman, as embodied in Elizabeth, passed her by, except where she could turn it into comedy, which she did best in her famous story about a seduction on a train, "The Man in the Brooks Brothers Shirt." At her best her characters can surprise us because, even as a satirist, she avoids reducing them to a formula or idea. "You are, after all, a human being, with a hundred tricks up your sleeve."[10]

McCarthy's fiction most resembles *The Unpossessed* in her "Portrait of the Intellectual as a Yale Man," the longest story in *The Company She Keeps* (1942). The protagonist, Jim Barnett, and his complaisant wife, Nancy, remind us strikingly of Jeffrey Blake and his Norah; both men are fashionable radicals with passive, accommodating wives. But McCarthy's story sets Jim against the formidable Meg Sargent, who is as annoyingly intense in her anti-Stalinist radicalism as he is mild and commonsensical. For him going left was simply the sensible thing to do. Barnett is less a portrait of an intellectual than the facsimile of an intellectual. Unlike Meg, he gets on well with his Stalinist friends, and when he resigns on principle from a job on a liberal magazine and tries to write a book, he finds he has nothing to say. In the end he takes a job with *Destiny*, a magazine like *Fortune*, and cares little about what happens to his copy once he submits it. Finally, he becomes a family man, keeping down his spiritual expenses, while Meg Sargent soldiers on. Now "a comfortable man," he can't forgive her for showing him "the cage of his own nature."[11] Her intransigence, her convictions, make her a genuine intellectual—and leave her unemployed. McCarthy brings Slesinger's satirical take on the New York intellectuals to perfection but inverts its point of view. She attacks men like Jim Barnett not for their misplaced passion for ideas but for having no passion at all, for not really caring. If fiction and satire lean toward the anti-intellectual, McCarthy's work, bracing in its sheer intelligence, is one of the bright exceptions that prove the rule. Even in its deft mockery, it conveys how exciting the intellectual ferment of the 1930s could be.

CHAPTER 17

Conclusion:

THE WORK OF CULTURE IN DEPRESSION AMERICA

THE DEPRESSION EVENTUALLY CAME to an end, not mainly because of the New Deal programs, despite their enormous impact, but thanks to the mobilization of manpower and industry after America's entry into the war in 1941. The Depression had unfolded roughly in three phases: the critical years culminating in the winter of despair in 1932–33, when the business activity, banking, and employment hit bottom; the prime years of the New Deal from

1933 to 1937, highlighted by the legislation of the First Hundred Days in 1933 and the so-called Second Hundred Days (or Second New Deal) of 1935; and a final phase that began in 1937 with a premature effort to balance the federal budget, a jarring nine-month recession, the failure of FDR's plan to enlarge the Supreme Court, and major Democratic losses in the congressional elections of 1938, which cost the president his legislative majorities. But as the economy improved and unemployment eased, international concerns came to a head with the growing threat of European fascism and Japanese militarism.

The cultural changes of the 1930s are harder to pin down but, surprisingly, they parallel the effects of the New Deal. The initial sense of crisis and personal isolation gave way to a dream of community, a vision of interdependence, just as it did in the political world. In those early years the individual was usually shown either as a victim, as in *I Am a Fugitive from a Chain Gang*, or as an aggressive loner, as in the classic gangster films of 1930–32 or the hard-boiled novels of Dashiell Hammett, such as *Red Harvest*, *The Maltese Falcon*, or *The Glass Key*. This is also when writers discovered poverty, a time when ordinary Americans, feeling helpless and ashamed, had nothing to fall back on but their own shrunken resources. But by 1933 the arts too began to reflect a new collective awareness, a sense of solidarity that contributed to a tempered optimism about the future. We see it in organizations like the Group Theatre, a commune-like extended family, at once fractious and idealistic, that came into its own with Clifford Odets's plays of 1935, works that climaxed with punchy messages of youthful hope. A different sort of collective vision could be seen in the exhilaratingly surreal choreography of Busby Berkeley, with its abstract design and impersonal group formations, or in the communal world of King Vidor's 1934 film about a collective farm, *Our Daily Bread*, which takes its cues from the new Soviet cinema. This pressing social purpose dominated Upton Sinclair's quixotic campaign for the governorship of California in the same year, on a platform to End Poverty in California (EPIC), and it was brought closer to reality by the major legislative achievements of 1935, such as Social Security, the Wagner Act, entitling labor unions to organize, and far-reaching welfare programs such as the Works Progress Administration. In that year the Communists widened their appeal to liberals, including many artists and writers, by shifting from class warfare to the Popular Front, a collaborative strategy highlighting the progressive traditions of American folklore, history, and institutions. They also encouraged artists, writers, and composers to form their own front organizations, which paralleled the WPA arts projects. Similar group feelings sparked those who were opposed to the Popular Front, such as the Southern Agrarians and the young New York intellectuals who revived *Partisan Review* in 1937 as an anti-Stalinist journal of politics and the arts.

You can feel this collective energy even in the most unlikely places, as in one of the last major films of the thirties, *The Wizard of Oz* (1939). It begins in a monochromatic world of rural poverty, spiced by ill will (Miss Gulch's hatred of Toto, Dorothy's dog) and then disrupted by natural disaster (the twister that stands in for other Depression catastrophes). Amid this calamity Dorothy is transported to another world, at once ravishingly beautiful and oppressed by fear. Dreaming of a trouble-free world, "somewhere over the rainbow," cheered on by the Munchkins, the local proletariat, targeted by the Wicked Witch, who is yet another fierce incarnation of Miss Gulch (Margaret Hamilton), she finds that she can get home only by working with others who also need help: the Cowardly Lion, who wants courage, the Tin Man, who needs a heart, the Scarecrow, in need of a brain. Though all these characters go back to L. Frank Baum's original novel, the qualities they demanded were precisely the ones needed to get through the Depression, those FDR was trying to instill: courage to face up to the social crisis, empathy for the sufferings of others, a break with past thinking about how we ought to live. Together, through many trials, they follow the Yellow Brick Road to the Emerald City much the way the Joads travel along Route 66 to another promised land, California; this too is a Depression road movie. Once there the benign Wizard, perhaps a stand-in for FDR, convinces them they already have these powers within themselves. By working together they discovered their own strength and found their way home.

This sense of community, of collective action in the face of social disaster, combined with the lessening economic effects of the Depression, helps explain why the last years of the 1930s were a strangely hopeful period—despite the run of bad news from overseas, including the Spanish Civil War of 1936–39, which attracted passionate international volunteers, and the intensifying persecution of the Jews of Germany, both of them rehearsals for much worse to come. Roosevelt and the New Deal stimulated the feeling that we were all in the same boat, though we needed someone we could trust at the rudder. The era of the common man was also the era of the trusted leader, the benevolent father figure. Growing up in the 1940s, I could feel the reverence for FDR among the second-generation immigrant Jews around me. The forgotten men he had evoked in his 1932 campaign trusted that he had not forgotten them.

The president had devoted his first inaugural address to boosting morale and building a constituency for reform. At that low point of the Depression, he said that "the only thing we have to fear is fear itself— nameless, unreasoning, unjustified terror which paralyzes needed efforts to convert retreat into advance." As the Hoover era ended, the American people still felt like hapless, isolated victims, responsible for their own fate, living in dread of what the future would bring. Four years later, in his second inaugural address (1937), with major legislation behind him, he described how a new way of thinking had enabled the helpless to become hopeful, the victims to become agents. He credited an activist conception of government. We now understand, he said, "the need to find through government the instrument of our united purpose to solve for the individual the ever-rising problems of a complex civilization. Repeated attempts at their solution without the aid of government had left us baffled and bewildered." This was the New Deal message that was rediscovered during the financial meltdown of 2008, after decades of free-market ideology.

But Roosevelt aimed to change not only the role of government but the relation between individuals and their society.

> Old truths have been relearned; untruths have been unlearned. We have always known that heedless self-interest was bad morals; we know now that it is bad economics. . . . This new understanding undermines the old admiration of worldly success as such. We are beginning to abandon our tolerance of the abuse of power by those who betray for profit the elementary decencies of life.

Roosevelt went on to his famous vision of tens of millions of Americans denied the basic decencies of life, "one-third of a nation ill-housed, ill-clad, ill-nourished." He demanded universal inclusion in the fruits of prosperity and education, and added, "The test of our progress is not whether we add more to the abundance of those who have much; it is whether we provide enough for those who have too little." His peroration drove this point home:

> Today we reconsecrate our country to long-cherished ideals in a sud-
> denly changed civilization. In every land there are always at work
> forces that drive men apart and forces that draw men together. In our
> personal ambitions we are individualists. But in our seeking for eco-
> nomic and political progress as a nation, we all go up, or else we all
> go down, as one people.[1]

Roosevelt's outlook, like his enigmatic personality, was at once patrician and egalitarian. It was democratic yet grounded in noblesse oblige.
He preached an ethic of responsibility that altered the way Americans
viewed their government.

In this book I've tried to show how that the expressive culture of the
thirties—the books, films, murals, photographs, reportage, radio programs, dance, and music—besides telling us much about the inner life of
the Depression years, played a role parallel to the leadership of FDR and
the programs of the New Deal. This went well beyond the new government sponsorship of the arts: the arts bound people together in a collaborative effort to interpret and alleviate their plight. These works could
traffic in harsh exposure, warm empathy, fizzy distraction, or energetic
uplift. They could resonate with the moods of the Depression by portraying dismal failure, as in *Tender Is the Night*, *Studs Lonigan*, or *Miss Lonelyhearts*, or they could feed the nation's hopes and dreams with a shot of
adrenaline, as in screwball comedy or swing music, creating a remarkably buoyant, graceful, even giddy culture against a bleak background.
They offered a stimulus of optimism and energy. They could appeal to
the masses, paradoxically, by tuning in to the lives of exceptional people,
such as the warring couples in romantic comedy, and by resolving scenes
of conflict into moments of concord. At the other end of the spectrum,
the folkways of ordinary people brought out the best in Woody Guthrie
and John Steinbeck, Walker Evans and Frank Capra, Aaron Copland and
George Gershwin, James Agee and John Ford. But such populist sentiments fueled the corrosive skepticism of naysayers like Nathanael West,
who worried about the latent savagery of the common man, a forebod-

ing borne out by the terrific carnage of the Second World War, abetted by deadly new technology.

Brought together by the challenge of the Depression, the American people were primed for the patriotism, sacrifice, and collective effort of the war, a time of emergency when individual needs were set aside for dire national priorities. (Such an enforced unity would take a darker turn with the social conformity and political intolerance of the early cold war years.) But the symbolic end of the Depression came not with the attack on Pearl Harbor but with the New York World's Fair of 1939–40, the last major collective event of the Depression years. First conceived as a way of stimulating business activity, it was built on the dump site that figured ominously as "the valley of ashes" in *The Great Gatsby*. Over two seasons, on the cusp between Depression and war, it provided 45 million visitors with an immense cabinet of wonders, pointing the way to a brighter tomorrow. It combined elements of a trade show, a county fair, an amusement park, a science fair, a design exhibition, and a concourse of nations. In separate zones around an uplifting Theme Center, symbolized by the Trylon and Perisphere, the fair brought together many strands of thirties culture: Transportation (to get the country moving again), Food (in a world where many were still poor and hungry), Amusement (to take people's minds off their troubles), Government (to help get them *out* of trouble), Communications (ranging from high art—a collection of Old Masters—to new inventions like television and FM radio), and a Hall of Nations (a world soon to descend into war).

The big corporate pavilions, led by General Motors, promoted not only their own wares but a way of life, a vision of the future as a utopia of advanced technology, streamlined modernity, and consumer abundance. (FDR's speech opening the fair was the nation's first regular television broadcast, which few could then receive.) The fair's most popular exhibit, GM's Futurama, offered a vast diorama of the American landscape; it envisioned an automotive paradise for the year 1960, a nation crisscrossed by highways, with traffic monitored and controlled from central locations. In moving seats accompanied by sound commentary, spectators were swept across the whole terrain of the exhibit in a trip that took fifteen minutes and covered a third of a mile. From above they saw a miniaturized world in dazzling detail, smoothly functioning and free of real-world conflict.

It combined capitalist commerce (the auto industry) with public works (a national road network), and the individual family, each in its own conveyance, with central planning worthy of Le Corbusier. All through the fair, a battalion of architects and all the great industrial designers of the 1930s—including Norman Bel Geddes, Walter Dorwin Teague, and Raymond Loewy, the avatars of streamlined Deco—created a sense of the World of Tomorrow as a consumer's dream made possible by the energies of industry and the marvels of technology.

Another group experience of the fair was the crowd itself, the masses of people moving through the fairgrounds or along the Helicline, a curved, visually striking elevated walkway that led away from the Perisphere. There they would have seen another planned environment called Democracity, an accurate forecast of the postwar suburban world, with the cities as workplaces and the surrounding towns, linked by roads, as pastoral bedroom communities. On the other hand, in the City of Light diorama at the Con Ed Building, they could see a brilliantly lit miniature of New York itself, a nocturnal playground that revealed a vast potential for the uses of electricity. According to a 1940 editorial in *Architectural Record*, "the greatest discovery in New York was the discovery of the crowd both as actor and as decoration of great power. The designers found out that the crowd's greatest pleasure is in the crowd."[2] The same year the fair opened, Nathanael West concluded *The Day of the Locust* with a gawking crowd rioting at a movie premiere, an apocalyptic metaphor for the mass potential for fascism. It would be hard to find a better illustration of the antitheses of thirties culture: at the fair, ordinary folk amusing themselves or dreaming the future as consumers within an ingeniously planned public space; in West's novel the restless mob, unsatisfied, irrational, venting its boredom and desperation in spontaneous violence.

Historians like C. Vann Woodward and David Kennedy note with surprise that hard times did not incite the American people to rise up and rebel or take up extreme collectivist ideologies, as in Europe and the Far East. "More surprising than people's despair was their prevailing submissiveness," writes Woodward in his introduction to Kennedy's *Freedom from Fear*. "Much more common than rebellion among Americans of those years was a sense of shame and a loss of self-respect."[3] This points less to some special fiber in the national character than to American traditions of inclusion, popular sovereignty, and democratic leadership, which deflected the influence of demagogues like Huey Long. Woodward attributes it to our patterns of individualism, which led people to blame themselves for the reverses in their lives—precisely the reaction the president and the New Deal worked hard to combat. Instead, they encouraged a sense of common problems and common purpose. "We're going to make a country in which no one is left out," FDR once told his secretary of labor, Frances Perkins.[4]

In their own way, the art and entertainment of the thirties had a similar impact. Radio, movies, and popular music left few people out, especially with the tremendous advances in rural electrification, one of the New Deal's most far-reaching programs. The high arts, once the preserve of the white, Anglo-Saxon, Protestant majority, began to embrace a crazy quilt of ethnic, religious, and regional populations. As Alfred Kazin wrote in *Starting Out in the Thirties*, "the banked-up experience of the plebes, of Jews, Irishmen, Negroes, Armenians, Italians, was coming into American books."[5] And not just books but mass culture as well. The energies of such outsiders, especially blacks and Jews, propelled popular music to the center of this new hybrid culture, while immigrant Jews and their children confected a Hollywood version of the American Dream. Moviegoing then was nothing if not a collective activity, a genuine mass act.

Writers, painters, composers, and photographers took on timely subjects with the same zeal that their predecessors of the 1920s searched out advanced techniques. The modernists of the earlier decade prized difficulty, instinctively separating the creative spirit from the philistine masses. Their successors had a more common touch as they worked to incite, amuse, inform, or console a beleaguered nation. If the popular culture helped people cope with their lives, the serious culture helped them make sense of their lives. But such lines were not easily drawn, for some serious works (like *The Grapes of Wrath*) became hugely popular while many popular artists (such as Astaire, Gershwin, and Ellington) proved deeply serious. They sought (but did not always find) a universal audience, binding disparate people together, as Roosevelt did with his fireside chats, and helping them weather the economic storm.

Artists and performers rarely succeed in changing the world, but they can change our feelings about the world, our understanding of it, the way we live in it. They produced a rich, sometimes paradoxical culture by keeping their eyes trained on the ups and downs of individual lives within the larger social crisis, to which they bore eloquent witness. Their work and serious play did much to ease the national trauma. They were dancing in the dark, moving in time to a music of their own, but the steps were magical.

ACKNOWLEDGMENTS

This book was long in the making, and it's a pleasure to acknowledge the many debts I incurred along the way, including some to friends who are no longer here to be thanked. Erwin Glikes, who edited my work on the 1960s, was the first who believed in the book and urged me to write it. With his usual gusto, Alfred Kazin shared with me his vivid memories of the thirties. Stanley Burnshaw, who always identified with the period, cheered me on with his enthusiasm. I regret that none of them lived to read it.

My agents and friends, Georges and Anne Borchardt, showed wonderful patience laced with Georges's wry amusement, which helped keep things in perspective. I'm also grateful for the help of their assistants, including Barbara Galletly, DeAnna Heindel, and Jonathan Berman. Bob Weil at Norton was everything an editor should be. His assistant, Lucas Wittmann, was helpful in a hundred ways, while Don Rifkin gave the book an exceptionally close in-house reading. I want to thank those who invited me to lecture on some facet of the 1930s or to adapt parts of this book into essays or articles, including Eric Banks, William Boelhower, Daniel Born, Maria DiBattista, Ronald Gottesman, Frank Lentricchia, Bill Mullen, Kent Mullikin, Carol Oja, the late William Phillips, Richard Pollak, Ruth Prigozy, Harold Schechter, Ben Sonnenberg, and Judith Tick. A lecture invitation from Tom Staley, the director of the Ransom

Center at the University of Texas at Austin, gave me an opportunity to focus on some leading poets of the thirties. Timely fellowships from the National Endowment for the Humanities and the National Humanities Center and a month's residency at the Rockefeller Foundation Bellagio Center enabled me to write large parts of the first, second, and third sections of this book, respectively, under ideal working conditions.

Many friends and colleagues were generous with their assistance and encouragement. At the CUNY Graduate Center, President Bill Kelly provided me with a semester without teaching that proved crucial as I was completing the book. Marc Dolan's knowledge of popular music and his extraordinary collection of CDs were a renewable resource. Gary Giddins offered a close reading of the chapter on swing and big bands and made some acute suggestions. David Yaffe provided discographies and bibliographical suggestions, as did Phillip Lopate. Trevor Lee furnished indispensable aid through a maze of computer problems in the preparation of the manuscript. Bridget McGovern was helpful in tracking down illustrations and references. Otto Sonntag proved to be an eagle-eyed copy editor, and Elyse Rieder was resourceful in searching out apt illustrations. Robert Kimball and Jim Steinblatt helped guide me through the maze of song permissions. Marshall Berman, Vicki Goldberg, Eugene Goodheart, Molly Haskell, Richard Locke, Gerald Monroe, Anne Roiphe, and Dan and Toby Talbot proffered warm support when I most needed it. My former teacher Jeffrey Hart combined enthusiasm with graphic recollections of a childhood in New York during the Great Depression.

My dearest friend and first reader, Lore Dickstein, has lived with this book as long as I have. Without her support, wise counsel, and love it would never have been written.

NOTES

PREFACE

1. Quoted in Richard M. Cook, *Alfred Kazin: A Biography* (New Haven: Yale University Press, 2007), 22.
2. Matthew Baigell, *The American Scene: American Painting of the 1930's* (New York: Praeger, 1974), 18.
3. Caroline Bird, *The Invisible Scar* (1966; New York: Longman, 1978), 39, 40.
4. David M. Kennedy, *Freedom from Fear: The American People in Depression and War, 1929–1945* (New York: Oxford University Press, 1999), 377.

INTRODUCTION: DEPRESSION CULTURE

1. This led in 2008 to a series of bank failures, mergers, and bailouts, beginning with the takeover of a private securities firm, Bear Stearns, barely averting a major banking crisis. This was the work of Federal Reserve chair Ben Bernanke, whose reputation as an economist rested largely on his close study of the causes of the Great Depression. This and the crises that followed, which required a huge infusion of public funds, revealed major gaps in the regulatory safety net put in place then to monitor and restrain the banking industry, which had now been transformed almost beyond recognition.
2. Caroline Bird, *The Invisible Scar* (1966; New York: Longman, 1978), 59.
3. William Stott, *Documentary Expression and Thirties America* (New York: Oxford University Press, 1973), 68. Though his public relations were bad, many of Hoover's programs—such as the Reconstruction Finance Corporation of 1931—anticipated the efforts of the New Deal, though he largely put his faith in the private sector.

4. Ibid., 67–68n.

5. *Nothing to Fear: The Selected Addresses of Franklin Delano Roosevelt, 1932–1945*, ed. B. D. Zevin (Boston: Houghton Mifflin, 1946), 91.

6. Feminist scholarship on the Depression years includes books by Paula Rabinowitz, Constance Coiner, and Nora Roberts, drawing attention to the work of women writers such as Josephine Herbst, Tillie Olsen, Tess Slesinger, and Meridel Le Sueur. Books aiming to revive interest in radical, proletarian, and Popular Front culture include works by James Bloom, Michael Denning, Barbara Foley, Cary Nelson, Robert Shulman, and Alan Wald. See the bibliography for details.

7. One of the striking but lesser-known exceptions was the work of Herman Melville, who was forgotten by the 1890s and rediscovered only in the 1920s. On Melville's remarkable explorations of poverty, see the dense but rewarding book by Gavin Jones, *American Hungers: The Problem of Poverty in U.S. Literature, 1840–1945* (Princeton, N.J.: Princeton University Press, 2007), 21–61.

2. THE TENEMENT AND THE WORLD: IMMIGRANT LIVES

1. "Detroit counted 30 former bank tellers on its relief rolls. The universities graduated thousands of engineers, architects, and lawyers who had not the slightest prospect of a job." William E. Leuchtenburg, *The Perils of Prosperity, 1914–32* (Chicago: University of Chicago Press, 1958), 248.

2. Edmund Wilson, "The Literary Consequences of the Crash," in *The Shores of Light* (1952; New York: Vintage, 1961), 498–99. As Granville Hicks recalled, "the twenties was a decade of revolt in literature and, indeed, in all the arts. . . . [M]uch of the literature written in the twenties was somber and even tragic, but the spirit of the decade was one of exhilaration." Hicks, "Writers in the Thirties," in *As We Saw the Thirties*, ed. Rita James Simon (Urbana: University of Illinois Press, 1967), 78, 81.

3. This is especially true of the final version, which appeared in book form in 1898, for Crane removed the opening and closing passages in which the young man plans his masquerade and emerges to comment on it. Without this frame he seems swallowed up by his experiences, less detached and more like the outcasts he has encountered. Stephen Crane, *Prose and Poetry* (New York: Library of America, 1984), 547–48. For the deleted text as first printed in the New York *Press* (April 22, 1894), see pp. 1366–67.

4. "Towards Proletarian Art," in Michael Folsom, ed., *Mike Gold: A Literary Anthology* (New York: International Publishers, 1972), 67. Hereafter cited in text.

5. There is no genuine biography of Gold, who did not encourage interest in his checkered private life. The first biographical research was the work of Michael Folsom. See his article "The Education of Michael Gold," in *Proletarian Writers of the Thirties*, ed. David Madden (Carbondale: Southern Illinois University Press, 1968), 222–51. This should be supplemented by the much ampler account of Alan M. Wald, "Inventing Mike Gold," in *Exiles from a Future Time: The Forging of the Mid-Twentieth-Century Literary Left* (Chapel Hill: University of North Carolina Press, 2002), 39–70.

6. Michael Gold, *Jews without Money* (1930; New York: Carroll & Graf, 1984), 309. Hereafter cited in text. This is a reprint of the 1935 edition, which includes a brief new introduction by Gold.

7. Allen Guttmann, *The Jewish Writer in America* (New York: Oxford University Press, 1971), 140.

8. See Michael Harrington on the voluntary poverty of "the intellectual poor" in *The Other America: Poverty in the United States* (Harmondsworth: Penguin, 1963), 84–89. Hereafter cited in text. Harrington had cut his teeth in the Catholic Worker movement around Dorothy Day, also based on the Lower East Side.

9. Oscar Lewis, *La Vida: A Puerto Rican Family in the Culture of Poverty—San Juan and New York* (New York: Random House, 1966), xliii.

10. See Donald Reiman, ed., *The Romantics Reviewed*, vol. 2 (New York: Garland, 1972), 117.

11. As Linda Nochlin writes in *Realism*, "Courbet's paintings were socially inflammatory not so much because of what they said—they contain no overt message at all—but because of what they did not say. His unidealized, startlingly direct and matter-of-fact representations of contemporary lower-class subjects, utterly devoid of the small-scale, patronizingly picturesque charm which had made genre painting of similar themes acceptable, even if not theoretically admirable, in the eyes of right-thinking Frenchmen, made their Salon debut in 1850–51, at the very moment when the triumphant bourgeoisie had deprived these very lower classes of most of the advantages they had won on the barricades of 1848. . . . Courbet's 1850–51 Salon paintings, simply because of their scale, their style, and their subject matter, were seen as a threat to the as yet shakily re-established power of the middle-classes." Linda Nochlin, *Realism* (Harmondsworth: Penguin, 1971), 46–48.

12. Alfred Kazin, *Starting Out in the Thirties* (Boston: Atlantic Monthly Press, 1965), 12.

13. Some of the material from these interviews with Roth can be found in my profile "Call It an Awakening," *New York Times Book Review*, November 29, 1987. Other interviews as well as short fiction and autobiographical pieces were collected in Henry Roth, *Shifting Landscape*, ed. Mario Materassi (Philadelphia: Jewish Publication Society, 1987).

14. Quoted in Walter B. Rideout, *The Radical Novel in the United States, 1900–1954* (Cambridge: Harvard University Press, 1956), 189. With extraordinary insight for a time when the Roth's book was virtually unknown, Rideout called it "the most distinguished single proletarian novel" (186).

15. I have discussed this in my account of this late novel, "Memory Unbound," *Three-penny Review* (Summer 2007): 10–11, www.threepennyreview.com/samples/dickstein_ou07.html.

16. Bonnie Lyons, *Henry Roth: The Man and His Work* (New York: Cooper Square Publishers, 1976), 168. Hereafter cited in text. Before the publication of *Shifting Landscape*, this was the key source of information about Roth and his work. More recently there has appeared a lively and readable biography by Steven G. Kellman, *Redemption: The Life of Henry Roth* (New York: W. W. Norton, 2005).

17. Jean-Paul Sartre, "John Dos Passos and *1919*," in *Literary and Philosophical Essays*, trans. Annette Michelson (1955; New York: Collier Books, 1962), 100.

18. Henry Roth, *Call It Sleep* (1934; New York: Avon Books, 1964), 83. Hereafter cited in text. The page numbers are the same in the paperback edition of 1991.

19. Henry James, *The American Scene*, ed. Leon Edel (1907; Bloomington: Indiana University Press, 1968), 139.

20. Henry James, "The Art of Fiction," in *Literary Criticism: Essays on Literature, American Writers, English Writers*, ed. Leon Edel, with Mark Wilson (New York: Library of America, 1984), 61–62.

21. On this subject, see Hana Wirth-Nesher's afterword to a later edition of *Call It Sleep* (New York: Farrar, Straus and Giroux, 1991), 443–62.

3. THE STARVATION ARMY

1. Malcolm Cowley, *The Dream of the Golden Mountains* (New York: Viking, 1980), 250–51.

2. Philip Rahv, "Proletarian Literature: A Political Autopsy," in *Essays on Literature and Politics, 1932–1972*, ed. Arabel J. Porter and Andrew J. Dvosin (Boston: Houghton Mifflin, 1978), 299–300.

3. Murray Kempton, *Part of Our Time: Some Ruins and Monuments of the Thirties* (New York: Simon & Schuster, 1955), 136–37.

4. See Walter Rideout, *The Radical Novel in the United States, 1900–1954* (Cambridge: Harvard University Press, 1956), 185–90.

5. James T. Farrell, *Sam Holman* (Buffalo, N.Y.: Prometheus Books, 1983), 44. In chapter 16 I discuss the circle of writers on whom this novel was based.

6. D. H. Lawrence, *Phoenix: The Posthumous Papers of D. H. Lawrence*, ed. Edward D. McDonald (1936; London: Heinemann, 1961), 267, 271, 272.

7. See H. E. F. Donohue, *Conversations with Nelson Algren* (1964; New York: Berkly, 1965), 32–51. Hereafter cited in text.

8. Murray Kempton neatly avoids precise class origins by paying tribute to "plebeian" writers like Farrell who carried the freight of early poverty through their whole writing lives. He cites an epigraph that Farrell borrowed from Chekhov: "What writers belonging to the upper class have received from nature for nothing, plebeians acquire at the cost of their youth." *Part of Our Time*, 128.

9. Andrew Bergman, *We're in the Money* (1971; New York: Harper & Row, 1972), 94.

10. The most fully conceived film version of such a utopia is King Vidor's portrayal of a Soviet-style agricultural commune in *Our Daily Bread* (1934). But there are also fantasy versions of such a dream in works like *Lost Horizon* and *You Can't Take It with You*, both directed by Frank Capra. See also the technological utopia of H. G. Wells's *Things to Come* (1936).

11. Edward Anderson, *Hungry Men* (1935; New York: Penguin, 1985), 122, 123. Hereafter cited in text.

12. Kromer, whose own novel *Waiting for Nothing*, published by Knopf the same year, was beyond grim, insisted that Anderson had not shown how bad it could get to be down and out in Depression America. "You'll see no Jesus Christ looks in the eyes of Edward Anderson's *Hungry Men*, no working stiffs dying of malnutrition on lice-infested blankets of three-decker bunks in the missions, no soup-lines that stretch for blocks in the city streets and never start moving. In a word, you find no Hungry Men." See Kromer, "A Very Sad Blurb," in *Waiting for Nothing and Other Writings*, ed. Arthur D. Casciato and James L. W. West III (Athens: University of Georgia Press,

1986), 237. On Anderson and Kromer, see Woody Haut's Weblog: http://woody haut.blogspot.com/2007/01/edward-anderson-from-hungry-men-to.html.

13. William E. Leuchtenburg, *Franklin D. Roosevelt and the New Deal, 1932–1940* (New York: Harper & Row, 1963), 142.

14. Lincoln Kirstein, "James Cagney and the American Hero," in *American Film Criticism: From the Beginnings to* Citizen Kane, ed. Stanley Kauffmann, with Bruce Henstell (New York: Liveright, 1972), 264.

15. *Steinbeck: A Life in Letters,* ed. Elaine Steinbeck and Robert Wallsten (1975; New York: Penguin, 1976), 92–93. Hereafter cited in text.

16. Jackson J. Benson, *The True Adventures of John Steinbeck, Writer* (New York: Viking, 1984). Hereafter cited in text.

17. John Steinbeck, *In Dubious Battle* (1936; New York: Penguin, 1979), 130, 131.

18. Frederick Lewis Allen, *Since Yesterday: The 1930s in America, September 3, 1929–September 3, 1939* (1940; New York: Harper & Row, 1972), 161.

19. *American Film Criticism,* ed. Kauffmann, 207.

20. Alfred Kazin, *On Native Grounds: An Interpretation of Modern American Prose Literature* (1942; Garden City, N.Y.: Doubleday Anchor, 1956), 305. In a 1986 conversation, Kazin vigorously retracted this charge as youthful harshness, praising instead the sheer "physicality" of Steinbeck's writing. Yet as we see from Busby Berkeley—and from numberless pornographers—physicality and dehumanization aren't inconsistent effects. In its search for quintessential features of American culture, *On Native Grounds* was itself a typical offshoot of the 1930s.

21. These works have been scrutinized closely by Nicolaus Mills in his suggestive book *The Crowd in American Literature* (Baton Rouge: Louisiana University Press, 1986). Gide's comments can be found in *The Journals of André Gide,* trans. Justin O'Brien (New York: Alfred A. Knopf, 1951), 4:48. Hereafter cited in text.

22. Richard Astro, *John Steinbeck and Edward F. Ricketts* (Minneapolis: University of Minnesota Press, 1973), 120–21.

23. Carey McWilliams, *Factories in the Field: The Story of Migratory Farm Labor in California* (1939; Berkeley: University of California Press, 2000).

24. Vivian Gornick, *The Romance of American Communism* (New York: Basic Books, 1977), 100.

4. THE COUNTRY AND THE CITY

1. William E. Leuchtenburg, *The Perils of Prosperity, 1914–1932* (Chicago: University of Chicago Press, 1958), 101.

2. Arthur M. Schlesinger Jr., *The Coming of the New Deal* (Boston: Houghton Mifflin, 1958), 27.

3. William E. Leuchtenburg, *Franklin D. Roosevelt and the New Deal, 1932–1940* (New York: Harper & Row, 1963), 136–42.

4. See the indispensable study by William Stott, *Documentary Expression and Thirties America* (New York: Oxford University Press, 1973).

5. H. L. Mencken wrote some famously entertaining diatribes on the cultural backwardness, the philistinism of the South, insisting that "it is impossible for intelligence to flourish in such an atmosphere. Free inquiry is blocked by the idiotic

certainties of ignorant men." This was years before the 1925 Scopes trial brought national attention to the South's religious fundamentalism. Of the older culture of the South, Mencken said, "what remains . . . is simply a certain charming civility in private intercourse." See "The Sahara of the Bozart," in Mencken, *Prejudices: Second Series* (New York: Alfred A. Knopf, 1920), 136–54.

6. See Cowley, "A Farewell to the 1930's," in *Think Back on Us*, ed. Henry Dan Piper (Carbondale: Southern Illinois University Press, 1967), 349. This article first appeared in *The New Republic* on November 8, 1939.

7. In *The Caldwell Caravan* (New York: World Publishing, 1946), a selection of his novels and stories, Caldwell typically disclaimed any social significance: "The present writer has no delusions concerning his work. I can only say that the pieces on the following pages are readable, honest, and the result of hard work. I do not consider them to be examples of artistry, or of earth-shaking importance; they are not indicative of a trend in fiction; they were not written to make propaganda. The one and only thing they do is tell stories; if they do anything else, something is wrong somewhere." Of course this was written when "social significance" was far less fashionable than it had been in the preceding decade.

8. Erskine Caldwell, *Tobacco Road* (New York: Scribner's, 1932), 119. Hereafter cited in text.

9. Erskine Caldwell and Margaret Bourke-White, *You Have Seen Their Faces* (New York: Modern Age Books, 1937), 48. Hereafter cited in text.

10. Of course, Evans has more than one style. In 1938, two years after the sharecropper pictures, he took a famous series of candid shots with a concealed camera on the New York subways. Curiously, even here he makes little intrusion into the private space of his subjects, for the faces we see are almost expressionless: these are eerie yet revealing portraits of calm vacancy, with life's concerns bracketed and suspended.

11. Lionel Trilling, "An American Classic," in *Speaking of Literature and Society*, ed. Diana Trilling (New York: Harcourt Brace Jovanovich, 1980), 376. First published as "Greatness with One Fault in It," *Kenyon Review* (Winter 1942): 99–102.

12. James Agee and Walker Evans, *Let Us Now Praise Famous Men: Three Tenant Families* (1941, 1960; New York: Ballantine, 1966), 11. Hereafter cited in text.

13. See Stott, *Documentary Expression and Thirties America*, 273. This remains one of the best accounts of both Evans and Agee, with separate discussions of each of their contributions to the sharecropper book. Stott's comments on Evans are extremely perceptive, especially his analysis of some significant differences between the 1941 edition, which had thirty-one photographs, and the 1960 edition, which had twice as many. He makes much of Evans's choices and revealingly discusses several related pictures not included in either edition.

14. John Szarkowski, *Walker Evans* (New York: Museum of Modern Art, 1971), 17.

15. Trilling, "An American Classic," 376.

16. Vicki Goldberg, *Margaret Bourke-White* (New York: Harper & Row, 1986), 189.

17. Ibid., 88, 111. Describing some of these striking abstractions, Goldberg concludes that "in this respect as in some others, photography outpaced American painting in the thirties."

18. Trilling, "An American Classic," 378.

19. Sylvia Jenkins Cook, *Tobacco Road to Route 66: The Southern Poor White in Fiction* (Chapel Hill: University of North Carolina Press, 1976), 81.

20. Quoted in Jay Martin, *Nathanael West: The Art of His Life* (New York: Farrar, Straus and Giroux, 1970), 257. Hereafter cited in text.

21. See Alan M. Wald, *The New York Intellectuals: The Rise and Decline of the Anti-Stalinist Left from the 1930s to the 1980s* (Chapel Hill: University of North Carolina Press, 1987), 132.

22. W. H. Auden, "West's Disease" (1957), in *Nathanael West: A Collection of Critical Essays*, ed. Jay Martin (Englewood Cliffs, N.J.: Prentice-Hall, 1971), 149.

23. Nathanael West, *Miss Lonelyhearts & The Day of the Locust* (New York: New Directions, 1962), 32. Hereafter cited in text.

24. Clement Greenberg, "Avant-Garde and Kitsch" (1939), in *Art and Culture: Critical Essays* (Boston: Beacon Press, 1961), 10.

25. West, "Some Notes on Miss L.," in Martin, ed., *Nathanael West: A Collection of Critical Essays*, 66.

26. *Steinbeck: A Life in Letters*, ed. Elaine Steinbeck and Robert Wallsten (1975; New York: Penguin, 1976), 159. Hereafter cited in text.

27. I quote from the pamphlet printed in April 1938, a month before Steinbeck began the final version of *The Grapes of Wrath*, John Steinbeck, *"Their Blood Is Strong"* (San Francisco: Simon J. Lubin Society of California, 1938), 3. Hereafter cited in text.

28. John Steinbeck, *The Grapes of Wrath* (1939; New York: Viking, 1958), 477. Hereafter cited in text.

29. Cowley, "A Farewell to the 1930's" (1939), in *Think Back on Us*, 350. Cowley also points out the influence of Dos Passos, "the drawling conversation of *Tobacco Road*," and Pare Lorentz's films, as well as proletarian writing. "A whole literature is summarized in this book," he writes, "and much of it is carried to a new level of excellence."

30. The renewal of immigration in the 1960s and the migrations from the industrial cities of the Northeast to the Sun Belt have given new life to this westering motif. In his witty academic novel *Stepping Westward* (1965), Malcolm Bradbury associates an Englishman's westward journey with the quest for freedom. Yet the mildly liberated American world of the early 1960s is mercilessly satirized as a scene of rootless anarchy and absurdity, and the protagonist returns at the end to the cozy, predictable constraints of home and family in the red-brick provinces of Little England.

31. Quoted in Jackson J. Benson, *The True Adventures of John Steinbeck, Writer* (New York: Viking, 1984), 376.

32. George Bluestone, *Novels into Film* (1957; Berkeley: University of California Press, 1968), 161.

33. Ibid., 166.

34. After the trouble he had in publishing *Flags in the Dust*, the manuscript that became *Sartoris*, Faulkner decided to please himself with *The Sound and the Fury*, even at the cost of never publishing again. He first achieved considerable popularity— and notoriety—with the lurid *Sanctuary* in 1931, a book he rewrote in galleys, at great expense, "trying to make out of it something which would not shame *The Sound and the Fury* and *As I Lay Dying* too much." Even as the book caused scandal and debate about the new "sadism" in American letters, Faulkner remained the prototype of the difficult, idiosyncratic "artist" conscientiously going his own

way—definitely *not* the model preferred by left-leaning critics and middlebrow reviewers in the 1930s.

35. Quoted in Joseph Blotner, *Faulkner: A Biography*, vol. 1 (New York: Random House, 1974), 634.

36. Edmund Wilson, *Classics and Commercials* (New York: Farrar, Straus, 1950), 42.

37. William Faulkner, *As I Lay Dying* (1930; New York: Vintage, 1964), 121. Hereafter cited in text.

38. Flannery O'Connor, "Some Aspects of the Grotesque in Southern Fiction" (1960), in Flannery O'Connor, *Collected Works*, ed. Sally Fitzgerald (New York: Library of America, 1988), 818.

39. "In Faulkner's work there is never any progression, never anything which comes from the future," Sartre writes. By contrast with the flickering, often formless present, "the past takes on a sort of super-reality; its contours are hard and clear, unchangeable. The present, nameless and fleeting, is helpless before it. It is full of gaps, and, through these gaps, things of the past, fixed, motionless and silent as judges or glances, come to invade it." Many modern writers have distorted time, Sartre says, but "Proust and Faulkner have simply decapitated it. They have deprived it of its future, that is, its dimension of deeds and freedom." Sartre, "On *The Sound and the Fury*: Time in the Work of Faulkner" (1939), in *Literary and Philosophical Essays*, trans. Annette Michelson (1955; New York: Collier Books, 1962), 86, 97, 90.

5. HARD TIMES FOR POETS

1. Cary Nelson, *Repression and Recovery: Modern American Poetry and the Politics of Cultural Memory, 1910–1945* (Madison: University of Wisconsin Press, 1989), 51, 69.

2. Langston Hughes, "A New Song," in *The Collected Poems of Langston Hughes*, ed. Arnold Rampersad, with David Roessel (New York: Alfred A. Knopf, 1994), 170. Hereafter cited in text.

3. Robert Frost, "Build Soil—A Political Pastoral," delivered at Columbia University during the presidential election campaign of 1932 and collected in *A Further Range* (1936). See Robert Frost, *Collected Poems, Prose, and Plays*, ed. Richard Poirier and Mark Richardson (New York: Library of America, 1995). Hereafter cited in text.

4. Quoted in Louis L. Martz, *The Poem of the Mind* (New York: Oxford University Press, 1969), 145.

5. *The Collected Poems of William Carlos Williams*, vol. 1, *1909–1939*, ed. A. Walton Litz and Christopher MacGowan (New York: New Directions, 1986), 203. As he writes later, "Poetry has to do with the crystallization of the imagination—the perfection of new forms as additions to nature" (226). Hereafter cited in text.

6. Williams describes the sources of his two extraordinary collections of stories *The Knife of the Times* (1932) and *Life along the Passaic River* (1938) in *I Wanted to Write a Poem* (1958; New York: New Directions, 1978), 49–51, 63. Langston Hughes turned impressively to short fiction during the same period in *The Ways of White Folk* (1934). Michael Denning notes the influence of both Williams and Hughes on proletarian writing in *The Cultural Front: The Laboring of American Culture in the Twentieth Century* (London and New York: Verso, 1997), 212–14, 217–19.

7. These stories have appeared in a number of collections, among them *The Doctor Stories*, comp. Robert Coles (New York: New Direction, 1984), which also includes a handful of poems, a key excerpt from Williams's 1951 autobiography, and a memoir by one of Williams's sons, himself a doctor.

8. Williams, "The Girl with a Pimply Face," in *The Doctor Stories*, 44. Compare Williams's description, from the autobiographical excerpt, of our own "lying habits of speech and thought" (122–23).

9. The poet Louis Simpson describes Williams's way of "starting from a point outside or above the material, then being dragged down into it." In *Paterson*, "he immerses himself in the 'filthy' river and is reborn." Simpson, *Three on the Tower: The Lives and Works of Ezra Pound, T. S. Eliot, and William Carlos Williams* (New York: Macmillan, 1975), 288.

10. Frost, October 27, 1917, in *The Letters of Robert Frost to Louis Untermeyer* (New York: Holt, Rinehart and Winston, 1963), 59. Hereafter cited in text. In the same letter he adds, "The conviction closes in on me that I was cast for gloom as the sparks fly upward."

11. This may have been because he really believed in the war. Pritchard's commentary emphasizes something quite different, Frost's sister's sexual recoil from "the coarseness and brutality of the world," including his own. William H. Pritchard, *Frost: A Literary Life Reconsidered* (New York: Oxford University Press, 1984), 135–36.

12. Frost to B. F. Skinner, April 7, 1926, in *Selected Letters of Robert Frost*, ed. Lawrance Thompson (New York: Holt, Rinehart and Winston, 1964), 327. See also Pritchard, *Frost*, 171–72. Earlier he had written to Louis Untermeyer, "What I love best in man is definiteness of position. I don't care what position so long as it is definite enough. I mean I don't half care. . . . My God how I adore some people who stand right out in history with distinct meaning" (U58).

13. See "Poverty and Poetry," a lecture and reading Frost gave at Haverford College in 1937 in the wake of the controversy over *A Further Range*. The original 1914 dedication of *North of Boston* described it as a "Book of People," and Frost uses both this and his more recent poems to claim the proletarian mantle for his own. *Collected Poems, Prose, and Plays*, 759–67.

14. See his introduction to Edwin Arlington Robinson's *King Jasper* (1935), one of his sharpest rejoinders to the New Deal and the literary Left. "Grievances are a form of impatience. Griefs are a form of patience. . . . The day of perfection waits on unanimous social action. Two or three more good national elections should do the business." *Collected Poems, Prose, and Plays*, 742–43.

15. See Pritchard's comments on this letter in *Frost*, 182–83.

16. Wallace Stevens, "Esthétique du Mal," in *Collected Poetry and Prose*, ed. Frank Kermode and Joan Richardson (New York: Library of America, 1997), 286. Hereafter cited in text.

17. Burnshaw's review is reprinted with his own valuable commentary in *A Stanley Burnshaw Reader* (Athens: University of Georgia Press, 1990), 22–32.

18. Alan Filreis, *Modernism from Right to Left: Wallace Stevens, the Thirties, and Literary Radicalism* (New York: Cambridge University Press, 1994).

19. Quoted by Denis Donoghue, *Reading America: Essays on American Literature* (New York: Alfred A. Knopf, 1987), 223.

20. Joan Richardson, *Wallace Stevens: The Later Years, 1923–1955* (New York: William Morrow, 1988), 121. Richardson sees in the poems of the period "how deeply involved the poet seems to have become with things outside himself" as he "began to be preoccupied with 'anonymity' and the 'common man' " (117–18).

21. Wallace Stevens, "Williams," in *Opus Posthumous*, ed. Milton J. Bates (New York: Alfred A. Knopf, 1989), 213–14.

22. *Letters of Wallace Stevens*, ed. Holly Stevens (1966; Berkeley: University of California Press, 1996), 286.

6. BLACK GIRLS AND NATIVE SONS

1. Zora Neale Hurston, *Dust Tracks on a Road* (1942), in Hurston, *Forklore, Memoirs, and Other Writings*, ed. Cheryl A. Wall (New York: Library of America, 1995), 635. Unless otherwise indicated, Hurston's work is cited in the text from this edition or from the companion volume, Hurston, *Novels and Stories*.

2. William E. Leuchtenburg, *Franklin D. Roosevelt and the New Deal, 1932–1940* (New York: Harper & Row, 1963), 187.

3. Richard Wright, "Blueprint for Negro Writing," in David Levering Lewis, ed., *The Portable Harlem Renaissance Reader* (New York: Viking, 1994), 198–99.

4. Richard Wright, *Uncle Tom's Children* (New York: Harper Perennial, 1993), 64. This reprints the expanded edition of 1940, adding a fifth story and an autobiographical preface that was a sketch for his 1945 memoir *Black Boy*.

5. Richard Wright, "How 'Bigger' Was Born," a lecture given at Columbia University in 1940 and subsequently published as a pamphlet. Here quoted from Richard Wright, *Early Works*, ed. Arnold Rampersad (New York: Library of America, 1991), 874.

6. Richard Wright, *12 Million Black Voices: A Folk History of the Negro in the United States*, with photographs selected by Edwin Rosskam (New York: Viking, 1941), 50–55.

7. Richard Wright, *Native Son*, in *Early Works*, ed. Rampersad, 452. Hereafter cited in text.

8. Richard Wright, *Black Boy: A Record of Childhood and Youth* (New York: Harper, 1945), 222.

9. Richard Wright, *Black Boy (American Hunger)*, in Wright, *Later Works*, ed. Arnold Rampersad (New York: Library of America, 1991), 254.

10. James Baldwin, *Collected Essays*, ed. Toni Morrison (New York: Library of America, 1998), 27.

11. Ibid., 581.

12. Hazel Rowley, *Richard Wright: The Life and Times* (New York: Henry Holt, 2001), 138.

13. In his portrait of her in his roman à clef, *Infants of the Spring*, Wallace Thurman says "she was a great favorite among those whites who went in for Negro prodigies." He describes the character based on her as "a master of Southern dialect, and an able raconteur, but she was too indifferent to literary creation to transfer to paper that which she told so well." Quoted by Robert E. Hemenway, *Zora Neale Hurston: A Literary Biography* (Urbana: University of Illinois Press, 1977), 64.

14. Zora Neale Hurston, "Stories of Conflict," in Hurston, *Folklore, Memoirs, and Other Writings*, 912–13. First appeared in the *Saturday Review*, April 2, 1938.

15. Baldwin, *Collected Essays*, 27.

16. Zora Neale Hurston. "How It Feels to Be Colored Me," in *Folklore, Memoirs, and Other Writings*, 826–29. First appeared in *The World Tomorrow*, May 1928.

17. Zora Neale Hurston, Introduction to *Mules and Men*, in *Folklore, Memoirs, and Other Writings*, 10.

18. Richard Wright, "Between Laughter and Tears," in *Critical Essays on Zora Neale Hurston*, ed. Gloria L. Cronin (New York: G. K. Hall, 1998), 76.

19. Richard Wright, "Blueprint for Negro Writing," in Lewis, ed., *The Portable Harlem Renaissance Reader*, 194–95.

20. Zora Neale Hurston, *Their Eyes Were Watching God* (Urbana: University of Illinois Press, 1978), 24. Hereafter cited in text.

7. BEYOND THE AMERICAN DREAM

1. Caroline Bird, *The Invisible Scar* (1966; New York: Longman, 1978), 37.

2. Robert S. Lynd and Helen Merrell Lynd, *Middletown in Transition: A Study in Cultural Conflicts* (New York: Harcourt, Brace, 1937), 472. Hereafter cited in text.

3. T. H. Watkins, *The Great Depression: America in the 1930s* (Boston: Little, Brown, 1993), 13.

4. Bird, *The Invisible Scar*, 277, 274.

5. For a good summary of such assumptions, see Frederick Lewis Allen, *Since Yesterday* (1940; New York: Harper & Row, 1972), 125.

6. Benjamin Franklin, *Autobiography and Other Writings*, ed. Russel B. Nye (Boston: Houghton Mifflin/Riverside, 1958), 167.

7. John G. Cawelti, *Apostles of the Self-made Man: Changing Concepts of Success in America* (Chicago: University of Chicago Press, 1965), 120–22.

8. Quoted in Richard M. Huber, *The American Idea of Success* (New York: McGraw-Hill, 1971), 440.

9. Ibid., 34, 35.

10. See Irvin G. Wyllie, *The Self-made Man in America: The Myth of Rags to Riches* (New Brunswick, N.J.: Rutgers University Press, 1954), 55–74.

11. Quoted in Huber, *The American Idea of Success*, 97, 95.

12. Wilbur F. Crafts, *Successful Men of To-day and What They Say of Success* (1883; New York: Arno Press, 1973), 38. Like many of his contemporaries, Crafts gave a strong religious spin to the idea of success, arguing that religion paid off in worldly advancement and that success itself was a spiritual imperative. "Yes, *it pays, it pays* to serve God." On the other hand, "most of the suffering poor are the victims of vice." See Huber, *The American Idea of Success*, 62–64.

13. Quoted in Huber, *The American Idea of Success*, 59.

14. Roland Marchand, *Advertising the American Dream: Making Way for Modernity, 1920–1940* (Berkeley: University of California Press, 1985), 301.

15. Leuchtenburg, *Franklin D. Roosevelt and the New Deal*, 39.

16. In Studs Terkel, *Hard Times: An Oral History of the Great Depression* (1970; New York: Avon, 1971), 289.

17. Elisha Friedman, "Business Psychosis," *New York Times*, May 15, 1932, cited by Leuchtenburg, *Franklin D. Roosevelt and the New Deal*, 29.

18. Terkel, *Hard Times*, 102, 121.

19. Susan Ware, *Holding Their Own: American Women in the 1930s* (Boston: G. K. Hall, 1982), 8.

20. Quoted in Robert S. McElvaine, *The Great Depression: America, 1929–1941* (New York: Times Books, 1984), 180. See *One Third of a Nation: Lorena Hickok Reports on the Great Depression*, ed. Richard Lowitt and Maurine Beasley (Urbana: University of Illinois Press, 1981), 325.

21. McElvaine, *The Great Depression*, 180–81. This is part of a chapter called "'Fear Itself': Depression Life," a fine essay in the tradition of Frederick Lewis Allen and other social historians of everyday life. See "Poverty, Shame and Self-Reliance," my review of McElvaine's book, *New York Times Book Review*, January 22, 1984, 9–10, as well as McElvaine's valuable selection from these unpublished letters, *Down and Out in the Great Depression: Letters from the "Forgotten Man"* (Chapel Hill: University of North Carolina Press, 1983), with a good introduction. See also the letters and commentary in Lawrence W. Levine and Cornelia R. Levine, *The People and the President: America's Conversation with FDR* (Boston: Beacon Press, 2002).

22. McElvaine, *The Great Depression*, 176–77.

23. Quoted by Milton Meltzer, *Brother, Can You Spare a Dime?: The Great Depression, 1929–1933* (1969; New York: New American Library, 1977), 102.

24. McElvaine, *The Great Depression*, 185, 183, citing Alice Kessler-Harris, *Out of Work: A History of Wage-Earning Women in the United States* (New York: Oxford University Press, 1982).

25. Tillie Olsen, *Yonnondio: From the Thirties* (1974; New York: Dell/Laurel, 1975), 70.

26. Andrew Bergman, *We're in the Money: Depression America and Its Films* (1971; New York: Harper & Row, 1972), 6–7.

27. Carlos Clarens, *Crime Movies: From Griffith to the Godfather and Beyond* (New York: W. W. Norton, 1980), 86.

28. Robert Warshow, "The Gangster as Tragic Hero," in *The Immediate Experience* (Garden City, N.Y.: Doubleday, 1962), 132–33, 129.

29. Bergman, *We're In the Money*, 13.

30. For a good early study of the influence of radio on the American public, with special emphasis on its power of "extending the social environment," see Hadley Cantril and Gordon Allport, *The Psychology of Radio* (New York: Harper & Brothers, 1935).

31. The great French film critic André Bazin once remarked that Hollywood had usually been most serious in its comedies. As Richard H. Pells insists, "the 'serious' melodramas of the 1930s often turned out to be less insightful than the comedies; the cinema of social protest was frequently more unrealistic than the 'escapist' films of crime or horror or romance." Pells, *Radical Visions and American Dreams: Culture and Social Thought in the Depression Years* (New York: Harper & Row, 1973), 287.

32. For some excellent corporate history illuminating the emergence of the style of individual studios, including Warner Brothers, see Thomas Schatz, *The Genius of the System: Hollywood Filmmaking in the Studio Era* (New York: Pantheon, 1989). See

also Peter Roffman and Jim Purdy, *The Hollywood Social Problem Film: Madness, Despair, and Politics from the Depression to the Fifties* (Bloomington: Indiana University Press, 1981).

33. Tony Thomas and Jim Terry, with Busby Berkeley, *The Busby Berkeley Book* (Greenwich, Conn.: New York Graphic Society, 1973), 28, 58–59. It's hard to tell what role Berkeley played in putting together this useful catalogue raisonné of his work.

34. Clarens, *Crime Movies*, 168.

35. Jack Shadoian, *Dreams and Dead Ends: The American Gangster/Crime Film* (Cambridge: MIT Press, 1977), 82.

36. Abraham Cahan, *The Rise of David Levinsky* (1917; New York: Harper & Row, 1966), 530.

37. *New York Times* obituary, December 23, 1940, 19, reprinted by Matthew J. Bruccoli, *Some Sort of Epic Grandeur: The Life of F. Scott Fitzgerald* (New York: Harcourt Brace Jovanovich, 1981), 4–6.

38. See, for example, James R. Mellow's *Invented Lives: F. Scott and Zelda Fitzgerald* (Boston: Houghton Mifflin, 1984), where Fitzgerald's life in the thirties half his writing life—is sketched in little more than the last hundred pages.

39. Quoted in Bruccoli, *Some Sort of Epic Grandeur*, 307.

40. F. Scott Fitzgerald, "Early Success," in *The Crack-Up*, ed. Edmund Wilson (New York: New Directions, 1945), 87.

41. F. Scott Fitzgerald, "Absolution," in *Babylon Revisited and Other Stories* (New York: Scribner's, 1960), 142, 144. "The Rich Boy" and "Babylon Revisited" also cited in text from this volume.

42. *The Fitzgerald Reader*, ed. Arthur Mizener (New York: Scribner's, 1963), 405.

43. F. Scott Fitzgerald, "Winter Dreams," in ibid., 58. "'The Sensible Thing'" also cited in text from this volume.

44. On Ginevra King, and on Fitzgerald's pursuit of the impossible woman in life as well as fiction, see, for example, Scott Donaldson's fine *Fool for Love: F. Scott Fitzgerald* (New York: Congdon & Weed, 1983), especially the chapters "'I Love you, Miss X'" and "The Glittering Things."

45. Fitzgerald, *The Great Gatsby* (1925; Harmondsworth: Penguin, 1950), 105. Hereafter cited in text.

46. Edith Wharton, *The Age of Innocence* (1920; New York: Signet, 1964), 97, 195, 183.

47. The word "single" occupies no fewer than seven columns of the *OED*, which reminds us that "single life" was once commonly used to mean the celibate life. The shadow of this meaning survives in Fitzgerald's phrase; without quite intending to do so, Anson completely walls himself in.

48. Fitzgerald, "Echoes of the Jazz Age," in *The Fitzgerald Reader*, ed. Mizener, 329.

49. Quoted by Bruccoli, *Some Sort of Epic Grandeur*, 367.

50. In 1933, for example, when the Fitzgeralds were living in Baltimore, there were regular joint sessions at Zelda's clinic, and Fitzgerald took to writing long letters to her doctor. As James R. Mellow describes it, "he and Zelda . . . were involved in a contest of proving their credibility to the doctors." Following Nancy Milford's corrective biography *Zelda*, Mellow gives us a fascinating stenographer's account of one of their joint sessions. It suggests that Fitzgerald behaved abominably, dismissing her attempts to write and dance, and claiming as usual that "she

was poaching on his material." See Mellow, *Invented Lives*, 408–12. Also Milford, *Zelda* (1970; New York: Avon, 1971), 323–31.

51. *The Fitzgerald Reader*, ed. Mizener, 420.

52. Quoted by Richard D. Lehan in *Tender Is the Night: Essays in Criticism*, ed. Marvin J. LaHood (Bloomington: Indiana University Press, 1969), 70.

53. Alfred Kazin, *Starting Out in the Thirties* (Boston: Atlantic Monthly Press, 1965), 12.

54. Wharton's letter, which highlights both the link and the gap between the realist and modernist generations, is reprinted by Edmund Wilson in *The Crack-Up*, 309.

55. This story first appeared in the *Saturday Evening Post* on October 11, 1930, a few months after the death of D. H. Lawrence, who had made something of a specialty of stories built on short, swift takes on the emotional life of a couple. (See, for example, his late story "Things.") The woman in Fitzgerald's story is called Nicole, and Arthur Mizener suggests that Fitzgerald never reprinted it because it's "almost a precis of the novel." It's also an example of the double take, for it ends oddly with a doppelgänger twist: the couple, having lost both love and health, see another pair they recognize, horribly, as an image of themselves. The story was first reprinted by Mizener in *Afternoon of an Author* (1957; New York: Scribner's, 1958).

56. Mellow, *Invented Lives*, 410, 422.

57. Jeffrey Berman, *The Talking Cure: Literary Representations of Psychoanalysis* (New York: New York University Press, 1985), 60–86.

58. F. Scott Fitzgerald, *Tender Is the Night: A Romance* (1934; rev ed., Harmondsworth: Penguin, 1955), 57. Hereafter cited in text. This is the restructured version of the novel, edited by Malcolm Cowley along lines Fitzgerald suggested.

59. Edward Anderson, *Hungry Men* (1935; New York: Penguin, 1985), 157, 52.

60. *The Fitzgerald Reader*, ed. Mizener, 418–19.

61. Quoted by Bruccoli, *Some Sort of Epic Grandeur*, 312.

62. See Donaldson, *Fool For Love*, 99.

63. James T. Farrell, "How *Studs Lonigan* Was Written," in *The League of Frightened Philistines and Other Papers* (New York: Vanguard Press, 1945), 82–83.

64. James T. Farrell, *Studs Lonigan* (New York: Signet, 1958), 431.

65. Farrell, *The Short Stories of James T. Farrell* (New York: Vanguard Press, 1937), 354.

66. Lionel Trilling, "Studs Lonigan's World," *Nation* 141 (Oct. 23, 1935): 485.

67. Norman Podhoretz, *Making It* (New York: Random House, 1967), xi, xvii. He also "discovers" that "it was better to be rich than to be poor," that power "was desirable," that "it was better to give orders than to take them," and so on.

68. Pare Lorentz, "A Young Man Goes to Work," *Scribner's Magazine* 89 (1931): 205–8.

69. Gary Scharnhorst, with Jack Bales, *The Lost Life of Horatio Alger, Jr.* (Bloomington: Indiana University Press, 1985), 152–53.

70. Nathanael West, with Boris Ingster, "A Cool Million: A Screen Story," in *Novels and Other Writings*, ed. Sacvan Bercovitch (New York: Library of America, 1997), 745.

71. S. J. Perelman, "Nathanael West: A Portrait," reprinted in Jay Martin, ed., *Nathanael West: A Collection of Critical Essays* (Englewood Cliffs, N.J.: Prentice-Hall, 1971), 11–12.

72. Scharnhorst and Bales, *The Lost Life of Horatio Alger, Jr.*, 162.

73. Lionel Trilling, "The Princess Casamassima," in *The Liberal Imagination: Essays on Literature and Society* (New York: Viking, 1950), 64.

74. Ralph D. Gardner, foreword to Horatio Alger Jr., *Silas Snobden's Office Boy* (Garden City, N.Y.: Doubleday, 1973), 9.

75. Nathanael West, *A Cool Million* (1934), in *Miss Lonelyhearts and A Cool Million* (Harmondsworth: Penguin, 1961), 85. Hereafter cited in text.

76. See Edward Pessen, *The Log Cabin Myth: The Social Background of Presidents* (New Haven: Yale University Press, 1984). The Alger myth resurfaced in the obsequies for Richard Nixon in 1994, as it had in his own memoirs. They evoked his humble origins, and there were glowing tributes to his never-say-die determination, though Nixon was no doubt a morally problematic example of the self-made man. For a good discussion of West's burlesque of success myths and a rare appreciation of this neglected novel, see Charles R. Hearn, *The American Dream in the Great Depression* (Westport, Conn.: Greenwood Press, 1977), 166–73. See also Jonathan Veitch, *American Superrealism: Nathanael West and the Politics of Representation in the 1930s* (Madison: University of Wisconsin Press, 1997), 88–112. This is one of the few books that sets West effectively in a Depression context.

77. Harold Clurman, *The Fervent Years: The Story of the Group Theatre and the Thirties* (1945; New York: Harcourt Brace Jovanovich, 1975), 147–48. Hereafter cited in text.

78. Done everywhere throughout the 1930s, sometimes with scenes dropped and the text changed, *Waiting for Lefty* has a complex production history, which Garrett Eisler has reconstructed in an unpublished essay.

79. Clifford Odets, *Six Plays of Clifford Odets* (New York: Random House, 1939), 22. Hereafter cited in text.

80. Margaret Brenman-Gibson, *Clifford Odets, American Playwright: The Years from 1906 to 1940* (New York: Atheneum, 1981), 321. For one revealing episode, in which Clurman throws an epileptic fit in response to an Odets revision, see p. 482. See also the striking exchange of letters reprinted on pp. 553–59.

81. Quoted ibid., 649.

82. Kazin, *Starting Out in the Thirties*, 80–82.

83. John Howard Lawson, *Success Story: A Play* (New York: Farrar & Rinehart, 1932), 111. Hereafter cited in text.

84. See Brenman-Gibson, *Clifford Odets*, 477, 485.

85. Ibid., 10, 13.

86. Gerald Weales, *Clifford Odets: Playwright* (New York: Pegasus, 1971), 163.

87. Quoted by Brenman-Gibson, *Clifford Odets*, 552, 3.

8. WHAT PRICE HOLLYWOOD?

1. Josephine Herbst, "Moralist's Progress," *Kenyon Review* 27 (Autumn 1965): 772.

2. Arthur M. Schlesinger Jr., *A Life in the Twentieth Century: Innocent Beginnings, 1917–1950* (Boston: Houghton Mifflin, 2000), 142.

3. Budd Schulberg, *What Makes Sammy Run?* (1941; New York: Bantam, 1961), 213.

4. Christopher Ames, *Movies about the Movies: Hollywood Reflected* (Lexington: University Press of Kentucky, 1997), 22.

5. Kevin Starr, *Inventing the Dream: California through the Progressive Era* (New York: Oxford University Press, 1985), 336, 335.

6. David Thomson, *Showman: The Life of David O. Selznick* (New York: Alfred A. Knopf, 1992), 134.

7. Elizabeth Kendall, *The Runaway Bride: Hollywood Romantic Comedy of the 1930's* (New York: Alfred A. Knopf, 1990), 162. Includes a superb chapter on *Stage Door*.

8. James Harvey, *Romantic Comedy in Hollywood, from Lubitsch to Sturges* (New York: Alfred A. Knopf, 1987), 178.

9. Matthew J. Bruccoli, *"The Last of the Novelists": F. Scott Fitzgerald and* The Last Tycoon (Carbondale: Southern Illinois University Press, 1977), 135. Contains a good selection of Fitzgerald's working notes, cited in the text from this volume.

10. F. Scott Fitzgerald, *The Last Tycoon: An Unfinished Novel*, ed. Edmund Wilson (New York: Charles Scribner's, 1941), 35. Hereafter cited in text.

11. Scott Donaldson, *Fool for Love: F. Scott Fitzgerald* (New York: Congdon & Weed, 1983), 207–8.

12. Bruccoli, *"The Last of the Novelists,"* 145.

13. Matthew J. Bruccoli, *Some Sort of Epic Grandeur: The Life of F. Scott Fitzgerald* (New York: Harcourt Brace Jovanovich, 1981), 493.

14. Bruccoli, *"The Last of the Novelists,"* 140.

15. Schulberg, *What Makes Sammy Run?*, 194. Hereafter cited in text.

16. Andrew Turnbull, *Scott Fitzgerald* (New York: Scribner's, 1962), 320.

9. THE LAST FILM OF THE 1930s; OR, NOTHING FAILS LIKE SUCCESS

1. Pauline Kael, "Raising Kane," in *The Citizen Kane Book* (1971; New York: Bantam, 1974), 1–124. Robert L. Carringer, *The Making of* Citizen Kane (Berkeley: University of California Press, 1985), 34.

2. F. Scott Fitzgerald, *The Great Gatsby* (Harmondsworth: Penguin, 1950), 186.

3. Terry Comito, ed., *Touch of Evil* (New Brunswick, N.J.: Rutgers University Press, 1985), 204–5.

4. One notable exception was Robert L. Carringer, "*Citizen Kane, The Great Gatsby*, and Some Conventions of American Narrative," *Critical Inquiry* 2 (1975): 307–25.

5. Robert Warshow, *The Immediate Experience: Movies, Comics, Theatre and Other Aspects of Popular Culture* (Garden City, N.Y.: Doubleday, 1962), 132–33.

10. FANTASY, ELEGANCE, MOBILITY: THE DREAM LIFE OF THE 1930s

1. Edward Jablonski, *Gershwin* (New York: Doubleday, 1987), 86–87.

2. See Michael Rogin's study of blackface minstrelsy, Al Jolson, and *The Jazz Singer*, "Blackface, White Noise: The Jewish Jazz Singer Finds His Voice," *Critical Inquiry* 18 (Spring 1992): 417–53, later developed into a book, *Blackface, White Noise: Jewish Immigrants in the Hollywood Melting Pot* (Berkeley: University of California Press, 1996). For a much more sympathetic view of the Jewish fascination with black

identity, including *The Jazz Singer*, see Marshall Berman, *On the Town: One Hundred Years of Spectacle in Times Square* (New York: Random House, 2006). See also Alex Ross, *The Rest Is Noise: Listening to the Twentieth Century* (New York: Farrar, Straus and Giroux, 2007), 122–23, 142–43.

3. Quoted by Rogin, "Blackface, White Noise," 437–38.

4. Quoted by Jablonski, *Gershwin*, 230.

5. Quoted in Howard Pollack, *George Gershwin: His Life and Work* (Berkeley: University of California Press, 2006), 330. Pollack, also the biographer of Copland, notes that "Fascinating Rhythm" became "paradigmatic not only of a certain side of Gershwin's work but of the Jazz Age itself."

6. According to Howard Pollack, "But Not for Me" became a popular standard after Judy Garland sang it in the 1943 MGM film version of *Girl Crazy*, the second of at least three times the musical was filmed. As with the many stage revivals, culminating in the Broadway hit *Crazy for You* in 1992, the book was extensively rewritten to accommodate the times and the performers. See Pollack, *George Gershwin*, 474–78.

7. One side of Porter, says Wilfrid Sheed, is the "sentimental country boy who can tug your heartstrings without any tricks at all." See Sheed's savvy and witty book *The House That George Built* (New York: Random House, 2007), 143.

8. Philip Furia, *The Poets of Tin Pan Alley* (New York: Oxford University Press, 1990), 168.

9. Quoted in Robert Kimball, ed., *The Complete Lyrics of Cole Porter* (1983; New York: Da Capo Press, 1992), 205.

10. Arlene Croce, *The Fred Astaire and Ginger Rogers Book* (New York: Galahad Books, 1972), 33.

11. Ibid., 56.

12. Bob Thomas, *Astaire: The Man, the Dancer* (New York: St. Martin's Press, 1984), 121.

13. James M. Cain, *The Postman Always Rings Twice* (New York: Alfred A. Knopf, 1934), 15. Hereafter cited in text.

11. CLASS FOR THE MASSES: ELEGANCE DEMOCRATIZED

1. Richard Schickel, *Cary Grant: A Celebration* (Boston: Little, Brown, 1983), 63.

2. David Thomson, *The New Biographical Dictionary of Film* (New York: Alfred A. Knopf, 2002), 351.

3. Pauline Kael, "The Man from Dream City," in *When the Lights Go Down* (New York: Holt, Rinehart and Winston, 1980), 9. Kael's brilliant profile first appeared in *The New Yorker*, July 14, 1975. It includes many acute remarks on screwball comedy and its leading performers.

4. Gary Giddins, *Bing Crosby: A Pocketful of Dreams: The Early Years, 1903–1940* (Boston: Little, Brown, 2001), 366.

5. Will Friedwald, *Jazz Singing* (New York: Da Capo Press, 1996), 11.

6. Quoted ibid., 49.

7. With *Pennies from Heaven* Burke became his in-house songwriter and close friend.

Over the next seventeen years he wrote 23 film scores and more than 120 songs for Crosby, including "I've Got a Pocketful of Dreams," based on a phrase he'd heard Crosby say. See Giddins, *Bing Crosby*, 422.

8. Whiteman's stock as a jazz pioneer has been rising recently after he was virtually excluded from jazz history. See Joshua Berrett's dual biography, *Louis Armstrong and Paul Whiteman: Two Kings of Jazz* (New Haven: Yale University Press, 2004).

9. Ted Gioia, *The History of Jazz* (New York: Oxford University Press, 1997), 50.

10. Quoted by Robert G. O'Meally in the booklet accompanying Louis Armstrong, *The Complete Hot Five and Hot Seven Recordings* (Columbia, 2000), 66.

11. O'Meally, "An Appreciation," in *The Complete Hot Five*, 56–67.

12. Rex Stewart, *Jazz Masters of the Thirties* (1972; New York: Da Capo Press, 1980), 99–100.

13. Ted Fox, quoted by Lewis A. Erenberg, *Swingin' the Dream: Big Band Jazz and the Rebirth of American Culture* (Chicago: University of Chicago Press, 1998), 97. As Erenberg writes, "He lived in an elegant apartment in the Sugar Hill district of Harlem, mixed with best of black society, and superbly created elegant music in a stable orchestra" (96).

14. Quoted ibid., 9.

15. Martin Williams, *The Jazz Tradition* (New York: Oxford University Press, 1993), 105, 112.

16. Gary Giddins reminds me that this barrier had already been breached by Ellington in his two-sided "Creole Rhapsody" of 1931, "for which Decca fired him from the label."

17. The parallels between the music scene and the New Deal have recently been developed in convincing detail by social historians knowledgeable about jazz. See especially David W. Stowe, *Swing Changes: Big-Band Jazz in New Deal America* (Cambridge: Harvard University Press, 1994), and Erenberg, *Swingin' the Dream.*

18. Quoted in John Edward Hasse, *Beyond Category: The Life and Genius of Duke Ellington* (New York: Simon & Schuster, 1993), 203.

19. Gioia, *The History of Jazz*, 135. Erenberg *Swingin' the Dream*, 14, gives the figure of 104 million for 1927.

20. Gary Giddins, "The Mirror of Swing," in *Faces in the Crowd* (1992; New York: Da Capo Press, 1996), 120.

21. Quoted by Giddins, *Bing Crosby*, 259.

22. On the contributions of Ray Nance (who replaced Cootie Williams), Strayhorn, and others to Ellington's band in the early 1940s, see Gary Giddins, *Visions of Jazz: The First Century* (New York: Oxford University Press, 1998), 233–57.

23. Quoted by Erenberg, *Swingin' the Dream*, 46.

24. Alastair Duncan, *Art Deco* (London: Thames & Hudson, 1988), 15.

25. Cervin Robinson and Rosemarie Haag Bletter, *Skyscraper Style: Art Deco New York* (New York: Oxford University Press, 1975), 41. I'm indebted to this book and to my friend and colleague Rosemarie Bletter for introducing me to the wealth of Deco architecture in New York.

26. Quoted in Robert Heide and John Gilman, *Popular Art Deco: Depression Era Style and Design* (New York: Abbeville Press, 1991), 157.

27. Quoted by Robinson and Bletter, *Skyscraper Style*, 69.

28. See Heide and Gilman, *Popular Art Deco*, 200–202. The write-up appeared in *Hollywood* magazine, August 1931, under the title "Dolores del Rio Goes Moderne."

29. Howard Mandelbaum and Eric Myers, *Screen Deco* (1985; Santa Monica: Hennessey & Ingalls, 2000), 32. This is essentially a picture book, spectacularly illustrated but also nicely comprehensive. For a more scholarly and searching study of screen decor, focused on New York, see the indispensable work by James Sanders, *Celluloid Skyline: New York and the Movies* (New York: Alfred A. Knopf, 2002). I'm grateful to Phillip Lopate for directing me to this work.

30. For a valuable account of the economics of the swing craze and the reasons for its decline, see Scott DeVeaux, *The Birth of Bebop: A Social and Musical History* (Berkeley: University of California Press, 1997), 116–64.

31. The headline writer made the parallel even more explicit. See Ken Johnson, "The Essence of Wit/And Cool as Jazz," *New York Times*, August 20, 2004, E28.

12. THE POPULIST TURN: COPLAND AND THE POPULAR FRONT

1. First published in 1934 by a publisher that soon went bankrupt, it was reprinted in hardcover by a small publisher in 1960 but did not gain wide attention until a paperback edition by Avon Books in 1964. Reviewed by Irving Howe on the front page of the *New York Times Book Review*, a first for a paperback, it went on to sell a million copies.

2. See F. Scott Fitzgerald, "Echoes of the Jazz Age," in *The Fitzgerald Reader*, ed. Arthur Mizener (New York: Scribner's, 1963), 323–31, and Malcolm Cowley, *Exile's Return: A Literary Odyssey of the 1920s* (1934; New York: Viking, 1956).

3. For a detailed history of the Federal Writers' Project see Jerre Mangione, *The Dream and the Deal: The Federal Writers' Project, 1935–1943* (Boston: Little, Brown, 1972). A general introduction to the New Deal arts projects can be found in Milton Meltzer, *Violins and Shovels: The WPA Arts Projects* (New York: Delacorte, 1976). See also William E. Leuchtenburg, *Franklin D. Roosevelt and the New Deal, 1932–1940* (New York: Harper & Row, 1963), 124–28. Among public works Leuchtenburg records that the WPA built 2,500 hospitals, 5,900 school buildings, 1,000 airport landing fields, and nearly 13,000 playgrounds—in short, the precious public infrastructure for the next half century and beyond. For a broad narrative history of the WPA, not simply the arts programs, see Nick Taylor, *American-Made: The Enduring Legacy of the WPA: When FDR Put the Nation to Work* (New York: Bantam, 2008).

4. On the variety of creative work associated with the Popular Front, see especially Michael Denning, *The Cultural Front: The Laboring of American Culture in the Twentieth Century* (London: Verso, 1997), though Denning, to counteract old stereotypes about realism and documentary, casts his net perhaps *too* widely, turning even *Citizen Kane* into a Popular Front movie. The emphasis on documentary is best formulated in William Stott, *Documentary Expression and Thirties America* (New York: Oxford University Press, 1973). A much more jaundiced view of the Popular Front, reflecting both the early critiques of anti-Stalinist intellectuals and a post-sixties New Left radicalism, is developed by Richard H. Pells, *Radical Visions and American Dreams* (New York: Harper & Row, 1973), 292–329.

5. Alfred Kazin, *On Native Grounds: An Interpretation of Modern American Prose Literature* (1942; Garden City, N.Y.: Doubleday Anchor, 1956), 378.

6. Aaron Copland and Vivian Perlis, *Copland: 1900 through 1942* (New York: St. Martin's/Marek, 1984), 55. Hereafter cited in text as C-P 1.

7. Howard Pollack, *Aaron Copland: The Life and Work of an Uncommon Man* (New York: Henry Holt, 1999), 129. Hereafter cited in text as C-Pol.

8. Paul Rosenfeld, "Aaron Copland," in *Musical Impressions: Selections from Paul Rosenfeld's Criticism*, ed. Herbert A. Leibowitz (New York: Hill and Wang, 1969), 249, 250, 252.

9. Arnold Rampersad, ed., *The Collected Poems of Langston Hughes* (New York: Vintage, 1994), 50. Hereafter cited in text as *CP*.

10. Virgil Thomson, "Aaron Copland," in *A Virgil Thomson Reader* (1981; New York: E. P. Dutton, 1984), 22. Thomson's piece is at once shrewd, competitive, and marginally anti-Semitic, with its undue emphasis on Copland's Jewish origins. "His melodic material is of a markedly Hebrew cast," says Thomson, strangely. "Its tendency to return upon itself is penitential" (20). But the unflappable Copland hardly ever took offense. Moreover, Thomson's essay includes incisive comments such as these: "By coloristic I mean it is made out of harmonic and instrumental rather than melodic devices. This compilation is picturesque and cumulative. It tends to augment its excitement, to add to weight and tension. His dominant idea of form is crescendo" (20). Some of this could readily be applied to music Copland had not yet written.

11. Karal Ann Marling, *Wall-to-Wall America: A Cultural History of the Post-Office Murals in the Great Depression* (Minneapolis: University of Minnesota Press, 1982), 14.

12. Though Thomson was a Paris-trained cosmopolitan who based his first two operas on witty librettos by Gertrude Stein, his music took strength from his deep midwestern roots.

13. See Marshall Berman, "Studs Terkel: Living in the Mural," in *Adventures in Marxism* (New York: Verso, 1999), 65–68.

14. See Benjamin Appel, *The People Talk: American Voices from the Great Depression* (1940; New York: Touchstone, 1982).

15. James Agee and Walker Evans, *Let Us Now Praise Famous Men* (1941, 1960; New York: Ballantine Books, 1966), 12.

16. Quoted in Daniel Aaron, *Writers on the Left: Episodes in American Literary Communism* (1961; New York: Columbia University Press, 1992), 290–91.

13. WHO CARES?: THE WORLD OF *PORGY AND BESS*

1. Virgil Thomson, "George Gershwin," in *A Virgil Thomson Reader* (1981; New York: E. P. Dutton, 1984), 25.

2. On *Four Saints in Three Acts* as a cultural event see Steven Watson, *Prepare for Saints: Gertrude Stein, Virgil Thomson, and the Mainstreaming of American Modernism* (New York: Random House, 1998).

3. Quoted in Edward Jablonski, *Gershwin* (New York: Doubleday, 1987), 268.

4. Quoted ibid., 256.

5. Mark Tucker, ed., *The Duke Ellington Reader* (New York: Oxford University Press, 1993), 115.

6. Fitzgerald, clearly fascinated by the piece, evoked a performance in *The Great Gatsby*, as his friend Edmund Wilson later did in his novel *I Thought of Daisy*. On Fitzgerald's response, see Howard Pollack, *George Gershwin: His Life and Work* (Berkeley: University of California Press, 2006), 305–6. On Wilson's intriguing reaction, see Deena Rosenberg, *Fascinating Rhythm: The Collaboration of George and Ira Gershwin* (1991; London: Lime Tree Books, 1992), 71–72.

7. In a lively profile of Gershwin, in which she ingeniously compares this self-made man to Fitzgerald's Gatsby, Claudia Roth Pierpont points out that when this piece first appeared in *Modern Music* in 1935, the editor—Minna Lederman, who was otherwise quite terrified of Thomson—changed this last phrase to "plum-pudding orchestration." Pierpont, "Jazzbo: Why We Still Listen to Gershwin," *The New Yorker*, January 10, 2005, www.newyorker.com/archive/2005/01/10/050110crat_atlarge. Thomson's more pointed phrase was restored in his own essay collections. Even half a century later, in a published conversation with Diana Trilling, Thomson was still insisting that the "Jewish Mafia" dominating the music and literary scene had kept his work from getting its due (*Virgil Thomson Reader*, 549).

8. Jablonski, *Gershwin*, 271.

9. Ibid., 267.

10. For a definitive account of the production history of *Porgy and Bess*, see Pollack, *George Gershwin*, 592–664. See also Hollis Alpert, *The Life and Times of Porgy and Bess: The Story of an American Classic* (New York: Alfred A. Knopf, 1990).

14. THE PEOPLE VS. FRANK CAPRA: POPULISM AGAINST ITSELF

1. Graham Greene, reviewing *Mr. Smith Goes to Washington* in the *Spectator*, January 5, 1940. See *Graham Greene on Film*, ed. John Russell Taylor (New York: Simon & Schuster, 1972), 260. Earlier Greene had written that "his screen always seems twice as big as other people's, and he cuts as brilliantly as Eisenstein" (204).

2. Leonard Quart, "Frank Capra and the Popular Front," *Cineaste* 8, no. 1 (1977): 4–5.

3. Richard Griffith, *Frank Capra* (London: British Film Institute, 1951), 18. He describes the Capra hero as "a messianic innocent, not unlike the classic simpletons of literature, [who] pits himself against the forces of entrenched greed. His experience defeats him strategically, but his gallant integrity in the face of temptation calls forth the goodwill of the 'little people,' and through their combined protest, he triumphs."

4. John G. Cawelti, *Adventure, Mystery, and Romance: Formula Stories as Art and Popular Culture* (Chicago: University of Chicago Press, 1976), 38.

5. Robert Warshow, "Father and Son—and the FBI," *The Immediate Experience* (Garden City, N.Y.: Doubleday, 1962), 163–64.

6. Frank Capra, *The Name above the Title* (New York: Macmillan, 1971), 186. Capra adds that "it was the rebellious cry of the individual against being trampled to an ort by massiveness—mass production, mass thought, mass education, mass politics, mass wealth, mass conformity." This suggests the political ambiguity, or perhaps the confusion, of this outlook, caught between populism and individualism, and hardly sympathetic to the administrative liberalism of the New Deal.

7. Lionel Trilling, *Prefaces to The Experience of Literature* (1967; New York: Harcourt Brace Jovanovich, 1979), 69.

8. Compare John Ford's more subtle and understated treatment of Lincoln's depression in *Young Mr. Lincoln*, made in the same year. We often see Lincoln surrounded by shadows or brooding with eyes sunken in shadows, all conveyed with a silent reserve. The trial scenes, in which Lincoln defends two boys accused of murder and almost lynched, parallel Jimmy Stewart's ordeal before the Senate. Ford's period of populist filmmaking, beginning with his films with Will Rogers and embracing a series of literary adaptations, coincides with Capra's. Neither of them was connected to the Popular Front or the organized Left, though some of their screenwriters were.

9. Raymond Carney, *American Vision: The Films of Frank Capra* (1986; Cambridge: Cambridge University Press, 1996), xiii.

10. According to McBride, "Capra insisted on starting over from scratch, and [Harry] Cohn readily agreed. . . . But Capra had no time—or inclination—to make many changes in the screenplay. . . . Capra followed Riskin's story and dialogue almost to the letter, and he also adhered closely to the screenplay's unusually detailed visual plan." Joseph McBride, *Frank Capra: The Catastrophe of Success* (New York: Simon & Schuster, 1992), 251–52. McBride's biographical research seems definitive, but his dislike of Capra colors everything he writes. Nevertheless, he convincingly shows that Capra, with his "one man, one film" approach, loathed sharing credit with the people he worked with, especially Riskin, his longtime cameraman Joseph Walker, and even Eugene Vale, the writer who helped turn Capra's long, shapeless autobiography into a book.

11. Richard Hofstadter, *The Age of Reform* (New York: Vintage, 1955), 64–65.

12. Robert Warshow, *"Monsieur Verdoux,"* in *The Immediate Experience*, 208–9.

15. SHAKESPEARE IN OVERALLS: AN AMERICAN TROUBADOUR

1. According to a recent article, Woody Guthrie left behind some 2,400 lyrics, some of which have been used by these groups to write new songs. See Geoffrey Himes, "Dead 40 Years, Woody Guthrie Stays Busy," *New York Times*, Arts and Leisure section, September 2, 2007, p. 15. The Jewish songs were the product of his second marriage, to Marjorie Greenblatt Mazia. He also was inspired by her mother, Aliza Waitzman Greenblatt, who wrote poetry and songs in Yiddish.

2. Joe Klein, *Woody Guthrie: A Life* (New York: Alfred A. Knopf, 1980). Hereafter cited in text. In 2004 this novelistic account would be supplemented by a well-researched though overly detailed biography by Ed Cray, *Ramblin' Man: The Life and Times of Woody Guthrie* (New York: W. W. Norton, 2004).

16. GENDER TROUBLE: EXPOSING THE INTELLECTUALS

1. Philip Rahv, "The Cult of Experience in American Writing," in *Essays on Literature and Politics, 1932–1972*, ed. Arabel J. Porter and Andrew J. Dvosin (Boston: Houghton Mifflin, 1978), 11.

2. *Partisan Review* was founded in 1934 in association with the party-linked John Reed Clubs, an organization of left-wing writers. It stopped publishing in 1936 and reappeared as an independent radical journal toward the end of 1937, when it proclaimed its commitment to literary modernism and strong opposition to the cultural and political policies of the party. In its new anti-Stalinist incarnation it was coedited by Philip Rahv and William Phillips, two founding editors, along with Dwight Macdonald, George L. K. Morris, and F. W. Dupee, who were soon joined by Clement Greenberg and Delmore Schwartz.

3. Murray Kempton, *Part of Our Time: Some Ruins and Monuments of the Thirties* (New York: Simon & Schuster, 1955), 122. Kempton describes the book as "almost our only surviving document on a group of intellectuals who were drawn to the Communists early in the thirties and left them very soon." James T. Farrell later documented the same group in a posthumously published novel, *Sam Holman* (Buffalo, N.Y.: Prometheus Books, 1983), as did Alan M. Wald in his well-researched history, *The New York Intellectuals: The Rise and Decline of the Anti-Stalinist Left from the 1930s to the 1980s* (Chapel Hill: University of North Carolina Press, 1987).

4. Tess Slesinger, *The Unpossessed* (New York: Simon & Schuster, 1934), 32. Hereafter cited in text.

5. Lionel Trilling, "A Novel of the Thirties," in *The Last Decade: Essays and Reviews, 1965–75*, ed. Diana Trilling (New York: Harcourt Brace Jovanovich, 1979), 6–7.

6. Diana Trilling, *The Beginning of the Journey* (New York: Harcourt Brace, 1993), 92.

7. Paula Rabinowitz, *Labor and Desire: Women's Revolutionary Fiction in Depression America* (Chapel Hill: University of North Carolina Press, 1991), 147.

8. Lionel Trilling, "A Novel of the Thirties," 7.

9. Sidney Hook, quoted in Wald, *The New York Intellectuals*, 40.

10. Mary McCarthy, "Portrait of the Intellectual as a Yale Man," in *The Company She Keeps* (1942; New York: Dell, 1955), 159.

11. McCarthy, *The Company She Keeps*, 180, 181. For more extended comments on this book, see my essay "A Glint of Malice," in *A Mirror in the Roadway: Literature and the Real World* (Princeton: Princeton University Press, 2005), 96–103.

17. CONCLUSION: THE WORK OF CULTURE IN DEPRESSION AMERICA

1. *Nothing to Fear: The Selected Addresses of Franklin Delano Roosevelt, 1932–1945*, ed. B. D. Zevin (Boston: Houghton Mifflin, 1946), 13, 87–92.

2. Quoted by Warren I. Susman, "The People's Fair: Cultural Contradictions of a Consumer Society," in *Dawn of a New Day: The New York World's Fair, 1939–40* (New York: Queens Museum, 1980), 22.

3. C. Vann Woodward, "Editor's Introduction," in David M. Kennedy, *Freedom from Fear: The American People in Depression and War, 1929–1945* (New York: Oxford University Press, 1999), xiv.

4. Quoted in Kennedy, *Freedom from Fear*, 378.

5. Alfred Kazin, *Starting Out in the Thirties* (Boston: Houghton Mifflin, 1965), 13.

SELECTED BIBLIOGRAPHY

Aaron, Daniel. *Writers on the Left: Episodes in American Literary Communism*. 1961. Reprint, New York: Columbia University Press, 1992.

Allen, Frederick Lewis. *Since Yesterday: The 1930s in America, September 3, 1929–September 3, 1939*. 1940. Reprint, New York: Harper & Row, 1972.

Alter, Jonathan. *The Defining Moment: FDR's Hundred Days and the Triumph of Hope*. New York: Simon & Schuster, 2006.

Ames, Christopher. *Movies about the Movies: Hollywood Reflected*. Lexington: University Press of Kentucky, 1997.

Appel, Benjamin. *The People Talk: American Voices from the Great Depression*. 1940. Reprint, New York: Touchstone, 1982.

Astro, Richard. *John Steinbeck and Edward F. Ricketts*. Minneapolis: University of Minnesota Press, 1973.

Baigell, Matthew. *The American Scene: American Painting of the 1930's*. New York: Praeger, 1974.

Baldwin, James. *Collected Essays*. Edited by Toni Morrison. New York: Library of America, 1998.

Banks, Ann. *First-Person America*. New York: Alfred A. Knopf, 1980.

Bazin, André. *Orson Welles: A Critical View*. Translated by Jonathan Rosenbaum. New York: Harper & Row, 1978.

Benson, Jackson J. *The True Adventures of John Steinbeck, Writer*. New York: Viking, 1984.

Bergman, Andrew. *We're in the Money: Depression America and Its Films*. 1971. Reprint, New York: Harper & Row, 1972.

Bergreen, Laurence. *James Agee: A Life*. New York: E. P. Dutton, 1984.

———. *Louis Armstrong: An Extravagant Life*. New York: Broadway, 1997.

Berman, Marshall. *On the Town: One Hundred Years of Spectacle in Times Square*. New York: Random House, 2006.

———. "Studs Terkel: Living in the Mural." In *Adventures in Marxism*. New York: Verso, 1999.

Berrett, Joshua. *Louis Armstrong and Paul Whiteman: Two Kings of Jazz*. New Haven: Yale University Press, 2004.

Bird, Caroline. *The Invisible Scar*. 1966. Reprint, New York: Longman, 1978.

Bloom, James D. *Left Letters: The Culture Wars of Mike Gold and Joseph Freeman*. New York: Columbia University Press, 1992.

Bluestone, George. *Novels into Film*. 1957. Reprint, Berkeley: University of California Press, 1968.

Bourke-White, Margaret. *Portrait of Myself*. New York: Simon & Schuster, 1963.

Brenman-Gibson, Margaret. *Clifford Odets: American Playwright: The Years from 1906–1940*. New York: Atheneum, 1981.

Brinkley, Alan. *The End of Reform: New Deal Liberalism in Recession and War*. New York: Alfred A. Knopf, 1995.

———. *Voices of Protest: Huey Long, Father Coughlin, and the Great Depression*. New York: Alfred A. Knopf, 1982.

Bruccoli, Matthew J. *"The Last of the Novelists": F. Scott Fitzgerald and* The Last Tycoon. Carbondale: Southern Illinois University Press, 1977.

———. *Some Sort of Epic Grandeur: The Life of F. Scott Fitzgerald*. New York: Harcourt Brace Jovanovich, 1981.

Burnshaw, Stanley. *Robert Frost Himself*. New York: George Braziller, 1986.

———. *A Stanley Burnshaw Reader*. Athens: University of Georgia Press, 1990.

Capra, Frank. *The Name above the Title*. New York: Macmillan, 1971.

Carney, Raymond. *American Vision: The Films of Frank Capra*. 1986. Reprint, Cambridge: Cambridge University Press, 1996.

Carringer, Robert L. "*Citizen Kane*, The Great Gatsby, and Some Conventions of American Narrative." *Critical Inquiry* 2 (1975): 307–25.

———. *The Making of* Citizen Kane. Berkeley: University of California Press, 1985.

Cavell, Stanley. *Pursuits of Happiness: The Hollywood Comedy of Remarriage*. Cambridge: Harvard University Press, 1981.

Cawelti, John. *Apostles of the Self-made Man: Changing Concepts of Success in America*. Chicago: University of Chicago Press, 1965.

———. *Adventure, Mystery, and Romance: Formula Stories as Art and Popular Culture*. Chicago: University of Chicago Press, 1976.

Clarens, Carlos. *Crime Movies: From Griffith to the Godfather and Beyond*. New York: W. W. Norton, 1980.

Clurman, Harold. *The Fervent Years: The Story of the Group Theatre and the Thirties*. 1945. Reprint, New York: Harcourt Brace Jovanovich, 1975.

Cook, Sylvia Jenkins. *Erskine Caldwell and the Fiction of Poverty: The Flesh and the Spirit*. Baton Rouge: Louisiana State University Press, 1991.

———. *Tobacco Road to Route 66: The Southern Poor White in Fiction*. Chapel Hill: University of North Carolina Press, 1976.

Copland, Aaron, and Vivian Perlis, *Copland: 1900 through 1942*. New York: St. Martin's/ Marek, 1984.

Cowley, Malcolm. *The Dream of the Golden Mountains*. New York: Viking, 1980.

———. *Exile's Return: A Literary Odyssey of the 1920s*. 1934, 1951. Reprint, New York: Viking, 1956.

———. *Think Back on Us: A Contemporary Chronicle of the 1930's*. Edited by Henry Dan Piper. Carbondale: Southern Illinois University Press, 1967.

Cray, Ed. *Ramblin' Man: The Life and Times of Woody Guthrie*. New York: W. W. Norton, 2004.

Croce, Arlene. *The Fred Astaire and Ginger Rogers Book*. New York: Galahad Books, 1972.

Dardis, Tom. *Some Time in the Sun*. New York: Scribner's, 1976.

Davis, Mike. *City of Quartz: Excavating the Future in Los Angeles*. 1990. Reprint, New York: Vintage, 1992.

Dawn of a New Day: The New York World's Fair, 1939–40. New York: Queens Museum, 1980.

Denning, Michael. *The Cultural Front: The Laboring of American Culture in the Twentieth Century*. London: Verso, 1997.

DeVeaux, Scott. *The Birth of Bebop: A Social and Musical History*. Berkeley: University of California Press, 1997.

DiBattista, Maria. *Fast-Talking Dames*. New Haven: Yale University Press, 2001.

Dickstein, Morris. "Call It an Awakening." *New York Times Book Review*, November 29, 1987.

———. "Poverty, Shame and Self-Reliance." *New York Times Book Review*, January 22, 1984.

Donaldson, Scott. *Fool for Love: F. Scott Fitzgerald*. New York: Congdon & Weed, 1983.

Donohue, H. E. F. *Conversations with Nelson Algren*. 1964. Reprint, New York: Berkley, 1965.

Dorothea Lange. New York: Museum of Modern Art, 1966.

Duncan, Alastair. *Art Deco*. New York: Thames & Hudson, 1988.

Ely, Melvin Patrick. *The Adventures of Amos 'n' Andy: A Social History of an American Phenomenon*. New York: Free Press, 1991.

Erenberg, Lewis A. *Swingin' the Dream: Big Band Jazz and the Rebirth of American Culture*. Chicago: University of Chicago Press, 1998.

Filreis, Alan. *Modernism from Right to Left: Wallace Stevens, the Thirties, and Literary Radicalism*. New York: Cambridge University Press, 1994.

Foley, Barbara. *Radical Representations: Politics and Form in U.S. Proletarian Fiction, 1929–1941*. Durham, N.C.: Duke University Press, 1993.

Friedwald, Will. *Jazz Singing*. New York: Da Capo Press, 1996.

Furia, Philip. *The Poets of Tin Pan Alley*. New York: Oxford University Press, 1990.

Galbraith, John Kenneth. *The Great Crash: 1929*. 1955. 3rd ed. Boston: Houghton Mifflin, 1972.

Gallafent, Edward. *Astaire and Rogers*. New York: Columbia University Press, 2000.

Garraty, John A. *The Great Depression*. New York: Harcourt Brace Jovanovich, 1986.

Gelernter, David. *1939: The Lost World of the Fair*. New York: Free Press, 1995.

Giddins, Gary. *Bing Crosby: A Pocketful of Dreams: The Early Years, 1903–1940*. Boston: Little, Brown, 2001.

————. "The Mirror of Swing." In *Faces in the Crowd*. 1992. Reprint, New York: Da Capo Press, 1996.

————. *Visions of Jazz: The First Century*. New York: Oxford University Press, 1998.

Gilbert, James. *Writers and Partisans: A History of Literary Radicalism in America*. 1968. Reprint, New York: Columbia University Press, 1992.

Gioia, Ted. *The History of Jazz*. New York: Oxford University Press, 1997.

Glatzer, Richard, and John Raeburn, ed. *Frank Capra: The Man and His Films*. Ann Arbor: University of Michigan Press, 1975.

Goldberg, Vicki. *Margaret Bourke-White: A Biography*. New York: Harper & Row, 1986.

Goldstein, Malcolm. *The Political Stage: American Drama and Theater of the Great Depression*. New York: Oxford University Press, 1974.

Gottesman, Ronald, ed. *Perspectives on* Citizen Kane. New York: G. K. Hall, 1996.

Greif, Martin. *Depression Modern: The Thirties Style in America*. New York: Universe Books, 1975.

Guttmann, Allen. *The Jewish Writer in America*. New York: Oxford University Press, 1971.

Halper, Albert. *Good-bye, Union Square: A Writer's Memoir of the Thirties*. Chicago: Quadrangle, 1970.

Harrington, Michael. *The Other America: Poverty in the United States*. 1962. Reprint, Harmondsworth: Penguin, 1963.

Harvey, James. *Romantic Comedy in Hollywood, from Lubitsch to Sturges*. New York: Alfred A. Knopf, 1987.

Haskell, Molly. *From Reverence to Rape: The Treatment of Women in the Movies*. 1974. Reprint, New York: Penguin, 1975.

Hasse, John Edward. *Beyond Category: The Life and Genius of Duke Ellington*. New York: Simon & Schuster, 1993.

Hearn, Charles R. *The American Dream in the Great Depression*. Westport, Conn.: Greenwood Press, 1977.

Heide, Robert, and John Gilman. *Popular Art Deco: Depression Era Style and Design*. New York: Abbeville Press, 1991.

Hemenway, Robert E. *Zora Neale Hurston: A Literary Biography*. Urbana: University of Illinois Press, 1977.

Herbst, Josephine. *The Starched Blue Sky of Spain and Other Memoirs*. New York: HarperCollins, 1991.

Himmelfarb, Gertrude. *The Idea of Poverty: England in the Early Industrial Age*. New York: Alfred A. Knopf, 1984.

Huber, Richard M. *The American Idea of Success*. New York: McGraw-Hill, 1971.

Jablonski, Edward. *Gershwin*. New York: Doubleday, 1987.

Jones, Gavin. *American Hungers: The Problem of Poverty in U.S. Literature, 1840–1945*. Princeton: Princeton University Press, 2007.

Kael, Pauline. "Raising Kane." In *The Citizen Kane Book*. 1971. Reprint, New York: Bantam, 1974.

————, "The Man from Dream City." In *When the Lights Go Down*. New York: Holt, Rinehart and Winston, 1980.

Kauffmann, Stanley, with Bruce Henstell, eds. *American Film Criticism: From the Beginnings to* Citizen Kane. New York: Liveright, 1972.

Kazin, Alfred. *On Native Grounds: An Interpretation of Modern American Prose Literature.* 1942. Reprint, Garden City, N.Y.: Doubleday Anchor, 1956.

———. *Starting Out in the Thirties.* Boston: Atlantic Monthly Press, 1965.

Kellman, Steven G. *Redemption: The Life of Henry Roth.* New York: W. W. Norton, 2005.

Kempton, Murray. *Part of Our Time: Some Ruins and Monuments of the Thirties.* New York: Simon & Schuster, 1955.

Kendall, Elizabeth. *The Runaway Bride: Hollywood Romantic Comedy of the 1930's.* New York: Alfred A. Knopf, 1990.

Kennedy, David M. *Freedom from Fear: The American People in Depression and War, 1929–1945.* New York: Oxford University Press, 1999.

Klehr, Harvey. *The Heyday of American Communism: The Depression Decade.* New York: Basic Books, 1984.

Klein, Joe. *Woody Guthrie: A Life.* New York: Alfred A. Knopf, 1980.

Klein, Marcus. *Foreigners: The Making of American Literature, 1900–1940.* Chicago: University of Chicago Press, 1981.

Lawrence, D. H. *Phoenix: The Posthumous Papers of D. H. Lawrence.* Edited by Edward D. McDonald. 1936. Reprint, London: Heinemann, 1961.

Leibowitz, Herbert A., ed. *Musical Impressions: Selections from Paul Rosenfeld's Criticism.* New York: Hill and Wang, 1969.

Leuchtenburg, William E. *Franklin D. Roosevelt and the New Deal, 1932–1940.* New York: Harper & Row, 1963.

———. *The Perils of Prosperity, 1914–32.* Chicago: University of Chicago Press, 1958.

Levine, Lawrence W. "American Culture and the Great Depression." *Yale Review* 74 (Winter 1985).

———. "Jazz and American Culture." In *The Jazz Cadence of American Culture.* Edited by Robert G. O'Meally. New York: Columbia University Press, 1998.

Lewis, David Levering, ed. *The Portable Harlem Renaissance Reader.* New York: Viking, 1994.

Lynd, Robert S., and Helen Merrell Lynd. *Middletown in Transition: A Study in Cultural Conflicts.* New York: Harcourt, Brace, 1937.

Lyons, Bonnie. *Henry Roth: The Man and His Work.* New York: Cooper Square, 1976.

McBride, Joseph. *Frank Capra: The Catastrophe of Success.* New York: Simon & Schuster, 1992.

McBrien, William. *Cole Porter: A Biography.* 1998. Reprint, New York: Vintage, 2000.

McCann, Sean. *Gumshoe America: Hard-Boiled Crime Fiction and the Rise and Fall of New Deal Liberalism.* Durham, N.C.: Duke University Press, 2000.

McElvaine, Robert S., ed. *Down and Out in the Great Depression: Letters from the "Forgotten Man."* Chapel Hill: University of North Carolina Press, 1983.

———. *The Great Depression: America, 1929–1941.* New York: Times Books, 1984.

McGilligan, Patrick. *George Cukor: A Double Life.* New York: St. Martin's Press, 1991.

McKinzie, Richard D. *The New Deal for Artists.* Princeton: Princeton University Press, 1973.

McWilliams, Carey. *Factories in the Field: The Story of Migratory Farm Labor in California.* 1939. Reprint, Berkeley: University of California Press, 2000.

Madden, David, ed. *Proletarian Writers of the Thirties.* Carbondale: Southern Illinois University Press, 1968.

Mandelbaum, Howard, and Eric Myers. *Screen Deco.* 1985. Reprint, Santa Monica: Hennessey & Ingalls, 2000.

Maney, Patrick J. *The Roosevelt Presence: The Life and Legacy of FDR.* Berkeley: University of California Press, 1992.

Mangione, Jerre. *The Dream and the Deal: The Federal Writers' Project, 1935–1943.* Boston: Little, Brown, 1972.

Marchand, Roland. *Advertising the American Dream: Making Way for Modernity, 1920–1940.* Berkeley: University of California Press, 1985.

Mariani, Paul. *William Carlos Williams: A New World Naked.* New York: McGraw-Hill, 1981.

Marling, Karal Ann. *Wall-to-Wall America: A Cultural History of Post-Office Murals in the Great Depression.* Minneapolis: University of Minnesota Press, 1982.

Marquis, Alice G. *Hopes and Ashes: The Birth of Modern Times, 1929–1939.* New York: Free Press, 1986.

Martin, Jay. *Nathanael West: The Art of His Life.* New York: Farrar, Straus and Giroux, 1970.

———, ed. *Nathanael West: A Collection of Critical Essays.* Englewood Cliffs, N.J.: Prentice-Hall, 1971.

Mellow, James R. *Invented Lives: F. Scott and Zelda Fitzgerald.* Boston: Houghton Mifflin, 1984.

Meltzer, Milton. *Brother, Can You Spare a Dime?: The Great Depression, 1929–1933.* 1969. Reprint, New York: Mentor, 1977.

———. *Violins and Shovels: The WPA Arts Projects.* New York: Delacorte, 1976.

Milford, Nancy. *Zelda.* 1970. Reprint, New York: Avon, 1971.

Mordden, Ethan. *The Hollywood Musical.* New York: St. Martin's Press, 1981.

Mueller, John. *Astaire Dancing: The Musical Films.* New York: Alfred A. Knopf, 1991.

Mullen, Bill, and Sherry Linkon, eds. *Radical Revisions: Rereading 1930s Culture.* Urbana: University of Illinois Press, 1996.

Nekola, Charlotte, and Paula Rabinowitz, eds. *Writing Red: An Anthology of American Women Writers, 1930–1940.* New York: Feminist Press, 1987.

Nelson, Cary. *Repression and Recovery: Modern American Poetry and the Politics of Cultural Memory, 1910–1945.* Madison: University of Wisconsin Press, 1989.

Oja, Carol J., and Judith Tick, eds. *Aaron Copland and His World.* Princeton: Princeton University Press, 2005.

Parini, Jay. *Robert Frost: A Life.* New York: Henry Holt, 1999.

———. *John Steinbeck: A Biography.* New York: Henry Holt, 1996.

Park, Marlene, and Gerald E. Markowitz. *Democratic Vistas: Post Offices and Public Art in the New Deal.* Philadelphia: Temple University Press, 1984.

Parrish, Michael E. *Anxious Decades: America in Prosperity and Depression, 1920–1941.* New York: W. W. Norton, 1992.

Peeler, David P. *Hope among Us Yet: Social Criticism and Social Solace in Depression America.* Athens: University of Georgia Press, 1987.

Pells, Richard H. *Radical Visions and American Dreams: Culture and Social Thought in the Depression Years.* New York: Harper & Row, 1973.

Pessen, Edward. *The Log Cabin Myth: The Social Background of Presidents.* New Haven: Yale University Press, 1984.

Phillips, Cabell. *From the Crash to the Blitz: 1929–1939.* New York: Macmillan, 1969.

Pierpont, Claudia Roth. "Jazzbo: Why We Still Listen to Gershwin." *The New Yorker*, January 10, 2005.

Poirier, Richard. *Robert Frost: The Work of Knowing*. New York: Oxford University Press, 1977.

Pollack, Howard. *Aaron Copland: The Life and Work of an Uncommon Man*. New York: Henry Holt, 1999.

———. *George Gershwin: His Life and Work*. Berkeley: University of California Press, 2006.

Pritchard, William H. *Frost: A Literary Life Reconsidered*. New York: Oxford University Press, 1984.

Proletarian Literature in the United States: An Anthology. Edited by Granville Hicks, et al. New York: International Publishers, 1935.

Quart, Leonard. "Frank Capra and the Popular Front." *Cineaste* 8, no. 1 (1977).

Rabinowitz, Paula. *Labor and Desire: Women's Revolutionary Fiction in Depression America*. Chapel Hill: University of North Carolina Press, 1991.

Rahv, Philip. *Essays on Literature and Politics, 1932–1972*. Edited by Arabel J. Porter and Andrew J. Dvosin. Boston: Houghton Mifflin, 1978.

Rampersad, Arnold. *The Life of Langston Hughes*. Volume 1, *1902–1941: I, Too, Sing America*. New York: Oxford University Press, 1986.

Richardson, Joan. *Wallace Stevens: The Later Years, 1923–1955*. New York: William Morrow, 1988.

Rideout, Walter. *The Radical Novel in the United States, 1900–1954*. 1956. Reprint, New York: Columbia University Press, 1992.

Roberts, Nora Ruth. *Three Radical Women Writers: Class and Gender in Meridel Le Sueur, Tillie Olson, and Josephine Herbst*. New York: Garland, 1996.

Robinson, Cervin, and Rosemarie Haag Bletter. *Skyscraper Style: Art Deco New York*. New York: Oxford University Press, 1975.

Roffman, Peter, and Jim Purdy. *The Hollywood Social Problem Film: Madness, Despair, and Politics from the Depression to the Fifties*. Bloomington: Indiana University Press, 1981.

Rosenberg, Deena. *Fascinating Rhythm: The Collaboration of George and Ira Gershwin*. 1991. Reprint, London: Lime Tree Books, 1992.

Ross, Alex. *The Rest Is Noise: Listening to the Twentieth Century*. New York: Farrar, Straus and Giroux, 2007.

Rowley, Hazel. *Richard Wright: The Life and Times*. New York: Henry Holt, 2001.

Salzman, Jack, and Barry Wallenstein, eds. *Years of Protest: A Collection of American Writings of the 1930's*. New York: Pegasus, 1967.

Salzman, Jack, and Leo Zanderer, eds. *Social Poetry of the 1930s: A Selection*. New York: Burt Franklin, 1978.

Sanders, James. *Celluloid Skyline: New York and the Movies*. New York: Alfred A. Knopf, 2002.

Scharnhorst, Gary, with Jack Bales, *The Lost Life of Horatio Alger, Jr.* Bloomington: Indiana University Press, 1985.

Schatz, Thomas. *The Genius of the System: Hollywood Filmmaking in the Studio Era*. New York: Pantheon, 1988.

Schickel, Richard. *Cary Grant: A Celebration*. Boston: Little, Brown, 1983.

Schlesinger, Arthur M., Jr. *The Age of Roosevelt*. 3 vols. Boston: Houghton Mifflin, 1957–60.

———. *A Life in the Twentieth Century: Innocent Beginnings, 1917–1950*. Boston: Houghton Mifflin, 2000.

Shadoian, Jack. *Dreams and Dead Ends: The American Gangster/Crime Film*. Cambridge: MIT Press, 1977.

Sheed, Wilfrid. *The House That George Built: With a Little Help from Irving, Cole, and a Crew of About Fifty*. New York: Random House, 2007.

Shulman, Robert. *The Power of Political Art: The 1930s Literary Left Reconsidered*. Chapel Hill: University of North Carolina Press, 2000.

Simon, Rita James, ed. *As We Saw the Thirties*. Urbana: University of Illinois Press, 1967.

Simpson, Louis. *Three on the Tower: The Lives and Works of Ezra Pound, T. S. Eliot, and William Carlos Williams*. New York: Macmillan, 1975.

Sklar, Robert. *Movie-Made America: A Cultural History of American Movies*. 1975. Reprint, New York: Vintage, 1976.

Smith, Gene. *The Shattered Dream: Herbert Hoover and the Great Depression*. New York: William Morrow, 1970.

Smith, Jean Edward. *FDR*. New York: Random House, 2007.

Smith, Wendy. *Real Life Drama: The Group Theatre and America, 1931–1940*. New York: Alfred A. Knopf, 1990.

Snowman, Daniel. *America since 1920*. 1968. Reprint, New York: Harper & Row, 1970.

Starr, Kevin. *Endangered Dreams: The Great Depression in California*. New York: Oxford University Press, 1996.

———. *Inventing the Dream: California through the Progressive Era*. New York: Oxford University Press, 1985.

Staub, Michael E. *Voices of Persuasion: Politics of Representation in 1930s America*. Cambridge: Cambridge University Press, 1994.

Stewart, Rex. *Jazz Masters of the Thirties*. 1972. Reprint, New York: Da Capo Press, 1980.

Stott, William. *Documentary Expression and Thirties America*. New York: Oxford University Press, 1973.

Stowe, David W. *Swing Changes: Big-Band Jazz in New Deal America*. Cambridge: Harvard University Press, 1994.

Susman, Warren I. *Culture as History: The Transformation of American Society in the Twentieth Century*. New York: Pantheon, 1984.

Swados, Harvey, ed. *The American Writer and the Great Depression*. Indianapolis: Bobbs-Merrill, 1966.

Taylor, Nick. *American Made: The Enduring Legacy of the WPA: When FDR Put the Nation to Work*. New York: Bantam, 2008.

Terkel, Studs. *Hard Times: An Oral History of the Great Depression*. 1970. Reprint, New York: Avon, 1971.

These Are Our Lives. 1939. New York: W. W. Norton, 1975.

Thomas, Bob. *Astaire: The Man, the Dancer*. New York: St. Martin's Press, 1984.

Thomas, Tony, and Jim Terry, with Busby Berkeley. *The Busby Berkeley Book*. Greenwich, Conn.: New York Graphic Society, 1973.

Thomson, Virgil. *A Virgil Thomson Reader*. New York. E. P. Dutton, 1981.

———. *Virgil Thomson*. New York: Alfred A. Knopf, 1966.

Trilling, Diana. *The Beginning of the Journey*. New York: Harcourt Brace, 1993.

Trilling, Lionel. "A Novel of the Thirties." In *The Last Decade: Essays and Reviews, 1965–75*, edited by Diana Trilling. New York: Harcourt Brace Jovanovich, 1979.

Veitch, Jonathan. *American Superrealism: Nathanael West and the Politics of Representation in the 1930s*. Madison: University of Wisconsin Press, 1997.

Wald, Alan M. *Exiles from a Future Time: The Forging of the Mid-Twentieth-Century Literary Left*. Chapel Hill: University of North Carolina Press, 2002.

———. *James T. Farrell: The Revolutionary Socialist Years*. New York: New York University Press, 1978.

———. *The New York Intellectuals: The Rise and Decline of the Anti-Stalinist Left from the 1930s to the 1980s*. Chapel Hill: University of North Carolina Press, 1987.

Ware, Susan. *Beyond Suffrage: Women in the New Deal*. Cambridge: Harvard University Press, 1981.

———. *Holding Their Own: American Women in the 1930s*. Boston: G. K. Hall, 1982.

Warren, Harris Gaylord. *Herbert Hoover and the Great Depression*. New York: Oxford University Press, 1959.

Warshow, Robert. *The Immediate Experience: Movies, Comics, Theatre and Other Aspects of Popular Culture*. Garden City, N.Y.: Doubleday, 1962.

Watkins, T. H. *The Great Depression: America in the 1930s*. Boston: Little, Brown, 1993.

———. *The Hungry Years: A Narrative History of the Great Depression in America*. New York: Henry Holt, 1999.

Watson, Steven. *Prepare for Saints: Gertrude Stein, Virgil Thomson, and the Mainstreaming of American Modernism*. New York: Random House, 1998.

Weales, Gerald. *Clifford Odets: Playwright*. New York: Pegasus, 1971.

———. *Canned Goods as Caviar: American Film Comedies of the 1930s*. Chicago: University of Chicago Press, 1985.

Webb, Constance. *Richard Wright: A Biography*. New York: Putnam's, 1968.

Weber, Eva. *Art Deco in America*. New York: Exeter Books, 1985.

Wilder, Alec. *American Popular Song: The Great Innovators, 1900–1950*. New York: Oxford University Press, 1972.

Williams, Martin. *The Jazz Tradition*. Rev. ed. New York: Oxford University Press, 1993.

Wilson, Edmund. *The American Earthquake: A Documentary of the Twenties and Thirties*. Garden City, N.Y.: Doubleday Anchor, 1958.

———. *Classics and Commercials: A Literary Chronicle of the Forties*. New York: Farrar, Straus, 1950.

———. *The Shores of Light: A Literary Chronicle of the Twenties and Thirties*. 1952. Reprint, New York: Vintage, 1961.

Wyllie, Irvin G. *The Self-made Man in America: The Myth of Rags to Riches*. New Brunswick, N.J.: Rutgers University Press, 1954.

ILLUSTRATIONS AND PERMISSIONS

Railroad's S-1 locomotive, Wilmington, Delaware. (Library of Congress, LC-DIG-mmnsca-06611)

p. 357—They're hungry, too: Clark Gable and Claudette Colbert on the road in Frank Capra's *It Happened One Night*, 1934. (Columbia Pictures / Ohlinger's)

p. 408—Top of the world: The glorious spire of the Chrysler Building. (Margaret Bourke-White / Time Life Pictures / Getty Images)

p. 439—Busby Berkeley's "Remember My Forgotten Man," from *Gold Diggers of 1933*. (Warner Bros. / Ohlinger's)

p. 441—Thomas Hart Benton's *The Ballad of the Jealous Lover of Lone Green Valley*, 1934. (Copyright T. H. Benton and R. P. Benton Testamentary Trusts /UMB Bank Trustee / Licensed by VAGA, New York, NY. Spencer Art Museum, purchase Elizabeth M. Watkins Fund, 1958. 0055)

p. 464—Sheet music for "It Ain't Necessarily So," from *Porgy and Bess*, by George and Ira Gershwin and DuBose Heyward, 1935. (Museum of the City of New York)

p. 477—Scene of humiliation and despair: Jimmy Stewart on the floor of the Senate in Frank Capra's *Mr. Smith Goes to Washington*, 1939. (Columbia Pictures / Ohlinger's)

p. 496—Man with a guitar: Woody Guthrie performing. (Al Aumuller / Library of Congress, LC-USZ62–113276)

p. 507—*The National Hunger March in Pictures*, 1932. (Unemployed Councils of United States, Hunger March 1931, Labadie Collection, Special Collections, University of Michigan Library)

p. 522—Trylon and Perisphere, abstracted: New York World's Fair Poster, 1939. (Library of Congress, LC-USZC4–4856)

endpiece—Hitting the road again: migrant on California highway, 1935. (Library of Congress, LC-USF347–003801-ZE)

"Build Soil," "To a Thinker," "An Old Man's Winter Night," " 'Out, Out—,' " "Provide, Provide," "The Oven Bird," and "Two Tramps in Mud Time" copyright © 1916, 1936, 1944 by Robert Frost, copyright © 1964, 1969 by Lesley Frost Ballantine. Reprinted by permission of Henry Holt and Comany, LLC.

"A New Song," "Let America Be America Again," "Call to Creation," "Park Bench," and "The Weary Blues" from *The Collected Poems of Langston Hughes* by Langston Hughes, edited by Arnold Rampersad with David Roessel, associate editor, copyright © 1994 by the Estate of Langston Hughes. Used by permission of Alfred A. Knopf, a division of Random House, Inc.

"Ésthetique du Mal," "Sailing After Lunch," "Farewell to Florida," "Mozart, 1935," "Anglais Mort à Florence," "The Sun This March," "Autumn Refrain," "Sad Strains of a Gay Waltz," "Botanist on Alp (no. 1)," "The Man with the Blue Guitar," "The Poems of Our Climate," and "Like Decorations in a Nigger Cemetery" from *The Collected Poems of Wallace Stevens* by Wallace Stevens, copyright © 1954 by Wallace Stevens and renewed 1982 by Holly Stevens. Used by permission of Alfred A. Knopf, a division of Random House, Inc.

"Pastoral," "Spring and All (XX)," "The Red Wheelbarrow," and "The Yachts" from *The Collected Poems: Volume I, 1909–1939* by William Carlos Williams, copyright

INDEX

ABOUT THE AUTHOR

Born in 1940, Morris Dickstein grew up in New York. He received his education at Columbia, the Jewish Theological Seminary, Cambridge, and Yale, where he worked with distinguished critics such as Lionel Trilling, F. R. Leavis, Raymond Williams, and Harold Bloom. Returning to New York, he taught first at Columbia, closely observing the 1968 student uprising, and then at Queens College and the Graduate Center of the City University of New York, where he is currently Distinguished Professor of English and Theatre and senior fellow of the Center for the Humanities, which he founded in 1993.

Dickstein's interests have ranged from English Romantic poetry to the history of criticism, from American cultural history to modern and contemporary fiction. He began teaching film courses in 1975 and writing about film in the late 1970s for publications like *American Film, Bennington Review, Partisan Review,* and *Dissent.* His connection to the tumultuous world of the New York intellectuals began with a book review for *Partisan Review* in 1962, when he was a year out of college. He was a member of the editorial board from 1972 until it ceased publication in 2003. A longstanding contributor to the *New York Times Book Review* and the *Times Literary Supplement,* he has also written for the *American Scholar, Bookforum,* the *Nation,* and many other publications, combining a career as a teacher and scholar with the activities of a public intellectual.

His books include a widely known cultural history of the 1960s, *Gates of Eden,* nominated for a National Book Critics Circle award in criticism in 1978 and selected as one of the best books of the year by the *New York Times Book Review.* Among his other books are a study of modern criticism, *Double Agent* (1992), a social history of postwar American fiction, *Leopards in the Temple* (2002), and a collection of essays on realism and literature, *A Mirror in the Roadway* (2005). Dickstein has served on the boards of the National Book Critics Circle and the New York Council for the Humanities, and as president of the Association of Literary Scholars and Critics. He lives in New York with his wife, Lore, also a writer. The late Norman Mailer described him as "one of our best and most distinguished critics of American literature."